CRIC

EDIT
All statistics by the Editor unless otherwise stated

Playfair Competition	2
Sponsor's Message	5
Foreword by Barry Richards	6
Editorial Preface	9
The 1999 Season	
England v New Zealand – Records and Register	11
County Register, Records and 1998 Championship Averages	14
Ireland, Scotland and Universities Register	108
Umpires – ECB First-Class and ICC International Panels	110
The 1998 Season	
Statistical Highlights	113
First-Class Averages	117
Britannic Assurance County Championship	132
NatWest Trophy	134
Benson and Hedges Cup	140
AXA Sunday League	143
County Caps Awarded	145
Minor Counties Championship and Averages	145
Second XI Championship	149
Current Career Records	
First-Class Cricket	150
Leading Current Players	168
Limited-Overs Internationals (England)	169
Test Matches	171
Cricket Records	
First-Class Cricket	181
Limited-Overs Internationals	190
Women's Cricket	196
Test Matches	200
Test Match Scores and Averages – January 1998 to January 1999	209
ECB Tours Programme	270
Young Cricketers of the Year	270
1999 Fixtures	
Second XI	271
Minor Counties Championship	273
ECB 38 County Competition	275
Test Match, World Cup, First-Class and Limited-Overs	277
Fielding Chart	287

PLAYFAIR CRICKET COMPETITION 1999
CRICKET QUIZ
£1500 TO BE WON

PLUS NATWEST FINAL TICKETS AND HOSPITALITY
PLUS 25 CONSOLATION PRIZES

First Prize £500 + overnight accommodation (B and B) at the Regents Park Hilton Hotel (opposite Lord's) on 28 and 29 August + TWO tickets to the 1999 NatWest Trophy Final + NatWest hospitality

Second Prize £400 + TWO tickets to the 1999 NatWest Trophy Final

Third Prize £300 + TWO tickets to the 1999 NatWest Trophy Final

Fourth Prize £200

Fifth Prize £100

Consolation prizes

Senders of the next 25 correct entries will each receive a signed copy of

FROM OUTBACK TO OUTFIELD

by Justin Langer, published by Headline at £16.99

Closing date for entries:
12.00 noon on 23 July 1999

Winning entries will be drawn by the Man of the Match Adjudicator at one of the NatWest semi-finals on 14/15 August.

SPONSOR'S MESSAGE FROM
♻ NatWest

As we approach the millennium, NatWest will embark on the most exciting year of its nineteen-year cricket sponsorship to date. Not only will NatWest be a GlobalPartner of the 1999 ICC Cricket World Cup, but we have also launched a new-look NatWest Trophy Competition. For the first time, sixty teams will compete for the NatWest Trophy throughout seven rounds of one-day, 50-over competition.

Starting on 4 May, the NatWest Trophy will see teams from the Minor Counties and the County Boards begin their quest to topple their first-class county counterparts over four months of competition. A week earlier, we will have already opened the futuristic NatWest Media Centre at Lord's with a weekend set aside for the semi-finals for the first time and a Bank Holiday Sunday final on 29 August, this year's NatWest Trophy Competition is set to surpass all of the excitement the competition has seen in previous years.

Along with the excitement of the new NatWest Trophy and the Cricket World Cup, there will also be one other major international cricket series taking place this year. The Ashes will once again be hosted by England, albeit the NatWest England Under-19s, as they play host to a young touring Australian side over One-Day International and Test series.

As NatWest's commitment to cricket continues, 1999 will be very much a season of new experiences. As we look forward to hailing the new world champions, celebrating the first winners of the new format NatWest Trophy, this year promises to be a fitting finale to a wonderful century of cricket.

Martin Gray
Chief Executive, NatWest UK

FOREWORD

by Barry Richards

Cricket has had a tumultuous year and much that has happened has not been as positive as one would like. Bribery, throwing, dissent and umpiring standards are some unwanted headlines over the year.

The bribery scandal will just not go away and cricket really has to put it together globally and ensure the ICC has meaningful powers that are stringent and enforceable. For far too long the ICC, whose diversity is both a plus and a minus, has tiptoed around issues for fear of upsetting different interest groups. It cannot be tolerated any longer if cricket is to be successful in 2000 and beyond. Cultural differences are never more evident than with the cricket-playing nations, but that should not be a barrier to the powers that be to prevent further erosion of cricket's image. It will take hard and honest negotiation by all nations to fashion a global strategic plan that gives the ICC the muscle it needs. For some countries that might be painful as it will be perceived by them as loss of internal power and no doubt egos will be dented, but it is the only way forward.

Litigation is the bane of sport at the moment and, whilst everyone wants to ensure fairness, the advent of teams of lawyers has muddied the waters in many areas of sport. Cricket's laws, for so long the basis of the game, are under threat from legal teams hellbent on challenging every aspect which is at odds with long held traditions of the game. It is sad, but in Australia litigation has hit at the very core of the game. No longer can dads (and mums for that matter) just turn up and look after the Under-10s on a Saturday morning. Injuries will always occur both on and off the field with a hard ball. Parents are threatened with legal action should injury occur and they are not prepared to take that risk.

If we wanted further proof of where we are going, the handling of the Arjuna Ranatunga affair in Australia is an example. Ross Emerson, under the laws, had every right to challenge Muttiah Muralitharan's action as he saw it. One could argue it was inopportune given the findings of an internationally renowned panel, but it was the umpire's right. What followed was a sad reflection of the direction we are going. Arjuna himself will reflect on it and in time realise that it will change the game, perhaps forever. Governments, in time, might be compelled to have separate and specific legislation for sport to ensure that the traditions of the game are upheld and that the sport can be effectively run by people who really love and care for the game. Perhaps the answer might be a panel of independent judges appointed by the ICC for a certain term to have final arbitration on cricket matters. The present course will be destructive and is a potential minefield for cricket, but one thing is for sure: cricket's laws must take precedent over any political considerations.

International players are starting to take a bigger interest in the running of the game and not just on the playing field. In the not-too-distant future there will be an international players' body so that the voice of players can be heard in decisions which will affect the game. In the past players were notoriously slack and were also conveniently overlooked by administration in making decisions. Previously this may have been put down to amateurism, but these days TV, in its many formats, has raised the level of awareness amongst the players. They want a slice of the action, and also a say in formats, international itineraries and the like. It is very positive for cricket so long as the players and their representatives have the long-term vision in mind as well as the timespan that affects their playing careers. An internationally endorsed body will go a long way to defusing any potential problems between boards and players.

Throwing has again reared its ugly head, although solutions are much harder to find. Sri Lankan double-jointed wizard Muttiah Muralitharan has been subjected to humiliation in Australia, causing much heartache for their officials. You can understand the Sri Lankans being upset given the findings of an international panel but the 'behind the hand' talking has not ceased. Whether it is pure skill or an unfair advantage has been debated for several years now. Why has it been so long? It is not easy to cater for players who are different. Muralitharan has an arm defect much the same as the South African bowler Geoff Griffen, who was no-balled out the game in 1960. He, too, could not straighten his elbow to the full extent due to a boyhood accident. Ironically he got a hat-trick in this same Test, perhaps some consolation for an unfulfilled career. Muralitharan is different and gains enormous turn but if he is deemed to be unfair it must be signalled now, otherwise cricket-mad Sri Lanka will have a plethora of young bowlers imitating the action even though they have no structural arm problems. Technology could provide the answer with extra slow-motion cameras. A final decision will need to be made and, if necessary, an alteration to the law to ensure we have no repeat of what happened in Australia.

Talk of technology always leads to the debate as to whether it should be used more in cricket. I'm all in favour of it provided it does not affect the flow of the game. We are at pains to increase the over rate so we must be sure that more technology doesn't encroach. Players would prefer the correct decision and spectators have come to love the replays which are so much part and parcel of international cricket. It can, however, only be realistically used at international level. Umpires, like players, want to achieve the highest level possible and to have that prospect taken away because of technology could cause a real dearth of umpires at grass roots where they are most needed. Technology is in its infancy but I'm sure in time it will enhance the game and provide an exciting aspect to the promotion of the game.

I hope that it is embraced by groundsmen around the world as well so they can tap into knowledge from all countries. Whilst ultimate responsibility for good Test matches rests with captains, groundsmen can also play their part in ensuring that there is a fair balance between bat and ball. Too often in the past we have seen batting marathons that do nothing for the game. Statistics play a part in the rich heritage but, with so much TV and six hours a day to fill, it is becoming all encompassing and players, realising the commercial advantages of good averages, have not always had the course of the game in mind. I have for long believed that we would get the truly best players if we had a separate section for statistics on the games that have been won. The players who go for it provide the spectacle that people want in modern times. They deserve more recognition. That's digressing but my firm belief is that, whilst we don't want uniform wickets around the world, we do want a great contest. It is an art to produce a good wicket, but technology can help and it is another area which has to be addressed on an international scale.

Financially, cricket has never been in better shape and there is a real opportunity to enhance the game, especially in the areas in which it is already played. We must ensure that all ICC member nations have the opportunity to develop so that they can compete on the world stage. There is a perception that the affluent and well populated countries will forge ahead at the expense of the others. This must not happen on or off the field, so officials have a challenge to ensure resources are used wisely and that all nations can tap into the expertise that is available around the world. If a powerful and committed ICC takes the lead we have a rosy future.

Barry Richards
February 1999

EDITORIAL PREFACE

Our final edition of this century heralds a summer of records and change. The first-class season's very span sets records for both the longest in England and also for the earliest start (8 April). It will also be the last summer in which the County Championship is played in a single division and the first under a sponsor other than Britannic Assurance. Gone are the Benson and Hedges Cup and the Sunday League. Foremost in a schedule featuring two new limited-overs competitions, a substantially revised NatWest Trophy and four Test matches against New Zealand, will be the seventh World Cup. The latter, staged in Europe (at least one match will be played in Holland) for the first time since 1983, is the subject of a companion publication: *NatWest Playfair Cricket World Cup 1999*.

Starting with warm-up matches early in May and culminating in a Lord's final on Sunday 20 June, the World Cup will consume much of the first half of the season. Then the four-match Cornhill Insurance series against New Zealand will be completed within eight weeks to allow the season's final four weeks to be dominated by the counties' battle for those nine places in the first division of next year's Championship. Last season's competition provided a climax stirring enough, with Leicestershire worthy and emphatic winners, Jack Birkenshaw's skilful team-building bringing a second success in the space of three summers.

Sandwiched between these high profile contests will be the limited-overs competitions. Numerous unsatisfactory September finals have at last persuaded the planners to stage the NatWest Trophy showpiece a little earlier. Moving it forward a single week is unlikely to make too much difference but trimming 20 overs off the match certainly will. The competition's organisers are going to be fully stretched by a format featuring 60 teams and an extra two rounds. The National League is a revamped version of the Sunday slog which will be staged on a confusing variety of days with 20 of its 144 games under floodlights. Played in two divisions with each of the nine members playing its associates twice, it will feature 45-over matches (an unsatisfactory compromise between the Sunday League 40 and the international 50) and involve everyone concerned with a considerable increase in travelling. The last innovation is the peculiar Super Cup which involves the top eight counties in last year's Championship in a seven-match 50-over tournament. No one has managed to justify the selection of the top eight teams at real cricket for a limited-overs thrash.

The merits of dividing the counties into two has been debated heatedly for many years, the erratic performances of our national team having compelled a close examination of the county structure. How can England A achieve such consistent success against their overseas counterparts, with Michael Vaughan's recent expedition to southern Africa extending their unbeaten overseas run to 29 matches within five years, while their seniors continue to blow hot and cold? Many have decided that county cricket is far too cosy and that its intensity and competitive strength can only be improved by culling its participants by half. Amalgamating counties was considered too drastic so we are on the threshold of a two-tier system. However, with second division sides guaranteed their customary share of the Board's annual hand-out and a promotion/relegation system involving a third of the counties, one wonders whether the penalty for wearing second division sackcloth is severe enough to persuade every player to raise his personal targets.

Future seasons will remove the top players from all these domestic competitions for most of the summer. Soon the front runners are likely to be contracted directly to the Board. Even if that does not occur, our leading cricketers will be fully extended by a revised format featuring seven Test matches and ten limited-overs internationals.

One change that was long overdue in the view of this MCC member, was the admission of women to the ranks of cricket's most prestigious club. In addition England's female cricketers are at long last being supported by both the national board and by sponsors. I apologise for their feats going unheeded in early editions and I am greatly indebted to Marion Collin, honorary women's cricket statistician to the international and national boards, for compiling a section on Women's Test Cricket.

I am delighted that Barry Richards has honoured us with this edition's foreword. His rapid advances as a radio and television pundit mirror his forthright performances with the bat. International cricket's loss proved to be Hampshire's gain and scoring some of his spectacular innings for John Arlott's sublime commentary remains high on my list of cherished memories.

NatWest have again done us proud, continuing their sponsorship of this annual, its quiz and the World Cup guide. Remember that the answers to the quiz can all be found from within these covers. Again my thanks to Barbara Quinn and her team who receive and mark all the entries.

Playfair continues to benefit from many kindnesses. The county and university clubs' administrators, scorers and statisticians have again been extremely helpful, as have Clive Hitchcock (ICC), Kate Hansen (ECB), Alex Ritchie (Scottish Cricket Union), Gerard Byrne (Ireland) and David Armstrong (Minor Counties). In addition to compiling the first-class career records, Philip Bailey has again researched birth registrations of new players, while Debbie Frindall has continued to find time to update numerous records and compile scorecards.

My final thanks go to our publishers, Headline, for their expertise in all departments (after nine editions, Ian Marshall's growing responsibilities have led to his delegating most of his responsiblities to Andrew Kinsman, whose efficiency has made the handover the envy of any relay runner), and to Chris Leggett and his unflappable team of typesetters.

BILL FRINDALL
Urchfont
11 March 1999

ENGLAND v NEW ZEALAND

1929-30 to 1996-97

RESULTS SUMMARY

ENGLAND v NEW ZEALAND – IN ENGLAND

	Tests	Series E NZ D	Lord's E NZ D	Oval E NZ D	Man E NZ D	Leeds E NZ D	B'ham E NZ D	N'ham E NZ D
1931	3	1 – 2	– – 1	1 – –	– – 1	– – –	– – –	– – –
1937	3	1 – 2	– – 1	– – 1	1 – –	– – –	– – –	– – –
1949	4	– – 4	– – 1	– – 1	– – 1	– – 1	– – –	– – –
1958	5	4 – 1	1 – –	– – 1	1 – –	1 – –	1 – –	– – –
1965	3	3 – –	1 – –	– – –	– – –	1 – –	1 – –	– – –
1969	3	2 – 1	1 – –	– – –	– – –	1 – –	– – –	– – 1
1973	3	2 – 1	– – 1	– – –	– – –	1 – –	1 – –	– – –
1978	3	3 – –	1 – –	– – –	– – –	1 – –	1 – –	– – –
1983	4	3 1 –	– 1 –	1 – –	– – –	1 – –	1 – –	– – –
1986	3	– 1 2	– 1 –	– – 1	– – –	– – –	– – 1	– – –
1990	3	1 – 2	– – 1	– – 1	– – –	– – 1	– – –	1 – –
1994	3	1 – 2	– – 1	– – 1	– – –	1 – –	– – 1	– – –
	40	21 2 17	5 – 7	4 – 4	2 – 3	3 1 1	3 – –	4 1 2

ENGLAND v NEW ZEALAND – IN NEW ZEALAND

	Tests	Series E NZ D	Christchurch E NZ D	Wellington E NZ D	Auckland E NZ D	Dunedin E NZ D
1929-30	4	1 – 3	1 – –	– – –	1 – 2	– – –
1932-33	2	– – 2	– – 1	– – –	– – 1	– – –
1946-47	1	– – 1	– – –	– – 1	– – –	– – –
1950-51	2	1 – 1	– – 1	1 – –	– – –	– – –
1954-55	2	2 – –	– – –	– – –	1 – –	1 – –
1958-59	2	1 – 1	1 – –	– – –	– – 1	– – –
1962-63	3	3 – –	1 – –	1 – –	1 – –	– – –
1965-66	3	– – 3	– – 1	– – –	– – 1	– – 1
1970-71	2	1 – 1	1 – –	– – –	– – 1	– – –
1974-75	2	1 – 1	1 – –	– – 1	– – –	– – –
1977-78	3	1 1 1	1 – –	– 1 –	1 – –	– – –
1983-84	3	– 1 2	– 1 –	– – 1	– – 1	– – –
1987-88	3	– – 3	– – 1	– – 1	– – 1	– – –
1991-92	3	2 – 1	1 – –	– – 1	1 – –	– – –
1996-97	3	2 – 1	– – 1	1 – –	1 – –	– – –
	38	15 2 21	7 1 6	3 1 5	4 – 10	1 – 1

| Totals | 78 | 36 | 4 | 38 |

ENGLAND v NEW ZEALAND SERIES RECORDS

HIGHEST INNINGS TOTALS

England	in England	567-8d	Nottingham	1994
	in New Zealand	593-6d	Auckland	1974-75
New Zealand	in England	551-9d	Lord's	1973
	in New Zealand	537	Wellington	1983-84

LOWEST INNINGS TOTALS

England	in England	158	Birmingham	1990
	in New Zealand	64	Wellington	1977-78
New Zealand	in England	47	Lord's	1958
	in New Zealand	26	Auckland	1954-55

HIGHEST MATCH AGGREGATE   1293 for 34 wickets   Lord's   1931
LOWEST MATCH AGGREGATE   390 for 30 wickets   Lord's   1958

HIGHEST INDIVIDUAL INNINGS

England	in England	310*	J.H.Edrich	Leeds	1965
	in New Zealand	336*	W.R.Hammond	Auckland	1932-33
New Zealand	in England	206	M.P.Donnelly	Lord's	1949
	in New Zealand	174*	J.V.Coney	Wellington	1983-84

HIGHEST AGGREGATE OF RUNS IN A SERIES

England	in England	469	(av 78.16)	L.Hutton	1949
	in New Zealand	563	(av 563.00)	W.R.Hammond	1932-33
New Zealand	in England	462	(av 77.00)	M.P.Donnelly	1949
	in New Zealand	341	(av 85.25)	C.S.Dempster	1929-30

RECORD WICKET PARTNERSHIPS – ENGLAND

1st	223	G.Fowler (105)/C.J.Tavaré (109)	The Oval	1983
2nd	369	J.H.Edrich (310*)/K.F.Barrington (163)	Leeds	1965
3rd	245	J.Hardstaff jr (114)/W.R.Hammond (140)	Lord's	1937
4th	266	M.H.Denness (188)/K.W.R.Fletcher (216)	Auckland	1974-75
5th	242	W.R.Hammond (227)/L.E.G.Ames (103)	Christchurch	1932-33
6th	240	P.H.Parfitt (131*)/B.R.Knight (125)	Auckland	1962-63
7th	149	A.P.E.Knott (104)/P.Lever (64)	Auckland	1970-71
8th	246	L.E.G.Ames (137)/G.O.B.Allen (122)	Lord's	1931
9th	163*	M.C.Cowdrey (128*)/A.C.Smith (69*)	Wellington	1962-63
10th	59	A.P.E.Knott (49)/N.Gifford (25*)	Nottingham	1973

RECORD WICKET PARTNERSHIPS – NEW ZEALAND

1st	276	C.S.Dempster (136)/J.E.Mills (117)	Wellington	1929-30
2nd	241	J.G.Wright (116)/A.H.Jones (143)	Wellington	1991-92
3rd	210	B.A.Edgar (83)/M.D.Crowe (106)	Lord's	1986
4th	155	M.D.Crowe (143)/M.J.Greatbatch (68)	Wellington	1987-88
5th	180	M.D.Crowe (142)/S.A.Thomson (69)	Lord's	1994
6th	141	M.D.Crowe (115)/A.C.Parore (71)	Manchester	1994
7th	117	D.N.Patel (99)/C.L.Cairns (61)	Christchurch	1991-92
8th	104	D.A.R.Moloney (64)/A.W.Roberts (66*)	Lord's	1937
9th	118	J.V.Coney (174*)/B.L.Cairns (64)	Wellington	1983-84
10th	106*	N.J.Astle (102*)/D.K.Morrison (14*)	Auckland	1996-97

BEST INNINGS BOWLING ANALYSIS

England	in England	7- 32	D.L.Underwood	Lord's	1969
	in New Zealand	7- 47	P.C.R.Tufnell	Christchurch	1991-92
New Zealand	in England	7- 74	B.L.Cairns	Leeds	1983
	in New Zealand	7-143	B.L.Cairns	Wellington	1983-84

BEST MATCH BOWLING ANALYSIS

England	in England	12-101	D.L.Underwood	The Oval	1969
	in New Zealand	12- 97	D.L.Underwood	Christchurch	1970-71
New Zealand	in England	11-169	D.J.Nash	Lord's	1994
	in New Zealand	10-100	R.J.Hadlee	Wellington	1977-7

HIGHEST AGGREGATE OF WICKETS IN A SERIES

England	in England	34	(av 7.47)	G.A.R.Lock	1958
	in New Zealand	19	(av 19.00)	D.Gough	1996-97
New Zealand	in England	21	(av 26.61)	R.J.Hadlee	1983
	in New Zealand	15	(av 19.53)	R.O.Collinge	1977-78
		15	(av 24.73)	R.J.Hadlee	1977-78

1999 NEW ZEALANDERS

The New Zealand touring team had not been selected at the time of going to press. The following players represented New Zealand in international cricket during 1998:

Full Names	Birthdate	Birthplace	Team	Type	F-C Debut
ALLOTT, Geoffrey Ian	24.12.71	Christchurch	Canterbury	RHB/LFM	1994-95
ASTLE, Nathan John	15. 9.71	Christchurch	Canterbury	RHB/RM	1991-92
BAILEY, Mark David	26.11.70	Hamilton	N Districts	RHB/RM	1989-90
BELL, Matthew David	25. 2.77	Dunedin	Wellington	RHB/OB	1993-94
CAIRNS, Christopher Lance	13. 6.70	Picton	Canterbury	RHB/RFM	1988
DOULL, Simon Blair	6. 8.69	Pukekohe	N Districts	RHB/RMF	1989-90
FLEMING, Stephen Paul	1. 4.73	Christchurch	Canterbury	LHB/RSM	1991-92
HARRIS, Chris Zinzan	20.11.69	Christchurch	Canterbury	LHB/RM	1989-90
HORNE, Matthew Jeffery	5.12.70	Auckland	Otago	RHB/RM	1992-93
HOWELL, Llorne Gregory	8. 7.72	Napier	Canterbury	RHB/RM	1990-91
McMILLAN, Craig Douglas	13. 9.76	Christchurch	Canterbury	RHB/RM	1994-95
NASH, Dion Joseph	20.11.71	Auckland	N Districts	RHB/RFM	1990-91
O'CONNOR, Shayne Barry	15.11.73	Hastings	Otago	LHB/LFM	1994-95
PARORE, Adam Craig	23. 1.71	Auckland	Auckland	RHB/WK	1988-89
PRIEST, Mark Wellings	12. 8.61	Greymouth	Canterbury	LHB/SLA	1984-85
SPEARMAN, Craig Murray	4. 7.72	Auckland	C Districts	RHB	1993-94
TAIT, Alex Ross	13. 6.72	Paparoa	N Districts	RHB/RM	1994-95
TWOSE, Roger Graham	17. 4.68	Torquay	Wellington	LHB/RM	1989
VETTORI, Daniel Luca	27. 1.79	Auckland	N Districts	RHB/SLA	1996-97
WISEMAN, Paul John	4. 5.70	Auckland	Otago	RHB/OB	1991-92
YOUNG, Bryan Andrew	3.11.64	Whangarei	N Districts	RHB/WK	1983-84

THE FIRST-CLASS COUNTIES REGISTER, RECORDS AND 1998 AVERAGES

Career statistics deadlines: Test Matches to 27 Jan 1999; LOI to 13 Feb 1999; first-class to end of 1998 English season.

ABBREVIATIONS
General

*	not out/unbroken partnership	f-c	first-class
b	born	HS	Highest Score
BB	Best innings bowling analysis	LOI	Limited-Overs Internationals
Cap	Awarded 1st XI County Cap	Tests	Official Test Matches
Tours	Overseas tours involving first-class appearances		

Awards

BHC	Benson and Hedges Cup 'Gold' Award
NWT	NatWest Trophy/Gillette Cup 'Man of the Match' Award
Wisden 1998	One of *Wisden Cricketers' Almanack's* Five Cricketers of 1998
YC 1998	Cricket Writers' Club Young Cricketer of 1998

Competitions
BHC   Benson and Hedges Cup
CC   County Championship
NWT   NatWest Trophy
SL   AXA Sunday League

Playing Categories
LBG   Bowls right-arm leg-breaks and googlies
LF   Bowls left-arm fast
LFM   Bowls left-arm fast-medium
LHB   Bats left-handed
LM   Bowls left-arm medium pace
LMF   Bowls left-arm medium fast
OB   Bowls right-arm off-breaks
RF   Bowls right-arm fast
RFM   Bowls right-arm fast-medium
RHB   Bats right-handed
RM   Bowls right-arm medium pace
RMF   Bowls right-arm medium-fast
RSM   Bowls right-arm slow-medium
SLA   Bowls left-arm leg-breaks
SLC   Bowls left-arm 'Chinamen'
WK   Wicket-keeper

Education
BHS   Boys' High School
BS   Boys' School
C   College
CE   College of Education
CFE   College of Further Education
CHE   College of Higher Education
CS   Comprehensive School
GS   Grammar School
HS   High School
IHE   Institute of Higher Education
LSE   London School of Economics
RGS   Royal Grammar School
S   School
SFC   Sixth Form College
SM   Secondary Modern School
SS   Secondary School
TC   Technical College
T(H)S Technical (High) School
U   University
UMIST University of Manchester Institute of Science and Technology

Teams (see also p 117)

B	Bangladesh	NT	Northern Transvaal
CD	Central Districts	OFS	(Orange) Free State
DHR	D.H.Robins' XI	PIA	Pakistan International Airlines
Eng Co	English Counties XI	Q	Queensland
EP	Eastern Province	RW	Rest of the World XI
GW	Griqualand West	SAB	South African Breweries XI
IW	International Wanderers	SAU	South African Universities
K	Kenya	WA	Western Australia
ND	Northern Districts	WP	Western Province
NSW	New South Wales	Z	Zimbabwe (Rhodesia)

DERBYSHIRE

Formation of Present Club: 4 November 1870
Colours: Chocolate, Amber and Pale Blue
Badge: Rose and Crown
Championships: (1) 1936
NatWest Trophy/Gillette Cup Winners: (1) 1981
Benson and Hedges Cup Winners: (1) 1993
Sunday League Champions: (1) 1990
Match Awards: NWT 43; BHC 67

Secretary/General Manager: J.Smedley
County Cricket Ground, Nottingham Road, Derby DE2 6DA (Tel 01332 383211)
Captain: D.G.Cork. **Vice-Captain:** K.M.Krikken. **Overseas Player:** M.J.Slater.
1999 Beneficiary: None. **Scorer:** S.W.Tacey.

ALDRED, Paul (Lady Manner's S, Bakewell), b Chellaston 4 Feb 1969. 5'10". RHB, RM. Debut 1995. Cheshire 1994. HS 83 v Hants (Chesterfield) 1997. BB 3-28 v Notts (Nottingham) 1997. **NWT:** HS 4. BB 4-30 v Lincs (Lincoln) 1997. **BHC:** HS 24* v Yorks (Derby) 1998. BB 2-35 v Warwks (Birmingham) 1996. **SL:** HS 17 v Warwks (Birmingham) 1997. BB 4-41 v Leics (Derby) 1996.

BLACKWELL, Ian David (Brookfield Community S), b Chesterfield 10 Jun 1978. 6'1". LHB, SLA. Debut 1997. HS 57 v Durham (Derby) 1998. BB 5-115 v Surrey (Oval) 1998. **NWT:** HS 4. **BHC:** HS 27 v Yorks (Derby) 1998. **SL:** HS 89 v Notts (Derby) 1998. BB 3-47 v Surrey (Oval) 1998.

CASSAR, Matthew Edward (Sir Joseph Banks HS, Sydney), b Sydney, Australia 16 Oct 1972. Husband of Jane Cassar (England). 6'0". RHB, RFM. Debut 1994. Qualified for England/D.G debut 1997. HS 121 v Sussex (Horsham) 1998. BB 4-54 v OU (Oxford) 1995. CC BB 3-26 v Glam (Cardiff) 1998. Award: NWT 1. **NWT:** HS 90* v Cumb (Derby) 1998. **SL:** HS 134 v Northants (Northampton) 1998. BB 1-11.

CLARKE, Vincent Paul (Sacred Heart C, Perth, Australia; Perth C), b Liverpool, Lancs 11 Nov 1971. 6'3". RHB, RM/LB. Somerset 1994. Leicestershire 1995-96. Derbyshire debut 1997. HS 99 v Warwks (Birmingham) 1997. BB 3-47 v CU (Cambridge) 1997. CC BB 3-72 Le v Worcs (Worcester) 1995. Award: BHC 1. **NWT:** HS 24* v Northants (Derby) 1997. BB 2-29 v Scot (Edinburgh) 1998. **BHC:** HS 52 v Worcs (Worcester) 1997. BB 4-49 v Warwks (Derby) 1997. **SL:** HS 77* v Yorks (Derby) 1997. BB 3-47 v Glam (Cardiff) 1998.

CORK, Dominic Gerald (St Joseph's C, Stoke-on-Trent), b Newcastle-under-Lyme, Staffs 7 Aug 1971. 6'2". RHB, RFM. Debut 1990; cap 1993; captain 1998 to date. *Wisden* 1995. Staffordshire 1989-90. **Tests:** 27 (1995 to 1998-99); HS 59 v NZ (Auckland) 1996-97; BB 7-43 v WI (Lord's) 1995 – on debut (named England analysis by Test match debutant); hat-trick v WI (Manchester) 1995 – the first in Test history to occur in the opening over of a day's play. **LOI:** 25 (1992 to 1996-97); HS 31*; BB 3-27. Tours: A 1992-93 (Eng A), 1998-99; SA 1993-94 (Eng A), 1995-96; WI 1991-92 (Eng A), 1997-98; I 1994-95 (Eng A). HS 104 v Glos (Cheltenham) 1993. 50 wkts (4); most – 90 (1995). BB 9-43 (13-93 match) v Northants (Derby) 1995. Took 8-53 before lunch on his 20th birthday v Essex (Derby) 1991. 2 hat-tricks: 1994 and 1995 (see *Tests*). Awards: NWT 3; BHC 3. **NWT:** HS 62 v Kent (Derby) 1994. BB 5-18 v Berks (Derby) 1992. **BHC:** HS 92* v Lancs (Lord's) 1993. BB 5-49 v Lancs (Chesterfield) 1996. **SL:** HS 66 v Sussex (Eastbourne) 1994. BB 6-21 v Glam (Chesterfield) 1997.

DEAN, Kevin James (Leek HS; Leek C), b Derby 16 Oct 1975. 6'5". LHB, LMF. Debut 1996. Cap 1998. HS 27* v SA (Derby) 1998. CC HS 25* v Essex (Derby) 1998. 50 wkts (1): 74 (1998). BB 6-63 (12-133 match) v Somerset (Taunton) 1998. Hat-trick 1998. Award: NWT 1. **NWT:** HS 0*. BB 3-13 v Scot (Edinburgh) 1998. **BHC:** HS 14* and BB 3-62 v Yorks (Derby) 1998. **SL:** HS 16* v Glam (Cardiff) 1998. BB 5-32 v Glos (Derby) 1996.

DeFREITAS, Phillip Anthony Jason (Willesden HS, London), b Scotts Head, Dominica 18 Feb 1966. 6'0". RHB, RFM. UK resident since 1976. Leicestershire 1985-88; cap 1986. Lancashire 1989-93; cap 1989. Boland 1993-94 and 1995-96. Derbyshire debut/cap 1994; captain 1997 (part). *Wisden* 1991. MCC YC. **Tests:** 44 (1986-87 to 1995-96); HS 88 v A (Adelaide) 1994-95; BB 7-70 v SL (Lord's) 1991. **LOI:** 103 (1986-87 to 1997); HS 67; BB 4-35. Tours: A 1986-87, 1990-91, 1994-95; WI 1989-90; NZ 1987-88, 1991-92; P 1987-88; I 1992-93; Z 1988-89 (La). HS 113 Le v Notts (Worksop) 1988. De HS 108 v Leics (Derby) 1994. 50 wkts (11); most – 94 (1986). BB 7-21 La v Middx (Lord's) 1989. De BB 7-64 v Kent (Canterbury) 1997. Hat-trick 1994. Awards: NWT 5; BHC 4. **NWT:** HS 69 Le v Lancs (Leicester) 1986. BB 5-13 La v Cumb (Kendal) 1989. **BHC:** HS 75* La v Hants (Manchester) 1990. BB 5-16 La v Essex (Chelmsford) 1992. **SL:** HS 72* v Kent (Derby) 1996. BB 5-26 La v Hants (Southampton) 1993.

GRIFFITHS, Steven Paul (Beechen Cliff S, Bath; Brunel C of Art & Technology, Bristol), b Hereford 31 May 1973. RHB, WK. 5'11". Debut 1995. HS 20 v Surrey (Derby) 1995. **SL:** HS –.

HARRIS, Andrew James (Hadfield CS; Glossopdale Community C), b Ashton-under-Lyne, Lancs 26 Jun 1973. 6'1". RHB, RM. Debut 1994; cap 1996. Tour: A 1996-97 (Eng A). HS 36 v Worcs (Worcester) 1997. BB 6-40 (12-83 match) v Middx (Derby) 1996. 50 wkts (1): 72 (1996). **NWT:** HS 11* and BB 3-58 v Kent (Derby) 1996. **BHC:** HS 5. BB 3-41 v Warwks (Derby) 1997. **SL:** HS 10* v Lancs (Derby) 1997. BB 4-22 v Yorks (Derby) 1997.

KRIKKEN, Karl Matthew (Rivington & Blackrod HS & SFC), b Bolton, Lancs 9 Apr 1969. Son of B.E. (Lancs and Worcs 1966-69). 5'9". RHB, WK. GW 1988-89. Derbyshire debut 1989; cap 1992. HS 104 v Lancs (Manchester) 1996. **NWT:** HS 55 v Kent (Derby) 1996. **BHC:** HS 42* v Lancs (Derby) 1997. **SL:** HS 44* v Essex (Chelmsford) 1991.

LACEY, Simon James (Aldercar CS; Ripley Mill Hill SFC), b Nottingham 9 Mar 1975. 5'11". RHB, OB. Debut 1997. HS 50 v Somerset (Derby) 1997. BB 3-97 v Essex (Southend) 1997. **SL:** HS 9. BB 1-38.

MAY, Michael Robert (The Bolsover S; NE Derbyshire CFE), b Chesterfield 22 Jul 1971. 5'9". RHB, OB. Debut 1996. HS 116 v Glam (Chesterfield) 1997. **NWT:** HS 5.

ROBERTS, Glenn Martin (King James's HS and Greenhead C, Huddersfield; Leeds Met U), b Huddersfield, Yorks 4 Nov 1973. 5'11". LHB, SLA. Debut 1996. HS 52 v Somerset (Taunton) 1996 – on debut. BB 4-105 v Durham (Derby) 1998. **NWT:** HS –. BB 1-30. **BHC:** HS 12 v Warwks (Derby) 1997. BB 3-45 v Lancs (Manchester) 1997. **SL:** HS 9. BB 3-34 v Surrey (Oval) 1998.

ROLLINS, Adrian Stewart (Little Ilford CS), b Barking, Essex 8 Feb 1972. Brother of R.J. (*see* ESSEX). 6'5". RHB, occ WK, occ RM. Debut 1993; cap 1995. 1000 runs (3); most – 1142 (1997). HS 210 v Hants (Chesterfield) 1997. BB 1-19. **NWT:** HS 58 v Cumb (Derby) 1998. **BHC:** HS 70* v Worcs (Worcester) 1998. **SL:** HS 126* v Surrey (Derby) 1995.

SLATER, Michael Jonathon (Wagga Wagga HS), b Wagga Wagga, NSW, Australia 21 Feb 1970. 5'9". RHB, RM. NSW 1991-92 to date. Derbyshire debut/cap 1998. **Tests** (A): 45 (1993 to 1998-99); HS 219 v SL (Perth) 1995-96; BB 1-4. **LOI** (A): 42 (1993-94 to 1997); HS 73. Tours (A): E 1993, 1995 (NSW), 1997; SA 1993-94; WI 1994-95, 1998-99; I 1996-97, 1997-98; P 1994-95, 1998-99. 1000 runs (1+1); most – 1472 (1994-95). HS 219 (see *Tests*). De HS 185 v SA (Derby) 1998. CC HS 99 v Surrey (Oval) 1998. BB 1-4 (see *Tests*). **NWT:** HS 82 v Surrey (Oval) 1998. **SL:** HS 110 v Worcs (Derby) 1998.

SMITH, Trevor Mark (Friesland S, Sandiacre; Broxtowe C, Chilwell), b Derby 18 Jan 1977. 6'3". LHB, RFM. Debut 1997. HS 29 and BB 6-32 v Essex (Derby) 1998. **SL:** HS 6.
SPENDLOVE, Benjamin Lee (Trent C), b Belper 4 Nov 1978. 6'1". RHB, OB. Debut 1997. HS 49 v Somerset (Taunton) 1998. **NWT:** HS 58 v Leics (Leicester) 1998. **BHC:** HS 11 v Yorks (Derby) 1998. **SL:** HS 25 v Essex (Derby) 1998.
STUBBINGS, Stephen David (Frankston HS; Swinburne U), b Huddersfield, Yorks 31 Mar 1978. 6'3". LHB, OB. Debut 1997. HS 22 v Worcs (Worcester) 1997. **BHC:** HS 7. **SL:** HS 4.
TWEATS, Timothy Andrew (Endon HS; Stoke-on-Trent SFC), b Stoke-on-Trent, Staffs 18 Apr 1974. 6'3". RHB, RM. Debut 1992. HS 189 v Yorks (Derby) 1997. BB 1-23. Award: BHC 1. **NWT:** HS 16 v Warwks (Derby) 1995. **BHC:** HS 42* v Scot (Forfar) 1998. **SL:** HS 35 v Warwks (Derby) 1998.
WESTON, Robin Michael Swann (Durham S; Loughborough U), b Durham 7 Jun 1975. Brother of W.P.C. (*see WORCESTERSHIRE*). 5'10". RHB, LB. Durham 1995-97. Derbyshire debut 1998. Minor C debut 1991 when aged 15yr 355d (Durham record). HS 97 v Kent (Derby) 1998. BB (Du) 1-41. **NWT:** HS 56 v Leics (Leicester) 1998. **SL:** HS 41 v Surrey (Oval) 1998.

NEW REGISTRATIONS

DEANE, Michael John, b Chesterfield 9 Mar 1977. RHB, RM.
TITCHARD, Stephen Paul (Lymm County HS; Priestley C), b Warrington, Lancs 17 Dec 1967. 6'3". RHB, RM. Lancashire 1990-98; cap 1995. HS 163 La v Essex (Chelmsford) 1996. BB 1-11 (La – twice). Award: NWT 1. **NWT:** HS 92 La v Worcs (Manchester) 1995. **BHC:** HS 82 La v Surrey (Oval) 1992. **SL:** HS 96 La v Essex (Chelmsford) 1994.
WOOLLEY, Anthony Paul (Spondon S), b Derby 4 Dec 1971. RHB, RM.

RELEASED/RETIRED
(Having made a first-class County appearance in 1998)

BARNETT, K.J. – *see GLOUCESTERSHIRE*.

BILL FRINDALL'S SCORING SHEETS AND BINDERS

For illustrated instructions and price list send a large S.A.E. to

THE BEECHES, URCHFONT, DEVIZES, WILTSHIRE SN10 4RD

DERBYSHIRE 1998

RESULTS SUMMARY

	Place	Won	Lost	Tied	Drew	No Result
Britannic Assurance Championship	10th	6	7		4	
All First-Class Matches		6	7		5	1
NatWest Trophy	Finalist					
Benson and Hedges Cup	4th in Group B					
Sunday League	15th	6	8			3

BRITANNIC ASSURANCE CHAMPIONSHIP AVERAGES

BATTING AND FIELDING

Cap		M	I	NO	HS	Runs	Avge	100	50	Ct/St
1982	K.J.Barnett	17	32	6	162	1229	47.26	1	7	8
–	R.M.S.Weston	8	15	–	97	524	34.93	–	4	4
1995	A.S.Rollins	10	19	–	107	618	32.52	1	4	11
1993	D.G.Cork	10	16	3	102*	393	30.23	1	3	9
1998	M.J.Slater	13	22	–	99	600	27.27	–	2	8
–	M.E.Cassar	16	29	4	121	616	24.64	1	4	8
–	G.M.Roberts	7	12	3	44	197	21.88	–	–	7
1994	P.A.J.DeFreitas	14	23	3	87	435	21.75	–	2	6
1992	K.M.Krikken	16	26	5	83	432	20.57	–	3	34/2
–	B.L.Spendlove	9	17	–	49	318	18.70	–	–	3
–	T.A.Tweats	8	16	–	161	295	18.43	1	–	8
–	M.R.May	12	22	–	54	372	16.90	–	1	4
–	P.Aldred	6	8	3	37*	80	16.00	–	–	6
1998	K.J.Dean	14	20	12	25*	127	15.87	–	–	1
–	I.D.Blackwell	11	18	–	57	254	14.11	–	2	6
–	T.M.Smith	6	9	1	29	81	10.12	–	–	4
–	V.P.Clarke	4	7	–	26	67	9.57	–	–	4

Also batted: S.P.Griffiths (1 match) 12, 3 (5 ct); A.J.Harris (cap 1996)(2) 4, 0, 5; S.J.Lacey (3) 11, 0, 17 (1 ct).

BOWLING

	O	M	R	W	Avge	Best	5wI	10wM
K.J.Dean	441.2	92	1486	71	20.92	6- 63	5	1
T.M.Smith	124.3	36	396	16	24.75	6- 32	1	–
D.G.Cork	332.2	77	914	36	25.38	5- 72	1	–
P.A.J.DeFreitas	482.4	114	1363	52	26.21	5- 38	3	–
I.D.Blackwell	156.2	32	524	14	37.42	5-115	1	–
P.Aldred	164.4	34	470	12	39.16	3- 30	–	–

Also bowled: K.J.Barnett 54-10-148-4; M.E.Cassar 137-26-524-9; V.P.Clarke 41-4-173-2; A.J.Harris 32-3-136-4; S.J.Lacey 88-19-274-4; M.R.May 3-0-51-0; G.M.Roberts 169-27-629-9; T.A.Tweats 3-0-29-0.

The First-Class Averages (pp 117-131) give the records of Derbyshire players in all first-class county matches (Derbyshire's other opponents being the South Africans and Cambridge University, the latter match being abandoned), with the exception of D.G.Cork, whose full county figures are as above.

DERBYSHIRE RECORDS

FIRST-CLASS CRICKET

Highest Total	For 645		v Hampshire	Derby	1898
	V 662		by Yorkshire	Chesterfield	1898
Lowest Total	For 16		v Notts	Nottingham	1879
	V 23		by Hampshire	Burton upon T	1958
Highest Innings	For 274	G.A.Davidson	v Lancashire	Manchester	1896
	V 343*	P.A.Perrin	for Essex	Chesterfield	1904

Highest Partnership for each Wicket

1st	322	H.Storer/J.Bowden	v Essex	Derby	1929
2nd	417	K.J.Barnett/T.A.Tweats	v Yorkshire	Derby	1997
3rd	316*	A.S.Rollins/K.J.Barnett	v Leics	Leicester	1997
4th	328	P.Vaulkhard/D.Smith	v Notts	Nottingham	1946
5th	302*†	J.E.Morris/D.G.Cork	v Glos	Cheltenham	1993
6th	212	G.M.Lee/T.S.Worthington	v Essex	Chesterfield	1932
7th	241*	G.H.Pope/A.E.G.Rhodes	v Hampshire	Portsmouth	1948
8th	198	K.M.Krikken/D.G.Cork	v Lancashire	Manchester	1996
9th	283	A.Warren/J.Chapman	v Warwicks	Blackwell	1910
10th	132	A.Hill/M.Jean-Jacques	v Yorkshire	Sheffield	1986

† *346 runs were added for this wicket in two separate partnerships*

Best Bowling	For 10- 40	W.Bestwick	v Glamorgan	Cardiff	1921
(Innings)	V 10- 45	R.L.Johnson	for Middlesex	Derby	1994
Best Bowling	For 17-103	W.Mycroft	v Hampshire	Southampton	1876
(Match)	V 16-101	G.Giffen	for Australians	Derby	1886

Most Runs – Season	2165	D.B.Carr	(av 48.11)	1959
Most Runs – Career	23854	K.J.Barnett	(av 41.12)	1979-98
Most 100s – Season	8	P.N.Kirsten		1982
Most 100s – Career	53	K.J.Barnett		1979-98
Most Wkts – Season	168	T.B.Mitchell	(av 19.55)	1935
Most Wkts – Career	1670	H.L.Jackson	(av 17.11)	1947-63

LIMITED-OVERS CRICKET

Highest Total	NWT	365-3		v Cornwall	Derby	1986
	BHC	366-4		v Combined U	Oxford	1991
	SL	292-9		v Worcs	Knypersley	1985
Lowest Total	NWT	79		v Surrey	The Oval	1967
	BHC	98		v Worcs	Derby	1994
	SL	61		v Hampshire	Portsmouth	1990
Highest Innings	NWT	153	A.Hill	v Cornwall	Derby	1986
	BHC	142	D.M.Jones	v Minor C	Derby	1996
	SL	141*	C.J.Adams	v Kent	Chesterfield	1992
Best Bowling	NWT	8-21	M.A.Holding	v Sussex	Hove	1988
	BHC	6-33	E.J.Barlow	v Glos	Bristol	1978
	SL	6- 7	M.Hendrick	v Notts	Nottingham	1972

DURHAM

Formation of Present Club: 10 May 1882
Colours: Navy blue, yellow and maroon
Badge: Coat of Arms of the County of Durham
Championships: (0) 14th 1998
NatWest Trophy/Gillette Cup Winners: (0) Quarter-Finalist 1992
Benson and Hedges Cup Winners: (0) Quarter-Finalist 1998
Sunday League Champions: (0) Seventh 1993
Match Awards: NWT 20; BHC 13.

Chief Executive: M.Candlish
County Ground, Riverside, Chester-le-Street, Co Durham DH3 3QR (Tel 0191 387 1717)
Captain/Overseas Player: D.C.Boon. **Vice-Captain:** N.J.Speak.
1999 Beneficiary: J.E.Morris. **Scorer:** B.Hunt

BETTS, Melvyn Morris (Fyndoune CS, Sacriston), b Sacriston 26 Mar 1975. 5'10". RHB, RFM. Debut 1993; cap 1998. Tour: Z 1998-99. HS 57* v Sussex (Hove) 1996. BB 9-64 (Durham record; 13-143 match) v Northants (Northampton) 1997. **NWT:** HS 14 v Middx (Southgate) 1998. BB 3-33 v Scot (Chester-le-St) 1996. **BHC:** HS 20* and BB 2-26 v Worcs (Chester-le-St) 1998. **SL:** HS 21 v Hants (Chester-le-St) 1997. BB 3-22 v Derbys (Chester-le-St) 1997.

BOON, David Clarence (Launceston GS), b Launceston, Australia 29 Dec 1960. 5'7½". RHB, OB. Tasmania 1978-79 to date. Durham debut 1997; captain 1997 to date; cap 1998. MBE. **Tests** (A): 107, inc 60 in succession (1984-85 to 1995-96); HS 200 v NZ (Perth) 1989-90. **LOI** (A): 181 (1983-84 to 1994-95); HS 122. Tours: E 1985, 1989, 1993; SA 1993-94; WI 1990-91, 1994-95; NZ 1985-86, 1989-90, 1992-93; I 1986-87; P 1988-89, 1994-95; SL 1992-93; Z 1995-96 (Tas – captain). 1000 runs (4+2); most – 1437 (1993). HS 227 Tasmania v Victoria (Melbourne) 1983-84. Du HS 139* v Yorks (Chester-le-St) 1998. BB 2-18 v Kent (Darlington) 1997. **NWT:** HS 80* v Norfolk (Lakenham) 1998. **BHC:** HS 103 v Northants (Chester-le-St) 1997. **SL:** HS 76 v Sussex (Chester-le-St) 1997 and 76 v Glam (Chester-le-St) 1998. BB 2-44 v Derbys (Derby) 1998.

BROWN, Simon John Emmerson (Boldon CS), b Cleadon 29 Jun 1969. 6'3". RHB, LFM. Northamptonshire 1987-90. Durham debut 1992; captain 1996 (part); cap 1998. **Tests**: 1 (1996); HS 10* and BB 1-60 v P (Lord's) 1996. HS 69 v Leics (Durham) 1994. 50 wkts (5); most – 79 (1996). BB 7-70 v A (Durham) 1993. CC BB 7-105 v Kent (Canterbury) 1992. Awards: NWT 1; BHC 1. **NWT:** HS 7*. BB 5-22 v Cheshire (Bowdon) 1994. **BHC:** HS 12 v Warwks (Birmingham) 1995. BB 6-30 v Northants (Chester-le-St) 1997. **SL:** HS 18 v Derbys (Derby) 1996. BB 4-20 v Yorks (Leeds) 1995.

CHAPMAN, Steven (Willington Parkside CS), b Crook 2 Oct 1971. 6'4". RHB, SLA. Debut 1998. Cumberland 1997. HS 11 v Sussex (Eastbourne) 1998. **SL:** HS 14 v Glam (Chester-le-St) 1998. BB 2-57 v Surrey (Chester-le-St) 1998.

COLLINGWOOD, Paul David (Blackfyne CS; Derwentside C), b Shotley Bridge 26 May 1976. 5'11". RHB, RMF. Debut 1996 v Northants (Chester-le-St) taking wicket of D.J.Capel with his first ball before scoring 91 and 16; cap 1998. HS 107 v OU (Oxford) 1996. CC HS 105 v Warwks (Birmingham) 1998. BB 3-46 v Lancs (Manchester) 1997. Award: BHC 1. **NWT:** HS 28 v Essex (Chelmsford) 1996. BB 1-25. **BHC:** HS 49 v Notts (Nottingham) 1997. BB 3-28 v Minor C (Chester-le-St) 1996. **SL:** HS 62 v Kent (Canterbury) 1998. BB 3-20 v Derys (Derby) 1998.

DALEY, James Arthur (Hetton CS), b Sunderland 24 Sep 1973. 5'10". RHB, RM. Debut 1992. MCC YC. HS 159* v Hants (Portsmouth) 1994. BB 1-12. **BHC:** HS 33 v Lancs (Manchester) 1996. **SL:** HS 98* v Kent (Canterbury) 1994.

DAVIES, Anthony **Mark** (Northfield CS, Billingham), b Stockton-on-Tees 4 Oct 1980. 6'2". RHB. RM. Non-contracted Durham Academy player awaiting f-c debut. **SL:** HS 0 and BB 2-44 v Surrey (Chester-le-St) 1998.

FOSTER, Michael James (New C, Pontefract), b Leeds, Yorks 17 Sep 1972. 6'1". RHB, RFM. Yorkshire 1993-94. Northamptonshire staff 1995. Durham debut 1996. HS 129 v Glam (Cardiff) 1997. BB 4-21 v Middx (Lord's) 1996. Award: BHC 1. **NWT:** HS 56* and BB 2-37 v Surrey (Oval) 1997. **BHC:** HS 73* v Scot (Forfar) 1997. BB 3-26 v Worcs (Chester-le-St) 1998. **SL:** HS 118 Y v Leics (Leicester) 1993. BB 3-34 v Essex (Chester-le-St) 1998.

GOUGH, Michael Andrew (English Martyrs CS; Hartlepool SFC), b Hartlepool 18 Dec 1979. 6'5". Son of M.P. (Durham 1974-77). RHB, OB. Debut 1998. HS 123 v CU (Cambridge) 1998. CC HS 62 v Essex (Chester-le-St) 1998 – on debut. BB 1-4.

GRAHAM, John Alexander (Seaton Burn HS; Leeds U), b Newcastle upon Tyne, Northumb 4 Mar 1978. 6'1½". RHB, RM. Non-contracted player awaiting f-c debut.

HARMISON, Stephen James (Ashington HS), b Ashington, Northumb 23 Oct 1978. 6'4". RHB, RF. Debut 1996. Northumberland 1996. Tours (Eng A): SA 1998-99; Z 1998-99. HS 36 v Kent (Canterbury) 1998. 50 wkts (1): 51 (1998). BB 5-70 v Glos (Chester-le-St) 1998. **BHC:** HS 1. **SL:** HS 1*.

KILLEEN, Neil (Greencroft CS; Derwentside C; Teesside U), b Shotley Bridge 17 Oct 1975. 6'2". RHB, RFM. Debut 1995. HS 48 v Somerset (Chester-le-St) 1995. BB 5-49 v Lancs (Chester-le-St) 1998. **NWT:** HS 1* and BB 2-46 v Middx (Southgate) 1998. **BHC:** HS 24* and BB 2-28 v Worcs (Chester-le-St) 1998. **SL:** HS 32 v Middx (Lord's) 1996. BB 5-26 v Northants (Northampton) 1995.

LEWIS, Jonathan James Benjamin (King Edward VI S, Chelmsford; Roehampton IHE), b Isleworth, Middx 31 May 1970. 5'9½". RHB. Essex 1990-96; cap 1994; scored 116* on debut v Surrey (Oval). Durham debut 1997; cap 1998. 1000 runs (1): 1252 (1997). HS 210* v OU (Oxford) 1997 – on Du debut. CC HS 160* v Derbys (Chester-le-St) 1997. BB 1-73. Award: BHC 1. **NWT:** HS 24* Ex v Sussex (Hove) 1994. **BHC:** HS 67 v Yorks (Leeds) 1998. **SL:** HS 102 v Glos (Cheltenham) 1997.

MORRIS, John Edward (Shavington CS; Dane Bank CFE), b Crewe, Cheshire 1 Apr 1964. 5'10". RHB, RM. Derbyshire 1982-93; cap 1986. GW 1988-89 and 1993-94. Durham debut 1994; cap 1998; benefit 1999. **Tests:** 3 (1990); HS 32 v I (Oval) 1990. **LOI:** 8 (1990-91); HS 63*. Tour: A 1990-91. 1000 runs (11); most – 1739 (1986). HS 229 De v Glos (Cheltenham) 1993. Du HS 204 v Warwks (Birmingham) 1994. BB 1-6. Du BB 1-37. Awards: NWT 2; BHC 2. **NWT:** HS 109 v Scot (Chesterfield) 1996. **BHC:** HS 145 v Leics (Leicester) 1996. **SL:** HS 134 De v Somerset (Taunton) 1990.

PHILLIPS, Nicholas Charles (Wm Parker S, Hastings), b Pembury, Kent 10 May 1974. 5'10½". RHB, OB. Sussex 1993-97. HS 53 Sx v Young A (Hove) 1995. CC HS 52 Sx v Lancs (Lytham) 1995. Du HS 35 v Glos (Chester-le-St) 1998. BB 5-56 v Derbys (Derby) 1998. Award: NWT 1. **NWT:** HS 1. BB 2-16 v Norfolk (Lakenham) 1998. **BHC:** HS 13 v Yorks (Leeds) 1998. BB 3-48 Sx v Glos (Hove) 1997. **SL:** HS 38* Sx v Essex (Chelmsford) 1996. BB 4-24 v Somerset (Taunton) 1998.

PRATT, Andrew (Willington Parkside CS; Durham New C), b Helmington Row, Crook 4 Mar 1975. 6'0". LHB, WK. Debut 1997. MCC YC. HS 34 v Lancs (Chester-le-St) 1998. **SL:** HS 5*.

SPEAK, Nicholas Jason (Parrs Wood HS, Manchester), b Manchester 21 Nov 1966. 6'0". RHB, LB. Lancashire 1986-87 to 1996; cap 1992. Durham debut 1997; cap 1998. Tours (La): WI 1986-87, 1995-96. 1000 runs (3); most – 1892 (1992). HS 232 La v Leics (Leicester) 1992. Du HS 124* v CU (Cambridge) 1997. BB 1-0. Award: BHC 1. **NWT:** HS 83 La v Oxon (Aston Rowant) 1996. **BHC:** HS 82 La v Hants (Manchester) 1992. **SL:** HS 102* La v Yorks (Leeds) 1992.

SPEIGHT, Martin Peter (Hurstpierpoint C; Durham U), b Walsall, Staffs 24 Oct 1967. 5'9". RHB, WK. Sussex 1986-96; cap 1991. Wellington 1989-90 to 1992-93. Durham debut 1997; cap 1998. 1000 runs (3); most – 1375 (1990). HS 184 Sx v Notts (Eastbourne) 1993. Du HS 97* v Hants (Southampton) 1998. BB 1-2. Awards: BHC 2. **NWT:** HS 50 Sx v Warwks (Lord's) 1993. **BHC:** HS 83 Comb U v Glos (Bristol) 1988. **SL:** HS 126 Sx v Somerset (Taunton) 1993.

SYMINGTON, Marc Joseph (St Michaels, Billingham; Stockton SFC), b Newcastle upon Tyne, Northumb 10 Jan 1980. 5'8". RHB, RM. Debut 1998. HS 8*. CC HS –. BB 3-55 v Derbys (Derby) 1998. **SL:** HS 7. BB 1-51.

WOOD, John (Crofton HS; Wakefield District C; Leeds Poly), b Crofton, Yorks 22 Jul 1970. 6'3". RHB, RFM. GW in Nissan Shield 1990-91. Debut 1992; cap 1998. HS 63* v Notts (Chester-le-St) 1993. 50 wkts (1): 62 (1998). BB 6-110 v Essex (Stockton) 1994. **NWT:** HS 8*. BB 2-22 v Ireland (Dublin) 1992. **BHC:** HS 27 v Leics (Stockton) 1995. BB 3-50 v Warwicks (Birmingham) 1995. **SL:** HS 28 v Worcs (Worcester) 1994. BB 4-17 v Kent (Darlington) 1997.

NEW REGISTRATIONS

ALI, Syed Muazam (Chigwell S), b Whipps Cross, Essex 23 Oct 1979. 5'7". RHB, LB.

HATCH, Nicholas Guy (Barnard Castle S; Hull U), b Darlington 21 Apr 1979. 6'8". RHB, RMF. Joins staff on summer contract in vacation.

ROBINSON, Ryan (Shelley HS & SFC), b Huddersfield, Yorks 19 Oct 1976. 6'0". Cousin of A.Walker (Northamptonshire 1983-93 and Durham 1994-98). RHB, RM. Yorkshire Academy.

RELEASED/RETIRED
(Having made a first-class County appearance in 1998)

HUTTON, Stewart (De Brus S, Skelton; Cleveland TC), b Stockton-on-Tees 30 Nov 1969. 6'0". LHB, RSM. Durham 1992-98. HS 172* v OU (Oxford) 1996. CC HS 101 v Northants (Hartlepool) 1994. Award: NWT 1. **NWT:** HS 125 v Herefords (Chester-le-St) 1995. **BHC:** HS 38 v Yorks (Leeds) 1998. **SL:** HS 81 v Leics (Chester-le-St) 1996.

LUGSDEN, S. – see *HAMPSHIRE*.

ROSEBERRY, M.A. – see *MIDDLESEX*.

SAGGERS, Martin John (Springwood HS, King's Lynn; Huddersfield U), b King's Lynn, Norfolk 23 May 1972. 6'2". RHB, RMF. Durham 1996-98. Norfolk 1995-96. HS 18 v Somerset (Weston-s-M) 1996. BB 6-65 v Glam (Chester-le-St) 1996. Award: BHC 1. **NWT:** HS O (Norfolk). **BHC:** BB 2-42 v Middx (Southgate) 1998. **BHC:** (Minor C) HS 34* v Leics (Jesmond) 1996. BB 2-49 v Durham (Chester-le-St) 1996. **SL:** HS 13 v Warwks (Birmingham) 1996. BB 4-35 v Essex (Chelmsford) 1997.

SEARLE, Jason Paul (John Bentley S, Calne; Swindon C), b Bath, Somerset 16 May 1976. 5'9". RHB, OB. Durham 1994-98. HS 5*. BB 3-92 v Lancs (Chester-le-St) 1998. **BHC:** HS –.

WALKER, Alan (Shelley HS), b Emley, Yorks 7 Jul 1962. 5'11". LHB, RFM. Northamptonshire 1983-93; cap 1987. Durham 1994-98. Tour: SA 1991-92 (Nh). HS 41* Nh v Warwks (Birmingham) 1987. Du HS 29 v WI (Chester-le-St) 1995. 50 wkts (1): 54 (1988). BB 8-118 (14-177 match) v Essex (Chelmsford) 1995. Award: NWT 1. **NWT:** HS 13 v Derbys (Darlington) 1994. BB 4-7 Nh v Ire (Northampton) 1987. **BHC:** HS 15* Nh v Notts (Nottingham) 1987. BB 4-42 v Minor C (Jesmond) 1995. **SL:** HS 30 Nh v Durham (Northampton) 1993. BB 4-18 v Kent (Darlington) 1997. Appointed Durham 2nd XI coach/captain.

DURHAM 1998

RESULTS SUMMARY

	Place	Won	Lost	Tied	Drew	No Result
Britannic Assurance Championship	14th	3	9		5	
All First-Class Matches		4	9		6	
NatWest Trophy	2nd Round					
Benson and Hedges Cup	Quarter-Finalist					
Sunday League	17th	4	9	1		3

BRITANNIC ASSURANCE CHAMPIONSHIP AVERAGES

BATTING AND FIELDING

Cap		M	I	NO	HS	Runs	Avge	100	50	Ct/St
1998	D.C.Boon	15	27	3	139*	953	39.70	3	5	12
–	J.A.Daley	10	19	2	157	554	32.58	1	1	4
1998	P.D.Collingwood	17	30	4	105	793	30.50	1	5	16
1998	J.E.Morris	12	23	1	163	657	29.86	2	1	5
1998	N.J.Speak	14	25	2	77*	638	27.73	–	6	9
1998	M.A.Roseberry	6	11	–	97	295	26.81	–	2	2
–	M.J.Foster	8	13	1	76*	321	26.75	–	2	2
1998	M.P.Speight	16	28	4	97*	581	24.20	–	4	58/3
1998	J.J.B.Lewis	14	26	1	72	578	23.12	–	4	10
–	M.A.Gough	8	15	–	62	329	21.93	–	2	9
–	S.J.Harmison	13	21	4	36	214	12.58	–	–	1
1998	M.M.Betts	11	17	7	29*	125	12.50	–	–	3
–	M.J.Saggers	2	4	2	10	25	12.50	–	–	1
–	N.C.Phillips	15	24	2	35	225	10.22	–	–	6
1998	J.Wood	16	25	3	37	225	10.22	–	–	2
–	S.Lugsden	3	5	2	8*	15	5.00	–	–	1

Also played: S.Chapman (1 match) 2, 11; N.Killeen (2) 12, 0 (2ct); A.Pratt (1) 0, 34 (2 ct); J.P.Searle (1) 0, 0 (1 ct); M.J.Symington did not bat; A.Walker (1) 3*, 2*.

BOWLING

	O	M	R	W	Avge	Best	5wI	10wM
M.J.Foster	113	23	351	17	20.64	4-41	–	–
M.M.Betts	331	76	944	44	21.45	6-83	4	–
N.Killeen	76.2	19	275	10	27.50	5-49	1	–
S.J.Harmison	415.5	85	1400	49	28.57	5-70	1	–
J.Wood	543.5	108	1800	61	29.50	5-52	2	–
P.D.Collingwood	170	42	519	12	43.25	3-89	–	–
N.C.Phillips	360.4	78 1037	1037	23	45.08	5-56	1	–

Also bowled: D.C.Boon 27.4-8-107-1; S.Chapman 29-6-79-0; M.A.Gough 24.2-4-109-1; J.J.B.Lewis 8-0-73-1; S.Lugsden 72.2-6-325-8; M.J.Saggers 58.2-14-149-7; J.P.Searle 20.4-4-92-3; N.J.Speak 2-0-13-0; M.J.Symington 23.2-5-87-3; A.Walker 23.5-5-51-1.

The First-Class Averages (pp 117-131) give the records of Durham players in all first-class county matches (Durham's other opponents being the South Africans and Cambridge University).

DURHAM RECORDS

FIRST-CLASS CRICKET

Highest Total	For 625-6d		v	Derbyshire	Chesterfield	1994
	V 810-4d		by	Warwicks	Birmingham	1994
Lowest Total	For 67		v	Middlesex	Lord's	1996
	V 73		by	Oxford U	Oxford	1994
Highest Innings	For 210*	J.J.B.Lewis	v	Oxford U	Oxford	1997
	V 501*	B.C.Lara	for	Warwicks	Birmingham	1994

Highest Partnership for each Wicket

1st	334*	S.Hutton/M.A.Roseberry	v	Oxford U	Oxford	1996
2nd	206	W.Larkins/D.M.Jones	v	Glamorgan	Cardiff	1992
3rd	205	G.Fowler/S.Hutton	v	Yorkshire	Leeds	1993
4th	204	J.J.B.Lewis/J.Boiling	v	Derbyshire	Chester-le-St[2]	1997
5th	185	P.W.G.Parker/J.A.Daley	v	Warwicks	Darlington	1993
6th	193	D.C.Boon/P.D.Collingwood	v	Warwickshire	Birmingham	1998
7th	110	P.D.Collingwood/M.J.Foster	v	Notts	Nottingham	1998
8th	134	A.C.Cummins/D.A.Graveney	v	Warwicks	Birmingham	1994
9th	127	D.G.C.Ligertwood/S.J.E.Brown	v	Surrey	Stockton	1996
10th	103	M.M.Betts/D.M.Cox	v	Sussex	Hove	1996

Best Bowling	For	9- 64	M.M.Betts	v	Northants	Northampton	1997
(Innings)	V	8- 22	D.Follett	for	Middlesex	Lord's,	1996
Best Bowling	For	14-177	A.Walker	v	Essex	Chelmsford	1995
(Match)	V	12- 68	J.N.B.Bovill	for	Hampshire	Stockton	1995

Most Runs – Season	1536	W.Larkins	(av 37.46)		1992
Most Runs – Career	4878	J.E.Morris	(av 32.95)		1994-98
Most 100s – Season	4	D.M.Jones			1992
	4	W.Larkins			1992
	4	J.E.Morris			1994
Most 100s – Career	12	J.E.Morris			1994-98
Most Wkts – Season	77	S.J.E.Brown	(av 25.87)		1996
Most Wkts – Career	383	S.J.E.Brown	(av 30.31)		1992-98

LIMITED-OVERS CRICKET

Highest Total	NWT	326-4		v	Herefords	Chester-le-St[2]	1995
	BHC	287-5		v	Leics	Leicester	1996
	SL	281-2		v	Derbyshire	Durham	1993
Lowest Total	NWT	82		v	Worcs	Chester-le-St[1]	1968
	BHC	162		v	Derbyshire	Chesterfield	1996
	SL	99		v	Warwicks	Birmingham	1996
Highest Innings	NWT	125	S.Hutton	v	Herefords	Chester-le-St[2]	1995
	BHC	145	J.E.Morris	v	Leics	Leicester	1996
	SL	131*	W.Larkins	v	Hampshire	Portsmouth	1993
Best Bowling	NWT	7-32	S.P.Davis	v	Lancashire	Chester-le-St[1]	1983
	BHC	6-30	S.J.E.Brown	v	Northants	Chester-le-St[2]	1997
	SL	5-23	J.Boiling	v	Notts	Nottingham	1998

[1] Chester-le-Street CC (Ropery Lane)   [2] Riverside Ground

ESSEX

Formation of Present Club: 14 January 1876
Colours: Blue, Gold and Red
Badge: Three Seaxes above Scroll bearing 'Essex'
Championships: (6) 1979, 1983, 1984, 1986, 1991, 1992
NatWest Trophy/Gillette Cup Winners: (2) 1985, 1997
Benson and Hedges Cup Winners: (2) 1979, 1998
Sunday League Champions: (3) 1981, 1984, 1985
Match Awards: NWT 47; BHC 84

Secretary/General Manager: P.J.Edwards
 County Ground, New Writtle Street, Chelmsford CM2 0PG (Tel 01245 252420)
Captain: N.Hussain. **Vice-Captain:** R.C.Irani. **Overseas Player:** S.G.Law.
1999 Beneficiary: N.Hussain. **Scorer:** C.F.Driver

COWAN, Ashley Preston (Framlingham C), b Hitchin, Herts 7 May 1975. 6'4". RHB, RFM. Debut 1995; cap 1997. Cambridgeshire 1993. Tour: WI 1997-98. HS 94 v Leics (Leicester) 1998. 50 wkts (1): 52 (1997). BB 5-45 v Sussex (Hove) 1997. Hat-trick 1996. Award: BHC 1. **NWT:** HS 17* v Notts (Nottingham) 1997. BB 3-29 v Warwks (Lord's) 1997. **BHC:** HS 15* v Yorks (Leeds) 1998. BB 5-28 v Middx (Lord's) 1998. **SL:** HS 40* v Notts (Chelmsford) 1998. BB 4-31 v Middx (Chelmsford) 1997.

FLANAGAN, Ian Nicholas (Colne Community S), b Colchester 5 Jun 1980. 6'0". LHB, OB. Debut 1997. HS 61 v Warwks (Birmingham) 1998.

GRAYSON, Adrian **Paul** (Bedale CS), b Ripon, Yorks 31 Mar 1971. 6'1". RHB, SLA. Yorkshire 1990-95. Essex debut/cap 1996. Tour: SA 1991-92 (Y). 1000 runs (2); most – 1046 (1994). HS 140 v Middx (Lord's) 1996. BB 4-53 v Northants (Northampton) 1997. **NWT:** HS 82* v Worcs (Chelmsford) 1997. BB 3-24 v Lancs (Lord's) 1996. **BHC:** HS 49* v Surrey (Chelmsford) 1997. BB 3-30 v Kent (Chelmsford) 1996. **SL:** HS 69* v Northants (Northampton) 1997. BB 4-25 Y v Glam (Cardiff) 1994.

GROVE, Jamie Oliver (Bury St Edmunds County Upper S), b Bury St Edmunds, Suffolk 3 Jul 1979. 6'1". RHB, RMF. Debut 1998. HS 33 and BB 3-74 v Surrey (Chelmsford) 1998.

HODGSON, Timothy Philip (Wellington C; Durham U), b Guildford, Surrey 27 Mar 1971. Brother of J.S. (Cambridge U 1994); great-nephew of N.A.Knox (Surrey and England 1904-10). 5'10". LHB, RM. Debut 1997. HS 54 v Yorks (Scarborough) 1998. **NWT:** HS 2. **BHC:** (Brit U) HS 113 v Hants (Oxford) 1997. **SL:** HS 21 v Glos (Colchester) 1996.

HUSSAIN, Nasser (Forest S, Snaresbrook; Durham U), b Madras, India 28 Mar 1968. Son of J. (Madras 1966-67); brother of M. (Worcs 1985). 5'11". RHB, LB. Debut 1987; cap 1989; captain 1999; benefit 1999. YC 1989. **Tests:** 39 (1989-90 to 1998-99); HS 207 v A (Birmingham) 1997. **LOI:** 28 (1989-90 to 1998-99, 1 as captain); HS 93. Tours: A 1998-99; WI 1989-90, 1991-92 (Eng A), 1993-94, 1997-98; NZ 1996-97; P 1990-91 (Eng A), 1995-96 (Eng A – captain); SL 1990-91 (Eng A); Z 1996-97. 1000 runs (5); most – 1854 (1995). HS 207 (see *Tests*). Ex HS 197 v Surrey (Oval) 1990. BB 1-38. Awards: NWT 3; BHC 3. **NWT:** HS 108 v Cumb (Chelmsford) 1992. **BHC:** HS 118 Comb U v Somerset (Taunton) 1989. **SL:** HS 83 v Kent (Canterbury) 1995.

HYAM, Barry James (Havering SFC), b Romford 9 Sep 1975. RHB, WK. Debut 1993. MCC YC. HS 49 v P (Chelmsford) 1996. CC HS 26 v Glam (Cardiff) 1997. **SL:** HS 11 v Yorks (Scarborough) 1998.

ILOTT, Mark Christopher (Francis Combe S, Garston), b Watford, Herts 27 Aug 1970. 6'0½". LHB, LFM. Debut 1988; cap 1993. Hertfordshire 1987-88 (at 16, the youngest to represent that county). **Tests:** 5 (1993 to 1995-96); HS 15 v A (Oval) 1993; BB 3-48 v SA (Durban) 1995-96. Tours: A 1992-93 (Eng A); SA 1993-94 (Eng A), 1995-96; I 1994-95 (Eng A – part); SL 1990-91 (Eng A). HS 60 Eng A v Warwks (Birmingham) 1995. Ex HS 58 v Worcs (Worcester) 1996. 50 wkts (6); most – 78 (1995). BB 9-19 (14-105 match; inc hat-trick – all lbw) v Northants (Luton) 1995. Hat-trick 1995. Awards: BHC 2. **NWT:** HS 54* v Cheshire (Chester) 1995. BB 2-23 v Cumb (Chelmsford) 1992 and 2-23 v Cheshire (Chester) 1998. **BHC:** HS 21 v Glam (Chelmsford) 1995. BB 5-21 v Scot (Forfar) 1993. **SL:** HS 56* v Sussex (Hove) 1995. BB 4-15 v Derbys (Derby) 1992.

IRANI, Ronald Charles (Smithills CS, Bolton), b Leigh, Lancs 26 Oct 1971. 6'3". RHB, RMF. Lancashire 1990-93. Essex debut/cap 1994. **Tests:** 2 (1996); HS 41 v I (Lord's) 1996; BB 1-22. **LOI:** 10 (1996 to 1996-97); HS 45*; BB 1-23. Tours: NZ 1996-97; P 1995-96 (Eng A); Z 1996-97. 1000 runs (3); most – 1165 (1995). HS 127* Somerset (Bath) 1996. BB 5-19 Eng A v Comb XI (Karachi) 1995-96. BB 5-27 v Notts (Chelmsford) 1996. Awards: NWT 3; BHC 2. **NWT:** HS 124 v Durham (Chelmsford) 1996. BB 4-41 v Hants (Southampton) 1998. **BHC:** HS 82* v Glam (Chelmsford) 1997. BB 4-30 v Brit U (Chelmsford) 1996. **SL:** HS 101* v Glos (Cheltenham) 1995. BB 4-26 v Glam (Chelmsford) 1998.

LAW, Danny Richard (Steyning GS), b Lambeth, London 15 Jul 1975. 6'5". RHB, RFM. Sussex 1993-96; cap 1996. Essex debut 1997. HS 115 Sx v Young A (Hove) 1995. CC HS 97 Sx v Glos (Bristol) 1996. Ex HS 81 v CU (Cambridge) 1997. BB 5-33 Sx v Durham (Hove) 1996. Ex BB 5-46 (inc hat-trick) v Durham (Chester-le-St) 1998. Hat-trick 1998. **NWT:** HS 47 v Hants (Southampton) 1998. BB 1-2 (Sx). **BHC:** HS 36* v Yorks (Leeds) 1998. BB 1-44 (Sx). **SL:** HS 82 v Durham (Chelmsford) 1997. BB 3-34 Sx v Worcs (Worcester) 1996.

LAW, Stuart Grant (Craigslea State HS), b Herston, Brisbane, Australia 18 Oct 1968. 6'2". RHB, RM/LB. Queensland 1988-89 to date; captain 1994-95 to date. Essex debut/cap 1996. *Wisden* 1997. **Tests** (A): 1 (1995-96); HS 54* v SL (Perth) 1995-96. **LOI** (A): 54 (1994-95 to 1998-99); HS 110; BB 2-22. Tours: E 1995 (Young A); Z 1991-92 (Aus B). 1000 runs (2+1); most – 1545 (1996). HS 179 Q v Tasmania (Brisbane) 1988-89. Ex HS 175 v Leics (Colchester) 1996. BB 5-39 Q v Tasmania (Brisbane) 1995-96. Ex BB 3-27 v Worcs (Chelmsford) 1997. Awards: NWT 4; BHC 1. **NWT:** HS 107 v Hants (Southampton) 1996. BB 2-36 v Devon (Chelmsford) 1996. **BHC:** HS 116 v Somerset (Taunton) 1996. BB 2-13 v Leics (Lord's) 1998. **SL:** HS 126 v Kent (Southend) 1998. BB 4-37 v Worcs (Chelmsford) 1997.

NAPIER, Graham Richard (The Gilberd S, Colchester), b Colchester 6 Jan 1980. 5'9½". RHB, RM. Debut 1997. HS 35* v Notts (Worksop) 1997. BB 2-25 v CU (Cambridge) 1997. CC BB 2-59 v Sussex (Chelmsford) 1998. **BHC:** HS –. **SL:** HS 16 v Lancs (Chelmsford) 1998. BB 3-22 v Derbys (Derby) 1998.

PETERS, Stephen David (Coopers Coborn & Co S), b Harold Wood 10 Dec 1978. 5'9". RHB. Debut 1996 scoring 110 and 12* v CU (Cambridge) 1996. HS 110 (as above). CC HS 64 v Notts (Ilford) 1998. **NWT:** HS 6. **BHC:** HS 58* v Middx (Lord's) 1998. **SL:** HS 54 v Middx (Uxbridge) 1998.

PHILLIPS, Timothy James (Felsted S), b Cambridge 13 Mar 1981. 6'1". LHB, SLA. Staff 1998 – awaiting f-c debut.

POWELL, Jonathan Christopher (Chelmsford C), b Harold Wood 13 Jun 1979. 5'10". RHB, OB. Debut 1997. Tour (Eng A): SL 1997-98. HS (Eng A) 6. Ex HS 4*. BB (Ex) 1-109. **SL:** HS 2. BB 2-10 v Northants (Northampton) 1997.

PRICHARD, Paul John (Brentwood HS), b Billericay 7 Jan 1965. 5'10". RHB, RSM. Debut 1984; cap 1986; captain 1995-98; benefit 1996. Tour (Eng A): A 1992-93. 1000 runs (8); most – 1485 (1992). HS 245 v Leics (Chelmsford) 1990. BB 1-28. Awards: NWT 1; BHC 4. **NWT:** HS 94 v Oxon (Chelmsford) 1985. **BHC:** HS 114 v Somerset (Chelmsford) 1997. **SL:** HS 107 v Notts (Nottingham) 1993.

ROBINSON, Darren David John (Tabor HS, Braintree; Chelmsford CFE), b Braintree 2 Mar 1973. 5'10½". RHB, RMF. Debut 1993; cap 1997. HS 148 v Worcs (Chelmsford) 1997. Awards: BHC 2. **NWT:** HS 62 v Glam (Chelmsford) 1997. **BHC:** HS 137* v Sussex (Hove) 1998. **SL:** HS 129* v Sussex (Chelmsford) 1998. BB 1-7.

ROLLINS, Robert John (Little Ilford CS), b Plaistow 30 Jan 1974. 5'9". RHB, RM, WK. Brother of A.S. (*see DERBYSHIRE*). Debut 1992; cap 1995. HS 133* v Glam (Swansea) 1995. Award: NWT 1. **NWT:** HS 67* v Bucks (Beaconsfield) 1997. **BHC:** HS 28 v Middx (Lord's) 1998. **SL:** HS 38 v Somerset (Chelmsford) 1997.

SUCH, Peter Mark (Harry Carlton CS, Ex Leake, Notts), b Helensburgh, Dunbartonshire 12 Jun 1964. 5'11". RHB, OB. Nottinghamshire 1982-86. Leicestershire 1987-89. Essex debut 1990; cap 1991. **Tests:** 10 (1993 to 1998-99); HS 14* and BB 6-67 v A (Manchester) 1993 – on debut. Tours: A 1992-93 (Eng A), 1998-99; SA 1993-94 (Eng A). HS 54 v Worcs (Chelmsford) 1993 and 54 v Notts (Chelmsford) 1996. 50 wkts (5); most – 82 (1996). BB 8-93 (11-160 match) v Notts (Chelmsford) 1996. **NWT:** HS 8*. BB 3-56 v Durham (Chelmsford) 1996. **BHC:** HS 10* v Glam (Cardiff) 1996. BB 4-43 v Northants (Northampton) 1992. **SL:** HS 19* v Notts (Ilford) 1994. BB 5-29 v Glam (Cardiff) 1997.

NEW REGISTRATIONS

BISHOP, Justin Edward, b Bury St Edmunds 4 Jan 1982. RHB, RFM.
FOSTER, James Savin (Forest S), b Whipps Cross 15 Apr 1980. RHB, WK.
JEFFERSON, William Ingleby, b Derby 25 Oct 1979. RHB, RFM.

RELEASED/RETIRED
(Having made a first-class County appearance in 1998)

BRINKLEY, James Edward (Marist C, Canberra; Trinity C, Perth), b Helensburgh, Scotland 13 Mar 1974. 6'3". RHB, RFM. Worcestershire 1993-94 (Z tour) to 1995. Matabeleland 1994-95. Scotland 1998. Essex (one SL appearance) 1998. Tour: Z 1993-94 (Wo). HS 29 Matabeleland v Mashonaland U-24 (Harare) 1994-95. CC HS 5. BB 6-35 Matabeleland v Mashonaland CD (Harare South) 1994-95. CC BB 6-98 Wo v Surrey (Oval) 1994 on UK debut. **BHC:** HS 30* Scot v Yorks (Linlithgow) 1998. BB 2-35 Wo v Yorks (Leeds) 1997. **SL:** HS 7. BB 2-26 Wo v Hants (Worcester) 1996.

COUSINS, Darren Mark (Netherhall CS; Impington Village C), b Cambridge 24 Sep 1971. 6'2". RHB, RMF. Essex 1993-98. Cambridgeshire 1990. HS 18* v Durham (Chelmsford) 1995. BB 6-35 v CU (Cambridge) 1994. CC BB 3-73 v Leics (Chelmsford) 1995. **NWT:** HS 1*. BB 1-33. **BHC:** HS 12* v Glam (Chelmsford) 1995. BB 1-33. **SL:** HS 6. BB 3-18 v Warwks (Birmingham) 1994.

HIBBERT, Andrew James Edward (St Edward's CS and SFC, Romford), b Harold Wood 17 Dec 1974. 5'11½". RHB, RM. Essex 1995-98. HS 85 v CU (Cambridge) 1996. CC HS 47 v Lancs (Chelmsford) 1998. BB 3-16 v Hants (Portsmouth) 1998. **SL:** HS 25 v Glos (Colchester) 1996.

WILLIAMS, Neil FitzGerald (Acland Burghley CS), b Hope Well, St Vincent 2 Jul 1962. 5'11". RHB, RFM. Middlesex 1982-94; cap 1984; benefit 1994. Essex 1995-98; cap 1996. Windward Is 1982-83 and 1989-90 to 1991-92. Tasmania 1983-84. MCC YC. **Tests:** 1 (1990); HS 38 and BB 2-148 v I (Oval) 1990. Tour: Z 1984-85 (EC). HS 77 M v Warwks (Birmingham) 1991. Ex HS 39 v Worcs (Worcester) 1996. 50 wkts (3); most – 63 (1983). BB 8-75 (12-139 match) M v Glos (Lord's) 1992. Ex BB 5-43 v Glos (Colchester) 1996. Award: BHC 1. **NWT:** HS 11* v Lancs (Lord's) 1996. BB 4-36 M v Derbys (Derby) 1983. **BHC:** HS 29* M v Surrey (Lord's) 1985. BB 3-16 M v Comb U (Cambridge) 1982. **SL:** HS 43 M v Somerset (Lord's) 1988. BB 4-39 M v Surrey (Oval) 1988.

WILSON, Daniel Graeme (St Mary's S, Bishop's Stortford; Cheltenham & Gloucester U), b Paddington, London 18 Feb 1977. RHB, RM. Essex 1997-98. Scored 52* and took 2-40 v SA A (limited-overs match) 1996. HS 14* and BB 1-22 v Durham (Chester-le-St) 1998. **SL:** HS 7*. BB 3-40 v Sussex (Chelmsford) 1996.

ESSEX 1998

RESULTS SUMMARY

	Place	Won	Lost	Tied	Drew	No Result
Britannic Assurance Championship	18th	2	11		4	
All First-Class Matches		2	11		5	
NatWest Trophy	2nd Round					
Benson and Hedges Cup	Winners					
Sunday League	3rd	9	5	1		2

BRITANNIC ASSURANCE CHAMPIONSHIP AVERAGES
BATTING AND FIELDING

Cap		M	I	NO	HS	Runs	Avge	100	50	Ct/St
1996	S.G.Law	14	26	2	165	982	40.91	2	3	19
1994	R.C.Irani	17	32	2	127*	968	32.26	2	2	6
1989	N.Hussain	5	9	–	68	244	27.11	–	2	7
–	I.N.Flanagan	5	10	–	61	248	24.80	–	2	9
–	S.D.Peters	13	23	2	64	484	23.04	–	3	7
1991	P.M.Such	15	24	17	25	133	19.00	–	–	5
–	D.R.Law	14	25	–	66	466	18.64	–	3	10
–	A.J.E.Hibbert	2	4	–	47	72	18.00	–	–	2
–	B.J.Hyam	9	18	3	47*	269	17.93	–	–	31/2
1996	N.F.Williams	8	15	6	36	161	17.88	–	–	2
1997	D.D.J.Robinson	13	24	–	85	429	17.87	–	1	11
1997	A.P.Cowan	8	13	–	94	228	17.53	–	2	4
1996	A.P.Grayson	16	30	–	59	507	16.90	–	4	9
–	T.P.Hodgson	6	12	–	54	190	15.83	–	1	3
–	J.O.Grove	4	7	1	33	88	14.66	–	–	–
1995	R.J.Rollins	8	12	–	42	171	14.25	–	–	13
1986	P.J.Prichard	10	18	–	24	237	13.16	–	–	7
1993	M.C.Ilott	16	29	4	38	281	11.24	–	–	3

Also batted: D.M.Cousins (1 match) 8, 6; G.R.Napier (2) 4, 7, 4; D.G.Wilson (1) 14, 14*.

BOWLING

	O	M	R	W	Avge	Best	5wI	10wM
M.C.Ilott	486.5	131	1293	56	23.08	6-20	2	–
N.F.Williams	227.5	45	763	26	29.34	4-42	–	–
R.C.Irani	431.5	102	1348	40	33.70	5-47	1	–
D.R.Law	247.5	34	1045	29	36.03	5-46	1	–
P.M.Such	503	129	1398	38	36.78	5-73	2	–
A.P.Grayson	234.2	58	674	18	37.44	3-13	–	–
A.P.Cowan	238.3	54	859	19	45.21	3-18	–	–

Also bowled: D.M.Cousins 15-5-52-1; I.N.Flanagan 1-0-1-0; J.O.Grove 74.1-8-347-9; A.J.E.Hibbert 11.3-3-29-3; G.R.Napier 17-4-72-2; D.G.Wilson 10-2-38-1.

The First-Class Averages (pp 117-131) give the records of Essex players in all first-class county matches (Essex's other opponents being the South Africans), with the exception of N.Hussain, whose full county figures are as above.

ESSEX RECORDS

FIRST-CLASS CRICKET

Highest Total	For	761-6d	v	Leics	Chelmsford	1990
	V	803-4d	by	Kent	Brentwood	1934
Lowest Total	For	30	v	Yorkshire	Leyton	1901
	V	14	by	Surrey	Chelmsford	1983
Highest Innings	For	343*	P.A.Perrin	v	Derbyshire	Chesterfield	1904
	V	332	W.H.Ashdown	for	Kent	Brentwood	1934

Highest Partnership for each Wicket

1st	316	G.A.Gooch/P.J.Prichard	v	Kent	Chelmsford	1994
2nd	403	G.A.Gooch/P.J.Prichard	v	Leics	Chelmsford	1990
3rd	347*	M.E.Waugh/N.Hussain	v	Lancashire	Ilford	1992
4th	314	Salim Malik/N.Hussain	v	Surrey	The Oval	1991
5th	316	N.Hussain/M.A.Garnham	v	Leics	Leicester	1991
6th	206	J.W.H.T.Douglas/J.O'Connor	v	Glos	Cheltenham	1923
	206	B.R.Knight/R.A.G.Luckin	v	Middlesex	Brentwood	1962
7th	261	J.W.H.T.Douglas/J.Freeman	v	Lancashire	Leyton	1914
8th	263	D.R.Wilcox/R.M.Taylor	v	Warwicks	Southend	1946
9th	251	J.W.H.T.Douglas/S.N.Hare	v	Derbyshire	Leyton	1921
10th	218	F.H.Vigar/T.P.B.Smith	v	Derbyshire	Chesterfield	1947

Best Bowling	For	10- 32	H.Pickett	v	Leics	Leyton	1895
(Innings)	V	10- 40	E.G.Dennett	for	Glos	Bristol	1906
Best Bowling	For	17-119	W.Mead	v	Hampshire	Southampton	1895
(Match)	V	17- 56	C.W.L.Parker	for	Glos	Gloucester	1925

Most Runs – Season	2559	G.A.Gooch	(av 67.34)		1984
Most Runs – Career	30701	G.A.Gooch	(av 51.77)		1973-97
Most 100s – Season	9	J.O'Connor			1934
	9	D.J.Insole			1955
Most 100s – Career	94	G.A.Gooch			1973-97
Most Wkts – Season	172	T.P.B.Smith	(av 27.13)		1947
Most Wkts – Career	1610	T.P.B.Smith	(av 26.68)		1929-51

LIMITED-OVERS CRICKET

Highest Total	NWT	386-5		v	Wiltshire	Chelmsford	1988
	BHC	388-7		v	Scotland	Chelmsford	1992
	SL	310-5		v	Glamorgan	Southend	1983
Lowest Total	NWT	57		v	Lancashire	Lord's	1996
	BHC	61		v	Lancashire	Chelmsford	1992
	SL	69		v	Derbyshire	Chesterfield	1974
Highest Innings	NWT	144	G.A.Gooch	v	Hampshire	Chelmsford	1990
	BHC	198*	G.A.Gooch	v	Sussex	Hove	1982
	SL	176	G.A.Gooch	v	Glamorgan	Southend	1983
Best Bowling	NWT	5- 8	J.K.Lever	v	Middlesex	Westcliff	1972
		5- 8		v	Cheshire	Chester	1995
	BHC	5-13	J.K.Lever	v	Middlesex	Lord's	1985
	SL	8-26	K.D.Boyce	v	Lancashire	Manchester	1971

GLAMORGAN

Formation of Present Club: 6 July 1888
Colours: Blue and Gold
Badge: Gold Daffodil
Championships: (3) 1948, 1969, 1997
NatWest Trophy/Gillette Cup Winners: (0) Finalists 1977
Benson and Hedges Cup Winners: (0) Semi-Finalists 1988
Sunday League Champions: (1) 1993
Match Awards: NWT 40; BHC 51

Secretary: G.R.Stone. **Cricket Secretary:** M.J.Fatkin
 Sophia Gardens, Cardiff, CF1 9XR (Tel 01222 343478)
Captain: M.P.Maynard. **Vice-Captain:** S.P.James. **Overseas Player:** J.H.Kallis.
1999 Beneficiary: None. **Scorer:** B.T.Denning

CHERRY, Daniel David (Tonbridge S; U of Wales, Swansea), b Newport, Gwent 7 Feb 1980. 5'9". LHB, RM. Debut 1998. HS 11 v Derbys (Cardiff) 1998 – on debut.

COSKER, Dean Andrew (Millfield S), b Weymouth, Dorset 7 Jan 1978. 5'11". RHB, SLA. Debut 1996. Tours (Eng A): SA 1998-99, SL 1997-98; Z 1998-99, K 1997-98. HS 37 v Essex (Chelmsford) 1998. BB 6-140 v Lancs (Colwyn Bay) 1998. **NWT:** HS 4*. BB 3-26 v Yorks (Cardiff) 1997. **BHC:** HS 1*. BB 2-26 v Ire (Dublin) 1998. **SL:** HS 19 v Surrey (Swansea) 1998. BB 3-18 v Warwks (Birmingham) 1998.

CROFT, Robert Damien Bale (St John Lloyd Catholic CS; W Glam IHE), b Morriston 25 May 1970. 5'10½". RHB, OB. Debut 1989; cap 1992. **Tests:** 15 (1996 to 1998-99); HS 37* v SA (Manchester) 1998; BB 5-95 v NZ (Christchurch) 1996-97. **LOI:** 40 (1996 to 1998-99); HS 32; BB 3-51. Tours: A 1998-99; SA 1993-94 (Eng A), 1995-96 (Gm); WI 1991-92 (Eng A), 1997-98; NZ 1996-97; Z 1990-91 (Gm), 1994-95 (Gm), 1996-97 (Gm). HS 143 v Somerset (Taunton) 1995. 50 wkts (5); most – 76 (1996). BB 8-66 (14-169 match) v Warwks (Swansea) 1992. Awards: NWT 1; BHC 1. **NWT:** HS 64 v Beds (Cardiff) 1997. BB 3-30 v Lincs (Swansea) 1998. **BHC:** HS 77 v Essex (Cardiff) 1998. BB 4-30 v Essex (Cardiff) 1996. **SL:** HS 68 v Northants (Northampton) 1998. BB 6-20 v Worcs (Cardiff) 1994.

DALE, Adrian (Chepstow CS; Swansea U), b Germiston, SA 24 Oct 1968 (to UK at 6 mths). 5'11½". RHB, RM. Debut 1989; cap 1992. Tours (Gm): SA 1993-94 (Eng A), 1995-96; Z 1990-91, 1994-95. 1000 runs (3); most – 1472 (1993). HS 214* v Middx (Cardiff) 1993. BB 6-18 v Warwks (Cardiff) 1993. Awards: NWT 2; BHC 2. **NWT:** HS 110 v Lincs (Swansea) 1994. BB 3-54 v Worcs (Swansea) 1993. **BHC:** HS 100 v Middx (Cardiff) 1997. BB 5-41 v Middx (Lord's) 1996. **SL:** HS 82 v Derbys (Cardiff) 1998. BB 6-22 v Durham (Colwyn Bay) 1993.

DAVIES, Andrew Philip (Dwr-y-Felin CS; Christ C, Brecon), b Neath 7 Nov 1976. 5'11". LHB, RMF. Debut 1995. Wales (MC). HS 34 v Essex (Chelmsford) 1998. BB 2-22 v Sussex (Hove) 1998. **SL:** HS 18 v Essex (Chelmsford) 1998. BB 2-17 v Warwks (Birmingham) 1998.

DAWOOD, Ismail (Batley GS), b Dewsbury, Yorks 23 Jul 1976. 5'8". RHB, WK. Northamptonshire 1994. Worcestershire 1996-97. Glamorgan debut 1998. HS 40 v Somerset (Cardiff) 1998. **SL:** HS 57 v Essex (Chelmsford) 1998.

EVANS, Alun Wyn (Fishguard SS; Neath Tertiary C), b Glanamman, Dyfed 20 Aug 1975. 5'8". RHB, RM. Debut 1996 v OU (Oxford), scoring 66* and 71*. MCC YC. HS 125 v CU (Cambridge) 1998. CC HS 87 v Hants (Southampton) 1998. **BHC:** HS 14 v Middx (Cardiff) 1998. **SL:** HS 50* v Glos (Bristol) 1996.

JAMES, Stephen Peter (Monmouth S; Swansea U; Hughes Hall, Cambridge), b Lydney, Glos 7 Sep 1967. 6'0". RHB. Debut 1985; cap 1992. Cambridge U 1989-90; blue 1989-90. Mashonaland 1993-94 to date. **Tests**: 2 (1998); HS 36 v SL (Oval) 1998. Tours: SA 1995-96 (Gm); SL 1997-98; Z 1990-91 (Gm); K 1997-98. 1000 runs (6); most – 1775 (1997). HS 235 v Notts (Worksop) 1996. Awards: NWT 2; BHC 2. **NWT:** HS 123 v Lincs (Swansea) 1994. **BHC:** HS 135 v Comb U (Cardiff) 1992. **SL:** HS 107 v Sussex (Llanelli) 1993.

JONES, Simon Philip (Coedcae CS; Millfield S), b Swansea 25 Dec 1978. Son of I.J. (Glamorgan and England 1960-68). 6'3½". LHB, RF. Debut 1998. HS 2* and BB 3-94 v Yorks (Cardiff) 1998.

LAW, Wayne Lincoln (Graig CS; Graig SFC, Llanelli), b Swansea 4 Sep 1978. 5'11". RHB, OB. Debut 1997 – awaiting CC debut. MCC YC. HS 131 v Lancs (Colwyn Bay) 1998. BB 2-29 v CU (Cambridge) 1998. CC BB 1-31. **SL:** HS 24 v Leics (Pontypridd) 1998.

MAYNARD, Matthew Peter (David Hughes S, Anglesey), b Oldham, Lancs 21 Mar 1966. 5'10½". RHB, RM. Debut 1985 v Yorks (Swansea), scoring 102 out of 117 in 87 min, reaching 100 with 3 sixes off successive balls; cap 1987; captain 1996 to date; benefit 1996. *Wisden* 1997. N Districts 1990-91/1991-92. Otago 1996-97/1997-98. YC 1988. **Tests:** 4 (1988 to 1993-94); HS 35 v WI (Kingston) 1993-94. **LOI:** 10 (1993-94 to 1996); HS 41. Tours: SA 1989-90 (Eng XI), 1995-96 (Gm – captain); WI 1993-94; Z 1994-95 (Gm). 1000 runs (11); most – 1803 (1991). HS 243 v Hants (Southampton) 1991. BB 3-21 v OU (Oxford) 1987. CC BB 1-3. Awards: NWT 4; BHC 7. **NWT:** HS 151* v Durham (Darlington) 1991. **BHC:** HS 151* v Middx (Lord's) 1996. **SL:** HS 132 v Surrey (Oval) 1997.

PARKIN, Owen Thomas (Bournemouth GS, Bath U), b Coventry, Warwks 24 Sep 1972. 6'2". RHB, RFM. Dorset 1992. Debut 1994. HS 24* v Essex (Chelmsford) 1998. BB 5-24 v Somerset (Cardiff) 1998. **NWT:** HS 2. BB 3-23 v Worcs (Cardiff) 1996. **BHC:** HS 8 and BB 3-42 v Somerset (Taunton) 1997. **SL:** HS 2. BB 5-28 v Sussex (Hove) 1996.

POWELL, Michael John (Crickhowell HS; Pontypool CFE), b Abergavenny 3 Feb 1977. 6'1". RHB, RSM. Debut 1997 scoring 200* v OU (Oxford). HS 200 (*see above*). CC HS 106 v Northants (Northampton) 1998. **NWT:** HS 11 v Leics (Cardiff) 1998. **SL:** HS 55 v Derbys (Cardiff) 1998.

SHAW, Adrian David (Neath Tertiary C), b Neath 17 Feb 1972. 5'11". RHB, WK. Wales (MC) 1990-92. Debut 1994. HS 74 v Surrey (Cardiff) 1996. **NWT:** HS 47 v Beds (Cardiff) 1998. **BHC:** HS 25 v Sussex (Hove) 1998. **SL:** HS 48 v Glos (Swansea) 1997.

THOMAS, Ian James (Bassaleg CS), b Newport, Gwent 9 May 1979. 5'11". LHB, OB. Debut 1998. Non-contracted player awaiting CC debut. HS 9*.

THOMAS, Stuart Darren (Graig CS, Llanelli; Neath Tertiary C), b Morriston 25 Jan 1975. 6'0". LHB, RFM. Debut v Derbys (Chesterfield) 1992, taking 5-80 when aged 17yr 217d; cap 1997. Tours (Eng A): SA 1995-96 (Gm), 1998-99; Z 1994-95 (Gm), 1998-99. HS 78* v Glos (Abergavenny) 1995. 50 wkts (2); most – 71 (1998). BB 5-24 v Sussex (Swansea) 1997. Award: BHC 1. **NWT:** HS 28* v Beds (Cardiff) 1998. BB 5-74 v Essex (Chelmsford) 1997. **BHC:** HS 29 v Middx (Cardiff) 1998. BB 6-20 v Comb U (Cardiff) 1995. **SL:** HS 21 v Somerset (Cardiff) 1998 and 21 v Essex (Chelmsford) 1998. BB 7-16 v Surrey (Swansea) 1998.

TOMLINSON, Steven Charles Benjamin (Oratory S; U of Wales Institute), b Bridgetown, Barbados 21 Dec 1978. 5'11". RHB, RMF. Non-contracted player awaiting f-c debut. **SL:** HS 2.

WATKIN, Steven Llewellyn (Cymer Afan CS; S Glamorgan CHE), b Maesteg 15 Sep 1964. 6'3". RHB, RMF. Debut 1986; cap 1989. Benefit 1998. *Wisden* 1993. **Tests:** 3 (1991 to 1993); HS 13 and BB 4-65 v A (Oval) 1993. **LOI:** 4 (1993-94); HS 4; BB 4-49. Tours: SA 1995-96 (Gm); WI 1991-92 (Eng A), 1993-94; P 1990-91 (Eng A); Z 1989-90 (Eng A), 1990-91 (Gm), 1994-95 (Gm). HS 41 v Worcs (Worcester) 1992. 50 wkts (9); most – 94 (1989). BB 8-59 v Warwks (Birmingham) 1988. Awards: NWT 1; BHC 1. **NWT:** HS 13 v Worcs (Cardiff) 1996. BB 4-26 v Middx (Cardiff) 1995. **BHC:** HS 15 v Hants (Southampton) 1991. BB 4-31 v Kent (Canterbury) 1996. **SL:** HS 31* v Derbys (Checkley) 1991. BB 5-23 v Warwks (Birmingham) 1990.

NEW REGISTRATIONS

DAVIES, Adam James, b Cardiff 26 Oct 1980. RHB, RMF.

HARRISON, David Stuart, b Newport, Gwent 31 Jul 1981. RHB, RM.

HUGHES, Jonathan (Coed-y-Lan CS, Pontypridd), b Pontypridd 30 Jun 1981. RHB, RM.

KALLIS, Jacques Henry (Wynberg HS), b Pinelands, SA 16 Oct 1975. RHB, RMF. Western Province 1993-94 to date. Middlesex 1997; cap 1997. **Tests** (SA): 24 (1996-97 to 1998-99); HS 132 v E (Manchester) 1998; BB 5-90 v WI (Cape Town) 1998-99. **LOI** (SA): 58 (1995-96 to 1998-99); HS 113*; BB 5-30. Tours: E 1996 (SA A), 1998; A 1995-96 (WP), 1997-98; NZ 1998-99; P 1997-98; SL 1995-96 (SA U-24). 1000 runs (1): 1034 (1997). HS 186* WP v Queensland (Brisbane) 1995-96. UK HS 172* M v Worcs (Kidderminster) 1997. BB 5-54 M v Kent (Lord's) 1997. Award: NWT 1. **NWT:** HS 100 and BB 4-47 M v Glos (Uxbridge) 1997. **BHC:** HS 72 M v Glam (Cardiff) 1997. BB 2-49 M v Somerset (Lord's) 1997. **SL:** HS 24 M v Leics (Lord's) 1997. BB 2-19 M v Sussex (Lord's) 1997.

NEWELL, Keith (Ifield Community C), b Crawley, Sussex 25 Mar 1972. Brother of M. (Sussex 1996-98). 6'0". RHB, RM. Sussex 1995-98. Matabeleland 1995-96. HS 135 Sx v WI (Hove) 1995. CC HS 112 and BB 4-61 Sx v Kent (Horsham) 1997. **NWT:** HS 52 Sx v Derbys (Hove) 1995. BB 1-61. **BHC:** HS 62* Sx v Middx (Lord's) 1998. BB 1-25. **SL:** HS 97 and BB 5-33 Sx v Worcs (Worcester) 1998.

WALLACE, Mark Alexander, b Crickhowell, Powys 19 Nov 1981. LHB, WK.

RELEASED/RETIRED
(Having made a first-class County appearance in 1998)

BUTCHER, G.P. – *see SURREY*.

COTTEY, P.A. – *see SUSSEX*.

WAQAR YOUNIS (Government C, Vehari), b Vehari, Pakistan 16 Nov 1969. 6'0". RHB, RF. Multan 1987-88 to 1990-91. United Bank 1988-89 to date. Surrey 1990-91 and 1993; cap 1990. Glamorgan 1997-98; cap 1998. *Wisden* 1991. **Tests** (P): 55 (1989-90 to 1998-99, 1 as captain); HS 45 v SA (Rawalpindi) 1997-98; BB 7-76 v NZ (Faisalabad) 1990-91. **LOI** (P): 172 (1989-90 to 1998-99, 1 as captain); HS 37; BB 6-26. Tours (P): E 1992, 1996; A 1989-90, 1995-96; SA 1997-98; WI 1992-93; NZ 1992-93, 1993-94, 1995-96; I 1998-99; SL 1994-95. HS 55 P v Natal (Durban) 1994-95. CC HS 47 Gm v Kent (Canterbury) 1997.50 wkts (4+1) inc 100 (1): 113 (1991). BB 8-17 Gm v Sussex (Swansea) 1997. Hat-trick 1997. Awards: NWT 3. **NWT:** HS 34* Gm v Yorks (Cardiff) 1997. BB 5-40 Sy v Northants (Oval) 1991. **BHC:** HS 45 and BB 4-43 Gm v Sussex (Hove) 1998. **SL:** HS 39 Sy v Hants (Oval) 1993. BB 5-26 Sy v Kent (Oval) 1990.

GLAMORGAN 1998

RESULTS SUMMARY

	Place	Won	Lost	Tied	Drew	No Result
Britannic Assurance Championship	13th	4	6		7	
All First-Class Matches		6	6		7	
NatWest Trophy		2nd Round				
Benson and Hedges Cup		3rd in Group D				
Sunday League	10th	7	8			2

BRITANNIC ASSURANCE CHAMPIONSHIP AVERAGES

BATTING AND FIELDING

Cap		M	I	NO	HS	Runs	Avge	100	50	Ct/St
1992	S.P.James	13	24	1	227	1268	55.13	4	5	9
–	W.L.Law	7	11	1	131	414	41.40	1	2	2
–	M.J.Powell	14	23	2	106	783	37.28	1	5	8
1989	S.L.Watkin	12	15	12	25*	107	35.66	–	–	4
1992	P.A.Cottey	17	28	2	123	901	34.65	2	4	17
1992	A.Dale	17	30	1	92	969	33.41	–	8	9
1987	M.P.Maynard	16	27	2	94	672	26.88	–	4	20
1997	S.D.Thomas	17	25	3	74	492	22.36	–	3	10
–	A.W.Evans	7	13	1	87	261	21.75	–	1	5
1992	R.D.B.Croft	9	14	3	63*	222	20.18	–	1	8
–	I.Dawood	6	10	1	40	168	18.66	–	–	16/1
–	G.P.Butcher	8	12	1	85	186	16.90	–	1	4
–	A.P.Davies	4	5	1	34	54	13.50	–	–	–
–	A.D.Shaw	10	15	1	51	177	12.64	–	1	24
–	O.T.Parkin	10	13	4	24*	85	9.44	–	–	2
–	D.A.Cosker	13	20	3	37	123	7.23	–	–	10
1997	Waqar Younis	4	6	–	15	39	6.50	–	–	1

Also batted: D.D.Cherry (1 match) 11; S.P.Jones (2) 0*, 0*, 2* (1 ct).

BOWLING

	O	M	R	W	Avge	Best	5wI	10wM
S.L.Watkin	346.4	96	866	39	22.20	5- 30	1	–
O.T.Parkin	276.3	69	699	31	22.54	5- 24	2	–
S.D.Thomas	525.1	92	1687	66	25.56	5- 84	3	–
A.P.Davies	124.5	37	369	13	28.38	2- 22	–	–
G.P.Butcher	132	18	494	15	32.93	4- 22	–	–
Waqar Younis	100.1	13	397	12	33.08	3-147	–	–
A.Dale	217.1	38	696	21	33.14	3- 23	–	–
D.A.Cosker	429.5	114	1126	32	35.18	6-140	1	–
R.D.B.Croft	352.5	91	895	19	47.10	4- 76	–	–

Also bowled: P.A.Cottey 40-9-92-3; S.P.Jones 63-8-261-5; W.L.Law 14-1-50-1; M.P.Maynard 5.4-0-46-0; M.J.Powell 0.2-0-8-0; A.D.Shaw 1-0-7-0.

The First-Class Averages (pp 117-131) give the records of Glamorgan players in all first-class county matches (Glamorgan's other opponents being the Sri Lankans and Cambridge University), with the exception of S.P.James, whose full county figures are as above, and:
R.D.B.Croft 10-16-3-63*-253-19.46-0-1-8. 366.5-97-933-20-46.65-4/76.

GLAMORGAN RECORDS

FIRST-CLASS CRICKET

Highest Total	For 597-8d		v	Durham	Cardiff	1997
	V 712		by	Northants	Northampton	1998
Lowest Total	For 22		v	Lancashire	Liverpool	1924
	V 33		by	Leics	Ebbw Vale	1965
Highest Innings	For 287*	D.E.Davies	v	Glos	Newport	1939
	V 322*	M.B.Loye	for	Northants	Northampton	1998

Highest Partnership for each Wicket

1st	330	A.Jones/R.C.Fredericks	v	Northants	Swansea	1972
2nd	249	S.P.James/H.Morris	v	Oxford U	Oxford	1987
3rd	313	D.E.Davies/W.E.Jones	v	Essex	Brentwood	1948
4th	425*	A.Dale/I.V.A.Richards	v	Middlesex	Cardiff	1993
5th	264	M.Robinson/S.W.Montgomery	v	Hampshire	Bournemouth	1949
6th	230	W.E.Jones/B.L.Muncer	v	Worcs	Worcester	1953
7th	211	P.A.Cottey/O.D.Gibson	v	Leics	Swansea	1996
8th	202	D.Davies/J.J.Hills	v	Sussex	Eastbourne	1928
9th	203*	J.J.Hills/J.C.Clay	v	Worcs	Swansea	1929
10th	143	T.Davies/S.A.B.Daniels	v	Glos	Swansea	1982

Best Bowling	For	10- 51	J.Mercer	v	Worcs	Worcester	1936
(Innings)	V	10- 18	G.Geary	for	Leics	Pontypridd	1929
Best Bowling	For	17-212	J.C.Clay	v	Worcs	Swansea	1937
(Match)	V	16- 96	G.Geary	for	Leics	Pontypridd	1929

Most Runs – Season	2276	H.Morris	(av 55.51)	1990
Most Runs – Career	34056	A.Jones	(av 33.03)	1957-83
Most 100s – Season	10	H.Morris		1990
Most 100s – Career	52	A.Jones		1957-83
	52	H.Morris		1981-97
Most Wkts – Season	176	J.C.Clay	(av 17.34)	1937
Most Wkts – Career	2174	D.J.Shepherd	(av 20.95)	1950-72

LIMITED-OVERS CRICKET

Highest Total	NWT	373-7		v	Beds	Cardiff	1998
	BHC	318-3		v	Combined U	Cardiff	1995
	SL	287-8		v	Middlesex	Cardiff	1993
Lowest Total	NWT	76		v	Northants	Northampton	1968
	BHC	68		v	Lancashire	Manchester	1973
	SL	42		v	Derbyshire	Swansea	1979
Highest Innings	NWT	162*	I.V.A.Richards	v	Oxfordshire	Swansea	1993
	BHC	151*	M.P.Maynard	v	Middlesex	Lord's	1996
	SL	132	M.P.Maynard	v	Surrey	The Oval	1997
Best Bowling	NWT	5-13	R.J.Shastri	v	Scotland	Edinburgh	1988
	BHC	6-20	S.D.Thomas	v	Comb Us	Cardiff	1995
	SL	7-16	S.D.Thomas	v	Surrey	Swansea	1998

GLOUCESTERSHIRE

Formation of Present Club: 1871
Colours: Blue, Gold, Brown, Silver, Green and Red
Badge: Coat of Arms of the City and County of Bristol
Championships (since 1890): (0) Second 1930, 1931, 1947, 1959, 1969, 1986
NatWest Trophy/Gillette Cup Winners: (1) 1973
Benson and Hedges Cup Winners: (1) 1977
Sunday League Champions: (0) Second 1988
Match Awards: NWT 43; BHC 56

Chief Executive: C.Sextone.
County Ground, Nevil Road, Bristol BS7 9EJ (Tel 0117 910 8000)
Captain: M.W.Alleyne. **Vice-Captain:** tba. **Overseas Player:** I.J.Harvey (tbc).
1999 Beneficiary: M.W.Alleyne. **Scorer:** K.T.Gerrish

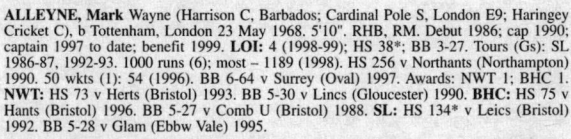

ALLEYNE, Mark Wayne (Harrison C, Barbados; Cardinal Pole S, London E9; Haringey Cricket C), b Tottenham, London 23 May 1968. 5'10". RHB, RM. Debut 1986; cap 1990; captain 1997 to date; benefit 1999. **LOI:** 4 (1998-99); HS 38*; BB 3-27. Tours (Gs): SL 1986-87, 1992-93. 1000 runs (6); most – 1189 (1998). HS 256 v Northants (Northampton) 1990. 50 wkts (1): 54 (1996). BB 6-64 v Surrey (Oval) 1997. Awards: NWT 1; BHC 1. **NWT:** HS 73 v Herts (Bristol) 1993. BB 5-30 v Lincs (Gloucester) 1990. **BHC:** HS 75 v Hants (Bristol) 1996. BB 5-27 v Comb U (Bristol) 1988. **SL:** HS 134* v Leics (Bristol) 1992. BB 5-28 v Glam (Ebbw Vale) 1995.

AVERIS, James Maxwell Michael (Cathedral S, Bristol; Portsmouth U; St Cross C, Oxford), b Bristol 28 May 1974. 5'11". RHB, RMF. Oxford U 1997; blue 1997; rugby blue 1996-97. Gloucestershire debut 1997. HS 42 OU v Durham (Oxford) 1997 – on debut. Gs HS 6*. BB 5-98 OU v Hants (Oxford) 1997. Gs BB 2-40 v SA (Bristol) 1998. **SL:** HS 2*. BB 2-33 v Notts (Nottingham) 1998.

BALL, Martyn Charles John (King Edmund SS; Bath CFE), b Bristol 26 Apr 1970. 5'8". RHB, OB. Debut 1988; cap 1996. Tour (Gs): SL 1992-93. HS 71 v Notts (Bristol) 1993. BB 8-46 (14-169 match) v Somerset (Taunton) 1993. **NWT:** HS 31 v Lincs (Sleaford) 1996. BB 3-42 v Lancs (Gloucester) 1989. **BHC:** HS 28 v Hants (Southampton) 1997. BB 4-23 v Brit U (Bristol) 1998. **SL:** HS 36* v Northants (Cheltenham) 1998. BB 4-26 v Glam (Swansea) 1997.

CAWDRON, Michael John (Cheltenham C), b Luton, Beds 7 Oct 1974. 6'2". LHB, RM. Staff 1994 – awaiting f-c debut. **BHC:** HS 5*. BB 4-28 v Hants (Bristol) 1998. **SL:** HS 50 v Essex (Cheltenham) 1995. BB 2-46 v Surrey (Cheltenham) 1998.

CHURCH, Matthew John (St George's C, Weybridge), b Guildford, Surrey 26 Jul 1972. 6'2". RHB, RM. Worcestershire 1994-96. Gloucestershire debut 1997. MCC YC. HS 152 and BB 4-50 Wo v OU (Oxford) 1996. Gs HS 53 v Pak A (Bristol) 1997. CC HS 38 Wo v Yorks (Worcester) 1994. CC BB 2-27 Wo v Yorks (Worcester) 1996. Award: BHC 1. **NWT:** HS 35 Wo v Hants (Worcester) 1996. **BHC:** HS 64* v Hants (Bristol) 1998. **SL:** HS 25 v Warwks (Birmingham) 1997 and 25 v Kent (Bristol) 1998.

CUNLIFFE, Robert John (Banbury C; Banbury TC), b Oxford 8 Nov 1973. 5'10". RHB, RM. Debut 1994. Oxfordshire 1991-94. HS 190* v OU (Bristol) 1995. CC HS 92* v Lancs (Cheltenham) 1998. Awards: BHC 2. **NWT:** HS 40 v Durham (Chester-le-St) 1995. **BHC:** HS 137* v Surrey (Oval) 1996. **SL:** HS 56 v Yorks (Leeds) 1997.

DAWSON, Robert Ian (Millfield S; Newcastle Poly), b Exmouth, Devon 29 Mar 1970. 5'11". RHB, RM. Debut 1992. Devon 1988-91. 1000 runs (1): 1112 (1994). HS 127* v CU (Bristol) 1994. CC HS 101 v Worcs (Gloucester) 1995. BB 3-15 v Lancs (Manchester) 1998. **NWT:** HS 60 v Devon (Bristol) 1994. BB 1-37. **BHC:** HS 38 v Middx (Bristol) and v Somerset (Bristol) 1995. **SL:** HS 85 v Worcs (Worcester) 1996. BB 1-19.

GANNON, Benjamin Ward (Dragon S, Oxford; Abingdon S; Cheltenham & Gloucester CHE), b Oxford 5 Sep 1975. 6'3". RHB, RMF. Herefordshire 1996. Awaiting f-c debut.

HANCOCK, Timothy Harold Coulter (St Edward's S, Oxford; Henley C), b Reading, Berks 20 Apr 1972. 5'10". RHB, RM. Debut 1991; cap 1998. Oxfordshire 1990. Tour: SL 1992-93 (Gs). 1000 runs (1): 1227 (1998). HS 220* v Notts (Nottingham) 1998. BB 3-5 v Essex (Colchester) 1998. Award: NWT 1. **NWT:** HS 60 v Northants (Bristol) 1998. BB 6-58 v Scot (Bristol) 1997. **BHC:** HS 71* v Sussex (Bristol) 1996. BB 3-13 v Hants (Bristol) 1996. **SL:** HS 73 v Notts (Nottingham) 1998. BB 3-18 v Durham (Chester-le-St) 1998.

HEWSON, Dominic Robert (Cheltenham C), b Cheltenham 3 Oct 1974. 5'8". RHB, occ RM. Debut 1996. HS 87 v Hants (Southampton) 1996 (on CC debut). BB 1-7. **NWT:** HS 45 v Northants (Bristol) 1998. **SL:** HS 25 v Lancs (Manchester) 1998.

LEWIS, Jonathan (Churchfields S, Swindon; Swindon C), b Aylesbury, Bucks 26 Aug 1975. 6'2". RHB, RMF. Debut 1995; cap 1998. Wiltshire 1993. Northamptonshire staff 1994. HS 54* and BB 6-48 v Derbys (Chesterfield) 1998. 50 wkts (2); most – 59 (1998). Award: BHC 1. **NWT:** HS 6*. BB 3-27 v Somerset (Taunton) 1998. **BHC:** HS 33* v Somerset (Bristol) 1998. BB 3-31 v Ireland (Dublin) 1996. **SL:** HS 26* v Leics (Bristol) 1998. BB 3-27 v Warwks (Birmingham) 1995.

RUSSELL, Robert Charles (*'Jack'*) (Archway CS), b Stroud 15 Aug 1963. 5'8½". LHB, WK, occ OB. Debut 1981 – youngest Glos wicket-keeper (17yr 307d), setting record for most match dismissals on f-c debut – 8 v SL (Bristol); cap 1985; benefit 1994; captain 1995. *Wisden* 1989. MBE 1996. **Tests:** 54 (1988 to 1997-98); HS 128* v A (Manchester) 1989; 11 ct v SA (Jo'burg) 1995-96 (Test record); 27 dis 1995-96 series v SA (Eng record). **LOI:** 40 (1987-88 to 1998-99); HS 50. Tours: A 1990-91, 1992-93 (Eng A); SA 1995-96; WI 1989-90, 1993-94, 1997-98; NZ 1991-92, 1996-97; P 1987-88; SL 1986-87 (Gs). 1000 runs (1): 1049 (1997). HS 129* Eng XI v Boland (Paarl) 1995-96. BB Gs 124 v Notts (Nottingham) 1996. BB 1-4. Awards: BHC 2. **NWT:** HS 59* v Suffolk (Bristol) 1995. **BHC:** HS 119* v Brit U (Bristol) 1998. **SL:** HS 108 v Worcs (Hereford) 1986.

SMITH, Andrew Michael (Queen Elizabeth GS, Wakefield; Exeter U), b Dewsbury, Yorks 1 Oct 1967. 5'9". RHB, LMF. Debut 1991; cap 1995. **Tests:** 1 (1997); HS 4*; BB –. Tour: P 1995-96 (Eng A – *part*). HS 61 v Yorks (Gloucester) 1998. 50 wkts (4); most – 83 (1997). BB 8-73 (10-118 match) v Middx (Lord's) 1996. Award: BHC 1. **NWT:** HS 13 v Somerset (Taunton) 1996. BB 4-46 v Surrey (Bristol) 1998. **BHC:** HS 15* Comb U v Surrey (Oxford) 1990. BB 6-39 v Hants (Southampton) 1995. **SL:** HS 26* v Kent (Moreton-in-M) 1996. BB 4-29 v Yorks (Gloucester) 1998.

TRAINOR, Nicholas James (St Edmund Campion S, Low Fell), b Gateshead, Co Durham 29 Jun 1975. 6'1". RHB, OB. Debut 1996. Northumberland 1995. HS 121 v A (Bristol) 1997. CC HS 67 v Surrey (Gloucester) 1996 – on debut. **NWT:** HS 143 and BB 2-25 v Scot (Bristol) 1997. **BHC:** HS 62 v Brit U (Bristol) 1997. **SL:** HS 25 v Durham (Chester-le-St) 1998.

WILLIAMS, Richard Charles James (*'Reggie'*) (Millfield S), b Southmead, Bristol 8 Aug 1969. 5'8". LHB, WK. Debut 1990; cap 1996. Tour: SL 1992-93 (Gs). HS 90 v OU (Bristol) 1995. CC HS 55* v Derbys (Gloucester) 1991. **BHC:** HS –. **SL:** HS 19 v Essex (Cheltenham) 1995.

WINDOWS, Matthew Guy Newman (Clifton C; Durham U), b Bristol 5 Apr 1973. Son of A.R. (Glos and CU 1960-68). 5'7". RHB, RSM. Debut 1992; cap 1998. Combined U 1995. Tours (Eng A): SA 1998-99; Z 1998-99. 1000 runs (1): 1173 (1998). HS 184 v Warwks (Cheltenham) 1996. BB 1-6 (Comb U). **NWT:** HS 33 v Devon (Bristol) 1994. **BHC:** HS 24 v Somerset (Bristol) 1998. **SL:** HS 72 v Somerset (Bristol) 1994.

NEW REGISTRATIONS

BARNETT, Kim John (Leek HS), b Stoke-on-Trent, Staffs 17 Jul 1960. 6'1". RHB, RM/LB. Derbyshire 1979-98; cap 1982; captain 1983-95; benefit 1992. Boland 1982-83 to 1987-88. Staffordshire 1976. *Wisden* 1988. **Tests:** 4 (1988 to 1989); HS 80 v A (Leeds) 1989. **LOI:** 1 (1988); HS 84. Tours: SA 1989-90 (Eng XI); NZ 1979-80 (DHR); SL 1985-86 (Eng B). 1000 runs (15); most – 1734 (1984). HS 239* De v Leics (Leicester) 1988. BB 6-28 De v Glam (Chesterfield) 1991. Awards: NWT 4; BHC 11. **NWT:** HS 113* De v Glos (Bristol) 1994. BB 6-24 De v Cumb (Kendal) 1984. **BHC:** HS 115 De v Glos (Derby) 1987. BB 3-52 De v Yorks (Derby) 1997. **SL:** HS 131* De v Essex (Derby) 1984. BB 4-25 De v Notts (Derby) 1998.

COOMBES, Mark Andrew (Hengrove S), b Bristol 19 Apr 1978. LHB, RM.

HARDINGES, Mark Andrew (Malvern C; Bath U), b Gloucester 5 Feb 1978. RHB, RFM.

HARVEY, Ian Joseph, b Wonthaggi, Australia 10 Apr 1972. RHB, RM. Victoria 1993-94 to date. **LOI** (A): 11 (1997-98); HS 43; BB 3-17. Tour: NZ 1994-95 (Aus Academy). HS 136 Victoria v S Aus (Melbourne) 1995-96. BB 7-44 Victoria v S Aus (Melbourne) 1996-97.

LAZENBURY, Paul Stuart (Malmesbury S), b Bath, Somerset 10 Aug 1978. LHB, RM.

POPE, Stephen Patrick, b Cheltenham 25 Jan 1983. RHB, WK.

SNAPE, Jeremy Nicholas (Denstone C; Durham U), b Stoke-on-Trent, Staffs 27 Apr 1973. 5'8½". RHB, OB. Northamptonshire 1992-97. Combined U 1994. Tour: Z 1994-95 (Nh). HS 87 Nh v Mashonaland Select XI (Harare) 1994-95. CC HS 66 Nh v Notts (Northampton) 1997. BB 5-65 Nh v Durham (Northampton) 1995. Awards: BHC 2. **NWT:** HS 54 Nh v Derbys (Derby) 1997. BB 2-43 Nh v Glos (Bristol) 1995. **BHC:** HS 52 Comb U v Hants (Southampton) 1993. BB 5-32 Nh v Leics (Northampton) 1997. **SL:** HS 77* Nh v Glos (Northampton) 1998. BB 4-31 Nh v Sussex (Hove) 1997.

RELEASED/RETIRED
(Having made a first-class County appearance in 1998)

MACMILLAN, Gregor Innes (Guildford Grammar S; Charterhouse; Southampton U; Keble C, Oxford), b Guildford, Surrey 7 Aug 1969. 6'5". RHB, OB. Oxford U 1993-95; blue 1993-94-95; captain 1995. Leicestershire 1995-97, scoring 103 v Sussex (Hove) on debut. Gloucestershire 1998. HS 122 Le v Surrey (Leicester) 1995. Gs HS 53 v Yorks (Gloucester) 1998. BB 3-13 OU v CU (Lord's) 1993. CC BB 2-44 Le v Glam (Swansea) 1996. **NWT:** HS 9. BB 1-13. **BHC:** HS 77 Comb U v Hants (Oxford) 1995. BB 1-18. **SL:** HS 58 Le v Glos (Cheltenham) 1996. BB 2-37 Le v Glam (Swansea) 1996.

WALSH, Courtney Andrew (Excelsior HS), b Kingston, Jamaica 30 Oct 1962. 6'5½". RHB, RF. Jamaica 1981-82 to date (captain 1990-91 to date). Gloucestershire 1984-96, 1998; cap 1985; captain 1993-94 and 1996; benefit 1992; testimonial 1998. *Wisden* 1986. **Tests** (WI): 106 (1984-85 to 1998-99, 22 as captain); HS 30* v A (Melbourne) 1988-89; BB 7-37 (13-55 match) v NZ (Wellington) 1994-95. **LOI** (WI): 185 (1984-85 to 1997-98, 43 as captain); HS 30; BB 5-1. Tours (WI)(C=captain): E 1984, 1988, 1991, 1995; A 1984-85, 1986-87, 1988-89, 1992-93, 1995-96, 1996-97C; SA 1998-99; NZ 1986-87, 1994-95C; I 1987-88, 1994-95C; P 1986-87, 1990-91, 1997-98C; SL 1993-94 (Young WI). HS 66 v Kent (Cheltenham) 1994. 50 wkts (10+1) inc 100 (2); most – 118 (1986). BB 9-72 v Somerset (Bristol) 1986. Hat-trick 1988-89 (WI). Awards: NWT 2. **NWT:** HS 37 v Herts (Bristol) 1993. BB 6-21 v Kent (Bristol) 1990 and v Cheshire (Bristol) 1997. **BHC:** HS 28 v Comb U (Bristol) 1989. BB 3-36 v Kent (Canterbury) 1998. **SL:** HS 38 v Derbys (Derby) 1996. BB 5-23 v Leics (Bristol) 1996.

WRIGHT, Anthony John (Alleyn's GS) b Stevenage, Herts 27 Jun 1962. 6'0". RHB, RM. Gloucestershire 1982-98; cap 1987; captain 1990-93; benefit 1996. Tours (Gs): SL 1986-87, 1992-93 (captain). 1000 runs (6); most – 1596 (1991). HS 193 v Notts (Bristol) 1995. BB 1-16. Awards: NWT 4; BHC 2. **NWT:** HS 177 v Scot (Bristol) 1997. **BHC:** HS 123 v Ireland (Dublin) 1996. **SL:** HS 96 v Sussex (Bristol) 1996.

GLOUCESTERSHIRE 1998

RESULTS SUMMARY

	Place	Won	Lost	Tied	Drew	No Result
Britannic Assurance Championship	4th	11	5		1	
All First-Class Matches		11	6		1	
NatWest Trophy		2nd Round				
Benson and Hedges Cup		4th in Group C				
Sunday League	6th	7	6			4

BRITANNIC ASSURANCE CHAMPIONSHIP AVERAGES

BATTING AND FIELDING

Cap		M	I	NO	HS	Runs	Avge	100	50	Ct/St
1998	M.G.N.Windows	15	27	2	151	1083	43.32	4	4	11
1998	T.H.C.Hancock	17	32	2	220*	1181	39.36	2	7	15
1990	M.W.Alleyne	17	31	2	137	1076	37.10	2	6	22
1996	M.C.J.Ball	17	28	5	67*	589	25.60	–	3	21
–	D.R.Hewson	11	20	3	78*	428	25.17	–	3	4
1995	A.M.Smith	17	28	11	61	353	20.76	–	2	5
1985	R.C.Russell	16	28	2	63*	527	20.26	–	2	56
–	G.I.Macmillan	4	7	–	53	121	17.28	–	1	3
1987	A.J.Wright	11	20	–	57	345	17.25	–	1	5
–	R.J.Cunliffe	11	20	–	53	336	16.80	–	2	13
–	N.J.Trainor	4	8	–	52	109	13.62	–	1	4
–	R.I.Dawson	8	15	2	46	177	13.61	–	–	3
1998	J.Lewis	17	29	2	54*	356	13.18	–	1	5
–	M.J.Church	4	7	–	30	85	12.14	–	–	5
1985	C.A.Walsh	17	23	10	25	111	8.53	–	–	4

Also batted: R.C.J.Williams (cap 1996)(1 match) 5 (1 ct).

BOWLING

	O	M	R	W	Avge	Best	5wI	10wM
T.H.C.Hancock	53	14	155	12	12.91	3- 5	–	–
C.A.Walsh	633	162	1835	106	17.31	6-36	7	2
A.M.Smith	489.3	132	1336	67	19.94	6-32	4	–
J.Lewis	425.1	105	1277	58	22.01	6-48	3	–
M.C.J.Ball	390	95	1042	31	33.61	4-26	–	–
M.W.Alleyne	248.1	70	718	20	35.90	3-16	–	–

Also bowled: R.I.Dawson 14.3-0-67-5; D.R.Hewson 3-1-7-1; G.I.Macmillan 5-2-14-0.

The First-Class Averages (pp 117-131) give the records of Gloucestershire players in all first-class county matches (Gloucestershire's other opponents being the South Africans).

GLOUCESTERSHIRE RECORDS

FIRST-CLASS CRICKET

Highest Total	For	653-6d		v	Glamorgan	Bristol	1928
	V	774-7d		by	Australians	Bristol	1948
Lowest Total	For	17		v	Australians	Cheltenham	1896
	V	12		by	Northants	Gloucester	1907
Highest Innings	For	318*	W.G.Grace	v	Yorkshire	Cheltenham	1876
	V	296	A.O.Jones	for	Notts	Nottingham	1903

Highest Partnership for each Wicket
1st	395	D.M.Young/R.B.Nicholls	v	Oxford U	Oxford	1962
2nd	256	C.T.M.Pugh/T.W.Graveney	v	Derbyshire	Chesterfield	1960
3rd	336	W.R.Hammond/B.H.Lyon	v	Leics	Leicester	1933
4th	321	W.R.Hammond/W.L.Neale	v	Leics	Gloucester	1937
5th	261	W.G.Grace/W.O.Moberley	v	Yorkshire	Cheltenham	1876
6th	320	G.L.Jessop/J.H.Board	v	Sussex	Hove	1903
7th	248	W.G.Grace/E.L.Thomas	v	Sussex	Hove	1896
8th	239	W.R.Hammond/A.E.Wilson	v	Lancashire	Bristol	1938
9th	193	W.G.Grace/S.A.P.Kitcat	v	Sussex	Bristol	1896
10th	131	W.R.Gouldsworthy/J.G.Bessant	v	Somerset	Bristol	1923

Best Bowling	For	10-40	E.G.Dennett	v	Essex	Bristol	1906
(Innings)	V	10-66	A.A.Mailey	for	Australians	Cheltenham	1921
		10-66	K.Smales	for	Notts	Stroud	1956
Best Bowling	For	17-56	C.W.L.Parker	v	Essex	Gloucester	1925
(Match)	V	15-87	A.J.Conway	for	Worcs	Moreton-in-M	1914

Most Runs – Season	2860	W.R.Hammond	(av 69.75)		1933
Most Runs – Career	33664	W.R.Hammond	(av 57.05)		1920-51
Most 100s – Season	13	W.R.Hammond			1938
Most 100s – Career	113	W.R.Hammond			1920-51
Most Wkts – Season	222	T.W.J.Goddard	(av 16.80)		1937
	222	T.W.J.Goddard	(av 16.37)		1947
Most Wkts – Career	3170	C.W.L.Parker	(av 19.43)		1903-35

LIMITED-OVERS CRICKET

Highest Total	NWT	351-2		v	Scotland	Bristol	1997
	BHC	308-3		v	Ireland	Dublin	1996
	SL	284-4		v	Leics	Cheltenham	1996
Lowest Total	NWT	82		v	Notts	Bristol	1987
	BHC	62		v	Hampshire	Bristol	1975
	SL	49		v	Middlesex	Bristol	1978
Highest Innings	NWT	177	A.J.Wright	v	Scotland	Bristol	1997
	BHC	154*	M.J.Procter	v	Somerset	Taunton	1972
	SL	146*	S. Young	v	Yorkshire	Leeds	1997
Best Bowling	NWT	6-21	C.A.Walsh	v	Kent	Bristol	1990
		6-21	C.A.Walsh	v	Cheshire	Bristol	1992
	BHC	6-13	M.J.Procter	v	Hampshire	Southampton	1977
	SL	6-52	J.N.Shepherd	v	Kent	Bristol	1983

HAMPSHIRE

Formation of Present Club: 12 August 1863
Colours: Blue, Gold and White
Badge: Tudor Rose and Crown
Championships: (2) 1961, 1973
NatWest Trophy/Gillette Cup Winners: (1) 1991
Benson and Hedges Cup Winners: (2) 1988, 1992
Sunday League Champions: (3) 1975, 1978, 1986
Match Awards: NWT 58; BHC 63

Chief Executive: A.F.Baker
County Cricket Ground, Northlands Road, Southampton SO15 2UE (Tel 01703 333788)
Captain: R.A.Smith. **Vice-Captain:** S.D.Udal. **Overseas Player:** N.A.M.McLean.
1999 Beneficiary: K.D.James. **Scorer:** V.H Isaacs

AYMES, Adrian Nigel (Bellemoor SM, Southampton), b Southampton 4 Jun 1964. 6'0". RHB, WK. Debut 1987; cap 1991. HS 133 v Leics (Leicester) 1998. BB 2-135 v Northants (Southampton) 1998. Award: NWT 1. **NWT:** HS 73* v Middx (Lord's) 1998. **BHC:** HS 46* v Kent (Southampton) 1998. **SL:** HS 60 v Durham (Southampton) 1998.

FRANCIS, Simon Richard George (Yardley Court, Tonbridge; King Edward VI S, Southampton; Durham U), b Bromley, Kent 15 Aug 1978. 6'2". RHB, RMF. Debut 1997. British U 1998. HS 6* (Brit U). H HS 4. BB 2-21 v SL (Southampton) 1998. **SL:** HS – and BB 2-31 v Sussex (Southampton) 1997.

GARAWAY, Mark (Sandown HS, IoW), b Swindon, Wilts 20 Jul 1973. 5'8". RHB, WK. Debut 1996. MCC YC. Awaiting CC debut. HS 44 v CU (Cambridge) 1996.

HANSEN, Thomas Munkholt (Norregaard, Falkonergaarden), b Glostrup, Denmark 25 Mar 1976. 6'3". RHB, LFM. Debut 1997. Denmark 1996 to date. HS 19 v Worcs (Southampton) 1997.

HARTLEY, Peter John (Greenhead GS; Bradford C), b Keighley, Yorks 18 Apr 1960. 6'0". RHB, RMF. Warwickshire 1982. Yorkshire 1985-97; cap 1987; benefit 1996. Hampshire debut/cap 1998. Tours (Y): SA 1991-92; WI 1986-87; Z 1995-96. HS 127* Y v Lancs (Manchester) 1988. H HS 29 v Warwks (Birmingham) 1998. 50 wkts (6); most – 81 (1995). BB 9-41 (inc hat-trick, 4 wkts in 5 balls and 5 in 9; 11-68 match) Y v Derbys (Chesterfield) 1995. H BB 4-42 v Essex (Portsmouth) 1998. Hat-trick 1995. Awards: NWT 1; BHC 2. **NWT:** HS 83 Y v Ire (Leeds) 1997. BB 5-46 Y v Hants (Southampton) 1990. **BHC:** HS 29* Y v Notts (Nottingham) 1986. BB 5-43 Y v Scot (Leeds) 1986. **SL:** HS 52 Y v Glos (Bristol) 1996. BB 5-36 Y v Sussex (Scarborough) 1993.

JAMES, Kevan David (Edmonton County HS), b Lambeth, London 18 Mar 1961. 6'0". LHB, LMF. Middlesex 1980-84. Wellington 1982-83. Hampshire debut 1985; cap 1989; benefit 1999. 1000 runs (2); most – 1274 (1991). HS 162 v Glam (Cardiff) 1989. BB 8-49 (13-93 match) v Somerset (Basingstoke) 1997. Achieved unique double of 4 wkts in 4 balls and a hundred (103) v I (Southampton) 1996. **NWT:** HS 52 v Lancs (Southampton) 1998. BB 4-42 v Worcs (Worcester) 1996. **BHC:** HS 56 v Glos (Bristol) 1996. BB 3-31 v Middx 1987 and v Glam 1988. **SL:** HS 66 v Glos (Trowbridge) 1989. BB 6-35 v Notts (Southampton) 1996.

KEECH, Matthew (Northumberland Park S), b Hampstead 21 Oct 1970. 6'0". RHB, RM. Middlesex 1991-93. Hampshire debut 1994. MCC YC. Hants F/C 1997. CC HS 104 v Sussex (Arundel) 1996. BB 2-28 M v Glos (Bristol) 1993. H BB 1-12. Scored 251 (256 balls) v Glam 2nd XI (Usk) – Hants 2nd XI record. **NWT:** HS 34 v Glam (Southampton) 1997. **BHC:** HS 74 v Brit U (Oxford) 1998. BB 1-37. **SL:** HS 98 v Worcs (Southampton) 1995. BB 2-22 M v Northants (Lord's) 1993.

40

KENDALL, William Salwey (Bradfield C; Keble C, Oxford), b Wimbledon, Surrey 18 Dec 1973. 5'10". RHB, RM. Oxford U 1994-96; blue 1995-96. Hampshire debut 1996. 1000 runs (1): 1045 (1996). HS 145* OU v CU (Lord's) 1996. H HS 103* and BB 2-46 v Notts (Southampton) 1996. BB 3-37 OU v Derbys (Oxford) 1995. **NWT:** HS 16 v Glam (Southampton) 1997. **BHC:** HS 26 v Kent (Canterbury) 1997. **SL:** HS 55 v Essex (Chelmsford) 1997.

KENWAY, Derek Anthony (St George's S, Southampton; Barton Peveril C, Eastleigh), b Fareham 12 Jun 1978. 5'11". RHB, RM, occ WK. Debut 1997. HS 57 v Lancs (Manchester) 1998. BB 1-5. **SL:** HS 5.

LANEY, Jason Scott (Pewsey Vale SS; St John's SFC, Marlborough; Leeds U), b Winchester 27 Apr 1973. 5'10". RHB, OB. Debut 1995; cap 1996. Matabeleland 1995-96. 1000 runs (1): 1163 (1996). HS 112 v OU (Oxford) 1996. CC HS 105 v Kent (Canterbury) 1996. Award: NWT 1. **NWT:** HS 153 v Norfolk (Southampton) 1996. **BHC:** HS 41 v Surrey (Oval) 1996. **SL:** HS 69 v Notts (Nottingham) 1997.

LOUDON, Hugo John Hope (Eton C; Durham U), b Westminster, London 11 Dec 1978. 6'2". RHB, SLA. Awaiting f-c debut.

McLEAN, Nixon Alexei McNamara (Carapan SS, St Vincent), b Stubbs, St Vincent 20 Jul 1973. 6'4". LHB, RF. Windward Is 1991-92 to date. Hampshire debut/cap 1998. **Tests** (WI): 8 (1997-98 to 1998-99); HS 39 and BB 3-53 v SA (Cape Town) 1998-99. **LOI** (WI): 16 (1996-97 to 1998-99); HS 23; BB 3-32 v I (Margao). Tours (WI): A 1996-97; SA 1997-98 (WI A), 1998-99. HS 52 Windward Is v Barbados (St George's) 1997-98. H HS 43 v Glos (Southampton) 1998. 50 wkts (1): 62 (1998). BB 6-28 WI A v EP (Port Elizabeth) 1997-98. H BB 6-101 v Leics (Leicester) 1998. **NWT:** HS 36 v Lancs (Southampton) 1998. BB 2-23 v Middx (Lord's) 1998. **BHC:** HS 28* v Somerset (Taunton) 1998. BB 1-54. **SL:** HS 30 v Worcs (Worcester) 1998. BB 3-39 v Lancs (Manchester) 1998.

MASCARENHAS, Adrian Dimitri (Trinity C, Perth, Australia), b Hammersmith, London 30 Oct 1977. Resident in Australia 1979-96. RHB, RMF. Debut 1996, taking 6-88 v Glamorgan (Southampton); took 16 wickets in first two CC matches; cap 1998. Dorset 1996. HS 89 v Notts (Portsmouth) 1998. BB 6-88 (*see above*). Award: NWT 1. **NWT:** HS 73 and BB 3-28 v Lancs (Southampton) 1998. **BHC:** HS 52* v Brit U (Oxford) 1998. BB 4-28 v Surrey (Southampton) 1998. **SL:** HS 65 v Kent (Canterbury) 1998. BB 3-9 v Glam (Southampton) 1998.

MORRIS, Alexander Corfield (Holgate S; Barnsley C), b Barnsley, Yorks 4 Oct 1976. Elder brother of Z.C. 6'3". LHB, RMF. Yorkshire 1995-97. Yorks 2nd XI debut when 16yr 332d. Hampshire debut 1998. Tour: Z 1995-96 (Y). HS 60 Y v Lancs (Manchester) 1996 (not CC). H HS 51 v Essex (Portsmouth) 1998. 50 wkts (1): 50 (1998). BB 4-30 v Durham (Southampton) 1998. **NWT:** HS 1*. BB 1-43. **BHC:** –. **SL:** HS 48* Y v Durham (Chester-le-St) 1996. BB 4-49 Y v Leics (Leeds) 1997.

MORRIS, Zachary Clegg (Holgate S, Barnsley), b Barnsley, Yorks 4 Sep 1978. Younger brother of A.C. 6'1". RHB, SLA. Debut 1998. HS 10 v Glos (Southampton) 1998.

RENSHAW, Simon John (Birkenhead S; Leeds U), b Bebington, Cheshire 6 Mar 1974. 6'3". RHB, RMF. Combined U 1995. Hampshire debut 1996. Cheshire 1994-95. HS 56 v Surrey (Guildford) 1997. BB 5-110 v Derbys (Chesterfield) 1997. **NWT:** HS –. BB 2-71 v Glam (Southampton) 1997. **BHC:** HS 23 v Surrey (Southampton) 1998. BB 6-25 v Surrey (Southampton) 1997. **SL:** HS 25 v Surrey (Guildford) 1997. BB 4-44 v Northants (Southampton) 1998.

SAVIDENT, Lee (Guernsey GS; Guernsey CFE), b Guernsey 22 Oct 1976. 6'5". RHB, RM. Debut 1997. HS 6 and BB 2-86 v Yorks (Portsmouth) 1997. **SL:** HS 39 v Somerset (Taunton) 1998. BB 3-41 v Middx (Lord's) 1997.

SMITH, Robin Arnold (Northlands BHS), b Durban, SA 13 Sep 1963. Brother of C.L. (Natal, Glam, Hants and England 1977-78 to 1992) and grandson of Dr V.L.Shearer (Natal). 5'11". RHB, LB. Natal 1980-81 to 1984-85. Hampshire debut 1982; cap 1985; benefit 1996; captain 1998 to date. *Wisden* 1989. **Tests:** 62 (1988 to 1995-96); HS 175 v WI (St John's) 1993-94. **LOI:** 71 (1988 to 1995-96); HS 167* – Eng record. Tours: A 1990-91; SA 1995-96; WI 1989-90, 1993-94; NZ 1991-92; I/SL 1992-93. 1000 runs (10); most – 1577 (1989). HS 209* v Essex (Southend) 1987. BB 2-11 v Surrey (Southampton) 1985. Awards: NWT 9; BHC 5. **NWT:** HS 158 v Worcs (Worcester) 1996. BB 2-13 v Berks (Southampton) 1985. **BHC:** HS 155* v Glam (Southampton) 1989. **SL:** HS 131 v Notts (Nottingham) 1989. BB 1-0.

STEPHENSON, John Patrick (Felsted S; Durham U), b Stebbing, Essex 14 Mar 1965. 6'1". RHB, RM. Essex 1985-94 (cap 1989). Hampshire debut/cap 1995; captain 1996-97. Boland 1988-89. **Tests:** 1 (1989); HS 25 v A (Oval) 1989. Tours: WI 1991-92 (Eng A); Z 1989-90 (Eng A). 1000 runs (5); most – 1887 (1990). HS 202* Ex v Somerset (Bath) 1990. H HS 140 v OU (Oxford) 1997. BB 7-51 v Middx (Lord's) 1995. Awards: BHC 5. **NWT:** HS 107 v Norfolk (Southampton) 1996. BB 5-34 v Cambs (Wisbech) 1997. **BHC:** HS 142 Ex v Warwks (Birmingham) 1991. BB 3-22 Ex v Northants (Northampton) 1990. **SL:** HS 110* v Essex (Southampton) 1996. BB 6-33 v Worcs (Southampton) 1997.

UDAL, Shaun David (Cove CS), b Cove, Farnborough 18 Mar 1969. Grandson of G.F.U. (Middx 1932 and Leics 1946); great-great-grandson of J.S. (MCC 1871-75). 6'2". RHB, OB. Debut 1989; cap 1992. **LOI:** 10 (1994 to 1995); HS 11*; BB 2-37. Tours: A 1994-95; P 1995-96 (Eng A). HS 117* v Warwks (Southampton) 1997. 50 wkts (4); most – 74 (1993). BB 8-50 v Sussex (Southampton) 1992. Awards: NWT 1; BHC 1. **NWT:** HS 39* v Glam (Southampton) 1997. BB 4-20 v Dorset (Bournemouth) 1998. **BHC:** HS 34 v Glos (Southampton) 1997. BB 4-40 v Middx (Southampton) 1992. **SL:** HS 78 v Surrey (Guildford) 1997. BB 5-43 v Surrey (Oval) 1998.

WHITE, Giles William (Millfield S; Loughborough U), b Barnstaple, Devon 23 Mar 1972. 6'0". RHB, LB. Somerset 1991 (one match). Combined U 1994. Hampshire debut 1994; cap 1998. Devon 1988-94. 1000 runs (1): 1211 (1998). HS 156 v SL (Southampton) 1998. CC HS 145 v Yorks (Portsmouth) 1997. BB 1-4. **NWT:** HS 69 v Middx (Lord's) 1998. BB 1-45 Devon v Kent (Canterbury) 1992. **BHC:** HS 56 v Brit U (Oxford) 1997. **SL:** HS 76 v Glam (Southampton) 1998.

NEW REGISTRATIONS

LUGSDEN, Steven (St Edmund Campion S, Low Fell), b Gateshead, Co Durham 10 Jul 1976. 6'2". RHB, RFM. Durham 1993-98 (youngest Durham f-c player – 17yr 27d on debut). HS 9. BB 3-45 Du v Lancs (Chester-le-St) 1996. **SL:** HS –. BB 1-55.

RELEASED/RETIRED
(Having made a first-class County appearance in 1998)

CONNOR, Cardigan Adolphus (The Valley SS, Anguilla; Langley C, Berkshire), b The Valley, Anguilla 24 Mar 1961. 5'9". RHB, RFM. Debut 1984; cap 1988; benefit 1997. Buckinghamshire 1979-83. HS 59 v Surrey (Oval) 1993. 50 wkts (5); most – 72 (1994). BB 9-38 v Glos (Southampton) 1996. Awards: NWT 2. **NWT:** HS 13 v Yorks (Southampton) 1990. BB 4-11 v Cambs (March) 1994. **BHC:** HS 11 v Glos (Southampton) 1995. BB 4-19 v Sussex (Hove) 1989. **SL:** HS 25 v Middx (Lord's) 1993. BB 5-25 v Northants (Basingstoke) 1996.

continued on p 106

HAMPSHIRE 1998

RESULTS SUMMARY

	Place	Won	Lost	Tied	Drew	No Result
Britannic Assurance Championship	6th	6	5		6	
All First-Class Matches		6	6		7	
NatWest Trophy	Semi-Finalist
Benson and Hedges Cup	6th in Group C
Sunday League	8th	8	8			1

BRITANNIC ASSURANCE CHAMPIONSHIP AVERAGES

BATTING AND FIELDING

Cap		M	I	NO	HS	Runs	Avge	100	50	Ct/St
1985	R.A.Smith	15	23	2	138	841	40.04	3	2	10
1991	A.N.Aymes	17	26	5	133	741	35.28	2	3	52/2
–	W.S.Kendall	6	9	2	78*	245	35.00	–	1	6
1989	K.D.James	17	25	9	57	559	34.93	–	3	4
1998	G.W.White	17	29	2	106	905	33.51	2	5	12
1992	S.D.Udal	13	18	5	62	404	31.07	–	1	9
1995	J.P.Stephenson	15	23	1	114	681	30.95	2	4	14
–	P.R.Whitaker	7	11	1	74	309	30.90	–	2	7
1998	A.D.Mascarenhas	16	24	2	89	645	29.31	–	6	11
–	M.Keech	10	12	–	67	262	21.83	–	2	9
–	D.A.Kenway	2	4	–	57	80	20.00	–	1	1
–	A.C.Morris	11	14	4	51	184	18.40	–	1	6
1998	N.A.M.McLean	16	22	2	43	288	14.40	–	–	5
1998	P.J.Hartley	12	16	3	29	160	12.30	–	–	3
1996	J.S.Laney	7	12	–	67	123	10.25	–	1	8

Also batted: C.A.Connor (cap 1988)(3 matches) 0*; R.J.Maru (1) 13, 14 (cap 1986)(1 ct); Z.C.Morris (1) 0, 10; S.J.Renshaw (1) 10*.

BOWLING

	O	M	R	W	Avge	Best	5wI	10wM
A.C.Morris	296	61	944	47	20.08	4- 30	–	–
N.A.M.McLean	518.5	105	1575	62	25.40	6-101	2	–
A.D.Mascarenhas	266.5	58	934	30	31.13	4- 31	–	–
K.D.James	320	67	1005	31	32.41	4- 22	–	–
J.P.Stephenson	271.4	66	735	22	33.40	4- 29	–	–
P.J.Hartley	348.5	65	1102	31	35.54	4- 42	–	–
S.D.Udal	176.2	34	542	13	41.69	4- 37	–	–

Also bowled: A.N.Aymes 11-0-166-2; C.A.Connor 35-5-122-2; W.S.Kendall 4-0-16-0; D.A.Kenway 2-0-17-0; J.S.Laney 2-0-14-0; R.J.Maru 31-5-112-2; Z.C.Morris 1-0-5-0; S.J.Renshaw 6-1-9-1; R.A.Smith 21-1-197-2; P.R.Whitaker 6-1-15-1; G.W.White 11-1-47-0.

The First-Class Averages (pp 117-131) give the records of Hampshire players in all first-class county matches (Hampshire's other opponents being the Sri Lankans and Oxford University), with the exception of:

S.R.G.Francis 1 match; did not bat; 0 ct. 21-3-68-4-17.00-2/21.

HAMPSHIRE RECORDS

FIRST-CLASS CRICKET

Highest Total	For	672-7d		v Somerset	Taunton	1899
	V	742		by Surrey	The Oval	1909
Lowest Total	For	15		v Warwicks	Birmingham	1922
	V	23		by Yorkshire	Middlesbrough	1965
Highest Innings	For	316	R.H.Moore	v Warwicks	Bournemouth	1937
	V	303*	G.A.Hick	for Worcs	Southampton	1997

Highest Partnership for each Wicket

1st	347	V.P.Terry/C.L.Smith	v Warwicks	Birmingham	1987
2nd	321	G.Brown/E.I.M.Barrett	v Glos	Southampton	1920
3rd	344	C.P.Mead/G.Brown	v Yorkshire	Portsmouth	1927
4th	263	R.E.Marshall/D.A.Livingstone	v Middlesex	Lord's	1970
5th	235	G.Hill/D.F.Walker	v Sussex	Portsmouth	1937
6th	411	R.M.Poore/E.G.Wynyard	v Somerset	Taunton	1899
7th	325	G.Brown/C.H.Abercrombie	v Essex	Leyton	1913
8th	227	K.D.James/T.M.Tremlett	v Somerset	Taunton	1985
9th	230	D.A.Livingstone/A.T.Castell	v Surrey	Southampton	1962
10th	192	H.A.W.Bowell/W.H.Livsey	v Worcs	Bournemouth	1921

Best Bowling	For	9- 25	R.M.H.Cottam	v Lancashire	Manchester	1965
(Innings)	V	10- 46	W.Hickton	for Lancashire	Manchester	1870
Best Bowling	For	16- 88	J.A.Newman	v Somerset	Weston-s-Mare	1927
(Match)	V	17-119	W.Mead	for Essex	Southampton	1895

Most Runs – Season	2854	C.P.Mead	(av 79.27)	1928
Most Runs – Career	48892	C.P.Mead	(av 48.84)	1905-36
Most 100s – Season	12	C.P.Mead		1928
Most 100s – Career	138	C.P.Mead		1905-36
Most Wkts – Season	190	A.S.Kennedy	(av 15.61)	1922
Most Wkts – Career	2669	D.Shackleton	(av 18.23)	1948-69

LIMITED-OVERS CRICKET

Highest Total	NWT	371-4		v Glamorgan	Southampton	1975
	BHC	321-1		v Minor C (S)	Amersham	1973
	SL	313-2		v Sussex	Portsmouth	1993
Lowest Total	NWT	98		v Lancashire	Manchester	1975
	BHC	50		v Yorkshire	Leeds	1991
	SL	43		v Essex	Basingstoke	1972
Highest Innings	NWT	177	C.G.Greenidge	v Glamorgan	Southampton	1975
	BHC	173*	C.G.Greenidge	v Minor C (S)	Amersham	1973
	SL	172	C.G.Greenidge	v Surrey	Southampton	1987
Best Bowling	NWT	7-30	P.J.Sainsbury	v Norfolk	Southampton	1965
	BHC	6-25	S.J.Renshaw	v Surrey	Southampton	1997
	SL	6-20	T.E.Jesty	v Glamorgan	Cardiff	1975

KENT

Formation of Present Club: 1 March 1859
Substantial Reorganisation: 6 December 1870
Colours: Maroon and White
Badge: White Horse on a Red Ground
Championships: (6) 1906, 1909, 1910, 1913, 1970, 1978
Joint Championship: (1) 1977
NatWest Trophy/Gillette Cup Winners: (2) 1967, 1974
Benson and Hedges Cup Winners: (3) 1973, 1976, 1978
Sunday League Champions: (4) 1972, 1973, 1976, 1995
Match Awards: NWT 48; BHC 90

Chief Executive: P.E.Millman
  St Lawrence Ground, Canterbury, CT1 3NZ (Tel 01227 456886)
Captain: M.V.Fleming. **Vice-Captain:** tba. **Overseas Player:** tba.
1999 Beneficiary: T.R.Ward. **Scorer:** J.C.Foley

De la PENA, Jason Michael (Stowe S; Bournside S), b London 16 Sep 1972. 6'5". RHB, RMF. Gloucestershire 1991-93. Surrey 1995. Kent 1998 (non-contracted). Hertfordshire 1997. HS 7* (Gs). CC HS 2* (Sy). K HS 0*. BB 4-77 Gs v A (Bristol) 1993. CC BB 3-53 v Yorks (Oval) 1995. K BB 2-44 v Notts (Canterbury) 1998. **SL:** HS 2* (Sy).

EALHAM, Mark Alan (Stour Valley SS, Chartham), b Willesborough, Ashford 27 Aug 1969. Son of A.G.E. (Kent 1966-82). 5'9". RHB, RMF. Debut 1989; cap 1992. **Tests:** 8 (1996 to 1998); HS 53* v A (Birmingham) 1997; BB 4-21 v I (Nottingham) 1996. **LOI:** 30 (1996 to 1998); HS 45; BB 5-32. Tours: A 1996-97 (Eng A); SL 1997-98; Z 1992-93 (K); K 1997-98. 1000 runs (1): 1055 (1997). HS 139 v Leics (Canterbury) 1997. BB 8-36 (10-74 match) v Warwks (Birmingham) 1996. Awards: NWT 2; BHC 5. **NWT:** HS 58* v Warwks (Birmingham) 1993. BB 4-10 v Derbys (Derby) 1994. **BHC:** HS 75 v Brit U (Oxford) 1996. BB 4-29 v Somerset (Canterbury) 1992. **SL:** HS 112 v Derbys (Maidstone) 1995 (off 44 balls – SL record). BB 6-53 v Hants (Basingstoke) 1993.

FLEMING, Matthew Valentine (St Aubyns S, Rottingdean; Eton C), b Macclesfield, Cheshire 12 Dec 1964. 5'11½". RHB, RM. Debut 1989; cap 1990; captain 1999. **LOI:** 11 (1997-98 to 1998); HS 34; BB 4-45 – on debut. Tour: Z 1992-93 (K). HS 138 v Essex (Canterbury) 1997. BB 5-51 v Notts (Nottingham) 1997. Awards: NWT 1; BHC 7. **NWT:** HS 53 v Devon (Canterbury) 1992. BB 3-28 v Warwks (Birmingham) 1994. **BHC:** HS 105* v Brit U (Oxford) 1998. BB 5-27 v Hants (Canterbury) 1998. **SL:** HS 112 v Essex (Ilford) 1996. BB 4-13 v Yorks (Canterbury) 1996.

FORD, James Antony (Tonbridge S; Durham U), b Pembury 30 Mar 1976. 5'8". RHB, SLA. Debut 1996. Awaiting CC debut. HS –. **BHC:** (Brit U) HS 38 v Surrey (Oval) 1997.

FULTON, David Paul (The Judd S; Kent U), b Lewisham 15 Nov 1971. 6'2". RHB, SLA, occ WK. Debut 1992; cap 1998. HS 207 v Yorks (Maidstone) 1998. BB 1-37. **NWT:** HS 19 v Staffs (Stone) 1995. **BHC:** HS 25 v Lancs (Lord's) 1995. **SL:** HS 29 v Lancs (Manchester) 1993.

HEADLEY, Dean Warren (Oldswinford Hospital S; Worcester RGS), b Norton, Stourbridge, Worcs 27 Jan 1970. Son of R.G.A. (Worcs, Jamaica and WI 1958-74); grandson of G.A. (Jamaica and WI 1927-28 to 1953-54). 6'4". RHB, RFM. Middlesex 1991-92; took 5-46 on CC debut, including wicket of A.A.Metcalfe with his first ball. Kent debut 1993; cap 1993. Staffordshire 1990. **Tests:** 13 (1997 to 1998-99); HS 31 v WI (Bridgetown) 1997-98; BB 6-60 v A (Melbourne) 1998-99. **LOI:** 13 (1996 to 1998-99); HS 10*; BB 2-38. Tours: A 1996-97 (Eng A), 1998-99; WI 1997-98; P 1995-96 (Eng A); Z 1992-93 (K). HS 91 M v Leics (Leicester) 1992. K HS 81 v Hants (Canterbury) 1998. 50 wkts (2); most – 54 (1998). BB 8-98 (inc hat-trick; 11-165 match) v Derbys (Derby) 1996. 3 hat-tricks (v Derbys, Worcs and Hants) 1996. Awards: BHC 3. **NWT:** HS 24* v Warwks (Birmingham)

45

HEADLEY, D.W. *continued*
1995. BB 5-20 M v Salop (Telford) 1992. **BHC:** HS 26 M v Surrey (Lord's) 1991. BB 4-19 M v Sussex (Hove) 1992. **SL:** HS 29* v Glos (Moreton-in-M) 1996. BB 6-42 v Surrey (Canterbury) 1995.

HOCKLEY, James Bernard (Kelsey Park S, Beckenham), b Beckenham 16 Apr 1979. 6'2". RHB, OB. Debut 1998. Awaiting CC debut. HS 21 v OU (Canterbury) 1998.

HOUSE, William John (Sevenoaks S; Gonville & Caius C, Cambridge), b Sheffield, Yorks 16 Mar 1976. 5'11". LHB, RM. Cambridge U 1996-98, scoring 136 v Derbys on debut; blue 1996-97-98. Kent debut 1997. British U 1998. HS 136 (*see above*). K HS 20 v A (Canterbury) 1997. CC HS 5. BB 1-34 (CU). Awards: BHC 2. **BHC:** HS 93 Brit U v Surrey (Oval) 1997. BB 5-58 Brit U v Glos (Bristol) 1998. **SL:** HS 38 v Derbys (Derby) 1998. BB 1-4.

KEY, Robert William Trevor (Colfe's S), b East Dulwich, London 12 May 1979. 6'1". RHB, RM/OB. His mother played for Kent Ladies. Debut 1998. Tours (Eng A): SA 1998-99; Z 1998-99. HS 115 v Notts (Canterbury) 1998. **NWT:** HS 18 v Cambs (Canterbury) 1998. **BHC:** HS 4. **SL:** HS 68 v Essex (Southend) 1998.

LLONG, Nigel James (Ashford North S), b Ashford 11 Feb 1969. 6'0". LHB, OB. Debut 1990; cap 1993. Tour: Z 1992-93 (K). HS 130 v Hants (Canterbury) 1996. BB 5-21 v Middx (Canterbury) 1996. Awards: NWT 1; BHC 1. **NWT:** HS 115* and BB 3-36 v Cambs (March) 1996. **BHC:** HS 75 v Brit U (Canterbury) 1997. BB 2-38 v Brit U (Oxford) 1996. **SL:** HS 70 v Sussex (Tunbridge W) 1996. BB 4-24 v Sussex (Hove) 1993.

McCAGUE, Martin John (Hedland Sr HS; Carine Tafe C), b Larne, N Ireland 24 May 1969. 6'5". RHB, RFM. W Australia 1990-91 to 1991-92. Kent debut 1991; cap 1992. **Tests:** 3 (1993 to 1994-95); HS 11 v A (Leeds) 1993; BB 4-121 v A (Nottingham) 1993. Tours: A 1994-95 (part), SA 1993-94 (Eng A). HS 63* v Surrey (Oval) 1996. 50 wkts (4); most – 76 (1996). BB 9-86 (15-147 match) v Derbys (Derby) 1994. Hat-trick 1996. Award: NWT 1. **NWT:** HS 31* v Staffs (Stone) 1995. BB 5-26 v Middx (Canterbury) 1993. **BHC:** HS 30 v Derbys (Canterbury) 1992. BB 5-43 v Somerset (Canterbury) 1992. **SL:** HS 22* v Glam (Swansea) 1992. BB 5-40 v Essex (Canterbury) 1995.

MARSH, Steven Andrew (Walderslade SS; Mid-Kent CFE), b Westminster, London 27 Jan 1961. 5'10". RHB, WK. Debut 1982; cap 1986; benefit 1995; captain 1996-98. Tour: Z 1992-93 (K – captain). HS 142 v Sussex (Horsham) 1997. BB 2-20 v Warwks (Birmingham) 1990. Set world f-c record by holding eight catches in an innings AND scoring a hundred (v Middx at Lord's) 1991. **NWT:** HS 55 v Warwks (Birmingham) 1995. BB 1-3. **BHC:** HS 71 v Lancs (Manchester) 1991. **SL:** HS 59 v Leics (Canterbury) 1991.

MASTERS, David Daniel (Fort Luton HS; Mid-Kent CHE), b Chatham 22 Apr 1978. Son of K.D. (Kent 1981-85, Surrey 1986). 6'4". RHB, RMF. Staff 1998 – awaiting f-c debut.

PATEL, Minal Mahesh (Dartford GS; Erith TC), b Bombay, India 7 Jul 1970. 5'9". RHB, SLA. Debut 1989; cap 1994. **Tests:** 2 (1996); HS 27 and BB 1-101 v I (Nottingham) 1996. Tour: I 1994-95 (Eng A). HS 58* v Hants (Canterbury) 1998. 50 wkts (2); most – 90 (1994). BB 8-96 v Lancs (Canterbury) 1994. **NWT:** HS 5*. BB 2-29 v Oxon (Oxford) 1990. **BHC:** HS 18* v Glam (Canterbury) 1996. BB 2-29 v Somerset (Canterbury) 1995. **SL:** HS 5. BB 3-50 v Northants (Northampton) 1994.

PHILLIPS, Ben James (Langley Park S and SFC, Beckenham), b Lewisham 30 Sep 1974. 6'6". RHB, RFM. Debut 1996. HS 100* v Lancs (Manchester) 1997. BB 5-47 v Sussex (Horsham) 1997. Award: NWT 1. **NWT:** HS 9*. BB 3-14 v Cambs (Canterbury) 1996. **BHC:** HS 1*. BB 3-34 v Brit U (Oxford) 1998. **SL:** HS 29 v Glam (Cardiff) 1996. BB 3-31 v Glos (Bristol) 1998.

SCOTT, Darren Anthony (Geoffrey Chaucer GS; Christ Church C, Canterbury), b Canterbury 26 Aug 1972. 6'2". LHB, OB. Debut 1998. HS 17* v OU (Canterbury) 1998. CC HS 3*. BB 1-48

SMITH, Edward Thomas (Tonbridge S; Peterhouse, Cambridge), b Pembury 19 Jul 1977. 6'2". RHB, RM. Cambridge U 1996-98, scoring 101 v Glam (Cambridge) on debut; blue 1996-97 (injured 1998). Kent debut 1996. British U 1998. 1000 runs (1): 1163 (1997). HS 190 CU v Leics (Cambridge) 1997. K HS 102 v Hants (Portsmouth) 1997. **BHC:** (Brit U) HS 43 v Sussex (Cambridge) 1997. **SL:** HS 72* v Hants (Portsmouth) 1997.

THOMPSON, Dr Julian Barton deCourcy (The Judd S; Guy's Hospital Medical S, London U), b Cape Town, SA 28 Oct 1968. 6'4". RHB, RMF. Debut 1994. HS 65* v OU (Canterbury) 1998. CC HS 59* v Warwks (Tunbridge Wells) 1997. BB 5-72 v Surrey (Oval) 1996. Awards: BHC 2. **BHC:** HS 12* v Glam (Canterbury) 1996. BB 3-29 v Middx (Canterbury) 1996. **SL:** HS 30 v Glam (Cardiff) 1996. BB 3-17 v Somerset (Taunton) 1997.

WALKER, Matthew Jonathan (King's S, Rochester), b Gravesend 2 Jan 1974. Grandson of Jack (Kent 1949). 5'8". LHB, RM. Debut 1992-93 (Z tour). UK debut 1994. Tour: Z 1992-93 (K). HS 275* v Somerset (Canterbury) 1996. Awards: BHC 2. **NWT:** HS 51 v Derbys (Derby) 1996. **BHC:** HS 117 v Warwks (Canterbury) 1997. **SL:** HS 80 v Derbys (Canterbury) 1997.

WALSH, Christopher David (Tonbridge S; Exeter U), b Pembury 6 Nov 1975. Son of D.R. (Oxford U 1966-69). 6'1". RHB, LB. Debut 1996. Awaiting CC debut. HS 56* v OU (Canterbury) 1996 (on debut). CC HS 20 v Northants (Northampton) 1998.

WARD, Trevor Robert (Hextable CS, nr Swanley), b Farningham 18 Jan 1968. 5'11". RHB, OB. Debut 1986; cap 1989; benefit 1999. Tour: Z 1992-93 (K). 1000 runs (6); most – 1648 (1992). HS 235* v Middx (Canterbury) 1991. BB 2-10 v Yorks (Canterbury) 1996. Awards: NWT 1; BHC 2. **NWT:** HS 120 v Berks (Finchampstead) 1994. BB 1-28. **BHC:** HS 125 v Surrey (Canterbury) 1995. **SL:** HS 131 v Notts (Nottingham) 1993. BB 3-20 v Glam (Canterbury) 1989.

WELLS, Alan Peter (Tideway CS, Newhaven), b Newhaven, Sussex 2 Oct 1961. Younger brother of C.M. (Sussex, Derbyshire, Border and WP 1979-96). 6'0". RHB, RM. Sussex 1981-96; cap 1986; captain 1992-96; benefit 1996. Border 1981-82. Kent debut/cap 1997. **Tests:** 1 (1995); HS 3*. **LOI:** 1 (1995); HS 15. Tours (Eng A): SA 1989-90 (Eng XI), 1993-94; I 1994-95 (captain). 1000 runs (11); most – 1784 (1991). HS 253* Sx v Yorks (Middlesbrough) 1991. K HS 109 v Essex (Canterbury) 1997. BB 3-67 Sx v Worcs (Worcester) 1987. Awards: NWT 3; BHC 1. **NWT:** HS 119 Sx v Bucks (Beaconsfield) 1992. **BHC:** HS 111* v Hants (Southampton) 1998. BB 1-17. **SL:** HS 127 Sx v Hants (Portsmouth) 1993. BB 1-0.

WILLIS, Simon Charles (Wilmington GS), b Greenwich, London 19 Mar 1974. 5'8". RHB, WK. Debut 1993. HS 82 v CU (Folkestone) 1995. CC HS 78 v Northants (Northampton) 1996. **NWT:** HS 19* v Staffs (Stone) 1995. **SL:** HS 31* v Worcs (Canterbury) 1996.

NEW REGISTRATIONS

BANES, Matthew John, b Pembury 10 Dec 1979. RHB, OB.

BROADHURST, Mark (Kingstone S, Barnsley), b Worsborough Common, Barnsley, Yorks 20 Jun 1974. 6'0". RHB, RFM. Yorkshire 1991-94. Tour: SA 1992-93 (Y). Nottinghamshire 1996. No CC appearances. HS 6 (Y). BB 3-61 Y v OU (Oxford) 1991. **SL:** HS –.

WATSON, James David, b Ashford 21 Apr 1981. RHB, RMF. Non-contracted player.

continued on p 106

KENT 1998

RESULTS SUMMARY

	Place	Won	Lost	Tied	Drew	No Result
Britannic Assurance Championship	11th	5	5		7	
All First-Class Matches		5	6		7	
NatWest Trophy	2nd Round					
Benson and Hedges Cup	Quarter-Finalist					
Sunday League	5th	8	6			3

BRITANNIC ASSURANCE CHAMPIONSHIP AVERAGES

BATTING AND FIELDING

Cap		M	I	NO	HS	Runs	Avge	100	50	Ct/St
1992	C.L.Hooper	15	28	1	203	1215	45.00	6	1	15
1998	D.P.Fulton	17	31	1	207	954	31.80	1	7	21
1992	M.A.Ealham	10	18	3	121	437	29.13	1	2	2
1997	A.P.Wells	15	26	1	95	684	27.36	–	5	3
–	R.W.T.Key	13	23	–	115	612	26.60	2	1	11
1986	S.A.Marsh	16	28	4	92	620	25.83	–	5	42/4
–	M.J.Walker	7	12	–	68	276	23.00	–	2	5
–	E.T.Smith	7	14	–	58	321	22.92	–	1	1
1990	M.V.Fleming	16	29	4	51	571	22.84	–	1	9
1994	M.M.Patel	13	19	5	58*	303	21.64	–	2	7
1992	M.J.McCague	10	15	7	38	166	20.75	–	–	8
1989	T.R.Ward	12	22	–	94	416	18.90	–	1	8
1993	D.W.Headley	13	19	5	81	262	18.71	–	1	5
–	B.J.Phillips	10	19	3	54	193	12.06	–	1	1
–	J.B.D.Thompson	3	5	3	8*	24	12.00	–	–	–
–	C.D.Walsh	2	4	–	20	38	9.50	–	–	–
1989	A.P.Igglesden	3	4	3	4*	8	8.00	–	–	2

Also batted (1 match each): J.M.de la Pena 0*; W.J.House 5, 0 (1 ct); N.J.Llong (cap 1993) 4, 0 (1 ct); D.A.Scott 3*, 2*; S.C.Willis 0* (1 ct).

BOWLING

	O	M	R	W	Avge	Best	5wI	10wM
D.W.Headley	388.2	86	1106	52	21.26	6-71	4	–
J.B.D.Thompson	76.4	17	251	11	22.81	4-52	–	–
M.A.Ealham	204.4	73	488	21	23.23	5-23	3	–
M.V.Fleming	404.4	115	1008	38	26.52	4-24	–	–
M.J.McCague	235.1	45	758	27	28.07	4-40	–	–
C.L.Hooper	386.2	104	957	31	30.87	7-93	1	–
M.M.Patel	387.3	96	1015	29	35.00	5-73	1	–
B.J.Phillips	275	53	839	13	64.53	3-66	–	–

Also bowled: J.M.de la Pena 33-2-126-3; A.P.Igglesden 70-13-202-2; R.W.T.Key 1-0-1-0; D.A.Scott 41-13-103-1; M.J.Walker 12-0-51-0; T.R.Ward 2-0-4-0.

The First-Class Averages (pp 117-131) give the records of Kent players in all first-class county matches (Kent's other opponents being Oxford University), with the exception of M.A.Ealham, D.W.Headley, W.J.House and E.T.Smith, whose full county figures are as above.

KENT RECORDS

FIRST-CLASS CRICKET

Highest Total	For 803-4d		v	Essex	Brentwood 1934
	V 676		by	Australians	Canterbury 1921
Lowest Total	For 18		v	Sussex	Gravesend 1867
	V 16		by	Warwicks	Tonbridge 1913
Highest Innings	For 332	W.H.Ashdown	v	Essex	Brentwood 1934
	V 344	W.G.Grace	for	MCC	Canterbury 1876

Highest Partnership for each Wicket

1st	300	N.R.Taylor/M.R.Benson	v	Derbyshire	Canterbury 1991
2nd	366	S.G.Hinks/N.R.Taylor	v	Middlesex	Canterbury 1990
3rd	321*	A.Hearne/J.R.Mason	v	Notts	Nottingham 1899
4th	368	P.A.de Silva/G.R.Cowdrey	v	Derbyshire	Maidstone 1995
5th	277	F.E.Woolley/L.E.G.Ames	v	New Zealand	Canterbury 1931
6th	315	P.A.de Silva/M.A.Ealham	v	Notts	Nottingham 1995
7th	248	A.P.Day/E.Humphreys	v	Somerset	Taunton 1908
8th	157	A.L.Hilder/A.C.Wright	v	Essex	Gravesend 1924
9th	171	M.A.Ealham/P.A.Strang	v	Notts	Nottingham 1997
10th	235	F.E.Woolley/A.Fielder	v	Worcs	Stourbridge 1909

Best Bowling	For	10- 30	C.Blythe	v	Northants	Northampton 1907
(Innings)	V	10- 48	C.H.G.Bland	for	Sussex	Tonbridge 1899
Best Bowling	For	17- 48	C.Blythe	v	Northants	Northampton 1907
(Match)	V	17-106	T.W.J.Goddard	for	Glos	Bristol 1939

Most Runs – Season	2894	F.E.Woolley	(av 59.06)	1928
Most Runs – Career	47868	F.E.Woolley	(av 41.77)	1906-38
Most 100s – Season	10	F.E.Woolley		1928
	10	F.E.Woolley		1934
Most 100s – Career	122	F.E.Woolley		1906-38
Most Wkts – Season	262	A.P.Freeman	(av 14.74)	1933
Most Wkts – Career	3340	A.P.Freeman	(av 17.64)	1914-36

LIMITED-OVERS CRICKET

Highest Total	NWT	384-6		v	Berkshire	Finchampstead 1994
	BHC	338-6		v	Somerset	Maidstone 1996
	SL	327-6		v	Leics	Canterbury 1993
Lowest Total	NWT	60		v	Somerset	Taunton 1979
	BHC	73		v	Middlesex	Canterbury 1979
	SL	83		v	Middlesex	Lord's 1984
Highest Innings	NWT	136*	C.L.Hooper	v	Berkshire	Finchampstead 1994
	BHC	143	C.J.Tavaré	v	Somerset	Taunton 1985
	SL	145	C.L.Hooper	v	Leics	Leicester 1996
Best Bowling	NWT	8-31	D.L.Underwood	v	Scotland	Edinburgh 1987
	BHC	6-41	T.N.Wren	v	Somerset	Canterbury 1995
	SL	6- 9	R.A.Woolmer	v	Derbyshire	Chesterfield 1979

LANCASHIRE

Formation of Present Club: 12 January 1864
Colours: Red, Green and Blue
Badge: Red Rose
Championships (since 1890): (7) 1897, 1904, 1926, 1927, 1928, 1930, 1934
Joint Championship: (1) 1950
NatWest Trophy/Gillette Cup Winners: (7) 1970, 1971, 1972, 1975, 1990, 1996, 1998
Benson and Hedges Cup Winners: (4) 1984, 1990, 1995, 1996
Sunday League Champions: (4) 1969, 1970, 1989, 1998
Match Awards: NWT 67; BHC 77

Cricket Secretary: D.M.R.Edmundson
Old Trafford, Manchester M16 0PX (Tel 0161 282 4021)
Captain: J.P.Crawley. **Vice-Captain:** tba. **Overseas Player:** M.Muralitharan.
1999 Beneficiary: W.K.Hegg. **Scorer:** A.West.

ATHERTON, Michael Andrew (Manchester GS; Downing C, Cambridge), b Failsworth, Manchester 23 Mar 1968. 5'11". RHB, LB. Cambridge U 1987-89; blue 1987-88-89; captain 1988-89. Lancashire debut 1987; cap 1989; benefit 1997. YC 1990. *Wisden* 1990. OBE 1997. **Tests:** 88 (1989 to 1998-99, 52 as captain − England record); HS 185* v SA (Johannesburg) 1995-96; BB 1-20. **LOI:** 54 (1990 to 1998, 43 as captain); HS 127. Tours (C=captain): A 1990-91, 1994-95C, 1998-99; SA 1995-96C; WI 1993-94C, 1995-96 (La); 1997-98C; NZ 1996-97C; I/SL 1992-93; Z 1989-90 (Eng A), 1996-97C. 1000 runs (6); most − 1924 (1990). Scored 1193 in season of f-c debut. HS 199 v Durham (Gateshead) 1992. BB 6-78 v Notts (Nottingham) 1990. Awards: NWT 4; BHC 3. **NWT:** HS 115 v Derbys (Manchester) 1996. BB 2-15 v Glos (Manchester) 1990. **BHC:** HS 121* v Durham (Manchester) 1996. BB 4-42 Comb U v Somerset (Taunton) 1989. **SL:** HS 111 v Essex (Colchester) 1990. BB 3-33 v Notts (Nottingham) 1990.

AUSTIN, Ian David (Haslingden HS), b Haslingden 30 May 1966. 5'10". LHB, RM. Debut 1987; cap 1990. **LOI:** 4 (1998 to 1998-99); HS 11*; BB 2-37. Tours (Eng A): WI 1995-96; Z 1988-89. HS 115* v Derbys (Blackpool) 1992. BB 5-23 (10-60 match) v Middx (Manchester) 1994. Awards: NWT 2; BHC 2. **NWT:** HS 97 v Sussex (Hove) 1997. BB 3-14 v Derbys (Lord's) 1989. **BHC:** HS 80 v Worcs (Worcester) 1987. BB 4-8 v Minor C (Leek) 1995. **SL:** HS 48 v Middx (Lord's) 1991. BB 5-56 v Derbys (Derby) 1991.

CHAPPLE, Glen (West Craven HS; Nelson & Colne C), b Skipton, Yorks 23 Jan 1974. 6'1". RHB, RFM. Debut 1992; cap 1994. Tours (Eng A): WI 1996-97; SL 1997-98 (La); I 1994-95. HS 109* v Glam (Manchester) 1993 (100 off 27 balls in contrived circumstances). HS (authentic) 69 v Glos (Manchester) 1998. 50 wkts (2); most − 55 (1994). BB 6-48 v Durham (Stockton) 1994. Awards: NWT 1; BHC 1. **NWT:** HS 6. BB 6-18 v Essex (Lord's) 1996. **BHC:** HS 8. BB 5-7 v Minor C (Lakenham) 1998. **SL:** HS 43 v Worcs (Manchester) 1996. BB 6-25 v Yorks (Leeds) 1998.

CHILTON, Mark James (Manchester GS; Durham U), b Sheffield, Yorks 2 Oct 1976. 6'3". RHB, RM. Debut 1997. British U 1998. HS 47 v Glam (Colwyn Bay) 1998. Awards: BHC 2. **NWT:** HS 41 v Notts (Manchester) 1998. BB **BHC:** (Brit U) HS 56 v Kent (Oxford) 1998. BB 5-26 v Sussex (Cambridge) 1997. **SL:** HS 22 v Middx (Uxbridge) 1997. BB 2-27 v Hants (Southampton) 1997.

CRAWLEY, John Paul (Manchester GS; Trinity C, Cambridge), b Maldon, Essex 21 Sep 1971. Brother of M.A. (Oxford U, Lancs and Notts 1987-94) and P.M. (Cambridge U 1992). 6'1". RHB, RM, occ WK. Debut 1990; cap 1994; captain 1999. Cambridge U 1991-93; blue 1991-92-93; captain 1992-93. YC 1994. **Tests:** 29 (1994 to 1998-99); HS 156* v SL (Oval)

CRAWLEY, J.P. *continued*
1998. **LOI:** 13 (1994-95 to 1998-99); HS 73. Tours: A 1994-95, 1998-99; SA 1993-94 (Eng A), 1995-96; WI 1995-96 (La), 1997-98; NZ 1996-97; Z 1996-97. 1000 runs (7); most – 1851 (1998). HS 286 England A v E Province (Port Elizabeth) 1993-94. La HS 281* v Somerset (Southport) 1994. BB 1-90. Award: BHC 1. **NWT:** HS 113* v Sussex (Hove) 1997. **BHC:** HS 114 v Notts (Manchester) 1995. **SL:** HS 100 v Kent (Canterbury) 1998.

FAIRBROTHER, Neil Harvey (Lymm GS), b Warrington 9 Sep 1963. 5'8". LHB, LM. Debut 1982; cap 1985; captain 1992-93; benefit 1995. Transvaal 1994-95. **Tests:** 10 (1987 to 1992-93); HS 83 v I (Madras) 1992-93. **LOI:** 66 (1986-87 to 1998-99); HS 113. Tours: NZ 1987-88, 1991-92; I/SL 1992-93; P 1987-88, 1990-91 (Eng A); SL 1990-91 (Eng A). 1000 runs (10); most – 1740 (1990). HS 366 v Surrey (Oval) 1990 (ground record), including 311 in a day and 100 or more in each session. BB 2-91 v Notts (Manchester) 1987. Awards: NWT 6; BHC 9. **NWT:** HS 93* v Leics (Leicester) 1986. BB 1-28. **BHC:** HS 116* v Scot (Manchester) 1988. BB 1-17. **SL:** HS 116* v Notts (Nottingham) 1988. BB 1-33.

FLINTOFF, Andrew (Ribbleton Hall HS), b Preston 6 Dec 1977. 6'4". RHB, RM. Debut 1995; cap 1998. **Tests:** 2 (1998); HS 17 and BB 1-52 v SA (Nottingham) 1998. Tours (Eng A): SA 1998-99; SL 1997-98; Z 1998-99; K 1997-98. HS 124 v Northants (Northampton) 1998. BB 3-51 v Worcs (Lytham) 1998. Award: BHC 1. **NWT:** HS 35 v Sussex (Manchester) 1998. BB 1-4. **BHC:** HS 92 v Northants (Manchester) 1998. BB 1-10. **SL:** HS 93* v Notts (Nottingham) 1998. BB 1-9.

GREEN, Richard James (Bridgewater HS, Cheshire; Mid-Cheshire C), b Warrington 13 Mar 1976. 6'1". RHB, RM. Debut 1995. HS 51 v Essex (Manchester) 1997. BB 6-41 v Yorks (Manchester) 1996 (non-CC match). BB 4-78 v Northants (Northampton) 1996. **NWT:** HS 0. BB 1-35. **BHC:** HS 7. BB 2-33 v Minor C (Walsall) 1997. **SL:** HS 0*. BB 3-18 v Yorks (Manchester) 1997.

HARVEY, Mark Edward (Habergham HS; Loughborough U), b Burnley 26 Jun 1974. 5'9". RHB, RM/LB. Debut 1994. Combined U 1995. HS 25 v Glos (Bristol) 1997. Award: NWT 1. **NWT:** HS 86 v Berks (Manchester) 1997. **BHC:** (Brit U) HS 5. **SL:** HS 39 v Warwks (Birmingham) 1998.

HAYNES, Jamie Jonathan (St Edmunds C, Canberra; Canberra U), b Bristol 5 Jul 1974. 5'11". RHB, WK. Debut 1996. Represented Australian Capital Territory at cricket and Australian Rules football. HS 21 v Yorks (Leeds) 1997 (non-CC match). CC HS 18 v Kent (Manchester) 1997. **SL:** HS –.

HEGG, Warren Kevin (Unsworth HS, Bury; Stand C, Whitefield), b Whitefield 23 Feb 1968. 5'8". RHB, WK. Debut 1986; cap 1989; benefit 1999. **Tests:** 2 (1998-99); HS 15 v A (Sydney) 1998-99. Tours: A 1996-97 (Eng A), 1998-99; WI 1986-87 (La), 1995-96 (La); SL 1990-91 (Eng A); Z 1988-89 (La). HS 134 v Leics (Manchester) 1996. Held 11 catches (equalling world f-c match record) v Derbys (Chesterfield) 1989. Award: NWT 1. **NWT:** HS 37 v Berks (Manchester) 1997. **BHC:** HS 81 v Yorks (Manchester) 1996. **SL:** HS 52 v Glam (Colwyn Bay) 1994.

KEEDY, Gary (Garforth CS), b Wakefield, Yorks 27 Nov 1974. 6'0". LHB, SLA. Yorkshire 1994 (one match). Lancashire debut 1995. Tour: WI 1995-96 (La). HS 26 v Essex (Chelmsford) 1996. BB 6-79 (10-173 match) v Surrey (Oval) 1997. **SL:** HS –. BB 1-40.

LLOYD, Graham David (Hollins County HS), b Accrington 1 Jul 1969. Son of D. (Lancs and England 1965-83). 5'9". RHB, RM. Debut 1988; cap 1992. **LOI:** 6 (1996 to 1998-99); HS 22. Tours: A 1992-93 (Eng A); WI 1995-96 (La). 1000 runs (4); most – 1389 (1992). HS 241 v Essex (Chelmsford) 1996. BB 1-4. Awards: BHC 2. **NWT:** HS 96 v Berks (Manchester) 1997. BB 1-23. **BHC:** HS 81* v Leics (Manchester) 1995. **SL:** HS 134 v Durham (Manchester) 1997.

McKEOWN, Patrick Christopher (Merchant Taylors S; Rossall S), b Liverpool 1 Jun 1976. 6'3". RHB, OB. Debut 1996. HS 64 v Warwks (Birmingham) 1996. **NWT:** HS 42 v Berks (Manchester) 1997. **BHC:** HS 10 v Minor C (Walsall) 1997. **SL:** HS 69 v Northants (Northampton) 1996.

MARTIN, Peter James (Danum S, Doncaster), b Accrington 15 Nov 1968. 6'4". RHB, RFM. Debut 1989; cap 1994. **Tests:** 8 (1995 to 1997); HS 29 v WI (Lord's) 1995; BB 4-60 v SA (Durban) 1995-96. **LOI:** 20 (1995 to 1998-99); HS 6; BB 4-44. Tour: SA 1995-96. HS 133 v Durham (Gateshead) 1992. 50 wkts (2); most – 58 (1997). BB 8-32 (13-79 match) v Middx (Uxbridge) 1997. Awards: NWT 2. **NWT:** HS 16 v Surrey (Oval) 1994. BB 5-30 v Sussex (Manchester) 1998. **BHC:** HS 10* (twice). BB 3-31 v Yorks (Manchester) 1997. **SL:** HS 35* v Worcs (Manchester) 1996. BB 5-21 v Northants (Manchester) 1997.

RIDGWAY, Paul Mathew (Settle HS), b Airedale, Yorks 13 Feb 1977. 6'4". RHB, RFM. Debut 1997. HS 35 and BB 3-51 v Durham (Chester-le-St) 1998.

SCHOFIELD, Christopher Paul (Wardle HS), b Birch Hill, Rochdale 6 Oct 1978. 6'2". LHB, LB. Debut 1998. HS 4*. BB 4-56 (8-116 match) v Glos (Manchester) 1998.

SHADFORD, Darren James (Breeze Hill HS; Oldham TC), b Oldham 4 Mar 1975. 6'3". RHB, RMF. Debut 1995. HS 30 v Hants (Southampton) 1997. BB 5-80 v Warwks (Blackpool) 1997. **NWT:** HS –. **SL:** HS 2. BB 3-30 v Middx (Uxbridge) 1997.

WATKINSON, Michael (Rivington and Blackrod HS, Horwich), b Westhoughton 1 Aug 1961. 6'1". RHB, RMF/OB. Debut 1982; cap 1987; captain 1994-97; benefit 1996. Cheshire 1982. **Tests:** 4 (1995 to 1995-96); HS 82* v WI (Nottingham) 1995; BB 3-64 v WI (Manchester) 1995 – on debut. **LOI:** 1 (1995-96); HS –. Tours: SA 1995-96; WI 1995-96 (La – captain). 1000 runs (1): 1016 (1993). HS 161 v Essex (Manchester) 1995. 50 wkts (7); most – 66 (1992). BB 8-30 (11-87 match) v Hants (Manchester) 1994 – completing match 'double' with 128 runs. Hat-trick 1992. Awards: NWT 2; BHC 3. **NWT:** HS 90 and BB 3-14 v Glos (Manchester) 1990. **BHC:** HS 76 v Northants (Northampton) 1992. BB 5-44 v Derbys (Chesterfield) 1996. **SL:** HS 121 v Notts (Nottingham) 1996. BB 5-46 v Warwks (Manchester) 1990.

WOOD, Nathan Theodore (Wm Hulme's GS), b Thornhill Edge, Yorks 4 Oct 1974. Son of B. (Yorks, Lancs, Derbys and England 1964-83). 5'8". LHB, OB. Debut 1996. HS 155 v Surrey (Oval) 1997. **SL:** HS 23 v Sussex (Hove) 1998.

YATES, Gary (Manchester GS), b Ashton-under-Lyne 20 Sep 1967. 6'0". RHB, OB. Debut 1990; cap 1994. HS 134* v Northants (Manchester) 1993. BB 5-34 v Hants (Manchester) 1994. **NWT:** HS 34* and BB 2-15 v Berks (Manchester) 1997. **BHC:** HS 26 v Yorks (Manchester) 1996. BB 3-42 v Warwks (Birmingham) 1995. **SL:** HS 38 v Essex (Chelmsford) 1996. BB 4-34 v Warwks (Birmingham) 1994.

NEW REGISTRATIONS

MURALITHARAN, Muttiah (St Anthony's C, Kandy), b Kandy, Sri Lanka 17 Apr 1972. 5'5". RHB, OB. Central Province 1989-90 to date. Tamil Union 1991-92 to date. **Tests** (SL): 42 (1992-93 to 1998); HS 39 v I (Colombo) 1997-98; BB 9-65 (16-220 match) v E (Oval) 1998. **LOI** (SL): 110 (1993-94 to 1998-99); HS 18; BB 5-23. Tours (SL): E 1991, 1998; A 1995-96; SA 1992-93 (SL U-24), 1994-95, 1997-98; WI 1996-97; NZ 1994-95, 1996-97; I 1993-94, 1997-98; P 1995-96; Z 1994-95. 50 wkts (0+2); most – 66 (1996-97). HS 39 (*see Tests*). BB 9-65 (*see Tests*).

SMETHURST, Michael Paul, b Oldham 11 Oct 1976. RHB, RFM.

RELEASED/RETIRED
(Having made a first-class County appearance in 1998)

TITCHARD, S.P. – *see DERBYSHIRE.*

continued on p 106

LANCASHIRE 1998

RESULTS SUMMARY

	Place	Won	Lost	Tied	Drew	No Result
Britannic Assurance Championship	2nd	11	1		5	
All First-Class Matches		11	1		5	
NatWest Trophy	Winners					
Benson and Hedges Cup	Quarter-Finalist					
Sunday League	1st	12	2			3

BRITANNIC ASSURANCE CHAMPIONSHIP AVERAGES

BATTING AND FIELDING

Cap		M	I	NO	HS	Runs	Avge	100	50	Ct/St
1994	J.P.Crawley	17	26	2	239	1681	70.04	7	5	6
1985	N.H.Fairbrother	12	17	2	138	759	50.60	3	3	11
1992	G.D.Lloyd	15	22	1	212*	831	39.57	2	3	11
1989	W.K.Hegg	15	21	4	85	628	36.94	–	6	34/3
1994	G.Yates	4	6	1	55	174	34.80	–	1	2
–	M.J.Chilton	2	4	–	47	125	31.25	–	–	–
1989	Wasim Akram	13	18	1	155	531	31.23	1	2	8
1989	M.A.Atherton	8	14	1	152	381	29.30	1	–	7
1987	M.Watkinson	10	12	1	87	318	28.90	–	2	6
–	N.T.Wood	12	19	3	80*	457	28.56	–	2	1
1998	A.Flintoff	15	22	–	124	591	26.86	1	3	22
–	P.C.McKeown	5	7	–	42	186	26.57	–	–	6
1990	I.D.Austin	13	17	4	64	304	23.38	–	2	7
1994	G.Chapple	14	18	3	69	282	18.80	–	1	7
1994	P.J.Martin	14	15	5	26	154	15.40	–	–	3
–	G.Keedy	7	10	5	13	44	8.80	–	–	1

Also played: R.J.Green (6 matches) 14, 0*, 0 (1 ct); M.E.Harvey (1) 0, 0*; P.M.Ridgway (1) 35, 4; C.P.Schofield (2) 1*, 4*, 0 (1 ct); D.J.Shadford (1) 13*; S.P.Titchard (cap 1995)(1) did not bat.

BOWLING

	O	M	R	W	Avge	Best	5wI	10wM
Wasim Akram	335.5	75	1025	48	21.35	5-56	1	–
G.Chapple	313	58	942	44	21.40	5-49	1	–
P.J.Martin	388	94	1062	48	22.12	4-21	–	–
G.Yates	131.3	26	432	18	24.00	4-64	–	–
I.D.Austin	345.4	80	978	36	27.16	4-21	–	–
C.P.Schofield	79.4	9	299	10	29.90	4-56	–	–
G.Keedy	182.3	43	563	18	31.27	5-35	1	–
M.Watkinson	175.4	22	607	18	33.72	5-45	1	–

Also bowled: M.J.Chilton 8-2-24-0; J.P.Crawley 1-0-21-0; A.Flintoff 104-25-317-6; R.J.Green 126-25-424-4; M.E.Harvey 5-0-48-0; G.D.Lloyd 7.3-1-49-0; P.M.Ridgway 18-2-83-4; D.J.Shadford 30.5-4-90-1; N.T.Wood 5.1-0-80-0.

The First-Class Averages (pp 117-131) give the records of Lancashire players in all first-class county matches, with the exception of M.A.Atherton, M.J.Chilton, J.P.Crawley and A.Flintoff, whose full county figures are as above.

LANCASHIRE RECORDS

FIRST-CLASS CRICKET

Highest Total	For	863		v Surrey	The Oval	1990
	V	707-9d		by Surrey	The Oval	1990
Lowest Total	For	25		v Derbyshire	Manchester	1871
	V	22		by Glamorgan	Liverpool	1924
Highest Innings	For	424	A.C.MacLaren	v Somerset	Taunton	1895
	V	315*	T.W.Hayward	for Surrey	The Oval	1898

Highest Partnership for each Wicket

1st	368	A.C.MacLaren/R.H.Spooner		v Glos	Liverpool	1903
2nd	371	F.B.Watson/G.E.Tyldesley		v Surrey	Manchester	1928
3rd	364	M.A.Atherton/N.H.Fairbrother		v Surrey	The Oval	1990
4th	358	S.P.Titchard/G.D.Lloyd		v Essex	Chelmsford	1996
5th	249	B.Wood/A.Kennedy		v Warwicks	Birmingham	1975
6th	278	J.Iddon/H.R.W.Butterworth		v Sussex	Manchester	1932
7th	248	G.D.Lloyd/I.D.Austin		v Yorks	Leeds	1997
8th	158	J.Lyon/R.M.Ratcliffe		v Warwicks	Manchester	1979
9th	142	L.O.S.Poidevin/A.Kermode		v Sussex	Eastbourne	1907
10th	173	J.Briggs/R.Pilling		v Surrey	Liverpool	1885

Best Bowling	For	10-46	W.Hickton	v Hampshire	Manchester	1870
(Innings)	V	10-40	G.O.B.Allen	for Middlesex	Lord's	1929
Best Bowling	For	17-91	H.Dean	v Yorkshire	Liverpool	1913
(Match)	V	16-65	G.Giffen	for Australians	Manchester	1886

Most Runs – Season	2633	J.T.Tyldesley	(av 56.02)	1901
Most Runs – Career	34222	G.E.Tyldesley	(av 45.20)	1909-36
Most 100s – Season	11	C.Hallows		1928
Most 100s – Career	90	G.E.Tyldesley		1909-36
Most Wkts – Season	198	E.A.McDonald	(av 18.55)	1925
Most Wkts – Career	1816	J.B.Statham	(av 15.12)	1950-68

LIMITED-OVERS CRICKET

Highest Total	NWT	372-5		v Glos	Manchester	1990
	BHC	353-7		v Notts	Manchester	1995
	SL	300-7		v Leics	Leicester	1993
Lowest Total	NWT	59		v Worcs	Worcester	1963
	BHC	82		v Yorkshire	Bradford	1972
	SL	71		v Essex	Chelmsford	1987
Highest Innings	NWT	131	A.Kennedy	v Middlesex	Manchester	1978
	BHC	136	G.Fowler	v Sussex	Manchester	1991
	SL	134*	C.H.Lloyd	v Somerset	Manchester	1970
Best Bowling	NWT	6-18	G.Chapple	v Essex	Lord's	1996
	BHC	6-10	C.E.H.Croft	v Scotland	Manchester	1982
	SL	6-25	G.Chapple	v Yorkshire	Leeds	1998

LEICESTERSHIRE

Formation of Present Club: 25 March 1879
Colours: Dark Green and Scarlet
Badge: Gold Running Fox on Green Ground
Championships: (3) 1975, 1996, 1998
NatWest Trophy/Gillette Cup Winners: (0) Finalist 1992
Benson and Hedges Cup Winners: (3) 1972, 1975, 1985
Sunday League Champions: (2) 1974, 1977
Match Awards: NWT 41; BHC 72

Chief Executive: D.G.Collier. **Administrative Secretary:** K.P.Hill
County Ground, Grace Road, Leicester LE2 8AD (Tel 0116 283 2128)
Captain: J.J.Whitaker. **Vice-Captain:** C.C.Lewis. **Overseas Player:** M.S.Kasprowicz.
1999 Beneficiary: D.J.Millns. **Scorer:** G.A.York

BRIMSON, Matthew Thomas (Chislehurst & Sidcup GS; Durham U), b Plumstead, London 1 Dec 1970. 6'0". RHB, SLA. Kent staff 1991. Debut 1993; cap 1998. Tour (Le): SA 1996-97. HS 54* v Warwks (Birmingham) 1998. BB 5-12 v Sussex (Leicester) 1996. **NWT:** HS 9 and BB 3-34 v Sussex (Leicester) 1996. **BHC:** HS 0 and BB 2-36 v Somerset (Leicester) 1997. **SL:** HS 12* v Glos (Leicester) 1997. BB 3-23 v Glam (Swansea) 1996 and 3-23 v Northants (Leicester) 1998.

CROWE, Carl Daniel (Lutterworth GS), b Leicester 25 Nov 1975. 6'0". RHB, OB. Debut 1995. HS 29* v Lancs (Manchester) 1998. BB 3-49 v Durham (Darlington) 1998. **SL:** HS 4*.

DAKIN, Jonathan Michael (King Edward VII S, Johannesburg) b Hitchin, Herts 28 Feb 1973. 6'4". LHB, RM. Debut 1993. Tour (Le): SA 1996-97. HS 190 v Northants (Northampton) 1997. BB 4-45 v CU (Cambridge) 1993 (on debut). CC BB 3-38 v Hants (Leicester) 1998. Award: BHC 1. **NWT:** HS 26 v Hants (Leicester) 1995 and 26 v Berks (Leicester) 1996. BB 1-63. **BHC:** HS 108* v Durham (Leicester) 1996. BB 3-68 v Lancs (Leicester) 1998. **SL:** HS 45 v Notts (Leicester) 1995. BB 4-14 v Hants (Leicester) 1998.

HABIB, Aftab (Millfield S; Taunton S), b Reading, Berkshire 7 Feb 1972. 5'11". Cousin of Zahid Sadiq (Surrey and Derbys 1988-9). RHB, RMF. Middlesex 1992 (one match). Leicestershire debut 1995; cap 1998. HS 215 v Worcs (Leicester) 1996. Award: BHC 1. **NWT:** HS 67 v Glam (Cardiff) 1998. **BHC:** HS 111 v Durham (Chester-le-St) 1997. **SL:** HS 99* v Glos (Cheltenham) 1996.

KIRBY, Steven P. (Elton HS; Bury C), b Bury, Lancs 4 Oct 1977. 6'3½". RHB, RFM. Staff 1998 – awaiting f-c debut.

LEWIS, Clairmonte Christopher (Willesden HS, London), b Georgetown, Guyana 14 Feb 1968. 6'2½". RHB, RFM. Leicestershire 1987-91, 1998; cap 1990. Nottinghamshire 1992-94; cap 1994. Surrey 1996-97; cap 1996. **Tests:** 32 (1990 to 1996); HS 117 v I (Madras) 1992-93; BB 6-111 v WI (Birmingham) 1991. **LOI:** 51 (1989-90 to 1996); HS 33; BB 4-30. Tours: A 1990-91 (part), 1994-95 (part); WI 1989-90 (part), 1993-94; NZ 1991-92; I/SL 1992-93. HS 247 Nt v Durham (Chester-le-St) 1993. Le HS 189* v Essex (Chelmsford) 1990. 50 wkts (2); most – 56 (1990). BB 6-22 v OU (Oxford) 1988. CC BB 6-55 v Glam (Cardiff) 1990. Award: NWT 1. **NWT:** HS 89 Nt v Northumb (Jesmond) 1994. BB 5-19 v Staffs (Leicester) 1998. **BHC:** HS 55* v Minor C (Leicester) 1998. BB 5-46 Nt v Kent (Nottingham) 1992. **SL:** HS 93* v Essex (Leicester) 1990. BB 4-13 v Essex (Leicester) 1988.

MADDY, Darren Lee (Wreake Valley C), b Leicester 23 May 1974. 5'9". RHB, RM/OB. Debut 1994; cap 1996. **LOI:** 2 (1998): HS 1. Tours (Eng A): SA 1996-97 (Le), 1998-99; SL 1997-98; Z 1998-99; K 1997-98. 1000 runs (1): 1047 (1997). Le HS 202 Eng A v Kenya (Nairobi) 1997-98. Le HS 162 v Durham (Darlington) 1998. BB 2-21 v Lancs (Manchester) 1996. Awards: BHC 7 (inc 5 in 1998). **NWT:** HS 34 and BB 2-38 v Hants (Leicester) 1995. **BHC:** HS 151 v Minor C (Leicester) 1998. BB 3-32 v Leics (Leicester) 1996. **SL:** HS 106* v Durham (Chester-le-St) 1996. BB 3-11 v Hants (Leicester) 1997.

MASON, Timothy James (Denstone C), b Leicester 12 Apr 1975. 5'8". RHB, OB. Debut 1994. HS 4. BB 2-21 v A (Leicester) 1997. CC BB 1-22. **NWT:** HS 36 v Yorks (Leicester) 1997. BB 3-29 v Devon (Exmouth) 1997. **BHC:** HS 30 v Surrey (Oval) 1997. BB 3-41 v Northants (Northampton) 1998. **SL:** HS 17* v Somerset (Weston-s-M) 1995 and 17* v Kent (Canterbury) 1997. BB 4-12 v Essex (Leicester) 1998.

MILLNS, David James (Garibaldi CS), b Clipstone, Notts 27 Feb 1965. 6'3". LHB, RF. Nottinghamshire 1988-89. Leicestershire debut 1990; cap 1991; benefit 1999. Boland 1996-97. Tours: A 1992-93 (Eng A); SA 1996-97 (Le). HS 121 v Northants (Northampton) 1997. 50 wkts (4); most – 76 (1994). BB 9-37 (12-91 match) v Derbys (Derby) 1991. Awards: NWT 1; BHC 1. **NWT:** HS 29* v Derbys (Derby) 1992. BB 3-22 v Norfolk (Leicester) 1992. **BHC:** HS 39* v Warwks (Birmingham) 1996. BB 4-26 v Durham (Stockton) 1995. **SL:** HS 20* v Notts (Leicester) 1991. BB 2-11 v Somerset (Leicester) 1994.

MULLALLY, Alan David (Cannington HS, Perth, Australia; Wembley TC), b Southend-on-Sea, Essex 12 Jul 1969. 6'5". RHB, LFM. W Australia 1987-88 to 1989-90. Victoria 1990-91. Hampshire (1 match) 1988. Leicestershire debut 1990; cap 1993. **Tests:** 13 (1996 to 1998-99); HS 24 v P (Oval) 1996; BB 5-105 v A (Brisbane) 1998-99. **LOI:** 22 (1996 to 1998-99); HS 20; BB 4-18. Tours: A 1998-99; NZ 1996-97. HS 75 v Middx (Leicester) 1996. 50 wkts (4); most – 70 (1996). BB 7-55 (11-89 match) v Notts (Worksop) 1998. Award: NWT 1. **NWT:** HS 19* v Bucks (Marlow) 1993. BB 5-18 v Warwks (Leicester) 1998. **BHC:** HS 11 v Surrey (Leicester) 1992. BB 3-33 v Somerset (Leicester) 1997. **SL:** HS 38 v Kent (Leicester) 1994. BB 5-15 v Warwks (Birmingham) 1996.

NIXON, Paul Andrew (Ullswater HS, Penrith), b Carlisle, Cumberland 21 Oct 1970. 6'0". LHB, WK. Debut 1989; cap 1994. Cumberland 1987. MCC YC. Tours: I 1994-95 (Eng A); SA 1996-97 (Le). 1000 runs (1): 1046 (1994). HS 131 v Hants (Leicester) 1994. **NWT:** HS 39 v Sussex (Leicester) 1996. **BHC:** HS 53 v Surrey (Oval) 1997. **SL:** HS 84 v Sussex (Hove) 1995.

ORMOND, James (St Thomas More S, Nuneaton), b Walsgrave, Coventry, Warwks 20 Aug 1977. 6'3". RHB, RFM. Debut 1995. Tours (Eng A): SL 1997-98; K 1997-98. HS 49 Eng A v President's XI (Colombo) 1997-98. Le HS 35 v Glos (Leicester) 1997. BB 6-33 (9-62 match) v Somerset (Leicester) 1998. HS 1-58. **NWT:** HS –. BB 3-31 v Kent (Leicester) 1998. **SL:** HS 18 v Notts (Leicester) 1997. BB 4-12 v Middx (Leicester) 1998.

SMITH, Benjamin Francis (Kibworth HS), b Corby, Northants 3 Apr 1972. 5'9". RHB, RM. Debut 1990; cap 1995. Tour (Le): SA 1996-97. 1000 runs (2); most – 1243 (1996). HS 204 v Surrey (Oval) 1998. BB 1-5. Award: NWT 1. **NWT:** HS 63* v Cumb (Netherfield) 1994. **BHC:** HS 90 v Lancs (Leicester) 1998. **SL:** HS 115 v Somerset (Weston-s-M) 1995.

STEVENS, Darren Ian (Hinkley C), b Leicester 30 Apr 1976. 5'11". RHB, RM. Debut 1997. Tour (Eng A): I 1997-98. CC HS 8 and BB 1-5 v Sussex (Eastbourne) 1997. **SL:** HS 21 v Derbys (Derby) 1998.

SUTCLIFFE, Iain John (Leeds GS; Queen's C, Oxford), b Leeds, Yorks 20 Dec 1974. 6'2". LHB, occ OB. Oxford U 1994-96; blue 1995-96. Leicestershire debut 1995; cap 1997. Tour (Le): SA 1996-97. HS 167 v Middx (Leicester) 1998. BB 2-21 OU v CU (Lord's) 1996. CC BB 1-17. Awards: NWT 1; BHC 1. **NWT:** HS 103* v Devon (Exmouth) 1997. **BHC:** HS 105* v Notts (Nottingham) 1998. **SL:** HS 96 v Durham (Leicester) 1997. Boxing blue 1993-94.

WELLS, Vincent John (Sir William Nottidge S, Whitstable), b Dartford, Kent 6 Aug 1965. 6'0". RHB, RMF. Kent 1988-91. Leicestershire debut 1992; cap 1994. **LOI:** 7 (1998-99); HS 39; BB 3-30. Tour (Le): SA 1996-97. 1000 runs (2); most – 1331 (1996). HS 224 v Middx (Lord's) 1997. BB 5-18 v Notts (Worksop) 1998. Hat-trick 1994. Awards: NWT 3; BHC 1. **NWT:** 201 v Berks (Leicester) 1996. BB 3-30 v Devon (Exmouth) 1997. **BHC:** HS 90 v Durham (Chester-le-St) 1997. BB 6-25 v Minor C (Leicester) 1998. **SL:** HS 101 v Middx (Leicester) 1994. BB 5-10 v Surrey (Oval) 1994.

WHITAKER, John James (Uppingham S), b Skipton, Yorks 5 May 1962. 5'10". RHB, OB. Debut 1983; cap 1986; benefit 1993; captain 1996 to date. *Wisden* 1986. YC 1986. **Tests:** 1 (1986-87); HS 11 v A (Adelaide) 1986-87. **LOI:** 2 (1986-87); HS 44*. Tours: A 1986-87; SA 1996-97 (Le); Z 1989-90 (Eng A). 1000 runs (10); most – 1767 (1990). HS 218 v Yorks (Bradford) 1996. BB 1-29. Awards: NWT 1; BHC 2. **NWT:** HS 155 v Wilts (Swindon) 1984. **BHC:** HS 100 v Kent (Canterbury) 1991. **SL:** HS 132 v Glam (Swansea) 1984.

WILLIAMSON, Dominic (St Leonard's CS, Durham; Durham SFC), b Durham City 15 Nov 1975. 5'8". RHB, RM. Debut 1996. MCC YC. HS 41 v Hants (Leicester) 1998. BB 3-19 v Glam (Leicester) 1997 – on CC debut. **NWT:** HS 19* v Derbys (Leicester) 1998. BB 5-37 v Glam (Cardiff) 1998. **BHC:** HS 11 and BB 2-49 v Essex (Lord's) 1998. **SL:** HS 32* v Northants (Leicester) 1998. BB 5-32 v Sussex (Eastbourne) 1997.

WRIGHT, Ashley Spencer (King Edward VII S, Melton Mowbray), b Grantham, Lincs 21 Oct 1980. 6'0". RHB, RM. Staff 1998 – awaiting f-c debut.

NEW REGISTRATIONS

BOSWELL, Scott Antony John (Pocklington S; Wolverhampton U), b Fulford, Yorks 11 Sep 1974. 6'5". RHB, RFM. Debut (British U) 1996. Northamptonshire 1996-98. HS 35 Nh v Leics (Northampton) 1997. BB 5-94 Nh v Worcs (Northampton) 1997. **BHC** (Brit U): HS 14 v Essex (Chelmsford) 1996. BB 3-39 v Kent (Canterbury) 1997. **SL:** HS 2. BB 1-20.

KASPROWICZ, Michael Scott (Brisbane State HS), b South Brisbane, Australia 10 Feb 1972. 6'4". RHB, RF. Queensland 1989-90 to date. Essex 1994; cap 1994. **Tests** (A): 14 (1996-97 to 1998-99); HS 25 v I (Calcutta) 1997-98; BB 7-36 v E (Oval) 1997. **LOI** (A): 16 (1995-96 to 1998-99); HS 28*; BB 3-50. Tours (A): E 1995 (Young A), 1997; I 1997-98; P 1998-99. HS 49 Q v WA (Perth) 1989-90. BAC HS 44 Ex v Middx (Uxbridge) 1994. 50 wkts (1+2); most: 64 (1995-96). BB 7-36 (see Tests). BAC BB 7-83 Ex v Somerset (Weston-s-M) 1994. **NWT:** HS 13 and BB 5-60 Ex v Glam (Cardiff) 1994. **BHC:** HS 2. BB 2-52 Ex v Leics (Chelmsford) 1994. **SL:** HS 17 Ex v Glos (Chelmsford) 1994. BB 2-38 Ex v Glam (Southend) and 2-38 Ex v Northants (Chelmsford) 1994.

KHAN, Amer Ali (Muslim Modle HS, Lahore; MAO C, Lahore), b Lahore, Pakistan 5 Nov 1969. 5'9½". RHB, LB. Rawalpindi 1987-88 (one match as AAMER ALI). Middlesex 1995. Sussex 1997-98. HS 52 Sx v Hants (Southampton) 1997. BB 5-137 Sx v Middx (Lord's) 1997. **NWT:** HS 4. BB 1-13. **BHC:** HS BB 3-31 Sx v Hants (Hove) 1997. **SL:** HS 22* Sx v Middx (Lord's) 1997. BB 5-40 Sx v Kent (Horsham) 1997.

SACHDEVA, Atul (Lancaster GS), b Preston, Lancs 22 Aug 1980. RHB, LB.

RELEASED/RETIRED

SIMMONS, Philip Verant (Holy Cross C, Arima), b Arima, Trinidad 18 Apr 1963. 6'3½". RHB, RM. Debut for N Trinidad 1982-83. Trinidad 1982-83 to date; captain 1988-89. Durham 1989-90 (NWT only). Leicestershire 1994-96, 1998; cap 1994. Eastern (SA) 1996-97. *Wisden* 1996. **Tests** (WI): 26 (1987-88 to 1997-98); HS 110 and BB 2-34 v A (Melbourne) 1992-93. **LOI** (WI): 133 (1987-88 to 1998-99); HS 122; BB 4-3. Tours (WI): E 1988 (*part*), 1991, 1992 (RW), 1993 (RW), 1995; A 1992-93, 1995-96; I 1987-88, 1994-95; P 1997-98; SL 1993-94; Z 1983-84 (Young WI), 1986-87 (Young WI). 1000 runs (2); most – 1244 (1996). HS 261 v Northants (Leicester) 1994 – on Le debut (county record). 50 wkts (1): 56 (1996). BB 7-49 v Durham (Darlington) 1998. Awards: NWT 1; BHC 2. **NWT:** HS 107* v Staffs (Leicester) 1998. BB 3-31 v Cumb (Netherfield) 1994. **BHC:** HS 89 v Warwks (Leicester) 1998. BB 5-33 v Kent (Leicester) 1998. **SL:** HS 140 v Middx (Leicester) 1994. BB 5-37 v Middx (Leicester) 1996.

LEICESTERSHIRE 1998

RESULTS SUMMARY

	Place	Won	Lost	Tied	Drew	No Result
Britannic Assurance Championship	1st	11			6	
All First-Class Matches		11	1		7	
NatWest Trophy	Semi-Finalist					
Benson and Hedges Cup	Finalist					
Sunday League	4th	9	6			2

BRITANNIC ASSURANCE CHAMPIONSHIP AVERAGES

BATTING AND FIELDING

Cap		M	I	NO	HS	Runs	Avge	100	50	Ct/St
1995	B.F.Smith	17	22	4	204	1165	64.72	4	3	13
1998	A.Habib	17	20	5	198	929	61.93	3	3	12
1991	D.J.Millns	10	8	3	99	229	45.80	–	1	4
1994	P.A.Nixon	17	19	4	101*	580	38.66	2	1	37/5
1994	V.J.Wells	16	24	1	171	826	35.91	3	3	10
1990	C.C.Lewis	12	14	3	71*	367	33.36	–	4	10
1997	I.J.Sutcliffe	17	23	3	167	659	32.95	1	2	11
1994	P.V.Simmons	17	19	–	194	464	24.42	1	2	23
1996	D.L.Maddy	16	23	2	162	512	24.38	2	–	16
–	C.D.Crowe	5	4	1	29*	63	21.00	–	–	3
1998	M.T.Brimson	16	12	5	54*	112	16.00	–	1	3
1993	A.D.Mullally	15	11	2	38*	132	14.66	–	–	3
–	J.Ormond	5	5	–	9	15	3.00	–	–	–
–	J.M.Dakin	5	4	–	7	7	1.75	–	–	2

Also played (1 match each): T.J.Mason did not bat; D.Williamson 41* (1 ct).

BOWLING

	O	M	R	W	Avge	Best	5wI	10wM
V.J.Wells	199.1	66	514	36	14.27	5-18	1	–
J.Ormond	133.3	51	311	19	16.36	6-33	2	–
A.D.Mullally	448.5	156	1128	60	18.80	7-55	3	1
P.V.Simmons	170.5	44	491	23	21.34	7-49	1	–
D.J.Millns	232.3	53	754	34	22.17	4-60	–	–
C.C.Lewis	266.4	53	972	39	24.92	6-60	2	–
M.T.Brimson	345	126	810	31	26.12	4- 4	–	–

Also bowled: C.D.Crowe 21-5-61-4; J.M.Dakin 89-25-243-3; A.Habib 4-0-15-0; D.L.Maddy 24-7-83-2; T.J.Mason 45.2-9-139-0; B.F.Smith 5-0-11-0; I.J.Sutcliffe 9-0-51-1; D.Williamson 23-4-73-1.

The First-Class Averages (pp 117-131) give the records of Leicestershire players in all first-class county matches (their other opponents being the Sri Lankans and Cambridge University).

LEICESTERSHIRE RECORDS

FIRST-CLASS CRICKET

Highest Total	For	701-4d		v	Worcs	Worcester	1906
	V	761-6d		by	Essex	Chelmsford	1990
Lowest Total	For	25		v	Kent	Leicester	1912
	V	24		by	Glamorgan	Leicester	1971
		24		by	Oxford U	Oxford	1985
Highest Innings	For	261	P.V.Simmons	v	Northants	Leicester	1994
	V	341	G.H.Hirst	for	Yorkshire	Leicester	1905

Highest Partnership for each Wicket

1st	390	B.Dudleston/J.F.Steele	v	Derbyshire	Leicester	1979
2nd	289*	J.C.Balderstone/D.I.Gower	v	Essex	Leicester	1981
3rd	316*	W.Watson/A.Wharton	v	Somerset	Taunton	1961
4th	290*	P.Willey/T.J.Boon	v	Warwicks	Leicester	1984
5th	322	B.F.Smith/P.V.Simmons	v	Notts	Worksop	1998
6th	284	P.V.Simmons/P.A.Nixon	v	Durham	Chester-le-St	1996
7th	219*	J.D.R.Benson/P.Whitticase	v	Hampshire	Bournemouth	1991
8th	172	P.A.Nixon/D.J.Millns	v	Lancashire	Manchester	1996
9th	160	W.W.Odell/R.T.Crawford	v	Worcs	Leicester	1902
10th	228	R.Illingworth/K.Higgs	v	Northants	Leicester	1977

Best Bowling	For	10-18	G.Geary	v	Glamorgan	Pontypridd	1929
(Innings)	V	10-32	H.Pickett	for	Essex	Leyton	1895
Best Bowling	For	16-96	G.Geary	v	Glamorgan	Pontypridd	1929
(Match)	V	16-102	C.Blythe	for	Kent	Leicester	1909

Most Runs – Season	2446	L.G.Berry	(av 52.04)		1937
Most Runs – Career	30143	L.G.Berry	(av 30.32)		1924-51
Most 100s – Season	7	L.G.Berry			1937
	7	W.Watson			1959
	7	B.F.Davison			1982
Most 100s – Career	45	L.G.Berry			1924-51
Most Wkts – Season	170	J.E.Walsh	(av 18.96)		1948
Most Wkts – Career	2130	W.E.Astill	(av 23.19)		1906-39

LIMITED-OVERS CRICKET

Highest Total	NWT	406-5		v	Berkshire	Leicester	1996
	BHC	382-6		v	Minor C	Leicester	1998
	SL	344-4		v	Durham	Chester-le-St	1996
Lowest Total	NWT	56		v	Northants	Leicester	1964
	BHC	56		v	Minor C	Wellington	1982
	SL	36		v	Sussex	Leicester	1973
Highest Innings	NWT	201	V.J.Wells	v	Berkshire	Leicester	1996
	BHC	158*	B.F.Davison	v	Warwicks	Coventry	1972
	SL	152	B.Dudleston	v	Lancashire	Manchester	1975
Best Bowling	NWT	6-20	K.Higgs	v	Staffs	Longton	1975
	BHC	6-25	V.J.Wells	v	Minor C	Leicester	1998
	SL	6-17	K.Higgs	v	Glamorgan	Leicester	1973

MIDDLESEX

Formation of Present Club: 2 February 1864
Colours: Blue
Badge: Three Seaxes
Championships (since 1890): (10) 1903, 1920, 1921, 1947, 1976, 1980, 1982, 1985, 1990, 1993
Joint Championships: (2) 1949, 1977
NatWest Trophy/Gillette Cup Winners: (4) 1977, 1980, 1984, 1988
Benson and Hedges Cup Winners: (2) 1983, 1986
Sunday League Champions: (1) 1992
Match Awards: NWT 56; BHC 60

Secretary: V.J.Codrington
  Lord's Cricket Ground, London NW8 8QN (Tel 0171 289 1300/286 1310)
Captain: M.R.Ramprakash. **Vice-Captain/Overseas Player:** J.L.Langer.
1999 Beneficiary: P.C.R.Tufnell. **Scorer:** M.J.Smith

BATT, Christopher James (Cox Green CS), b Taplow, Bucks 22 Sep 1976. 6'4". LHB, LMF. Sussex 1997 – no CC appearances. Middlesex debut 1998. Berkshire 1997. HS 43 v Warwks (Lord's) 1998. BB 6-101 v Notts (Nottingham) 1998. **NWT:** HS 0. BB 1-37. **SL:** HS –. BB 3-26 v Yorks (Lord's) 1998.

BLANCHETT, Ian Neale (Downham Market SFC; Luton U), b Melbourne, Australia 2 Oct 1975. 6'4". RHB, RMF. Debut 1998. Norfolk 1993-94. HS 18 v Worcs (Uxbridge) 1998 – on debut. BB 2-38 v Glam (Lord's) 1998. **BHC:** HS –. BB 1-44. **SL:** HS 9*. BB 1-16.

BLOOMFIELD, Timothy Francis (Halliford S, Shepperton), b Ashford 31 May 1973. 6'2". RHB, RMF. Debut 1997. Berkshire 1996. HS 20* v Sussex (Hove) 1998. BB 5-67 v Northants (Northampton) 1998. **NWT:** HS 0. BB 1-25. **BHC:** HS –. **SL:** HS 15 v Warwks (Lord's) 1998. BB 2-8 v Surrey (Lord's) 1998.

COOK, Simon James (Matthew Arnold S), b Oxford 15 Jan 1977. 6'4". RHB, RM. Awaiting f-c debut. **BHC:** HS 6.

DUTCH, Keith Philip (Nower Hill HS; Weald C), b Harrow 21 Mar 1973. 5'10". RHB, OB. Debut 1993. MCC YC. HS 79 v Glos (Bristol) 1997. BB 3-25 v Somerset (Uxbridge) 1996. **NWT:** HS 49* v Durham (Southgate) 1998. BB 2-30 v Herefords (Lord's) 1998. **BHC:** HS 20 v Somerset (Lord's) 1997. BB 4-42 v Glam (Cardiff) 1997. **SL:** HS 58 v Kent (Lord's) 1997. BB 4-22 v Yorks (Lord's) 1998.

FRASER, Alastair Gregory James (Gayton HS, John Lyon S, Harrow; Harrow Weald SFC), b Edgware 17 Oct 1967. Brother of A.R.C. (Middlesex and England). 6'1". RHB, RFM. Middlesex 1986-89 and 1998 (L-O matches). Essex 1991-92. HS 52* Ex v Sussex (Horsham) 1991. M HS 19* v Warwks (Uxbridge) 1986. BB 3-46 v NZ (Lord's) 1986. BAC BB 2-12 v Lancs (Lord's) 1986. Award: BHC 1. **NWT:** HS 18 and BB 1-39 v Durham (Southgate) 1998. **BHC:** HS 6 (Ex). BB 4-45 v Essex (Chelmsford) 1998. **SL:** HS 14 v Surrey (Guildford) 1998. BB 4-19 v Durham (Lord's) 1998.

FRASER, Angus Robert Charles (Gayton HS, Harrow; Orange Sr HS, Edgware), b Billinge, Lancs 8 Aug 1965. Brother of A.G.J. (Middx and Essex 1986-92). 6'5". RHB, RMF. Debut 1984; cap 1988; benefit 1994. MBE 1999. *Wisden* 1995. **Tests:** 46 (1989 to 1998-99); HS 32 v SL (Oval) 1998; BB 8-53 (11-110 match) v WI (P-of-S) 1997-98 – record England innings analysis v WI. **LOI:** 37 (1989-90 to 1998); HS 38*; BB 4-22. Tours: A 1990-91, 1994-95 (part), 1998-99; SA 1995-96; WI 1989-90, 1993-94, 1997-98. HS 92 v Surrey (Oval) 1990. 50 wkts (7); most – 92 (1989). BB 8-53 (*Tests*). M BB 7-40 v Leics (Lord's) 1993. **NWT:** HS 19 v Durham (Darlington) 1989. BB 4-34 v Yorks (Leeds) 1988. **BHC:** HS 30* v Ire (Dublin) 1997. BB 4-49 v Kent (Canterbury) 1995. **SL:** HS 33 v Essex (Chelmsford) 1997. BB 5-32 v Derbys (Lord's) 1995.

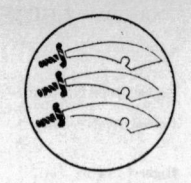

GOODCHILD, David John (Whitmore HS; Weald C; N London U), b Harrow 17 Sep 1976. 6'2". RHB, RM. Debut 1996. HS 105 v SL (Lord's) 1998. CC HS 83* v Yorks (Lord's) 1998. **SL:** HS 38* v Hants (Southampton) 1998.

HEWITT, James Peter (Teddington S; Richmond C; City of Westminster C), b Southwark, London 26 Feb 1976. 6'2½". LHB, RMF. Debut 1996; cap 1998. HS 75 v Essex (Chelmsford) 1997. 50 wkts (1): 60 (1997). BB 6-14 v Glam (Cardiff) 1997. Took wicket of R.I.Dawson (Glos) with first ball in f-c cricket. **NWT:** HS 14* v Kent (Lord's) 1997. BB 1-37. **BHC:** HS 14 v Ire (Dublin) 1997. BB 2-49 v Somerset (Lord's) 1997. **SL:** HS 32* v Glos (Bristol) 1997. BB 4-24 v Worcs (Uxbridge) 1998.

HUTTON, Benjamin Leonard (Radley C; Durham U), b Johannesburg, SA 29 Jan 1977. 6'2". Elder son of R.A. (Yorkshire, Transvaal and England 1962 to 1975-76); grandson of Sir Leonard (Yorkshire and England 1934-60). LHB, RMF. British U 1998. Awaiting Middlesex debut. HS 10 Brit U v SA (Cambridge) 1998. **BHC** (Brit U): HS 4 and BB 2-43 v Surrey (Oval) 1998.

JOHNSON, Richard Leonard (Sunbury Manor S; S Pelthorne C), b Chertsey, Surrey 29 Dec 1974. 6'2". RHB, RMF. Debut 1992; cap 1995. Tour: I 1994-95 (Eng A – part). **HS** 50* v CU (Cambridge) 1994. CC HS 47 v Hants (Southampton) 1994. 50 wkts (2); most – 50 (1997, 1998). BB 10-45 v Derbys (Derby) 1994 (second youngest to take all ten wickets in any f-c match). Award: NWT 1. **NWT:** HS 45* v Durham (Southgate) 1998. BB 5-50 v Kent (Lord's) 1997. **BHC:** HS 26 v Ire (Lord's) 1998. BB 3-33 v Glam (Cardiff) 1998. **SL:** HS 29 v Worcs (Lord's) 1996 and 29 v Essex (Chelmsford) 1997. BB 4-45 v Leics (Leicester) 1998.

KETTLEBOROUGH, Richard Allan (Worksop C), b Sheffield, Yorks 15 Mar 1973. 6'0". LHB, RM. Yorkshire 1994-97. Middlesex debut 1998. Tour: Z 1995-96 (Y). HS 108 Y v Essex (Leeds) 1996. M HS 92* v OU (Oxford) 1998. BB 2-26 Y v Notts (Scarborough) 1996. **SL:** HS 48 v Hants (Southampton) 1998. BB 2-43 Y v Surrey (Oval) 1995.

LANGER, Justin Lee (Aquinas C; U of WA), b perth, Australia 21 Nov 1970. 5'8". LHB, RM. W Australia 1991-92 to date. Middlesex debut/cap 1998. **Tests** (A): 16 (1992-93 to 1998-99); HS 179* v E (Adelaide) 1998-99. **LOI:** 8 (1993-94 to 1997); HS 36. Tours (A): E 1995 (Young A), 1997; SA 1996-97; WI 1994-95, 1998-99; NZ 1992-93; P 1994-95, 1998-99. 1000 runs (1+2); most – 1448 (1998). HS 274* WA v S Australia (Perth) 1996-97. M HS 233* v Somerset (Lord's) 1998. BB 2-17 Aus A v SA A (Brisbane) 1997-98. M BB 1-10. Award: NWT 1. **NWT:** HS 114* v Herefords (Lord's) 1998. BB 1-45. **BHC:** HS 71 v Essex (Lord's) 1998. **SL:** HS 87* v Northants (Northampton) 1998. BB 3-51 v Surrey (Guildford) 1998.

LARAMAN, Aaron William (Enfield GS), b Enfield 10 Jan 1979. 6'5". RHB, RM. Debut 1998. Awaiting CC debut. HS –. **SL:** HS 3.

MARTIN, Neil Donald (Verulam S, St Albans), b Enfield 19 Aug 1979. 5'10". RHB, RFM. Debut 1998. HS –. BB 1-22. CC BB –. **SL:** HS –. BB 2-28 v Essex (Uxbridge) 1998.

NASH, David Charles (Sunbury Manor S; Malvern C), b Chertsey, Surrey 19 Jan 1978. 5'8". RHB, occ LB, WK. Debut 1997. Tour: SL 1997-98 (Eng A). HS 114 v Somerset (Lord's) 1998. **BHC:** HS 9*. **SL:** HS 36 v Surrey (Guildford) 1998.

RAMPRAKASH, Mark Ravin (Gayton HS; Harrow Weald SFC), b Bushey, Herts 5 Sep 1969. 5'9". RHB, RM. Debut 1987; cap 1990; captain 1997 to date. YC 1991. **Tests**: 34 (1991 to 1998-99); HS 154 v WI (Bridgetown) 1997-98. **LOI:** 13 (1991 to 1997-98); HS 51. Tours: A 1994-95 (*part*), 1998-99; SA 1995-96; WI 1991-92 (Eng A), 1993-94, 1997-98; NZ 1991-92; I 1994-95 (Eng A); P 1990-91 (Eng A); SL 1990-91 (Eng A). 1000 runs (8) inc 2000 (1): 2258 (1995). HS 235 v Yorks (Leeds) 1995. BB 3-32 v Glam (Lord's) 1998. Awards: NWT 2; BHC 3. **NWT:** HS 104 v Surrey (Uxbridge) 1990. BB 2-15 v Ire (Dublin) 1991. **BHC:** HS 119* v Northants (Northampton) 1994. BB 3-35 v Brit U (Cambridge) 1996. **SL:** HS 147* v Worcs (Lord's) 1990. BB 5-38 v Leics (Lord's) 1993.

ROSEBERRY, Michael Anthony (Durham S), b Sunderland 28 Nov 1966. Elder brother of A. (Leics and Glam 1992-94). 6'1". RHB, RM. Middlesex 1986-94; cap 1990. Durham 1995-98; captain 1995-96; cap 1998. Tour: A 1992-93 (Eng A). 1000 runs (4) inc 2000 (1): 2044 (1992). HS 185 M v Leics (Lord's) 1993. Du HS 145* v OU (Oxford) 1996. BB 1-1. Awards: NWT 1; BHC 1. **NWT:** HS 121 Du v Herefords (Chester-le-St) 1995. BB 1-22. **BHC:** HS 84 M v Minor C (of's) 1992. **SL:** HS 119* M v Surrey (Oval) 1994.

SHAH, Owais Alam (Isleworth & Syon S), b Karachi, Pakistan 22 Oct 1978. 6'0". RHB, OB. Debut 1996. Tours (Eng A): A 1996-97; SL 1997-98. HS 140 v Yorks (Lord's) 1998. BB 1-24 v Somerset (Uxbridge) 1996. **NWT:** HS 37 v Herefords (Lord's) 1998. **BHC:** HS 43 v Essex (Lord's) 1998. BB 2-2 v Glam (Cardiff) 1998. **SL:** HS 87* v Glam (Lord's) 1998. BB 1-4.

STRAUSS, Andrew John (Radley C; Durham U), b Johannesburg, SA 2 Mar 1977. 5'11". LHB, LM. Debut 1998. Oxfordshire 1996. HS 83 v Hants (Southampton) 1998 – on debut. **BHC:** (Brit U) HS 29 v Kent (Oxford) 1998. **SL:** HS 15 v Glos (Lord's) 1998.

TUFNELL, Philip Clive Roderick (Highgate S), b Barnet, Herts 29 Apr 1966. 6'0". RHB, SLA. Debut 1986; cap 1990; benefit 1999. MCC YC. **Tests:** 34 (1990-91 to 1997-98); HS 22* v I (Madras) 1992-93; BB 7-47 (11-147 match) v NZ (Christchurch) 1991-92, took 11-93 v A (Oval) 1997. **LOI:** 20 (1990-91 to 1996-97); HS 5*; BB 4-22. Tours: A 1990-91, 1994-95; WI 1993-94, 1997-98; NZ 1991-92, 1996-97; I/SL 1992-93, Z 1996-97. HS 67* v Worcs (Lord's) 1996. 50 wkts (7); most – 88 (1991). BB 8-29 v Glam (Cardiff) 1993. Award: NWT 1. **NWT:** HS 8. BB 3-29 v Herts (Lord's) 1988. **BHC:** HS 18 v Warwks (Lord's) 1991. BB 3-32 v Northants (Lord's) 1994. **SL:** HS 13* v Glam (Merthyr Tydfil) 1989. BB 5-28 v Leics (Lord's) 1993.

WEEKES, Paul Nicholas (Homerton House SS, Hackney), b Hackney, London 8 Jul 1969. 5'10". LHB, OB. Debut 1990; cap 1998. Tour: I 1994-95 (Eng A). MCC YC. 1000 runs (1): 1218 (1996). HS 171* v Somerset (Uxbridge) 1996. BB 8-39 v Glam (Lord's) 1996. Awards: NWT 2; BHC 3. **NWT:** HS 143* v Cornwall (St Austell) 1995. BB 3-35 v Cumb (Carlisle) 1996. **BHC:** HS 77 v Somerset (Lord's) 1997. BB 3-32 v Warwks (Lord's) 1994. **SL:** HS 119* v Glam (Lord's) 1996. BB 4-29 v Glos (Lord's) 1996 and 4-29 v Essex (Lord's) 1996.

NEW REGISTRATIONS

ALLEYNE, David (Enfield GS), b York 17 Apr 1976. RHB, WK.

BROWN, Michael James (Queen Elizabeth GS, Blackburn), b Burnley, Lancs 9 Feb 1980. RHB, OB.

BRYAN, Russell Barnaby, b Maidstone, Kent 14 Feb 1981. RHB, RFM.

HUNT, Thomas 'Thos', b Melbourne, Australia 19 Jan 1982. Resident in UK since 1985 (English parents). LHB, LFM. Registration tbc.

MAUNDERS, John Kenneth (Ashford S), b Ashford 4 Apr 1981. LHB, LM. Middx 2nd XI debut aged 16y 19d.

RELEASED/RETIRED
(Having made a first-class County appearance in 1998)

BROWN, Keith Robert (Chace S, Enfield), b Edmonton 18 Mar 1963. Brother of G.K. (Middx 1986 and Durham 1992). 5'11". RHB, WK, RSM. Middlesex 1984-98; cap 1990; benefit 1998. MCC YC. 1000 runs (2); most – 1505 (1990). HS 200* v Notts (Lord's) 1990. BB 2-7 v Glos (Bristol) 1987. Awards: NWT 2; BHC 3. **NWT:** HS 103* v Surrey (Uxbridge) 1990. **BHC:** HS 114 v Sussex (Lord's) 1998. **SL:** HS 102 v Somerset (Lord's) 1988.

continued on p 107

MIDDLESEX 1998

RESULTS SUMMARY

	Place	Won	Lost	Tied	Drew	No Result
Britannic Assurance Championship	17th	2	9		6	
All First-Class Matches		2	9		8	
NatWest Trophy	Quarter-Finalist					
Benson and Hedges Cup	Quarter-Finalist					
Sunday League	12th	7	8			2

BRITANNIC ASSURANCE CHAMPIONSHIP AVERAGES

BATTING AND FIELDING

Cap		M	I	NO	HS	Runs	Avge	100	50	Ct/St
1998	J.L.Langer	14	26	5	233*	1393	66.33	4	6	11
1990	M.R.Ramprakash	9	15	2	128*	635	48.84	4	–	5
1977	M.W.Gatting	16	28	3	241	1077	43.08	2	6	18
1993	P.N.Weekes	15	24	5	139	811	42.68	1	5	18
–	O.A.Shah	14	22	2	140	707	35.35	2	3	10
1990	K.R.Brown	16	23	5	59*	511	28.38	–	2	40/5
–	A.J.Strauss	3	6	–	83	146	24.33	–	1	3
–	R.A.Kettleborough	10	19	3	62*	373	23.31	–	2	6
–	D.C.Nash	12	17	–	114	361	21.23	1	1	7/1
–	D.J.Goodchild	6	12	1	83*	213	19.36	–	2	1
1998	J.P.Hewitt	15	19	2	53	268	15.76	–	1	5
1995	R.L.Johnson	13	19	3	43	230	14.37	–	–	5
–	C.J.Batt	7	12	1	43	121	11.00	–	–	1
1988	A.R.C.Fraser	8	9	2	30	63	9.00	–	–	1
1990	P.C.R.Tufnell	16	21	6	19	131	8.73	–	–	2
–	T.F.Bloomfield	7	9	4	20*	35	7.00	–	–	–
–	I.N.Blanchett	3	4	–	18	25	6.25	–	–	1

Also played: K.P.Dutch (2 matches) 11, 6, 16 (1 ct); N.D.Martin (1) did not bat.

BOWLING

	O	M	R	W	Avge	Best	5wI	10wM
A.R.C.Fraser	252	64	618	34	18.17	6- 23	1	–
R.L.Johnson	355.2	72	1297	49	26.46	7- 86	1	–
T.F.Bloomfield	146.5	25	586	20	29.30	5- 67	2	–
J.P.Hewitt	377.3	64	1378	41	33.60	6- 71	2	–
C.J.Batt	170	21	712	19	37.47	6-101	2	–
P.C.R.Tufnell	607.5	158	1512	36	42.00	4- 24	1	–
P.N.Weekes	237	37	702	13	54.00	3-113	–	–

Also bowled: I.N.Blanchett 78-9-285-5; K.P.Dutch 27-7-63-1; M.W.Gatting 5-1-9-1; D.J.Goodchild 11-1-42-0; R.A.Kettleborough 23-1-89-0; J.L.Langer 13-5-34-1; N.D.Martin 12-1-61-0; D.C.Nash 0.1-0-0-0; M.R.Ramprakash 42.2-8-112-5; O.A.Shah 17.5-1-79-1.

The First-Class Averages (pp 117-131) give the records of Middlesex players in all first-class county matches (Middlesex's other opponents being the Sri Lankans and Oxford University), with the exception of A.R.C.Fraser and M.R.Ramprakash, whose full county figures are as above. B.L.Hutton appeared in one match for the British Universities.

MIDDLESEX RECORDS

FIRST-CLASS CRICKET

Highest Total	For 642-3d		v	Hampshire	Southampton	1923
	V 665		by	W Indians	Lord's	1939
Lowest Total	For 20		v	MCC	Lord's	1864
	V 31		by	Glos	Bristol	1924
Highest Innings	For 331*	J.D.B.Robertson	v	Worcs	Worcester	1949
	V 316*	J.B.Hobbs	for	Surrey	Lord's	1926

Highest Partnership for each Wicket

1st	372	M.W.Gatting/J.L.Langer	v	Essex	Southgate	1998
2nd	380	F.A.Tarrant/J.W.Hearne	v	Lancashire	Lord's	1914
3rd	424*	W.J.Edrich/D.C.S.Compton	v	Somerset	Lord's	1948
4th	325	J.W.Hearne/E.H.Hendren	v	Hampshire	Lord's	1919
5th	338	R.S.Lucas/T.C.O'Brien	v	Sussex	Hove	1895
6th	270	J.D.Carr/P.N.Weekes	v	Glos	Lord's	1994
7th	271*	E.H.Hendren/F.T.Mann	v	Notts	Nottingham	1925
8th	182*	M.H.C.Doll/H.R.Murrell	v	Notts	Lord's	1913
9th	160*	E.H.Hendren/T.J.Durston	v	Essex	Leyton	1927
10th	230	R.W.Nicholls/W.Roche	v	Kent	Lord's	1899

Best Bowling	For 10- 40	G.O.B.Allen	v	Lancashire	Lord's	1929
(Innings)	V 9- 38	R.C.R-Glasgow†	for	Somerset	Lord's	1924
Best Bowling	For 16-114	G.Burton	v	Yorkshire	Sheffield	1888
(Match)	16-114	J.T.Hearne	v	Lancashire	Manchester	1898
	V 16-109	C.W.L.Parker	for	Glos	Cheltenham	1930

Most Runs – Season	2669	E.H.Hendren	(av 83.41)	1923
Most Runs – Career	40302	E.H.Hendren	(av 48.81)	1907-37
Most 100s – Season	13	D.C.S.Compton		1947
Most 100s – Career	119	E.H.Hendren		1907-37
Most Wkts – Season	158	F.J.Titmus	(av 14.63)	1955
Most Wkts – Career	2361	F.J.Titmus	(av 21.27)	1949-82

LIMITED-OVERS CRICKET

Highest Total	NWT	304-7		v	Surrey	The Oval	1995
		304-8		v	Cornwall	St Austell	1995
	BHC	325-5		v	Leics	Leicester	1992
	SL	290-6		v	Worcs	Lord's	1990
Lowest Total	NWT	41		v	Essex	Westcliff	1972
	BHC	73		v	Essex	Lord's	1985
	SL	23		v	Yorkshire	Leeds	1974
Highest Innings	NWT	158	G.D.Barlow	v	Lancashire	Lord's	1984
	BHC	143*	M.W.Gatting	v	Sussex	Hove	1985
	SL	147*	M.R.Ramprakash	v	Worcs	Lord's	1990
Best Bowling	NWT	6-15	W.W.Daniel	v	Sussex	Hove	1980
	BHC	7-12	W.W.Daniel	v	Minor C (E)	Ipswich	1978
	SL	6- 6	R.W.Hooker	v	Surrey	Lord's	1969

† R.C.Robertson-Glasgow

NORTHAMPTONSHIRE

Formation of Present Club: 31 July 1878
Colours: Maroon
Badge: Tudor Rose
Championships: (0) Second 1912, 1957, 1965, 1976
NatWest Trophy/Gillette Cup Winners: (2) 1976, 1992
Benson and Hedges Cup Winners: (1) 1980
Sunday League Champions: (0) Third 1991
Match Awards: NWT 50; BHC 55

Chief Executive: S.P.Coverdale
County Ground, Wantage Road, Northampton, NN1 4TJ (Tel 01604 32917)
Captain/Overseas Player: M.L.Hayden. **Vice-Captain:** D.Ripley.
1999 Beneficiary: K.M.Curran. **Scorer:** A.C.Kingston

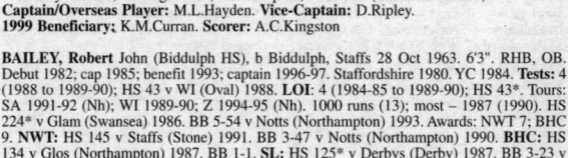

BAILEY, Robert John (Biddulph HS), b Biddulph, Staffs 28 Oct 1963. 6'3". RHB, OB. Debut 1982; cap 1985; benefit 1993; captain 1996-97. Staffordshire 1980. YC 1984. **Tests:** 4 (1988 to 1989-90); HS 43 v WI (Oval) 1988. **LOI:** 4 (1984-85 to 1989-90); HS 43*. **Tours:** SA 1991-92 (Nh); WI 1989-90; Z 1994-95 (Nh). 1000 runs (13); most – 1987 (1990). HS 224* v Glam (Swansea) 1986. BB 5-54 v Notts (Northampton) 1993. Awards: NWT 7; BHC 9. **NWT:** HS 145 v Staffs (Stone) 1991. BB 3-47 v Notts (Northampton) 1990. **BHC:** HS 134 v Glos (Northampton) 1987. BB 1-1. **SL:** HS 125* v Derbys (Derby) 1987. BB 3-23 v Leics (Leicester) 1987.

BAILEY, Tobin Michael Barnaby (Bedford S; Loughborough U), b Kettering 28 Aug 1976. 5'10". RHB, WK. Debut 1996. British U 1998. Bedfordshire 1994-96. HS 31* v Lancs (Northampton) 1996. **BHC:** (Brit U) HS 52 v Glos (Bristol) 1997. **SL:** HS –.

BLAIN, John Angus Rae (Penicuik HS; Jewel & Esk Valley C), b Edinburgh, Scotland 4 Jan 1979. 6'1". RHB, RMF. Scotland 1996. Northamptonshire debut 1997. HS 0 and BB 1-18 v Worcs (Northampton) 1997. **NWT:** (Scot) HS –. BB 2-56 v Durham (Chester-le-St) 1996. **BHC:** (Scot) HS 10* v Notts (Nottingham) 1996. BB 2-82 v Leics (Leicester) 1997. **SL:** HS –. BB 5-24 v Derbys (Derby) 1997.

BROWN, Jason Fred (St Margaret Ward HS & SFC), b Newcastle-under-Lyme, Staffs 10 Oct 1974. 6'0". RHB, OB. Debut 1996. Staffordshire 1994 to date. HS 16* v Durham (Northampton) 1997. BB 6-53 (11-102 match) v Somerset (Taunton) 1998. **SL:** HS –. BB 4-26 v Leics (Northampton) 1997.

CURRAN, Kevin Malcolm (Marandellas HS), b Rusape, S Rhodesia 7 Sep 1959. Son of K.P. (Rhodesia 1947-48 to 1953-54). 6'1". RHB, RMF. Zimbabwe 1980-81 to 1987-88. Qualified for England 1994. Natal 1988-89. Gloucestershire 1985-90; cap 1985. Northamptonshire debut 1991; cap 1992; captain 1998; benefit 1999. Boland 1994-95 and 1997-98. **LOI:** (Z): 11 (1983 to 1987-88); HS 73; BB 3-65. Tours (Z): E 1982; SL 1983-84. 1000 runs (7); most – 1353 (1986). HS 159 v Glam (Abergavenny) 1997. 50 wkts (5); most – 67 (1993). BB 7-47 Natal v Transvaal (Johannesburg) 1988-89 and v Yorks (Harrogate) 1993. Awards: NWT 2; BHC 2. **NWT:** HS 78* v Cambs (Northampton) 1992. BB 4-34 Gs v Northants (Bristol) 1985. **BHC:** HS 71 v Notts (Northampton) 1998. BB 4-38 v Worcs (Northampton) 1995. **SL:** HS 119* v Kent (Canterbury) 1990. BB 5-15 Gs v Leics (Gloucester) 1988.

DAVIES, Michael Kenton (Loughborough GS, Loughborough U), b Ashby-de-la-Zouch, Leics 17 Jul 1976. 6'0". RHB, SLA. Debut 1997. British U 1998. HS 17 v Glam (Abergavenny) 1997. BB 5-19 v Sussex (Northampton) 1998. **BHC:** (Brit U) HS 2*. BB 3-11 v Somerset (Taunton) 1998.

FOLLETT, David (Moorland Road HS, Burslem; Stoke-on-Trent TC), b Newcastle-under-Lyme, Staffs 14 Oct 1968. 6'2". RHB, RFM. Middlesex 1995-96. Northamptonshire debut 1997. Staffordshire 1994. HS 17 M v Yorks (Lord's) 1996. Nh HS 7. BB 8-22 (10-87 match) M v Durham (Lord's) 1996. Nh BB 3-48 v Glos (Bristol) 1998. **BHC:** HS 4 (twice). BB 4-39 v Scot (Northampton) 1997. **SL:** HS 3*. BB 3-26 v Worcs (Worcester) 1998.

INNES, Kevin John (Weston Favell Upper S), b Wellingborough 24 Sep 1975. 5'10". RHB, RM. 2nd XI debut 1990 (aged 14yr 8m – Northamptonshire record). Debut 1994. HS 63 and BB 4-61 v Lancs (Northampton) 1996. **NWT:** HS 25 v Cumb (Barrow) 1997. **BHC:** HS 1. BB 1-25. **SL:** HS 19* v Worcs (Northampton) 1997. BB 1-35.

LOGAN, Richard James (Wolverhampton GS), b Stone, Staffs 28 Jan 1980. 6'1". RHB, RMF. Staff 1997 – awaiting f-c debut.

LOYE, Malachy Bernhard (Moulton S), b Northampton 27 Sep 1972. 6'2". RHB, OB. Debut 1991; cap 1994. Tours (Eng A): SA 1993-94, 1998-99; Z 1994-95 (Nh), 1998-99. 1000 runs (2); most – 1198 (1998). HS 322* v Glam (Northampton) 1998 – record Northants score. Award: NWT 1. **NWT:** HS 65 v Essex (Chelmsford) 1993. **BHC:** HS 68* v Middx (Lord's) 1994. **SL:** HS 122 v Somerset (Luton) 1993.

MALCOLM, Devon Eugene (St Elizabeth THS; Richmond C, Sheffield; Derby CHE), b Kingston, Jamaica 22 Feb 1963. Qualified for England 1987. 6'2". RHB, RF. Derbyshire 1984-97; cap 1989; benefit 1997. Northamptonshire debut 1998. *Wisden* 1994. **Tests:** 40 (1989 to 1997); HS 29 v A (Sydney) 1994-95; BB 9-57 v SA (Oval) 1994 – sixth best analysis in Test cricket. **LOI:** 10 (1990 to 1993-94); HS 4; BB 3-40. Tours: A 1990-91, 1994-95; SA 1995-96; WI 1989-90, 1991-92 (Eng A), 1993-94; I 1992-93; SL 1992-93. HS 51 De v Surrey (Derby) 1989. Nh HS 42 v Glam (Northampton) 1998. 50 wkts (6); most – 82 (1996). BB 9-57 (*see Tests*). CC BB 6-23 De v Lancs (Derby) 1997. Nh BB 6-54 v Yorks (Northampton) 1998. Awards: NWT 1; BHC 1. **NWT:** HS 10* De v Leics (Derby) 1992. BB 7-35 De v Northants (Derby) 1997. **BHC:** HS 16 v Warwks (Birmingham) 1998. BB 5-27 De v Middx (Derby) 1988. **SL:** HS 42 De v Surrey (Oval) 1996. BB 4-21 De v Surrey (Derby) 1989 and De v Leics (Knypersley) 1990.

PENBERTHY, Anthony Leonard (Camborne CS), b Troon, Cornwall 1 Sep 1969. 6'1". LHB, RM. Debut 1989; cap 1994. Cornwall 1987-89. Tours (Nh): SA 1991-92; Z 1994-95. HS 128 v Warwks (Northampton) 1998. BB 5-37 v Glam (Swansea) 1993. Took wicket of M.A.Taylor (A) with his first ball in f-c cricket. Award: NWT 1. **NWT:** HS 79 v Lancs (Manchester) 1996. BB 5-56 v Cumb (Barrow) 1997. **BHC:** HS 62 v Leics (Northampton) 1998. BB 3-22 v Notts (Northampton) 1998. **SL:** HS 81* v Surrey (Northampton) 1997. BB 5-36 v Glos (Northampton) 1993.

RIPLEY, David (Royds SS, Leeds), b Leeds, Yorks 13 Sep 1966. 5'9". RHB, WK. Debut 1984; cap 1987; benefit 1997. Tours (Nh): SA 1991-92; Z 1994-95. HS 209 v Glam (Northampton) 1998. BB 2-89 v Essex (Ilford) 1987. Award: BHC 1. **NWT:** HS 27* v Durham (Darlington) 1984. **BHC:** HS 36* v Glos (Bristol) 1991. **SL:** HS 52* v Surrey (Northampton) 1993.

ROBERTS, David James (Mullion CS), b Truro, Cornwall 29 Dec 1976. Cousin of C.K.Bullen (Surrey 1982-91). 5'11". RHB, RSM. Debut 1996. HS 117 v Essex (Northampton) 1997.

SALES, David John Grimwood (Caterham S; Cumnor House S), b Carshalton, Surrey 3 Dec 1977. 6'0". RHB, RM. Debut 1996 v Worcs (Kidderminster) scoring 0 and 210* – record Championship score on f-c debut; youngest (18yr 237d) to score 200 in a Championship match. Tours (Eng A): SL 1997-98; K 1997-98. HS 210* (as above). BB 1-28. **NWT:** HS 53 v Cumb (Barrow) 1997. **BHC:** HS 26 v Notts (Northampton) 1998. **SL:** HS 70* (off 56 balls) v Essex (Chelmsford) 1994, when 16yr 289d (youngest to score a Sunday League fifty).

SWANN, Alec James (Risade S; Sponne S, Towcester), b Northampton 26 Oct 1976. Son of R. (Northumberland 1969-72; Bedfordshire 1988-95); elder brother of G.P. 6'1". RHB, RM/OB. Debut 1996. Bedfordshire 1994. HS 136 v Warwks (Birmingham) 1997.

SWANN, Graeme Peter (Sponne SS, Towcester), b Northampton 24 Mar 1979. Son of R. (Northumberland 1969-72; Bedfordshire 1988-95); younger brother of A.J. 6'0". RHB, OB. Debut 1998. Bedfordshire 1996. Tours (Eng A): SA 1998-99; Z 1998-99. HS 111 v Leics (Leicester) 1998. **BB** 5-29 v Sussex (Northampton) 1998. **BHC:** HS –. BB 1-14. **SL:** HS 10* and BB 2-5 v Sussex (Northampton) 1998.

TAYLOR, Jonathan **Paul** (Pingle S, Swadlincote), b Ashby-de-la-Zouch, Leics 8 Aug 1964. 6'2". LHB, LFM. Derbyshire 1984-86. Northamptonshire debut 1991; cap 1992. Staffordshire 1989-90. **Tests:** 2 (1992-93 to 1994); HS 17* v I (Calcutta) 1992-93. BB 1-18. **LOI:** 1 (1992-93); HS 1. Tours: SA 1993-94 (Eng A – part); I 1992-93; Z 1994-95 (Nh). HS 86 v Durham (Northampton) 1995. 50 wkts (6); most – 69 (1993). BB 7-23 v Hants (Bournemouth) 1992. Award: BHC 1. **NWT:** HS 9. BB 4-34 v Glos (Bristol) 1995. **BHC:** HS 14 v Lancs (Manchester) 1998. BB 5-45 v Notts (Northampton) 1996. **SL:** HS 24 v Worcs (Northampton) 1993. BB 3-14 De v Glos (Gloucester) 1986.

WARREN, Russell John (Kingsthorpe Upper S), b Northampton 10 Sep 1971. 6'1". RHB, OB. Debut 1992; cap 1995. HS 201* v Glam (Northampton) 1996. Award: NWT 1. **NWT:** HS 100* v Ire (Northampton) 1994. **BHC:** HS 23 v Derbys (Derby) 1995. **SL:** HS 71* v Leics (Northampton) 1993.

NEW REGISTRATIONS

COOK, Jeffrey William, b Sydney, Australia 2 Feb 1972. LHB, RM. Resident in UK since 1993. Qualifies 2000.

DOBSON, Martyn Colin, b Scunthorpe, Lincs 28 May 1982. Brother of A.M. (Northamptonshire staff 1997-98). RHB, OB.

HAYDEN, Matthew Lawrence (Marist C, Ashgrove; Queensland U of Tech), b Kingaroy, Queensland, Australia 29 Oct 1971. 6'2". LHB, RM. Queensland 1991-92 to date. Hampshire 1997; cap 1997. Joins Northamptonshire as captain 1999 on two-year contract. **Tests** (A): 7 (1993-94 to 1996-97); HS 125 v WI (Adelaide) 1996-97. **LOI** (A): 13 (1993 to 1993-94); HS 67. Tours (A): E 1993, 1995 (Young A), 1998 (Aus A); SA 1993-94, 1996-97. 1000 runs (2+3); most – 1446 (1997). HS 235* H v Warwks (Southampton) 1997. BB 2-17 H v Sussex (Southampton) 1997. Award: BHC 1. **NWT:** HS 90 H v Cambs (Wisbech) 1997. **BHC:** HS 120* and BB 2-45 H v Brit U (Oxford) 1997. **SL:** HS 118 H v Warwks (Southampton) 1997. BB 2-38 H v Leics (Southampton) 1997.

INIFF, Dale Lee (U of Wales), b Penrith, Cumb 18 Sep 1977. RHB, LFM. Cumberland 1996.

POWELL, Mark John (Kingsthorpe S, Northampton), b Northampton 4 Nov 1980. RHB, OB.

RELEASED/RETIRED
(Having made a first-class County appearance in 1998)

BOSWELL, S.A.J. – *see LEICESTERSHIRE.*

CAPEL, David John (Roade CS), b Northampton 6 Feb 1963. 5'11". RHB, RMF. Northamptonshire 1981-98; cap 1986; benefit 1994. E Province 1985-86 to 1986-87. **Tests:** 15 (1987 to 1989-90); HS 98 v P (Karachi) 1987-88; BB 3-88 v WI (Bridgetown) 1989-90. **LOI:** 23 (1986-87 to 1989-90); HS 50*; BB 3-38. Tours: A 1987-88, 1992-93 (Eng A); WI 1989-90; NZ 1987-88; P 1987-88. 1000 runs (3); most – 1311 (1989). HS 175 v Leics (Northampton) 1995. 50 wkts (4); most – 63 (1986). BB 7-44 v Warwks (Birmingham) 1995. Awards: NWT 3; BHC 2. **NWT:** HS 101 v Notts (Northampton) 1990. BB 3-21 v Glam (Swansea) 1992. **BHC:** HS 97 v Yorks (Lord's) 1987. BB 5-51 v Yorks (Leeds) 1997. **SL:** HS 121 v Glam (Northampton) 1990. BB 4-30 v Yorks (Middlesbrough) 1982.

MONTGOMERIE, R.R. – *see SUSSEX.*

continued on p 107

NORTHAMPTONSHIRE 1998

RESULTS SUMMARY

	Place	Won	Lost	Tied	Drew	No Result
Britannic Assurance Championship	15th	4	5		8	
All First-Class Matches		4	5		9	
NatWest Trophy	1st Round					
Benson and Hedges Cup	5th in Group A					
Sunday League	13th	6	7	1		3

BRITANNIC ASSURANCE CHAMPIONSHIP AVERAGES

BATTING AND FIELDING

Cap		M	I	NO	HS	Runs	Avge	100	50	Ct/St
1994	M.B.Loye	14	21	2	322*	1184	62.31	4	4	7
1987	D.Ripley	16	22	2	209	805	40.25	1	5	30/1
1994	A.L.Penberthy	13	21	2	128	755	39.73	2	4	14
1985	R.J.Bailey	16	24	2	188	759	34.50	1	2	10
–	G.P.Swann	13	18	2	111	548	34.25	1	2	7
1992	K.M.Curran	17	25	3	90*	668	30.36	–	6	23
1992	J.P.Taylor	15	20	3	58	371	21.82	–	3	5
–	D.J.G.Sales	13	20	1	60	337	17.73	–	2	10
1995	R.R.Montgomerie	9	15	2	54	222	17.07	–	1	4
–	A.J.Swann	10	16	–	85	249	15.56	–	1	6
–	D.E.Malcolm	14	16	5	42	114	10.36	–	–	3
–	F.A.Rose	14	17	2	21	133	8.86	–	–	–
1995	R.J.Warren	5	8	–	11	30	3.75	–	–	1
–	J.F.Brown	8	11	5	6*	18	3.00	–	–	1
–	D.Follett	5	7	1	7	13	2.16	–	–	2

Also played (1 match each): T.M.B.Bailey 12 (2 ct); D.J.Capel (cap 1986) did not bat; M.K.Davies 3*, 4; K.J.Innes 6, 31 (2 ct); D.J.Roberts 39, 0 (3 ct).

BOWLING

	O	M	R	W	Avge	Best	5wI	10wM
J.F.Brown	280.2	68	726	33	22.00	6-53	4	1
J.P.Taylor	436.5	105	1337	54	24.75	4-31	–	–
F.A.Rose	373.2	59	1367	50	27.34	7-39	3	1
G.P.Swann	199.4	41	666	22	30.27	5-29	1	–
D.Follett	103	17	325	10	32.50	3-48	–	–
D.E.Malcolm	334	48	1331	40	33.27	6-54	2	–

Also bowled: R.J.Bailey 66-14-178-6; D.J.Capel 13-1-66-1; K.M.Curran 78-20-265-2; M.K.Davies 39-17-54-7; M.B.Loye 2-0-42-0; A.L.Penberthy 65-13-204-0; D.J.G.Sales 11-2-36-1; A.J.Swann 6.3-0-59-0.

The First-Class Averages (pp 117-131) give the records of Northamptonshire players in all first-class county matches (Northamptonshire's other opponents being Cambridge University), with the exception of T.M.B.Bailey and M.K.Davies, whose full county figures are as above.

NORTHAMPTONSHIRE RECORDS

FIRST-CLASS CRICKET

Highest Total	For 781-7d		v	Notts	Northampton	1995
	V 670-9d		by	Sussex	Hove	1921
Lowest Total	For 12		v	Glos	Gloucester	1907
	V 33		by	Lancashire	Northampton	1977
Highest Innings	For 322	M.B.Loye	v	Glamorgan	Northampton	1998
	V 333	K.S.Duleepsinhji	for	Sussex	Hove	1930

Highest Partnership for each Wicket

1st	372	R.R.Montgomerie/M.B.Loye	v	Yorkshire	Northampton	1996
2nd	344	G.Cook/R.J.Boyd-Moss	v	Lancashire	Northampton	1986
3rd	393	A.Fordham/A.J.Lamb	v	Yorkshire	Leeds	1990
4th	370	R.T.Virgin/P.Willey	v	Somerset	Northampton	1976
5th	401	M.B.Loye/D.Ripley	v	Glamorgan	Northampton	1998
6th	376	R.Subba Row/A.Lightfoot	v	Surrey	The Oval	1958
7th	229	W.W.Timms/F.A.Walden	v	Warwicks	Northampton	1926
8th	164	D.Ripley/N.G.B.Cook	v	Lancashire	Manchester	1987
9th	156	R.Subba Row/S.Starkie	v	Lancashire	Northampton	1955
10th	148	B.W.Bellamy/J.V.Murdin	v	Glamorgan	Northampton	1925

Best Bowling	For 10-127	V.W.C.Jupp	v	Kent	Tunbridge W	1932
(Innings)	V 10- 30	C.Blythe	for	Kent	Northampton	1907
Best Bowling	For 15- 31	G.E.Tribe	v	Yorkshire	Northampton	1958
(Match)	V 17- 48	C.Blythe	for	Kent	Northampton	1907

Most Runs – Season	2198	D.Brookes	(av 51.11)	1952
Most Runs – Career	28980	D.Brookes	(av 36.13)	1934-59
Most 100s – Season	8	R.A.Haywood		1921
Most 100s – Career	67	D.Brookes		1934-59
Most Wkts – Season	175	G.E.Tribe	(av 18.70)	1955
Most Wkts – Career	1097	E.W.Clark	(av 21.31)	1922-47

LIMITED-OVERS CRICKET

Highest Total	NWT	360-2	v	Staffs	Northampton	1990
	BHC	304-6	v	Scotland	Northampton	1995
	SL	306-2	v	Surrey	Guildford	1985
Lowest Total	NWT	62	v	Leics	Leicester	1974
	BHC	85	v	Sussex	Northampton	1978
	SL	41	v	Middlesex	Northampton	1972
Highest Innings	NWT	145	R.J.Bailey	v	Staffs	Stone	1991
	BHC	134	R.J.Bailey	v	Glos	Northampton	1987
	SL	172*	W.Larkins	v	Warwicks	Luton	1983
Best Bowling	NWT	7-37	N.A.Mallender	v	Worcs	Northampton	1984
	BHC	5-14	F.A.Rose	v	Minor C	Luton	1998
	SL	7-39	A.Hodgson	v	Somerset	Northampton	1976

NOTTINGHAMSHIRE

Formation of Present Club: March/April 1841
Substantial Reorganisation: 11 December 1866
Colours: Green and Gold
Badge: Badge of City of Nottingham
Championships (since 1890): (4) 1907, 1929, 1981, 1987
NatWest Trophy/Gillette Cup Winners: (1) 1987
Benson and Hedges Cup Winners: (1) 1989
Sunday League Champions: (1) 1991
Match Awards: NWT 41; BHC 67

Secretary/General Manager: B.Robson
Trent Bridge, Nottingham NG2 6AG (Tel 0115 982 1525)
Captain: J.E.R.Gallian. **Vice-Captain:** tba. **Overseas Player:** V.C.Drakes.
1999 Beneficiary: M.Newell. **Scorer:** G.Stringfellow.

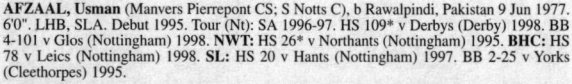

AFZAAL, Usman (Manvers Pierrepont CS; S Notts C), b Rawalpindi, Pakistan 9 Jun 1977. 6'0". LHB, SLA. Debut 1995. Tour (Nt): SA 1996-97. HS 109* v Derbys (Derby) 1998. BB 4-101 v Glos (Nottingham) 1998. **NWT:** HS 26* v Northants (Nottingham) 1995. **BHC:** HS 78 v Leics (Nottingham) 1998. **SL:** HS 20 v Hants (Nottingham) 1997. BB 2-25 v Yorks (Cleethorpes) 1995.

ARCHER, Graeme Francis (Heron Brook Middle S; King Edward VI HS, Stafford), b Carlisle, Cumberland 26 Sep 1970. 6'1". RHB, OB. Debut 1992; cap 1995. Staffordshire 1990. Tour (Nt): SA 1996-97. 1000 runs (1): 1171 (1995). HS 168 v Glam (Worksop) 1994. BB 3-18 v Hants (Southampton) 1996. Awards: BHC 2. **NWT:** HS 39 v Cheshire (Warrington) 1993. BB 1-17. **BHC:** HS 111* v Durham (Nottingham) 1997. BB 1-34. **SL:** HS 104* v Derbys (Nottingham) 1997. BB 2-16 v Surrey (Guildford) 1995.

BATES, Richard Terry (Bourne GS; Stamford CFE), b Stamford, Lincs 17 Jun 1972. 6'1". RHB, OB. Debut 1993. Lincolnshire 1990-91. HS 34 v Worcs (Worcester) 1996. BB 5-88 v Durham (Chester-le-St) 1996. Award: BHC 1. **NWT:** HS 11 v Surrey (Oval) 1997. BB 2-32 v Wales MC (Colwyn Bay) 1998. **BHC:** HS 27 v Yorks (Leeds) 1996. BB 3-21 v Scot (Nottingham) 1996. **SL:** HS 28* v Derbys (Derby) 1998. BB 3-30 v Glam (Nottingham) 1996.

BOWEN, Mark Nicholas (Sacred Heart, Redcar; St Mary's C; Tees Side Poly), b Redcar, Yorks 6 Dec 1967. 6'2". RHB, RM. Northamptonshire 1991-92/1994. Nottinghamshire debut 1996; cap 1997. Tours: SA 1991-92 (Nh), 1996-97 (Nt). HS 32 Nh v Northants (Northampton) 1997 and 32 v Durham (Nottingham) 1998. BB 7-73 v Somerset (Taunton) 1998. **NWT:** HS 8* and BB 3-38 v Surrey (Oval) 1997. **BHC:** HS 9. BB 2-40 v Minor C (Nottingham) 1998. **SL:** HS 27* Nh v Kent (Northampton) 1994. BB 4-29 v Warwks (Nottingham) 1997.

DOWMAN, Mathew Peter (St Hugh's CS; Grantham C), b Grantham, Lincs 10 May 1974. 5'10". LHB, RMF. Debut 1994; cap 1998. Scored 267 for England YC v WI YC (Hove) 1993 – record score in youth 'Tests'. 1000 runs (1): 1091 (1997). HS 149 v Leics (Leicester) 1997. BB 3-10 v Pak A (Nottingham) 1997. CC BB 2-10 v Kent (Canterbury) 1998. **NWT:** HS 47 v Lancs (Manchester) 1998. BB 1-23. **BHC:** HS 92 v Northants (Nottingham) 1997. BB 3-21 v Worcs (Nottingham) 1996. **SL:** HS 74* v Glam (Nottingham) 1996. BB 2-31 v Lancs (Manchester) 1997.

EVANS, Kevin Paul (Colonel Frank Seely S) b Calverton 10 Sep 1963. Elder brother of R.J. (Notts 1987-90). 6'2". RHB, RMF. Debut 1984; cap 1990; benefit 1998. HS 104 v Surrey (Nottingham) 1992 and v Sussex (Nottingham) 1994. BB 6-40 v Lancs (Manchester) 1997. Awards: BHC 2. **NWT:** HS 21 v Worcs (Worcester) 1994. BB 6-10 v Northumb (Jesmond) 1994. **BHC:** HS 47 v Lancs (Manchester) 1995. BB 4-19 v Minor C (Leek) 1995. **SL:** HS 30 v Kent (Canterbury) 1990 and 30 v Hants (Southampton) 1992. BB 5-29 v Glam (Nottingham) 1994.

FRANKS, Paul John (Southwell Minster CS), b Mansfield 3 Feb 1979. 6'2". LHB, RMF. Debut 1996. Tour: SA 1998-99 (Eng A). HS 66* v Kent (Canterbury) 1998. 50 wkts (1): 52 (1998). BB 6-63 v Worcs (Kidderminster) 1998. Hat-trick 1997. **NWT:** HS 26* v Wales MC (Colwyn Bay) 1998. BB 3-40 v Somerset (Nottingham) 1998. **SL:** HS 17* v Hants (Portsmouth) 1998. BB 4-21 v Yorks (Scarborough) 1998.

GALLIAN, Jason Edward Riche (Pittwater House S, Sydney; Keble C, Oxford), b Manly, Sydney, Australia 25 Jun 1971. Qualified for England 1994. 6'0". RHB, RM. Lancashire 1990-97, taking wicket of D.A.Hagan (OU) with his first ball; cap 1994. Oxford U 1992-93; blue 1992-93; captain 1993. Nottinghamshire debut/cap 1998; captain 1998 (part) to date. Captained Australia YC v England YC 1989-90, scoring 158* in 1st 'Test'. **Tests:** 3 (1995 to 1995-96); HS 28 v SA (Pt Elizabeth) 1995-96. Tours: A 1996-97 (Eng A); I 1995-96 (La); SA 1995-96 (part); I 1994-95 (Eng A); P 1995-96 (Eng A). 1000 runs (2); most – 1156 (1996). HS 312 La v Derbys (Manchester) 1996 (record score at Old Trafford). Nt HS 113* v Hants (Portsmouth) 1998. BB 6-115 La v Surrey (Southport) 1996. Nt BB 1-14. Awards: NWT 2; BHC 2. **NWT:** HS 101* La v Norfolk (Manchester) 1995. BB 1-11. **BHC:** HS 134 La v Notts (Manchester) 1995. BB 5-15 La v Minor C (Leek) 1995. **SL:** HS 104 La v Leics (Leicester) 1997. BB 2-10 La v Somerset (Manchester) 1994.

GIE, Noel Addison (Trent C), b Pretoria, SA 12 Apr 1977. UK resident since 1984. Son of C.A. (WP and SAU 1970-71 to 1980-81). 6'0". RHB, RM. Debut 1995. HS 50 v OU (Oxford) 1997 and 50 v Glos (Nottingham) 1998. Award: BHC 1. **BHC:** HS 70 v Warwks (Birmingham) 1998. **SL:** HS 75* v Kent (Nottingham) 1997.

HART, Jamie Paul (Millfield S), b Blackpool, Lancs 31 Dec 1975. Son of P. (Nottingham Forest footballer). 6'3". RHB, RM. Debut 1996. HS 18* v Yorks (Scarborough) 1996 (on debut). **SL:** HS –. BB 1-48.

JOHNSON, Paul (Grove CS, Balderton), b Newark 24 Apr 1965. 5'7". RHB, RM. Debut 1982; cap 1986; benefit 1995; captain 1996-98. Tours: SA 1996-97 (Nt); WI 1991-92 (Eng A). 1000 runs (8); most – 1518 (1990). HS 187 v Lancs (Manchester) 1993. BB 1-9. CC BB 1-14. Awards: NWT 2; BHC 3. **NWT:** HS 146 v Northumb (Jesmond) 1994. **BHC:** HS 104* v Essex (Chelmsford) 1990. **SL:** HS 167* v Kent (Nottingham) 1993.

NEWELL, Michael (West Bridgford CS), b Blackburn, Lancs 25 Feb 1965. 5'8". RHB, LB. Debut 1984; cap 1987; benefit 1999. No f-c appearances since 1992. 1000 runs (1): 1054 (1987). HS 203* v Derbys (Derby) 1987. BB 2-38 v SL (Nottingham) 1988. CC BB 1-0. **NWT:** HS 60 v Derbys (Derby) 1987. **BHC:** HS 39 v Somerset (Taunton) 1989. **SL:** HS 109* v Essex (Southend) 1990.

NOON, Wayne Michael (Caistor S), b Grimsby, Lincs 5 Feb 1971. 5'9". RHB, WK. Northamptonshire 1989-93. Nottinghamshire debut 1994; cap 1995. Canterbury 1994-95. Worcs 2nd XI debut when aged 15yr 199d. Tours: SA 1991-92 (Nh), 1996-97 (Nt). HS 83 v Northants (Northampton) 1997. **NWT:** HS 34 v Worcs (Worcester) 1994. **BHC:** HS 46 v Warwks (Birmingham) 1998. **SL:** HS 38 v Durham (Chester-le-St) 1995.

ORAM, Andrew Richard (Roade CS), b Northampton 7 Mar 1975. 6'2". RHB, RM. Debut 1997. HS 13 and BB 4-37 v Surrey (Nottingham) 1998. **NWT:** HS –. BB 1-51. **BHC:** HS 1*. BB 1-19. **SL:** HS 0*. BB 4-45 v Glam (Colwyn Bay) 1997.

READ, Christopher Mark Wells (Torquay GS; Bath U), b Paignton, Devon 10 Aug 1978. 5'8". RHB, WK. Gloucestershire (L-O) 1997. Nottinghamshire debut 1998. Devon 1995-97. Tours (Eng A): SA 1998-99; SL 1997-98; Z 1998-99; K 1997-98. HS 76 v Middx (Nottingham) 1998. **NWT:** HS 37 Devon v Essex (Chelmsford) 1996. **SL:** HS 19 v Northants (Nottingham) 1998.

ROBINSON, Robert Timothy (Dunstable GS; High Pavement SFC; Sheffield U), b Sutton in Ashfield 21 Nov 1958. 6'0". RHB, RM. Debut 1978; cap 1983; captain 1988-95; benefit 1992. *Wisden* 1985. **Tests:** 29 (1984-85 to 1989); HS 175 v A (Leeds) 1985. **LOI:** 26 (1984-85 to 1988); HS 83. Tours: A 1987-88; SA 1989-90 (Eng XI), 1996-97 (Nt); NZ 1987-88; WI 1985-86 (E); P 1987-88. 1000 runs (14) inc 2000 (2): 2032 (1984). HS 220* v Yorks (Nottingham) 1990. BB 1-22. Awards: NWT 4; BHC 7. **NWT:** HS 139 v Worcs (Worcester) 1985. **BHC:** HS 120 v Scot (Glasgow) 1985. **SL:** HS 119* v Lancs (Nottingham) 1994.

TOLLEY, Christopher Mark (King Edward VI C, Stourbridge; Loughborough U), b Kidderminster, Worcs 30 Dec 1967. 5'9". RHB, LMF. Worcestershire 1989-95; cap 1993. Nottinghamshire debut 1996; cap 1997. Tours (Wo): SA 1996-97 (Nt); Z 1990-91, 1993-94. HS 84 Wo v Derbys (Derby) 1994. Nt HS 78 v Glos (Nottingham) 1998. BB 7-45 v Worcs (Kidderminster) 1998. Hat-trick 1997. Awards: NWT 1; BHC 1. **NWT:** HS 77 v Somerset (Nottingham) 1998. BB 3-21 v Surrey (Oval) 1997. **BHC:** HS 77 Comb U v Lancs (Cambridge) 1990. BB 1-12. **SL:** HS 44 v Sussex (Nottingham) 1998. BB 5-16 v Hants (Southampton) 1996.

WELTON, Guy Edward (Healing CS; Grimsby C), b Grimsby, Lincs 4 May 1978. 6'1". RHB, OB. Debut 1997. MCC YC. HS 95 v Sussex (Hove) 1997. **SL:** HS 68 v Middx (Lord's) 1997.

WHARF, Alexander George (Buttershaw Upper S), b Bradford, Yorks 4 Jun 1975. 6'5". RHB, RMF. Yorkshire 1994-97. Nottinghamshire debut 1998. HS 62 Y v Glam (Cardiff) 1996. Nt HS 3. Debut 1998 v Lancs (Manchester) 1996 (not CC). Nt BB 3-25 v Sussex (Nottingham) 1998. **BHC:** HS 20 v Warwks (Birmingham) 1998. BB 4-29 Y v Notts (Leeds) 1996. **SL:** HS 12 v Durham (Nottingham) 1998. BB 3-26 v Somerset (Taunton) 1998.

WHILEY, Matthew Jeffrey Allen (Harry Carlton CS, Nottingham), b Clifton, Nottingham 6 May 1980. 6'5½". RHB, LMF. Debut 1997. HS 0*. BB 1-66.

NEW REGISTRATIONS

DRAKES, Vasbert Conneil (St Lucy SS), b St James, Barbados 5 Aug 1969. 6'2". RHB, RFM. Barbados 1991-92 to date. Sussex 1996-97; cap 1996. Border 1996-97 to date. **LOI** (WI): 5 (1994-95); HS 16; BB 1-36. Tour (WI): E 1995. HS 180* Barbados v Leeward Is (Anguilla) 1994-95. UK HS 145* Sx v Essex (Chelmsford) 1996. 50 wkts (1): 50 (1996). BB 8-59 Border v Natal (Durban) 1996-97. UK BB 5-20 WI v Kent (Canterbury) 1995. CC BB 5-47 Sx v Derbys (Hove) 1996. **NWT:** HS 35 Sx v Yorks (Hove) 1996. BB 4-62 Sx v Derbys (Derby) 1997. **BHC:** HS 58 Sx v Brit U (Cambridge) 1996. BB 5-19 Sx v Ire (Hove) 1996. **SL:** HS 37 Sx v Hants (Arundel) 1996. BB 4-50 Sx v Surrey (Guildford) 1996.

LUCAS, David Scott (Djangoly CTC, Nottingham), b Nottingham 19 Aug 1978. RHB, LMF.

RANDALL, Stephen John (W Bridgford S), b Nottingham 9 Jun 1980. RHB, OB.

STEMP, Richard David (Britannia HS, Rowley Regis), b Erdington, Birmingham 11 Dec 1967. 6'0". RHB, SLA. Worcestershire 1990-92. Yorkshire 1993-98; cap 1996. Tours (Eng A): SA 1992-93 (Y); I 1994-95; P 1995-96. HS 65 Y v Durham (Chester-le-St) 1996. BB 6-37 Y v Durham (Durham) 1994. Award: BHC 1. **NWT:** HS 1*. BB 4-45 Y v Notts (Leeds) 1996. **BHC:** HS 2. BB 3-22 Y v Minor C (Leeds) 1997. **SL:** HS 23* Y v Warwks (Birmingham) 1993. BB 4-25 Y v Glos (Bristol) 1996.

RELEASED/RETIRED
(Having made a first-class County appearance in 1998)

POLLARD, P.R. – see *WORCESTERSHIRE*.

STRANG, Paul Andrew (Falcon C; Cape Town U), b Bulawayo, Rhodesia 28 Jul 1970. Elder brother of B.C. (Mashonaland and Zimbabwe 1994-95 to date). RHB, LBG. Debut (Zimbabwe B) 1992-93. Mashonaland Country Districts 1993-94 to 1995-96. Mashonaland 1996-97. Kent 1997; cap 1997. Nottinghamshire 1998. **Tests** (Z): 20 (1994-95 to 1997-98); HS 106* v P (Sheikhupura) 1996-97; BB 5-106 v SL (Colombo) 1996-97. **LOI** (Z): 69 (1994-95 to 1998-99); HS 47; BB 5-21. Tours (Z): E 1996 (MCC); A 1994-95; SA 1993-94 (Z Board), 1994-95 (Z Board), 1995-96 (Z A); NZ 1995-96, 1997-98; P 1996-97; SL 1996-97, 1997-98. HS 106* *(see Tests)*. UK HS 148 K v Leics (Canterbury) 1997. Nt HS 48 (twice) v Sussex (Nottingham) 1998. 50 wkts (1): 63 (1997). BB 7-75 Mashonaland CD v Mashonaland U-24 (Harare South) 1994-95. CC BB 7-118 (11-186 match) K v Lancs (Manchester) 1997. Nt BB 5-166 v Kent (Canterbury) 1998. **NWT:** HS 40 v Somerset (Nottingham) 1998. BB 2-33 v Wales MC (Colwyn Bay) 1998. **BHC:** HS 38* K v Glos (Bristol) 1997. BB 4-27 K v Sussex (Canterbury) 1997. **SL:** HS 40 K v Warwks (Tunbridge Wells) 1997. BB 6-32 v Warwks (Birmingham) 1998.

NOTTINGHAMSHIRE 1998

RESULTS SUMMARY

	Place	Won	Lost	Tied	Drew	No Result
Britannic Assurance Championship	16th	3	10		4	
All First-Class Matches		3	10		4	
NatWest Trophy	Quarter-Finalist					
Benson and Hedges Cup	4th in Group A					
Sunday League	11th	7	8	1		1

BRITANNIC ASSURANCE CHAMPIONSHIP AVERAGES

BATTING AND FIELDING

Cap		M	I	NO	HS	Runs	Avge	100	50	Ct/St
1986	P.Johnson	15	26	1	139	976	39.04	2	4	14
1983	R.T.Robinson	11	18	2	114	553	34.56	1	4	6
1995	G.F.Archer	13	23	–	107	647	28.13	1	5	23
1998	J.E.R.Gallian	14	25	3	113*	592	26.90	1	3	8
–	U.Afzaal	17	30	3	109*	686	25.40	2	4	7
–	C.M.W.Read	13	22	6	76	401	25.06	–	2	39/3
1997	C.M.Tolley	11	19	2	78	374	22.00	–	2	5
–	P.J.Franks	12	20	2	66*	390	21.66	–	2	6
–	P.A.Strang	13	18	3	48	300	20.00	–	–	19
1998	M.P.Dowman	13	24	1	63	451	19.60	–	2	7
1997	M.N.Bowen	10	13	5	32	142	17.75	–	–	2
1992	P.R.Pollard	4	7	–	69	121	17.28	–	1	3
–	G.E.Welton	5	9	–	55	152	16.88	–	1	3
–	N.A.Gie	4	8	–	50	128	16.00	–	1	3
1990	K.P.Evans	9	13	–	36	129	9.92	–	–	3
–	R.T.Bates	2	4	2	17	17	8.50	–	–	–
1995	W.M.Noon	4	5	1	16*	22	5.50	–	–	9
–	A.R.Oram	11	19	8	13	39	3.54	–	–	–
–	A.G.Wharf	5	6	1	3	8	1.60	–	–	6

Also batted: M.J.A.Whiley (1 match) 0, 0*.

BOWLING

	O	M	R	W	Avge	Best	5wI	10wM
P.J.Franks	404.2	87	1375	52	26.44	6- 63	4	–
K.P.Evans	273	73	735	27	27.22	5- 92	2	–
M.N.Bowen	309.1	76	875	31	28.22	7- 73	1	–
C.M.Tolley	324.3	76	960	34	28.23	7- 45	3	–
A.R.Oram	305.5	75	969	31	31.25	4- 37	–	–
P.A.Strang	353.3	105	983	30	32.76	5-166	1	–
M.P.Dowman	139	31	397	12	33.08	2- 10	–	–

Also bowled: U.Afzaal 75.4-9-292-7; R.T.Bates 21-2-98-0; J.E.R.Gallian 47.1-13-103-2; A.G.Wharf 83.1-14-333-9; M.J.A.Whiley 29-4-124-1;

The First-Class Averages (pp 117-131) give the records of Nottinghamshire players in all first-class county matches.

NOTTINGHAMSHIRE RECORDS

FIRST-CLASS CRICKET

Highest Total	For	739-7d	v	Leics	Nottingham	1903
	V	781-7d	by	Northants	Northampton	1995
Lowest Total	For	13	v	Yorkshire	Nottingham	1901
	V	16	by	Derbyshire	Nottingham	1879
		16	by	Surrey	The Oval	1880
Highest Innings	For	312*	W.W.Keeton	v	Middlesex	The Oval	1939
	V	345	C.G.Macartney	for	Australians	Nottingham	1921

Highest Partnership for each Wicket

1st	391	A.O.Jones/A.Shrewsbury	v	Glos	Bristol	1899
2nd	398	A.Shrewsbury/W.Gunn	v	Sussex	Nottingham	1890
3rd	369	W.Gunn/J.R.Gunn	v	Leics	Nottingham	1903
4th	361	A.O.Jones/J.R.Gunn	v	Essex	Leyton	1905
5th	266	A.Shrewsbury/W.Gunn	v	Sussex	Hove	1884
6th	303*	F.H.Winrow/P.F.Harvey	v	Derbyshire	Nottingham	1947
7th	301	C.C.Lewis/B.N.French	v	Durham	Chester-le-St	1993
8th	220	G.F.H.Heane/R.Winrow	v	Somerset	Nottingham	1935
9th	170	J.C.Adams/K.P.Evans	v	Somerset	Taunton	1994
10th	152	E.B.Alletson/W.Riley	v	Sussex	Hove	1911

Best Bowling	For	10-66	K.Smales	v	Glos	Stroud	1956
(Innings)	V	10-10	H.Verity	for	Yorkshire	Leeds	1932
Best Bowling	For	17-89	F.C.Matthews	v	Northants	Nottingham	1923
(Match)	V	17-89	W.G.Grace	for	Glos	Cheltenham	1877

Most Runs – Season	2620	W.W.Whysall	(av 53.46)	1929
Most Runs – Career	31592	G.Gunn	(av 35.69)	1902-32
Most 100s – Season	9	W.W.Whysall		1928
	9	M.J.Harris		1971
	9	B.C.Broad		1990
Most 100s – Career	65	J.Hardstaff jr		1930-55
Most Wkts – Season	181	B.Dooland	(av 14.96)	1954
Most Wkts – Career	1653	T.G.Wass	(av 20.34)	1896-1920

LIMITED-OVERS CRICKET

Highest Total	NWT	344-6		v	Northumb	Jesmond	1994
	BHC	296-6		v	Kent	Nottingham	1989
	SL	329-6		v	Derbyshire	Nottingham	1993
Lowest Total	NWT	123		v	Yorkshire	Scarborough	1969
	BHC	74		v	Leics	Leicester	1987
	SL	66		v	Yorkshire	Bradford	1969
Highest Innings	NWT	149*	D.W.Randall	v	Devon	Torquay	1988
	BHC	130*	C.E.B.Rice	v	Scotland	Glasgow	1982
	SL	167*	P.Johnson	v	Kent	Nottingham	1993
Best Bowling	NWT	6-10	K.P.Evans	v	Northumb	Jesmond	1994
	BHC	6-22	M.K.Bore	v	Leics	Leicester	1980
		6-22	C.E.B.Rice	v	Northants	Northampton	1981
	SL	6-12	R.J.Hadlee	v	Lancashire	Nottingham	1980

SOMERSET

Formation of Present Club: 18 August 1875
Colours: Black, White and Maroon
Badge: Somerset Dragon
Championships: (0) Third 1892, 1958, 1963, 1966, 1981
NatWest Trophy/Gillette Cup Winners: (2) 1979, 1983
Benson and Hedges Cup Winners: (2) 1981, 1982
Sunday League Champions: (1) 1979
Match Awards: NWT 51; BHC 65

Chief Executive: P.W.Anderson
The County Ground, Taunton TA1 1JT (Tel 01823 272946)
Captain/Overseas Player: J.Cox. **Vice-Captain:** M.E.Trescothick.
1999 Beneficiary: A.R.Caddick. **Scorer:** G.A.Stickley.

BOULTON, Nicholas Ross (King's C, Taunton), b Johannesburg, SA 22 Mar 1979. 6'1½". LHB, RM. Debut 1997 – awaiting CC debut. HS 14 v Pak A (Taunton) 1997.

BOWLER, Peter Duncan (Educated at Canberra, Australia), b Plymouth, Devon 30 Jul 1963. 6'1". RHB, OB, occ WK. Leicestershire 1986 – first to score hundred on f-c debut for Leics (100* and 62 v Hants). Tasmania 1986-87. Derbyshire 1988-94; cap 1989; scored 155* v CU (Cambridge) on debut – first instance of hundreds on debut for two counties. Somerset debut/cap 1995; captain 1997-98. 1000 runs (8) inc 2000 (1): 2044 (1992). HS 241* De v Hants (Portsmouth) 1992. Sm HS 207 v Surrey (Taunton) 1996. BB 3-25 v Northants (Taunton) 1998. Sm BB 2-48 v Yorks (Taunton) 1997. Awards: BHC 4. **NWT:** HS 111 De v Berks (Derby) 1992. **BHC:** HS 109 De v Somerset (Taunton) 1990. BB 1-15. **SL:** HS 138* De v Somerset (Derby) 1993. BB 3-31 De v Glos (Cheltenham) 1991.

BULBECK, Matthew Paul Leonard (Taunton S; Richard Huish C), b Taunton 8 Nov 1979. 6'3½". LHB, LMF. Debut 1998. HS 35 v Warwks (Taunton) 1998. BB 4-40 v Derbys (Taunton) 1998.

BURNS, Michael (Walney CS), b Barrow-in-Furness, Lancs 6 Jun 1969. 6'0". RHB, RM, WK. Cumberland 1988-90. Warwickshire 1992-96. Somerset debut 1997. HS 96 v Glos (Bristol) 1998. BB 2-18 v Kent (Taunton) 1997. Award: BHC 1. **NWT:** HS 84* v Holland (Taunton) 1998. **BHC:** HS 95 v Surrey (Oval) 1998. BB 3-18 v Glam (Taunton) 1997. **SL:** HS 115* v Middx (Taunton) 1997. BB 4-39 v Glos (Taunton) 1997.

CADDICK, Andrew Richard (Papanui HS), b Christchurch, NZ 21 Nov 1968. Son of English emigrants – qualified for England 1992. 6'5". RHB, RFM. Debut 1991; cap 1992; benefit 1999. Represented NZ in 1987-88 Youth World Cup. **Tests:** 21 (1993 to 1997-98); HS 29* v WI (Kingston) 1993-94; BB 6-65 v WI (P-o-S) 1993-94. **LOI:** 9 (1993 to 1996-97); HS 20*; BB 3-35. Tours: A 1992-93 (Eng A); WI 1993-94, 1997-98; NZ 1996-97; Z 1996-97. HS 92 v Worcs (Worcester) 1995. 50 wkts (6) inc 100 (1): 105 (1998) BB 9-32 (12-120 match) v Lancs (Taunton) 1993. Award: NWT 1. **NWT:** HS 8. BB 6-30 v Glos (Taunton) 1992. **BHC:** HS 38 v Leics (Leicester) 1997. BB 5-51 v Brit U (Taunton) 1996. **SL:** HS 39 v Hants (Taunton) 1996. BB 4-18 v Lancs (Manchester) 1997.

HOLLOWAY, Piran Christopher Laity (Millfield S; Taunton S; Loughborough U), b Helston, Cornwall 1 Oct 1970. 5'8". LHB, WK. Warwickshire 1988-93. Somerset debut 1994; cap 1998. HS 168 v Middx (Uxbridge) 1996. **NWT:** HS 90 v Herefords (Taunton) 1997. **BHC:** HS 27 Comb U v Derbys (Oxford) 1991. **SL:** HS 117 v Glos (Taunton) 1997.

JONES, Philip Steffan (Stradey CS, Llanelli; Neath TC; Homerton C; Cambridge), b Llanelli, Wales 9 Feb 1974. 6'2". RHB, RMF. Cambridge U 1997; blue 1997. Somerset debut 1997. Wales MC 1992-96. HS 36 v Essex (Cambridge) 1997. Sm HS 22* v Worcs (Taunton) 1998. BB 6-67 v OU (Lord's) 1997. Sm BB 3-30 v Glos (Taunton) 1998. **NWT:** HS 26* Wales MC v Middx (Northop Hall) 1994. BB 2-36 v Holland (Taunton) 1998. **BHC:** (Brit U) HS 12 v Surrey (Oval) 1997. BB 2-51 v Hants (Oxford) 1997. **SL:** HS 6*. BB 5-23 v Warwks (Taunton) 1998.

KERR, Jason Ian Douglas (Withins HS; Bolton C), b Bolton, Lancs 7 Apr 1974. 6'2". RHB, RMF. Debut 1993. HS 80 and BB 5-82 v WI (Taunton) 1995. CC HS 68* v Derbys (Taunton) 1996. CC BB 4-68 v Sussex (Bath) 1995. **NWT:** HS 3. BB 3-32 v Herefords (Taunton) 1997. **BHC:** HS 17 v Essex (Chelmsford) 1997. BB 3-34 v Middx (Lord's) 1997. **SL:** HS 33 v Warwks (Birmingham) 1997. BB 4-28 v Hants (Basingstoke) 1997.

LATHWELL, Mark Nicholas (Braunton S, Devon), b Bletchley, Bucks 26 Dec 1971. 5'8". RHB, RM. Debut 1991; cap 1992. YC 1993. MCC YC. **Tests:** 2 (1993); HS 33 v A (Nottingham) 1993. Tours (Eng A): A 1992-93; SA 1993-94. 1000 runs (5); most – 1230 (1994). HS 206 v Surrey (Bath) 1994. BB 2-21 v Sussex (Hove) 1994. Awards: NWT 1; BHC 2. **NWT:** HS 103 and BB 1-23 v Salop (Telford) 1993. **BHC:** HS 121 v Middx (Lord's) 1996. **SL:** HS 117 v Notts (Taunton) 1994.

PARSONS, Keith Alan (The Castle S, Taunton; Richard Huish SFC), b Taunton 2 May 1973. Identical twin brother of K.J. (Somerset staff 1992-94). 6'1". RHB, RM. Debut 1992. HS 105 v Young A (Taunton) 1995. CC HS 83* v Middx (Uxbridge) 1996. BB 2-4 v OU (Taunton) 1997. CC BB 2-11 v Derbys (Derby) 1995. **NWT:** HS 51 v Suffolk (Taunton) 1996. BB 3-34 v Warwks (Birmingham) 1997. **BHC:** HS 33* v Brit U (Taunton) 1996. BB 2-60 v Kent (Maidstone) 1996. **SL:** HS 56 v Sussex (Hove) 1996. BB 3-36 v Leics (Leics) 1996.

PIERSON, Adrian Roger Kirshaw (Kent C, Canterbury; Hatfield Poly), b Enfield, Middx 21 Jul 1963. 6'4". RHB, OB. Warwickshire 1985-91. Leicestershire 1993-97; cap 1995. Somerset debut 1998. Cambridgeshire 1992. MCC YC. Tour (Le): SA 1996-97. HS 108* v Sussex (Hove) 1998. 50 wkts (1): 69 (1995). BB 8-42 Le v Warwks (Birmingham) 1994. Sm BB 5-117 v Glam (Cardiff) 1998. Awards: NWT 1; BHC 1. **NWT:** HS 20* Le v Hants (Leicester) 1995. BB 3-20 Wa v Wilts (Birmingham) 1989. **BHC:** HS 11 Wa v Minor C (Walsall) 1986. BB 3-34 Wa v Lancs (Birmingham) 1988. **SL:** HS 29* Le v Kent (Leicester) 1994. BB 5-36 Le v Derbys (Leicester) 1995.

ROSE, Graham David (Northumberland Park S, Tottenham), b Tottenham, London 12 Apr 1964. 6'4". RHB, RM. Middlesex 1985-86. Somerset debut 1987; cap 1988; benefit 1997. 1000 runs (1): 1000 (1990). HS 191 v Sussex (Taunton) 1997. 50 wkts (5); most – 63 (1997). BB 7-47 (13-88 match) v Notts (Taunton) 1996. Awards: BHC 4. **NWT:** HS 110 v Devon (Torquay) 1990. BB 3-11 v Salop (Telford) 1993. **BHC:** HS 79 v Surrey (Taunton) 1995. BB 4-21 v Ire (Erlington) 1995. **SL:** HS 148 v Glam (Neath) 1990. BB 4-26 v Kent (Taunton) 1993.

SHINE, Kevin James (Maiden Erlegh CS), b Bracknell, Berks 22 Feb 1969. 6'2½". RHB, RFM. Hampshire 1989-93. Middlesex 1994-95. Somerset debut 1996; cap 1997. Berkshire 1986. HS 40 v Surrey (Taunton) 1996 (on Sm debut). 50 wkts (1): 55 (1997). BB 8-47 (8 wkts in 38 balls inc hat-trick and 4 in 5; 13-105 match) H v Lancs (Manchester) 1992. Sm BB 7-43 (11-97 match) v Lancs (Taunton) 1997. **NWT:** HS – . BB 3-31 M v Wales MC (Northop Hall) 1994. **BHC:** HS 38* v Kent (Maidstone) 1996. BB 4-68 H v Surrey (Oval) 1990. **SL:** HS 3. BB 4-31 v Northants (Taunton) 1996.

SUTTON, Luke David (Millfield S; Durham U), b Keynsham 4 Oct 1976. 5'11". RHB, WK. Debut 1997. HS 16* v SL (Taunton) 1998. CC HS 5. **BHC:** HS 60 Brit U v Kent (Oxford) 1998.

TRESCOTHICK, Marcus Edward (Sir Bernard Lovell S), b Keynsham 25 Dec 1975. 6'2". LHB, RM. Debut 1993. HS 178 v Hants (Taunton) 1996. BB 4-36 (inc hat-trick) v Young A (Taunton) 1995. CC BB 4-82 v Yorks (Leeds) 1998. Hat-trick 1995. Award: NWT 1. **NWT:** HS 116 v Oxon (Aston Rowant) 1994. BB 2-49 v Notts (Nottingham) 1998. **BHC:** HS 122 v Ire (Erlington) 1995. BB 3-46 v Surrey (Oval) 1998. **SL:** HS 74 v Yorks (Leeds) 1994. BB 2-14 v Surrey (Taunton) 1998.

TROTT, Benhamin James (Court Fields Community S; Richard Huish C, Taunton; Plymouth U), b Wellington 14 Mar 1975. 6'5". RHB, RFM. Debut 1997. HS 1* and BB 3-74 v Glam (Taunton) 1997. **SL:** HS –. BB 1-29.

TUCKER, Joseph Peter (Colson Collegiate S; Richard Huish C), b Bath 14 Sep 1979. 6'3". RHB, RMF. Awaiting f-c debut.

TURNER, Robert Julian (Millfield S; Magdalene C, Cambridge), b Malvern, Worcs 25 Nov 1967. 6'1½". RHB, WK. Brother of S.J. (Somerset 1984-85). Cambridge U 1988-91; blue 1988-89-90-91; captain 1991. Somerset debut 1991; cap 1994. 1000 runs (1): 1069 (1997). HS 144 v Kent (Taunton) 1997. Award: BHC 1. **NWT:** HS 40 v Suffolk (Taunton) 1996. **BHC:** HS 70 v Glam (Cardiff) 1996. **SL:** HS 67 v Worcs (Worcester) 1997.

Van TROOST, Adrianus Pelrus ('*Andre*') (Spieringshoek C, Schiedam), b Schiedam, Holland Oct 1972. 6'7". RHB, RF. Debut 1991; cap 1997. Holland 1990 and 1997. HS 35 v Lancs (Taunton) 1993. BB 6-48 v Essex (Taunton) 1992. **NWT:** HS 17* v Surrey (Taunton) 1993. BB 5-22 v Oxon (Aston Rowant) 1994. **BHC:** HS 9* and BB 2-38 v Notts (Nottingham) 1993. **SL:** HS 9*. BB 4-23 v Notts (Taunton) 1994.

NEW REGISTRATIONS

COX, Jamie, b Burnie, Tasmania, Australia 15 Oct 1969. RHB. Tasmania 1987-88 to date; vice-captain 1996-97 to date. Joins Somerset 1999 as captain. Tours: Z 1991-92 (Aus B), 1995-96 (Tas). 1000 runs (0+1): 1349 (1996-97). HS 200 Tasmania v P (Hobart) 1996-97.

JARVIS, Paul William (Bydales CS, Marske), b Redcar, Yorks 29 Jun 1965. 5'10". RHB, RFM. Yorkshire 1981-93; cap 1986; youngest Yorkshire debutant at 16yr 75d. Sussex 1994-98; cap 1994. **Tests:** 9 (1987-88 to 1992-93); HS 29* and BB 4-107 v WI (Lord's) 1988. **LOI:** 16 (1987-88 to 1993); HS 16*; BB 5-35. Tours: SA 1989-90 (Eng XI); WI 1986-87 (Y); NZ 1987-88; I/SL 1992-93; P 1987-88. HS 80 Y v Northants (Scarborough) 1992. 50 wkts (4); most – 81 (1987). BB 7-55 Y v Surrey (Leeds) 1986. Hat-trick 1985 (Y). Award: BHC 1. **NWT:** HS 34* Sx v Yorks (Hove) 1996. BB 4-41 Y v Leics (Leeds) 1987. **BHC:** HS 63 Sx v Kent (Canterbury) 1997. BB 4-34 Y v Warwks (Birmingham) 1992. **SL:** HS 43 Sx v Surrey (Guildford) 1996. BB 6-27 Y v Somerset (Taunton) 1989.

MAHMOOD, Saqib, b Kettering, Northants 24 Aug 1977. RHB, LB.

RELEASED/RETIRED
(Having made a first-class County appearance in 1998)

ECCLESTONE, Simon Charles (Bryanston S; Durham U; Keble C, Oxford), b Great Dunmow, Essex 16 Jul 1971. 6'3". LHB, RM. Oxford U 1994; blue 1994. Somerset 1994-98; cap 1997. Cambridgeshire 1990-94. HS 133 v OU (Oxford) 1997. CC HS 123 v Kent (Taunton) 1997. BB 4-66 OU v Surrey (Oval) 1994. CC BB 2-48 v Notts (Nottingham) 1995. Awards: NWT 2; BHC 1. **NWT:** HS 101 v Herefords (Taunton) 1997. **BHC:** HS 112* v Middx (Lord's) 1996. BB 2-44 v Kent (Canterbury) 1995. **SL:** HS 130 v Surrey (Taunton) 1996. BB 4-31 v Essex (Weston-s-M) 1994.

HARDEN, R.J. – *see YORKSHIRE*.

KENNIS, Gregor John (Tiffin S), b Yokohama, Japan 9 Mar 1974. 6'1". RHB, OB. MCC YC. Surrey 1994-97. Scored Surrey 2nd XI record 258 (395 balls, 41 fours) v Leics 2nd XI (Kibworth) 1995. Somerset 1998. HS 49 v Derbys (Taunton) 1998. **SL:** HS 5 (Sy).

MUSHTAQ AHMED, b Sahiwal, Pakistan 28 Jun 1970. 5'5". RHB, LBG. Multan 1986-87 to 1990-91. United Bank 1986-87 to date. Somerset 1993-95, 1997-98; cap 1993. *Wisden* 1996. **Tests** (P): 41 (1989-90 to 1998-99); HS 59 v SA (Rawalpindi) 1997-98; BB 7-56 (10-171 match) v NZ (Christchurch) 1995-96. **LOI:** 130 (1988-89 to 1997-98); HS 26; BB 5-36. Tours: E 1992, 1996; A 1989-90, 1991-92, 1992-93, 1995-96, 1996-97; SA 1997-98; WI 1992-93; NZ 1992-93, 1993-94, 1995-96; I 1998-99; SL 1994-95, 1996-97. HS 90 and Sm BB 7-91 (12-175 match) v Sussex (Taunton) 1993. 50 wkts (4+1); most – 95 (1995). BB 9-93 Multan v Peshawar (Sahiwal) 1990-91. Awards: NWT 2; BHC 2. **NWT:** HS 35 v Surrey (Taunton) 1993. BB 5-26 v Holland (Taunton) 1998. **BHC:** HS 31 v Essex (Chelmsford) 1997. BB 7-24 v Ire (Taunton) 1997. **SL:** HS 41 v Durham (Taunton) 1998. BB 3-17 v Glos (Taunton) 1993.

SOMERSET 1998

RESULTS SUMMARY

	Place	Won	Lost	Tied	Drew	No Result
Britannic Assurance Championship	9th	6	7		4	
All First-Class Matches		6	7		5	
NatWest Trophy	2nd Round					
Benson and Hedges Cup	3rd in Group C					
Sunday League	14th	6	8	1		2

BRITANNIC ASSURANCE CHAMPIONSHIP AVERAGES

BATTING AND FIELDING

Cap		M	I	NO	HS	Runs	Avge	100	50	Ct/St
1992	M.N.Lathwell	11	17	–	106	513	30.17	1	4	7
–	M.E.Trescothick	17	27	2	98	726	29.04	–	5	19
–	M.Burns	9	15	–	96	424	28.26	–	3	15/1
–	M.P.L.Bulbeck	7	11	6	35	141	28.20	–	–	2
1994	R.J.Turner	14	22	2	105	558	27.90	1	2	43
1997	S.C.Ecclestone	5	7	–	94	186	26.57	–	1	4
–	A.R.K.Pierson	12	18	3	108*	396	26.40	1	1	6
1988	G.D.Rose	17	26	2	76	606	25.25	–	4	3
1997	P.C.L.Holloway	16	28	3	123	624	24.96	1	1	7
1995	P.D.Bowler	17	30	2	104	696	24.85	2	2	18
1992	A.R.Caddick	17	25	8	37	322	18.94	–	–	5
1989	R.J.Harden	11	19	2	63	293	17.23	–	2	13
1993	Mushtaq Ahmed	6	9	1	37	121	15.12	–	–	1
1997	K.J.Shine	3	5	2	18	44	14.66	–	–	–
–	G.J.Kennis	3	6	–	49	71	11.83	–	–	5
–	P.S.Jones	3	4	2	22*	23	11.50	–	–	–
–	K.A.Parsons	13	21	–	58	241	11.47	–	1	14
1997	A.P.van Troost	5	7	1	23	61	10.16	–	–	–

Also batted: L.D.Sutton (1 match) 0, 5 (1 ct).

BOWLING

	O	M	R	W	Avge	Best	5wI	10wM
M.P.L.Bulbeck	124.4	23	485	26	18.65	4-40	–	–
A.R.Caddick	687.2	156	2082	105	19.82	8-64	10	3
G.D.Rose	480.3	132	1399	52	26.90	5-48	2	–
A.P.van Troost	118	24	415	15	27.66	4-18	–	–
Mushtaq Ahmed	136	40	411	14	29.35	3-26	–	–
A.R.K.Pierson	243.1	50	788	21	37.52	5-117	1	–
M.E.Trescothick	162.3	38	546	14	39.00	4-82	–	–

Also bowled: P.D.Bowler 22.5-4-71-4; M.Burns 2-0-8-0; P.S.Jones 42.5-11-129-2; K.A.Parsons 107.4-27-357-5; K.J.Shine 57.4-10-216-4.

The First-Class Averages (pp 117-131) give the records of Somerset players in all first-class county matches (Somerset's other opponents being the Sri Lankans).

SOMERSET RECORDS

FIRST-CLASS CRICKET

Highest Total	For 675-9d		v	Hampshire	Bath	1924
	V 811		by	Surrey	The Oval	1899
Lowest Total	For 25		v	Glos	Bristol	1947
	V 22		by	Glos	Bristol	1920
Highest Innings	For 322	I.V.A.Richards	v	Warwicks	Taunton	1985
	V 424	A.C.MacLaren	for	Lancashire	Taunton	1895

Highest Partnership for each Wicket

1st	346	H.T.Hewett/L.C.H.Palairet	v	Yorkshire	Taunton	1892
2nd	290	J.C.W.MacBryan/M.D.Lyon	v	Derbyshire	Buxton	1924
3rd	319	P.M.Roebuck/M.D.Crowe	v	Leics	Taunton	1984
4th	310	P.W.Denning/I.T.Botham	v	Glos	Taunton	1980
5th	235	J.C.White/C.C.C.Case	v	Glos	Taunton	1927
6th	265	W.E.Alley/K.E.Palmer	v	Northants	Northampton	1961
7th	279	R.J.Harden/G.D.Rose	v	Sussex	Taunton	1997
8th	172	I.V.A.Richards/I.T.Botham	v	Leics	Leicester	1983
9th	183	C.H.M.Greetham/H.W.Stephenson	v	Leics	Weston-s-Mare	1963
	183	C.J.Tavaré/N.A.Mallender	v	Sussex	Hove	1990
10th	143	J.J.Bridges/A.H.D.Gibbs	v	Essex	Weston-s-Mare	1919

Best Bowling	For 10- 49	E.J.Tyler	v	Surrey	Taunton	1895
(Innings)	V 10- 35	A.Drake	for	Yorkshire	Weston-s-Mare	1914
Best Bowling	For 16- 83	J.C.White	v	Worcs	Bath	1919
(Match)	V 17-137	W.Brearley	for	Lancashire	Manchester	1905

Most Runs – Season	2761	W.E.Alley	(av 58.74)		1961
Most Runs – Career	21142	H.Gimblett	(av 36.96)		1935-54
Most 100s – Season	11	S.J.Cook			1991
Most 100s – Career	49	H.Gimblett			1935-54
Most Wkts – Season	169	A.W.Wellard	(av 19.24)		1938
Most Wkts – Career	2166	J.C.White	(av 18.02)		1909-37

LIMITED-OVERS CRICKET

Highest Total	NWT	413-4		v	Devon	Torquay	1990
	BHC	349-7		v	Ireland	Taunton	1997
	SL	360-3		v	Glamorgan	Neath	1990
Lowest Total	NWT	59		v	Middlesex	Lord's	1977
	BHC	98		v	Middlesex	Lord's	1982
	SL	58		v	Essex	Chelmsford	1977
Highest Innings	NWT	162*	C.J.Tavaré	v	Devon	Torquay	1990
	BHC	177	S.J.Cook	v	Sussex	Hove	1990
	SL	175*	I.T.Botham	v	Northants	Wellingborough	1986
Best Bowling	NWT	7-15	R.P.Lefebvre	v	Devon	Torquay	1990
	BHC	7-24	Mushtaq Ahmed	v	Ireland	Taunton	1997
	SL	6-24	I.V.A.Richards	v	Lancashire	Manchester	1983

SURREY

Formation of Present Club: 22 August 1845
Colours: Chocolate
Badge: Prince of Wales' Feathers
Championships (since 1890): (15) 1890, 1891, 1892, 1894, 1895, 1899, 1914, 1952, 1953, 1954, 1955, 1956, 1957, 1958, 1971. Joint: (1) 1950
NatWest Trophy/Gillette Cup Winners: (1) 1982
Benson and Hedges Cup Winners: (2) 1974, 1997
Sunday League Champions: (1) 1996
Match Awards: NWT 47; BHC 67

Chief Executive: P.C.J.Sheldon
Kennington Oval, London, SE11 5SS (Tel 0171 582 6660)
Captain: A.J.Hollioake. **Vice-Captain:** M.A.Butcher. **Overseas Player:** Saqlain Mushtaq (tbc). **1999 Beneficiary:** D.J.Bicknell. **Scorer:** K.R.Booth

AMIN, Rupesh Mahesh (Riddlesdown HS; John Ruskin C; Croydon C), b Clapham, London 20 Aug 1977. 6'0". RHB, SLA. Debut 1997. HS 12 v Leics (Oval) 1998. BB 3-58 v Durham (Oval) 1997 – on debut. **SL:** HS –. BB 2-43 v Lancs (Oval) 1997.

BATTY, Gareth Jon (Bingley GS), b Bradford, Yorks 13 Oct 1977. Younger brother of J.D. (Yorkshire and Somerset 1989-96). 5'11". RHB, OB. Yorkshire 1997. Surrey (L-O matches) 1998. Awaiting debut. HS 18 and BB 1-11 Y v Lancs (Leeds) 1997 (non-CC match). **SL:** HS 37 v Derbys (Oval) 1998. BB 1-32.

BATTY, Jonathan Neil (Wheatley Park S, Oxon; Repton S; Durham U; Keble C, Oxford), b Chesterfield, Derbys 18 Apr 1974. 5'10". RHB, WK. Minor C 1994. Comb U 1995. Oxford U 1996; blue 1996. Surrey debut 1997. Oxfordshire 1993 to date. HS 63 v Hants (Southampton) 1998. **NWT:** (Oxon) HS 1. **BHC:** (Minor C) HS 26* v Warwks (Jesmond) 1996. **SL:** HS 38* v Kent (Oval) 1998.

BELL, Michael Anthony Vincent (Bishop Milner CS; Dudley TC), b Birmingham 19 Dec 1966. 6'2". RHB, LMF. Warwickshire 1992-97. Surrey 1998 (L-O matches). MCC YC. Tour (Wa): Z 1993-94. HS 30 Wa v Notts (Nottingham) 1997. BB 7-48 Wa v Glos (Birmingham) 1993. **NWT:** HS –. BB 2-41 Wa v Northants (Lord's) 1995. **BHC:** HS –. BB 2-34 Wa v Middx (Lord's) 1994. **SL:** HS 16 v Derbys (Oval) 1998. BB 5-19 Wa v Leics (Birmingham) 1994.

BENJAMIN, Joseph Emmanuel (Cayon HS, St Kitts; Mount Pleasant S, Highgate, Birmingham), b Christ Church, St Kitts 2 Feb 1961. 6'2". RHB, RMF. Warwickshire 1988-91. Surrey debut 1992; cap 1993. Staffordshire 1986-88. **Tests:** 1 (1994); HS 0 and BB 4-42 v SA (Oval) 1994. **LOI:** 2 (1994-95); HS 0; BB 1-22. Tour: A 1994-95. HS 49 v Essex (Oval) 1995. 50 wkts (3); most – 80 (1994). BB 6-19 v Notts (Nottingham) 1993. Awards: NWT 2; BHC 1. **NWT:** HS 25 v Worcs (Oval) 1994. BB 4-20 v Berks (Oval) 1995. **BHC:** HS 20 Wa v Worcs (Birmingham) 1990. BB 4-19 v Hants (Southampton) 1997. **SL:** HS 24 Wa v Lancs (Manchester) 1990. BB 4-44 v Middx (Oval) 1992.

BICKNELL, Darren John (Robert Haining SS; Guildford TC), b Guildford 24 Jun 1967. Elder brother of M.P. 6'4". LHB, SLA. Debut 1987; cap 1990; benefit 1999. Tours (Eng A): WI 1991-92; P 1990-91; SL 1990-91; Z 1989-90. 1000 runs (6); most – 1888 (1991). HS 235* v Notts (Nottingham) 1994. BB 3-7 v Sussex (Guildford) 1996. Awards: NWT 1; BHC 3. **NWT:** HS 135* v Yorks (Oval) 1989. **BHC:** HS 119 v Hants (Oval) 1990. **SL:** HS 125 v Durham (Durham) 1992. BB 1-11.

BICKNELL, Martin Paul (Robert Haining SS), b Guildford 14 Jan 1969. Younger brother of D.J. 6'3". RHB, RFM. Debut 1986; cap 1989; benefit 1997. **Tests:** 2 (1993); HS 14 and BB 3-99 v A (Birmingham) 1993. **LOI:** 7 (1990-91); HS 31*; BB 3-55. Tours: A 1990-91; SA 1993-94 (Eng A); Z 1989-90 (Eng A). HS 88 v Hants (Southampton) 1992. 50 wkts (7); most – 71 (1992). BB 9-45 v CU (Oxford) 1988. CC BB 7-52 v Sussex (Oval) 1991. Awards: BHC 3. **NWT:** HS 66* v Northants (Oval) 1991. BB 4-35 v Somerset (Taunton) 1993. **BHC:** HS 43 v Kent (Canterbury) 1995. BB 4-38 v Hants (Southampton) 1998. **SL:** HS 57* v Worcs (Worecester) 1997. BB 5-12 v Northants (Oval) 1994.

BROWN, Alistair Duncan (Caterham S), b Beckenham, Kent 11 Feb 1970. 5'10". RHB, occ LB. Debut 1992; cap 1994. **LOI:** 13 (1996 to 1998-99); HS 118. 1000 runs (4); most – 1382 (1993). HS 187 v Glos (Oval) 1995. Awards: BHC 2. **NWT:** HS 72 v Holland (Oval) 1996. **BHC:** HS 117* v Sussex (Hove) 1996. **SL:** HS 203 v Hants (Guildford) 1997.

BUTCHER, Mark Alan (Trinity S; Archbishop Tenison's S, Croydon), b Croydon 23 Aug 1972. Son of A.R. (see RETIRED/RELEASED below); brother of G.P. (see NEW REGISTRATIONS below). 5'11". LHB, RM. Debut 1992; cap 1996. **Tests:** 19 (1997 to 1998-99); HS 116 v SA (Leeds) 1998 and 116 v A (Brisbane) 1998-99. Tours: A 1996-97 (Eng A), 1998-99; WI 1997-98. 1000 runs (4); most – 1604 (1996). HS 167 v Durham (Oval) 1995. BB 4-31 v Worcs (Oval) 1994. Awards: NWT 1; BHC 1. **NWT:** HS 91 v Somerset (Oval) 1996. BB 2-57 v Somerset (Taunton) 1993. **BHC:** HS 67 v Hants (Southampton) 1998. BB 3-37 v Somerset (Oval) 1994. **SL:** HS 85* v Durham (Chester-le-St) 1998. BB 3-23 v Sussex (Oval) 1992.

GREENIDGE, Carl Gary (Lodge S and St Michael S, Barbados; Heathcote S, Chingford; W Hatch HS; City of Westminster C), b Basingstoke, Hants 20 Apr 1978. Son of CG (Hampshire, Barbados and West Indies 1970-92). 5'10". RHB, RM. MCC YC. Awaiting f-c debut. **SL:** HS –.

HOLLIOAKE, Adam John (St George's C, Weybridge), b Melbourne, Australia 5 Sep 1971. Brother of B.C. 5'11". RHB, RMF. Debut 1993, scoring 13 and 123 v Derbys (Ilkeston); cap 1995. Qualified for England 1992. **Tests:** 4 (1997 to 1997-98); HS 45 and BB 2-31 v A (Nottingham) 1997 – on debut. **LOI:** 31 (1996 to 1998-99, 14 as captain); HS 83*; BB 4-23. Tours: A 1996-97 (Eng A – captain); WI 1997-98. 1000 runs (2); most – 1522 (1996). HS 182 v Middx (Lord's) 1997. BB 5-62 v Glam (Swansea) 1998. Awards: NWT 1; BHC 1. **NWT:** HS 88 v Glos (Bristol) 1998. BB 4-53 v Middx (Oval) 1995. **BHC:** HS 85 v Leics (Leicester) 1998. BB 4-34 v Hants (Oval) 1996. **SL:** HS 93 v Kent (Canterbury) 1995. BB 5-38 v Kent (Canterbury) 1997.

HOLLIOAKE, Benjamin Caine (Millfield S), b Melbourne, Australia 11 Nov 1977. Brother of A.J. 6'2". RHB, RFM. Debut 1996. YC 1997. **Tests:** 2 (1997 to 1998); HS 28 v A (Nottingham) 1997 on debut; BB 2-105 v SL (Oval) 1998. **LOI:** 7 (1997 to 1998-99); HS 63 – on debut; BB 2-43. Tours: A 1998-99; SL (Eng A) 1997-98. HS 163 Eng A v SL A (Moratuwa) 1997-98. Sy 76 v Middx (Lord's) 1997. BB 4-28 v Notts (Nottingham) 1998. Awards: BHC 2. **NWT:** HS 33 and BB 2-28 v Bucks (Oval) 1998. **BHC:** HS 98 v Kent (Lord's) 1997. BB 3-23 v Brit U (Oval) 1998. **SL:** HS 61 v Lancs (Oval) 1997. BB 5-10 v Derbys (Oval) 1996.

KNOTT, James Alan (City of Westminster C), b Canterbury, Kent 14 Jun 1975. Son of A.P.E. (Kent, Tasmania and England 1964-85). 5'6". RHB, occ LB, WK. Debut 1995. MCC YC. HS 49* v SA A (Oval) 1996. CC HS 41* v Derbys (Oval) 1988. **BHC:** HS 10 v Hants (Southampton) 1997. **SL:** HS 98 v Glos (Cheltenham) 1998.

PATTERSON, Mark William (Belfast Royal Academy; Ulster U), b Belfast, N Ireland 2 Feb 1974. Elder brother of A.D. (Ireland 1996). 6'1". RHB, RFM. Debut 1996, taking 6-80 v SA A (Oval). Awaiting CC debut. HS 4 and BB 6-80 (as above). **NWT:** HS 2. BB 3-66 Ire v Yorks (Leeds) 1995. **BHC:** HS 9. BB 3-48 Ire v Somerset (Eglington) 1995.

RATCLIFFE, Jason David (Sharman's Cross SS; Solihull SFC), b Solihull, Warwks 19 Jun 1969. Son of D.P. (Warwks 1957-68). 6'4". RHB, RM. Warwickshire 1988-94. Surrey debut 1995; cap 1998. Tours (Wa): SA 1991-92, 1992-93; Z 1993-94. HS 135 v Worcs (Worcester) 1997. BB 2-26 v Yorks (Middlesbrough) 1996. Awards: NWT 2. **NWT:** HS 105 Wa v Yorks (Leeds) 1993. **BHC:** HS 41 v Leics (Leicester) 1998. BB 2-42 v Sussex (Oval) 1997. **SL:** HS 82 v Northants (Northampton) 1997. BB 2-11 Wa v Glam (Neath) 1993.

SALISBURY, Ian David Kenneth (Moulton CS), b Northampton 21 Jan 1970. 5'11". RHB, LBG. Sussex 1989-96; cap 1991. Surrey debut 1997; cap 1998. MCC YC. YC 1992. *Wisden* 1992. **Tests:** 12 (1992 to 1998); HS 50 v P (Manchester) 1992; BB 4-163 v WI (Georgetown) 1993-94. **LOI:** 4 (1992-93 to 1993-94); HS 5; BB 3-41. Tours: WI 1991-92 (Eng A), 1993-94; I 1992-93; 1994-95 (Eng A); P 1990-91 (Eng A), 1995-96 (Eng A); SL 1990-91 (Eng A). HS 86 Eng A v Pak A (Rawalpindi) 1995-96. CC HS 83 Sx v Glam (Hove) 1996. Sy HS 61 v Middx (Guildford) 1998. 50 wkts (4); most – 87 (1992). BB 8-75 (11-169 match) Sx v Essex (Chelmsford) 1996. Sy BB 7-65 v Glam (Swansea) 1998. Awards: NWT 1; BHC 2. **NWT:** HS 34* Derbys (Oval) 1998. BB 3-28 Sx v Bucks (Beaconsfield) 1992. **BHC:** HS 19 Sx v Hants (Southampton) 1996. BB 4-53 v Sussex (Oval) 1997. **SL:** HS 48* Sx v Glam (Swansea) 1995. BB 5-30 Sx v Leics (Leicester) 1992.

SAQLAIN MUSHTAQ (Govt Muslim League HS, M.A.O. College, Lahore), b Lahore, Pakistan 29 Dec 1976. Brother of Sibtain Mushtaq (Lahore 1988-89). 5'11". RHB, OB. Islamabad 1994-95. PIA 1994-95 to date. Surrey debut 1997; cap 1998. **Tests** (P): 17 (1995-96 to 1998-99); HS 79 v Z (Sheikhupura) 1996-97; BB 5-32 v Z (Lahore) 1998-99. **LOI** (P): 88 (1995-96 to 1998-99); HS 30*; BB 5-29. Tours (P): E 1996; A 1995-96, 1996-97; SA 1997-98; I 1998-99, SL 1996-97. HS 79 (*see Tests*). Sy HS 45* v Essex (Chelmsford) 1998. 50 wkts (1+1); most – 63 (1998). BB 8-65 (11-107 match) v Derbys (Oval) 1988. Hat-trick 1997. **NWT:** HS 6* and BB 3-30 v Notts (Oval) 1997. **BHC:** HS 11 v Leics (Leicester) 1998. BB 4-46 v Lancs (Oval) 1998. **SL:** HS 29* v Warwks (Birmingham) 1997. BB 3-31 v Northants (Northampton) 1997.

SHAHID, Nadeem (Ipswich S), b Karachi, Pakistan 23 Apr 1969. 6'0". RHB, LB. Essex 1989-94. Surrey debut 1995; cap 1998. Suffolk 1988. 1000 runs (1): 1003 (1990). HS 139 v Yorks (Oval) 1995. BB 3-91 Ex v Surrey (Oval) 1990. Sy BB 3-93 v SA A (Oval) 1994. **NWT:** HS 85* Ex v Glam (Cardiff) 1994. BB 3-30 v Bucks (Oval) 1998.**BHC:** HS 65* and BB 1-59 v Kent (Canterbury) 1995. **SL:** HS 101 v Derbys (Derby) 1995.

STEWART, Alec James (Tiffin S), b Merton 8 Apr 1963. Son of M.J. (Surrey and England 1954-72). 5'11". RHB, WK. Debut 1981; cap 1985; captain 1992-97; benefit 1994. *Wisden* 1992. MBE 1998. **Tests:** 86 (1989-90 to 1998-99, 13 as captain); HS 190 v P (Birmingham) 1992. **LOI:** 116 (1989-90 to 1998-99, 21 as captain); HS 116. Tours (C=captain): A 1990-91, 1994-95, 1998-99C; SA 1995-96; WI 1989-90, 1993-94, 1997-98; NZ 1991-92, 1996-97; I 1992-93; SL 1992-93C; Z 1996-97. 1000 runs (8); most – 1665 (1986). HS 271* v Yorks (Oval) 1997. BB 1-7. Held 11 catches (equalling world f-c match record) v Leics (Leicester) 1989. Awards: NWT 5; BHC 5. **NWT:** HS 125* v Essex (Oval) 1991. **BHC:** HS 167* v Somerset (Oval) 1994. **SL:** HS 125 v Lancs (Oval) 1990.

THORPE, Graham Paul (Weydon CS; Farnham SFC), b Farnham 1 Aug 1969. 5'11". LHB, RM. Debut 1988; cap 1991. *Wisden* 1991. **Tests:** 53 (1993 to 1998-99); HS 138 v A (Birmingham) 1997; scored 114* v A (Nottingham) 1993 on debut. **LOI:** 44 (1993 to 1997-98); HS 89 – twice. Tours: A 1992-93 (Eng A), 1994-95, 1998-99 (*part*); SA 1995-96; WI 1991-92 (Eng A), 1993-94, 1997-98; NZ 1996-97; P 1990-91 (Eng A); SL 1990-91 (Eng A); Z 1996-97 (Eng A), 1996-97. 1000 runs (6); most – 1895 (1992). HS 222 v Glam (Oval) 1997. BB 4-40 v A (Oval) 1993. CC BB 2-14 v Derbys (Oval) 1996. Awards: NWT 2; BHC 1. **NWT:** HS 145* v Lancs (Oval) 1994. **BHC:** HS 103 v Lancs (Oval) 1993. BB 3-35 v Middx (Lord's) 1989. **SL:** HS 115* v Lancs (Manchester) 1991. BB 3-21 v Somerset (Oval) 1991.

TUDOR, Alex Jeremy (St Mark's S, Hammersmith; City of Westminster C), b West Brompton, London 23 Oct 1977. 6'5". RHB, RF. Debut 1995. **Tests:** 2 (1998-99); HS 18* and BB 4-89 v A (Perth) 1998-99 – on debut. Tour: A 1998-99. HS 56 v Leics (Leicester) 1995. BB 6-101 v Glos (Oval) 1997. **NWT:** HS 1 and BB 4-39 v Bucks (Oval) 1998. **SL:** HS 29* v Essex (Oval) 1995. BB 3-38 v Leics (Oval) 1998.

WARD, Ian James (Millfield S), b Plymouth, Devon 30 Sep 1972. 5'8½". LHB, RM. Surrey 1992 and 1996. HS 81* v Lancs (Manchester) 1998. **NWT:** HS 27 v Derbys (Oval) 1998. **SL:** HS 91 v Middx (Guildford) 1998.

NEW REGISTRATIONS

BARRETT, Kevin Andrew Owen, b Swansea, Glam 16 Nov 1975. LHB, RM.

BISHOP, Ian Emlyn (Castle S; Somerset C of Art & Tech), b Taunton, Somerset 26 Aug 1977. 6'1". RHB, RFM. Somerset 1996. Awaiting CC debut. HS 2 (Sm).

BUTCHER, Gary Paul (Trinity S; Riddlesdown S; Heath Clark C), b Clapham, London 11 Mar 1975. Son of A.R. (Surrey, Glam and England 1972-92); brother of M.A. 5'9". RHB, RM. Glamorgan 1994-98. Tours (Gm): SA 1994-95; Z 1994-95. HS 101* Gm v OU (Oxford) 1997. CC HS 89 Gm v Northants (Northampton) 1996. BB 7-77 Gm v Glos (Bristol) 1996. **NWT:** HS 48 and BB Gm 2-33 v Beds (Cardiff) 1997. **BHC:** HS 17 Gm v Somerset (Taunton) 1997. BB 2-21 Gm v Warwks (Cardiff) 1996. **SL:** HS 47 Gm v Worcs (Worcester) 1997. BB 4-32 Gm v Glos (Bristol) 1996.

CARBERRY, Michael Alexander, b Croydon 29 Sep 1980. LHB. Summer contract.

MURTAGH, Timothy James, b Lambeth 2 Aug 1981. LHB, RFM. Summer contract.

RELEASED/RETIRED
(Having made a first-class County appearance in 1998)

BUTCHER, Alan Raymond (Heath Clark GS), b Croydon, Surrey 7 Jan 1954. Brother of I.P. (Leics 1980-87 and Glos 1988-90) and M.S. (Surrey 1982); father of G.P. and M.A. 5'8½". LHB, SLA/LM. Surrey 1972-86 and 1998 (cap 1975; benefit 1985). Glamorgan 1987-92 (cap 1987; captain 1989-92). *Wisden* 1990. **Tests:** 1 (1979); HS 20 v I (Oval) 1979. **LOI:** 1 (1980); HS 14. Tours: WI 1982-83 (Int); I 1980-81 (Overseas XI); Z 1990-91 (Gm – captain). 1000 runs (12) inc 2000 (1): 2116 (1990). HS 216* v CU (Cambridge) 1980. CC HS 188 v Sussex (Hove) 1978. Gm HS 171* v Warwks (Birmingham) 1989. BB 6-48 v Hants (Guildford) 1972. Gm BB 3-35 v Middx (Cardiff) 1987. Awards: NWT 3; BHC 6. **NWT:** HS 104* v Middx (Lord's) 1990. BB 1-27. **BHC:** HS 127 v Yorks (Cardiff) 1991. BB 4-36 v Middx (Lord's) 1985. **SL:** HS 113* v Warwks (Birmingham) 1978. BB 5-19 v Glos (Bristol) 1975.

SURREY 1998

RESULTS SUMMARY

	Place	Won	Lost	Tied	Drew	No Result
Britannic Assurance Championship	5th	10	5		2	
All First-Class Matches		10	5		2	
NatWest Trophy	Quarter-Finalist					
Benson and Hedges Cup	Semi-Finalist					
Sunday League	18th	3	12			2

BRITANNIC ASSURANCE CHAMPIONSHIP AVERAGES

BATTING AND FIELDING

Cap		M	I	NO	HS	Runs	Avge	100	50	Ct/St
1994	A.D.Brown	15	22	1	155	1036	49.33	4	6	20
1985	A.J.Stewart	8	12	1	96	464	42.18	–	4	15
1991	G.P.Thorpe	6	7	1	114	251	41.83	1	1	10
1996	M.A.Butcher	12	18	1	109*	661	38.88	2	4	10
1998	N.Shahid	12	22	3	126*	683	35.94	2	3	13
1995	A.J.Hollioake	15	22	2	112	684	34.20	1	4	15
1998	J.D.Ratcliffe	9	15	1	100	449	32.07	1	2	2
–	I.J.Ward	10	19	2	81*	529	31.11	–	5	9
1998	I.D.K.Salisbury	12	13	2	61	285	25.90	–	3	6
–	B.C.Hollioake	16	24	3	60	455	21.66	–	2	7
1989	M.P.Bicknell	17	21	1	81	433	21.65	–	1	5
–	J.N.Batty	16	19	2	63	351	20.64	–	2	39/6
1998	Saqlain Mushtaq	12	15	5	45*	176	17.60	–	–	7
–	J.A.Knott	5	9	3	41*	103	17.16	–	–	1
–	A.J.Tudor	10	13	3	48	167	16.70	–	–	3
1993	J.E.Benjamin	8	9	3	18*	57	9.50	–	–	1
–	R.M.Amin	3	4	2	12	14	7.00	–	–	–

Also batted: A.R.Butcher (cap 1975)(1 match) 22, 12.

BOWLING

	O	M	R	W	Avge	Best	5wI	10wM
Saqlain Mushtaq	475	136	1119	63	17.76	8-65	3	3
M.P.Bicknell	494.1	141	1340	65	20.61	5-27	2	–
I.D.K.Salisbury	337	99	766	36	21.27	7-65	2	–
B.C.Hollioake	248.4	49	792	34	23.29	4-28	–	–
A.J.Tudor	184.2	34	737	29	25.41	5-43	1	–
M.A.Butcher	94.4	22	287	11	26.09	4-41	–	–
J.E.Benjamin	189.1	42	626	22	28.45	6-35	1	–

Also bowled: R.M.Amin 59-9-176-3; J.N.Batty 1-0-22-0; A.D.Brown 2-1-2-0; A.J.Hollioake 92.5-29-247-8; J.A.Knott 1-0-2-0; J.D.Ratcliffe 2-1-4-0; N.Shahid 16-1-66-2.

The First-Class Averages (pp 117-131) give the records of Surrey players in all first-class county matches, with the exception of M.A.Butcher, B.C.Hollioake, I.D.K.Salisbury, A.J.Stewart and G.P.Thorpe, whose full county figures are as above.

SURREY RECORDS

FIRST-CLASS CRICKET

Highest Total	For 811		v	Somerset	The Oval	1899
	V 863		by	Lancashire	The Oval	1990
Lowest Total	For 14		v	Essex	Chelmsford	1983
	V 16		by	MCC	Lord's	1872
Highest Innings	For 357*	R.Abel	v	Somerset	The Oval	1899
	V 366	N.H.Fairbrother	for	Lancashire	The Oval	1990

Highest Partnership for each Wicket

1st	428	J.B.Hobbs/A.Sandham	v	Oxford U	The Oval	1926
2nd	371	J.B.Hobbs/E.G.Hayes	v	Hampshire	The Oval	1909
3rd	413	D.J.Bicknell/D.M.Ward	v	Kent	Canterbury	1990
4th	448	R.Abel/T.W.Hayward	v	Yorkshire	The Oval	1899
5th	308	J.N.Crawford/F.C.Holland	v	Somerset	The Oval	1908
6th	298	A.Sandham/H.S.Harrison	v	Sussex	The Oval	1913
7th	262	C.J.Richards/K.T.Medlycott	v	Kent	The Oval	1987
8th	205	I.A.Greig/M.P.Bicknell	v	Lancashire	The Oval	1990
9th	168	E.R.T.Holmes/E.W.J.Brooks	v	Hampshire	The Oval	1936
10th	173	A.Ducat/A.Sandham	v	Essex	Leyton	1921

Best Bowling	For	10-43	T.Rushby	v	Somerset	Taunton	1921
(Innings)	V	10-28	W.P.Howell	for	Australians	The Oval	1899
Best Bowling	For	16-83	G.A.R.Lock	v	Kent	Blackheath	1956
(Match)	V	15-57	W.P.Howell	for	Australians	The Oval	1899

Most Runs – Season	3246	T.W.Hayward	(av 72.13)	1906
Most Runs – Career	43554	J.B.Hobbs	(av 49.72)	1905-34
Most 100s – Season	13	T.W.Hayward		1906
	13	J.B.Hobbs		1925
Most 100s – Career	144	J.B.Hobbs		1905-34
Most Wkts – Season	252	T.Richardson	(av 13.94)	1895
Most Wkts – Career	1775	T.Richardson	(av 17.87)	1892-1904

LIMITED-OVERS CRICKET

Highest Total	NWT	350		v	Worcs	The Oval	1994
	BHC	333-6		v	Hampshire	The Oval	1996
	SL	375-4		v	Yorkshire	Scarborough	1994
Lowest Total	NWT	74		v	Kent	The Oval	1967
	BHC	89		v	Notts	Nottingham	1984
	SL	64		v	Worcs	Worcester	1978
Highest Innings	NWT	146	G.S.Clinton	v	Kent	Canterbury	1985
	BHC	167*	A.J.Stewart	v	Somerset	The Oval	1994
	SL	203	A.D.Brown	v	Hampshire	Guildford	1997
Best Bowling	NWT	7-33	R.D.Jackman	v	Yorkshire	Harrogate	1970
	BHC	5-15	S.G.Kenlock	v	Ireland	The Oval	1995
	SL	6-25	Intikhab Alam	v	Derbyshire	The Oval	1974

SUSSEX

Formation of Present Club: 1 March 1839
Substantial Reorganisation: August 1857
Colours: Dark Blue, Light Blue and Gold
Badge: County Arms of Six Martlets
Championships: (0) Second 1902, 1903, 1932, 1933, 1934, 1953, 1981
NatWest Trophy/Gillette Cup Winners: (4) 1963, 1964, 1978, 1986
Benson and Hedges Cup Winners: (0) Semi-Finalists 1982
Sunday League Champions: (1) 1982
Match Awards: NWT 55; BHC 54

Chief Executive: A.C.S.Pigott. **General Manager/Director of Cricket:** D.R.Gilbert County Ground, Eaton Road, Hove BN3 3AN (Tel 01273 827100)
Captain: C.J.Adams. **Vice-Captain:** tba. **Overseas Player:** M.J.Di Venuto.
1999 Beneficiary: N.J.Lenham. **Scorer:** L.V.Chandler

ADAMS, Christopher John (Repton S), b Whitwell, Derbyshire 6 May 1970. 6'0". RHB, RM/OB. Derbyshire 1988-97; cap 1992. Sussex debut/cap 1998; captain 1998 to date. **LOI:** 2 (1998); HS 25 – on debut. 1000 runs (4); most – 1742 (1996). HS 239 De v Hants (Southampton) 1996. Sx HS 170 v Middx (Hove) 1998. BB 4-29 De v Lancs (Derby) 1991. Awards: NWT 2; BHC 4. **NWT:** HS 129* De v Sussex (Derby) 1997. BB 1-15 De v Berks (Derby) 1992. **BHC:** HS 138 De v Minor C (Lakenham) 1997. **SL:** HS 141* De v Kent (Chesterfield) 1992. BB 5-16 v Middx (Hove) 1998.
BATES, Justin Jonathan (Hurstpierpoint C), b Farnborough, Hants 9 Apr 1976. 5'11". RHB, OB. Debut 1997. HS 47 v Glos (Hove) 1997. BB 5-67 (9-136 match) v Northants (Northampton) 1998. **SL:** HS 8. BB 2-42 v Northants (Northampton) 1998.
CAMPBELL, George Richard Angus (Lancing C), b Hammersmith, London 9 Feb 1979. 6'2". LHB, RM. Non-contracted player awaiting f-c debut.
CARPENTER, James Robert (Birkenhead S), b Birkenhead, Cheshire 20 Oct 1975. 6'1½". LHB, SLA. MCC YC. Debut 1997. HS 65 v Notts (Nottingham) 1998. BB 1-50. **BHC:** HS 31 v Middx (Lord's) 1998. **SL:** HS 53 v Lancs (Hove) 1998.
EDWARDS, Alexander David (Imberhorne CS, E Grinstead; Loughborough U), b Cuckfield 2 Aug 1975. 6'0". RHB, RFM. Combined U 1995. Sussex debut 1995. HS 22 v Young A (Hove) 1995. CC HS 20 and CC BB 4-94 v Surrey (Hove) 1997. BB 5-34 v Pak A (Hove) 1997. **BHC:** HS 43 v Essex (Hove) 1998. BB 2-51 Brit U v Middx (Lord's) 1995. **SL:** HS 20 and BB 3-34 v Notts (Nottingham) 1998.
GREENFIELD, Keith (Falmer HS), b Brighton 6 Dec 1968. 6'0". RHB, RM. Debut 1987; cap 1996. HS 154* v Glam (Hove) 1996. BB 2-40 v Essex (Hove) 1993. Awards: NWT 2. **NWT:** HS 129 v Lancs (Hove) 1997. BB 2-35 v Glam (Hove) 1993. **BHC:** HS 93* v Essex (Hove) 1998. BB 1-17. **SL:** HS 102 v Notts (Arundel) 1995. BB 3-34 v Northants (Hove) 1995.
HAYWOOD, Giles Ronald (Lancing C), b Chichester 8 Sep 1979. 6'1". LHB, RM. Awaiting f-c debut. **SL:** HS 14 v Essex (Chemsford) 1998.
HUMPHRIES, Shaun (The Weald, Billingshurst; Kingston C, London), b Horsham 11 Jan 1973. 5'9". RHB, WK. Debut 1993. HS 66 v Kent (Tunbridge W) 1998. **NWT:** HS 10 v Lancs (Manchester) 1998. **BHC:** HS 16 v Glam (Hove) 1998. **SL:** HS 13 v Glos (Cheltenham) 1998.
KHAN, Wasim Gulzar (Small Heath CS; Josiah Mason SFC, Erdington), b Birmingham 26 Feb 1971. 6'1". LHB, LB. Warwickshire 1995-97. Sussex debut 1998. HS 181 Wa v Hants (Southampton) 1995. Sx HS 125 v Derbys (Horsham) 1998. **NWT:** HS 2. **BHC:** HS 33 v Glam (Hove) 1998. **SL:** HS 33 v Warwks (Hove) 1998.

KIRTLEY, Robert James (Clifton C), b Eastbourne 10 Jan 1975. 6'0". RHB, RFM. Debut 1995; cap 1998. Mashonaland 1996-97. HS 59 v Durham (Eastbourne) 1998. 50 wkts (1): 54 (1998). BB 7-29 (10-88 match) v Notts (Nottingham) 1998. Took 5-53 (7-88 match) for Mashonaland v Eng XI (Harare) 1996-97. Award: NWT 1. **NWT:** HS 6. BB 5-39 v Salop (Hove) 1997. **BHC:** HS 2 and BB 2-57 v Glam (Hove) 1998. **SL:** HS 15* v Derbys (Horsham) 1998. BB 4-21 v Yorks (Hove) 1998.

LEWRY, Jason David (Durrington HS, Worthing), b Worthing 2 Apr 1971. 6'2". LHB, LFM. Debut 1994; cap 1996. Tour: Z 1998-99 (Eng A). HS 34 v Kent (Hove) 1995. 50 wkts (1): 62 (1998). BB 6-43 v Worcs (Eastbourne) 1995. Hat-trick 1998. **NWT:** HS 9. BB 4-42 v Lancs (Manchester) 1994. **BHC:** HS 14* v Ire (Hove) 1995. BB 2-52 v Glam (Hove) 1998. **SL:** HS 10 v Somerset (Hove) 1998. BB 4-29 v Somerset (Bath) 1995.

MARTIN-JENKINS, Robin Simon Christopher (Radley C; Durham U), b Guildford, Surrey 28 Oct 1975. Son of C.D.A. (Cricket Correspondent/Commentator). 6'5". RHB, RFM. Debut 1995. British U 1996. HS 78 and BB 7-54 (9-119 match) v Glam (Hove) 1998. Award: BHC 1. **BHC** (Brit U): HS 39 v Hants (Oxford) 1998. BB 4-57 v Glos (Bristol) 1997. **SL:** HS 44 and BB 2-12 v Yorks (Hove) 1998.

PEIRCE, Michael Toby Edward (Ardingly C; Durham U), b Maidenhead, Berks 14 Jun 1973. 5'10". LHB, SLA. Combined U 1994. Sussex debut 1995. HS 104 v Hants (Southampton) 1997. **NWT:** HS 1. **BHC:** HS 44 Comb U v Middx (Lord's) 1995. **SL:** HS 29 v Northants (Northampton) 1998.

RAO, Rajesh Krishnakant (Alperton HS; Brighton U), b Park Royal, Middlesex 9 Dec 1974. 5'10". RHB, LBG. Debut 1996. MCC YC. HS 89 v Essex (Hove) 1997. BB 1-1. Award: NWT 1. **NWT:** HS 158 v Derbys (Derby) 1997. **BHC:** HS 61 v Surrey (Oval) 1997. **SL:** HS 91 v Glos (Bristol) 1996. BB 3-31 v Worcs (Worcester) 1996.

ROBINSON, Mark Andrew (Hull GS), b Hull, Yorkshire 23 Nov 1966. 6'3". RHB, RFM. Northamptonshire 1987-90; cap 1990. Canterbury 1988-89. Yorkshire 1991-95; cap 1992. Sussex debut/cap 1997. Tours (Y): SA 1991-92, 1992-93. Failed to score in 12 successive f-c innings 1990 – world record. HS 27 v Lancs (Manchester) 1997. 50 wkts (1): 50 (1992). BB 9-37 (12-124 match) Y v Northants (Harrogate) 1993. Sx Debut BB 6-78 v Northants (Hove) 1997 on Sussex debut. Award: BHC 1. **NWT:** HS 4. BB 4-32 Nh v Somerset (Taunton) 1989. **BHC:** HS 3*. BB 3-53 v Glam (Hove) 1998. **SL:** HS 9* (twice). BB 4-23 Y v Northants (Leeds) 1993.

STRONG, Michael Richard (Brighton C; Brunel UC), b Cuckfield 28 Jun 1974. 6'1". LHB, RMF. Debut 1998. HS 2*. **SL:** HS 2*.

WILTON, Nicholas James (Beacon Community C and SFC; City of Westminster C), b Pembury, Kent 23 Sep 1978. 5'11". RHB, WK. Debut 1998. MCC YC. HS 19* v Hants (Hove) 1998 – on debut. **SL:** HS 3.

NEW REGISTRATIONS

COTTEY, Phillip Anthony (Bishopston CS, Swansea), b Swansea, Glamorgan 2 Jun 1966. 5'4". RHB, OB. Glamorgan 1992-98. E Transvaal 1991-92. Tours (Gm): SA 1995-96; Z 1990-91, 1994-95. 1000 runs (7); most – 1543 (1996). HS 203 and BB 4-49 Gm v Leics (Swansea) 1996. **NWT:** HS 68 Gm v Beds (Cardiff) 1998. BB 1-9. **BHC:** HS 96 Gm v Sussex (Hove) 1998. BB 1-49. **SL:** HS 92* Gm v Hants (Ebbw Vale) 1991. BB 4-56 Gm v Essex (Chelmsford) 1996.

Di VENUTO, Michael James, b Hobart, Australia 12 Dec 1973. LHB. Tasmania 1991-92 to date. **LOI** (A): 9 (1996-97 to 1997-98); HS 89. Tours: E 1998 (Aus A); Z 1995-96 (Tas). HS 189 Tasmania v WA (Perth) 1997-98.

HAVELL, Paul Matthew, b Melbourne, Australia 4 Jul 1980. LHB, RFM. Non-contracted player.

MONTGOMERIE, Richard Robert (Rugby S; Worcester C, Oxford), b Rugby, Warwks 3 Jul 1971. 5'10½". RHB, OB. Oxford U 1991-94; blue 1991-92-93-94; captain 1994; half blues for rackets and real tennis. Northamptonshire 1991-98; cap 1995. Tour: Z 1994-95 (Nh). 1000 runs (2); most – 1178 (1996). HS 192 Nh v Kent (Canterbury) 1995. **NWT:** HS 109 Nh v Notts (Nottingham) 1995. **BHC:** HS 75 Comb U v Worcs (Oxford) 1992. **SL:** HS 86* Nh v Durham (Northampton) 1997.

RASHID, Umer Bin Abdul (Ealing Green HS; Ealing Tertiary C; Southbank U), b Southampton, Hants 6 Feb 1976. 6'3". LHB, SLA. Middlesex 1996-98. HS 9. **BHC** (Brit U): HS 82 v Hants (Oxford) 1997. BB 2-57 v Essex (Chelmsford) 1996. **SL:** HS 8. BB 2-34 M v Yorks (Leeds) 1995.

YARDY, Michael Howard (William Parker S, Hastings), b Pembury, Kent 27 Nov 1980. LHB, LM. Non-contracted player.

ZUIDERENT, Bastiaan ('*Bas*'), b Utrecht, Holland 3 Mar 1977. RHB, OB. Holland 1994 to date. **LOI:** 4 (1995-96 World Cup); HS 91.

RELEASED/RETIRED
(Having made a first-class County appearance in 1998)

BEVAN, Michael Gwyl (Western Creek HS, Canberra), b Belconnen, ACT, Australia 8 May 1970. 5'11½". LHB, SLC. S Australia 1989-90. NSW 1990-91 to date. Yorkshire 1995-96; cap 1995. Sussex 1998; cap 1998. **Tests** (A): 18 (1994-95 to 1997-98); HS 91 v P (Lahore) 1994-95; BB 6-82 (10-113 match) v WI (Adelaide) 1996-97. **LOI** (A): 97 (1993-94 to 1998-99); HS 108*; BB 3-36. Tours (A): E 1997; SA 1996-97; I 1996-97; P 1994-95; Z 1991-92 (Aus B). 1000 runs (2); most – 1598 (1995). HS 203* NSW v WA (Sydney) 1993-94. UK HS 160* Y v Surrey (Middlesbrough) 1996. Sx HS 149* v Leics (Leicester) 1998. BB 6-82 (*see Tests*). UK BB 3-36 Y v Warwks (Leeds) 1996 and 3-36 v Kent (Tunbridge W) 1998. Awards: NWT 2; BHC 4. **NWT:** HS 91* Y v Essex (Chelmsford) 1995. BB 2-47 v Lancs (Manchester) 1996. **BHC:** HS 95* Y v Lancs (Manchester) 1996 and 95* v Glam (Hove) 1998. BB 1-25. **SL:** HS 103* Y v Glos (Middlesbrough) 1995. BB 5-29 Y v Sussex (Eastbourne) 1996. Returns 2000.

JARVIS, P.W. – *see* SOMERSET.

KHAN, A.A. – *see* LEICESTERSHIRE.

MOORES, Peter (King Edward VI S, Macclesfield), b Macclesfield, Cheshire 18 Dec 1962. 6'0". RHB, WK. Worcestershire 1983-84. Sussex 1985-98; cap 1989; captain 1997; benefit 1998. OFS 1988-89. HS 185 v CU (Hove) 1996. CC HS 119* v Surrey (Guildford) 1996. **NWT:** HS 45 v Warwks (Birmingham) 1997. **BHC:** HS 76 v Middx (Hove) 1990. **SL:** HS 89* v Leics (Hove) 1995. Appointed Sussex cricket manager/coach/2nd XI captain.

NEWELL, K. – *see* GLAMORGAN.

NEWELL, Mark (Hazelwick SS; City of Westminster C), b Crawley 19 Dec 1973. Brother of K. (*see* GLAMORGAN). 6'1½". RHB, OB. Sussex 1996-98. MCC YC. HS 135* v Derbys (Horsham) 1998. **NWT:** HS 79 v Warwks (Birmingham) 1997. **BHC:** HS 87 v Glos (Hove) 1997. **SL:** HS 77 v Worcs (Worcester) 1998.

TAYLOR, Neil Royston (Cray Valley THS), b Orpington, Kent 21 Jul 1959. 6'1". RHB, OB. Kent 1979-95, scoring 110 and 11 on debut v SL (Canterbury); cap 1982; benefit 1992. Sussex 1997-98; cap 1997. 1000 runs (11); most – 1979 (1990). HS 204 K v Surrey (Canterbury) 1990. Sx HS 127 v Northants (Hove) 1997 on Sussex debut. BB 2-20 K v Somerset (Canterbury) 1985. Awards: BHC 9. **NWT:** HS 86 K v Staffs (Stone) 1995. BB 3-29 K v Dorset (Canterbury) 1989. **BHC:** HS 137 K v Surrey (Oval) 1988. **SL:** HS 95 K v Hants (Canterbury) 1990.

SUSSEX 1998

RESULTS SUMMARY

	Place	Won	Lost	Tied	Drew	No Result
Britannic Assurance Championship	7th	6	7		4	
All First-Class Matches		6	7		6	
NatWest Trophy	1st Round					
Benson and Hedges Cup	4th in Group D					
Sunday League	16th	6	9			2

BRITANNIC ASSURANCE CHAMPIONSHIP AVERAGES

BATTING AND FIELDING

Cap		M	I	NO	HS	Runs	Avge	100	50	Ct/St
1998	M.G.Bevan	12	19	2	149*	935	55.00	3	4	10
1998	C.J.Adams	16	27	1	170	1116	42.92	4	4	30
–	M.Newell	8	12	1	135*	338	30.72	2	–	6
–	R.S.C.Martin-Jenkins	8	13	1	78	353	29.41	–	2	3
–	W.G.Khan	16	28	1	125	775	28.70	1	5	5
–	K.Newell	9	17	4	84	325	25.00	–	2	7
–	M.T.E.Peirce	17	30	1	96	725	25.00	–	5	7
–	N.J.Wilton	2	4	2	19*	46	23.00	–	–	5
1997	N.R.Taylor	5	7	–	51	153	21.85	–	1	4
1994	P.W.Jarvis	4	6	1	39	107	21.40	–	–	4
–	R.K.Rao	9	16	1	76	320	21.33	–	2	–
1998	R.J.Kirtley	17	26	10	59	320	20.00	–	1	2
–	S.Humphries	13	21	1	66	272	13.60	–	1	25
–	J.R.Carpenter	8	15	–	65	193	12.86	–	1	3
–	A.A.Khan	3	4	–	23	41	10.25	–	–	–
–	J.J.Bates	4	7	–	38	54	7.71	–	–	4
1996	J.D.Lewry	16	23	–	24	132	5.73	–	–	1
–	A.D.Edwards	3	6	–	10	26	4.33	–	–	3
1997	M.A.Robinson	15	21	8	7	40	3.07	–	–	1

Also batted: P.Moores (cap 1989)(2 matches) 20*, 36, 0* (2 ct).

BOWLING

	O	M	R	W	Avge	Best	5wI	10wM
J.J.Bates	102.5	24	273	14	19.50	5-67	2	–
R.S.C.Martin-Jenkins	141.5	43	437	22	19.86	7-54	1	–
J.D.Lewry	461.3	112	1409	62	22.72	6-72	3	–
M.A.Robinson	416.1	107	1126	42	26.80	4-72	–	–
R.J.Kirtley	490.4	116	1532	54	28.37	7-29	3	1
M.G.Bevan	175.4	27	653	19	34.36	3-36	–	–

Also bowled: C.J.Adams 30.5-5-109-0; A.D.Edwards 53-9-198-3; P.W.Jarvis 96-11-347-7; A.A.Khan 116-25-389-6; W.G.Khan 1.5-0-7-0; K.Newell 65.4-22-190-5; M.Newell 2-0-15-0; M.T.E.Peirce 43-18-99-1; R.K.Rao 27-2-119-1.

The First-Class Averages (pp 117-131) give the records of Sussex players in all first-class county matches (Sussex's other opponents being the South Africans and Oxford University). J.P.Pyemont appeared in six matches for Cambridge University.

SUSSEX RECORDS

FIRST-CLASS CRICKET

Highest Total	For 705-8d	v	Surrey	Hastings	1902
	V 726	by	Notts	Nottingham	1895
Lowest Total	For 19	v	Surrey	Godalming	1830
	19	v	Notts	Hove	1873
	V 18	by	Kent	Gravesend	1867
Highest Innings	For 333 K.S.Duleepsinhji	v	Northants	Hove	1930
	V 322 E.Paynter	for	Lancashire	Hove	1937

Highest Partnership for each Wicket

1st	490	E.H.Bowley/J.G.Langridge	v	Middlesex	Hove	1933
2nd	385	E.H.Bowley/M.W.Tate	v	Northants	Hove	1921
3rd	298	K.S.Ranjitsinhji/E.H.Killick	v	Lancashire	Hove	1901
4th	326*	J.Langridge/G.Cox	v	Yorkshire	Leeds	1949
5th	297	J.H.Parks/H.W.Parks	v	Hampshire	Portsmouth	1937
6th	255	K.S.Duleepsinhji/M.W.Tate	v	Northants	Hove	1930
7th	344	K.S.Ranjitsinhji/W.Newham	v	Essex	Leyton	1902
8th	229*	C.L.A.Smith/G.Brann	v	Kent	Hove	1902
9th	178	H.W.Parks/A.F.Wensley	v	Derbyshire	Horsham	1930
10th	156	G.R.Cox/H.R.Butt	v	Cambridge U	Cambridge	1908

Best Bowling	For	10- 48	C.H.G.Bland	v	Kent	Tonbridge	1899
(Innings)	V	9- 11	A.P.Freeman	for	Kent	Hove	1922
Best Bowling	For	17-106	G.R.Cox	v	Warwicks	Horsham	1926
(Match)	V	17- 67	A.P.Freeman	for	Kent	Hove	1922

Most Runs – Season	2850	J.G.Langridge	(av 64.77)	1949
Most Runs – Career	34152	J.G.Langridge	(av 37.69)	1928-55
Most 100s – Season	12	J.G.Langridge		1949
Most 100s – Career	76	J.G.Langridge		1928-55
Most Wkts – Season	198	M.W.Tate	(av 13.47)	1925
Most Wkts – Career	2211	M.W.Tate	(av 17.41)	1912-37

LIMITED-OVERS CRICKET

Highest Total	NWT	384-9		v	Ireland	Belfast	1996
	BHC	305-6		v	Kent	Hove	1982
	SL	312-8		v	Hampshire	Portsmouth	1993
Lowest Total	NWT	49		v	Derbyshire	Chesterfield	1969
	BHC	61		v	Middlesex	Hove	1978
	SL	59		v	Glamorgan	Hove	1996
Highest Innings	NWT	158	R.K.Rao	v	Derbyshire	Derby	1997
	BHC	118	C.W.J.Athey	v	Kent	Hove	1995
	SL	129	A.W.Greig	v	Yorkshire	Scarborough	1976
Best Bowling	NWT	6- 9	A.I.C.Dodemaide	v	Ireland	Downpatrick	1990
	BHC	5- 8	Imran Khan	v	Northants	Northampton	1978
	SL	7-41	A.N.Jones	v	Notts	Nottingham	1986

WARWICKSHIRE

Formation of Present Club: 8 April 1882
Substantial Reorganisation: 19 January 1884
Colours: Dark Blue, Gold and Silver
Badge: Bear and Ragged Staff
Championships: (5) 1911, 1951, 1972, 1994, 1995
NatWest Trophy/Gillette Cup Winners: (5) 1966, 1968, 1989, 1993, 1995
Benson and Hedges Cup Winners: (1) 1994
Sunday League Champions: (3) 1980, 1994, 1997
Match Awards: NWT 63; BHC 59

Chief Executive: D.L.Amiss MBE
County Ground, Edgbaston, Birmingham, B5 7QU (Tel 0121 446 4422)
Captain: N.M.K.Smith. **Vice-Captain:** N.V.Knight. **Overseas Player:** A.A.Donald.
1999 Beneficiary: A.A.Donald. **Scorer:** D.Wainwright

ALTREE, Darren Anthony (Ashlawn S, Rugby), b Rugby 30 Sep 1974. 5'11". RHB, LMF. Debut 1996. HS 2*. BB 3-41 v P (Birmingham) 1996. CC BB 2-108 v Hants (Southampton) 1997.

BROWN, Douglas Robert (Alloa Academy; W London IHE), b Stirling, Scotland 29 Oct 1969. 6'2". RHB, RFM. Scotland 1989. Warwickshire debut 1991-92 (SA tour); cap 1995. Wellington 1995-96. **LOI:** 9 (1997-98); HS 21; BB 2-28. Tours (Wa): SA 1991-92, 1994-95; SL 1997-98 (Eng A). HS 85 v Essex (Ilford) 1995. 50 wkts (2); most – 81 (1997). BB 8-89 (11-154 match) v F-C Counties Select XI v Pak A (Chelmsford) 1997. Wa BB 6-52 (11-120 match) v Kent (Birmingham) 1996. Award: BHC 1. **NWT:** HS 67 v Cornwall (St Austell) 1999. BB 2-34 v Middx (Lord's) 1997. **BHC:** HS 62 v Minor C (Birmingham) 1997. BB 5-31 v Worcs (Worcester) 1997. **SL:** HS 78* v Notts (Nottingham) 1997. BB 4-42 v Kent (Tunbridge W) 1997.

DONALD, Allan Anthony (Grey College HS), b Bloemfontein, SA 20 Oct 1966. 6'2". RHB, RF. OFS 1985-86 to date. Warwickshire 1987-93, 1995, 1997; cap 1989; benefit 1999. *Wisden* 1991. **Tests** (SA): 52 (1991-92 to 1998-99); HS 34 v WI (Pt Elizabeth) 1998-99; BB 8-71 (11-113 match) v Z (Harare) 1995-96. **LOI** (SA): 108 (1991-92 to 1998-99); HS 12; BB 6-23. Tours (SA): E 1994, 1998; A 1993-94, 1997-98; WI 1991-92; NZ 1994-95, 1998-99; I 1996-97; P 1997-98; SL 1993-94; Z 1995-96. HS 55* SA v Tasmania (Devonport) 1997-98. Wa HS 44 v Essex (Ilford) 1995. 50 wkts (5); most – 89 (1995). BB 8-37 OFS v Transvaal (Johannesburg) 1986-87. Wa BB 7-37 v Durham (Birmingham) 1992. Awards: NWT 3. **NWT:** HS 14* v Northants (Birmingham) 1992. BB 5-12 v Wilts (Birmingham) 1989. **BHC:** HS 23* v Leics (Leicester) 1989. BB 5-25 v Lancs (Birmingham) 1997. **SL:** HS 18* v Middx (Lord's) 1988. BB 6-15 v Yorks (Birmingham) 1995.

EDMOND, Michael Denis (Airds HS, Cambelltown, NSW, Australia), b Barrow-in-Furness, Lancs 30 Jul 1969. 6'1". RHB, RMF. Debut 1996. Indoor Cricket for Australia. Scored 100 off 48 balls for Warwks 2nd XI II v Somerset 2nd XI (Taunton) 1995. HS 32 v Durham (Birmingham) 1998. BB 2-26 v OU (Oxford) 1997. CC BB 1-6. **NWT:** HS 0. BB 1-24. **SL:** HS 19 v Kent (Tunbridge W) 1997. BB 2-4 v Derbys (Birmingham) 1997.

FROST, Tony (James Brinkley HS; Stoke-on-Trent C), b Stoke-on-Trent, Staffs 17 Nov 1975. 5'11". RHB, WK. Debut 1997. HS 111* v OU (Oxford) 1998. CC HS 56 v Somerset (Birmingham) 1997. **NWT:** HS 0. **BHC:** HS 10* v Minor C (Birmingham) 1997. **SL:** HS 2*.

GIDDINS, Edward Simon Hunter (Eastbourne C), b Eastbourne, Sussex 20 Jul 1971. 6'4½". RHB, RFM. Sussex 1991-96; cap 1994. Warwickshire debut/cap 1998. MCC YC. Tour: P 1995-96 (Eng A). HS 34 Sx v Essex (Hove) 1995. Wa HS 11* v Hants (Birmingham) 1998. 50 wkts (3); most – 84 (1998). BB 6-47 Sx v Yorks (Eastbourne) 1996. Wa BB 6-79 (11-164 match) vs Glos (Bristol) 1998. **NWT:** HS 13 Sx v Essex (Hove) 1994. BB 3-24 Sx v Ire (Belfast) 1996. **BHC:** HS 4*. BB 3-28 Sx v Surrey (Oval) 1995. **SL:** HS 9*. BB 4-23 Sx v Kent (Tunbridge W) 1994.

GILES, Ashley Fraser (George Abbot S, Guildford), b Chertsey, Surrey 19 Mar 1973. 6'3". RHB, SLA. Debut 1993; cap 1996. Tour: A 1996-97 (Eng A). HS 106* v Lancs (Birmingham) 1996. **Tests:** 1 (1998); HS 16* and BB 1-106 v SA (Manchester) 1998. **LOI:** 5 (1997 to 1998-99); HS 10*; BB 2-37. Tours (Eng A): SL 1997-98; K 1997-98. 50 wkts (1): 64 (1996). BB 6-45 v Durham (Birmingham) 1996. Awards: NWT 1; BHC 1. **NWT:** HS 69 and BB 5-21 v Norfolk (Birmingham) 1997. **BHC:** HS 37 v Lancs (Manchester) 1998. BB 3-22 v Lancs (Manchester) 1998. **SL:** HS 57 v Hants (Southampton) 1997. BB 5-36 v Worcs (Birmingham) 1996.

HEMP, David Lloyd (Olchfa CS; Millfield S; W Glamorgan C), b Bermuda 8 Nov 1970. UK resident since 1976. 6'0". LHB, RM. Glamorgan 1991-96; cap 1994. Warwickshire debut/cap 1997. Wales (MC) 1992-94. Tours: SA 1995-96 (Gm); I 1994-95 (Eng A); Z 1994-95 (Gm). 1000 runs (2); most – 1452 (1994). HS 157 Gm v Glos (Abergavenny) 1995. Wa HS 138 v Hants (Southampton) 1997. BB 3-23 Gm v SA A (Cardiff) 1994. CC BB 1-1. Wa BB 2-68 v Ou (Oxford) 1998. Awards: NWT 3; BHC 2. **NWT:** HS 112 v Middx (Lord's) 1997. BB 1-40. **BHC:** HS 121 Gm v Comb U (Cardiff) 1995. BB 4-32 v Minor C (Lakenham) 1998. **SL:** HS 74 Gm v Leics (Leicester) 1995. BB 2-43 v Susex (Hove) 1998.

KNIGHT, Nicholas Verity (Felsted S; Loughborough U), b Watford, Herts 28 Nov 1969. 6'0". LHB, occ RM. Essex 1991-94; cap 1994. Warwickshire debut 1994-95 (SA tour); cap 1995. **Tests:** 12 (1995 to 1998); HS 113 v P (Leeds) 1996. **LOI:** 40 (1996 to 1998-99); HS 125*. Tours: SA 1994-95 (Wa); NZ 1996-97; I 1994-95 (Eng A); SL 1997-98 (captain); P 1995-96 (Eng A); Z 1996-97; K 1997-98 (captain). 1000 runs (2); most – 1196 (1996). HS 192 v Lancs (Birmingham) 1998. BB 1-61. Awards: NWT 2; BHC 2. **NWT:** HS 151 v Somerset (Birmingham) 1995. **BHC:** HS 104 v Minor C (Jesmond) 1996. **SL:** HS 134 v Hants (Birmingham) 1996. BB 1-14.

MUNTON, Timothy Alan (Sarson HS; King Edward VII Upper S), b Melton Mowbray, Leics 30 Jul 1965. 6'5". RHB, RMF. Debut 1985; cap 1990; captain 1997 (no appearances – back injury); benefit 1998. *Wisden* 1994. **Tests:** 2 (1992); HS 25* v P (Manchester) 1992; BB 2-22 v P (Leeds) 1992. Tours: SA 1992-93 (Wa); WI 1991-92 (Eng A); P 1990-91 (Eng A), 1995-96 (Eng A – *part*); SL 1990-91 (Eng A); Z 1993-94 (Wa). 50 wkts: HS 54* v Worcs (Worcester) 1996. 50 wkts (5); most – 81 (1994). BB 8-89 (11-128 match) v Middx (Birmingham) 1991. Awards: NWT 2; BHC 1. **NWT:** HS 5. BB 3-36 v Kent (Canterbury) 1989. **BHC:** HS 13 v Leics (Leicester) 1989. BB 4-35 v Surrey (Oval) 1991. **SL:** HS 15* v Yorks (Scarborough) 1994. BB 5-23 v Glos (Moreton-in-M) 1990.

OSTLER, Dominic Piers (Princethorpe C; Solihull TC), b Solihull 15 Jul 1970. 6'3". RHB, occ RM. Debut 1990; cap 1991. Tours: SA 1992-93 (Wa); P 1995-96 (Wa). 1000 runs (4); most – 1284 (1991). HS 208 v Surrey (Birmingham) 1995. Awards: NWT 2; BHC 1. **NWT:** HS 104 and BB 1-4 v Norfolk (Lakenham) 1993. **BHC:** HS 87 v Notts (Nottingham) 1995. **SL:** HS 91* v Sussex (Hove) 1996.

PENNEY, Trevor Lionel (Prince Edward S, Salisbury), b Salisbury, Rhodesia 12 Jun 1968. 6'0". RHB, RM. Qualified for England 1992. Boland 1991-92. Warwickshire debut 1991-92 (SA tour); UK debut v CU (Cambridge) 1992, scoring 102*; cap 1994. Mashonaland 1993-94. Tours: SA 1991-92, 1992-93, 1994-95; Z 1993-94. 1000 runs (2); most – 1295 (1996). HS 151 v Middx (Lord's) 1992. BB 3-18 Mashonaland v Mashonaland U-24 (Harare) 1993-94. Wa BB 1-40 (Z tour). CC BB –. Award: NWT 1. **NWT:** HS 90 v Cornwall (St Austell) 1996. BB 1-8. **BHC:** HS 57* v Leics (Leicester) 1998. **SL:** HS 83* v Kent (Canterbury) 1993.

PIPER, Keith John (Haringey Cricket C), b Leicester 18 Dec 1969. 5'6". RHB, WK. Debut 1989; cap 1992. Tours (Wa): SA 1991-92, 1992-93, 1994-95; I 1994-95 (Eng A); P 1995-96 (Eng A); Z 1993-94. HS 116* v Durham (Birmingham) 1994. BB 1-57. **NWT:** HS 19 v Leics (Leicester) 1998. **BHC:** HS 13* v Lancs (Manchester) 1998. **SL:** HS 30 v Lancs (Manchester) 1990.

POWELL, Michael James (Lawrence Sheriff S, Rugby), b Bolton, Lancs 5 Apr 1975. 5'11". RHB, RM. Debut 1996. HS 132 v Sussex (Hove) 1998. BB 2-16 v OU (Oxford) 1998. CC BB 1-18.

SHEIKH, Mohammad Avez (Broadway S), b Birmingham 2 Jul 1973. 6'0". LHB, RM. Debut 1997. HS 30 v OU (Oxford) 1998. CC HS 25 v Notts (Birmingham) 1998. BB 2-14 v Middx (Birmingham) 1997. **NWT:** HS 5. **SL:** HS 8. BB 3-28 v Glam (Birmingham) 1998.

SINGH, Anurag (King Edward's, Birmingham; Gonville & Caius C, Cambridge), b Kanpur, India 9 Sep 1975. 5'11½". RHB, OB. Debut 1995. Cambridge U 1996-98; blue 1996-97-98; captain 1997-98. British U 1998 (captain). HS 157 CU v Sussex (Hove) 1996. Wa HS 56 v Northants (Northampton) 1998. Award: BHC 1. **BHC:** HS 123 v Somerset (Taunton) 1996. **SL:** HS 86 v Somerset (Birmingham) 1997.

SMALL, Gladstone Cleophas (Moseley S; Hall Green TC), b St George, Barbados 18 Oct 1961. 5'11". RHB, RFM. Debut 1979-80 (DHR XI in NZ). Warwickshire debut 1980; cap 1982; benefit 1992. S Australia 1985-86. **Tests:** 17 (1986 to 1990); HS 59 v A (Oval) 1989; BB 5-48 v A (Melbourne) 1986-87. **LOI:** 53 (1986-87 to 1992); HS 18*; BB 4-31. Tours: A 1986-87, 1990-91; SA 1992-93 (Wa), 1994-95 (Wa); WI 1989-90; NZ 1979-80 (DHR); P 1981-82 (Int); Z 1993-94 (Wa). HS 70 v Lancs (Manchester) 1988. 50 wkts (6); most – 80 (1988). BB 7-15 v Notts (Birmingham) 1988. Awards: NWT 1; BHC 2. **NWT:** HS 33 v Surrey (Lord's) 1982. BB 3-22 v Glam (Cardiff) 1982 and 3-22 v Somerset (Birmingham) 1997. **BHC:** HS 22 v Kent (Canterbury) 1990. BB 5-23 v Minor C (Birmingham) 1997. **SL:** HS 40* v Essex (Ilford) 1984. BB 5-18 v Middx (Lord's) 1998.

SMITH, Neil Michael Knight (Warwick S), b Birmingham 27 Jul 1967. Son of M.J.K. (Leics, Warwks and England 1951-75). 6'0". RHB, OB. Debut 1987; cap 1993; captain 1999. MCC YC. **LOI:** 7 (1995-96 to 1996); HS 31; BB 3-29. Tours (Wa): SA 1991-92, 1994-95; Z 1993-94. 1000 runs (1): 1002 (1998). HS 161 v Yorks (Leeds) 1989. BB 7-42 v Lancs (Birmingham) 1994. Awards: NWT 1; BHC 2. **NWT:** HS 72 v Sussex (Birmingham) 1997. BB 5-17 v Norfolk (Lakenham) 1993. **BHC:** HS 125 v Kent (Canterbury) 1997. BB 3-29 v Middx (Lord's) 1994. **SL:** HS 111* v Sussex (Hove) 1996. BB 6-33 v Sussex (Birmingham) 1995.

WAGH, Mark Anant (King Edward's S, Keble C, Oxford), b Birmingham 20 Oct 1976. 6'2". RHB, OB. Oxford U 1996-98; blue 1996-97-98; captain 1997. Warwickshire debut 1997. British U 1998. 1000 runs (1): 1156 (1997). HS 126 OU v Kent (Canterbury) 1998. Wa HS 124 v Durham (Chester-le-St) 1998. BB 4-11 v Middx (Lord's) 1998. **BHC:** (Brit U) HS 23 v Middx (Cambridge) 1996. BB 1-39 (twice).

WELCH, Graeme (Hetton CS), b Durham 21 Mar 1972. 5'11½". RHB, RM. Debut 1994; cap 1997. Tour: SA 1994-95 (Wa). HS 84* v Notts (Birmingham) 1994. 50 wkts (1): 65 (1997). BB 6-115 (11-140 match) v Lancs (Blackpool) 1997. **NWT:** HS 25 v Leics (Leicester) 1998. BB 4-31 v Kent (Birmingham) 1998. **BHC:** HS 55* v Lancs (Birmingham) 1997. BB 3-20 v Minor C (Lakenham) 1998. **SL:** HS 54 v Northants (Northampton) 1996. BB 3-37 v Yorks (Leeds) 1996.

NEW REGISTRATIONS

DAGNELL, Charles Edward (Bridgewater S; Worsley & UMIST), b Bury, Lancs 10 Jul 1976. RHB, RFM. Cumberland 1997-98.

RICHARDSON, Alan (Alleyne's HS; Stafford CFE), b Newcastle-under-Lyme, Staffs 6 May 1975. 6'2". RHB, RMF. Derbyshire 1995 (one match). Staffordshire 1996-98. HS 4 and BB 3-27 De v OU (Oxford) 1995. **SL:** HS –.

continued on p 107

WARWICKSHIRE 1998

RESULTS SUMMARY

	Place	Won	Lost	Tied	Drew	No Result
Britannic Assurance Championship	8th	6	8		3	
All First-Class Matches		6	8		4	
NatWest Trophy	Quarter-Finalist					
Benson and Hedges Cup	3rd in Group A					
Sunday League	2nd	9	5			3

BRITANNIC ASSURANCE CHAMPIONSHIP AVERAGES

BATTING AND FIELDING

Cap		M	I	NO	HS	Runs	Avge	100	50	Ct/St
1995	N.V.Knight	14	24	2	192	1057	48.04	4	4	18
1993	N.M.K.Smith	17	28	4	147	959	39.95	2	6	23
1994	B.C.Lara	15	26	–	226	1033	39.73	3	3	15
1996	A.F.Giles	13	19	4	83	472	31.46	–	3	7
1995	D.R.Brown	15	26	4	81*	658	29.90	–	5	7
–	A.Singh	5	7	–	56	185	26.42	–	1	2
–	M.A.Wagh	8	15	–	119	391	26.06	1	2	4
1997	D.L.Hemp	14	24	–	102	578	24.08	1	3	15
–	M.J.Powell	12	20	1	132	455	23.94	1	3	12
1994	T.L.Penney	9	16	2	53*	329	23.50	–	1	5
–	T.Frost	7	13	1	50	278	23.16	–	1	19
1997	G.Welch	11	17	1	54	323	20.18	–	1	6
–	M.D.Edmond	2	4	1	32	48	16.00	–	–	1
1992	K.J.Piper	13	23	5	44*	283	15.72	–	–	29/3
1989	T.A.Munton	8	12	2	20	72	7.20	–	–	4
1991	D.P.Ostler	5	8	–	18	38	4.75	–	–	4
1998	E.S.H.Giddins	17	23	8	11*	43	2.86	–	–	4

Also batted (1 match each): D.A.Altree 2*, 0; M.A.Sheikh 1, 25.

BOWLING

	O	M	R	W	Avge	Best	5wI	10wM
T.A.Munton	265.1	66	691	36	19.19	7- 66	3	–
E.S.H.Giddins	644.2	152	1952	83	23.51	6- 79	5	1
A.F.Giles	423.3	147	919	35	26.25	5- 48	1	–
D.R.Brown	430.2	92	1458	50	29.16	5- 40	2	–
N.M.K.Smith	299.3	72	914	21	43.52	5-128	1	–
G.Welch	295.3	65	961	22	43.68	4- 94	–	–

Also bowled: D.A.Altree 13-4-34-0; M.D.Edmond 20-5-52-1; T.Frost 1-0-6-0; D.L.Hemp 13-0-51-2; N.V.Knight 1.5-0-15-0; B.C.Lara 5-0-44-0; M.J.Powell 7-0-30-0; M.A.Sheikh 27-7-56-3; M.A.Wagh 33-9-95-7.

The First-Class Averages (pp 117-131) give the records of Warwickshire's players in all first-class county matches (Warwickshire's other opponents being Oxford University), with the exception of A.F.Giles, N.V.Knight, A.Singh and M.A.Wagh, whose full county figures are as above.

WARWICKSHIRE RECORDS

FIRST-CLASS CRICKET

Highest Total	For	810-4d		v	Durham	Birmingham	1994
	V	887		by	Yorkshire	Birmingham	1896
Lowest Total	For	16		v	Kent	Tonbridge	1913
	V	15		by	Hampshire	Birmingham	1922
Highest Innings	For	501*	B.C.Lara	v	Durham	Birmingham	1994
	V	322	I.V.A.Richards	for	Somerset	Taunton	1985

Highest Partnership for each Wicket

1st	377*	N.F.Horner/K.Ibadulla	v	Surrey	The Oval	1960
2nd	465*	J.A.Jameson/R.B.Kanhai	v	Glos	Birmingham	1974
3rd	327	S.P.Kinneir/W.G.Quaife	v	Lancashire	Birmingham	1901
4th	470	A.I.Kallicharran/G.W.Humpage	v	Lancashire	Southport	1982
5th	322*	B.C.Lara/K.J.Piper	v	Durham	Birmingham	1994
6th	220	H.E.Dollery/J.Buckingham	v	Derbyshire	Derby	1938
7th	250	H.E.Dollery/J.S.Ord	v	Kent	Maidstone	1953
8th	228	A.J.W.Croom/R.E.S.Wyatt	v	Worcs	Dudley	1925
9th	154	G.W.Stephens/A.J.W.Croom	v	Derbyshire	Birmingham	1925
10th	141	A.F.Giles/T.A.Munton	v	Worcs	Worcester	1996

Best Bowling	For	10-41	J.D.Bannister	v	Comb Servs	Birmingham	1959
(Innings)	V	10-36	H.Verity	for	Yorkshire	Leeds	1931
Best Bowling	For	15-76	S.Hargreave	v	Surrey	The Oval	1903
(Match)	V	17-92	A.P.Freeman	for	Kent	Folkestone	1932

Most Runs – Season	2417	M.J.K.Smith	(av 60.42)	1959
Most Runs – Career	35146	D.L.Amiss	(av 41.64)	1960-87
Most 100s – Season	9	A.I.Kallicharran		1984
	9	B.C.Lara		1994
Most 100s – Career	78	D.L.Amiss		1960-87
Most Wkts – Season	180	W.E.Hollies	(av 15.13)	1946
Most Wkts – Career	2201	W.E.Hollies	(av 20.45)	1932-57

LIMITED-OVERS CRICKET

Highest Total	NWT	392-5		v	Oxfordshire	Birmingham	1984
	BHC	369-8		v	Minor C	Jesmond	1996
	SL	301-6		v	Essex	Colchester	1982
Lowest Total	NWT	98		v	Leics	Leicester	1998
	BHC	96		v	Leics	Leicester	1972
	SL	65		v	Kent	Maidstone	1979
Highest Innings	NWT	206	A.I.Kallicharran	v	Oxfordshire	Birmingham	1984
	BHC	137*	T.A.Lloyd	v	Lancashire	Birmingham	1985
	SL	134	N.V.Knight	v	Hampshire	Birmingham	1996
Best Bowling	NWT	6-32	K.Ibadulla	v	Hampshire	Birmingham	1965
		6-32	A.I.Kallicharran	v	Oxfordshire	Birmingham	1984
	BHC	7-32	R.G.D.Willis	v	Yorkshire	Birmingham	1981
	SL	6-15	A.A.Donald	v	Yorkshire	Birmingham	1995

WORCESTERSHIRE

Formation of Present Club: 11 March 1865
Colours: Dark Green and Black
Badge: Shield Argent a Fess between three Pears Sable
Championships: (5) 1964, 1965, 1974, 1988, 1989
NatWest Trophy/Gillette Cup Winners: (1) 1994
Benson and Hedges Cup Winners: (1) 1991
Sunday League Champions: (3) 1971, 1987, 1988
Match Awards: NWT 44; BHC 67

Secretary: Revd M.D.Vockins OBE
County Ground, New Road, Worcester, WR2 4QQ (Tel 01905 748474)
Captain/Overseas Player: T.M.Moody. **Vice-Captain:** G.A.Hick.
1999 Beneficiary: G.A.Hick. **Scorer:** S.S.Hale

BATSON, Nathan Evan (Billericay SS; Mayflower County HS), b Basildon, Essex 24 Jul 1978. 6'2". RHB, OB. Debut 1998. HS 18 v Warwks (Worcester) 1998.

CATTERALL, Duncan Neil (Queen Elizabeth's GS, Blackburn; Loughborough U), b Preston, Lancs 19 Sep 1978. 5'11". RHB, RMF. Debut 1998. HS 0. **SL:** HS 11* and BB 1-28 v Hants (Worcester) 1998.

CHAPMAN, Robert James (Farnborough CS; S Notts CFE), b Nottingham 28 Jul 1972. Son of footballer R.O. ('Sammy') (Nottingham Forest, Notts County and Shrewsbury Town). 6'1". RHB, RMF. Nottinghamshire 1992-96. Worcestershire debut 1996-97 (on Zimbabwe tour). Tour (Wo): Z 1996-97. HS 43* v Durham (Worcester) 1998. BB 6-105 v Notts (Kidderminster) 1998. **NWT:** HS –. **BHC:** HS 0. **SL:** HS 4*. BB 5-30 v Yorks (Worcester) 1998.

DRIVER, Ryan Craig (Redruth Community C; Durham U), b Truro, Cornwall 30 Apr 1979. 6'3½". LHB, RM. Debut 1998. Cornwall 1996-97. HS 5.

HAFEEZ, Abdul (Handsworth GS; Solihull C), b Moseley, Birmingham 21 Mar 1977. 6'3". RHB, RM. Debut 1998. HS 55 v Glos (Worcester) 1998. **NWT:** HS 33 v Scot (Edinburgh) 1998. **SL:** HS 7.

HAYNES, Gavin Richard (High Park S; King Edward VI S, Stourbridge), b Stourbridge 29 Sep 1969. 5'10". RHB, RM. Debut 1991; cap 1994. Tours (Wo): Z 1993-94, 1996-97. 1000 runs (1): 1021 (1994). HS 158 v Kent (Worcester) 1993. BB 6-50 v Hants (Worcester) 1998. Awards: NWT 2; BHC 1. **NWT:** HS 116* v Cumb (Worcester) 1995. BB 1-9. **BHC:** HS 65 v Hants (Worcester) 1994. BB 3-17 v Derbys (Worcester) 1995. **SL:** HS 83 v Hants (Worcester) 1994. BB 4-13 v Surrey (Worcester) 1997.

HICK, Graeme Ashley (Prince Edward HS, Salisbury), b Salisbury, Rhodesia 23 May 1966. 6'3". RHB, OB. Zimbabwe 1983-84 to 1985-86. Worcestershire debut 1984; cap 1986; benefit 1999. N Districts 1987-88 to 1988-89. Queensland 1990-91. *Wisden* 1986. **Tests:** 53 (1991 to 1998-99); HS 178 v I (Bombay) 1992-93; BB 4-126 v NZ (Wellington) 1991-92. **LOI:** 87 (1991 to 1998-99); HS 126*; BB 3-41. Tours: E 1985 (Z); A 1994-95, 1998-99 (*part*); SA 1995-96; WI 1993-94; NZ 1991-92; I 1992-93; SL 1983-84 (Z), 1992-93; Z 1990-91 (Wo), 1996-97 (Wo). 1000 runs (14+1) inc 2000 (3); most – 2713 (1988); youngest to score 2000 (1986). Scored 1019 runs before June 1988, including a record 410 runs in April. Fewest innings for 10,000 runs in county cricket (179). Youngest (24) to score 50 f-c hundreds. Second-youngest (32) to score 100 f-c hundreds. Scored 645 runs without being dismissed (UK record) in 1990. HS 405* (Worcs record and then second highest in UK f-c matches) v Somerset (Taunton) 1988. BB 5-18 v Leics (Worcester) 1995. Awards: NWT 4; BHC 11. **NWT:** HS 172* v Devon (Worcester) 1987. BB 4-54 v Hants (Worcester) 1988 and v Surrey (Oval) 1994. **BHC:** HS 127* v Derbys (Worcester) 1995. BB 3-36 v Warwks (Birmingham) 1990. **SL:** HS 130 v Durham (Darlington) 1995. BB 4-21 v Somerset (Worcester) 1995.

ILLINGWORTH, Richard Keith (Salts GS), b Bradford, Yorks 23 Aug 1963. 5'11". RHB, SLA. Debut 1982; cap 1986; benefit 1997. Natal 1988-89. **Tests:** 9 (1991 to 1995-96); HS 28 v SA (Pt Elizabeth) 1995-96; BB 4-96 v WI (Nottingham) 1995. Took wicket of P.V.Simmons with his first ball in Tests – v WI (Nottingham) 1991. **LOI:** 25 (1991 to 1995-96); HS 14; BB 3-33. Tours: SA 1995-96; NZ 1991-92; P 1990-91 (Eng A); SL 1990-91 (Eng A); Z 1989-90 (Eng A), 1990-91 (Wo), 1993-94 (Wo), 1996-97 (Wo). HS 120* v Warwks (Worcester) 1987 – as night-watchman. Scored 106 for England A v Z (Harare) 1989-90 – also as night-watchman. 50 wkts (5); most – 75 (1990). BB 7-50 v OU (Oxford) 1985. CC BB 7-79 v Hants (Southampton) 1997. **NWT:** HS 29* v Hants (Worcester) 1996. BB 4-20 v Devon (Worcester) 1987. **BHC:** HS 36* v Kent (Worcester) 1990. BB 4-27 v Northants (Northampton) 1995. **SL:** HS 31 v Yorks (Worcester) 1994. BB 5-24 v Somerset (Worcester) 1983.

LAMPITT, Stuart Richard (Kingsinford S; Dudley TC), b Wolverhampton, Staffs 29 Jul 1966. 5'11". RHB, RMF. Debut 1985; cap 1989. Tours (Wo): Z 1990-91, 1993-94, 1996-97. HS 122 v Middx (Lord's) 1994. 50 wkts (6); most – 64 (1994). BB 5-32 v Kent (Worcester) 1989. Awards: NWT 1; BHC 4. **NWT:** HS 54 v Scot (Edinburgh) 1998. BB 5-22 v Suffolk (Bury St E) 1994. **BHC:** HS 41 v Glam (Worcester) 1990. BB 6-26 v Derbys (Derby) 1994. **SL:** HS 41* v Leics (Worcester) 1993. BB 5-67 v Middx (Lord's) 1990.

LEATHERDALE, David Anthony (Pudsey Grangefield S), b Bradford, Yorks 26 Nov 1967. 5'10½". RHB, RM. Debut 1988; cap 1994. Tours (Wo): Z 1993-94, 1996-97. 1000 runs (1): 1001 (1998). HS 157 v Somerset (Worcester) 1991. BB 5-20 v Glos (Worcester) 1998. **NWT:** HS 43 v Hants (Worcester) 1988. BB 3-14 v Norfolk (Lakenham) 1994. **BHC:** HS 66 v Northants (Worcester) 1996. BB 4-13 v Minor C (Worcester) 1997. **SL:** HS 62* v Kent (Folkestone) 1988. BB 4-19 v Derbys (Derby) 1998.

MIRZA, Maneer (*registered as 'Mohamed MANEER'*)(Sheldon Heath CS; Bournville CHE), b Birmingham 1 Apr 1978. Younger brother of the late Parvaz (Worcestershire 1994-95). 5'10". RHB, RFM. Debut 1997. HS 10* and BB 4-51 v Warwks (Birmingham) 1997. **SL:** HS –. BB 1-31.

MOODY, Thomas Masson (Guildford GS, WA), b Adelaide, Australia 2 Oct 1965. 6'6½". RHB, RM. W Australia 1985-86 to date; captain 1995-96 to date. Warwickshire 1990; cap 1990. Worcestershire debut/cap 1991; captain 2000 (*part*) to date. **Tests** (A): 8 (1989-90 to 1992-93); HS 106 v SL (Brisbane) 1989-90; BB 1-17. **LOI** (A): 58 (1987-88 to 1997-98); HS 89; BB 3-39. Tours (A): E 1989; I 1989-90 (WA); SL 1992-93; Z 1991-92 (Aus B). 1000 runs (5+1); most – 1887 (1991). HS 272 WA v Tasmania (Hobart) 1994-95. Wo HS 212 v Notts (Worcester) 1996. BB 7-38 WA v Tasmania (Hobart) 1995-96. Wo BB 7-92 (13-159 match) v Glos (Worcester) 1996. Awards: NWT 3; BHC 7. **NWT:** HS 180* v Surrey (Oval) 1994. BB 2-33 v Norfolk (Lakenham) 1994. **BHC:** HS 110* v Derbys (Worcester) 1991. BB 4-24 v Scot (Worcester) 1998. **SL:** HS 160 v Kent (Worcester) 1991 (on Wo debut). BB 4-46 v Lancs (Manchester) 1996.

NEWPORT, Philip John (High Wycombe RGS; Portsmouth Poly), b High Wycombe, Bucks 11 Oct 1962. 6'3". RHB, RFM. Debut 1982; cap 1986; benefit 1998. Boland 1987-88. N Transvaal 1992-93. Buckinghamshire 1981-82. **Tests:** 3 (1988 to 1990-91); HS 40* v A (Perth) 1990-91; BB 4-87 v SL (Lord's) 1988 – on debut. Tours: A 1990-91 (*part*); P 1990-91 (Eng A); SL 1990-91 (Eng A); Z 1993-94 (Wo), 1996-97 (Wo). Wo HS 98 v NZ (Worcester) 1990. CC HS 96 v Essex (Worcester) 1990. 50 wkts (8); most – 93 (1988). BB 8-52 v Middx (Lord's) 1988. Awards: BHC 2. **NWT:** HS 25 v Northants (Northampton) 1984. BB 4-30 v Northants (Worcester) 1994. **BHC:** HS 28* v Yorks (Leeds) 1998. BB 5-22 v Warwks (Birmingham) 1998. **SL:** HS 26* v Leics (Leicester) 1987 and 26* v Surrey (Worcester) 1993. BB 5-32 v Essex (Chelmsford) 1995.

PATEL, Depesh Balvant (Moseley Park GS; Bilston Community C), b Wolverhampton, Staffs 23 Sep 1981. 6'3". RHB, RFM. Awaiting f-c debut.

PIPE, David James (Queensbury S), b Bradford, Yorks 16 Dec 1977. 5'11". RHB, WK. Debut 1998. Awaiting CC debut. HS –.

RAWNSLEY, Matthew James (Shenley Court CS, Birmingham), b Birmingham 8 Jun 1976. 6'2". RHB, SLA. Debut 1996. HS 26 v Essex (Chelmsford) 1997. BB 6-44 (11-116 match) v OU (Oxford) 1998. CC BB 2-14 v Notts (Kidderminster) 1998. **NWT:** HS –. BB 2-50 v Holland (Worcester) 1997. **SL:** HS 7. BB 2-29 v Essex (Chelmsford) 1997.

RHODES, Steven John (Lapage Middle S; Carlton-Bolling S, Bradford), b Bradford, Yorks 17 Jun 1964. Son of W.E. (Notts 1961-64). 5'7". RHB, WK. Yorkshire 1981-84. Worcestershire debut 1985; cap 1986; benefit 1996. *Wisden* 1994. **Tests:** 11 (1994 to 1994-95); HS 65* v SA (Leeds) 1994. **LOI:** 9 (1989 to 1994-95); HS 56. Tours: A 1994-95; SA 1993-94 (Eng A); WI 1991-92 (Eng A); SL 1985-86 (Eng B), 1990-91 (Eng A); Z 1989-90 (Eng A), 1990-91 (Wo), 1993-94 (Wo), 1996-97 (Wo – captain). 1000 runs (2); most – 1018 (1995). HS 122* v Young A (Worcester) 1995. CC HS 116* v Warwks (Worcester) 1992. Awards: NWT 1; BHC 2. **NWT:** HS 61 v Derbys (Worcester) 1989. **BHC:** HS 51* v Warwks (Birmingham) 1987. **SL:** HS 48* v Kent (Worcester) 1989.

SHERIYAR, Alamgir (George Dixon S; Joseph Chamberlain SFC; Oxford Poly), b Birmingham 15 Nov 1973. 6'1". RHB, LFM. Leicestershire 1994-95. Worcestershire debut 1996; cap 1997. HS 21 v Notts (Nottingham) 1997 and 21 v Pak A (Worcester) 1997. 50 wkts (1): 62 (1997). BB 6-19 (10-63 match) v Sussex (Arundel) 1997. Hat-trick Le v Durham (Durham) 1994 (his second match). **NWT:** HS 10 v Hants (Worcester) 1996. BB 1-35. **BHC:** HS 15 v Durham (Chester-le-St) 1998. BB 3-40 v Northants (Worcester) 1996. BB 1-65. **SL:** HS 19 v Derbys (Chesterfield) 1996. BB 4-18 v Yorks (Leeds) 1997.

SOLANKI, Vikram Singh (Regis S, Wolverhampton), b Udaipur, India 1 Apr 1976. 6'0". RHB, OB. Debut 1995; cap 1998. Tours (Eng A): SA 1998-99; Z 1996-97 (Wo), 1998-99. HS 170 v Derbys (Derby) 1998. BB 5-69 v Middx (Lord's) 1996. **NWT:** HS 50 v Glam (Cardiff) 1996. BB 1-48. **BHC:** HS 25 v Durham (Chester-le-St) 1998. BB 1-17. **SL:** HS 120* v Derbys (Derby) 1998. BB 1-9.

SPIRING, Karl Reuben (Monmouth S; Durham U), b Southport, Lancs 13 Nov 1974. 5'11". RHB, OB. Debut 1994; cap 1997. 1000 runs (1): 1084 (1996). HS 150 v Essex (Chelmsford) 1997. **NWT:** HS 53 v Holland (Worcester) 1997. **BHC:** HS 35 Comb U v Essex (Cambridge) 1995. **SL:** HS 58* v Sussex (Arundel) 1997.

WESTON, William Philip Christopher (Durham S), b Durham 16 Jun 1973. Son of M.P. (Durham; England RFU); brother of R.M.S. (Durham 1995-97). 6'3". LHB, LM. Debut 1991; cap 1995. Tours (Wo): Z 1993-94, 1996-97. 1000 runs (3); most – 1389 (1996). HS 205 v Northants (Northampton) 1997. BB 2-39 v P (Worcester) 1992. CC BB –. **NWT:** HS 31 v Scot (Edinburgh) 1993. **BHC:** HS 54* v Scot (Worcester) 1995. **SL:** HS 80* v Durham (Worcester) 1996. BB 1-2.

WILSON, Elliott James (Felsted S; Durham U), b St Pancras, London 3 Nov 1976. 6'3". RHB, RM. Debut 1998. Cambridgeshire 1996. HS 27 v Warwks (Worcester) 1998. **SL:** HS 15 v Northants (Worcester) 1998.

NEW REGISTRATION

POLLARD, Paul Raymond (Gedling CS), b Carlton, Nottingham 24 Sep 1968. 5'11". LHB, RM. Nottinghamshire 1987-98; cap 1992. Tour (Nt): SA 1996-97. 1000 runs (3); most – 1463 (1993). HS 180 Nt v Derbys (Nottingham) 1993. BB 2-79 Nt v Glos (Bristol) 1993. **NWT:** HS 96 Nt v Northants (Nottingham) 1995. **BHC:** HS 104 Nt v Surrey (Nottingham) 1994. **SL:** HS 132* Nt v Somerset (Nottingham) 1995.

RELEASED/RETIRED
(Having made a first-class County appearance in 1998)

ELLIS, Scott William Kenneth (Shrewsbury S; Warwick U), b Newcastle-under-Lyme, Staffs 3 Oct 1975. 6'3". RHB, RMF. Debut (Combined U) v WI (Oxford) 1995 taking 5-59. Worcestershire 1996-98. HS 15 v Middx (Lord's) 1996. BB (*see above*). Wo BB 3-29 v Durham (Worcester) 1996. **NWT:** HS 0* and B 2-34 v Glam (Cardiff) 1996. **BHC:** (Brit U) HS 4. BB 1-50. **SL:** HS 20 v Leics (Leicester) 1998. BB 2-35 v Kent (Canterbury) 1996.

WORCESTERSHIRE 1998

RESULTS SUMMARY

	Place	Won	Lost	Tied	Drew	No Result
Britannic Assurance Championship	12th	4	6		7	
All First-Class Matches		5	7		7	
NatWest Trophy	1st Round					
Benson and Hedges Cup	3rd in Group B					
Sunday League	7th	7	6	1		3

BRITANNIC ASSURANCE CHAMPIONSHIP AVERAGES

BATTING AND FIELDING

Cap		M	I	NO	HS	Runs	Avge	100	50	Ct/St
1986	G.A.Hick	12	22	-	166	973	44.22	5	1	19
1991	T.M.Moody	13	23	2	132	886	42.19	4	2	10
1986	S.J.Rhodes	17	31	5	104*	952	36.61	1	6	42/2
1994	G.R.Haynes	11	19	5	86	506	36.14	-	4	2
1986	R.K.Illingworth	15	21	6	84	473	31.53	-	3	5
1995	W.P.C.Weston	15	27	2	95	731	29.24	-	5	9
1994	D.A.Leatherdale	16	29	1	137	795	28.39	1	3	8
1998	V.S.Solanki	17	32	-	170	904	28.25	2	3	26
1989	S.R.Lampitt	16	26	6	48	450	22.50	-	-	5
1986	P.J.Newport	12	15	3	56	261	21.75	-	1	3
-	A.Hafeez	9	17	-	55	270	15.88	-	1	5
-	R.J.Chapman	10	16	8	43*	102	12.75	-	-	2
1997	A.Sheriyar	10	9	3	20	61	10.16	-	-	1
-	E.J.Wilson	5	10	-	27	101	10.10	-	-	3
-	N.E.Batson	3	6	-	18	50	8.33	-	-	-
-	M.J.Rawnsley	4	7	-	21	55	7.85	-	-	4

Also batted (1 match each): D.N.Catterall 0; R.C.Driver 5, 0.

BOWLING

	O	M	R	W	Avge	Best	5wI	10wM
D.A.Leatherdale	107.4	20	404	21	19.23	5- 20	1	-
P.J.Newport	304	102	820	32	25.62	4- 44	-	-
G.R.Haynes	209.5	57	668	26	25.69	6- 50	2	-
S.R.Lampitt	375	81	1253	48	26.10	5- 33	4	-
R.J.Chapman	233.1	41	914	33	27.69	6-105	1	-
T.M.Moody	251.1	73	790	27	29.25	5- 64	1	-
A.Sheriyar	237.1	54	837	23	36.39	5- 85	1	-
R.K.Illingworth	305	81	853	13	65.61	3- 28	-	-

Also bowled: D.N.Catterall 13-2-31-0; G.A.Hick 45-6-152-1; M.J.Rawnsley 88.4-28-241-5; V.S.Solanki 96-19-350-7; W.P.C.Weston 2-0-20-0.

The First-Class Averages (pp 117-131) give the records of Worcestershire's players in all first-class county matches (Worcestershire's other opponents being the South Africans and Oxford University), with the exception of:

G.A.Hick 14-25-0-166-1188-47.52-6-2-1. 82-18-242-7-34.57-3/25.

WORCESTERSHIRE RECORDS

FIRST-CLASS CRICKET

Highest Total	For	670-7d		v	Somerset	Worcester	1995
	V	701-4d		by	Leics	Worcester	1906
Lowest Total	For	24		v	Yorkshire	Huddersfield	1903
	V	30		by	Hampshire	Worcester	1903
Highest Innings	For	405*	G.A.Hick	v	Somerset	Taunton	1988
	V	331*	J.D.B.Robertson	for	Middlesex	Worcester	1949

Highest Partnership for each Wicket

1st	309	F.L.Bowley/H.K.Foster	v	Derbyshire	Derby	1901
2nd	300	W.P.C.Weston/G.A.Hick	v	Indians	Worcester	1996
3rd	438*	G.A.Hick/T.M.Moody	v	Hampshire	Southampton	1997
4th	281	J A Ormrod/Younis Ahmed	v	Notts	Nottingham	1979
5th	393	E.G.Arnold/W.B.Burns	v	Warwicks	Birmingham	1909
6th	265	G.A.Hick/S.J.Rhodes	v	Somerset	Taunton	1988
7th	205	G.A.Hick/P.J.Newport	v	Yorkshire	Worcester	1988
8th	184	S.J.Rhodes/S.R.Lampitt	v	Derbyshire	Kidderminster	1991
9th	181	J.A.Cuffe/R.D.Burrows	v	Glos	Worcester	1907
10th	119	W.B.Burns/G.A.Wilson	v	Somerset	Worcester	1906

Best Bowling	For	9- 23	C.F.Root	v	Lancashire	Worcester	1931
(Innings)	V	10- 51	J.Mercer	for	Glamorgan	Worcester	1936
Best Bowling	For	15- 87	A.J.Conway	v	Glos	Moreton-in-M	1914
(Match)	V	17-212	J.C.Clay	for	Glamorgan	Swansea	1937

Most Runs – Season	2654	H.H.I.Gibbons	(av 52.03)	1934
Most Runs – Career	34490	D.Kenyon	(av 34.18)	1946-67
Most 100s – Season	10	G.M.Turner		1970
	10	G.A.Hick		1988
Most 100s – Career	75	G.A.Hick		1984-98
Most Wkts – Season	207	C.F.Root	(av 17.52)	1925
Most Wkts – Career	2143	R.T.D.Perks	(av 23.73)	1930-55

LIMITED-OVERS CRICKET

Highest Total	NWT	404-3		v	Devon	Worcester	1987
	BHC	314-5		v	Lancashire	Manchester	1980
	SL	307-4		v	Derbyshire	Worcester	1975
Lowest Total	NWT	98		v	Durham	Chester-le-St	1968
	BHC	81		v	Leics	Worcester	1983
	SL	86		v	Yorkshire	Leeds	1969
Highest Innings	NWT	180*	T.M.Moody	v	Surrey	The Oval	1994
	BHC	143*	G.M.Turner	v	Warwicks	Birmingham	1976
	SL	160	T.M.Moody	v	Kent	Worcester	1991
Best Bowling	NWT	7-19	N.V.Radford	v	Beds	Bedford	1991
	BHC	6- 8	N.Gifford	v	Minor C (S)	High Wycombe	1979
	SL	6-26	A.P.Pridgeon	v	Surrey	Worcester	1978

YORKSHIRE

Formation of Present Club: 8 January 1863
Substantial Reorganisation: 10 December 1891
Colours: Dark Blue, Light Blue and Gold
Badge: White Rose
Championships (since 1890): (29) 1893, 1896, 1898, 1900, 1901, 1902, 1905, 1908, 1912, 1919, 1922, 1923, 1924, 1925, 1931, 1932, 1933, 1935, 1937, 1938, 1939, 1946, 1959, 1960, 1962, 1963, 1966, 1967, 1968. Joint: (1) 1949
NatWest Trophy/Gillette Cup Winners: (2) 1965, 1969
Benson and Hedges Cup Winners: (1) 1987
Sunday League Champions: (1) 1983
Match Awards: NWT 34; BHC 69

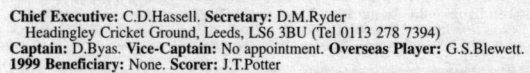

Chief Executive: C.D.Hassell. **Secretary:** D.M.Ryder
Headingley Cricket Ground, Leeds, LS6 3BU (Tel 0113 278 7394)
Captain: D.Byas. **Vice-Captain:** No appointment. **Overseas Player:** G.S.Blewett.
1999 Beneficiary: None. **Scorer:** J.T.Potter

BLAKEY, Richard John (Rastrick GS), b Huddersfield 15 Jan 1967. 5'9". RHB, WK. Debut 1985; cap 1987; benefit 1998. YC 1987. **Tests:** 2 (1992–93); HS 6. **LOI:** 3 (1992–93); HS 25. **Tours:** SA 1991-92 (Y); WI 1986-87 (Y); I 1992-93; P 1990-91 (Eng A); SL 1990-91 (Eng A); Z 1989-90 (Eng A), 1995-96 (Y). 1000 runs (5); most – 1361 (1987). HS 221 Eng A v Z (Bulawayo) 1989-90. Y HS 204* v Glos (Leeds) 1987. BB 1-68. Awards: BHC 2. **NWT:** HS 75 v Warwks (Leeds) 1993. **BHC:** HS 80* v Lancs (Manchester) 1996. **SL:** HS 130* v Kent (Scarborough) 1991.

BYAS, David (Scarborough C), b Kilham 26 Aug 1963. 6'4". LHB, RM. Debut 1986; cap 1991; captain 1996 to date. Tours (Y): SA 1991-92, 1992-93; Z 1995-96. 1000 runs (5); most – 1913 (1995). HS 213 v Worcs (Scarborough) 1995. BB 3-55 v Derbys (Chesterfield) 1990. Award: BHC 1. **NWT:** HS 73* v Middx (Leeds) 1996. **BHC:** HS 116* v Surrey (Oval) 1996. BB 2-38 v Somerset (Leeds) 1989. **SL:** HS 111* v Lancs (Leeds) 1996. BB 3-19 v Notts (Leeds) 1989.

CHAPMAN, Colin Anthony (Beckfoot GS, Bingley; Bradford & Ilkley Art C), b Bradford 8 Jun 1971. 5'8½". RHB, WK. Debut 1990. Tour: SA 1992-93 (Y). HS 80 v Lancs (Leeds) 1997 (non-CC match). CC HS 20 v Middx (Uxbridge) 1990. **NWT:** HS –. **SL:** HS 36* v Middx (Scarborough) 1990.

CLOUGH, Gareth David (Pudsey Grangefield S), b Leeds 23 May 1978. 6'0". RHB, RM. Debut 1998. HS 33 v Glam (Cardiff) 1998 – on debut.

FELLOWS, Gary Matthew (N Halifax GS), b Halifax 30 Jul 1978. 5'9". RHB, RM. Matabeleland 1996-97. Yorkshire debut 1998. HS 50 Matabeleland v Mashonaland (Bulawayo) 1996-97. Y HS 18 v Surrey (Leeds) 1998 – on Y debut. **SL:** HS 1.

FISHER, Ian Douglas (Beckfoot GS, Bingley; Thomas Danby C, Leeds), b Bradford 31 Mar 1976. 5'10½". LHB, SLA. Debut 1995-96 (Y tour). UK debut 1996. Tour: Z 1995-96 (Y). HS 37 v Derbys (Derby) 1997. BB 5-35 v Mashonaland Inv XI (Harare) 1995-96 (on debut). UK BB 1-26. CC BB –. **BHC:** HS –. BB 1-26. **SL:** HS 4*. BB 3-25 v Essex (Scarborough) 1998.

GOUGH, Darren (Priory CS, Lundwood), b Barnsley 18 Sep 1970. 5'11". RHB, RF. Debut 1989; cap 1993. **Tests:** 31 (1994 to 1998-99); HS 65 v NZ (Manchester) 1994 – on debut; BB 6-42 v SA (Leeds) 1998; hat-trick v A (Sydney) 1998-99 – first for E v A since 1899. **LOI:** 56 (1994 to 1998-99); HS 45; BB 5-44 – twice. Took wickets with his sixth balls in both Tests and LOIs. Tours: A 1994-95, 1998-99; SA 1991-92 (Y), 1992-93 (Y), 1993-94 (Eng A), 1995-96; NZ 1996-97; Z 1996-97. HS 121 v Warwks (Leeds) 1996. 50 wkts (4); most – 67 (1996). BB 7-28 (10-80 match) v Lancs (Leeds) 1995 (not CC). CC BB 7-42 (10-96 match) v Somerset (Taunton) 1993. 2 hat-tricks (1995, 1998-99); took 4 wkts in 5 balls v Kent (Leeds) 1995. Awards: NWT 2. **NWT:** HS 46 and BB 7-27 v Ire (Leeds) 1997. **BHC:** HS 48* v Scot (Leeds) 1996. BB 3-27 v Durham (Leeds) 1998. **SL:** HS 72* v Leics (Leicester) 1991. BB 5-13 v Sussex (Hove) 1994.

HAMILTON, Gavin Mark (Hurstmere S, Kent), b Broxburn, Scotland 16 Sep 1974. 6'1". LHB, RFM. Scotland 1993-94. Yorkshire debut 1994; cap 1998. Tour: Z 1995-96 (Y). HS 79 v Glam (Cardiff) 1998. 50 wkts (1): 59 (1998). BB 7-50 (11-72 match) v Surrey (Leeds) 1998. Match double (79, 70; 5-69, 5-43) v Glam (Cardiff) 1998 – first instance for Yorks since 1964 R.Illingworth). Award: BHC 1. **NWT:** HS 39 v Lancs (Manchester) 1998. BB 3-27 v Devon (Exmouth) 1998. **BHC:** HS 20 v Essex (Leeds) 1998. BB 4-33 v Worcs (Leeds) 1998. **SL:** HS 34* v Derbys (Leeds) 1998. BB 5-16 v Hants (Leeds) 1998.

HOGGARD, Matthew James (Grangefield S, Pudsey), b Leeds 31 Dec 1976. 6'2". RHB, RFM. Debut 1996. Awaiting CC debut. HS 13* v Durham (Chester-le-St) 1998. BB 5-57 v Essex (Scarborough) 1998. **SL:** HS 1. BB 2-12 v Sussex (Hove) 1998.

HUTCHISON, Paul Michael (Crawshaw HS, Pudsey), b Leeds 9 Jun 1977. 6'3". LHB, LFM. Debut 1995-96 (Y tour); cap 1998. The Rest 1996. Tours (Eng A): Sl 1997-98; Z 1995-96 (Y); K 1997-98. HS 30 v Essex (Scarborough) 1998. 50 wkts (1): 59 (1998). BB 7-31 v Sussex (Hove) 1998. Award: NWT 1. **NWT:** HS 4*. BB 3-18 v Devon (Exmouth) 1998. **BHC:** HS 4*. BB 3-14 v Durham (Leeds) 1998. **SL:** HS 2. BB 4-34 v Glos (Gloucester) 1998.

McGRATH, Anthony (Yorkshire Martyrs Collegiate S), b Bradford 6 Oct 1975. 6'2". RHB, OB. Debut 1995. Tours (Eng A): A 1996-97; P 1995-96; Z 1995-96 (Y). HS 141 v Worcs (Leeds) 1997. BB 2-33 v Lancs (Leeds) 1998. Award: BHC 1. **NWT:** HS 34 v Lancs (Manchester) 1996. **BHC:** HS 109* v Minor C (Leeds) 1997. BB 2-10 v Scot (Leeds) 1996. **SL:** HS 72 v Sussex (Scarborough) 1995. BB 2-20 v Worcs (Worcester) 1998.

MIDDLEBROOK, James Daniel (Pudsey Crawshaw S), b Leeds 13 May 1977. 6'1". RHB, OB. Debut 1998. HS 41 v Lancs (Leeds) 1998. BB 3-20 v Worcs (Worcester) 1998. **SL:** HS 5.

PARKER, Bradley (Bingley GS), b Mirfield 23 Jun 1970. 5'11". RHB, RM. Debut 1992. Tour: Z 1995-96 (Y). HS 138* v OU (Oxford) 1997. CC HS 127 v Surrey (Scarborough) 1994. **NWT:** HS 69 v Leics (Leicester) 1997. **BHC:** HS 58 v Northants (Leeds) 1997. **SL:** HS 42 v Warwks (Birmingham) 1997.

SIDEBOTTOM, Ryan Jay (King James's GS, Almondbury), b Huddersfield 15 Jan 1978. Son of A. (Yorks, OFS and England 1973-91). 6'3". LHB, LFM. Debut 1997. HS 54 v Glam (Cardiff) 1998. BB 3-13 v Durham (Chester-le-St) 1998. **NWT:** HS –. BB 3-15 v Devon (Exmouth) 1998. **BHC:** HS 4 and BB 2-42 v Essex (Leeds) 1998. **SL:** HS 2*. BB 6-40 v Glam (Cardiff) 1998.

SILVERWOOD, Christopher Eric Wilfred (Garforth CS), b Pontefract 5 Mar 1975. 6'1". RHB, RFM. Debut 1993; cap 1996. YC 1996. **Tests:** 1 (1996-97); HS 0 and BB 3-63 v Z (Bulawayo) 1996-97. **LOI:** 6 (1996-97 to 1997); HS 12; BB 2-27. Tours: WI 1997-98; NZ 1996-97; Z 1995-96 (Y), 1996-97. HS 58 v Lancs (Manchester) 1997. 50 wkts (1): 58 (1997). BB 7-93 (12-148 match) v Kent (Leeds) 1997. Awards: BHC 2. **NWT:** HS 12* v Lancs (Manchester) 1998. BB 3-24 v Ire (Leeds) 1997. **BHC:** HS 8. BB 5-28 v Scot (Leeds) 1996. **SL:** HS 14* v Northants (Northampton) 1996. BB 4-26 v Durham (Chester-le-St) 1996.

VAUGHAN, Michael Paul (Silverdale CS, Sheffield), b Manchester, Lancs 29 Oct 1974. 6'2". RHB, OB. Debut 1993; cap 1995. Tours (Eng A): A 1996-97; SA 1998-99 (captain); I 1994-95; Z 1995-96 (Y), 1998-99 (captain). 1000 runs (4); most – 1244 (1995). HS 183 v Glam (Cardiff) 1996. BB 4-39 v OU (Oxford) 1994. CC BB 4-62 v Surrey (Middlesbrough) 1996. Award: BHC 1. **NWT:** HS 64 v Notts (Leeds) 1996. BB 1-17. **BHC:** HS 88 v Warwks (Birmingham) 1997. BB 1-0. **SL:** HS 71* v Sussex (Eastbourne) 1996. BB 3-48 v Essex (Ilford) 1997.

WHITE, Craig (Flora Hill HS, Bendigo, Australia; Bendigo HS), b Morley 16 Dec 1969. 6'0". RHB, RFM. Debut 1990; cap 1993. Victoria 1990-91 (2 matches). **Tests:** 8 (1994 to 1996-97); HS 51 v NZ (Lord's) 1994; BB 3-18 v NZ (Manchester) 1994. **LOI:** 15 (1994-95 to 1996-97); HS 38; BB 4-37. Tours: A 1994-95, 1996-97 (Eng A); SA 1991-92 (Y), 1992-93 (Y); NZ 1996-97; P 1995-96 (Eng A); Z 1996-97 (*part*). HS 181 v Lancs (Leeds) 1996. BB 8-55 v Glos (Gloucester) 1998 – inc hat-trick. Hat-trick 1998. Awards: NWT 1; BHC 1. **NWT:** HS 113 and BB 3-38 v Ire (Leeds) 1995. **BHC:** HS 57* v Notts (Leeds) 1996. BB 4-29 v Derbys (Derby) 1998. **SL:** HS 148 v Leics (Leicester) 1997. BB 4-18 v Durham (Scarborough) 1997.

WILKINSON, Richard (Wombwell HS; Worksop C), b Barnsley 11 Nov 1977. 5'11". RHB, OB. Debut 1998. HS 9. BB 1-35.

WOOD, Matthew James (Shelley HS & SFC), b Huddersfield 6 Apr 1977. 5'9". RHB, OB. Debut 1997. 1000 runs (1): 108 (1998 – his first full season after playing one match in 1997). HS 200* v Warwks (Leeds) 1998. **NWT:** HS 25* v Devon (Exmouth) 1998. **SL:** HS 65* v Essex (Scarborough) 1998.

NEW REGISTRATIONS

BLEWETT, Gregory Scott (Prince Alfred C), b Adelaide, Australia 28 Oct 1971. Son of R.W. (South Australia 1975-76 to 1978-79). 6'0". RHB, RM. South Australia 1991-92 to date. **Tests** (A): 31 (1994-95 to 1997-98); HS 214 v SA (Johannesburg) 1996-97; scored 102* v E (Adelaide) on debut; first to score hundreds in his first 3 Ashes Tests; BB 2-25 v P (Hobart) 1995-96. **LOI** (A): 32 (1994-95 to 1998-99); HS 57*; BB 2-6. Tours: E 1997; SA 1996-97; WI 1994-95, 1998-99; I 1997-98. 1000 runs (0+2); most – 1173 (1995-96). HS 268 S Aus v Victoria (Melbourne) 1993-94. BB 5-29 Aus XI v WI (Hobart) 1996-97.

DAWSON, Richard Kevin James, b Doncaster 4 Aug 1980. RHB, OB.

ELLISON, Christopher John, b Sheffield 12 Apr 1979. LHB, SLA. Cornwall 1998.

GUY, Simon Mark (Wickersley CS), b Rotherham 17 Nov 1978. RHB, WK.

HARDEN, Richard John (King's C, Taunton), b Bridgwater, Somerset 16 Aug 1965. 5'11". RHB, SLA. Somerset 1985-98; cap 1989; benefit 1996. C Districts 1987-88. 1000 runs (7); most – 1460 (1990). HS 187 Sm v Notts (Taunton) 1992. BB 2-7 CD v Canterbury (Blenheim) 1987-88. CC BB 2-24 Sm v Hants (Taunton) 1986. Award: NWT 1. **NWT:** HS 108* Sm v Scot (Taunton) 1992. **BHC:** HS 76 Sm v Kent (Canterbury) 1992. **SL:** HS 100* Sm v Durham (Chester-le-St) 1995.

INGLIS, John William b Ripon 19 Oct 1979. RHB.

WIDDUP, Simon, b Doncaster 10 Nov 1977. RHB.

RELEASED/RETIRED
(Having made a first-class County appearance in 1998)

LEHMANN, Darren Scott (Gawler HS), b Gawler, South Australia 5 Feb 1970. 5'10. LHB, SLA. South Australia 1987-88 to 1989-90, 1993-94 to date; captain 1998-99. Victoria 1990-91 to 1992-93. Yorkshire 1997-98; cap 1997. **Tests** (A): 5 (1997-98 to 1998-99); HS 98 v P (Rawalpindi) 1998-99; BB 1-6. **LOI** (A): 38 (1996-97 to 1998-99); HS 103; BB 2-11. Tours (A): E 1991 (Vic); I 1997-98; P 1998-99. 1000 runs (1+4); most – 1575 (1997). HS 255 S Aus v Queensland (Adelaide) 1996-97. Y HS 200 v Worcs (Worcester) 1998. BB 4-42 v Kent (Maidstone) 1998. Awards: BHC 2. **NWT:** HS 105 v Glam (Cardiff) 1997. BB 1-14. **BHC:** HS 119 v Durham (Leeds) 1998. BB 2-17 v Scot (Linlithgow) 1998. **SL:** HS 99 v Kent (Maidstone) 1998. BB 3-43 v Northants (Leeds) 1998. Returns 2000.

STEMP, R.D. – *see NOTTINGHAMSHIRE*.

YORKSHIRE 1998

RESULTS SUMMARY

	Place	Won	Lost	Tied	Drew	No Result
Britannic Assurance Championship	3rd	9	3		5	
All First-Class Matches		9	3		7	
NatWest Trophy	2nd Round					
Benson and Hedges Cup	Semi-Finalist					
Sunday League	9th	8	8			1

BRITANNIC ASSURANCE CHAMPIONSHIP AVERAGES

BATTING AND FIELDING

Cap		M	I	NO	HS	Runs	Avge	100	50	Ct/St
1997	D.S.Lehmann	10	16	–	200	969	60.56	3	4	4
–	M.J.Wood	17	25	3	200*	991	45.04	4	4	15
–	R.J.Sidebottom	4	4	2	54	84	42.00	–	1	2
1995	M.P.Vaughan	17	28	3	177	1022	40.88	2	3	6
1993	C.White	8	12	3	104*	356	39.55	1	1	13
1998	G.M.Hamilton	14	18	1	79	572	33.64	–	6	3
1991	D.Byas	17	26	1	116	810	32.40	4	3	20
1993	D.Gough	5	6	–	89	186	31.00	–	2	1
–	B.Parker	6	7	1	41	154	25.66	–	–	2
1996	C.E.W.Silverwood	12	13	3	57*	239	23.90	–	1	2
–	A.McGrath	15	24	1	63*	518	22.52	–	2	5
1987	R.J.Blakey	17	23	2	67*	448	21.33	–	3	69/2
1998	P.M.Hutchison	16	18	8	30	127	15.87	–	–	3
1996	R.D.Stemp	11	15	8	43*	107	15.28	–	–	5
–	J.D.Middlebrook	7	11	2	41	132	14.66	–	–	7
–	M.J.Hoggard	8	10	3	13*	35	5.00	–	–	3

Also played (1 match each): G.D.Clough 33, 1 (1 ct); G.M.Fellows 3, 18; I.D.Fisher did not bat.

BOWLING

	O	M	R	W	Avge	Best	5wI	10wM
C.White	124.1	30	337	25	13.48	8- 55	2	–
G.M.Hamilton	387	91	1143	56	20.41	7- 50	4	2
M.J.Hoggard	227	46	805	36	22.36	5- 57	1	–
C.E.W.Silverwood	376.1	97	1085	46	23.58	5- 13	3	–
P.M.Hutchison	460.3	115	1397	57	24.50	7- 31	3	–
D.Gough	156.4	27	523	21	24.90	5- 36	1	–
J.D.Middlebrook	136.2	41	338	11	30.72	3- 20	–	–
R.D.Stemp	360	112	922	26	35.46	5-191	1	–

Also bowled: G.D.Clough 2-0-11-0; G.M.Fellows 3-0-21-0; I.D.Fisher 3-1-3-0; D.S.Lehmann 57-16-124-6; A.McGrath 36-8-135-3; R.J.Sidebottom 93-17-322-9; M.P.Vaughan 67-19-216-2.

The First-Class Averages (pp 117-131) give the records of Yorkshire players in all first-class county matches (Yorkshire's other opponents being Cambridge University and Oxford University), with the exception of:
  D.Gough 6-7-0-89-207-29.57-0-2-1. 179.4-34-577-23-25.08-5/36-1-0.

YORKSHIRE RECORDS

FIRST-CLASS CRICKET

Highest Total	For 887		v Warwicks	Birmingham	1896
	V 681-7d		by Leics	Bradford	1996
Lowest Total	For 23		v Hampshire	Middlesbrough	1965
	V 13		by Notts	Nottingham	1901
Highest Innings	For 341	G.H.Hirst	v Leics	Leicester	1905
	V 318*	W.G.Grace	for Glos	Cheltenham	1876

Highest Partnership for each Wicket

1st	555	P.Holmes/H.Sutcliffe	v Essex	Leyton	1932
2nd	346	W.Barber/M.Leyland	v Middlesex	Sheffield	1932
3rd	323*	H.Sutcliffe/M.Leyland	v Glamorgan	Huddersfield	1928
4th	312	D.Denton/G.H.Hirst	v Hampshire	Southampton	1914
5th	340	E.Wainwright/G.H.Hirst	v Surrey	The Oval	1899
6th	276	M.Leyland/E.Robinson	v Glamorgan	Swansea	1926
7th	254	W.Rhodes/D.C.F.Burton	v Hampshire	Dewsbury	1919
8th	292	R.Peel/Lord Hawke	v Warwicks	Birmingham	1896
9th	192	G.H.Hirst/S.Haigh	v Surrey	Bradford	1898
10th	149	G.Boycott/G.B.Stevenson	v Warwicks	Birmingham	1982

Best Bowling	For	10-10	H.Verity	v Notts	Leeds	1932
(Innings)	V	10-37	C.V.Grimmett	for Australians	Sheffield	1930
Best Bowling	For	17-91	H.Verity	v Essex	Leyton	1933
(Match)	V	17-91	H.Dean	for Lancashire	Liverpool	1913

Most Runs – Season	2883	H.Sutcliffe	(av 80.08)	1932
Most Runs – Career	38561	H.Sutcliffe	(av 50.20)	1919-45
Most 100s – Season	12	H.Sutcliffe		1932
Most 100s – Career	112	H.Sutcliffe		1919-45
Most Wkts – Season	240	W.Rhodes	(av 12.72)	1900
Most Wkts – Career	3608	W.Rhodes	(av 16.00)	1898-1930

LIMITED-OVERS CRICKET

Highest Total	NWT	345-5		v Notts	Leeds	1996
	BHC	317-5		v Scotland	Leeds	1986
	SL	318-7		v Leics	Leicester	1993
Lowest Total	NWT	76		v Surrey	Harrogate	1970
	BHC	88		v Worcs	Leeds	1995
	SL	56		v Warwicks	Birmingham	1995
Highest Innings	NWT	146	G.Boycott	v Surrey	Lord's	1965
	BHC	142	G.Boycott	v Worcs	Worcester	1980
	SL	148	C.White	v Leics	Leicester	1997
Best Bowling	NWT	7-27	D.Gough	v Ireland	Leeds	1997
	BHC	6-27	A.G.Nicholson	v Minor C (N)	Middlesbrough	1972
	SL	7-15	R.A.Hutton	v Worcs	Leeds	1969

HAMPSHIRE – RELEASED/RETIRED (continued from p 42)
(Having made a first-class County appearance in 1998)

MARU, Rajesh Jamandass (Rook's Heath HS, Harrow; Pinner SFC), b Nairobi, Kenya 28 Oct 1962. 5'6". RHB, SLA. Middlesex 1980-82. Hampshire 1984-98; cap 1986; benefit 1998. Tour: Z 1980-81 (Mx). HS 74 v Glos (Gloucester) 1988. 50 wkts (4); most – 73 (1985). BB 8-41 v Kent (Southampton) 1989. **NWT:** HS 22 v Yorks (Southampton) 1990. BB 3-46 v Leics (Leicester) 1990. **BHC:** HS 10* v Surrey (Southampton) 1997. BB 3-46 v Comb U (Southampton) 1990. **SL:** HS 33* v Glam (Ebbw Vale) 1991. BB 4-29 v Yorks (Southampton) 1997.

WHITAKER, Paul Robert (Whitcliffe Mount S), b Keighley, Yorks 28 Jun 1973. 5'9". LHB, OB. Hampshire 1994-98. Derbyshire staff 1992-93. HS 119 v Worcs (Southampton) 1995. BB 3-36 v OU (Oxford) 1996. CC BB 2-64 v Lancs (Manchester) 1996. Award: BHC 1. **NWT:** HS 13 v Leics (Leicester) 1995. BB 3-48 v Essex (Southampton) 1996. **BHC:** HS 53 v Sussex (Southampton) 1996. BB 2-33 v Surrey (Oval) 1996. **SL:** HS 97 v Worcs (Southampton) 1995. BB 3-44 v Surrey (Southampton) 1996.

KENT – RELEASED/RETIRED (continued from p 47)
(Having made a first-class County appearance in 1998)

HOOPER, Carl Llewellyn (Christchurch SS, Georgetown), b Georgetown, Guyana 15 Dec 1966. 6'1". RHB, OB. Demerara 1983-84. Guyana 1984-85 to date (captain 1996-97 to date). Kent 1992-94, 1996, 1998; cap 1992. **Tests** (WI): 78 (1987-88 to 1998-99); HS 178* v P (St John's) 1992-93; BB 5-26 v SL (Kingstown) 1996-97. **LOI** (WI): 177 (1986-87 to 1998-99, 4 as captain); HS 113*; BB 4-34. Tours (WI): E 1988, 1991, 1995; A 1988-89, 1991-92, 1992-93, 1995-96, 1996-97; SA 1998-99; NZ 1986-87; I 1987-88, 1994-95; P 1990-91, 1997-98; SL 1993-94; Z 1986-87 (Young WI), 1989-90 (Young WI). 1000 runs (7); most – 1579 (1994). HS 236* v Glam (Canterbury) 1993. BB 7-93 v Surrey (Oval) 1998. Awards: NWT 1; BHC 1. **NWT:** HS 136* v Berks (Finchampstead) 1994. BB 2-12 v Middx (Canterbury) 1993. **BHC:** HS 98 v Somerset (Maidstone) 1996. BB 3-28 v Yorks (Leeds) 1992. **SL:** HS 145 v Leics (Leicester) 1996. BB 5-41 v Essex (Maidstone) 1993.

IGGLESDEN, Alan Paul (Churchill S, Westerham), b Farnborough 8 Oct 1964. 6'6". RHB, RFM. Kent 1986-98; cap 1989; testimonial 1998. W Province 1987-88. Boland 1992-93. **Tests:** 3 (1989 to 1993-94); HS 3*; BB 2-91 v A (Oval) 1989. **LOI:** 4 (1993-94); HS 18; BB 2-12. Tours: WI 1993-94; Z 1989-90 (Eng A), 1992-93 (K). HS 41 v Surrey (Canterbury) 1988. 50 wkts (4); most – 56 (1989). BB 7-28 (12-66 match) Boland v GW (Kimberley) 1992-93. K BB 6-34 v Surrey (Canterbury) 1988. **NWT:** HS 12* v Oxon (Oxford) 1990. BB 4-29 v Cambs (Canterbury) 1991. **BHC:** HS 26* v Worcs (Worcester) 1991. BB 3-24 v Scot (Glasgow) 1991 and v Notts (Nottingham) 1992. **SL:** HS 13* (twice). BB 5-13 v Sussex (Hove) 1989. Joins Berkshire 1999.

LANCASHIRE – RELEASED/RETIRED (continued from p 52)
(Having made a first-class County appearance in 1998)

WASIM AKRAM (Islamia C), b Lahore, Pakistan 3 Jun 1966. 6'3". LHB, LF. PACO 1984-85 to 1985-86. Lahore 1985-86 to 1986-87. PIA 1987-88 to date. Lancashire 1988-98; cap 1989; captain 1998; benefit 1998. *Wisden* 1992. **Tests** (P): 83 (1984-85 to 1998-99, 17 as captain); HS 257* v Z (Sheikhupura) 1996-97; BB 7-119 v NZ (Wellington) 1993-94. **LOI** (P): 254 (1984-85 to 1998-99, 72 as captain); HS 86; BB 5-15. Tours (P)(C=captain): E 1987, 1992, 1996C; A 1988-89, 1989-90, 1991-92, 1992-93, 1995-96C, 1996-97C; SA 1997-98; WI 1987-88, 1992-93C; NZ 1984-85, 1992-93, 1993-94, 1995-96C; I 1986-87, 1998-99C; SL 1986-85 (P U-23), 1985-86, 1994-95. HS 257* *(see Tests)*. La HS 155 v Notts (Nottingham) 1998. 50 wkts (5); most – 82 (1992). BB 8-30 (13-147 match) v Somerset (Southport) 1994. Hat-trick 1988. Awards: NWT 1; BHC 4. **NWT:** HS 50 v Surrey (Oval) 1994. BB 4-27 v Lincs (Manchester) 1988. **BHC:** HS 89* v Notts (Nottingham) 1998. BB 5-10 v Leics (Leicester) 1993. **SL:** HS 75* v Glos (Manchester) 1998. BB 5-41 v Northants (Northampton) 1994. Joins Channel 4 commentary team and Smethwick CC (Birmingham Premier League).

MIDDLESEX – RELEASED/RETIRED (continued from p 62)
(Having made a first-class County appearance in 1998)

GATTING, Michael William (John Kelly HS), b Kingsbury 6 Jun 1957. 5'10". RHB, RM. Middlesex 1975-98; cap 1977; captain 1983-97; benefit 1988; testimonial 1996. YC 1981. *Wisden* 1983. OBE 1987. **Tests**: 79 (1977-78 to 1994-95, 23 as captain); HS 207 v I (Madras) 1984-85; BB 1-14. **LOI**: 92 (1977-78 to 1992-93, 37 as captain); HS 115*; BB 3-32. Tours (C=captain): A 1986-87C, 1987-88C; SA 1989-90C (Eng XI); WI 1980-81, 1985-86; NZ 1977-78, 1983-84, 1987-88C; I/SL 1981-82, 1984-85, 1992-93; P 1977-78, 1983-84, 1987-88C; Z 1980-81 (Mx). 1000 runs (19) inc 2000 (3); most – 2257 (1984). HS 258 v Somerset (Bath) 1984. BB 5-34 v Glam (Swansea) 1982. Awards: NWT 7; BHC 11. **NWT**: HS 132* v Sussex (Lord's) 1989. BB 2-14 (twice). **BHC**: HS 143* v Sussex (Hove) 1985. BB 4-49 v Sussex (Lord's) 1984. **SL**: HS 124* v Leics (Leicester) 1990. BB 4-30 v Glos (Bristol) 1989.

POOLEY, Jason Calvin (Acton HS), b Hammersmith 8 Aug 1969. 6'0". LHB, occ OB. Middlesex 1989-98; cap 1995. Tour: P 1995-96 (Eng A). 1000 runs (1): 1335 (1995). HS 138* v CU (Cambridge) 1996. CC HS 136 v Glos (Bristol) 1995. **NWT**: HS 79* v Glos (Uxbridge) 1997. **BHC**: HS 50* v Essex (Lord's) 1997. **SL**: HS 109 v Derbys (Lord's) 1991.

RASHID, U.B.A. – *see SUSSEX*.

NORTHAMPTONSHIRE – RELEASED/RETIRED (continued from p 67)
(Having made a first-class County appearance in 1998)

ROSE, Franklyn Albert (Ocho Rios SS; Holmwood THS), b St Ann's Bay, Jamaica 1 Feb 1972. RHB, RF. 6'5". Jamaica 1992-93 to date. Northamptonshire 1998. **Tests** (WI): 11 (1996-97 to 1998-99); HS 34 v I (P-of-S) 1996-97; BB 7-84 v SA (Durban) 1998-99. **LOI** (WI): 13 (1996-97 to 1997-98): HS 24; BB 3-25 – on debut. Tours (WI): A 1996-97; SA 1998-99; P 1997-98. HS 96 Jamaica v Leeward Is (Anguilla) 1996-97. Nh HS 21 v Somerset (Taunton) 1998. 50 wkts (1+1): most – 71 (1996-97). BB 7-39 (11-90 match) v Worcs (Worcester) 1998. Award: BHC 1. **NWT**: HS 19 and 3-43 v Glos (Bristol) 1998. **BHC**: HS 15 and BB 5-14 v Minor C (Luton) 1998. **SL**: HS 9*. BB 2-19 v Sussex (Northampton) 1998.

SNAPE, J.N. – *see GLOUCESTERSHIRE*.

WARWICKSHIRE – RELEASED/RETIRED (continued from p 93)
(Having made a first-class County appearance in 1998)

LARA, Brian Charles, b Santa Cruz, Trinidad 2 May 1969. 5'8". LHB, LB. Trinidad 1987-88 to date; captain 1995-96 to date. Warwickshire 1994, 1998; cap 1994; captain 1998. *Wisden* 1994. **Tests**: (WI) 59 (1990-91 to 1998-99, 12 as captain); HS 375 (world Test record) v E (St John's) 1993-94. **LOI** (WI): 137 (1990-91 to 1998-99, 14 as captain); HS 169; BB 2-5. Tours (WI): E 1991, 1995; A 1991-92, 1992-93, 1996-97; SA 1998-99 (captain); NZ 1994-95; I 1994-95; P 1990-91, 1997-98; SL 1993-94; Z 1989-90 (Young WI). 1000 runs (3+1) including 2000 (1): 2066 off 2262 balls in 1994. HS 501* (world f-c record) v Durham (Birmingham) 1994. Scored 6 hundreds in his first 7 innings for Warwks (147, 106, 120*, 136, 26, 140, 501*). BB 1-14 (T). Awards: NWT 1; BHC 1. **NWT**: HS 133 v Kent (Birmingham) 1998. **BHC**: HS 101 v Northants (Birmingham) 1998. **SL**: HS 75 v Notts (Birmingham) 1994.

IRELAND REGISTER 1998

Full Names	Birthdate	Birthplace	Bat/Bowl	F-C Debut
BUSHE, Jonathan Alexander	12.12.78	Craigavon	LHB/WK	1998
COOKE, Gordon	24. 7.75	Londonderry	RHB/RMF	1994
DUNLOP, Angus Richard	17. 3.67	Dublin	RHB/OB	1990
DWYER, Matthew Damian	22. 2.59	Dublin	LHB/SLA	1998
JOYCE, Edmund Christopher	22. 9.78	Dublin	LHB/RM	1997
McCALLAN, William Kyle	27. 8.75	Carrickfergus	RHB/OB	1996
MOLINS, Jason Adam Max	4.12.74	Dublin	RHB/RSM	1998
MOONEY, Paul John Kevin	15.10.76	Dublin	RHB/RM	1998
OLPHERT, David Mark	10. 1.69	Londonderry	RHB/LM	1998
SMYTH, Stephen Gordon	22.12.68	Londonderry	LHB	1991
WAUGH, Stephen Rodger	2. 6.65	Canterbury, NSW	RHB/RMF	1984-85

SCOTLAND REGISTER 1998

Full Names	Birthdate	Birthplace	Bat/Bowl	F-C Debut
ALLINGHAM, Michael James de Grey	6. 1.65	Inverness	RHB/RM	1996
ASIM BUTT	24.10.67	Lahore, Pakistan	RHB/LMF	1983-84
BRINKLEY, James Edward	13. 3.74	Helensburgh	RHB/RFM	1993
DAVIES, Alec George	14. 8.62	Rawalpindi, Pak	RHB/WK	1985
DYER, Nicholas Rayner	10. 6.69	Edinburgh	RHB/OB	1997
LOCKHART, Douglas Ross	19. 1.76	Glasgow	RHB	1996
LOCKIE, Bryn Gardner	5. 6.68	Alloa	RHB	1996
PATTERSON, Bruce Mathew Winston	29. 1.65	Ayr	RHB	1988
PHILIP, Iain Lindsay	9. 6.58	Falkirk	RHB	1986
SALMOND, George	1.12.69	Dundee	RHB	1991
SHERIDAN, Keith Lamont Paton	26. 3.71	Glasgow	RHB/SLA	1992
STANGER, Ian Michael	5.10.71	Glasgow	RHB/RMF	1997
STEINDL, Peter David	14. 6.70	Bundaberg, Aus	RHB/RM	1998
THOMSON, Kevin	24.12.71	Dundee	RHB/RMF	1992
WILLIAMSON, John Greig	28.12.68	Glasgow	RHB/RM	1994

UNIVERSITY REGISTER 1998

CAMBRIDGE

Full Names	Birthdate	Birthplace	College	Bat/Bowl	F-C Debut
BIRKS, Malcolm James	29. 7.75	Keighley	Jesus	RHB/WK	1995
COLLINS, Benjamin James	4.11.77	London	Girton	RHB	1998
HOUSE, William John	16. 3.76	Sheffield	Gonville & Caius	LHB/RM	1996
HUGHES, Quentin John	17.10.74	Durham City	St Edmund's	LHB/OB	1997
JANISCH, Adam Nicholas	21.10.75	Hammersmith	Trinity	RHB/RM	1995
LEWIS, Simon James Ward	9.10.78	Bolton	Jesus	RHB	1998
LOVERIDGE, Greg Riaka	15. 1.75	Palmerston N	St Edmund's	RHB/LBG	1994-95
LOWE, Jonathan Paul	13.11.77	Pontefract	Girton	RHB/RM	1998
MOFFAT, Philip John	29. 5.75	Lancaster	Hughes Hall	RHB/RM	1998
MOHAMMED, Imraan	31.12.76	Solihull	St Catharine's	RHB/OB	1997

Full Names	Birthdate	Birthplace	College	Bat/Bowl	F-C Debut
PYEMONT, James Patrick	10.4.78	Eastbourne	Trinity	RHB/OB	1997
SCHAFFTER, Prakash Anand	19.6.67	Colombo	King's	RHB/RFM	1997
SINGH, Anurag	9.9.75	Kanpur	Gonville & Caius	RHB/OB	1995
SMITH, Edward Thomas	19.7.77	Pembury	Peterhouse	RHB/RM	1996

OXFORD

Full Names	Birthdate	Birthplace	College	Bat/Bowl	F-C Debut
BARNES, Jeremy Paul Blissard	23. 3.70	Orpington	Wycliffe Hall	RHB/WK	1998
BUCHANAN, Laurence George	9. 3.76	Perivale	Keble	RHB	1997
BYRNE, Byron Walter	15. 2.72	Sydney	Balliol	RHB/OB	1997
CLAUGHTON, John Andrew	28.10.78	Southampton	Keble	RHB/RM	1998
COCKCROFT, Jonathan Richard	28. 5.77	Bradford	Oriel	RHB/LB	1997
EADIE, David John	2. 1.75	Cape Town	St Edmund Hall	RHB/RM	1998
FERGUSON, Stuart Hunter	13.10.74	Sonoma	Mansfield	RHB/RM	1998
FULTON, James Anthony Gervase	21. 9.77	Plymouth	Brasenose	LHB/RM	1997
GARLAND, Ross	26. 6.74	Durban	Pembroke	RHB/RM	1998
KHAN, Salman Haider	4. 6.71	Rawalpindi	Wadham	RHB/RM	1998
LIGHTFOOT, Charles Gordon Rufus	25. 2.76	Amersham	Keble	LHB/SLA	1996
LOCKHART, Douglas Ross	19. 1.76	Glasgow	Keble	RHB	1996
MATHER, David Peter	20.11.75	Bebington	St Hugh's	LHB/LM	1995
MOLINS, Jason Adam Max	4.12.74	Dublin	Oriel	RHB/RSM	1998
PARKER, Charles Rupert Camden	13.11.77	Auckland	Brasenose	RHB/RM	1998
PARKER, Joseph Timothy	23. 8.76	Bromley	St John's	RHB/OB	1998
PIRIHI, Nicholas Gordon	19. 4.97	Whangarei	Merton	RHB	1997
SCRINI, Alex Philip	18.11.76	Sheffield	Hertford	RHB/WK	1997
WAGH, Mark Anant	20.10.76	Birmingham	Keble	RHB/OB	1996

BRITISH UNIVERSITIES

(Excluding players listed either above or in the County Register)

Full Names	Birthdate	Birthplace	University	Bat/Bowl	F-C Debut
LEATHER, David	25.11.77	Whiston, Lancs	Loughborough	RHB/RFM	1998

FIRST-CLASS UMPIRES 1999

BALDERSTONE, John Christopher (Paddock Council S, Huddersfield), b Longwood, Huddersfield, Yorks 16 Nov 1940. RHB, SLA. Yorkshire 1961-69. Leicestershire 1971-86 (cap 1973; testimonial 1984). **Tests:** 2 (1976); HS 35 v WI (Leeds) 1976; BB 1-80. Tour: Z 1980-81 (Le). 1000 runs (11); most – 1482 (1982). HS 181* Le v Glos (Leicester) 1984. BB 6-25 Le v Hants (Southampton) 1978. Hat-trick 1976 (Le). F-c career: 390 matches; 19034 runs @ 34.11, 32 hundreds; 310 wickets @ 26.32; 210 ct. Soccer for Huddersfield Town, Carlisle United, Doncaster Rovers and Queen of the South. Appointed 1988. Umpired 2 LOI (1994 to 1998).

BURGESS, Graham Iefvion (Millfield S), b Glastonbury, Somerset 5 May 1943. RHB, RM. Somerset 1966-79 (cap 1968; testimonial 1978). HS 129 v Glos (Taunton) 1973. BB 7-43 (13-75 match) v OU (Oxford) 1975. F-c career: 252 matches; 7129 runs @ 18.90, 2 hundreds; 474 wickets @ 28.57. Appointed 1991.

CLARKSON, Anthony (Harrogate GS), b Killinghall, Harrogate, Yorks 5 Sep 1939. RHB, OB. Yorkshire 1963. Somerset 1966-71 (cap 1968). Devon. 1000 runs (2); most – 1246 (1970). HS 131 Sm v Northants (Northampton) 1969. BB 3-51 Sm v Essex (Yeovil) 1967. F-c career: 110 matches; 4458 runs @ 25.18, 2 hundreds; 13 wickets @ 28.23. Appointed 1996.

CONSTANT, David John, b Bradford-on-Avon, Wilts 9 Nov 1941. LHB, SLA. Kent 1961-63. Leicestershire 1965-68. HS 80 Le v Glos (Bristol) 1966. F-c career: 61 matches; 1517 runs @ 19.20; 1 wicket @ 36.00. Appointed 1969. Umpired 36 Tests (1971 to 1988) and 31 LOI (1972 to 1998). Represented Gloucestershire at bowls 1984-86.

DUDLESTON, Barry (Stockport S), b Bebington, Cheshire 16 Jul 1945. RHB, SLA. Leicestershire 1966-80 (cap 1969; benefit 1980). Gloucestershire 1981-83. Rhodesia 1976-80. 1000 runs (8); most – 1374 (1970). HS 202 Le v Derbys (Leicester) 1979. BB 4-6 Le v Surrey (Leicester) 1972. F-c career: 295 matches; 14747 runs @ 32.48, 32 hundreds; 47 wickets @ 29.04. Appointed 1984. Umpired 2 Tests (1991 to 1992) and 2 LOI (1992 to 1998).

HAMPSHIRE, John Harry (Oakwood THS, Rotherham), b Thurnscoe, Yorks 10 Feb 1941. RHB, LB. Son of J. (Yorks 1937); brother of A.W. (Yorks 1975). Yorkshire 1961-81 (cap 1963; benefit 1976; captain 1979-80). Derbyshire 1982-84 (cap 1982). Tasmania 1967-69, 1977-79. **Tests:** 8 (1969 to 1975); 403 runs @ 26.86, HS 107 v WI (Lord's) 1969 on debut (only England player to score hundred at Lord's on Test debut). Tours: A 1970-71; SA 1972-73 (DHR), 1974-75 (DHR); WI 1964-65 (Cav); NZ 1970-71; P 1967-68 (Cwlth XI); SL 1969-70; Z 1980-81 (Le XI). 1000 runs (15); most – 1596 (1978). HS 183* H v Sussex (Hove) 1971. BB 7-52 Y v Glam (Cardiff) 1963. F-c career: 577 matches; 28059 runs @ 34.55, 43 hundreds; 30 wickets @ 54.56; 445 ct. Appointed 1985. Umpired 11 Tests (1989 to 1993) and 8 LOI (1989 to 1998).

HARRIS, John Henry, b Taunton, Somerset 13 Feb 1936. LHB, RFM. Somerset 1952-59. Suffolk 1960-62. Devon 1975. HS 41 v Worcs (Taunton) 1957. BB 3-29 v Worcs (Bristol) 1959. F-c career: 15 matches; 154 runs @ 11.00; 19 wickets @ 32.57. Appointed 1983.

HARRIS, Michael John ('**Pasty**') (Gerrans S, nr Truro), b St Just-in-Roseland, Cornwall 25 May 1944. RHB, LB, WK. Middlesex 1964-68 (cap 1967). Nottinghamshire 1969-82 (cap 1970; benefit 1977). Eastern Province 1971-72. Wellington 1975-76. 1000 runs (11); most – 2238 (1971). Scored 9 hundreds in 1971 to equal Notts record. HS 201* Nt v Glam (Nottingham) 1973. BB 4-16 Nt v Warwks (Nottingham) 1969. F-c career: 344 matches; 19,196 runs @ 36.70, 41 hundreds; 79 wickets @ 43.78; 302 dismissals (288 ct, 14 st). Appointed 1998.

HOLDER, John Wakefield (Combermere S, Barbados), b St George, Barbados 19 Mar 1945. RHB, RFM. Hampshire 1968-72. Hat-trick 1972. HS 33 v Sussex (Hove) 1971. BB 7-79 v Glos (Gloucester) 1972. F-c career: 47 matches; 374 runs @ 10.68; 139 wickets @ 24.56. Appointed 1983. Umpired 10 Tests (1988 to 1991) and 15 LOI (1988 to 1998) including 1989-90 Nehru Cup and one Sharjah tournament.

HOLDER, Vanburn Alonza (Richmond SM, Barbados), b Bridgetown, Barbados 8 Oct 1945. RHB, RFM. Barbados 1966-78. Worcestershire 1968-80 (cap 1970; benefit 1979). Shropshire 1981. **Tests** (WI): 40 (1969 to 1978-79); 682 runs @ 14.20, HS 42 v NZ (P-o-S) 1971-72; 109 wkts @ 33.27, BB 6-28 v A (P-o-S) 1977-78. **LOI** (WI): 12. Tours (WI): E 1969, 1973, 1976; A 1975-76; I 1974-75, 1978-79; P 1973-74 (RW), 1974-75; SL 1974-75, 1978-79. HS 122 Barbados v Trinidad (Bridgetown) 1973-74. BB 7-40 Wo v Glam (Cardiff) 1974. F-c career: 311 matches; 3559 runs @ 13.03, 1 hundred; 947 wickets @ 24.48. Appointed 1992.

JESTY, Trevor Edward (Privet County SS, Gosport), b Gosport, Hants 2 Jun 1948. RHB, RM. Hampshire 1966-84 (cap 1971; benefit 1982). Surrey 1985-87 (cap 1985); captain 1985). Lancashire 1988-91 (cap 1989). Border 1973-74. GW 1974-76, 1980-81. Canterbury 1979-80. *Wisden* 1982. **LOI**: 10. Tours: WI 1982-83 (Int); Z 1988-89 (La). 1000 runs (10); most − 1645 (1982). HS 248 H v CU (Cambridge) 1984. Scored 122* La v OU (Oxford) 1991 in his final f-c innings. 50 wkts (2); most − 52 (1981). BB 7-75 H v Worcs (Southampton) 1976. F-c career: 490 matches; 21916 runs @ 32.71, 35 hundreds; 585 wickets @ 27.47. Appointed 1994.

JONES, Allan Arthur (St Johns C, Horsham), b Horley, Surrey 9 Dec 1947. RHB, RFM. Sussex 1966-69. Somerset 1970-75 (cap 1972). Middlesex 1976-79 (cap 1976). Glamorgan 1980-81. Northern Transvaal 1972-73. Orange Free State 1976-77. HS 33 M v Kent (Canterbury) 1978. BB 9-51 Sm v Sussex (Hove) 1972. F-c career: 214 matches; 799 runs @ 5.39; 549 wickets @ 28.07. Appointed 1985. Umpired 1 LOI (1996).

JULIAN, Raymond (Wigston SM), b Cosby, Leics 23 Aug 1936. RHB, WK. Leicestershire 1953-71 (cap 1961). HS 51 v Worcs (Worcester) 1962. F-c career: 192 matches; 2581 runs @ 9.73; 421 dismissals (382 ct, 39 st). Appointed 1972. Umpired 3 LOI (1996 to 1998).

KITCHEN, Mervyn John (Backwell SM, Nailsea), b Nailsea, Somerset 1 Aug 1940. LHB, RM. Somerset 1960-79 (cap 1966; testimonial 1973). Tour: Rhodesia 1972-73 (Int W). 1000 runs (7); most − 1730 (1968). HS 189 v Pakistanis (Taunton) 1967. BB 1-4. F-c career: 354 matches; 15230 runs @ 26.25, 17 hundreds; 2 wickets @ 54.50. Appointed 1982. Umpired 18 Tests (1990 to 1998) and 25 LOI (1983 to 1998), including tournaments in Sharjah (1) and Nairobi (1). **Appointed to International Panel 1995.**

LEADBEATER, Barrie (Harehills SS), b Harehills, Leeds, Yorks 14 Aug 1943. RHB, RM. Yorkshire 1966-79 (cap 1969; joint benefit with G.A.Cope 1980). Tour: WI 1969-70 (DN). HS 140* v Hants (Portsmouth) 1976. F-c career: 147 matches; 5373 runs @ 25.34, 1 hundred; 1 wicket @ 5.00. Appointed 1981. Umpired 4 LOI (1983).

LLOYDS, Jeremy William (Blundells S), b Penang, Malaya 17 Nov 1954. LHB, OB. Somerset 1979-84 (cap 1982). Gloucestershire 1985-91 (cap 1985). Orange Free State 1983-88. Tour (Glos): SL 1986-87. 1000 runs (3); most − 1295 (1986). HS 132* Sm v Northants (Northampton) 1982. BB 7-88 Sm v Essex (Chelmsford) 1982. F-c career: 267 matches; 10,679 runs @ 31.04, 10 hundreds; 333 wickets @ 38.86. Appointed 1998.

MALLENDER, Neil Alan (Beverley GS), b Kirk Sandall, Yorks 13 Aug 1961. RHB, RFM. Northamptonshire 1980-86 and 1995-96; cap 1984. Somerset 1987-94; cap 1987; benefit 1994. Otago 1983-84 to 1992-93; captain 1990-91 to 1992-93. **Tests**: 2 (1992); 8 runs @ 2.66, HS 4; 10 wkts @ 21.50, BB 5-50 v P (Leeds) 1992 − on debut. Tour: Z 1994-95 (Nh). HS 100* Otago v CD (Palmerston N) 1991-92, UK HS 87* Sm v Sussex (Hove) 1990. 50 wkts (1); most − 56 (1983). BB 7-27 Otago v Auckland (Auckland) 1984-85. UK BB 7-41 Nh v Derbys (Northampton) 1982. F-c career: 345 matches; 4,709 runs @ 17.18, 1 hundred; 937 wickets @ 26.31; 111 ct. Appointed 1999.

PALMER, Kenneth Ernest (Southbroom SM, Devizes), b Winchester, Hants 22 Apr 1937. RHB, RFM. Brother of R. (below) and father of G.V. (above). Somerset 1955-69 (cap 1958; testimonial 1968). Tours: WI 1963-64 (Cav); P 1963-64 (Cwlth XI). **Tests**: 1 (1964-65; while coaching in South Africa); 10 runs; 1 wicket. 1000 runs (1): 1036 (1961). 100 wickets (4); most − 139 (1963). HS 125* v Northants (Northampton) 1961. BB 9-57 v Notts (Nottingham) 1963. F-c career: 314 matches; 7761 runs @ 20.64, 2 hundreds; 866 wickets @ 21.34. Appointed 1972. Umpired 22 Tests (1978 to 1994) and 20 LOI (1977 to 1998). International Panel 1994.

PALMER, Roy (Southbroom SM, Devizes), b Devizes, Wilts 12 Jul 1942. RHB, RFM. Brother of K.E. (above). Somerset 1965-70. HS 84 v Leics (Taunton) 1967. BB 6-45 v Middx (Lord's) 1967. F-c career: 74 matches; 1037 runs @ 13.29; 172 wickets @ 31.62. Appointed 1980. Umpired 2 Tests (1992 to 1993) and 8 LOI (1983 to 1995).

PLEWS, Nigel Trevor (Mundella GS, Nottingham), b Nottingham 5 Sep 1934. Former policeman (Fraud Squad). No first-class appearances. Appointed 1982. Umpired 11 Tests (1988 to 1995-96) and 16 LOI (1986 to 1996), including 2 Sharjah tournaments. International Panel 1994 to 1995-96.

SHARP, George (Elwick Road SS, Hartlepool), b West Hartlepool, Co Durham 12 Mar 1950. RHB, WK, occ LM. Northamptonshire 1968-85 (cap 1973; benefit 1982). HS 98 v Yorks (Northampton) 1983. BB 1-47. F-c career: 306 matches; 6254 runs @ 19.85; 1 wicket @ 70.00; 655 dismissals (565 ct, 90 st). Appointed 1992. Umpired 7 Tests (1996 to 1998) and 12 LOI (1995-96 to 1998), including tournaments in Sharjah (1) and Singapore (1). **Appointed to International Panel 1996.**

SHEPHERD, David Robert (Barnstaple GS; St Luke's C, Exeter), b Bideford, Devon 27 Dec 1940. RHB, RM. Gloucestershire 1965-79 (cap 1969); joint benefit with J.Davey 1978). Scored 108 on debut (v OU). Devon 1959-64. 1000 runs (2); most – 1079 (1970). HS 153 v Middx (Bristol) 1968. F-c career: 282 matches; 10672 runs @ 24.47, 12 hundreds; 2 wickets @ 53.00. Appointed 1981. Umpired 42 Tests (1985 to 1998) and 71 LOI (1983 to 1998), including 1987-88, 1991-92 and 1995-96 World Cups (1 final), 1985-86 Asia Cup and tournaments in Sharjah (5) and Canada (1). **Appointed to International Panel 1994.**

STEELE, John Frederick (Endon SS), b Brown Edge, Staffs 23 Jul 1946. RHB, SLA. Brother of D.S. (Northants, Derbys and England 1963-84). Leicestershire 1970-83 (cap 1971; benefit 1983). Glamorgan 1984-86 (cap 1984). Natal 1973-78. Staffordshire 1965-74. Tour: SA 1974-75 (DHR). 1000 runs (6); most – 1347 (1972). HS 195 Le v Derbys (Leicester) 1971. BB 7-29 Natal B v GW (Umzinto) 1973-74, and Le v Glos (Leicester) 1980. F-c career: 379 matches; 15054 runs @ 28.95, 21 hundreds; 584 wickets @ 27.04. Appointed 1997.

WHITE, Robert Arthur (Chiswick GS), b Fulham, London 6 Oct 1936. LHB, OB. Middlesex 1958-65 (cap 1963). Nottinghamshire 1966-80 (cap 1966; benefit 1974). 1000 runs (1): 1355 (1963). HS 116* Nt v Surrey (Oval) 1967. BB 7-41 Nt v Derbys (Ilkeston) 1971. F-c career: 413 matches; 12452 runs @ 23.18, 5 hundreds; 693 wickets @ 30.50. Appointed 1983.

WHITEHEAD, Alan Geoffrey Thomas, b Butleigh, Somerset 28 Oct 1940. LHB, SLA. Somerset 1957-61. HS 15 v Hants (Southampton) 1959 and v Leics (Leicester) 1960. BB 6-74 v Sussex (Eastbourne) 1959. F-c career: 38 matches; 137 runs @ 5.70; 67 wickets @ 34.41. Appointed 1970. Umpired 5 Tests (1982 to 1987) and 13 LOI (1979 to 1996).

WILLEY, Peter (Seaham SS), b Sedgefield, Co Durham 6 Dec 1949. RHB, OB. Northamptonshire 1966-83 (cap 1971; benefit 1981). Leicestershire 1984-91 (cap 1984; captain 1987). E Province 1982-85. Northumberland 1992. **Tests:** 26 (1976 to 1986); 1184 runs @ 26.90, HS 102* v WI (St John's) 1980-81; 7 wkts @ 65.14, BB 2-73 v WI (Lord's) 1980. **LOI:** 26. Tours: A 1979-80; SA 1972-73 (DHR), 1981-82 (SAB); WI 1980-81, 1985-86; I 1979-80; SL 1977-78 (DHR). 1000 runs (10); most – 1783 (1982). HS 227 Nh v Somerset (Northampton) 1976. 50 wkts (3); most – 52 (1979). BB 7-37 Nh v OU (Oxford) 1975. F-c career: 559 matches; 24361 runs @ 30.56, 44 hundreds; 756 wickets @ 30.95. Appointed 1993. Umpired 11 Tests (1995-96 to 1998) and 5 LOI (1996 to 1998). **Appointed to International Panel 1996.**

RESERVE FIRST-CLASS LIST: P.Adams, M.R.Benson, P.Carrick, N.G.Cowley, J.H.Evans, K.J.Lyons, M.K.Reed, K.Shuttleworth.

CURRENT INTERNATIONAL PANEL: M.J.Kitchen, G.Sharp, D.R.Shepherd, P.Willey (England); D.B.Hair, D.J.Harper (Australia); V.K.Ramaswamy, S.Venkataraghavan (India); D.B.Cowie, R.S.Dunne (New Zealand); Javed Akhtar, Salim Badar (Pakistan); R.E.Koertzen, D.L.Orchard (South Africa); K.T.Francis, P.Manuel (Sri Lanka); S.A.Bucknor, E.A.Nicholls (West Indies); I.D.Robinson, R.B.Tiffin (Zimbabwe).

Test Match and LOI statistics to 25 September 1998. See page 14 for key to abbreviations.

THE 1998 FIRST-CLASS SEASON STATISTICAL HIGHLIGHTS

HIGHEST INNINGS TOTALS (* *Second innings*)
712*	Northamptonshire v Glamorgan	Northampton
627-6d	Worcestershire v Middlesex	Uxbridge
608-6d	Northamptonshire v Derbyshire	Northampton
593	Derbyshire v Sussex	Horsham
591	Surrey v Hampshire	Southampton
591	Sri Lanka v England	The Oval
585-6d	Leicestershire v Surrey	The Oval
580-9d*	Kent v Yorkshire	Maidstone
564	Gloucestershire v Essex	Colchester
563	Glamorgan v Northamptonshire	Northampton
552-5d	South Africa v England (3rd Test)	Manchester
544	Warwickshire v Worcestershire	Worcester
517*	Kent v Lancashire	Canterbury
509	Sri Lankans v Leicestershire	Leicester
505-6d	Leicestershire v Nottinghamshire	Worksop
502-7d	Surrey v Worcestershire	The Oval

LOWEST INNINGS TOTALS († *One man absent/retired hurt*)
54	Sri Lankans v Glamorgan	Cardiff
61	Nottinghamshire v Leicestershire	Worksop
65	Essex v Derbyshire	Derby
70	Derbyshire v Essex	Derby
72	Sussex v Northamptonshire	Northampton
72	Middlesex v Gloucestershire	Lord's
74	Durham v Yorkshire	Chester-le-Street
74	Somerset v Leicestershire	Leicester
77	Northamptonshire v Worcestershire	Worcester
80†	Hampshire v Warwickshire	Birmingham
84†	Warwickshire v Yorkshire	Leeds
86	Kent v Surrey	The Oval
86	Kent v Somerset	Canterbury
88	Gloucestershire v Middlesex	Lord's
89	Gloucestershire v Glamorgan	Bristol
90	Middlesex v Sussex	Hove
91	Durham v Surrey	Chester-le-Street
93	Somerset v Glamorgan	Cardiff
94	Worcestershire v Yorkshire	Worcester
95	Northamptonshire v Gloucestershire	Bristol
95	Essex v Leicestershire	Leicester
95†	Essex v Northamptonshire	Chelmsford
98	Derbyshire v Warwickshire	Derby

TEN BOWLERS IN AN INNINGS
Sri Lankans v Hampshire   Southampton

FIRST TO INDIVIDUAL TARGETS
1000 RUNS	J.L.Langer	Middlesex	27 June
2000 RUNS	–		
100 WICKETS	A.R.Caddick	Somerset	11 September

DOUBLE HUNDREDS (19)
R.P.Arnold   209   Sri Lankans v Somerset   Taunton

J.P.Crawley		239	Lancashire v Hampshire	Manchester
D.J.Cullinan		200*	South Africans v Durham	Chester-le-Street
D.P.Fulton		207	Kent v Yorkshire	Maidstone
M.W.Gatting		241	Middlesex v Essex	Southgate
T.H.C.Hancock		220*	Gloucestershire v Nottinghamshire	Nottingham
C.L.Hooper		203	Kent v Lancashire	Canterbury
S.P.James		227	Glamorgan v Northamptonshire	Northampton
S.T.Jayasuriya		213	Sri Lanka v England	The Oval
G.Kirsten	(2)	205*	South Africans v British Universities	Cambridge
		210	South Africa v England (3rd Test) *(Consecutive innings)*	Manchester
J.L.Langer		233*	Middlesex v Somerset	Lord's
B.C.Lara		226	Warwickshire v Middlesex	Lord's
D.S.Lehmann		200	Yorkshire v Worcestershire	Worcester
G.D.Lloyd		212*	Lancashire v Derbyshire	Manchester
M.B.Loye		322*	Northamptonshire v Glamorgan	Northampton
D.Ripley		209	Northamptonshire v Glamorgan	Northampton
B.F.Smith		204	Leicestershire v Surrey	The Oval
M.J.Wood		200*	Yorkshire v Warwickshire	Leeds

HUNDREDS IN FOUR CONSECUTIVE INNINGS
G.A.Hick (Worcestershire): 166 v Middlesex; 104 and 132 v Sussex; 119 v Surrey.

HUNDREDS IN THREE CONSECUTIVE INNINGS
J.P.Crawley (Lancashire): 108 v Worcestershire; 124 and 136 v Glamorgan.

HUNDRED IN EACH INNINGS OF A MATCH (5)
C.J.Adams	135	105	Sussex v Essex	Chelmsford
J.P.Crawley	124	136	Lancashire v Glamorgan	Colwyn Bay
G.A.Hick†	104	132	Worcestershire v Sussex	Worcester
G.Kirsten	125	131*	South Africans v Gloucestershire	Bristol
M.R.Ramprakash	122	108	Middlesex v Worcestershire	Uxbridge

†*His 99th and 100th first-class hundreds*

FASTEST HUNDRED (EDS WALTER LAWRENCE TROPHY)
| A.D.Brown | 72 balls | Surrey v Northamptonshire | The Oval |
| C.L.Hooper | 72 balls | Kent v Worcestershire | Canterbury |

HUNDRED BEFORE LUNCH
		Day		
V.S.Solanki	11*-119*	3	Worcestershire v Derbyshire	Derby
Wasim Akram	28*-150*	3	Lancashire v Nottinghamshire	Nottingham

HUNDRED ON FIRST-CLASS DEBUT IN BRITAIN
R.P.Arnold	209	Sri Lankans v Somerset	Taunton
M.J.Di Venuto	138	Australia A v Scotland	Edinburgh
D.F.Hills	118	Australia A v Scotland	Edinburgh

CARRYING BAT THROUGH COMPLETED INNINGS († *One man absent*)
M.A.Butcher		109*	Surrey (245) v Somerset	Taunton
J.E.R.Gallian		113*	Nottinghamshire (243†) v Hampshire	Portsmouth
N.V.Knight	(2)	67*	Warwickshire (129) v Somerset	Taunton
		130*	Warwickshire (297†) v Yorkshire	Leeds
J.J.B.Lewis		70*	Durham (158†) v Lancashire	Chester-le-Street
M.J.Powell		70*	Warwickshire (130) v Nottinghamshire	Birmingham
W.P.C.Weston		91*	Worcestershire (212) v Northamptonshire	Worcester

SCORING 30 RUNS OFF AN OVER
| 34 | A.Flintoff | Lancashire v Surrey | Manchester |

Hit 6 (nb), 4, 4, 4 (nb), 6, 6, 0 off A.J.Tudor – 38 runs including penalties

FIRST-WICKET PARTNERSHIP OF 100 IN EACH INNINGS
137	G.Kirsten/G.F.J.Liebenberg	South Africans v British U	Cambridge
141*	G.F.J.Liebenberg/D.J.Cullinan		

OTHER NOTABLE PARTNERSHIPS († *County record*)
First Wicket
372†	M.W.Gatting/J.L.Langer	Middlesex v Essex	Southgate
272	M.J.Powell/N.V.Knight	Warwickshire v Sussex	Hove

Second Wicket
296	R.J.Bailey/M.B.Loye	Northamptonshire v Derbyshire	Northampton
276*	J.L.Langer/M.R.Ramprakash	Middlesex v Glamorgan	Lord's
261	J.P.Crawley/N.H.Fairbrother	Lancashire v Hampshire	Manchester
257*	G.Kirsten/J.H.Kallis	South Africans v British U	Cambridge

Fourth Wicket
254	K.J.Barnett/M.E.Cassar	Derbyshire v Sussex	Horsham

Fifth Wicket
401†	M.B.Loye/D.Ripley	Northamptonshire v Glamorgan	Northampton
322†	B.F.Smith/P.V.Simmons	Leicestershire v Nottinghamshire	Worksop
252	B.F.Smith/A.Habib	Leicestershire v Surrey	The Oval
229	M.R.Ramprakash/P.N.Weekes	Middlesex v Leicestershire	Leicester

Sixth Wicket
193†	D.C.Boon/P.D.Collingwood	Durham v Warwickshire	Birmingham

Seventh Wicket
110†	P.D.Collingwood/M.J.Foster	Durham v Nottinghamshire	Nottingham

Tenth Wicket
123	D.W.Headley/M.M.Patel	Kent v Hampshire	Canterbury
109	D.J.Millns/M.T.Brimson	Leicestershire v Warwickshire	Birmingham
102	M.J.Foster/S.J.Harmison	Durham v Kent	Canterbury
102	A.P.Cowan/P.M.Such	Essex v Leicestershire	Leicester

EIGHT OR MORE WICKETS IN AN INNINGS (4)
A.R.Caddick		8-64	Somerset v Nottinghamshire	Taunton
M.Muralitharan		9-65	Sri Lanka v England	The Oval
Saqlain Mushtaq		8-65	Surrey v Derbyshire	The Oval
C.White		8-55	Yorkshire v Gloucestershire	Gloucester

TEN OR MORE WICKETS IN A MATCH (21)
J.F.Brown		11-102	Northamptonshire v Somerset	Taunton
A.R.Caddick	(3)	10-165	Somerset v Durham	Taunton
		11-111	Somerset v Worcestershire	Taunton
		10-101	Somerset v Kent	Canterbury
K.J.Dean		12-133	Derbyshire v Somerset	Taunton
A.R.C.Fraser		10-122	England v South Africa (4th Test)	Nottingham
E.S.H.Giddins		11-164	Warwickshire v Gloucestershire	Bristol
G.M.Hamilton	(2)	10-112	Yorkshire v Glamorgan	Cardiff
		11- 72	Yorkshire v Surrey	Leeds
R.J.Kirtley		10- 88	Sussex v Nottinghamshire	Nottingham
D.P.Mather		10-139	Oxford U v Cambridge U	Lord's
A.D.Mullally		11- 89	Leicestershire v Nottinghamshire	Worksop
M.Muralitharan	(2)	10- 94	Sri Lankans v Glamorgan	Cardiff
		16-220	Sri Lanka v England	The Oval
M.J.Rawnsley		11-116	Worcestershire v Oxford University	Oxford
F.A.Rose		11- 90	Northamptonshire v Worcestershire	Worcester
Saqlain Mushtaq	(3)	11-157	Surrey v Worcestershire	The Oval
		11-104	Surrey v Sussex	The Oval
		11-107	Surrey v Derbyshire	The Oval

C.A.Walsh		(2)	12-153	Gloucestershire v Warwickshire		Bristol
			10- 86	Gloucestershire v Northamptonshire		Bristol

HAT-TRICKS (4)
K.J.Dean		Derbyshire v Kent	Derby
D.R.Law		Essex v Durham	Chester-le-Street
J.D.Lewry		Sussex v Gloucestershire	Cheltenham
C.White		Yorkshire v Gloucestershire	Gloucester

OUTSTANDING INNINGS ANALYSIS
M.T.Brimson	8-6-4-4	Leicestershire v Glamorgan	Cardiff

60 OVERS IN AN INNINGS
R.D.Stemp	71-27-191-5	Yorkshire v Kent	Maidstone
Saqlain Mushtaq	60-17-116-4	Surrey v Worcestershire	The Oval

100 OVERS IN A MATCH
M.Muralitharan	113.5-41-220-16	Sri Lanka v England	The Oval

MATCH DOUBLE (100 RUNS AND 10 WICKETS)
G.M.Hamilton	79, 70; 5-69, 5-43	Yorkshire v Glamorgan	Cardiff

SIX OR MORE WICKET-KEEPING DISMISSALS IN AN INNINGS
W.K.Hegg	6 ct	Lancashire v Worcestershire	Lytham
B.J.Hyam	6 ct	Essex v Yorkshire	Scarborough
K.J.Piper	6 ct	Warwickshire v Sussex	Hove

NO BYES CONCEDED IN TOTAL OF 500 OR MORE
585-6d	A.J.Stewart	Surrey v Leicestershire	The Oval
505-6d	C.M.W.Read	Nottinghamshire v Leicestershire	Worksop

FIVE OR MORE CATCHES IN AN INNINGS IN THE FIELD
6	G.P.Thorpe	Surrey v Kent	The Oval

SEVEN OR MORE CATCHES IN A MATCH IN THE FIELD
7	G.P.Thorpe	Surrey v Kent	The Oval

SIXTY EXTRAS IN AN INNINGS
	B	LB	W	NB		
69	3	8	–	58	Durham (286) v South Africans	Chester-le-Street
69	15	18	2	34	Middlesex (437) v Hampshire	Southampton
65	4	22	5	34	Leicestershire (362) v Sri Lankans	Leicester
63	12	8	2	41	Durham (253-3d) v Surrey	Chester-le-Street
62	1	23	4	34	Northamptonshire (365) v Leicestershire	Leicester
61	8	27	4	22	Oxford University (269-9d) v Warwickshire	Oxford
61	15	13	15	18	Durham (396) v Glamorgan	Chester-le-Street
60	2	15	21	22	Sussex (245) v Hampshire	Hove

Under ECB regulations (Test matches excluded), two extras were scored for each no-ball, in addition to any runs scored off that ball, and two extras were also scored for each wide. There were a further 21 instances of 50-59 extras in an innings. The match between Hampshire and Middlesex at Southampton produced 195 extras: 45 byes, 33 leg-byes, 37 wides and 80 no-balls.

1998 FIRST-CLASS AVERAGES

These averages involve the 472 cricketers who played in the 188 first-class matches staged in the British Isles during the 1998 season.

'Cap' denotes the season in which the player was awarded a 1st XI cap by the county he represented in 1998. Durham, who formerly had awarded caps immediately their players joined the staff, revised their policy and capped 10 players on merit, past 'awards' being nullified.

Team abbreviations: AA – Australia A; BU – British Universities; CU – Cambridge University; De – Derbyshire; Du – Durham; E – England; Ex – Essex; Gm – Glamorgan; Gs – Gloucestershire; H – Hampshire; Ire – Ireland; K – Kent; La – Lancashire; Le – Leicestershire; M – Middlesex; Nh – Northamptonshire; Nt – Nottinghamshire; OU – Oxford University; SA – South Africa(ns); Sc – Scotland; SL – Sri Lanka(ns); Sm – Somerset; Sy – Surrey; Sx – Sussex; Wa – Warwickshire; Wo – Worcestershire; Y – Yorkshire.

† Left-handed batsman.

BATTING AND FIELDING

	Cap	M	I	NO	HS	Runs	Avge	100	50	Ct/St
Adams, C.J.(Sx)	1998	18	29	2	170	1174	41.92	4	4	30
Adams, P.R.(SA)	–	7	6	2	27	60	15.00	–	–	–
†Afzaal, U.(Nt)	–	17	30	3	109*	686	25.40	2	4	7
Aldred, P.(De)	–	7	9	3	37*	95	15.83	–	–	6
Alleyne, M.W.(Gs)	1990	18	33	2	137	1189	38.35	3	6	24
Allingham, M.J.D.(Sc)	–	2	3	–	45	88	29.33	–	–	1
Altree, D.A.(Wa)	–	1	2	1	2*	2	2.00	–	–	–
Amin, R.M.(Sy)	–	3	4	2	12	14	7.00	–	–	–
Archer, G.F.(Nt)	1995	13	23	–	107	647	28.13	1	5	23
†Arnold, R.P.(SL)	–	5	9	1	209	312	39.00	1	–	1
Asim Butt (Sc)	–	2	2	1	20*	29	29.00	–	–	–
Atapattu, M.S.(SL)	–	4	7	1	114	316	52.66	1	2	1
Atherton, M.A.(La/E)	1989	13	24	2	152	874	39.72	2	3	9
†Austin, I.D.(La)	1990	13	17	4	64	304	23.38	–	2	7
Averis, J.M.M.(Gs)	–	1	2	1	6*	6	6.00	–	–	–
Aymes, A.N.(H)	1991	18	27	6	133	754	35.90	2	3	53/2
Bacher, A.M.(SA)	–	2	2	1	43*	65	65.00	–	–	2
Bailey, R.J.(Nh)	1985	16	24	2	188	759	34.50	1	2	10
Bailey, T.M.B.(Nh/BU)	–	2	2	–	12	15	7.50	–	–	2
Ball, M.C.J.(Gs)	1996	18	30	5	67*	592	23.68	–	3	22
Bandaratilake, M.R.C.N.(SL)	–	2	1	–	11	11	11.00	–	–	–
Barnes, J.P.B.(OU)	–	5	6	3	38*	74	24.66	–	–	8
Barnett, K.J.(De)	1982	17	32	6	162	1229	47.26	1	7	8
Bates, J.J.(Sx)	–	4	7	–	38	54	7.71	–	–	4
Bates, R.T.(Nt)	–	2	4	–	17	34	8.50	–	–	–
Batson, N.E.(Wo)	–	3	6	–	18	50	8.33	–	–	–
†Batt, C.J.(M)	–	9	14	2	43	150	12.50	–	–	1
Batty, J.N.(Sy)	–	16	19	2	63	351	20.64	–	2	39/6
Benjamin, J.E.(Sy)	1993	8	13	–	18*	57	9.50	–	–	1
Betts, M.M.(Du)	1998	12	18	7	29*	135	12.27	–	–	3
†Bevan, M.G.(Sx)	1998	12	19	2	149*	935	55.00	3	4	10
Bichel, A.J.(AA)	–	1	2	2	4*	4	–	–	–	–
Bicknell, M.P.(Sy)	1989	17	21	1	81	433	21.65	–	1	5
Birks, M.J.(CU)	–	6	7	1	13	38	6.33	–	–	5/2
†Blackwell, I.D.(De)	–	11	18	–	57	254	14.11	–	2	6
Blain, J.A.R.(Nh)	–	1	–	–	–	–	–	–	–	–
Blakey, R.J.(Y)	1987	17	23	2	67*	448	21.33	–	3	69/2
Blanchett, I.N.(M)	–	4	4	–	18	25	6.25	–	–	1

117

	Cap	M	I	NO	HS	Runs	Avge	100	50	Ct/St
Bloomfield, T.F.(M)	–	8	10	5	20*	37	7.40	–	–	–
Boon, D.C.(Du)	1998	16	29	4	139*	1024	40.96	3	5	12
Boswell, S.A.J.(Nh)	–	1	–	–	–	–	–	–	–	–
Boucher, M.V.(SA)	–	11	10	1	46	211	23.44	–	–	43/1
Bowen, M.N.(Nt)	1997	10	13	5	32	142	17.75	–	–	2
Bowler, P.D.(Sm)	1995	18	32	2	104	789	26.30	2	3	18
Brimson, M.T.(Le)	1998	18	14	6	54*	115	14.37	–	1	3
Brinkley, J.E.(Sc)	–	1	1	–	0	0	0.00	–	–	–
Brown, A.D.(Sy)	1994	15	22	1	155	1036	49.33	4	6	20
Brown, D.R.(Wa)	1995	16	27	4	81*	691	30.04	–	5	9
Brown, J.F.(Nh)	–	8	11	5	6*	18	3.00	–	–	1
Brown, K.R.(M)	1990	17	25	6	59*	576	30.31	–	2	41/5
Brown, S.J.E.(Du)	1998	1	–	–	–	–	–	–	–	–
Buchanan, L.G.(OU)	–	2	1	–	2	2	2.00	–	–	1
†Bulbeck, M.P.L.(Sm)	–	8	11	6	35	141	28.20	–	–	2
Burns, M.(Sm)	–	10	17	–	96	450	26.47	–	3	16/1
‡Bushe, J.A.(Ire)	–	1	2	1	4*	6	6.00	–	–	3/1
Butcher, A.R.(Sy)	1975	2	2	–	22	34	17.00	–	–	–
Butcher, G.P.(Gm)	–	9	14	2	85	311	25.91	–	2	5
†Butcher, M.A.(Sy/E)	1996	16	26	1	116	1024	40.96	3	6	11
†Byas, D.(Y)	1991	18	28	1	116	842	31.18	4	3	20
Byrne, B.W.(OU)	–	8	12	4	69*	256	32.00	–	1	4
Caddick, A.R.(Sm)	1992	17	25	8	37	322	18.94	–	–	5
Campbell, R.J.(AA)	–	3	5	–	53	136	27.20	–	1	11/1
Capel, D.J.(Nh)	1986	2	–	–	–	–	–	–	–	–
†Carpenter, J.R.(Sx)	–	9	16	–	65	222	13.87	–	1	3
Cassar, M.E.(De)	–	17	31	5	121	708	27.23	1	5	4
Catterall, D.N.(Wo)	–	1	1	–	0	0	0.00	–	–	–
Chandana, U.D.U.(SL)	–	2	4	1	34	78	26.00	–	–	–
Chapman, C.A.(Y)	–	2	2	1	20	27	27.00	–	–	5
Chapman, R.J.(Wo)	–	11	16	8	43*	102	12.75	–	–	2
Chapman, S.(Du)	–	1	2	–	11	13	6.50	–	–	–
Chapple, G.(La)	1994	14	18	3	69	282	18.80	–	1	7
†Cherry, D.D.(Gm)	–	1	1	–	11	11	11.00	–	–	–
Chilton, M.J.(La/BU)	–	3	6	–	47	158	26.33	–	–	–
Church, M.J.(Gs)	–	4	7	–	30	85	12.14	–	–	5
Clarke, V.P.(De)	–	4	7	–	26	67	9.57	–	–	4
Claughton, J.A.(OU)	–	5	8	1	45	140	20.00	–	–	1
Clough, G.D.(Y)	–	1	2	–	33	34	17.00	–	–	1
Cockcroft, J.R.(OU)	–	2	1	1	18*	18	–	–	–	–
Collingwood, P.D.(Du)	1998	19	33	6	105	833	30.85	1	5	16
Collins, B.J.(CU)	–	3	5	–	36	79	15.80	–	–	5
Connor, C.A.(H)	1988	4	1	1	0*	0	–	–	–	–
Cooke, G.(Ire)	–	1	2	–	12	17	8.50	–	–	–
Cork, D.G.(De/E)	1993	16	27	4	102*	506	22.00	1	3	11
Cosker, D.A.(Gm)	–	15	21	3	37	123	6.83	–	–	11
Cottey, P.A.(Gm)	1992	19	32	3	123	1012	34.89	2	5	20
Cousins, D.M.(Ex)	–	1	2	–	8	14	7.00	–	–	–
Cowan, A.P.(Ex)	1997	8	13	–	94	228	17.53	–	2	4
Crawley, J.P.(La/E)	1994	18	28	3	239	1851	74.04	8	5	7
Croft, R.D.B.(Gm/E)	1992	13	22	7	63*	343	22.86	–	1	9
Cronje, W.J.(SA)	–	11	12	2	195	704	70.40	2	4	6
Crowe, C.D.(Le)	–	6	6	1	29*	88	17.60	–	–	3
Cullinan, D.J.(SA)	–	12	17	4	200*	900	69.23	2	6	9
Cunliffe, R.J.(Gs)	–	12	22	–	53	339	15.40	–	2	14
Curran, K.M.(Nh)	1992	18	26	4	90*	709	32.22	–	6	23
†Dakin, J.M. (Le)	–	6	6	–	79	128	21.33	–	1	2

118

	Cap	M	I	NO	HS	Runs	Avge	100	50	Ct/St
Dale, A.(Gm)	1992	19	33	1	92	1028	32.12	–	9	7
†Dale, A.C.(AA)	–	3	2	2	9*	12	–	–	–	–
Daley, J.A.(Du)	–	12	22	2	157	634	31.70	1	1	5
Davies, A.G.(Sc)	–	2	2	–	14	15	7.50	–	–	2
†Davies, A.P.(Gm)	–	5	6	1	34	55	11.00	–	–	1
Davies, M.K.(Nh/BU)	–	2	3	1	16	23	11.50	–	–	–
Dawood, I.(Gm)	–	7	12	1	40	194	17.63	–	–	19/1
Dawson, R.I.(Gs)	–	8	15	2	46	177	13.61	–	–	3
†Dean, K.J.(De)	1998	15	21	13	27*	154	19.25	–	–	1
DeFreitas, P.A.J.(De)	1994	14	23	3	87	435	21.75	–	2	6
De la Pena, J.M.(K)	–	2	1	1	0*	0	–	–	–	–
De Silva, P.A.(SL)	–	2	2	–	152	153	76.50	1	–	1
Dharmasena, H.D.P.K.(SL)	–	3	4	1	45*	68	22.66	–	–	3
Di Venuto, M.J.(AA)	–	3	4	–	138	213	53.25	1	1	2
Donald, A.A.(SA)	–	7	6	3	7*	29	9.66	–	–	1
†Dowman, M.P.(Nt)	1998	13	24	1	63	451	19.60	–	2	7
Driver, R.C.(Wo)	–	1	2	–	5	5	2.50	–	–	–
Dunlop, A.R.(Ire)	–	1	2	–	10	14	7.00	–	–	–
Dutch, K.P.(M)	–	4	5	–	16	41	8.20	–	–	3
†Dwyer, M.D.(Ire)	–	2	2	1	1*	1	1.00	–	–	–
Dyer, N.R.(Sc)	–	1	–	–	–	–	–	–	–	–
Eadie, D.J.(OU)	–	6	6	2	68*	84	21.00	–	1	2
Ealham, M.A.(K/E)	1992	12	22	3	121	461	24.26	1	2	2
†Ecclestone, S.C.(Sm)	1997	5	7	–	94	186	26.57	–	1	4
Edmond, M.D.(Wa)	–	3	5	1	32	64	16.00	–	–	–
Edwards, A.D.(Sx)	–	4	7	–	10	30	4.28	–	–	3
Ellis, S.W.K.(Wo)	–	2	2	1	0*	0	0.00	–	–	1
Elworthy, S.(SA)	–	5	2	–	48	58	29.00	–	–	2
Evans, A.W.(Gm)	–	8	14	1	125	386	29.69	1	1	7
Evans, K.P.(Nt)	1990	9	13	–	36	129	9.92	–	–	3
†Fairbrother, N.H.(La)	1985	12	17	2	138	759	50.60	3	3	11
Fellows, G.M.(Y)	–	1	2	–	18	21	10.50	–	–	–
Ferguson, S.H.(OU)	–	1	1	–	2	2	2.00	–	–	1
Fisher, I.D.(Y)	–	1	–	–	–	–	–	–	–	–
†Flanagan, I.N.(Ex)	–	6	11	–	61	254	23.09	–	2	9
Fleming, M.V.(K)	1990	17	30	4	51	612	23.53	–	1	9
Flintoff, A.(La/E)	1998	17	25	–	124	608	24.32	1	3	23
Follett, D.(Nh)	–	5	7	1	7	13	2.16	–	–	2
Foster, M.J.(Du)	–	8	13	1	76*	321	26.75	–	2	2
Francis, S.R.G.(H/BU)	–	2	1	1	6*	6	–	–	–	–
†Franks, P.J.(Nt)	–	12	20	2	66*	390	21.66	–	2	6
Fraser, A.R.C.(M/E)	1988	14	19	5	32	134	9.57	–	–	1
†Frost, T.(Wa)	–	8	14	2	111*	389	32.41	1	1	22
Fulton, D.P.(K)	1998	17	31	1	207	954	31.80	1	7	21
†Fulton, J.A.G.(OU)	–	8	12	1	78	180	16.36	–	1	4
Gallian, J.E.R.(Nt)	1998	14	25	2	113*	592	26.90	1	3	8
Garaway, M.(H)	–	1	1	–	19	19	19.00	–	–	–
Garland, R.(OU)	–	8	9	1	56*	158	31.60	–	1	1
Gatting, M.W.(M)	1977	17	29	3	241	1139	43.80	2	7	19
Giddins, E.S.H.(Wa)	1998	18	23	8	11*	43	2.86	–	–	4
Gie, N.A.(Nt)	–	4	8	–	50	128	16.00	–	1	3
Giles, A.F.(Wa/E)	–	14	21	5	83	489	30.56	–	3	7
Gillespie, J.N.(AA)	–	2	–	–	–	–	–	–	–	–
Goodchild, D.J.(M)	–	7	14	1	105	324	24.92	1	2	1
†Gough, D.(Y/E)	1993	11	15	1	89	269	19.21	–	2	1
Gough, M.A.(Du)	–	10	18	–	123	508	28.22	1	2	12
Grayson, A.P.(Ex)	1996	17	31	–	59	509	16.41	–	4	9

	Cap	M	I	NO	HS	Runs	Avge	100	50	Ct/St
Green, R.J.(La)	–	6	3	1	14	14	7.00	–	–	1
Griffiths, S.P.(De)	–	1	2	–	12	15	7.50	–	–	5
Grove, J.O.(Ex)	–	4	7	1	33	88	14.66	–	–	–
Habib, A.(Le)	1998	19	22	5	198	952	56.00	3	3	12
Hafeez, A.(Wo)	–	10	18	1	55	303	17.82	–	1	6
†Hamilton, G.M.(Y)	1998	15	19	1	79	578	32.11	–	6	3
Hancock, T.H.C.(Gs)	1998	18	34	2	220*	1227	38.34	2	7	16
Harden, R.J.(Sm)	1989	12	21	2	63	301	15.84	–	2	15
Harmison, S.J.(Du)	–	14	22	4	36	223	12.38	–	–	4
Harris, A.J.(De)	1996	2	3	–	5	9	3.00	–	–	1
Hartley, P.J.(H)	1998	13	16	3	29	160	12.30	–	–	3
Harvey, M.E.(La)	–	1	2	1	0*	0	0.00	–	–	–
Hathurusinghe, U.C.(SL)	–	5	8	3	108*	255	51.00	1	1	4
†Hayden, M.L.(AA)	–	3	3	–	123	241	80.33	1	2	3
Haynes, G.R.(Wo)	1994	12	21	5	86	532	33.25	–	4	2
Hayward, M.(SA)	–	6	4	3	1	46	50	50.00	–	3
Headley, D.W.(K/E)	1993	14	21	5	81	265	16.56	–	1	5
Hegg, W.K.(La)	1989	15	21	4	85	628	36.94	–	6	34/3
Hemp, D.L.(Wa)	1997	15	26	1	102	646	25.84	1	4	16
†Hewitt, J.P.(M)	1998	15	19	2	53	268	15.76	–	1	5
Hewson, D.R.(Gs)	–	12	22	3	78*	447	23.52	–	3	4
Hibbert, A.J.E.(Ex)	–	3	5	–	47	85	17.00	–	–	2
Hick, G.A.(Wo/E)	1986	17	30	–	166	1304	43.46	7	2	24
Hills, D.F.(AA)	–	3	5	1	118	264	66.00	2	–	3
Hockley, J.B.(K)	–	1	2	–	21	30	15.00	–	–	–
Hodgson, T.P.(Ex)	–	7	13	–	54	236	18.15	–	1	4
Hoggard, M.J.(Y)	–	9	10	3	13*	35	5.00	–	–	3
Holloioake, A.J.(Sy)	1995	15	22	2	112	684	34.20	1	4	15
Hollioake, B.C.(Sy/E)	–	17	26	3	60	469	20.39	–	2	8
†Holloway, P.C.L.(Sm)	1997	16	28	3	123	624	24.96	1	1	7
Hooper, C.L.(K)	1992	15	28	1	203	1215	45.00	6	1	15
†House, W.J.(K/CU/BU)	–	8	11	–	65	322	29.27	–	3	3
†Hughes, Q.J.(CU)	–	6	7	–	84	217	31.00	–	1	4
Humphries, S.(Sx)	–	14	22	1	66	286	13.61	–	1	25
Hussain, N.(Ex/E)	1989	10	19	–	105	591	31.10	1	4	9
†Hussey, M.E.(AA)	–	2	2	1	125*	192	192.00	1	1	–
†Hutchison, P.M.(Y)	1998	17	16	8	30	127	15.87	–	–	4
Hutton, B.L.(BU)	–	1	1	–	10	10	10.00	–	–	–
†Hutton, S.(Du)	–	1	1	–	100	100	100.00	1	–	–
Hyam, B.J.(Ex)	–	10	19	3	47*	307	19.18	–	–	32/2
Igglesden, A.P.(K)	1989	3	4	3	4*	8	8.00	–	–	2
Illingworth, R.K.(Wo)	1986	15	21	6	84	473	31.53	–	3	5
†Ilott, M.C.(Ex)	1993	17	30	4	38	307	11.80	–	–	5
Innes, K.J.(Nh)	–	1	2	–	31	37	18.50	–	–	2
Irani, R.C.(Ex)	1994	18	33	2	127*	1001	32.29	2	6	6
†James, K.D.(H)	1989	18	26	9	57	570	33.52	–	3	6
James, S.P.(Gm/E)	1992	15	28	1	227	1339	49.59	4	5	9
Janisch, A.N.(CU)	–	4	4	2	26*	83	41.50	–	–	1
Jarvis, P.W.(Sx)	1994	5	7	1	39	110	18.33	–	–	4
†Jayasuriya, S.T.(SL)	–	5	9	1	213	382	47.75	1	–	4
Jayawardena, D.P.M.D.(SL)	–	6	10	1	90	266	29.55	–	2	7
Jayawardena, H.P.W.(SL)	–	3	3	–	25	25	8.33	–	–	8
Johnson, P.(Nt)	1986	15	26	1	139	976	39.04	2	4	14
Johnson, R.L.(M)	1995	14	21	3	43	242	13.44	–	–	5
Jones, P.S.(Sm)	–	4	5	3	22*	31	15.50	–	–	–
†Jones, S.P.(Gm)	–	3	3	3	2*	5	–	–	–	1
†Joyce, E.C.(Ire)	–	1	2	–	15	26	13.00	–	–	–

	Cap	M	I	NO	HS	Runs	Avge	100	50	Ct/St
Julian, B.P.(AA)	–	3	4	1	60*	104	34.66	–	1	2
Kallis, J.H.(SA)	–	10	14	3	132	612	55.63	3	9	
Kaluwitharana, R.S.(SL)	–	3	4	–	73	152	38.00	–	1	11/2
Keech, M.(H)	–	12	14	–	70	335	23.92	–	3	12
†Keedy, G.(La)	–	7	10	5	13	44	8.80	–	–	2
Kendall, W.S.(H)	–	8	11	3	78*	340	42.50	–	2	8
Kennis, G.J.(Sm)	–	3	6	–	49	71	11.83	–	–	5
Kenway, D.A.(H)	–	3	5	–	57	118	23.60	–	1	1
†Kettleborough, R.A.(M)	–	12	22	4	92*	512	28.44	–	3	7
Key, R.W.T.(K)	–	13	23	–	115	612	26.60	2	1	11
Khan, A.A.(Sx)	–	4	4	–	23	41	10.25	–	–	4
Khan, S.H.(OU)	–	4	2	–	1	1	0.50	–	–	–
†Khan, W.G.(Sx)	–	18	30	1	125	837	28.86	1	6	5
Killeen, N.(Du)	–	3	3	1	15*	27	13.50	–	–	3
†Kirsten, G.(SA)	–	12	19	5	210	892	63.71	4	2	8
Kirtley, R.J.(Sx)	1998	18	26	10	59	320	20.00	–	1	2
Klusener, L.(SA)	–	5	5	2	73*	207	69.00	–	2	4
†Knight, N.V.(Wa/E)	1995	15	26	2	192	1069	44.54	4	4	18
Knott, J.A.(Sy)	–	5	9	3	41*	103	17.16	–	–	1
Krikken, K.M.(De)	1992	17	27	5	83	439	19.95	–	3	36/2
Lacey, S.J.(De)	–	3	3	–	17	28	9.33	–	–	–
Lampitt, S.R.(Wo)	1989	18	28	7	48	481	22.90	–	–	8
Laney, J.S.(H)	1996	8	13	–	101	224	17.23	1	1	10
†Langer, J.L.(M)	1998	15	28	5	233*	1448	62.95	4	6	12
†Lara, B.C.(Wa)	1994	15	26	–	226	1033	39.73	3	3	15
Laraman, A.W.(M)	–	1	–	–	–	–	–	–	–	–
Lathwell, M.N.(Sm)	1992	12	19	–	106	574	30.21	1	5	7
Law, D.R.(Ex)	1996	14	25	–	65	466	18.64	–	3	10
Law, S.G.(Ex)	1996	14	26	2	165	982	40.91	2	3	19
Law, W.L.(Gm)	–	9	14	2	131	444	37.00	1	2	4
Leather, D.(BU)	–	1	1	–	0	0	0.00	–	–	–
Leatherdale, D.A.(Wo)	1994	18	32	3	137	1001	33.36.	2	4	9
†Lehmann, D.S.(Y)	1997	10	16	–	200	969	60.56	3	4	4
Lewis, C.C.(Le)	1990	13	14	3	71*	367	33.36	–	4	10
Lewis, J.(Gs)	1998	18	31	2	54*	390	13.44	–	1	5
Lewis, J.J.B.(Du)	1998	15	28	1	72	622	23.03	–	4	10
Lewis, S.J.W.(CU)	–	1	2	–	3	3	1.50	–	–	–
†Lewry, J.D.(Sx)	1996	17	23	–	24	132	5.73	–	–	1
Liebenberg, G.F.J.(SA)	–	10	17	3	104*	642	45.85	1	5	11
†Lightfoot, C.G.R.(OU)	–	3	6	1	31	98	19.60	–	–	1
†Llong, N.J.(K)	1993	2	4	1	16	32	10.66	–	–	–
Lloyd, G.D.(La)	1992	15	22	1	212*	831	39.57	2	3	11
Lockhart, D.R.(OU/Sc)	–	9	15	–	46	241	16.06	–	–	7
Lockie, B.G.(Sc)	–	1	2	–	0	0	0.00	–	–	–
Loveridge, G.R.(CU/BU)	–	7	9	2	41	118	14.75	–	–	–
Lowe, J.P.(CU)	–	6	5	2	7*	13	4.33	–	–	1
Loye, M.B.(Nh)	1994	15	22	2	322*	1198	59.90	4	4	7
Lugsden, S.(Du)	–	3	5	2	8*	15	5.00	–	–	1
McCague, M.J.(K)	1992	10	15	7	38	166	20.75	–	–	8
McCallan, W.K.(Ire)	–	1	2	–	22	22	11.00	–	–	–
McGrath, A.(Y)	–	17	28	3	63*	612	24.48	–	3	5
McKeown, P.C.(La)	–	5	7	–	42	186	26.57	–	–	6
†McLean, N.A.M.(H)	1998	16	22	4	43	288	14.40	–	–	5
McMillan, B.M.(SA)	–	6	6	–	54	119	19.83	–	1	8
Macmillan, G.I.(Gs)	–	5	9	–	53	176	19.55	–	2	4
Maddy, D.L.(Le)	1996	18	26	2	162	569	23.70	2	–	17
Malcolm, D.E.(Nh)	–	14	16	5	42	114	10.36	–	–	3

121

	Cap	M	I	NO	HS	Runs	Avge	100	50	Ct/St
Marsh, S.A.(K)	1986	16	28	4	92	620	25.83	–	5	42/4
Martin, N.D.(M)	–	2	–	–	–	–	–	–	–	–
Martin, P.J.(La)	1994	14	15	5	26	154	15.40	–	–	3
Martin-Jenkins, R.S.C. (Sx)	–	8	13	1	78	353	29.41	–	2	3
Martyn, D.R.(AA)	–	2	4	2	60*	156	78.00	–	1	1
Maru, R.J.(H)	1986	2	3	1	14	27	13.50	–	–	2
Mascarenhas, A.D.(H)	1998	17	25	2	89	645	28.04	–	6	11
Mason, T.J.(Le)	–	2	–	–	–	–	–	–	–	–
†Mather, D.P.(OU)	–	7	2	–	–	–	–	–	–	4
May, M.R.(De)	–	13	24	–	101	473	19.70	1	1	4
Maynard, M.P.(Gm)	1987	17	29	2	99	776	28.74	–	5	21
Middlebrook, J.D.(Y)	–	8	12	2	41	139	13.90	–	–	7
Miller, C.R.(AA)	–	3	1	–	44	44	44.00	–	–	–
†Millns, D.J.(Le)	1991	11	10	4	99	289	48.16	–	1	4
Moffat, P.J.(CU)	–	5	6	1	12	34	6.80	–	–	–
I.Mohammed (CU)	–	6	7	1	136	237	39.50	1	–	–
Molins, J.A.M.(OU/Ire)	–	8	12	–	73	302	25.16	–	3	2
Montgomerie, R.R.(Nh)	1995	10	16	3	54	268	20.61	–	1	4
Moody, T.M.(Wo)	1991	13	23	2	132	886	42.19	4	2	10
Mooney, P.J.K.(Ire)	–	1	2	–	9	17	8.50	–	–	1
Moores, P.(Sx)	1989	3	3	2	36	56	56.00	–	–	7
†Morris, A.C.(H)	–	12	15	5	51	219	21.90	–	1	6
Morris, J.E.(Du)	1998	13	24	2	163	767	34.86	3	1	5
Morris, Z.C.(H)	–	1	2	–	10	10	5.00	–	–	–
Mullally, A.D.(Le)	1993	15	11	2	38*	132	14.66	–	–	3
Munton, T.A.(Wa)	1989	9	12	2	20	72	7.20	–	–	1
Muralitharan, M.(SL)	–	3	4	2	30	47	23.50	–	–	1
Mushtaq Ahmed (Sm)	1993	6	9	1	37	121	15.12	–	–	1
Napier, G.R.(Ex)	–	2	3	–	7	15	5.00	–	–	–
Nash, D.C.(M)	–	14	19	–	114	404	21.26	1	1	8/1
Newell, K.(Sx)	–	11	19	6	84	414	31.84	–	3	7
Newell, M.(Sx)	–	10	14	1	135*	386	29.69	2	–	6
Newport, D.P.(Wo)	1986	13	16	3	56	270	20.76	–	1	4
†Nixon, P.A.(Le)	1994	19	21	4	101*	638	37.52	2	1	41/5
Noon, W.M.(Nt)	1995	4	5	1	16*	22	5.50	–	–	9
Ntini, M.(SA)	–	7	2	1	4*	4	4.00	–	–	2
Olphert, D.M.(Ire)	–	1	2	–	1	1	0.50	–	–	–
Oram, A.R.(Nt)	–	11	19	8	13	39	3.54	–	–	–
Ormond, J.(Le)	–	6	5	–	9	15	3.00	–	–	1
Ostler, D.P.(Wa)	1991	6	10	1	133*	173	19.22	1	–	7
Parker, B.(Y)	–	8	10	2	41	180	22.50	–	–	3
Parker, C.R.C.(OU)	–	1	1	1	1*	1	–	–	–	–
Parker, J.T.(OU)	–	5	5	–	19	80	16.00	–	–	1
Parkin, O.T.(Gm)	–	11	13	4	24*	85	9.44	–	–	2
Parsons, K.A.(Sm)	–	14	23	1	101*	367	16.68	1	1	16
Patel, M.M.(K)	1994	14	20	5	58*	303	20.20	–	2	7
Patterson, B.M.W.(Sc)	–	1	2	1	17*	20	20.00	–	–	–
†Peirce, M.T.E.(Sx)	–	19	32	1	96	744	24.00	–	5	5
†Penberthy, A.L.(Nh)	1994	14	21	2	128	755	39.73	2	4	14
Penney, T.L.(Wa)	1994	9	16	2	53*	329	23.50	–	1	3
Perera, A.S.A.(SL)	–	3	3	1	43*	79	39.50	–	–	–
Peters, S.D.(Ex)	–	13	23	2	64	484	23.04	–	3	7
Philip, I.L.(Sc)	–	2	4	1	50*	83	27.66	–	1	1
Phillips, B.J.(K)	–	11	17	–	54	203	11.94	–	1	1
Phillips, N.C.(Du)	–	17	25	2	35	227	9.86	–	–	5
Pierson, A.R.K.(Sm)	–	13	20	3	108*	438	25.76	1	1	6
Pipe, D.J.(Wo)	–	1	–	–	–	–	–	–	–	2/1

	Cap	M	I	NO	HS	Runs	Avge	100	50	Ct/St
Piper, K.J.(Wa)	1992	13	23	5	44*	283	15.72	–	–	29/3
Pirihi, N.G.(OU)	–	3	5	1	23	70	17.50	–	–	1
†Pollard, P.R.(Nt)	1992	4	7	–	69	121	17.28	–	1	3
Pollock, S.M.(SA)	–	6	8	2	50	187	31.16	–	1	3
†Pooley, J.C.(M)	1995	1	–	–	–	–	–	–	–	–
Powell, M.J.(Gm)	–	16	27	3	106	840	35.00	1	5	10
Powell, M.J.(Wa)	–	13	22	1	132	511	24.33	1	3	13
Pratt, A.(Du)	–	2	3	–	34	40	13.33	–	–	4
Prichard, P.J.(Ex)	1986	10	18	–	24	237	13.16	–	–	7
Pushpakumara, K.R.(SL)	–	3	3	2	8*	15	15.00	–	–	–
Pyemont, J.P.(CU)	–	6	7	–	54	105	15.00	–	1	3
Ramprakash, M.R.(M/E)	1990	15	26	3	128*	979	42.56	4	2	10
†Ranatunga, A.(SL)	–	3	4	–	110	181	45.25	1	1	–
Rao, R.K.(Sx)	–	10	17	1	76	325	20.31	–	2	–
†Rashid, U.B.A.(M)	–	1	–	–	–	–	–	–	–	–
Ratcliffe, J.D.(Sy)	1998	9	15	1	100	449	32.07	1	2	2
Rawnsley, M.J.(Wo)	–	6	8	–	21	55	6.87	–	–	7
Read, C.M.W.(Nt)	–	13	22	6	76	401	25.06	–	2	39/3
Renshaw, S.J.(H)	–	2	1	1	10*	10	–	–	–	–
Rhodes, J.N.(SA)	–	11	14	1	123	562	43.23	2	3	4
Rhodes, S.J.(Wo)	1986	18	33	5	104*	1000	35.71	1	6	43/2
Ridgway, P.M.(La)	–	1	2	–	35	39	19.50	–	–	–
Ripley, D.(Nh)	1987	17	22	2	209	805	40.25	1	5	30/1
†Roberts, D.J.(Nh)	–	1	2	–	39	39	19.50	–	–	3
†Roberts, G.M.(De)	–	8	13	3	44	237	23.70	–	–	7
Robinson, D.D.J.(Ex)	1997	14	25	–	85	446	17.84	–	1	11
Robinson, M.A.(Sx)	1997	16	21	8	7	40	3.07	–	–	1
Robinson, R.T.(Nt)	1983	11	18	2	114	553	34.56	1	4	6
Rollins, A.S.(De)	1995	10	19	–	107	618	32.52	1	4	11
Rollins, R.J.(Ex)	1995	8	12	–	42	171	14.25	–	–	13
Rose, F.A.(Nh)	–	14	17	2	21	133	8.86	–	–	–
Rose, G.D.(Sm)	1988	17	26	2	76	606	25.25	–	4	3
Roseberry, M.A.(Du)	1998	6	11	–	97	295	26.81	–	2	2
†Russell, R.C.(Gs)	1985	16	28	2	63*	527	20.26	–	2	56
Saggers, M.J.(Du)	–	2	4	2	10	25	12.50	–	–	1
Sales, D.J.G.(Nh)	–	14	21	1	60	346	17.30	–	2	10
Salisbury, I.D.K.(Sy/E)	1998	15	18	2	61	314	19.62	–	3	8
Salmond, G.(Sc)	–	2	4	1	16	41	13.66	–	–	1
Saqlain Mushtaq (Sy)	1998	12	15	5	45*	176	17.60	–	–	7
Schaffter, P.A.(CU)	–	4	3	1	12	20	10.00	–	–	–
†Schofield, C.P.(La)	–	2	2	–	4*	5	5.00	–	–	1
†Scott, D.A.(K)	–	2	3	3	17*	22	–	–	–	–
Scrini, A.P.(OU)	–	1	–	–	–	–	–	–	–	–
Searle, J.P.(Du)	–	2	2	–	0	0	0.00	–	–	2
Shadford, D.J.(La)	–	1	1	1	13*	13	–	–	–	–
Shah, O.A.(M)	–	15	23	3	140	786	39.30	2	4	10
Shahid, N.(Sy)	1998	12	22	3	126*	683	35.94	2	3	13
Shaw, A.D.(Gm)	–	11	16	1	71	248	16.53	–	2	26
†Sheikh, M.A.(Wa)	–	2	3	–	30	56	18.66	–	–	–
Sheridan, K.L.P.(Sc)	–	1	1	1	12*	12	–	–	–	–
Sheriyar, A.(Wo)	1997	10	4	–	20	66	11.00	–	–	1
Shine, K.J.(Sm)	1997	3	5	2	18	44	14.66	–	–	–
†Sidebottom, R.J.(Y)	–	5	4	2	54	84	42.00	–	1	3
Silverwood, C.E.W.(Y)	1996	13	13	3	57*	239	23.90	–	1	2
Simmons, P.V.(Le)	1994	17	19	–	194	464	24.42	1	2	23
Singh, A.(Wa/CU/BU)	–	10	12	–	117	434	36.16	1	2	2
Slater, M.J.(De)	1998	14	24	–	185	848	35.33	1	3	9

	Cap	M	I	NO	HS	Runs	Avge	100	50	Ct/St
Smith, A.M.(Gs)	1995	18	30	13	61	384	22.58	–	2	5
Smith, B.F.(Le)	1995	19	24	4	204	1240	62.00	4	4	13
Smith, E.T.(K/CU/BU)	–	11	18	1	58	422	24.82	–	1	1
Smith, N.M.K.(Wa)	1993	18	29	5	147	1002	41.75	2	6	2
Smith, R.A.(H)	1985	17	25	2	138	853	37.08	3	2	10
†Smith, T.M.(De)	–	7	10	1	29	94	10.44	–	–	–
†Smyth, S.G.(Ire)	–	1	2	–	43	67	33.50	–	–	–
Solanki, V.S.(Wo)	1998	19	36	1	170	999	28.54	2	4	28
Speak, N.J.(Du)	1998	15	27	2	77*	658	26.32	–	6	9
Speight, M.P.(Du)	1998	17	29	4	97*	614	24.56	–	4	58/3
Spendlove, B.L.(De)	–	10	19	1	49	350	19.44	–	–	4
Stanger, I.M.(Sc)	–	2	3	1	52*	70	35.00	–	1	3
Steindl, P.D.(Sc)	–	1	1	–	14	14	14.00	–	–	–
Stemp, R.D.(Y)	1996	12	16	9	43*	133	19.00	–	–	6
Stephenson, J.P.(H)	1995	16	24	1	114	681	29.60	2	4	14
Stevens, D.I.(Le)	–	1	2	–	2	3	1.50	–	–	–
Stewart, A.J.(Sy/E)	1985	14	24	2	164	963	43.77	1	5	41
Strang, P.A.(Nt)	–	13	18	3	48	300	20.00	–	–	19
†Strauss, A.J.(M)	–	3	6	–	83	146	24.33	–	1	3
†Strong, M.R.(Sx)	–	1	1	1	2*	2	–	–	–	–
Such, P.M.(Ex)	1991	16	25	18	25	133	19.00	–	–	5
Sutcliffe, I.J.(Le)	1997	19	26	4	167	698	31.72	1	2	11
Sutton, L.D.(Sm)	–	2	4	2	16*	24	12.00	–	–	5
Swann, A.J.(Nh)	–	11	17	–	85	250	14.70	–	1	6
Swann, G.P.(Nh)	–	14	18	2	111	548	34.25	1	2	7
Symcox, P.L.(SA)	–	4	1	1	21*	21	–	–	–	2
Symington, M.J.(Du)	–	2	1	1	8*	8	–	–	–	–
Symonds, A.(AA)	–	2	3	1	33*	55	27.50	–	–	–
†Taylor, J.P.(Nh)	1992	15	20	3	58	371	21.82	–	3	5
Taylor, N.R.(Sx)	1997	6	8	1	74*	227	32.42	–	2	4
†Thomas, I.J.(Gm)	–	1	1	1	9*	9	–	–	–	–
†Thomas, S.D.(Gm)	1997	18	26	3	74	507	22.04	–	3	10
Thompson, J.B.D.(K)	–	4	6	4	65*	89	44.50	–	1	–
Thomson, K.(Sc)	–	1	1	–	22	22	22.00	–	–	–
†Thorpe, G.P.(Sy/E)	1991	9	13	1	114	314	26.16	1	1	10
†Tillekeratne, H.P.(SL)	–	6	9	1	120	317	39.62	1	1	6
Titchard, S.P.(La)	1995	1	–	–	–	–	–	–	–	–
Tolley, C.M.(Nt)	1997	11	19	2	78	374	22.00	–	2	5
Trainor, N.J.(Gs)	–	4	8	–	52	109	13.62	–	1	4
†Trescothick, M.E.(Sm)	–	18	29	2	98	847	31.37	–	6	20
Trott, B.J.(Sm)	–	1	–	–	–	–	–	–	–	–
Tudor, A.J.(Sy)	–	10	13	4	48	167	16.70	–	–	3
Tufnell, P.C.R.(M)	1990	17	22	6	24	155	9.68	–	–	2
Turner, R.J.(Sm)	1994	14	22	2	105	558	27.90	1	2	43
Tweats, T.A.(De)	–	9	18	–	161	332	18.44	1	–	8
Udal, S.D.(H)	1992	14	18	5	62	404	31.07	–	1	9
Van Troost, A.P.(Sm)	1997	5	7	1	23	61	10.16	–	–	–
Vaughan, M.P.(Y)	1995	19	31	3	177	1161	41.46	2	5	10
Villavarayen, M.S.(SL)	–	4	4	–	32	39	9.75	–	–	1
Wagh, M.A.(Wa/OU/BU)	–	14	23	2	126	686	32.66	2	3	6
†Walker, A.(Du)	–	1	2	2	3*	5	–	–	–	–
†Walker, M.J.(K)	–	8	14	1	68	341	26.23	–	2	6
Walsh, C.A.(Gs)	1985	18	23	10	25	111	8.53	–	–	4
Walsh, C.D.(K)	–	3	6	–	20	42	7.00	–	–	1
Waqar Younis (Gm)	1997	6	–	15	39	6.50	–	–	1	
†Ward, I.J.(Sy)	–	10	19	2	81*	529	31.11	–	5	9
Ward, T.R.(K)	1989	12	22	–	94	416	18.90	–	1	8

	Cap	M	I	NO	HS	Runs	Avge	100	50	Ct/St
Warren, R.J.(Nh)	1995	5	8	–	11	30	3.75	–	–	7
†Wasim Akram (La)	1989	13	18	1	155	531	31.23	1	2	8
Watkin, S.L.(Gm)	1989	13	16	13	25*	107	35.66	–	–	4
Watkinson, M.(La)	1987	10	12	1	87	318	28.90	–	2	6
Waugh, S.R.(Ire)	–	1	2	–	45	76	38.00	–	–	–
†Weekes, P.N.(M)	1993	16	26	5	139	903	43.00	1	5	20
Welch, G.(Wa)	1997	12	18	1	54	332	19.52	–	1	6
Wells, A.P.(K)	1997	15	26	1	95	684	27.36	–	5	3
Wells, V.J.(Le)	1994	17	25	2	171	836	36.34	3	3	10
Welton, G.E.(Nt)	–	5	9	–	55	152	16.88	–	1	3
Weston, R.M.S.(De)	–	9	17	–	97	537	31.58	–	4	5
†Weston, W.P.C.(Wo)	1995	17	31	3	95	829	29.60	–	5	9
Wharf, A.G.(Nt)	–	5	6	1	3	8	1.60	–	–	6
Whiley, M.J.A.(Nt)	–	1	2	1	0*	0	0.00	–	–	–
Whitaker, J.J.(Le)	1986	1	–	–	–	–	–	–	–	–
†Whitaker, P.R.(H)	–	7	11	1	74	309	30.90	–	2	7
White, C.(Y)	1993	10	15	3	104*	475	39.58	1	2	16
White, G.W.(H)	1998	19	31	2	156	1211	41.75	4	5	12
Wickremasinghe, G.P.(SL)	–	4	4	1	18	24	8.00	–	–	–
Wilkinson, R.(Y)	–	1	1	–	9	9	9.00	–	–	–
Williams, N.F.(Ex)	1996	9	16	6	36	171	17.10	–	–	2
†Williams, R.C.J.(Gs)	1996	2	3	–	67	72	24.00	–	1	3/1
Williamson, D.(Le)	–	2	3	1	41*	95	47.50	–	–	3
Williamson, J.G.(Sc)	–	1	1	–	6	6	6.00	–	–	1
Willis, S.C.(K)	–	2	2	1	58	58	58.00	–	1	3/2
Wilson, D.G.(Ex)	–	2	3	1	14*	31	15.50	–	–	–
Wilson, E.J.(Wo)	–	5	10	–	27	101	10.10	–	–	3
Wilton, N.J.(Sx)	–	2	4	2	19*	46	23.00	–	–	5
Windows, M.G.N.(Gs)	1998	16	29	2	151	1173	43.44	4	5	13
Wood, J.(Du)	1998	17	26	4	37	236	10.72	–	–	3
Wood, M.J.(Y)	–	19	29	6	200*	1080	46.95	4	4	17
†Wood, N.T.(La)	–	12	19	3	80*	457	28.56	–	2	1
Wright, A.J.(Gs)	1987	11	20	–	57	345	17.25	–	1	5
Yates, G.(La)	1994	4	6	1	55	174	34.80	–	1	2
Young, B.E.(AA)	–	3	3	1	41	63	31.50	–	–	4

BOWLING

See BATTING and FIELDING section for details of caps and teams

	Cat	O	M	R	W	Avge	Best	5wI	10wM
Adams, C.J.	RM/OB	30.5	5	109	0	–	–	–	–
Adams, P.R.	SLC	281.2	79	666	17	39.17	4- 63	–	–
Afzaal, U.	SLA	75.4	9	292	7	41.71	4-101	–	–
Aldred, P.	RM	181.4	38	556	12	46.33	3- 30	–	–
Alleyne, M.W.	RM	284.1	82	818	24	34.08	4- 63	–	–
Allingham, M.J.D.	RM	10	1	49	0	–	–	–	–
Altree, D.A.	LMF	13	4	34	0	–	–	–	–
Amin, R.M.	SLA	59	9	176	3	58.66	2- 32	–	–
Arnold, R.P.	OB	7	2	15	1	15.00	1- 4	–	–
Asim Butt	LMF	56	11	219	2	109.50	2- 57	–	–
Atapattu, M.S.	LB	1	0	4	0	–	–	–	–
Austin, I.D.	RM	345.4	80	978	36	27.16	4- 21	–	–
Averis, J.M.M.	RMF	35	0	127	2	63.50	2- 40	–	–
Aymes, A.N.	(WK)	11	0	166	2	83.00	2-135	–	–
Bailey, R.J.	OB	66	14	178	6	29.66	2- 20	–	–
Ball, M.C.J.	OB	433	108	1173	34	34.50	4- 26	–	–
Bandaratilake, M.R.C.N.	SLC	26	3	107	1	107.00	1- 53	–	–

125

	Cat	O	M	R	W	Avge	Best	5wI	10wM
Barnett, K.J.	RM/LB	54	10	148	4	37.00	2- 30	–	–
Bates, J.J.	OB	102.5	24	273	14	19.50	5- 67	2	–
Bates, R.T.	OB	21	2	98	0			–	–
Batt, C.J.	LMF	201.5	23	846	27	31.33	6-101	2	–
Batty, J.N.	(WK)	1	0	22	0			–	–
Benjamin, J.E.	RMF	189.1	42	626	22	28.45	6- 35	1	–
Betts, M.M.	RFM	363	81	1061	48	22.10	6- 83	4	–
Bevan, M.G.	SLC	175.4	27	653	19	34.36	3- 36	–	–
Bichel, A.J.	RFM	13	4	49	2	24.50	2- 49	–	–
Bicknell, M.P.	RFM	494.1	141	1340	65	20.61	5- 27	2	–
Blackwell, I.D.	SLA	156.2	32	524	14	37.42	5-115	1	–
Blanchett, I.N.	RMF	84	9	307	5	61.40	2- 38	–	–
Bloomfield, T.F.	RMF	168.5	27	660	22	30.00	5- 67	2	–
Boon, D.C.	OB	27.4	8	107	1	107.00	1- 33	–	–
Bowen, M.N.	RM	309.1	76	875	31	28.22	7- 73	1	–
Bowler, P.D.	OB	31.5	7	96	4	24.00	3- 25	–	–
Brimson, M.T.	SLA	369.5	129	901	33	27.30	4- 4	–	–
Brinkley, J.E.	RFM	30	7	100	1	100.00	1- 49	–	–
Brown, A.D.	LB	2	1	2	0			–	–
Brown, D.R.	RFM	438.2	93	1489	50	29.78	5- 40	2	–
Brown, J.F.	OB	280.2	68	726	33	22.00	6- 53	4	1
Brown, S.J.E.	LFM	31	12	54	7	7.71	6- 17	1	–
Bulbeck, M.P.L.	LMF	154.4	28	609	32	19.03	4- 40	–	–
Burns, M.	RM	8	1	52	0			–	–
Butcher, G.P.	RM	152.4	24	551	19	29.00	4- 14	–	–
Butcher, M.A.	RM	119.4	29	340	11	30.90	4- 41	–	–
Byrne, B.W.	OB	174.1	31	583	11	53.00	3-103	–	–
Caddick, A.R.	RFM	687.2	156	2082	105	19.82	8- 64	10	3
Capel, D.J.	RMF	13	1	66	1	66.00	1- 66	–	–
Cassar, M.E.	RFM	157	29	614	10	61.40	3- 26	–	–
Catterall, D.N.	RMF	13	2	31	0			–	–
Chandana, U.P.U.	LB	36.2	6	129	4	32.25	4- 45	–	–
Chapman, R.J.	RMF	246.1	44	943	33	28.57	6-105	1	–
Chapman, S.	SLA	29	6	79	0			–	–
Chapple, G.	RFM	313	58	942	44	21.40	5- 49	1	–
Chilton, M.J.	RM	14	3	48	0			–	–
Clarke, V.P.	RM/LB	41	4	173	2	86.50	1- 50	–	–
Clough, G.D.	RM	2	0	11	0			–	–
Cockcroft, J.R.	LB	20	1	74	0			–	–
Collingwood, P.D.	RMF	200.1	53	582	13	44.76	3- 89	–	–
Connor, C.A.	RFM	51	11	154	2	77.00	2- 23	–	–
Cooke, S.	RMF	23	5	90	2	45.00	2- 49	–	–
Cork, D.G.	RFM	545	111	1618	56	28.89	6-119	3	–
Cosker, D.A.	SLA	483.5	127	1265	36	35.13	6-140	1	–
Cottey, P.A.	OB	40	9	92	3	30.66	1- 14	–	–
Cousins, D.M.	RMF	15	5	52	1	52.00	1- 52	–	–
Cowan, A.P.	RFM	238.3	54	859	19	45.21	3- 18	–	–
Crawley, J.P.	RM	1	0	21	0			–	–
Croft, R.D.B.	OB	453.5	117	1144	20	57.20	4- 76	–	–
Cronje, W.J.	RM	42.1	16	97	1	97.00	1- 13	–	–
Crowe, C.D.	OB	61.4	10	201	6	33.50	3- 49	–	–
Cullinan, D.J.	OB	27	6	97	0			–	–
Curran, K.M.	RMF	78	20	265	2	132.50	1- 25	–	–
Dakin, J.M.	RM	132	31	374	8	46.75	4-110	–	–
Dale, A.	RMF	249.3	46	794	31	25.61	5- 25	1	–
Dale, A.C.	RM	83.5	30	183	18	10.16	6- 43	1	–
Daley, J.A.	RM	1	0	12	1	12.00	1- 12	–	–

	Cat	O	M	R	W	Avge	Best	5wI	10wM
Davies, A.P.	RMF	135.5	41	390	14	27.85	2- 22	–	–
Davies, M.K.	SLA	82	23	192	7	27.42	5- 19	1	–
Dawson, R.I.	RM	14.3	0	67	5	13.40	3- 15	–	–
Dean, K.J.	LMF	465.3	96	1572	74	21.24	6- 63	5	1
DeFreitas, P.A.J.	RFM	482.4	114	1363	52	26.21	5- 38	3	–
De la Pena, J.M.	RMF	42	6	154	3	51.33	2- 54	–	–
De Silva, P.A.	OB	19.3	6	30	1	30.00	1- 14	–	–
Dharmasena, H.D.P.K.	OB	112.3	31	258	3	86.00	1- 17	–	–
Donald, A.A.	RF	302.2	89	785	39	20.12	6- 56	5	–
Dowman, M.P.	RMF	139	31	397	12	33.08	2- 10	–	–
Dutch, K.P.	OB	49	11	131	2	65.50	1- 25	–	–
Dwyer, M.D.	SLA	19	4	84	5	16.80	4- 57	–	–
Dyer, N.R.	OB	32.5	7	128	4	32.00	4- 48	–	–
Eadie, D.J.	RM	113.5	19	434	13	33.38	2- 34	–	–
Ealham, M.A.	RMF	242.4	83	593	23	25.78	5- 23	3	–
Edmond, M.D.	RMF	33	8	94	2	47.00	1- 13	–	–
Edwards, A.D.	RFM	59	9	213	3	71.00	2- 60	–	–
Ellis, S.W.K.	RMF	21	7	48	1	48.00	1- 15	–	–
Elworthy, S.	RFM	127	31	415	16	25.93	4- 71	–	–
Evans, K.P.	RMF	273	73	735	27	27.22	5- 92	2	–
Fellows, G.M.	RM	3	0	21	0			–	–
Ferguson, S.H.	RM	26.2	1	141	3	47.00	3- 82	–	–
Fisher, I.D.	SLA	3	1	3	0			–	–
Flanagan, I.N.	OB	1	0	1	0			–	–
Fleming, M.V.	RM	404.4	115	1008	38	26.52	4- 24	–	–
Flintoff, A.	RM	139	29	429	7	61.28	3- 51	–	–
Follett, D.	RFM	103	17	325	10	32.50	3- 48	–	–
Foster, M.J.	RFM	113	23	351	17	20.64	4- 41	–	–
Francis, S.R.G.	RMF	43	8	141	4	35.25	2- 21	–	–
Franks, P.J.	RMF	404.2	87	1375	52	26.44	6- 63	4	–
Fraser, A.R.C.	RMF	480.3	122	1224	61	20.06	6- 23	4	1
Frost, A.	(WK)	1	0	6	0			–	–
Gallian, J.E.R.	RM	47.1	13	103	2	51.50	1- 14	–	–
Garland, R.	RM	102	14	452	8	56.50	2- 64	–	–
Gatting, M.W.	RM	5	1	9	1	9.00	1- 9	–	–
Giddins, E.S.H.	RFM	668.2	162	2006	84	23.88	6- 79	5	1
Giles, A.F.	SLA	459.3	154	1025	36	28.47	5- 48	1	–
Gillespie, J.N.	RF	31	4	109	6	18.16	3- 49	–	–
Goodchild, D.J.	RM	17	1	62	0			–	–
Gough, D.	RF	340.3	65	1067	42	25.40	6- 42	2	–
Gough, M.A.	OB	32.2	8	119	2	59.50	1- 4	–	–
Grayson, A.P.	SLA	248.2	59	734	19	38.63	3- 13	–	–
Green, R.J.	RM	126	28	424	4	106.00	1- 32	–	–
Grove, J.O.	RMF	74.1	8	347	9	38.55	3- 74	–	–
Habib, A.	RMF	4	0	15	0			–	–
Hamilton, G.M.	RFM	415	100	1212	59	20.54	7- 50	4	2
Hancock, T.H.C.	RM	68	16	214	13	16.46	3- 5	–	–
Harden, R.J.	SLA	4	1	12	0			–	–
Harmison, S.J.	RF	455.5	93	1545	51	30.29	5- 70	1	–
Harris, A.J.	RM	32	3	136	4	34.00	2- 53	–	–
Hartley, P.J.	RMF	353.5	66	1109	33	33.60	4- 42	–	–
Harvey, M.E.	RM/LB	5	0	48	0			–	–
Hathurusinghe, U.C.	RM	114	23	358	6	59.66	3- 64	–	–
Haynes, G.R.	RM	227.5	61	705	26	27.11	6- 50	2	–
Hayward, M.	RF	121	20	518	12	43.16	3- 34	–	–
Headley, D.W.	RFM	410.2	88	1175	54	21.75	6- 71	4	–
Hemp, D.L.	RM	31	3	140	4	35.00	2- 68	–	–

	Cat	O	M	R	W	Avge	Best	5wI	10wM
Hewitt, J.P.	RMF	377.3	64	1378	41	33.60	6- 71	2	–
Hewson, D.R.	RM	3	1	7	1	7.00	1- 7	–	–
Hibbert, A.J.E.	RM	16.3	4	48	3	16.00	3- 16	–	–
Hick, G.A.	OB	82	18	242	7	34.57	3- 25	–	–
Hoggard, M.J.	RFM	258	51	895	41	21.82	5- 57	1	–
Hollioake, A.J.	RMF	92.5	29	247	8	30.87	5- 62	1	–
Hollioake, B.C.	RFM	275.4	51	908	36	25.22	4- 28	–	–
Hooper, C.L.	OB	386.2	104	957	31	30.87	7- 93	1	–
House, W.J.	RM	44	8	135	1	135.00	1- 34	–	–
Hughes, Q.J.	OB	20.5	1	71	1	71.00	1- 11	–	–
Hutchison, P.M.	LFM	474.3	119	1432	59	24.27	7- 31	3	–
Hutton, B.L.	RMF	10	0	42	0				
Igglesden, A.P.	RFM	70	13	202	2	101.00	2- 36	–	–
Illingworth, R.K.	SLA	305	81	853	13	65.61	3- 28	–	–
Ilott, M.C.	LFM	506.5	138	1345	58	23.18	6- 20	2	–
Irani, R.C.	RMF	443.5	104	1392	41	33.95	5- 47	1	–
James, K.D.	LMF	340	70	1083	32	33.84	4- 22	–	–
Janisch, A.N.	RM	80	19	253	3	84.33	2- 36	–	–
Jarvis, P.W.	RFM	108	13	368	7	52.57	3- 67	–	–
Jayasuriya, S.T.	SLA	66	19	144	3	48.00	3- 42	–	–
Jayawardena, D.P.M.D.	RM	14	1	66	0				
Johnson, R.L.	RMF	377.2	77	1369	50	27.38	7- 86	3	–
Jones, P.S.	RMF	74.5	16	245	4	61.25	2- 25	–	–
Jones, S.P.	RF	86	11	345	7	49.28	3- 94	–	–
Joyce, E.C.	RM	12	1	58	0				
Julian, B.P.	LFM	63	10	230	9	25.55	3- 41	–	–
Kallis, J.H.	RMF	226.1	79	529	16	33.06	4- 24	–	–
Keedy, G.	SLA	182.3	43	563	18	31.27	5- 35	1	–
Kendall, W.S.	RM	4	0	16	0				
Kenway, D.A.	RM	2	0	17	0				
Kettleborough, R.A.	RM	23	1	89	0				
Key, R.W.T.	RM/OB	1	0	1	0				
Khan, A.A.	LB	116	25	389	6	64.83	2- 24	–	–
Khan, S.H.	RM	86.4	8	327	2	163.50	1- 41	–	–
Khan, W.G.	LB	1.5	0	7	0				
Killeen, N.	RFM	101.2	25	349	12	29.08	5- 49	1	–
Kirtley, R.J.	RFM	490.4	116	1532	54	28.37	7- 29	3	1
Klusener, L.	RFM	156	38	424	14	30.28	4- 66	–	–
Knight, N.V.	RM	1.5	0	15	0				
Knott, J.A.	LB	1	0	2	0				
Lacey, S.J.	OB	88	19	274	4	68.50	2- 89	–	–
Lampitt, S.R.	RMF	416	97	1330	50	26.60	5- 33	4	–
Laney, J.S.	OB	3	0	15	0				
Langer, J.L.	RM	13	5	34	1	34.00	1- 10	–	–
Lara, B.C.	LB	5	0	44	0				
Law, D.R.	RFM	247.5	34	1045	29	36.03	5- 46	1	–
Law, W.L.	OB	23	2	85	3	28.33	2- 29	–	–
Leather, D.	RFM	10	1	44	0				
Leatherdale, D.A.	RM	111.4	22	416	21	19.80	5- 20	1	–
Lehmann, D.S.	SLA	57	16	124	6	20.66	4- 42	–	–
Lewis, C.C.	RFM	266.4	53	972	39	24.92	6- 60	2	–
Lewis, J.	RMF	462.1	108	1447	59	24.52	6- 48	3	–
Lewis, J.J.B.	RSM	8	0	73	1	73.00	1- 73	–	–
Lewry, J.D.	LFM	461.3	112	1409	62	22.72	6- 72	3	–
Lightfoot, C.G.R.	SLA	38	10	132	2	66.00	1- 14	–	–
Lloyd, G.D.	RM	7.3	1	49	0				
Loveridge, G.R.	LBG	204	34	655	13	50.38	5- 59	1	–

	Cat	O	M	R	W	Avge	Best	5wI	10wM
Lowe, J.P.	RM	106	27	295	6	49.16	2- 42	–	–
Loye, M.B.	OB	2	0	42	0				
Lugsden, S.	RFM	72.2	6	325	8	40.62	3- 67	–	–
McCague, M.J.	RFM	235.1	45	758	27	28.07	4- 40	–	–
McCallan, W.K.	OB	29	7	105	1	105.00	1- 69	–	–
McGrath, A.	OB	42	10	159	3	53.00	2- 33	–	–
McLean, N.A.M.	RF	518.5	105	1575	62	25.40	6-101	2	–
McMillan, B.M.	RMF	85.5	26	210	8	26.25	3- 38	–	–
Macmillan, G.I.	OB	5	2	14	0				
Maddy, D.L.	RM/OB	34	9	130	2	65.00	1- 9	–	–
Malcolm, D.E.	RF	334	48	1331	40	33.27	6- 54	2	–
Martin, N.D.	RFM	18	2	83	1	83.00	1- 22	–	–
Martin, P.J.	RFM	388	94	1062	48	22.12	4- 21	–	–
Martin-Jenkins, R.S.C.	RFM	141.5	43	437	22	19.86	7- 54	1	–
Maru, R.J.	SLA	48	9	167	2	83.50	2-101	–	–
Mascarenhas, A.D.	RMF	280.5	58	1000	30	33.33	4- 31	–	–
Mason, T.J.	OB	45.2	9	139	0				
Mather, D.P.	LM	168.5	32	574	17	33.76	6- 74	1	1
May, M.R.	OB	3	0	51	0				
Maynard, M.P.	RM	5.4	0	46	0				
Middlebrook, J.D.	OB	164.1	45	422	13	32.46	3- 20	–	–
Miller, C.R.	RMF/OB	42.4	11	113	4	28.25	2- 22	–	–
Millns, D.J.	RF	243.3	55	817	34	24.02	4- 60	–	–
Moffat, P.J.	RM	91	24	232	7	33.14	3- 25	–	–
Mohammed, I.	OB	12	1	52	1	52.00	1- 13	–	–
Molins, J.A.M.	RSM	1	0	12	1	12.00	1- 12	–	–
Moody, T.M.	RM	251.1	73	790	27	29.25	5- 64	1	–
Mooney, P.J.K.	RM	22	4	72	2	36.00	2- 45	–	–
Morris, A.C.	RMF	314	64	1012	50	20.24	4- 30	–	–
Morris, Z.C.	SLA	1	0	5	0				
Mullally, A.D.	LFM	448.5	156	1128	60	18.80	7- 55	3	1
Munton, T.A.	RMF	278.5	72	708	37	19.13	7- 66	3	–
Muralitharan, M.	OB	226.3	77	463	34	13.61	9- 65	5	2
Mushtaq Ahmed	LBG	136	40	411	14	29.35	3- 26	–	–
Napier, G.R.	RM	17	4	72	2	36.00	2- 59	–	–
Nash, D.C.	LB	0.1	0	0	0				
Newell, K.	RM	65.4	22	190	5	38.00	3- 23	–	–
Newell, M.(Sx)	OB	2	0	15	0				
Newport, P.J.	RFM	335.1	117	893	36	24.80	4- 44	–	–
Ntini, M.	RFM	184.3	48	578	19	30.42	4- 72	–	–
Olphert, O.M.	LM	4	0	28	0				
Oram, A.R.	RM	305.5	75	969	31	31.25	4- 37	–	–
Ormond, J.	RFM	133.3	51	311	19	16.36	6- 33	2	–
Ostler, D.P.	RM	3	0	13	0				
Parker, C.R.C	RM	10	0	48	0				
Parkin, O.T.	RFM	300.3	99	757	34	22.26	5- 24	2	–
Parsons, K.A.	RM	129.2	34	412	8	51.50	2- 26	–	–
Patel, M.M.	SLA	418.3	102	1123	34	33.02	5- 73	1	–
Peirce, M.T.E.	SLA	43	18	99	1	99.00	1- 16	–	–
Penberthy, A.L.	RM	65	13	204	0				
Perera, A.S.A.	RMF	129.5	31	343	7	49.00	2- 60	–	–
Phillips, B.J.	RFM	294	55	928	17	54.58	3- 66	–	–
Phillips, N.C.	OB	425.4	101	1216	28	43.42	5- 56	1	–
Pierson, A.R.K.	OB	258.1	53	842	21	40.09	5-117	1	–
Pollock, S.M.	RFM	266.5	87	594	24	24.75	5- 53	1	–
Powell, M.J.(Gm)	RSM	0.2	0	8	0				
Powell, M.J.(Wa)	RM	16	5	46	2	23.00	2- 16	–	–

	Cat	O	M	R	W	Avge	Best	5wI	10wM
Pushpakumara, K.R.	RMF	57	7	224	6	37.33	3- 52	–	–
Pyemont, J.P.	OB	2	0	20	0				
Ramprakash, M.R.	RM	52.2	8	153	5	30.60	3- 32	–	–
Rao, R.K.	LBG	34	3	136	1	136.00	1- 12	–	–
Ratcliffe, J.D.	RM	2	1	4	0				
Rawnsley, M.J.	SLA	172.1	46	497	17	29.23	6- 44	2	1
Renshaw, S.J.	RMF	17	5	24	2	12.00	1- 9	–	–
Ridgway, P.M.	RFM	18	2	83	4	20.75	3- 51	–	–
Roberts, G.M.	SLA	185	27	729	9	81.00	4-105	–	–
Robinson, M.A.	RFM	416.1	107	1126	42	26.80	4- 72	–	–
Rose, F.A.	RF	373.2	59	1367	50	27.34	7- 39	3	1
Rose, G.D.	RM	480.3	132	1399	52	26.90	5- 48	2	–
Saggers, M.J.	RMF	58.2	14	149	7	21.28	3- 47	–	–
Sales, D.J.G.	RM	11	2	36	1	36.00	1- 28	–	–
Salisbury, I.D.K.	LBG	387.5	109	958	37	25.89	7- 65	2	–
Saqlain Mushtaq	OB	475	136	1119	63	17.76	8- 65	3	3
Schaffter, P.A.	RFM	44.3	16	118	2	59.00	1- 21	–	–
Schofield, C.P.	LB	79.4	9	299	10	29.90	4- 56	–	–
Scott, D.A.	OB	48	14	124	1	124.00	1- 48	–	–
Searle, J.P.	OB	42.5	10	158	5	31.60	3- 92	–	–
Shadford, D.J.	RMF	30.5	4	90	1	90.00	1- 56	–	–
Shah, O.A.	OB	17.5	1	79	1	79.00	1- 46	–	–
Shahid, N.	LB	16	1	66	2	33.00	1- 19	–	–
Shaw, A.D.	(WK)	1	0	7	0				
Sheikh, M.A.	RM	31.2	7	74	3	24.66	2- 18	–	–
Sheridan, K.L.P.	SLA	27.1	3	102	2	51.00	2- 77	–	–
Sheriyar, A.	LFM	286.1	69	962	24	40.08	5- 85	1	–
Shine, K.J.	RFM	57.4	10	216	4	54.00	2- 40	–	–
Sidebottom, R.J.	LFM	119	25	390	9	43.33	3- 13	–	–
Silverwood, C.E.W.	RFM	390.1	99	1123	48	23.39	5- 13	3	–
Simmons, P.V.	RM	170.5	44	491	23	21.34	7- 49	1	–
Singh, A.	OB	2	0	21	0				
Smith, A.M.	LMF	522.3	139	1440	68	21.17	6- 32	4	–
Smith, B.F.	RM	5	0	11	0				
Smith, N.M.K.	OB	329.3	84	957	24	39.87	5-128	1	–
Smith, R.A.	LB	21	1	197	2	98.50	1- 63	–	–
Smith, T.M.	RFM	150.3	42	484	21	23.04	6- 32	2	–
Solanki, V.S.	OB	106	23	375	8	46.87	2- 22	–	–
Speak, N.J.	LB	2	0	13	0				
Stanger, I.M.	RMF	33	4	167	3	55.66	3- 57	–	–
Steindl, P.D.	RM	21	6	98	0				
Stemp, R.D.	SLA	409	141	1001	27	37.07	5-191	1	–
Stephenson, J.P.	RM	286.4	71	770	24	32.08	4- 29	–	–
Strang, P.A.	LBG	353.3	105	983	30	32.76	5-166	1	–
Strong, M.R.	RMF	11	2	41	0				
Such, P.M.	OB	527	129	1479	38	38.92	5- 73	2	–
Sutcliffe, I.J.	OB	9	0	51	1	51.00	1- 17	–	–
Swann, A.J.	RM/OB	6.3	0	59	0				
Swann, G.P.	OB	199.4	41	666	22	30.27	5- 29	1	–
Symcox, P.L.	OB	92.3	26	207	12	17.25	5- 60	1	–
Symington, M.J.	RM	36.2	7	148	6	24.66	3- 55	–	–
Symonds, A.	OB	2	0	1	0				
Taylor, J.P.	LFM	436.5	105	1337	54	24.75	4- 31	–	–
Thomas, S.D.	RFM	544.1	94	1749	71	24.63	5- 84	3	–
Thompson, J.B.D.	RMF	95.4	20	335	11	30.45	4- 52	–	–
Thomson, K.	RMF	20	3	106	3	35.33	2- 52	–	–
Tillekeratne, H.P.	OB	3	0	16	0				

	Cat	O	M	R	W	Avge	Best	5wI	10wM
Tolley, C.M.	LMF	324.3	76	960	34	28.23	7- 45	3	–
Trescothick, M.E.	RM	193.3	45	654	17	38.47	4- 82	–	–
Trott, B.J.	RFM	17	4	56	2	28.00	2- 16	–	–
Tudor, A.J.	RF	184.2	34	737	29	25.41	5- 43	1	–
Tufnell, P.C.R.	SLA	631.5	162	1602	39	41.07	4- 24	–	–
Tweats, T.A.	RM	3	0	29	0				
Udal, S.D.	OB	191.2	44	549	16	34.31	4- 37	–	–
Van Troost, A.P.	RF	118	24	415	15	27.66	4- 18	–	–
Vaughan, M.P.	OB	118.1	30	412	9	45.77	3- 73	–	–
Villavarayen, M.S.	RMF	86.4	18	276	9	30.66	4- 36	–	–
Wagh, M.A.	OB	97	18	272	9	30.22	4- 11	–	–
Walker, A.	RFM	23.5	5	51	1	51.00	1- 51	–	–
Walker, M.J.	RM	12	0	51	0				
Walsh, C.A.	RF	633	162	1835	106	17.31	6- 36	7	2
Waqar Younis	RF	100.1	13	397	12	33.08	3-147	–	–
Ward, T.R.	OB	2	0	4	0				
Wasim Akram	LF	335.5	75	1025	48	21.35	5- 56	1	–
Watkin, S.L.	RMF	370.4	104	917	42	21.83	5- 30	1	–
Watkinson, M.	RMF/OB	175.4	22	607	18	33.72	5- 45	1	–
Waugh, S.R.	RMF	6	1	27	0				
Weekes, P.N.	OB	237	37	702	13	54.00	3-113	–	–
Welch, G.	RM	314.3	68	996	25	39.84	4- 94	–	–
Wells, V.J.	RMF	199.1	66	514	36	14.27	5- 18	1	–
Weston, W.P.C.	LM	2	0	20	0				
Wharf, A.G.	RMF	83.1	14	333	9	37.00	3- 25	–	–
Whiley, M.J.A.	LMF	29	4	124	1	124.00	1- 66	–	–
Whitaker, P.R.	OB	6	1	15	1	15.00	1- 2	–	–
White, C.	RFM	147.1	36	391	25	15.64	8- 55	2	–
White, G.W.	LB	12.1	2	51	1	51.00	1- 4	–	–
Wickremasinghe, G.P.	RMF	135.1	26	397	13	30.53	4- 69	–	–
Wilkinson, R.	OB	15	3	35	1	35.00	1- 35	–	–
Williams, N.F.	RFM	246.5	47	849	26	32.65	4- 42	–	–
Williamson, D.	RM	51	10	183	4	45.75	3-110	–	–
Williamson, J.G.	RM	17	1	73	1	73.00	1- 49	–	–
Wilson, D.G.	RM	25	4	114	2	57.00	1- 22	–	–
Windows, M.G.N.	RSM	1	0	7	0				
Wood, J.	RFM	572.5	113	1916	62	30.90	5- 52	2	–
Wood, N.T.	OB	5.1	0	80	0				
Yates, G.	OB	131.3	26	432	18	24.00	4- 64	–	–
Young, B.E.	SLA	44.4	18	110	5	22.00	2- 23	–	–

BRITANNIC ASSURANCE
COUNTY CHAMPIONSHIP 1998 FINAL TABLE

	P	W	L	D	Bonus Points Bat	Bonus Points Bowl	Total Points
1 LEICESTERSHIRE (10)	17	11	–	6	47	51	292
2 Lancashire (11)	17	11	1	5	30	56	277
3 Yorkshire (6)	17	9	3	5	47	63	269
4 Gloucestershire (7)	17	11	5	1	23	65	267
5 Surrey (8)	17	10	5	2	38	57	261
6 Hampshire (14)	17	6	5	6	27	61	202
7 Sussex (18)	17	6	7	4	30	63	201
8 Warwickshire (4)	17	6	8	3	35	60	200
9 Somerset (12)	17	6	7	4	30	54	192
10 Derbyshire (16)	17	6	7	4	28	55	191
11 Kent (2)	17	5	5	7	18	59	178
12 Worcestershire (3)	17	4	6	7	32	59	176
13 Glamorgan (1)	17	4	4	9	17	36	55	176
14 Durham (17)	17	3	9	5	30	65	158
15 Northamptonshire (15)	17	4	5	8	31	52	146
16 Nottinghamshire (13)	17	3	10	4	20	60	140
17 Middlesex (4)	17	2	9	6	28	52	130
18 Essex (8)	17	2	11	4	16	58	118

1997 final positions are shown in brackets. Northamptonshire were penalised 25 points for an 'unsuitable' pitch. The first eight counties qualified for the 1999 Benson and Hedges Super Cup.

SCORING OF POINTS 1998

(a) For a win, 16 points, plus any points scored in the first innings.
(b) In a tie, each side to score eight points, plus any points scored in the first innings.
(c) In a drawn match, each side to score three points, plus any points scored in the first innings (see also paragraph (f) below).
(d) If the scores are equal in a drawn match, the side batting in the fourth innings to score eight points plus any points scored in the first innings, and the opposing side to score three points plus any points scored in the first innings.
(e) **First Innings Points** (awarded only for the performances **in the first 120 overs** of each first innings and retained whatever the result of the match).

    (i) A maximum of four batting points to be available as under:-
        200 to 249 runs   – 1 point
        250 to 299 runs   – 2 points
        300 to 349 runs   – 3 points
        350 runs or over   – 4 points

    (ii) A maximum of four bowling points to be available as under:-
        3 to 4 wickets taken – 1 point
        5 to 6 wickets taken – 2 points
        7 to 8 wickets taken – 3 points
        9 to 10 wickets taken – 4 points

(f) If play starts when less than eight hours playing time remains (in which event a one innings match shall be played as provided for in First Class Playing Condition 20), no first innings points shall be scored. The side winning on the one innings to score 12 points. In a tie, each side to score six points. In a drawn match, each side to score three points. If the scores are equal in a drawn match, the side batting in the second innings to score six points and the opposing side to score three points.
(g) If a match is abandoned without a ball being bowled, each side to score three points.
(h) A County which is adjudged to have prepared a pitch which is 'unsuitable for four day First-Class Cricket' shall be liable to have 25 points deducted from its aggregate of points under the procedure agreed by the Board in December 1988 and revised in December 1993. In addition, a penalty of 10 or 15 points may in certain circumstances be imposed on a County in respect of a 'Poor' pitch under the procedure agreed by the Board in March 1995. There shall be no right of appeal against any points penalty provided for in this playing condition.
(i) The side which has the highest aggregate of points gained at the end of the season shall be the Champion County. Should any sides in the Championship table be equal on points, the following tie-breakers will be applied in the order stated; most wins, least losses, team achieving most points in contests between teams level on points, most wickets taken, most runs scored.

COUNTY CHAMPIONS

The English County Championship was not officially constituted until December 1889. Prior to that date there was no generally accepted method of awarding the title; although the 'least matches lost' method existed, it was not consistently applied. Rules governing playing qualifications were not agreed until 1873, and the first unofficial points system was not introduced until 1888.

Research has produced a list of champions dating back to 1826, but at least seven different versions exist for the period from 1864 to 1889 (see *The Wisden Book of Cricket Records*). Only from 1890 can any authorised list of county champions commence.

That first official Championship was contested between eight counties: Gloucestershire, Kent, Lancashire, Middlesex, Nottinghamshire, Surrey, Sussex and Yorkshire. The remaining counties were admitted in the following seasons: 1891 – Somerset, 1895 – Derbyshire, Essex, Hampshire, Leicestershire and Warwickshire, 1899 – Worcestershire, 1905 – Northamptonshire, 1921 – Glamorgan, and 1992 – Durham.

The Championship pennant was introduced by the 1951 champions, Warwickshire, and the Lord's Taverners' Trophy was first presented in 1973. The first sponsors, Schweppes (1977 to 1983), were succeeded by Britannic Assurance (1984 to 1998).

1890 Surrey	1928 Lancashire	1966 Yorkshire
1891 Surrey	1929 Nottinghamshire	1967 Yorkshire
1892 Surrey	1930 Lancashire	1968 Yorkshire
1893 Yorkshire	1931 Yorkshire	1969 Glamorgan
1894 Surrey	1932 Yorkshire	1970 Kent
1895 Surrey	1933 Yorkshire	1971 Surrey
1896 Yorkshire	1934 Lancashire	1972 Warwickshire
1897 Lancashire	1935 Yorkshire	1973 Hampshire
1898 Yorkshire	1936 Derbyshire	1974 Worcestershire
1899 Surrey	1937 Yorkshire	1975 Leicestershire
1900 Yorkshire	1938 Yorkshire	1976 Middlesex
1901 Yorkshire	1939 Yorkshire	1977 { Kent / Middlesex }
1902 Yorkshire	1946 Yorkshire	
1903 Middlesex	1947 Middlesex	1978 Kent
1904 Lancashire	1948 Glamorgan	1979 Essex
1905 Yorkshire	1949 { Middlesex / Yorkshire }	1980 Middlesex
1906 Kent		1981 Nottinghamshire
1907 Nottinghamshire	1950 { Lancashire / Surrey }	1982 Middlesex
1908 Yorkshire		1983 Essex
1909 Kent	1951 Warwickshire	1984 Essex
1910 Kent	1952 Surrey	1985 Middlesex
1911 Warwickshire	1953 Surrey	1986 Essex
1912 Yorkshire	1954 Surrey	1987 Nottinghamshire
1913 Kent	1955 Surrey	1988 Worcestershire
1914 Surrey	1956 Surrey	1989 Worcestershire
1919 Yorkshire	1957 Surrey	1990 Middlesex
1920 Middlesex	1958 Surrey	1991 Essex
1921 Middlesex	1959 Yorkshire	1992 Essex
1922 Yorkshire	1960 Yorkshire	1993 Middlesex
1923 Yorkshire	1961 Hampshire	1994 Warwickshire
1924 Yorkshire	1962 Yorkshire	1995 Warwickshire
1925 Yorkshire	1963 Yorkshire	1996 Leicestershire
1926 Lancashire	1964 Worcestershire	1997 Glamorgan
1927 Lancashire	1965 Worcestershire	1998 Leicestershire

THE LAST SEPTEMBER FINAL

Although it took them until 1pm on the second day to extend their record tally of Gillette Cup and NatWest Trophy titles to seven, Lancashire's demolition of Derbyshire was achieved in a mere 67 overs, the shortest of all the 36 September showpieces.

Rain delayed the start until 4.30pm and inevitably the toss proved crucial. With heavy cloud surrounding a sunlit Lord's, Lancashire surprised no one by opting to bowl first. Derbyshire's opening pair of Kim Barnett and Michael Slater, the latter showing no signs of jet lag despite returning from Australia the previous day, gave few hints of the disasters to come as they took full advantage of some wayward bowling by Wasim Akram and Peter Martin. Neither bowler could control the ball's erratic swing. Slater defied worsening light to drive Glen Chapple for six over extra-cover and pull his next ball for four. With the electronic scoreboards piercing the gloom like beacons and showing 70 for 0 after 18 overs, Derbyshire were defying history by appearing to be firmly in control.

Ian Austin, recently promoted to international status, achieved the breakthrough, winning umpire Sharp's approval for a leg before shout as Slater hit across his impeccable line. The dam was breached. In the space of 55 balls seven wickets fell for 11 runs, forcing some scorers to write with both hands. Peter Martin (four wickets) and Austin (three) shared the spoils. When bad light ended proceedings at 7.08pm, Derbyshire were 92 for 7 after 32.1 overs. They added only 16 from 5½ overs on Sunday morning, their total of 108 being the lowest in the first innings of any September final.

Derbyshire needed at least three early wickets to get back into the contest but, after Mike Atherton had lost his off stump to Dominic Cork's late outswing, John Crawley and Neil Fairbrother saw Lancashire home with almost half their overs in hand. It was fitting that Fairbrother, appearing in a Lord's final for a record tenth time, should make the winning hit.

This unequal contest marked the end of two eras. Future NatWest finals would be played on the last Sunday of August, with the competition dramatically revised to include 60 teams playing 50-over matches. It was also scheduled to be the last major match broadcast from the BBC's radio commentary box in a parapet of the Lord's pavilion, home of *Test Match Special* since 1973.

GILLETTE CUP WINNERS

1963	Sussex	1969	Yorkshire	1975	Lancashire
1964	Sussex	1970	Lancashire	1976	Northamptonshire
1965	Yorkshire	1971	Lancashire	1977	Middlesex
1966	Warwickshire	1972	Lancashire	1978	Sussex
1967	Kent	1973	Gloucestershire	1979	Somerset
1968	Warwickshire	1974	Kent	1980	Middlesex

NATWEST TROPHY WINNERS

1981	Derbyshire	1987	Nottinghamshire	1993	Warwickshire
1982	Surrey	1988	Middlesex	1994	Worcestershire
1983	Somerset	1989	Warwickshire	1995	Warwickshire
1984	Middlesex	1990	Lancashire	1996	Lancashire
1985	Essex	1991	Hampshire	1997	Essex
1986	Sussex	1992	Northamptonshire	1998	Lancashire

Lancashire crown Derby

Congratulations to
Lancashire on winning the
1998 NatWest Trophy.

⮔ NatWest

National Westminster Bank Plc, 41 Lothbury, London EC2P 2BP

1998 NATWEST TROPHY FINAL

DERBYSHIRE v LANCASHIRE

At Lord's, London on 5, 6 September 1998.
Result: LANCASHIRE won by 9 wickets.
Toss: Lancashire. Award: I.D.Austin.

DERBYSHIRE		Runs	Balls	4/6	Fall
M.J.Slater	lbw b Austin	34	62	3/1	1- 70
K.J.Barnett	b Martin	23	55	1	2- 70
A.S.Rollins	c Flintoff b Martin	1	10	–	4- 71
R.M.S.Weston	b Austin	0	4	–	3- 71
M.E.Cassar	c Chapple b Austin	6	18	–	6- 81
B.L.Spendlove	lbw b Martin	4	10	–	5- 81
* D.G.Cork	c Hegg b Wasim Akram	5	34	–	8- 81
P.A.J.DeFreitas	lbw b Martin	0	2	–	7- 81
† K.M.Krikken	c Hegg b Flintoff	2	16	–	9-102
V.P.Clarke	b Wasim Akram	13	7	3	10-108
K.J.Dean	not out	0	6	–	
Extras	(lb 5, w 7, nb 8)	20			
Total	(36.4 overs)	**108**			

LANCASHIRE		Runs	Balls	4/6	Fall
M.A.Atherton	b Cork	10	26	2	1-28
J.P.Crawley	not out	53	92	11	
N.H.Fairbrother	not out	38	64	5	
G.D.Lloyd					
A.Flintoff					
* Wasim Akram					
I.D.Austin					
† W.K.Hegg					
G.Yates					
G.Chapple					
P.J.Martin					
Extras	(lb 2, w 4, nb 2)	8			
Total	(30.2 overs; 1 wicket)	**109**			

LANCASHIRE	O	M	R	W	DERBYSHIRE	O	M	R	W
Wasim Akram	8.4	1	39	2	Cork	10.2	4	24	1
Martin	9	2	19	4	Dean	5	0	38	0
Chapple	6	0	27	0	DeFreitas	9	3	13	0
Austin	10	5	14	3	Cassar	6	0	32	0
Flintoff	3	1	4	1					

Umpires: K.E.Palmer and G.Sharp.

Unofficial Bank Holidays in 1999.

First Round – Tuesday 4th May

Second Round – Wednesday 19th May

Third Round – Wednesday 23rd June

Fourth Round – Wednesday 7th July

Quarter Finals – Wednesday 28th July

Semi Finals – Saturday 14th August

– Sunday 15th August

Final – Sunday 29th August

NatWest
TROPHY

National Westminster Bank Plc, 41 Lothbury, London EC2P 2BP

THE NATWEST TROPHY 1998 RESULTS CHART

FIRST ROUND 24, 25 June	SECOND ROUND 8 July	QUARTER-FINALS 28 July	SEMI-FINALS 11-12 August	FINAL 5, 6 September
LANCASHIRE†	LANCASHIRE†	LANCASHIRE	LANCASHIRE	**LANCASHIRE** (£47,000)
Sussex				
Devon†	Yorkshire			
YORKSHIRE				
NOTTINGHAMSHIRE	NOTTINGHAMSHIRE‡	Nottinghamshire (£5,750)		
MC Wales†				
SOMERSET†	Somerset			
Holland			Hampshire† (£11,750)	
HAMPSHIRE	HAMPSHIRE	HAMPSHIRE		
Dorset†				
ESSEX	Essex			
Cheshire†				
MIDDLESEX	MIDDLESEX	Middlesex† (£5,750)		
Herefordshire				
DURHAM	Durham			
Norfolk†			Leicestershire† (£11,750)	
WARWICKSHIRE	WARWICKSHIRE†	Warwickshire (£5,750)		
Ireland				
KENT†	Kent			
Cambridgeshire				
LEICESTERSHIRE†	LEICESTERSHIRE	LEICESTERSHIRE		
Staffordshire				
GLAMORGAN†	Glamorgan†			
Bedfordshire				Derbyshire (£23,500)
GLOUCESTERSHIRE‡	Gloucestershire†	Surrey† (£5,750)		
Northamptonshire				
SURREY†	SURREY		DERBYSHIRE	
Buckinghamshire				
Worcestershire	Scotland†	DERBYSHIRE		
SCOTLAND†				
DERBYSHIRE†	DERBYSHIRE			
Cumberland				

† Home team. Winning teams are in capitals. Prize-money shown in brackets.

NATWEST TROPHY
PRINCIPAL RECORDS 1963-98
(Including The Gillette Cup)

Highest Total		413-4	Somerset v Devon	Torquay 1990
Highest Total in a Final		322-5	Warwicks v Sussex	Lord's 1993
Highest Total by a Minor County		305-9	Durham v Glam	Darlington 1991
Highest Total Batting Second		350	Surrey v Worcs	The Oval 1994
Highest Total to Win Batting Second		329-5	Sussex v Derbyshire	Derby 1997
Lowest Total		39	Ireland v Sussex	Hove 1985
Lowest Total in a Final		57	Essex v Lancashire	Lord's 1996
Lowest Total to Win Batting First		98	Worcs v Durham	Chester-le-St 1968
Highest Score		206	A.I.Kallicharran	Warwicks v Oxon	Birmingham 1984
HS (Minor County)		132	G.Robinson	Lincs v Northumb	Jesmond 1971
Hundreds		314	(Gillette Cup 93; NatWest Trophy 221)		1963-98
Fastest Hundred		36 balls	G.D.Rose	Somerset v Devon	Torquay 1990
Most Hundreds		8	R.A.Smith	Hampshire	1985-98
Most Runs		2547	G.A.Gooch	Essex	1973-96
		(av 48.98)			

Highest Partnership for each Wicket

1st	311	A.J.Wright/N.J.Trainor	Glos v Scotland	Bristol 1997
2nd	286	I.S.Anderson/A.Hill	Derbys v Cornwall	Derby 1986
3rd	309*	T.S.Curtis/T.M.Moody	Worcs v Surrey	The Oval 1994
4th	234*	D.Lloyd/C.H.Lloyd	Lancashire v Glos	Manchester 1978
5th	166	M.A.Lynch/G.R.J.Roope	Surrey v Durham	The Oval 1982
6th	178	J.P.Crawley/I.D.Austin	Lancashire v Sussex	Hove 1997
7th	160*	C.J.Richards/I.R.Payne	Surrey v Lincs	Sleaford 1983
8th	112	A.L.Penberthy/J.E.Emburey	Northants v Lancs	Manchester 1996
9th	87	M.A.Nash/A.E.Cordle	Glamorgan v Lincs	Swansea 1974
10th	81	S.Turner/R.E.East	Essex v Yorkshire	Leeds 1982

Best Bowling		8-21	M.A.Holding	Derbys v Sussex	Hove 1988
		8-31	D.L.Underwood	Kent v Scotland	Edinburgh 1987
Most Wickets		81	G.G.Arnold	Surrey	1963-80
		(av 14.85)			

Hat-Tricks (11): J.D.F.Larter (Northamptonshire 1963), D.A.D.Sydenham (Surrey 1964), R.N.S.Hobbs (Essex 1968), N.M.McVicker (Warwickshire 1971), G.S.Le Roux (Sussex 1985), M.Jean-Jacques (Derbyshire 1987), J.F.M.O'Brien (Cheshire 1988), R.A.Pick (Nottinghamshire 1995), J.E.Emburey (Northamptonshire 1996), A.R.Caddick (Somerset 1996), D.Gough (Yorkshire 1997).

Most Wicket-Keeping Dismissals in an Innings
7 (7ct) A.J.Stewart Surrey v Glamorgan Swansea 1994

Most Catches in an Innings
4 – A.S.Brown (Gloucestershire 1963), G.Cook (Northamptonshire 1972), C.G.Greenidge (Hampshire 1981), D.C.Jackson (Durham 1984), T.S.Smith (Hertfordshire 1984), H.Morris (Glamorgan 1988), C.C.Lewis (Nottinghamshire 1992).

Most Appearances	67	M.W.Gatting	Middlesex	1975-98
Most Match Awards	9	G.A.Gooch	Essex	1973-96
	9	R.A.Smith	Hampshire	1985-98

Most Match Wins: 74 – Lancashire. **Most Cup/Trophy Wins:** 7 – Lancashire.

1998 BENSON AND HEDGES CUP FINAL

ESSEX v LEICESTERSHIRE

At Lord's, London on 11, 12 July 1998.
Result: ESSEX won by 192 runs.
Toss: Leicestershire. Award: P.J.Prichard.

ESSEX		Runs	Balls	4/6	Fall
* P.J.Prichard	c Simmons b Williamson	92	113	11/2	2-174
S.G.Law	c Mullally b Wells	6	24	–	1- 40
N.Hussain	c Smith b Lewis	88	102	8/1	3-234
R.C.Irani	c Maddy b Mullally	32	37	2/1	5-245
D.R.Law	c Lewis b Williamson	1	5	–	4-244
A.P.Grayson	not out	9	7	2	
† R.J.Rollins	c Brimson b Mullally	0	2	–	6-250
S.D.Peters	b Mullally	9	8	1	7-265
A.P.Cowan	not out	3	2	–	
M.C.Ilott					
P.M.Such					
Extras	(b 2, lb 8, w 18)	28			
Total	(50 overs; 7 wickets)	**268**			

LEICESTERSHIRE		Runs	Balls	4/6	Fall
D.L.Maddy	c S.G.Law b Cowan	5	41	–	6-31
I.J.Sutcliffe	c S.G.Law b Cowan	1	12	–	1- 6
B.F.Smith	c S.G.Law b Cowan	0	1	–	2- 6
P.V.Simmons	b Ilott	2	4	–	3-10
V.J.Wells	lbw b Ilott	1	10	–	4-17
A.Habib	lbw b Ilott	5	15	1	5-31
† P.A.Nixon	not out	21	36	3	
* C.C.Lewis	c Peters b Irani	0	14	–	7-36
D.Williamson	c Hussain b S.G.Law	11	18	2	8-67
A.D.Mullally	lbw b Irani	1	12	–	9-73
M.T.Brimson	b S.G.Law	0	5	–	10-76
Extras	(lb 8, w 17, nb 4)	29			
Total	(27.4 overs)	**76**			

LEICESTERSHIRE	O	M	R	W	ESSEX	O	M	R	W
Mullally	10	1	36	3	Ilott	8	2	10	3
Lewis	9	0	59	1	Cowan	10	2	24	3
Wells	10	0	34	1	Irani	6	2	21	2
Simmons	9	0	67	0	S.G.Law	3.4	0	13	2
Brimson	2	0	13	0					
Williamson	10	0	49	2					

Scores after 15 overs: Essex 61-1; Leicestershire 34-6.

Umpires: R.Julian and M.J.Kitchen.

1998 BENSON AND HEDGES CUP

FINAL GROUP TABLES

	P	W	L	NR	Pts	Net Run Rate
GROUP A						
LEICESTERSHIRE	5	4	1	–	8	23.32
LANCASHIRE	5	4	1	–	8	17.31
Warwickshire	5	4	1	–	8	16.35
Nottinghamshire	5	2	3	–	4	1.51
Northamptonshire	5	1	4	–	2	–10.40
Minor Counties	5	–	5	–	–	–50.57
GROUP B						
YORKSHIRE	4	4	–	–	8	13.13
DURHAM	4	3	1	–	6	–1.42
Worcestershire	4	2	2	–	4	3.66
Derbyshire	4	1	3	–	2	–3.27
Scotland	4	–	4	–	–	–10.51
GROUP C						
SURREY	5	5	–	–	10	13.16
KENT	5	3	1	1	7	14.17
Somerset	5	2	2	1	5	–0.43
Gloucestershire	5	2	3	–	4	2.89
British Universities	5	1	4	–	2	–13.26
Hampshire	5	1	4	–	2	–15.56
GROUP D						
MIDDLESEX	4	4	–	–	8	3.71
ESSEX	4	2	1	1	5	19.48
Glamorgan	4	1	2	1	3	10.33
Sussex	4	1	2	1	3	–1.53
Ireland	4	–	3	1	1	–33.29

FINAL ROUNDS

QUARTER-FINALS *27, 28 May*	SEMI-FINALS *9 June*	FINAL *11, 12 July*
LEICESTERSHIRE†		
Kent (£5,500)	LEICESTERSHIRE†	
SURREY†		Leicestershire (£22,000)
Lancshire (£5,500)	Surrey (£11,000)	
YORKSHIRE†		
Durham (£5,500)	Yorkshire† (£11,000)	
ESSEX		**ESSEX (£43,000)**
Middlesex† (£5,500)	ESSEX	

† *Home team. Winning teams are in capitals. Prize-money in brackets.*

BENSON AND HEDGES CUP
PRINCIPAL RECORDS 1972-98

Highest Total		388-7	Essex v Scotland	Chelmsford	1992
Highest Total Batting Second		318-5	Lancashire v Leics	Manchester	1995
Highest Total to Lose Batting 2nd		303-7	Derbys v Somerset	Taunton	1990
Lowest Total		50	Hampshire v Yorks	Leeds	1991
Highest Score	198*	G.A.Gooch	Essex v Sussex	Hove	1982
Hundreds	314				1972-98
Fastest Hundred	62 min	M.A.Nash	Glamorgan v Hants	Swansea	1976

Highest Partnership for each Wicket

1st	252*	V.P.Terry/C.L.Smith	Hants v Comb Us	Southampton	1990
2nd	285*	C.G.Greenidge/D.R.Turner	Hants v Minor C (S)	Amersham	1973
3rd	269*	P.M.Roebuck/M.D.Crowe	Somerset v Hants	Southampton	1987
4th	184*	D.Lloyd/B.W.Reidy	Lancashire v Derbys	Chesterfield	1980
5th	160	A.J.Lamb/D.J.Capel	Northants v Leics	Northampton	1986
6th	167*	M.G.Bevan/R.J.Blakey	Yorkshire v Lancs	Manchester	1996
7th	149*	J.D.Love/C.M.Old	Yorks v Scotland	Bradford	1981
8th	109	R.E.East/N.Smith	Essex v Northants	Chelmsford	1977
9th	83	P.G.Newman/M.A.Holding	Derbyshire v Notts	Nottingham	1985
10th	80*	D.L.Bairstow/M.Johnson	Yorkshire v Derbys	Derby	1981

Best Bowling	7-12	W.W.Daniel	Middx v Minor C (E)	Ipswich	1978
	7-22	R.Thomson	Middx v Hampshire	Lord's	1981
	7-24	Mushtaq Ahmed	Somerset v Ireland	Taunton	1997
	7-32	R.G.D.Willis	Warwicks v Yorks	Birmingham	1981
Four wickets in Four Balls		S.M.Pollock	Warwicks v Leics	Birmingham	1996
Hat-Tricks		G.D.McKenzie	Leics v Worcs	Worcester	1972
		K.Higgs	Leics v Surrey	Lord's	1974
		A.A.Jones	Middlesex v Essex	Lord's	1977
		M.J.Procter	Glos v Hampshire	Southampton	1977
		W.Larkins	Northants v Comb Us	Northampton	1980
		E.A.Moseley	Glamorgan v Kent	Cardiff	1981
		G.C.Small	Warwickshire v Leics	Leicester	1984
		N.A.Mallender	Somerset v Comb Us	Taunton	1987
		W.K.M.Benjamin	Leics v Notts	Leicester	1987
		A.R.C.Fraser	Middlesex v Sussex	Lord's	1988
		Saqlain Mushtaq	Surrey v Lancashire	The Oval	1998

Most Wicket-Keeping Dismissals in an Innings
8	(8ct)	D.J.S.Taylor	Somerset v Comb Us	Taunton	1982

Most Catches in an Innings
5	V.J.Marks	Comb Us v Kent	Oxford	1976

Most Match Awards
	22	G.A.Gooch	Essex	1973-97

BENSON AND HEDGES CUP WINNERS

1972	Leicestershire	1981	Somerset	1990	Lancashire
1973	Kent	1982	Somerset	1991	Worcestershire
1974	Surrey	1983	Middlesex	1992	Hampshire
1975	Leicestershire	1984	Lancashire	1993	Derbyshire
1976	Kent	1985	Leicestershire	1994	Warwickshire
1977	Gloucestershire	1986	Middlesex	1995	Lancashire
1978	Kent	1987	Yorkshire	1996	Lancashire
1979	Essex	1988	Hampshire	1997	Surrey
1980	Northamptonshire	1989	Nottinghamshire	1998	Essex

AXA SUNDAY LEAGUE
FINAL TABLE 1998

	P	W	L	T	NR	Pts	NRR
1 LANCASHIRE (3)	17	12	2	–	3	54	12.18
2 Warwickshire (1)	17	9	5	–	3	42	4.23
3 Essex (7)	17	9	5	1	2	42	1.27
4 Leicestershire (4)	17	9	6	–	2	40	15.13
5 Kent (2)	17	8	6	–	3	38	1.19
6 Gloucestershire (11)	17	7	6	–	4	36	–1.65
7 Worcestershire (8)	17	7	6	1	3	36	–4.60
8 Hampshire (15)	17	8	8	–	1	34	0.95
9 Yorkshire (10)	17	8	8	–	1	34	–2.47
10 Glamorgan (13)	17	7	8	–	2	32	–0.25
11 Nottinghamshire (12)	17	7	8	1	1	32	–0.67
12 Middlesex (16)	17	7	8	–	2	32	–4.90
13 Northamptonshire (9)	17	6	7	1	3	32	2.80
14 Somerset (6)	17	6	8	1	2	30	–0.10
15 Derbyshire (14)	17	6	8	–	3	30	–5.10
16 Sussex (18)	17	6	9	–	2	28	–1.84
17 Durham (17)	17	4	9	1	3	24	–7.89
18 Surrey (5)	17	3	12	–	2	16	–8.17

Win = 4 points. Tie (T)/No Result (NR) = 2 points. Positions of counties finishing equal on points are decided by most wins or, if equal, by higher net run-rate (NRR – overall run-rate in all matches, i.e. total runs scored x 100 divided by balls received, minus the run-rate of its opponents in those same matches).

1997 final positions are shown in brackets.

The Sunday League's sponsors were John Player & Sons (1969-86), Refuge Assurance (1987-91), TCCB (1992) and AXA Equity & Law Insurance (1993-98). Innings were limited to 40 overs (50 in 1993). This competition has been replaced by the 45-over, two-divisional National League, the top nine counties in the above table qualifying for the first division.

WINNERS

1969 Lancashire	1979 Somerset	1989 Lancashire
1970 Lancashire	1980 Warwickshire	1990 Derbyshire
1971 Worcestershire	1981 Essex	1991 Nottinghamshire
1972 Kent	1982 Sussex	1992 Middlesex
1973 Kent	1983 Yorkshire	1993 Glamorgan
1974 Leicestershire	1984 Essex	1994 Warwickshire
1975 Hampshire	1985 Essex	1995 Kent
1976 Kent	1986 Hampshire	1996 Surrey
1977 Leicestershire	1987 Worcestershire	1997 Warwickshire
1978 Hampshire	1988 Worcestershire	1998 Lancashire

SUNDAY LEAGUE
PRINCIPAL RECORDS 1969-98

Highest Total		375-4	Surrey v Yorkshire	Scarborough 1994
Highest Total Batting Second		317-6	Surrey v Notts	The Oval 1993
Lowest Total		23	Middlesex v Yorks	Leeds 1974

Highest Score	203	A.D.Brown	Surrey v Hampshire	Guildford 1997
Total Hundreds	592			1969-98
Fastest Hundred	44 balls	M.A.Ealham	Kent v Derbyshire	Maidstone 1995

Highest Partnership for each Wicket

1st	239	G.A.Gooch/B.R.Hardie	Essex v Notts	Nottingham 1985
2nd	273	G.A.Gooch/K.S.McEwan	Essex v Notts	Nottingham 1983
3rd	223	S.J.Cook/G.D.Rose	Somerset v Glam	Neath 1990
4th	219	C.G.Greenidge/C.L.Smith	Hampshire v Surrey	Southampton 1987
5th	190	R.J.Blakey/M.J.Foster	Yorkshire v Leics	Leicester 1993
6th	137	M.P.Speight/I.D.K.Salisbury	Sussex v Surrey	Guildford 1996
7th	132	K.R.Brown/N.F.Williams	Middx v Somerset	Lord's 1988
8th	110*	C.L.Cairns/B.N.French	Notts v Surrey	The Oval 1993
9th	105	D.G.Moir/R.W.Taylor	Derbyshire v Kent	Derby 1984
10th	82	G.Chapple/P.J.Martin	Lancashire v Worcs	Manchester 1996

Best Bowling

	8-26	K.D.Boyce	Essex v Lancashire	Manchester 1971
	7-15	R.A.Hutton	Yorkshire v Worcs	Leeds 1969
	7-16	S.D.Thomas	Glamorgan v Surrey	Swansea 1998
	7-39	A.Hodgson	Northants v Somerset	Northampton 1976
	7-41	A.N.Jones	Sussex v Notts	Nottingham 1986

Four Wkts in Four Balls	A.Ward	Derbyshire v Sussex	Derby	1970

Hat-Tricks (27): Derbyshire – A.Ward (1970), C.J.Tunnicliffe (1979); Essex – K.D.Boyce (1971); Glamorgan – M.A.Nash (1975), A.E.Cordle (1979), G.C.Holmes (1987), A.Dale (1993); Gloucestershire – K.M.Curran (1989), A.M.Smith (1998); Hampshire – J.M.Rice (1975), M.D.Marshall (1981); Kent – R.M.Ellison (1983), M.J.McCague (1992); Leicestershire – G.D.McKenzie (1972), J.M.Dakin (1998); Northamptonshire – A.Hodgson (1976); Nottinghamshire – K.Saxelby (1987), K.P.Evans (1994); Somerset – R.Palmer (1970), I.V.A.Richards (1982); Surrey – M.P.Bicknell (1992); Sussex – A.Buss (1974); Warwickshire – R.G.D.Willis (1973), W.Blenkiron (1974); Worcestershire – R.K.Illingworth (1993); Yorkshire – P.W.Jarvis (1982), D.Gough (1998).

Most Wicket-Keeping Dismissals in an Innings

7	(6ct, 1st)	R.W.Taylor	Derbyshire v Lancs	Manchester 1975

Most Catches in an Innings

5		J.M.Rice	Hampshire v Warwicks	Southampton 1978

COUNTY CAPS AWARDED IN 1998

Derbyshire	K.J.Dean, M.J.Slater.
Durham	M.M.Betts, D.C.Boon, S.J.E.Brown, P.D.Collingwood, J.J.B.Lewis, J.E.Morris, M.A.Roseberry, N.J.Speak, M.P.Speight, J.Wood.
	(Caps awarded on merit for the first time)
Essex	–
Glamorgan	–
Gloucestershire	T.H.C.Hancock, J.Lewis, M.G.N.Windows.
Hampshire	P.J.Hartley, N.A.M.McLean, A.D.Mascarenhas, G.W.White.
Kent	D.P.Fulton.
Lancashire	A.Flintoff.
Leicestershire	M.T.Brimson, A.Habib.
Middlesex	J.P.Hewitt, J.L.Langer.
Northamptonshire	–
Nottinghamshire	J.E.R.Gallian, M.P.Dowman.
Somerset	–
Surrey	J.D.Ratcliffe, I.D.K.Salisbury, Saqlain Mushtaq, N.Shahid.
Sussex	C.J.Adams, M.G.Bevan, R.J.Kirtley.
Warwickshire	E.S.H.Giddins.
Worcestershire	V.S.Solanki.
Yorkshire	G.M.Hamilton, P.M.Hutchison.

MINOR COUNTIES CHAMPIONSHIP

FINAL TABLE 1998

	Two Innings Matches				Bonus Points		Grade Rules		Total
	P	W	L	D	Bat	Bowl	P	Points	Points
EASTERN DIVISION									
Staffordshire	6	1	0	5(a)	11	13	3	59	104
Buckinghamshire	6	2	0	4(a)	5	9	3	38	89
Suffolk	6	1	1	4	15	14	3	29	74
Norfolk	6	1	0	5(a)	11	8	3	31	71
Bedfordshire	6	1	0	5(a)	14	12	3	20	67
Lincolnshire	6	1	3(d)	2	15	15	3	9	60
Northumberland	6	1	0	5(a)	9	9	3	20	59
Cambridgeshire	6	0	0	6	17	13	3	24	54
Hertfordshire	6	0	2(d)	4(a)	10	10	3	19	49
Cumberland	6	0	2	4(b)	6	14	3	17	47
WESTERN DIVISION									
Dorset	6	2	1(d)	3	15	14	3	39	105
Cheshire	6	1	0	5(a)	12	19	3	39	91
Shropshire	6	2	0	4(a)	10	13	3	27	87
Herefordshire	6	1	0	5	14	11	3	38	79
Devon	6	0	3	3	19	15	3	43	77
Cornwall	6	0	0	5	8	20	3	33	77
Wiltshire	6	1	1	4(a)	4	12	3	34	71
Berkshire	6	0	2	4(a)	8	12	3	45	70
Wales	6	1	2(d)	3(a)	8	11	3	15	60
Oxfordshire	6	0	0	6(c)	2	8	3	21	46

(a) Record includes 5 points gained in 1 'No Result' match
(b) Record includes 10 points gained in 2 'No Result' matches
(c) Record includes 15 points gained in 3 'No Result' matches
(d) Record includes 5 points gained in lost match reduced to one day

1998 CHAMPIONSHIP FINAL
DORSET v STAFFORDSHIRE

At Dean Park, Bournemouth on 6, 7 September.
Toss: Dorset. Result: **MATCH DRAWN: STAFFORDSHIRE** awarded Championship on run rate.
Debuts: None.

STAFFORDSHIRE

L.Potter	c Swarbrick b Shackleton	58	c Diment b Pike		52
*S.J.Dean	c Rintoul b Shackleton	0	c Richings b Cowley		59
P.E.Wellings	c Reynolds b Pike	15	c Lamb b Cowley		7
R.Mills	c Richings b Pike	12	lbw b Cowley		1
M.V.Steele	not out	40	c Hardy b Cowley		0
R.P.Harvey	run out	16	c Cowley b Pike		0
†M.I.Humphries	b Cowley	5	lbw b Cowley		0
D.R.Womble	not out	12	c Lamb b Cowley		20
D.J.Brock			not out		2
D.J.P.Boden			c sub b Cowley		9
A.Richardson			not out		2
Extras	(B 1, LB 8, W 2, NB 8)	19	(B 12, LB 2, W 4)		18
Total	(6 wickets, 50 overs)	**177**	(9 wickets)		**170**

DORSET

*J.J.E.Hardy	c Humphries b Brock	15
T.W.Richings	c Humphries b Boden	22
R.J.Scott	c Humphries b Richardson	1
†G.D.Reynolds	c Dean b Richardson	6
T.C.Z.Lamb	c Potter b Richardson	17
S.W.D.Rintoul	c Boden b Potter	5
N.G.Cowley	lbw b Richardson	1
M.Swarbrick	c Humphries b Potter	7
V.J.Pike	c Humphries b Potter	10
S.Diment	not out	1
J.H.Shackleton	c Humphries b Potter	0
Extras	(LB 3, W 2, NB 2)	7
Total		**92**

DORSET	O	M	R	W	O	M	R	W
Shackleton	22	6	54	2	9.1	2	17	0
Diment	6	2	20	0	3	0	16	0
Pike	19	1	74	2	30	12	68	2
Cowley	3	0	20	1	26	13	55	7

STAFFORDSHIRE	O	M	R	W
Richardson	18	7	49	4
Brock	11	2	29	1
Boden	1	0	5	1
Potter	7.5	5	6	4

FALL OF WICKETS

Wkt	S 1st	D 1st	S 2nd
1st	1	41	111
2nd	39	41	123
3rd	73	47	128
4th	112	58	128
5th	147	67	129
6th	156	70	132
7th	–	75	133
8th	–	89	155
9th	–	92	167
10th	–	92	–

Umpires: C.T.Puckett and M.K.Reed.

MINOR COUNTIES CHAMPIONS

1895	Norfolk / Durham / Worcestershire	1929	Oxfordshire	1968	Yorkshire II
1896	Worcestershire	1930	Durham	1969	Buckinghamshire
1897	Worcestershire	1931	Leicestershire II	1970	Bedfordshire
1898	Worcestershire	1932	Buckinghamshire	1971	Yorkshire II
1899	Northamptonshire / Buckinghamshire	1933	*Undecided*	1972	Bedfordshire
		1934	Lancashire II	1973	Shropshire
1900	Glamorgan / Durham / Northamptonshire	1935	Middlesex II	1974	Oxfordshire
		1936	Hertfordshire	1975	Hertfordshire
		1937	Lancashire II	1976	Durham
1901	Durham	1938	Buckinghamshire	1977	Suffolk
1902	Wiltshire	1939	Surrey II	1978	Devon
1903	Northamptonshire	1946	Suffolk	1979	Suffolk
1904	Northamptonshire	1947	Yorkshire II	1980	Durham
1905	Norfolk	1948	Lancashire II	1981	Durham
1906	Staffordshire	1949	Lancashire II	1982	Oxfordshire
1907	Lancashire II	1950	Surrey II	1983	Hertfordshire
1908	Staffordshire	1951	Kent II	1984	Durham
1909	Wiltshire	1952	Buckinghamshire	1985	Cheshire
1910	Norfolk	1953	Berkshire	1986	Cumberland
1911	Staffordshire	1954	Surrey II	1987	Buckinghamshire
1912	*In abeyance*	1955	Surrey II	1988	Cheshire
1913	Norfolk	1956	Kent II	1989	Oxfordshire
1920	Staffordshire	1957	Yorkshire II	1990	Hertfordshire
1921	Staffordshire	1958	Yorkshire II	1991	Staffordshire
1922	Buckinghamshire	1959	Warwickshire II	1992	Staffordshire
1923	Buckinghamshire	1960	Lancashire II	1993	Staffordshire
1924	Berkshire	1961	Somerset II	1994	Devon
1925	Buckinghamshire	1962	Warwickshire II	1995	Devon
1926	Durham	1963	Cambridgeshire	1996	Devon
1927	Staffordshire	1964	Lancashire II	1997	Devon
1928	Berkshire	1965	Somerset II	1998	Staffordshire
		1966	Lincolnshire		
		1967	Cheshire		

MINOR COUNTIES RECORDS

Highest Total	621		Surrey II v Devon	The Oval	1928
Lowest Total	14		Cheshire v Staffs	Stoke	1909
Highest Score	282	E.Garnett	Berkshire v Wiltshire	Reading	1908
Most Runs – Season	1212	A.F.Brazier	Surrey II		1949

Record Partnership
2nd 388* T.H.Clark and A.F.Brazier   Surrey II v Sussex II   The Oval   1949

Best Bowling – Innings	10-11	S.Turner	Cambs v Cumberland	Penrith	1987
– Match	18-100	N.W.Harding	Kent II v Wiltshire	Swindon	1937
Most Wickets – Season	119	S.F.Barnes	Staffordshire		1906

1998 MINOR COUNTIES CHAMPIONSHIP

LEADING BATTING AVERAGES 1998
(Qualification: 8 completed innings [or 500 runs] average 35.00)

		I	NO	HS	Runs	Avge
D.J.M.Mercer	Bedfordshire	15	8	103*	610	87.14
D.W.Randall	Suffolk	11	3	115	469	58.62
C.Amos	Norfolk	13	2	226*	632	57.45
N.A.Folland	Devon	13	2	123	631	57.36
J.B.R.Jones	Shropshire	14	2	147*	667	55.58
A.J.Pugh	Devon	11	3	163	439	54.87
A.C.H.Seymour	Suffolk	12	2	99	540	54.00
D.M.Ward	Hertfordshire	12	2	131	537	53.70
G.T.J.Townsend	Devon	14	2	129*	643	53.58
J.J.E.Hardy	Dorset	13	0	116	693	53.30
Asif Din	Shropshire	14	3	98	549	49.90
S.C.Goldsmith	Norfolk	13	2	157*	537	48.81
S.G.Plumb	Lincolnshire	15	4	115*	32	48.36
L.Potter	Staffordshire	14	1	143*	627	48.23
J.C.Harrison	Buckinghamshire	11	1	147	473	47.30
K.M.Wijesuriya	Suffolk	13	2	112	516	46.90
S.J.Dean	Staffordshire	15	2	131*	594	45.69
C.W.Boroughs	Herefordshire	9	1	103	362	45.25
G.E.Loveday	Berkshire	14	1	206*	562	43.23
M.J.Glasson	Wiltshire	12	1	86	464	42.18
M.E.Fell	Lincolnshire	11	2	92*	363	40.33
B.T.P.Donelan	Cambridgeshire	14	4	70*	401	40.10
P.R.J.Bryson	Cheshire	13	0	96	521	40.07
R.J.Catley	Suffolk	12	2	1308	395	39.50
J.L.Taylor	Wiltshire	13	0	101	512	39.38
R.G.Hignett	Cheshire	13	1	92	468	39.00
W.Falla	Northumberland	8	0	97	312	39.00
I.Cockbain	Cheshire	13	2	100*	407	37.00
C.Clark	Northumberland	9	0	108	329	36.55
A.R.Roberts	Bedfordshire	13	1	112*	428	35.66
P.M.Roebuck	Devon	10	2	90	283	35.37
T.A.Radford	Berkshire	12	1	96	389	35.36
J.Clarke	Lincolnshire	9	0	110	317	35.22

LEADING BOWLING AVERAGES
(Qualification: 20 wickets, average 30.00)

		O	M	R	W	Avge
A.Richardson	Staffordshire	150.4	60	337	31	10.87
D.B.Pennett	Cumberland	114.2	25	382	23	16.60
G.Kirk	Suffolk	141.2	42	416	23	18.08
P.J.Humphries	Herefordshire	172	35	560	29	19.31
C.J.Ellison	Cornwall	148.1	34	495	24	20.62
K.E.Cooper	Herefordshire	261.2	85	608	28	21.71
S.R.Barwick	Wales	217.5	61	606	27	22.44
P.M.Roebuck	Devon	293.2	95	596	26	22.92
A.Akhtar	Cambridgeshire	257.5	67	807	34	23.73
V.J.Pike	Dorset	334.5	75	1040	41	25.36
N.M.Kendrick	Berkshire	238.3	69	707	27	26.18
P.G.Newman	Norfolk	208	59	563	21	26.80
C.E.Shreck	Cornwall	246.2	52	828	30	27.60
S.W.Hampson	Cheshire	162.3	35	589	20	29.45
D.A.Christmas	Lincolnshire	160.4	24	600	20	30.00

SECOND XI CHAMPIONSHIP 1998
FINAL TABLE

		P	W	L	D	T	Bonus Points Bat	Bonus Points Bowl	Total Points	Avge
1	NORTHAMPTONSHIRE (7)	15	9	1	5	–	39	46	244	16.27
2	Sussex (9)	13	7	1	5	–	38	41	206	15.85
3	Somerset (13)	13	6	6	1	–	40	43	182	14.00
4	Gloucestershire (12)	14	6	5	3	–	41	39	185	13.21
5	Lancashire (1)	14	5	3	6	–	39	45	182	13.00
6	Leicestershire (8)	12	4	3	5	–	30	40	149	12.42
7	Hampshire (5)	14	5	5	4	–	38	36	166	11.86
8	Nottinghamshire (18)	17	5	2	10	–	41	50	201	11.82
9	Yorkshire (2)	15	4	2	9	–	37	40	168	11.20
10	Durham (14)	12	4	3	5	–	17	38	134	11.17
11	Worcestershire (15)	14	3	4	6	–	32	40	147	10.50
12	Derbyshire (3)	15	3	5	7	–	31	41	141	9.40
13	Kent (16)	14	2	3	9	–	33	33	125	8.93
14	Glamorgan (10)	14	2	4	7	1	28	32	121	8.64
15	Essex (17)	15	2	8	5	–	33	43	123	8.20
16	Warwickshire (4)	14	1	3	10	–	36	32	114	8.14
17	Middlesex (11)	13	1	4	8	–	31	30	101	7.77
18	Surrey (6)	14	1	8	5	–	26	45	102	7.29

Win = 16 points (12 when under 8 hours playing time remained).
1997 final positions are shown in brackets.

ECB SECOND XI AWARD 1998

Player of the Season　　　K.J.Innes　　　　　　　　Northamptonshire

SECOND XI CHAMPIONS

1959	Gloucestershire	1973	Essex	1987	Kent/Yorkshire
1960	Northamptonshire	1974	Middlesex	1988	Surrey
1961	Kent	1975	Surrey	1989	Middlesex
1962	Worcestershire	1976	Kent	1990	Sussex
1963	Worcestershire	1977	Yorkshire	1991	Yorkshire
1964	Lancashire	1978	Sussex	1992	Surrey
1965	Glamorgan	1979	Warwickshire	1993	Middlesex
1966	Surrey	1980	Glamorgan	1994	Somerset
1967	Hampshire	1981	Hampshire	1995	Hampshire
1968	Surrey	1982	Worcestershire	1996	Warwickshire
1969	Kent	1983	Leicestershire	1997	Lancashire
1970	Kent	1984	Yorkshire	1998	Northamptonshire
1971	Hampshire	1985	Nottinghamshire		
1972	Nottinghamshire	1986	Lancashire		

FIRST-CLASS CAREER RECORDS

Compiled by Philip Bailey

The following career records are for all players who appeared in first-class or limited-overs cricket during the 1998 season, and are complete to the end of that season. Some players who did not appear in 1998 but may do so in 1999, are also included.

BATTING AND FIELDING

'1000' denotes instances of scoring 1000 runs in a season. Where these have been achieved outside the UK, they are shown after a plus sign.

	M	I	NO	HS	Runs	Avge	100	50	1000	Ct/St
Adams, C.J.	173	282	21	239	9605	36.80	25	43	4	202
Adams, P.R.	42	44	19	38*	300	12.00	–	–	–	21
Afzaal, U.	48	83	8	109*	1845	24.60	2	11	–	22
Aldred, P.	27	34	7	83	375	13.88	–	1	–	19
Alleyne, M.W.	237	392	39	256	11428	32.37	16	60	6	193/2
Allingham, M.J.D.	4	7	2	50*	187	37.40	–	1	–	3
Altree, D.A.	5	7	3	2*	2	0.50	–	–	–	1
Amin, R.M.	7	10	5	12	25	5.00	–	–	–	2
Archer, G.F.	85	151	13	168	4719	34.19	9	25	1	100
Arnold, R.P.	62	94	9	217*	4023	47.32	12	14	0+1	57
Asim Butt	23	30	9	44	362	17.23	–	–	–	11
Atapattu, M.S.	126	177	35	253*	8012	56.42	27	31	0+3	91
Atherton, M.A.	271	471	41	199	17911	41.65	46	88	6	215
Austin, I.D.	118	163	35	115*	3653	28.53	2	20	–	33
Averis, J.M.M.	11	17	5	42	282	23.50	–	–	–	2
Aymes, A.N.	163	239	62	133	5525	31.21	5	26	–	374/33
Bacher, A.M.	49	88	8	210	2866	35.82	6	14	0+1	59
Bailey, R.J.	333	561	82	224*	19858	41.45	43	101	13	251
Bailey, T.M.B.	4	4	1	31*	48	16.00	–	–	–	6
Ball, M.C.J.	121	188	33	71	2823	18.21	–	7	–	144
Bandaratilake, M.R.C.N.	54	63	13	77	922	18.44	–	2	–	44
Barnes, J.P.B.	5	6	3	38*	74	24.66	–	–	–	8
Barnett, K.J.	431	702	68	238*	25556	40.30	53	138	15	250
Bates, J.J.	11	16	2	47	167	11.92	–	–	–	10
Bates, R.T.	32	47	12	34	450	12.85	–	–	–	18
Batson, N.E.	3	6	–	18	50	8.33	–	–	–	–
Batt, C.J.	10	14	2	43	150	12.50	–	–	–	2
Batty, G.J.	1	2	–	18	18	9.00	–	–	–	–
Batty, J.N.	31	38	7	63	747	24.09	–	4	–	57/9
Bell, M.A.V.	20	23	10	30	109	8.38	–	–	–	8
Benjamin, J.E.	124	143	43	49	1152	11.52	–	–	–	24
Betts, M.M.	49	75	17	57*	709	12.22	–	1	–	10
Bevan, M.G.	155	259	44	203*	11423	53.13	37	58	2	91
Bichel, A.J.	34	46	6	110	906	22.65	1	4	–	19
Bicknell, D.J.	200	352	34	235*	12696	39.92	30	59	6	75
Bicknell, M.P.	198	236	59	88	3412	19.27	–	11	–	68
Birks, M.J.	9	10	3	23*	81	11.57	–	–	–	8/1
Bishop, I.E.	1	2	–	2	4	2.00	–	–	–	1
Blackwell, I.D.	15	23	–	57	305	13.26	–	2	–	6
Blain, J.A.R.	3	1	–	0	0	0.00	–	–	–	2
Blakey, R.J.	275	436	67	221	11812	32.01	10	70	5	586/48
Blanchett, I.N.	4	4	–	18	25	6.25	–	–	–	1

	M	I	NO	HS	Runs	Avge	100	50	1000	Ct/St
Blewett, G.S.	106	183	11	268	7666	44.56	19	42	0+2	79
Bloomfield, T.F.	12	13	7	20*	41	6.83	–	–	–	2
Boiling, J.	88	125	38	69	1160	13.33	–	2	–	70
Boon, D.C.	324	543	50	227	22314	45.26	67	105	4+2	267
Boswell, S.A.J.	13	16	5	35	127	11.54	–	–	–	4
Boucher, M.V.	35	49	7	80	1354	32.23	–	10	–	124/9
Boulton, N.R.	1	2	–	14	15	7.50	–	–	–	–
Bowen, M.N.	52	65	18	32	604	12.85	–	–	–	13
Bowler, P.D.	230	400	35	241*	14227	38.97	31	78	8	158/1
Brimson, M.T.	52	50	21	54*	332	11.44	–	1	–	9
Brinkley, J.E.	15	17	4	29	89	6.84	–	–	–	5
Broadhurst, M.	6	3	–	6	7	2.33	–	–	–	1
Brown, A.D.	108	172	15	187	6664	42.44	18	29	4	112
Brown, D.R.	82	127	15	85	2857	25.50	–	17	–	44
Brown, J.F.	15	20	10	16*	43	4.30	–	–	–	4
Brown, K.R.	247	373	75	200*	10487	35.19	13	56	2	466/33
Brown, S.J.E.	125	172	50	69	1490	12.21	–	2	–	36
Buchanan, L.G.	10	15	4	43*	170	15.45	–	–	–	2
Bulbeck, M.P.L.	8	11	6	35	141	28.20	–	–	–	2
Burns, M.	44	72	3	96	1600	23.18	–	11	–	65/7
Bushe, J.A.	1	2	1	4*	6	6.00	–	–	–	3/1
Butcher, A.R.	402	684	60	216*	22667	36.32	46	123	12	185
Butcher, G.P.	40	58	10	101*	1357	28.27	1	8	–	16
Butcher, M.A.	101	177	13	167	6280	38.29	10	44	4	106
Byas, D.	218	365	33	213	12074	36.36	24	67	5	267
Byrne, B.W.	19	32	4	69*	610	21.78	–	1	–	6
Caddick, A.R.	128	167	31	92	2154	15.83	–	5	–	44
Campbell, R.J.	26	45	2	177	1580	36.74	4	10	–	49/3
Capel, D.J.	313	477	66	175	12202	29.68	16	72	3	156
Carpenter, J.R.	12	22	–	65	375	17.04	–	2	–	5
Cassar, M.E.	27	43	6	121	1069	28.89	1	8	–	8
Catterall, D.N.	1	1	–	0	0	0.00	–	–	–	–
Chandana, U.D.U.	76	97	9	163	3064	34.81	7	17	–	62
Chapman, C.A.	8	13	2	80	238	21.63	–	1	–	13/3
Chapman, R.J.	32	37	13	43*	233	9.70	–	–	–	7
Chapman, S.	1	2	–	11	13	6.50	–	–	–	–
Chapple, G.	88	120	41	109*	1668	21.11	1	4	–	31
Cherry, D.D.	1	1	–	11	11	11.00	–	–	–	–
Chilton, M.J.	4	7	–	47	167	23.85	–	–	–	–
Church, M.J.	20	36	1	152	629	17.97	1	1	–	13
Clarke, V.P.	30	50	7	99	1058	24.60	–	5	–	15
Claughton, J.A.	5	8	1	45	140	20.00	–	–	–	1
Clough, G.D.	1	2	–	33	34	17.00	–	–	–	1
Cockcroft, J.R.	3	2	1	18*	19	19.00	–	–	–	–
Collingwood, P.D.	38	66	7	107	1613	27.33	2	8	–	33
Collins, B.J.	3	5	–	36	79	15.80	–	–	–	5
Connor, C.A.	221	206	54	59	1814	11.93	–	2	–	61
Cooke, G.	3	3	–	12	17	5.66	–	–	–	1
Cork, D.G.	153	228	34	104	4722	24.34	3	27	–	97
Cosker, D.A.	42	42	13	37	209	7.20	–	–	–	21
Cottey, P.A.	203	329	49	203	10619	37.92	21	59	7	142
Cousins, D.M.	15	25	5	18*	159	7.95	–	–	–	5
Cowan, A.P.	44	66	14	94	936	18.00	–	3	–	20
Cowdrey, G.R.	179	284	29	147	8858	34.73	17	46	3	97
Cox, J.	103	188	12	200	7046	40.03	18	33	0+1	42

	M	I	NO	HS	Runs	Avge	100	50	1000	Ct/St
Crawley, J.P.	178	288	29	286	13083	50.51	30	74	7	134
Croft, R.D.B.	201	295	56	143	6054	25.33	2	25	–	105
Cronje, W.J.	156	266	29	251	10468	44.16	27	51	1	97
Crowe, C.D.	7	8	1	29*	98	14.00	–	–	–	4
Cullinan, D.J.	172	298	42	337*	10818	42.25	25	57	1	152
Cunliffe, R.J.	41	68	5	190*	1630	25.87	2	7	–	29
Curran, K.M.	323	508	83	159	15739	37.03	25	83	7	209
Dakin, J.M.	22	30	3	190	834	30.88	3	3	–	11
Dale, A.	165	273	24	214*	8157	32.75	14	43	3	64
Dale, A.C.	24	27	2	55	325	13.00	–	1	–	6
Daley, J.A.	58	101	10	159*	2858	31.40	2	14	–	31
Davies, A.G.	5	6	2	26*	80	20.00	–	–	–	10/2
Davies, A.S.	8	8	2	34	74	12.33	–	–	–	2
Davies, M.K.	8	12	5	17	72	10.28	–	–	–	2
Davis, R.P.	169	208	46	67	2452	15.13	–	4	–	155
Dawood, I	10	16	3	40	207	15.92	–	–	–	23/3
Dawson, R.I.	63	113	9	127*	2552	24.53	3	12	1	30
Dean, K.J.	33	41	19	27*	266	12.09	–	–	–	5
DeFreitas, P.A.J.	287	408	38	113	8059	21.78	6	40	–	102
De la Pena, J.M.	8	8	6	7*	10	5.00	–	–	–	–
De Silva, P.A.	178	279	27	267	12286	48.75	37	55	1+1	94
Dharmasena, H.D.P.K.	73	100	16	155*	2626	31.26	3	12	–	43
Di Venuto, M.J.	58	102	3	189	4043	40.83	9	22	–	42
Donald, A.A.	260	301	115	59	2281	12.26	–	1	–	98
Dowman, M.P.	53	94	4	149	2538	28.20	6	9	1	29
Drakes, V.C.	71	114	16	180*	2414	24.63	4	9	–	20
Driver, R.C.	1	2	–	5	5	2.50	–	–	–	–
Dunlop, A.R.	4	7	–	57	180	25.71	–	2	–	2
Dutch, K.P.	16	18	2	79	218	13.62	–	1	–	11
Dwyer, M.D.	1	2	1	1*	1	1.00	–	–	–	–
Dyer, N.R.	2	1	1	0*	0	–	–	–	–	1
Eadie, D.J.	6	6	2	68*	84	21.00	–	1	–	2
Ealham, M.A.	124	203	34	139	5432	32.14	5	35	1	50
Ecclestone, S.C.	46	74	9	133	2277	35.03	3	12	–	22
Edmond, M.D.	7	9	3	32	107	17.83	–	–	–	1
Edwards, A.D.	13	20	2	22	134	7.44	–	–	–	10
Ellis, S.W.K.	12	13	5	15	63	7.87	–	–	–	8
Elworthy, S.	92	143	20	89	2528	20.55	–	8	–	34
Evans, A.W.	17	30	4	125	823	31.65	1	3	–	13
Evans, K.P.	160	220	44	104	4198	23.85	3	21	–	111
Fairbrother, N.H.	315	500	70	366	17941	41.72	40	96	10	231
Fellows, G.M.	3	5	–	50	87	17.40	–	1	–	–
Ferguson, S.H.	1	1	–	2	2	2.00	–	–	–	1
Fisher, I.D.	6	5	1	37	75	18.75	–	–	–	–
Flanagan, I.N.	8	14	1	61	326	25.07	–	2	–	9
Fleming, M.V.	166	274	31	138	7301	30.04	9	37	–	69
Flintoff, A.	27	41	3	124	959	25.23	2	5	–	35
Follett, D.	13	17	7	17	43	4.30	–	–	–	5
Ford, J.A.	1	–	–	–	–	–	–	–	–	1
Foster, M.J.	30	50	2	129	1128	23.50	1	6	–	10
Francis, S.R.G.	3	3	1	6*	14	7.00	–	–	–	–
Franks, P.J.	27	39	8	66*	670	21.61	–	3	–	13
Fraser, A.G.J.	10	10	5	52*	137	27.40	–	1	–	6
Fraser, A.R.C.	242	286	69	92	2362	10.88	–	1	–	44
Frost, T.	17	25	4	111*	547	26.04	1	2	–	49/2

	M	I	NO	HS	Runs	Avge	100	50	1000	Ct/St
Fulton, D.P.	76	137	9	207	4059	31.71	5	23	–	111
Fulton, J.A.G.	18	31	1	78	631	21.03	–	5	–	10
Gallian, J.E.R.	105	184	16	312	6230	37.61	13	31	2	70
Garaway, M.	3	3	–	44	68	22.66	–	–	–	9/1
Garland, R	8	9	4	56*	158	31.60	–	1	–	1
Gatting, M.W.	551	861	123	258	36549	49.52	94	181	19	493
Giddins, E.S.H.	98	119	47	34	364	5.05	–	–	–	16
Gie, N.A.	11	20	–	50	311	15.55	–	2	–	7
Giles, A.F.	64	87	20	106*	2071	30.91	1	12	–	26
Gillespie, J.N.	37	49	10	58	455	11.66	–	1	–	15
Goodchild, D.J.	8	16	1	105	328	21.86	1	2	–	1
Gough, D.	147	197	32	121	2744	16.63	1	11	–	35
Gough, M.A.	10	18	–	123	508	28.22	1	2	–	12
Grayson, A.P.	105	169	16	140	4428	28.94	4	25	2	84
Green, R.J.	18	19	6	51	199	15.30	–	1	–	4
Greenfield, K.	78	135	15	154*	3550	29.58	9	13	–	65
Griffiths, S.P.	7	12	–	20	91	7.58	–	–	–	22
Grove, J.O.	4	7	1	33	88	14.66	–	–	–	–
Habib, A.	48	67	14	215	2390	45.09	6	6	–	26
Hafeez, A.	10	18	1	55	303	17.82	–	1	–	6
Hamilton, G.M.	40	51	8	79	1054	24.51	–	7	–	13
Hancock, T.H.C.	112	199	15	220*	5242	28.48	6	31	1	74
Hansen, T.M.	1	2	1	19	31	31.00	–	–	–	–
Harden, R.J.	241	395	60	187	12897	38.49	28	67	7	187
Harmison, S.J.	15	24	4	36	233	11.65	–	–	–	2
Harris, A.J.	39	54	11	36	344	8.00	–	–	–	12
Hart, J.P.	1	2	2	18*	18	–	–	–	–	–
Hartley, P.J.	211	257	55	127*	4035	19.97	2	13	–	65
Harvey, I.J.	34	61	3	136	1469	25.32	2	10	–	27
Harvey, M.E.	6	10	1	25	116	12.88	–	–	–	2
Hathurusinghe, U.C.	135	210	17	143	7206	37.33	12	43	–	101
Hayden, M.L.	122	216	23	235*	10455	54.17	33	45	2+3	107
Haynes, G.R.	92	143	14	158	3996	30.97	3	23	1	39
Haynes, J.J.	3	5	–	21	67	13.40	–	–	–	12/1
Hayward, M.	26	16	6	55*	222	22.20	–	1	–	12
Headley, D.W.	119	158	41	91	2007	17.15	–	5	–	47
Hegg, W.K.	238	346	67	134	7373	26.42	4	37	–	570/66
Hemp, D.L.	109	190	17	157	5630	32.54	10	31	2	75
Hewitt, J.P.	43	55	10	75	844	18.75	–	3	–	16
Hewson, D.R.	21	38	4	87	764	22.47	–	6	–	9
Hibbert, A.J.E.	7	12	1	85	236	21.45	–	1	–	5
Hick, G.A.	363	595	59	405*	29777	55.55	103	109	14+1	441
Hills, D.F.	80	149	8	265	6227	44.16	18	31	0+2	62
Hockley, J.B.	1	2	–	21	30	15.00	–	–	–	–
Hodgson, T.P.	10	19	–	54	337	17.73	–	1	–	4
Hoggard, M.J.	11	13	4	13*	47	5.22	–	–	–	3
Hollioake, A.J.	97	151	14	182	5557	40.56	12	32	2	80
Hollioake, B.C.	38	57	4	163	1502	28.33	2	6	–	30
Holloway, P.C.L.	75	127	21	168	3545	33.44	6	18	–	61/1
Hooper, C.L.	258	412	41	236*	16898	45.54	47	79	7	288
House, W.J.	26	40	6	136	1179	34.67	2	7	–	16
Hughes, Q.J.	14	19	3	84	414	25.87	–	1	–	5
Humphries, S.	18	25	2	66	338	14.69	–	1	–	34
Hussain, N.	230	367	37	207	14227	43.11	38	66	5	275
Hussey, M.E.	39	70	6	147	2996	46.81	8	12	–	17

	M	I	NO	HS	Runs	Avge	100	50	1000	Ct/St
Hutchison, P.M.	31	30	17	30	169	13.00	–	–	–	6
Hutton, B.L.	1	1	–	10	10	10.00	–	–	–	–
Hutton, S.	66	119	6	172*	3341	29.56	4	13	–	34
Hyam, B.J.	20	35	5	49	460	15.33	–	–	–	52/3
Igglesden, A.P.	154	170	65	41	876	8.34	–	–	–	40
Illingworth, R.K.	345	389	114	120*	6291	22.87	4	19	–	151
Ilott, M.C.	154	198	43	60	2190	14.12	–	4	–	35
Innes, K.J.	7	10	1	63	153	17.00	–	1	–	5
Irani, R.C.	104	172	18	127*	5335	34.64	9	31	3	43
James, K.D.	223	333	57	162	8498	30.77	10	42	2	76
James, S.P.	188	332	26	235	12109	39.57	35	46	6	146
Janisch, A.N.	18	23	7	26*	168	15.27	–	–	–	2
Jarvis, P.W.	206	259	67	80	3299	17.18	–	10	–	63
Jayasuriya, S.T.	138	207	23	340	7586	41.22	16	36	–	95
Jayawardena, D.P.M.D.	36	55	5	200*	2076	41.52	6	11	–	42
Jayawardena, H.P.W.	5	7	1	25	48	8.00	–	–	–	10/2
Johnson, P.	316	527	50	187	17731	37.17	36	102	8	202/1
Johnson, R.L.	70	98	11	50*	1247	14.33	–	1	–	28
Jones, P.S.	14	18	6	36	173	14.41	–	–	–	4
Jones, S.P.	3	3	3	2*	2	–	–	–	–	1
Joyce, E.C.	2	4	–	43	82	20.50	–	–	–	1
Julian, B.P.	117	157	27	124	3290	25.30	4	16	–	74
Kallis, J.H.	80	123	14	186*	4847	44.46	13	27	1	56
Kaluwitharana, R.S.	83	126	8	179	5184	43.93	12	33	0+2	171/29
Kasprowicz, M.S.	105	136	25	49	1565	14.09	–	–	–	39
Keech, M.	61	98	11	127	2471	28.40	3	14	–	48
Keedy, G.	45	50	32	26	202	11.22	–	–	–	12
Kendall, W.S.	52	79	14	145*	2508	38.58	4	12	1	40
Kennis, G.J.	9	17	1	49	211	13.18	–	–	–	11
Kenway, D.A.	4	7	1	57	140	23.33	–	1	–	2
Kerr, J.I.D.	32	47	9	80	730	19.21	–	3	–	10
Kettleborough, R.A.	25	41	6	108	958	27.37	1	5	–	16
Key, R.W.T.	13	23	–	115	612	26.60	2	1	–	11
Khan, A.A.	23	28	5	52	332	14.43	–	1	–	9
Khan, S.H.	4	2	–	1	1	0.50	–	–	–	–
Khan, W.G.	49	86	8	181	2524	32.35	5	14	–	35
Killeen, N.	18	26	7	48	228	12.00	–	–	–	10
Kirsten, G.	137	245	28	244	9793	45.12	27	45	–	102
Kirtley, R.J.	41	57	23	59	396	11.64	–	1	–	13
Klusener, L.	59	82	23	105	2036	34.50	3	9	–	34
Knight, N.V.	128	216	23	192	7842	40.63	20	38	2	176
Knott, J.A.	12	20	7	49*	273	21.00	–	–	–	12/2
Krikken, K.M.	168	248	51	104	4496	22.82	1	18	–	418/27
Lacey, S.J.	9	11	4	50	157	22.42	–	1	–	2
Lampitt, S.R.	194	252	56	122	4700	23.97	1	17	–	125
Laney, J.S.	51	91	2	112	2808	31.55	5	15	1	38
Langer, J.L.	104	182	24	274*	8443	53.43	24	33	1+2	79
Lara, B.C.	155	255	7	501*	12676	51.11	34	55	3+1	197
Laraman, A.W.	1	–	–	–	–	–	–	–	–	–
Lathwell, M.N.	134	237	9	206	7768	34.07	12	48	5	92
Law, D.R.	61	97	–	115	1836	18.92	1	8	–	34
Law, S.G.	153	259	27	179	10753	46.34	30	54	2+1	161
Law, W.L.	10	15	3	131	482	40.16	1	2	–	4
Leather, D.	1	1	–	0	0	0.00	–	–	–	–
Leatherdale, D.A.	143	225	26	157	6778	34.06	10	36	1	120

	M	I	NO	HS	Runs	Avge	100	50	1000	Ct/St
Lehmann, D.S.	133	228	11	255	11288	52.01	33	56	1+4	78
Lewis, C.C.	174	255	32	247	6806	30.52	7	32	–	141
Lewis, J.	46	69	12	54*	705	12.36	–	1	–	11
Lewis, J.J.B.	91	161	19	210*	4833	34.03	7	29	1	69
Lewis, S.J.W.	1	2	–	3	3	1.50	–	–	–	–
Lewry, J.D.	43	63	11	34	434	8.34	–	–	–	3
Liebenberg, G.F.J.	108	186	11	229	6257	35.75	14	31	–	102/4
Lightfoot, C.G.R.	16	26	2	61	402	16.75	–	1	–	3
Llong, N.J.	68	108	11	130	3024	31.17	6	16	–	59
Lloyd, G.D.	160	258	25	241	9137	39.21	20	51	4	106
Lockhart, D.R.	11	19	1	77*	377	20.94	–	1	–	9
Lockie, B.G.	2	5	–	32	38	9.50	–	–	–	2
Loveridge, G.R.	16	24	3	49*	349	16.61	–	–	–	3
Lowe, J.P.	6	5	2	7*	13	4.33	–	–	–	1
Loye, M.B.	97	155	17	322*	5305	38.44	11	25	2	55
Lugsden, S.	13	18	7	9	45	4.09	–	–	–	2
McCague, M.J.	116	161	43	63*	1857	15.73	–	4	–	66
McCallan, W.K.	3	6	–	65	196	32.66	–	2	–	1
McGrath, A.	66	112	7	141	3048	29.02	5	12	–	34
McKeown, P.C.	11	15	–	64	394	26.26	–	1	–	9
McLean, N.A.M.	41	62	13	52	858	17.51	–	1	–	8
McMillan, B.M.	143	224	37	140	7099	37.96	13	39	–	152
Macmillan, G.I.	53	85	9	122	2024	26.63	3	11	–	55
Maddy, D.L.	76	121	6	202	3657	31.80	9	15	1	72
Malcolm, D.E.	246	293	91	51	1638	8.10	–	1	–	36
Marsh, S.A.	276	407	67	142	9632	28.32	9	53	–	660/54
Martin, N.D.	2	–	–	–	–	–	–	–	–	–
Martin, P.J.	148	169	43	133	2470	19.60	1	5	–	37
Martin-Jenkins, R.S.C.	15	22	3	78	500	26.31	–	3	–	5
Martyn, D.R.	104	176	21	208*	6928	44.69	19	37	–	77/2
Maru, R.J.	229	232	58	74	2965	17.04	–	7	–	254
Mascarenhas, A.D.	25	35	3	89	719	22.46	–	6	–	11
Mason, T.J.	5	2	–	4	7	3.50	–	–	–	4
Mather, D.P.	25	13	4	8*	31	3.44	–	–	–	6
May, M.R.	25	45	4	116	1221	29.78	3	5	–	7
Maynard, M.P.	309	509	54	243	19496	42.84	43	107	11	300/5
Middlebrook, J.D.	8	12	2	41	139	13.90	–	–	–	1
Miller, C.R.	75	90	19	59	1020	14.36	–	1	–	23
Millns, D.J.	156	181	55	121	2744	21.77	3	7	–	68
Mirza, M.M.	6	4	2	10*	17	5.66	–	–	–	1
Moffat, P.J.	5	6	1	12	34	6.80	–	–	–	–
Mohammed, I.	7	8	1	136	249	35.57	1	–	–	–
Molins, J.A.M.	8	12	–	73	302	25.16	–	3	–	2
Montgomerie, R.R.	98	170	19	192	4943	32.73	9	27	2	84
Moody, T.M.	279	465	40	272	20143	47.50	63	89	5+1	276
Mooney, P.J.K.	1	2	–	9	17	8.50	–	–	–	1
Moores, P.	231	345	43	185	7351	24.34	7	31	–	502/44
Morris, A.C.	28	38	7	60	581	18.74	–	2	–	18
Morris, J.E.	326	551	33	229	19506	37.65	47	93	11	139
Morris, Z.C.	1	2	–	10	10	5.00	–	–	–	–
Mullally, A.D.	157	170	44	75	1166	9.25	–	2	–	31
Munton, T.A.	214	218	87	54*	1411	10.77	–	2	–	68
Muralitharan, M.	94	113	39	39	882	11.91	–	–	–	57
Mushtaq Ahmed	168	213	27	90	2648	14.23	–	9	–	82
Napier, G.R.	4	5	2	35*	54	18.00	–	–	–	–

	M	I	NO	HS	Runs	Avge	100	50	1000	Ct/St
Nash, D.C.	22	30	2	114	757	27.03	2	2	–	18/1
Newell, K.	44	80	11	135	2039	29.55	4	9	–	13
Newell, M. (Sx)	23	38	2	135*	857	23.80	3	3	–	16
Newell, M. (Nt)	102	178	26	203*	4636	30.50	6	24	1	93/1
Newport, P.J.	279	323	90	98	5715	24.52	–	21	–	76
Nixon, P.A.	163	227	52	131	5441	31.09	10	20	1	423/36
Noon, W.M.	85	133	22	83	2445	22.02	–	12	–	177/20
Ntini, M.	31	33	10	22	135	6.42	–	–	–	2
Olphert, D.M.	1	2	–	1	1	0.50	–	–	–	–
Oram, A.R.	19	28	13	13	53	3.53	–	–	–	6
Ormond, J.	25	21	2	49	208	10.94	–	–	–	7
Ostler, D.P.	153	256	21	208	7832	33.32	10	50	4	186
Parker, B.	44	71	10	138*	1839	30.14	2	9	–	19
Parker, C.R.C.	1	1	1	1*	1	–	–	–	–	–
Parker, J.T.	5	5	–	19	80	16.00	–	–	–	1
Parkin, O.T.	24	28	14	24*	152	10.85	–	–	–	7
Parsons, K.A.	57	97	9	105	2206	25.06	2	15	–	48
Patel, M.M.	94	134	30	58*	1534	14.75	–	4	–	50
Patterson, B.M.W.	9	16	1	114	776	51.03	3	4	–	10
Patterson, M.W.	1	2	–	4	6	3.00	–	–	–	–
Peirce, M.T.E.	38	67	1	104	1563	23.68	1	9	–	22
Penberthy, A.L.	115	172	21	128	3765	24.93	3	21	–	72
Penney, T.L.	124	198	37	151	6717	41.72	13	31	2	73
Perera, A.S.A.	15	17	5	45*	211	26.37	–	–	–	2
Peters, S.D.	20	33	4	110	761	26.24	2	3	–	15
Philip, I.L.	12	21	2	145	831	43.73	4	3	–	11
Phillips, B.J.	27	39	4	100*	584	16.68	1	2	–	8
Phillips, N.C.	36	51	12	53	677	17.35	–	3	–	17
Pierson, A.R.K.	160	200	63	108*	2386	17.41	1	4	–	78
Pipe, D.J.	1	–	–	–	–	–	–	–	–	2/1
Piper, K.J.	151	214	34	116*	3480	19.33	2	9	–	401/27
Pirihi, N.G.	5	8	1	23	85	12.14	–	–	–	1
Pollard, P.R.	157	275	20	180	8347	32.73	13	40	3	148
Pollock, S.M.	72	104	19	150*	2882	33.90	3	13	–	32
Pooley, J.C.	82	137	12	138*	3811	30.48	8	17	1	81
Powell, J.C.	2	2	1	6	10	10.00	–	–	–	–
Powell, M.J. (Gm)	21	35	6	200*	1126	38.82	2	5	–	11
Powell, M.J. (Wk)	18	31	1	132	713	23.76	1	3	–	17
Pratt, A.	3	3	–	34	40	13.33	–	–	–	4
Prichard, P.J.	290	472	46	245	15006	35.22	29	86	8	185
Pushpakumara, K.R.	56	61	19	27	388	9.23	–	–	–	16
Pyemont, J.P.	7	8	–	54	127	15.87	–	1	–	5
Ramprakash, M.R.	244	398	52	235	15964	46.13	44	76	8	134
Ranatunga, A.	180	259	25	238*	10033	43.27	22	53	–	95
Rao, R.K.	23	40	3	89	787	21.27	–	5	–	6
Rashid, U.B.A.	2	2	–	9	15	7.50	–	–	–	–
Ratcliffe, J.D.	120	218	12	135	6115	29.68	5	36	–	60
Rawnsley, M.J.	14	13	2	26	123	11.18	–	–	–	8
Read, C.M.W.	17	25	6	76	462	24.31	–	2	–	46/3
Reeve, D.A.	241	322	77	202*	8541	34.86	7	52	2	200
Renshaw, S.J.	23	28	13	56	289	19.26	–	1	–	6
Rhodes, J.N.	114	179	19	156*	5708	35.67	10	31	–	79
Rhodes, S.J.	346	483	131	122*	11837	33.62	10	63	2	864/110
Richardson, A.	1	1	–	4	4	4.00	–	–	–	–
Ridgway, P.M.	3	4	1	35	39	13.00	–	–	–	–

	M	I	NO	HS	Runs	Avge	100	50	1000	Ct/St
Rindel, M.J.R.	96	176	16	174	5902	36.88	11	31	–	60
Ripley, D.	264	345	89	209	7054	27.55	7	26	–	555/75
Roberts, D.J.	12	22	–	117	678	30.81	1	2	–	4
Roberts, G.M.	11	17	4	52	334	25.69	–	1	–	8
Robinson, D.D.J.	60	107	3	148	2781	26.74	4	14	–	58
Robinson, M.A.	188	207	85	27	466	3.81	–	–	–	36
Robinson, R.T.	413	717	84	220*	27046	42.72	63	137	14	247
Rollins, A.S.	86	159	15	210	5056	35.11	9	28	3	72/1
Rollins, R.J.	66	107	9	133*	2193	22.37	1	11	–	152/20
Rose, F.A.	53	69	12	96	736	12.91	–	1	–	8
Rose, G.D.	221	310	56	191	7776	30.61	8	39	1	110
Roseberry, M.A.	202	343	37	185	10498	34.30	19	53	4	146
Russell, R.C.	392	579	123	129*	13648	29.92	7	72	1	972/111
Saggers, M.J.	10	17	5	18	128	10.66	–	–	–	3
Sales, D.J.G.	37	57	5	210*	1353	26.01	2	4	–	23
Salisbury, I.D.K.	193	252	52	86	3649	18.24	–	13	–	139
Salmond, G.	8	14	2	181	709	59.08	2	3	–	5
Saqlain Mushtaq	63	91	26	79	1032	15.87	–	4	–	29
Savident, L.	3	4	1	6	15	5.00	–	–	–	1
Schaffter, P.A.	5	4	1	12	20	6.66	–	–	–	–
Schofield, C.P.	2	3	2	4*	5	5.00	–	–	–	1
Scott, D.A.	2	3	3	17*	22	–	–	–	–	–
Scrini, A.P.	12	18	6	58*	253	21.08	–	1	–	13
Searle, J.P.	4	6	3	5*	7	2.33	–	–	–	2
Shadford, D.J.	11	13	5	30	120	15.00	–	–	–	5
Shah, O.A.	34	53	6	140	1633	34.74	3	8	–	26
Shahid, N.	110	176	24	139	4878	32.09	7	26	1	102
Shaw, A.D.	47	62	9	74	956	18.03	–	5	–	115/9
Sheikh, M.A.	3	4	–	30	80	20.00	–	–	–	–
Sheridan, K.L.P.	4	2	1	12*	12	12.00	–	–	–	2
Sheriyar, A.	58	53	20	21	285	8.63	–	–	–	12
Shine, K.J	102	96	37	40	564	9.55	–	–	–	21
Sidebottom, R.J.	6	5	3	54	86	43.00	–	1	–	3
Silverwood, C.E.W.	70	92	22	58	1068	15.25	–	3	–	16
Simmons, P.V.	193	322	15	261	11095	36.14	23	60	2	226
Singh, A.	33	50	3	157	1519	32.31	4	4	–	14
Slater, M.J.	124	218	11	219	9286	44.85	21	51	1+1	61
Small, G.C.	315	404	97	70	4409	14.36	–	7	–	95
Smith, A.M.	110	145	37	61	1428	13.22	–	4	–	20
Smith, B.F.	128	191	29	204	5966	36.82	11	27	2	54
Smith, E.T.	36	60	4	190	2161	38.58	4	11	1	9
Smith, N.M.K.	145	211	30	161	5086	31.59	4	24	1	46
Smith, R.A.	350	593	80	209*	22498	43.85	56	109	10	202
Smith, T.M.	8	10	1	29	94	10.44	–	–	–	1
Smyth, S.G.	3	5	1	70	158	39.50	–	1	–	–
Snape, J.N.	39	56	11	87	1139	25.31	–	7	–	34
Solanki, V.S.	54	89	6	170	2516	30.31	3	13	–	57
Speak, N.J.	150	262	26	232	8484	35.94	13	50	3	99
Speight, M.P.	157	263	22	184	8001	33.19	13	42	3	212/1
Spendlove, B.L.	12	22	2	49	377	18.85	–	–	–	6
Spiring, K.R.	37	64	9	150	2072	37.67	4	13	1	19
Stanger, I.M.	3	4	1	52*	78	26.00	–	1	–	3
Steindl, P.D.	1	1	–	14	14	14.00	–	–	–	–
Stemp, R.D.	136	161	53	65	1425	13.19	–	2	–	59
Stephenson, J.P.	253	429	42	202*	13198	34.10	23	70	5	149

	M	I	NO	HS	Runs	Avge	100	50	1000	Ct/St
Stevens, D.I.	3	4	–	27	38	9.50	–	–	–	1
Stewart, A.J.	356	590	65	271*	21466	40.88	42	120	8	507/17
Strang, P.A.	82	123	24	106*	2685	27.12	2	13	–	75
Strauss, A.J.	3	6	–	83	146	24.33	–	1	–	3
Strong, M.R.	1	1	1	2*	2	–	–	–	–	–
Stubbings, S.D.	1	2	–	22	27	13.50	–	–	–	–
Such, P.M.	255	265	99	54	1339	8.06	–	2	–	103
Sutcliffe, I.J.	60	88	11	167	2734	35.50	4	15	–	29
Sutton, L.D.	3	6	3	16*	41	13.66	–	–	–	10
Swann, A.J.	16	25	1	136	512	21.33	1	2	–	7
Swann, G.P.	14	18	2	111	548	34.25	1	2	–	7
Symcox, P.L.	109	160	22	108	3751	27.18	2	22	–	65
Symington, M.J.	2	1	1	8*	8	–	–	–	–	1
Symonds, A.	72	120	11	254*	4550	41.74	14	18	–	35
Taylor, J.P.	147	165	59	86	1568	14.79	–	7	–	50
Taylor, N.R.	325	551	70	204	19031	39.56	45	91	11	158
Thomas, I.J.	1	1	1	9*	9	–	–	–	–	2
Thomas, S.D.	71	95	23	78*	1436	19.94	–	7	–	27
Thompson, J.B.D.	22	29	10	65*	370	19.47	–	2	–	4
Thomson, K.	3	2	1	22	31	31.00	–	–	–	–
Thorpe, G.P.	233	390	54	222	14965	44.53	32	87	8	186
Tillekeratne, H.P.	154	222	50	176*	7893	45.88	23	37	–	193/5
Titchard, S.P.	76	131	8	163	3945	32.07	4	25	–	52
Tolley, C.M.	96	131	30	84	2337	23.13	–	10	–	40
Trainor, N.J.	26	47	2	121	854	18.97	1	4	–	12
Trescothick, M.E.	72	122	4	178	3312	28.06	4	21	–	68
Trott, B.J.	3	2	1	1*	1	1.00	–	–	–	1
Tudor, A.J.	24	33	9	56	399	16.62	–	1	–	4
Tufnell, P.C.R.	248	266	104	67*	1611	9.94	–	1	–	96
Turner, R.J.	133	208	42	144	4989	30.05	6	23	1	315/36
Tweats, T.A.	29	55	5	189	1384	27.68	2	4	–	27
Udal, S.D.	140	198	35	117*	3756	23.04	1	17	–	69
Van Troost, A.P.	71	85	27	35	461	7.94	–	–	–	10
Vaughan M.P.	99	177	9	183	5840	34.76	12	27	4	41
Villavarayen, M.S.	45	46	13	61	585	17.72	–	2	–	17
Wagh, M.A.	43	67	7	126	2040	34.00	6	8	1	24
Walker, A.	128	142	63	41*	922	11.67	–	–	–	43
Walker, M.J.	41	69	6	275*	1756	27.87	2	7	–	22
Walsh, C.A.	386	489	132	66	4299	12.04	–	8	–	111
Walsh, C.D.	4	7	1	56*	98	16.33	–	1	–	3
Walton, T.C.	19	29	3	71	653	25.11	–	7	–	5
Waqar Younis	167	192	42	55	1875	12.50	–	2	–	39
Ward, I.J.	15	26	2	81*	650	27.08	–	6	–	16
Ward, T.R.	198	342	19	235*	11657	36.08	23	70	6	188
Warren, R.J.	61	100	12	201*	2743	31.17	3	15	–	82/3
Wasim Akram	219	299	34	257*	6044	22.80	6	21	–	78
Watkin, S.L.	223	248	87	41	1638	10.17	–	–	–	58
Watkinson, M.	300	446	48	161	10594	26.61	10	50	1	152
Waugh, S.R.	252	385	65	216*	16623	51.94	47	80	2	213
Weekes, P.N.	119	183	20	171*	5328	32.68	9	23	1	104
Welch, G.	57	80	11	84*	1453	21.07	–	7	–	24
Wells, A.P.	354	594	79	253*	20312	39.44	44	98	11	223
Wells, V.J.	132	207	16	224	6571	34.40	12	32	2	85
Welton, G.E.	11	20	–	95	447	22.35	–	2	–	4
Weston, R.M.S.	20	36	–	97	718	19.94	–	4	–	16

	M	I	NO	HS	Runs	Avge	100	50	1000	Ct/St
Weston, W.P.C.	123	213	23	205	6862	36.11	13	34	3	67
Wharf, A.G.	12	15	2	62	194	14.92	–	1	–	8
Whiley, M.J.A.	1	2	1	0*	0	0.00	–	–	–	–
Whitaker, J.J.	310	490	51	218	17068	38.87	38	80	10	171
Whitaker, P.R.	37	62	5	119	1734	30.42	1	11	–	15
White, C.	145	219	33	181	6057	32.56	8	32	–	103
White, G.W.	69	117	10	156	3607	33.71	6	20	1	59
Wickremasinghe, G.P.	93	107	18	76*	1177	13.22	–	3	–	40
Wilkinson, R.	1	1	–	9	9	9.00	–	–	–	–
Williams, N.F.	255	302	63	77	4457	18.64	–	13	–	67
Williams, R.C.J.	37	47	8	90	712	18.25	–	5	–	97/15
Williamson, D.	4	4	1	41*	98	32.66	–	–	–	3
Williamson, J.G.	4	4	–	55	115	28.75	–	1	–	1
Willis, S.C.	12	15	4	82	389	35.36	–	4	–	27/2
Wilson, D.G.	3	3	1	14*	31	15.50	–	–	–	1
Wilson, E.J.	5	10	–	27	101	10.10	–	–	–	3
Wilton, N.J.	2	4	2	19*	46	23.00	–	–	–	5
Windows, M.G.N.	56	104	6	184	3237	33.03	6	16	1	48
Wood, J.	68	102	19	63*	1015	12.22	–	2	–	17
Wood, M.J.	20	31	6	200*	1182	47.28	4	5	1	18
Wood, N.T.	23	35	5	155	927	30.90	1	4	–	4
Wright, A.J.	287	504	38	193	13440	28.84	18	67	6	218
Yates, G.	70	93	35	134*	1670	28.79	3	4	–	28
Young, B.E.	21	36	10	91*	896	34.46	–	5	–	18

BOWLING

'50wS' denotes instances of taking 50 or more wickets in a season. Where these have been achieved outside the UK, they are shown after a plus sign.

	Runs	Wkts	Avge	Best	5wI	10wM	50wS
Adams, C.J.	1197	18	66.50	4- 29	–	–	–
Adams, P.R.	4548	153	29.72	7- 69	7	–	–
Afzaal, U.	1829	32	57.15	4-101	–	–	–
Aldred, P.	1922	47	40.89	3- 28	–	–	–
Alleyne, M.W.	8825	280	31.51	6- 64	6	–	1
Allingham, M.J.D.	150	4	37.50	3- 53	–	–	–
Altree, D.A.	420	8	52.50	3- 41	–	–	–
Amin, R.M.	524	11	47.63	3- 58	–	–	–
Archer, G.F.	648	14	46.28	3- 18	–	–	–
Arnold, R.P.	2676	111	24.10	7- 84	4	–	–
Asim Butt	1023	38	26.92	5- 53	1	–	–
Atapattu, M.S.	692	19	36.42	3- 19	–	–	–
Atherton, M.A.	4733	108	43.82	6- 78	3	–	–
Austin, I.D.	7479	251	29.79	5- 23	5	1	–
Averis, J.M.M.	1231	18	68.38	5- 98	1	–	–
Aymes, A.N.	317	3	105.66	2-135	–	–	–
Bacher, A.M.	14	0					
Bailey, R.J.	4739	111	42.69	5- 54	2	–	–
Ball, M.C.J.	8510	229	37.16	8- 46	8	1	–
Bandaratilake, M.R.C.N.	3929	201	19.54	8- 78	13	1	0+1
Barnett, K.J.	6865	184	37.30	6- 28	3	–	–
Bates, J.J.	798	33	24.18	5- 67	3	–	–
Bates, R.T.	2437	50	48.74	5- 88	1	–	–
Batt, C.J.	946	33	28.66	6-101	2	–	–
Batty, G.J.	70	2	35.00	1- 11	–	–	–

	Runs	Wkts	Avge	Best	5wI	10wM	50wS
Batty, J.N.	31	0					
Bell, M.A.V.	1565	49	31.93	7- 48	3	–	–
Benjamin, J.E.	11510	386	29.81	6- 19	17	1	3
Betts, M.M.	4771	159	30.00	9- 64	9	1	–
Bevan, M.G.	4083	95	42.97	6- 82	1	1	–
Bichel, A.J.	3421	136	25.15	6- 56	8	1	–
Bicknell, D.J.	789	23	34.30	3- 7	–	–	–
Bicknell, M.P.	17745	695	25.53	9- 45	29	2	7
Bishop, I.E.	29	0					
Blackwell, I.D.	751	16	46.93	5-115	1	–	–
Blain, J.A.R.	208	2	104.00	1- 18	–	–	–
Blakey, R.J.	68	1	68.00	1- 68	–	–	–
Blanchett, I.N.	307	5	61.40	2- 38	–	–	–
Blewett, G.S.	2940	66	44.54	5- 29	1	–	–
Bloomfield, T.F.	918	35	26.22	5- 67	3	–	–
Boiling, J.	6633	140	47.37	6- 84	4	1	–
Boon, D.C.	676	13	52.00	2- 18	–	–	–
Boswell, S.A.J.	1012	22	46.00	5- 94	1	–	–
Boucher, M.V.	20	0					
Bowen, M.N.	4845	142	34.11	7- 73	6	1	–
Bowler, P.D.	1997	31	64.41	3- 25	–	–	–
Brimson, M.T.	3285	100	32.85	5- 12	2	–	–
Brinkley, J.E.	1215	35	34.71	6- 35	2	–	–
Broadhurst, M.	291	7	41.57	3- 61	–	–	–
Brown, A.D.	178	0					
Brown, D.R.	6418	257	24.97	8- 89	10	3	2
Brown, J.F.	1441	53	27.18	6- 53	4	1	–
Brown, K.R.	276	6	46.00	2- 7	–	–	–
Brown, S.J.E.	12746	415	30.71	7- 70	26	2	5
Bulbeck, M.P.L.	609	32	19.03	4- 40	–	–	–
Burns, M.	339	5	69.80	2- 18	–	–	–
Butcher, A.R.	5433	141	38.53	6- 48	1	–	–
Butcher, G.P.	2110	54	39.07	7- 77	1	–	–
Butcher, M.A.	2857	79	36.16	4- 31	–	–	–
Byas, D.	719	12	59.91	3- 55	–	–	–
Byrne, B.W.	1022	14	73.00	3-103	–	–	–
Caddick, A.R.	13959	543	25.70	9- 32	37	11	6
Campbell, R.J.	16	0					
Capel, D.J.	17573	546	32.18	7- 44	14	–	4
Carpenter, J.R.	81	1	81.00	1- 50	–	–	–
Cassar, M.E.	1023	26	39.34	4- 54	–	–	–
Catterall, D.N.	31	0					
Chandana, U.D.U.	3644	148	24.62	6- 25	4	–	–
Chapman, R.J.	2702	71	38.05	6-105	1	–	–
Chapman, S.	79	0					
Chapple, G.	7412	258	28.72	6- 48	9	–	2
Chilton, M.J.	71	0					
Church, M.J.	163	9	18.11	4- 50	–	–	–
Clarke, V.P.	1449	22	65.86	3- 47	–	–	–
Clough, G.D.	11	0					
Cockcroft, J.R.	74	0					
Collingwood, P.D.	966	22	43.90	3- 46	–	–	–
Connor, C.A.	19492	614	31.74	9- 38	18	4	5
Cooke, G.	218	6	36.33	2- 49	–	–	–
Cork, D.G.	13086	485	26.97	9- 43	15	2	4

	Runs	Wkts	Avge	Best	5wI	10wM	50wS
Cosker, D.A.	3509	100	35.09	6-140	1	–	–
Cottey, P.A.	859	16	53.68	4- 49	–	–	–
Cousins, D.M.	1138	27	42.14	6- 35	1	–	–
Cowan, A.P.	3970	113	35.13	5- 45	4	–	1
Cowdrey, G.R.	872	12	72.66	1- 5	–	–	–
Cox, J.	77	0					
Crawley, J.P.	129	1	129.00	1- 90	–	–	–
Croft, R.D.B.	19670	535	36.76	8- 66	22	3	5
Cronje, W.J.	3222	84	38.35	4- 47	–	–	–
Crowe, C.D.	205	6	34.16	3- 49	–	–	–
Cullinan, D.J.	200	3	66.66	2- 27	–	–	–
Curran, K.M.	16709	604	27.66	7- 47	15	4	5
Dakin, J.M.	1107	25	44.28	4- 45	–	–	–
Dale, A.	6152	163	37.74	6- 18	2	–	–
Dale, A.C.	1910	87	21.95	6- 38	4	–	–
Daley, J.A.	21	1	21.00	1- 12	–	–	–
Davies, A.P.	525	15	35.00	2- 22	–	–	–
Davies, M.K.	866	30	28.86	5- 19	2	–	–
Davis, R.P.	14543	414	35.12	7- 64	16	2	2
Dawson, R.I.	199	8	24.87	3- 15	–	–	–
Dean, K.J.	2854	118	24.18	6- 63	5	1	1
DeFreitas, P.A.J.	26979	968	27.87	7- 21	50	5	11
De la Pena, J.M.	656	16	41.00	4- 77	–	–	–
De Silva, P.A.	2763	80	34.53	7- 24	4	–	–
Dharmasena, H.D.P.K.	5140	222	23.15	7-111	15	3	0+1
Di Venuto, M.J.	157	0					
Donald, A.A.	23137	1043	22.18	8- 37	59	8	5
Dowman, M.P.	854	20	42.70	3- 10	–	–	–
Drakes, V.C.	6619	223	29.68	8- 59	7	1	1
Dunlop, A.R.	143	2	71.50	1- 8	–	–	–
Dutch, K.P.	547	14	39.07	3- 25	–	–	–
Dwyer, M.D.	84	5	16.80	4- 57	–	–	–
Dyer, N.R.	187	6	31.16	4- 48	–	–	–
Eadie, D.J.	434	13	33.38	2- 34	–	–	–
Ealham, M.A.	7853	266	29.52	8- 36	11	1	–
Ecclestone, S.C.	1208	33	36.60	4- 66	–	–	–
Edmond, M.D.	348	7	49.71	2- 26	–	–	–
Edwards, A.D.	912	23	39.65	5- 34	1	–	–
Ellis, S.W.K.	880	20	44.00	5- 59	1	–	–
Elworthy, S.	9087	298	30.49	7- 65	10	2	–
Evans, K.P.	12027	361	33.42	6- 40	10	–	–
Fairbrother, N.H.	440	5	88.00	2- 91	–	–	–
Fellows, G.M.	26	0					
Ferguson, S.H.	141	3	47.00	3- 82	–	–	–
Fisher, I.D.	288	12	24.00	5- 35	1	–	–
Flanagan, I.N.	1	0					
Fleming, M.V.	7734	211	36.65	5- 51	2	–	–
Flintoff, A.	479	8	59.87	3- 51	–	–	–
Follett, D.	1132	36	31.44	8- 22	3	1	–
Ford, J.	54	0					
Foster, M.J.	1839	61	30.14	4- 21	–	–	–
Francis, S.R.G.	238	4	59.50	2- 21	–	–	–
Franks, P.J.	2635	85	31.00	6- 63	4	–	1
Fraser, A.G.J.	386	12	32.16	3- 46	–	–	–
Fraser, A.R.C.	20049	753	26.62	8- 53	33	5	7

	Runs	Wkts	Avge	Best	5wI	10wM	50wS
Frost, T.	6	0					
Fulton, D.P.	65	1	65.00	1- 37	–	–	–
Fulton, J.A.G.	18	0					
Gallian, J.E.R.	3435	84	40.89	6-115	1	–	–
Garland, R.	452	8	56.50	2- 64	–	–	–
Gatting, M.W.	4703	158	29.76	5- 34	2	–	–
Giddins, E.S.H.	9433	332	28.41	6- 47	18	2	3
Giles, A.F.	5017	188	26.68	6- 45	6	–	1
Gillespie, J.N.	3178	135	23.54	7- 34	6	–	0+1
Goodchild, D.J.	88	0					
Gough, D.	13692	505	27.11	7- 28	21	3	4
Gough, M.A.	119	2	59.50	1- 4	–	–	–
Grayson, A.P.	3348	78	42.92	4- 53	–	–	–
Green, R.J.	1430	34	42.05	6- 41	1	–	–
Greenfield, K.	524	5	104.80	2- 40	–	–	–
Grove, J.O.	347	9	38.55	3- 74	–	–	–
Habib, A.	52	0					
Hamilton, G.M.	3245	118	27.50	7- 50	6	2	1
Hancock, T.H.C.	1159	31	37.38	3- 5	–	–	–
Hansen, T.M.	75	0					
Harden, R.J.	1023	20	51.15	2- 7	–	–	–
Harmison, S.J.	1622	51	31.80	5- 70	1	–	1
Harris, A.J.	3783	111	34.08	6- 40	2	1	1
Hart, J.P.	51	0					
Hartley, P.J.	18762	614	30.55	9- 41	21	2	6
Harvey, I.J.	2612	73	35.78	7- 44	3	–	–
Harvey, M.E.	48	0					
Hathurusinghe, U.C.	5798	237	24.46	8- 29	9	2	–
Hayden, M.L.	282	4	70.50	2- 17	–	–	–
Haynes, G.R.	3263	93	35.08	6- 50	2	–	–
Hayward, M.	2457	75	32.76	6- 51	1	–	–
Headley, D.W.	11186	400	27.96	8- 98	23	2	2
Hegg, W.K.	7	0					
Hemp, D.L.	590	14	42.14	3- 23	–	–	–
Hewitt, J.P.	3448	125	27.58	6- 14	4	–	1
Hewson, D.R.	7	1	7.00	1- 7	–	–	–
Hibbert, A.J.E.	49	3	16.33	3- 16	–	–	–
Hick, G.A.	9460	217	43.59	5- 18	5	1	–
Hills, D.F.	20	0					
Hoggard, M.J.	1091	44	24.79	5- 57	1	–	–
Hollioake, A.J.	3655	91	40.16	5- 62	1	–	–
Hollioake, B.C.	2265	79	28.67	4- 28	–	–	–
Holloway, P.C.L.	46	0					
Hooper, C.L.	14886	423	35.19	7- 93	14	–	–
House, W.J.	831	3	277.00	1- 34	–	–	–
Hughes, Q.J.	199	4	49.75	2- 73	–	–	–
Hussain, N.	307	2	153.50	1- 38	–	–	–
Hussey, M.E.	2	0					
Hutchison, P.M.	2655	119	22.31	7- 31	6	1	1
Hutton, B.L.	42	0					
Hutton, S.	18	0					
Igglesden, A.P.	13488	503	26.81	7- 28	23	4	4
Illingworth, R.K.	24647	793	31.08	7- 50	27	6	5
Ilott, M.C.	14353	526	27.28	9- 19	25	3	5
Innes, K.J.	275	8	34.37	4- 61	–	–	–

	Runs	Wkts	Avge	Best	5wI	10wM	50wS
Irani, R.C.	5939	176	33.74	5- 19	4	–	–
James, K.D.	12406	389	31.89	8- 49	11	1	–
James, S.P.	3	0					
Janisch, A.N.	1538	26	59.15	4- 71	–	–	–
Jarvis, P.W.	18154	628	28.90	7- 55	22	3	4
Jayasuriya, S.T.	2899	83	34.92	4- 44	–	–	–
Jayawardena, D.P.M.D.	750	23	32.60	5- 72	1	–	–
Johnson, P.	595	6	99.16	1- 9	–	–	–
Johnson, R.L.	5786	208	27.81	10- 45	5	2	2
Jones, P.S.	984	27	36.44	6- 67	1	–	–
Jones, S.P.	345	7	49.28	3- 94	–	–	–
Joyce, E.C.	78	0					
Julian, B.P.	11298	378	29.88	7- 39	21	2	1
Kallis, J.H.	3284	108	30.40	5- 54	2	–	–
Kasprowicz, M.S.	10967	400	27.41	7- 36	23	2	1+2
Keech, M.	383	8	47.87	2- 28	–	–	–
Keedy, G.	4266	107	39.86	6- 79	2	1	–
Kendall, W.S.	399	10	39.90	3- 37	–	–	–
Kennis, G.J.	4	0					
Kenway, D.A.	75	2	37.50	1- 5	–	–	–
Kerr, J.I.D.	2590	64	40.46	5- 82	1	–	–
Kettleborough, R.A.	242	3	80.66	2- 26	–	–	–
Key, R.W.T.	1	0					
Khan, A.A.	1946	47	41.40	5-137	1	–	–
Khan, S.H.	327	2	163.50	1- 41	–	–	–
Khan, W.G.	31	0					
Killeen, N.	1755	48	36.56	5- 49	2	–	–
Kirsten, G.	804	20	40.20	6- 68	1	–	–
Kirtley, R.J.	3657	128	28.57	7- 29	7	1	1
Klusener, L.	5049	199	25.37	8- 34	7	1	–
Knight, N.V.	191	1	191.00	1- 61	–	–	–
Knott, J.A.	2	0					
Krikken, K.M.	40	0					
Lacey, S.J.	565	11	51.36	3- 97	–	–	–
Lampitt, S.R.	14494	482	30.07	5- 32	17	–	6
Laney, J.S.	98	0					
Langer, J.L.	109	3	36.33	2- 17	–	–	–
Lara, B.C.	359	2	179.50	1- 14	–	–	–
Lathwell, M.N.	684	13	52.61	2- 21	–	–	–
Law, D.R.	3754	113	33.22	5- 33	4	–	–
Law, S.G.	3150	67	47.01	5- 39	1	–	–
Law, W.L.	85	3	28.33	2- 29	–	–	–
Leather, D.	44	0					
Leatherdale, D.A.	2063	68	30.33	5- 20	2	–	–
Lehmann, D.S.	1047	19	55.10	4- 42	–	–	–
Lewis, C.C.	15338	520	29.49	6- 22	20	3	2
Lewis, J.	3903	143	27.29	6- 48	6	–	2
Lewis, J.J.B.	121	1	121.00	1- 73	–	–	–
Lewry, J.D.	3913	157	24.92	6- 43	10	1	1
Liebenberg, G.F.J.	11	1	11.00	1- 10	–	–	–
Lightfoot, C.G.R.	387	4	96.75	2- 65	–	–	–
Llong, N.J.	1259	35	35.97	5- 21	2	–	–
Lloyd, G.D.	340	2	170.00	1- 4	–	–	–
Loveridge, G.R.	1430	33	43.33	5- 59	1	–	–
Lowe, J.P.	295	6	49.16	2- 42	–	–	–

	Runs	Wkts	Avge	Best	5wI	10wM	50wS
Loye, M.B.	43	0					
Lugsden, S.	1172	25	46.88	3-45	–	–	–
McCague, M.J.	11127	419	25.93	9-86	24	2	4
McCallan, W.K.	228	2	114.00	1-10	–	–	–
McGrath, A.	288	5	57.60	2-33	–	–	–
McLean, N.A.M.	3458	117	29.55	6-28	4	–	1
McMillan, B.M.	8752	304	28.78	5-35	4	–	–
Macmillan, G.I.	1217	23	52.91	3-13	–	–	–
Maddy, D.L.	446	8	55.75	2-21	–	–	–
Malcolm, D.E.	25578	833	30.70	9-57	33	7	6
Marsh, S.A.	240	2	120.00	2-20	–	–	–
Martin, N.D.	83	1	83.00	1-22	–	–	–
Martin, P.J.	11476	389	29.50	8-32	7	1	2
Martin-Jenkins, R.S.C.	790	28	28.21	7-54	1	–	–
Martyn, D.R.	931	22	42.31	4-46	–	–	–
Maru, R.J.	17714	527	33.61	8-41	15	1	4
Mascarenhas, A.D.	1714	54	31.74	6-88	2	–	–
Mason, T.J.	262	3	87.33	2-21	–	–	–
Mather, D.P.	2010	46	43.69	6-74	1	1	–
May, M.R.	120	0					
Maynard, M.P.	829	6	138.16	3-21	–	–	–
Middlebrook, J.D.	422	13	32.46	3-20	–	–	–
Miller, C.R.	8282	265	31.25	7-49	10	2	0+1
Millns, D.J.	13790	499	27.63	9-37	21	4	4
Mirza, M.M.	620	19	32.63	4-51	–	–	–
Moffat, P.J.	232	7	33.14	3-25	–	–	–
Mohammed, I.	52	1	52.00	1-13	–	–	–
Molins, J.A.M.	12	1	12.00	1-12	–	–	–
Montgomerie, R.R.	66	0					
Moody, T.M.	9879	318	31.06	7-38	9	2	–
Mooney, P.J.K.	72	2	36.00	2-45	–	–	–
Moores, P.	16	0					
Morris, A.C.	1520	59	25.76	4-30	–	–	1
Morris, J.E.	913	7	130.42	1- 6	–	–	–
Morris, Z.C.	5	0					
Mullally, A.D.	13736	453	30.32	7-55	16	3	4
Munton, T.A.	16285	631	25.80	8-89	29	6	5
Muralitharan, M.	9456	448	21.10	9-65	36	6	0+2
Mushtaq Ahmed	18770	741	25.33	9-93	52	15	4+1
Napier, G.R.	137	5	27.40	2-25	–	–	–
Nash, D.C.	19	1	19.00	1- 8	–	–	–
Newell, K.	837	17	49.23	4-61	–	–	–
Newell, M. (Sx)	15	0					
Newell, M. (Nt)	282	7	40.28	2-38	–	–	–
Newport, P.J.	22990	849	27.07	8-52	35	3	8
Nixon, P.A.	4	0					
Noon, W.M.	34	0					
Ntini, M.	2691	79	34.06	6-49	1	–	–
Olphert, D.M.	28	0					
Oram, A.R.	1653	57	29.00	4-37	–	–	–
Ormond, J.	1911	80	23.88	6-33	5	–	–
Ostler, D.P.	201	0					
Parker, B.	3	0					
Parker, C.R.C.	48	0					
Parkin, O.T.	1787	58	30.81	5-24	2	–	–

	Runs	Wkts	Avge	Best	5wI	10wM	50wS
Parsons, K.A.	1263	23	54.91	2- 4	–	–	–
Patel, M.M.	9241	284	32.53	8- 96	16	7	2
Patterson, M.W.	124	7	17.71	6- 80	1	–	–
Peirce, M.T.E.	205	1	205.00	1- 16	–	–	–
Penberthy, A.L.	6052	154	39.29	5- 37	3	–	–
Penney, T.L.	183	6	30.50	3- 18	–	–	–
Perera, A.S.A.	1040	43	24.18	4- 15	–	–	–
Philip, I.L.	47	0					
Phillips, B.J.	1914	65	29.44	5- 47	2	–	–
Phillips, N.C.	2859	55	51.98	5- 56	1	–	–
Pierson, A.R.K.	12657	343	36.90	8- 42	14	–	1
Piper, K.J.	57	1	57.00	1- 57	–	–	–
Pollard, P.R.	268	4	67.00	2- 79	–	–	–
Pollock, S.M.	5860	261	22.45	7- 33	11	1	–
Pooley, J.C.	68	0					
Powell, J.C.	137	1	137.00	1-109	–	–	–
Powell, M.J. (Gm)	11	0					
Powell, M.J. (Wk)	64	3	21.33	2- 16	–	–	–
Prichard, P.J.	497	2	248.50	1- 28	–	–	–
Pushpakumara, K.R.	4823	167	28.88	7-116	12	3	–
Pyemont, J.P.	20	0					
Ramprakash, M.R.	1455	26	55.96	3- 32	–	–	–
Ranatunga, A.	3045	92	33.09	5- 45	2	–	–
Rao, R.K.	243	3	81.00	1- 1	–	–	–
Rashid, U.B.A.	17	0					
Ratcliffe, J.D.	582	10	58.20	2- 26	–	–	–
Rawnsley, M.J.	934	28	33.35	6- 44	2	1	–
Reeve, D.A.	12232	456	26.82	7- 37	8	–	2
Renshaw, S.J.	2236	56	39.92	5-110	1	–	–
Rhodes, J.N.	56	1	56.11	1- 13	–	–	–
Rhodes, S.J.	30	0					
Richardson, A.	60	3	20.00	3- 27	–	–	–
Ridgway, P.M.	246	6	41.00	3- 51	–	–	–
Rindel, M.J.R.	1550	43	36.04	4- 17	–	–	–
Ripley, D.	103	2	51.50	2- 89	–	–	–
Roberts, G.M.	810	10	81.00	4-105	–	–	–
Robinson, D.D.J.	31	0					
Robinson, M.A.	14611	459	31.83	9- 37	9	2	1
Robinson, R.T.	289	4	72.25	1- 22	–	–	–
Rollins, A.S.	122	1	122.00	1- 19	–	–	–
Rose, F.A.	4703	188	25.01	7- 39	9	2	1+1
Rose, G.D.	16148	555	29.09	7- 47	14	1	5
Roseberry, M.A.	406	4	101.50	1- 1	–	–	–
Russell, R.C.	68	1	68.00	1- 4	–	–	–
Saggers, M.J.	769	27	28.48	6- 65	2	–	–
Sales, D.J.G.	64	1	64.00	1- 28	–	–	–
Salisbury, I.D.K.	18243	546	33.41	8- 75	28	4	4
Saqlain Mushtaq	5974	264	22.62	8- 65	18	6	1+1
Savident, L.	247	4	61.75	2- 86	–	–	–
Schaffter, P.A.	195	3	65.00	1- 21	–	–	–
Schofield, C.P.	299	10	29.90	4- 56	–	–	–
Scott, D.A.	124	1	124.00	1- 48	–	–	–
Searle, J.P.	291	7	41.57	3- 92	–	–	–
Shadford, D.J.	983	23	42.73	5- 80	1	–	–
Shah, O.A.	122	2	61.00	1- 24	–	–	–

	Runs	Wkts	Avge	Best	5wI	10wM	50wS
Shahid, N.	1993	43	46.34	3- 91	–	–	–
Shaw, A.D.	7	0					
Sheikh, M.A.	98	6	16.33	2- 14	–	–	–
Sheridan, K.L.P.	361	9	40.11	4- 43	–	–	–
Sheriyar, A.	5397	163	33.11	6- 19	7	2	1
Shine, K.J.	8988	249	36.09	8- 47	12	2	1
Sidebottom, R.J.	461	12	38.41	3- 13	–	–	–
Silverwood, C.E.W.	6127	219	27.97	7- 93	11	1	1
Simmons, P.V.	5563	193	28.82	7- 49	5	–	1
Singh, A.	45	0					
Slater, M.J.	26	1	26.00	1- 4	–	–	–
Small, G.C.	24392	852	28.62	7- 15	29	2	6
Smith, A.M.	9356	367	25.49	8- 73	17	5	4
Smith, B.F.	205	2	102.50	1- 5	–	–	–
Smith, E.T.	22	0					
Smith, N.M.K.	10921	289	37.78	7- 42	16	–	–
Smith, R.A.	965	14	68.92	2- 11	–	–	–
Smith, T.M.	535	22	24.31	6- 32	2	–	–
Smyth, S.G.	21	0					
Snape, J.N.	2931	65	45.09	5- 65	1	–	–
Solanki, V.S.	1925	40	48.12	5- 69	3	1	–
Speak, N.J.	191	2	95.50	1- 0	–	–	–
Speight, M.P.	32	2	16.00	1- 2	–	–	–
Spiring, K.R.	10	0					
Stanger, I.M.	228	4	57.00	3- 57	–	–	–
Steindl, P.D.	98	0					
Stemp, R.D.	10868	319	34.06	6- 37	13	1	–
Stephenson, J.P.	9541	278	34.32	7- 51	9	–	–
Stevens, D.I.	5	1	5.00	1- 5	–	–	–
Stewart, A.J.	417	3	139.00	1- 7	–	–	–
Strang, P.A.	8341	262	31.83	7- 75	16	2	1
Such, P.M.	21279	722	29.47	8- 93	41	7	5
Strong, M.R.	41	0					
Sutcliffe, I.J.	200	5	40.00	2- 21	–	–	–
Swann, A.J.	74	0					
Swann, G.P.	666	22	30.27	5- 29	1	–	–
Symcox, P.L.	7397	229	32.30	7- 93	5	–	–
Symington, M.J.	148	6	24.66	3- 55	–	–	–
Symonds, A.	1434	35	40.97	3- 77	–	–	–
Taylor, J.P.	13306	458	29.05	7- 23	16	3	6
Taylor, N.R.	891	16	55.68	2- 20	–	–	–
Thomas, S.D.	7001	220	31.82	5- 24	11	–	2
Thompson, J.B.D.	1838	58	31.68	5- 72	2	–	–
Thomson, K.	281	7	40.14	2- 41	–	–	–
Thorpe, G.P.	1248	25	49.92	4- 40	–	–	–
Tillekeratne, H.P.	757	21	36.04	4- 37	–	–	–
Titchard, S.P.	171	4	42.75	1- 11	–	–	–
Tolley, C.M.	6317	180	35.09	7- 45	5	–	–
Trescothick, M.E.	963	23	41.86	4- 36	–	–	–
Trainor, N.J.	93	0					
Trott, B.J.	184	7	26.28	3- 74	–	–	–
Tudor, A.J.	1664	60	27.73	6-101	3	–	–
Tufnell, P.C.R.	24573	828	29.67	8- 29	41	5	7
Turner, R.J.	29	0					
Tweats, T.A.	237	4	59.25	1- 23	–	–	–

	Runs	Wkts	Avge	Best	5wI	10wM	50wS
Udal, S.D.	13483	372	36.24	8- 50	20	4	4
Van Troost, A.P.	5614	146	38.45	6- 48	4	–	–
Vaughan, M.P.	3533	70	50.47	4- 39	–	–	–
Villavarayen, M.S.	3264	141	23.14	9- 15	5	1	–
Wagh, M.A.	1573	25	62.92	4- 11	–	–	–
Walker, A.	9667	299	32.33	8-118	6	1	1
Walker, M.J.	70	0					
Walsh, C.A.	35551	1621	21.93	9- 72	96	19	10+1
Walsh, C.D.	64	0					
Walton, T.C.	282	4	70.50	1- 26	–	–	–
Waqar Younis	15935	752	21.19	8- 17	57	14	4+1
Ward, I.J.	84	0					
Ward, T.R.	647	8	80.87	2- 10	–	–	–
Wasim Akram	19464	912	21.34	8- 30	64	15	5
Watkin, S.L.	21637	768	28.17	8- 59	25	4	9
Watkinson, M.	24547	727	33.76	8- 30	27	3	7
Waugh, S.R.	7627	240	31.77	6- 51	5	–	–
Weekes, P.N.	5607	133	42.15	8- 39	3	–	–
Welch, G.	4745	150	31.63	6-115	3	1	1
Wells, A.P.	820	10	82.00	3- 67	–	–	–
Wells, V.J.	5365	210	25.54	5- 18	3	–	–
Weston, R.M.S.	81	1	81.00	1- 41	–	–	–
Weston, W.P.C.	599	4	149.75	2- 39	–	–	–
Wharf, A.G.	787	20	39.35	4- 29	–	–	–
Whiley, M.J.A.	124	1	124.00	1- 66	–	–	–
Whitaker, J.J.	268	2	134.00	1- 29	–	–	–
Whitaker, P.R.	561	13	43.15	3- 36	–	–	–
White, C.	6293	230	27.36	8- 55	7	–	–
White, G.W.	240	2	120.00	1- 4	–	–	–
Wickremasinghe, G.P.	7463	260	28.70	10- 41	7	2	0+1
Wilkinson, R.	35	1	35.00	1- 35	–	–	–
Williams, N.F.	20448	675	30.29	8- 75	22	2	3
Williamson, D.	318	9	35.33	3- 19	–	–	–
Williamson, J.G.	357	5	71.40	2- 51	–	–	–
Wilson, D.G.	181	4	45.25	1- 22	–	–	–
Windows, M.G.N.	97	2	48.50	1- 6	–	–	–
Wood, J.	6796	191	35.58	6-110	6	–	1
Wood, N.T.	118	0					
Wright, A.J.	68	1	68.00	1- 16	–	–	–
Yates, G.	6253	155	40.34	5- 34	3	–	–
Young, B.E.	2342	62	37.77	5- 64	2	–	–

LEADING CURRENT PLAYERS

The leading career batting/bowling averages and wicket-keeping/fielding aggregates among players currently registered for first-class county cricket. All figures are to the end of the 1998 English season.

BATTING
(Qualification: 100 innings)

	Runs	Avge
G.A.Hick	29777	55.55
M.L.Hayden	10455	54.17
J.L.Langer	8443	53.43
J.P.Crawley	13083	50.51
T.M.Moody	20143	47.50
S.G.Law	10753	46.34
M.R.Ramprakash	15964	46.13
D.C.Boon	22314	45.26
M.J.Slater	9286	44.85
G.S.Blewett	7666	44.56
G.P.Thorpe	14965	44.53
J.H.Kallis	4847	44.46
R.A.Smith	22498	43.85
N.Hussain	14227	43.11
M.P.Maynard	19496	42.84
R.T.Robinson	27046	42.72
A.D.Brown	6664	42.44
N.H.Fairbrother	17941	41.723
T.L.Penney	6717	41.720
M.A.Atherton	17911	41.65
R.J.Bailey	19858	41.45
A.J.Stewart	21466	40.88
M.J.Di Venuto	4043	40.83
N.V.Knight	7842	40.63
A.J.Hollioake	5557	40.56
K.J.Barnett	25556	40.30
J.Cox	7046	40.03

BOWLING
(Qualification: 100 wickets)

	Wkts	Avge
M.Muralitharan	448	21.10
A.A.Donald	1043	22.18
P.M.Hutchison	119	22.31
Saqlain Mushtaq	264	22.62
K.J.Dean	118	24.18
J.D.Lewry	157	24.92
D.R.Brown	257	24.97
A.M.Smith	367	25.49
M.P.Bicknell	695	25.53
V.J.Wells	210	25.54
A.R.Caddick	543	25.70
T.A.Munton	631	25.80
M.J.McCague	419	25.93
A.R.C.Fraser	753	26.62
A.F.Giles	188	26.68
D.G.Cork	485	26.97
P.J.Newport	849	27.07
D.Gough	505	27.11
M.C.Ilott	526	27.28
J.Lewis	143	27.29
C.White	230	27.36
M.S.Kasprowicz	400	27.41
G.M.Hamilton	118	27.50
J.P.Hewitt	125	27.58
D.J.Millns	499	27.63
K.M.Curran	604	27.66
R.L.Johnson	208	27.81
P.A.J.DeFreitas	968	27.87
D.W.Headley	400	27.96
C.E.W.Silverwood	219	27.97

FIELDING

	Ct
G.A.Hick	441
M.P.Maynard	300
T.M.Moody	276
N.Hussain	275
D.C.Boon	267
D.Byas	267
R.J.Bailey	251
K.J.Barnett	250

WICKET-KEEPING

	Total	Ct	St
R.C.Russell	1083	972	111
S.J.Rhodes	974	864	110
S.A.Marsh	714	660	54
W.K.Hegg	636	570	66
R.J.Blakey	634	586	48
D.Ripley	630	555	75
A.J.Stewart	524	507	17

LIMITED-OVERS INTERNATIONALS CAREER RECORDS

These England records, complete to 7 April 1999 (prior to the start of the Sharjah Cup), include all players registered for county cricket in 1999. LOI career records for overseas countries will appear in *NatWest Playfair Cricket World Cup 1999*.

ENGLAND – BATTING AND FIELDING

	M	I	NO	HS	Runs	Avge	100	50	Ct/St
C.J.Adams	2	2	–	25	28	14.00	–	–	2
M.W.Alleyne	4	4	1	38*	76	25.33	–	–	–
M.A.Atherton	54	54	3	127	1791	35.11	2	12	15
I.D.Austin	4	3	1	11*	29	14.50	–	–	–
R.J.Bailey	4	4	2	43*	137	68.50	–	–	1
K.J.Barnett	1	1	–	84	84	84.00	–	1	–
J.E.Benjamin	2	1	–	0	0	0.00	–	–	–
M.P.Bicknell	7	6	2	31*	96	24.00	–	–	2
R.J.Blakey	3	2	–	25	25	12.50	–	–	2/1
A.D.Brown	13	13	–	118	333	25.61	1	1	6
D.R.Brown	9	8	4	21	99	24.75	–	–	1
A.R.Caddick	9	5	4	20*	35	35.00	–	–	2
D.G.Cork	25	15	2	31*	132	10.15	–	–	6
J.P.Crawley	13	12	1	73	235	21.36	–	2	1/1
R.D.B.Croft	40	28	11	32	274	16.11	–	–	9
P.A.J.DeFreitas	103	66	23	67	690	16.04	–	1	26
M.A.Ealham	30	22	1	45	380	18.09	–	–	3
N.H.Fairbrother	66	64	17	113	1918	40.80	1	15	32
M.V.Fleming	11	10	1	34	140	15.55	–	–	1
A.R.C.Fraser	37	16	7	38*	122	13.55	–	–	2
A.F.Giles	5	3	2	10*	17	17.00	–	–	1
D.Gough	56	37	13	45	269	11.20	–	–	7
D.W.Headley	13	6	4	10*	22	11.00	–	–	3
G.A.Hick	87	86	9	126*	2990	38.83	5	19	40
A.J.Hollioake	31	28	6	83*	582	26.45	–	3	12
B.C.Hollioake	7	6	–	63	122	20.33	–	1	1
N.Hussain	28	28	5	93	549	23.86	–	2	14
R.K.Illingworth	25	11	5	14	68	11.33	–	–	8
R.C.Irani	10	10	2	45*	78	9.75	–	–	2
P.W.Jarvis	16	8	2	16*	31	5.16	–	–	1
N.V.Knight	40	40	3	125*	1498	40.48	3	8	14
C.C.Lewis	53	40	4	33	374	14.38	–	–	20
G.D.Lloyd	6	5	1	22	39	9.75	–	–	2
D.L.Maddy	2	1	–	1	1	1.00	–	–	–
D.E.Malcolm	10	5	2	4	9	3.00	–	–	1
P.J.Martin	20	13	7	6	38	6.33	–	–	1
M.P.Maynard	10	10	4	41	153	17.00	–	–	1
J.E.Morris	8	8	1	63*	167	23.85	–	1	2
A.D.Mullally	22	9	2	20	42	6.00	–	–	5
M.R.Ramprakash	13	13	3	51	265	26.50	–	1	6
D.A.Reeve	29	21	9	35	291	24.25	–	–	12
S.J.Rhodes	9	8	2	56	107	17.83	–	1	9/2
R.T.Robinson	26	26	–	83	597	22.96	–	3	6
R.C.Russell	40	31	7	50	423	17.62	–	1	41/6
I.D.K.Salisbury	4	2	1	5	7	7.00	–	–	1
C.E.W.Silverwood	6	4	–	12	17	4.25	–	–	–
G.C.Small	53	24	9	18*	98	6.53	–	–	7
N.M.K.Smith	7	6	1	31	100	20.00	–	–	1

	M	I	NO	HS	Runs	Avge	100	50	Ct/St
R.A.Smith	71	70	8	167*	2419	39.01	4	15	26
A.J.Stewart	116	111	8	116	3211	31.17	2	18	101/11
J.P.Taylor	1	1	–	1	1	1.00	–	–	–
G.P.Thorpe	44	44	7	89	1482	40.05	–	14	23
P.C.R.Tufnell	20	10	9	5*	15	15.00	–	–	4
S.D.Udal	10	6	4	11*	35	17.50	–	–	1
S.L.Watkin	4	2	–	4	4	2.00	–	–	–
M.Watkinson	1	–	–	–	–	–	–	–	–
A.P.Wells	1	1	–	15	15	15.00	–	–	–
V.J.Wells	7	5	–	39	131	26.20	–	–	3
C.White	15	13	–	38	187	14.38	–	–	2
J.J.Whitaker	2	2	1	44*	48	48.00	–	–	1

ENGLAND – BOWLING

	O	R	W	Avge	Best	4wI	R/Over
M.W.Alleyne	15	58	3	19.33	3-27	–	3.86
I.D.Austin	37.3	179	3	59.66	2-37	–	4.77
R.J.Bailey	6	25	0	–	–	–	4.16
J.E.Benjamin	12	47	1	47.00	1-22	–	3.91
M.P.Bicknell	68.5	347	13	26.69	3-55	–	5.04
A.D.Brown	1	5	0	–	–	–	5.00
D.R.Brown	54	305	7	43.57	2-28	–	5.64
A.R.Caddick	87	398	15	26.53	3-35	–	4.57
D.G.Cork	240	1071	35	30.60	3-27	–	4.46
R.D.B.Croft	351	1464	40	36.60	3-51	–	4.17
P.A.J.DeFreitas	952	3775	115	32.82	4-35	1	3.96
M.A.Ealham	245.2	1047	30	34.90	5-32	1	4.26
N.H.Fairbrother	1	9	0	–	–	–	9.00
M.V.Fleming	87.1	434	17	25.52	4-45	1	4.97
A.R.C.Fraser	348.4	1245	42	29.64	4-22	1	3.57
A.F.Giles	38	197	5	39.40	2-37	–	5.18
D.Gough	519.2	2203	89	24.75	5-44	6	4.24
D.W.Headley	99	520	11	47.27	2-38	–	5.25
G.A.Hick	149.1	741	19	39.00	3-41	–	4.96
A.J.Hollioake	178.2	899	31	29.00	4-23	2	5.04
B.C.Hollioake	25	122	2	61.00	2-43	–	4.88
R.K.Illingworth	250.1	1059	30	35.30	3-33	–	4.23
R.C.Irani	54.5	246	4	61.50	1-23	–	4.48
P.W.Jarvis	146.3	672	24	28.00	5-35	2	4.58
C.C.Lewis	437.3	1942	66	29.42	4-30	4	4.43
D.E.Malcolm	87.4	404	16	25.25	3-40	–	4.60
P.J.Martin	174.4	806	27	29.85	4-44	1	4.61
A.D.Mullally	194.3	772	28	27.57	4-18	1	3.96
M.R.Ramprakash	2	14	0	–	–	–	7.00
D.A.Reeve	191.1	820	20	41.00	3-20	–	4.28
I.D.K.Salisbury	31	177	5	35.40	3-41	–	5.70
C.E.W.Silverwood	42	201	3	67.00	2-27	–	4.78
G.C.Small	465.3	1942	58	33.48	4-31	1	4.17
N.M.K.Smith	43.3	190	6	31.66	3-29	–	4.36
J.P.Taylor	3	20	0	–	–	–	6.66
G.P.Thorpe	20	97	2	48.50	2-15	–	4.85
P.C.R.Tufnell	170	699	19	36.78	4-22	1	4.11
S.D.Udal	95	371	8	46.37	2-37	–	3.90
S.L.Watkin	36.5	193	7	27.57	4-49	1	5.24
M.Watkinson	9	43	0	–	–	–	4.77
V.J.Wells	32.4	153	8	19.12	3-30	–	4.68
C.White	101.2	445	15	29.66	4-37	1	4.39

TEST CAREER RECORDS

These records, complete to 27 January 1999 prior to the start of Test No. 1442, include all players registered for county cricket in 1999 at the time of going to press, plus those who have played Test cricket since 1 August 1997.

ENGLAND – BATTING AND FIELDING

	M	I	NO	HS	Runs	Avge	100	50	Ct/St
M.A.Atherton	88	163	6	185*	6045	38.50	12	37	58
R.J.Bailey	4	8	–	43	119	14.87	–	–	–
K.J.Barnett	4	7	–	80	207	29.57	–	2	1
J.E.Benjamin	1	1	–	0	0	0.00	–	–	–
M.P.Bicknell	2	4	–	14	26	6.50	–	–	–
R.J.Blakey	2	4	–	6	7	1.75	–	–	2
S.J.E.Brown	1	2	1	10*	11	11.00	–	–	1
M.A.Butcher	19	37	1	116	1001	27.80	2	4	18
A.R.Caddick	21	33	4	29*	291	10.03	–	–	8
D.G.Cork	27	42	6	59	634	17.61	–	2	13
J.P.Crawley	29	47	5	156*	1329	31.64	3	7	26
R.D.B.Croft	15	24	6	37*	295	16.38	–	–	8
P.A.J.DeFreitas	44	68	5	88	934	14.82	–	4	14
M.A.Ealham	8	13	3	53*	210	21.00	–	2	4
N.H.Fairbrother	10	15	1	83	219	15.64	–	1	4
A.Flintoff	2	3	–	17	17	5.66	–	–	1
A.R.C.Fraser	46	67	15	32	388	7.46	–	–	9
J.E.R.Gallian	3	6	–	28	74	12.33	–	–	1
A.F.Giles	1	2	1	16*	17	17.00	–	–	–
D.Gough	31	47	6	65	468	11.41	–	2	9
D.W.Headley	13	23	4	31	152	8.00	–	–	7
W.K.Hegg	2	4	–	15	30	7.50	–	–	8
G.A.Hick	53	93	6	178	2993	34.40	5	17	76
A.J.Hollioake	4	6	–	45	65	10.83	–	–	4
B.C.Hollioake	2	4	–	28	44	11.00	–	–	2
N.Hussain	39	71	6	207	2440	37.53	7	10	31
R.K.Illingworth	9	14	7	28	128	18.28	–	–	5
M.C.Ilott	5	6	2	15	28	7.00	–	–	–
R.C.Irani	2	3	–	41	76	25.33	–	–	–
S.P.James	2	4	–	36	71	17.75	–	–	–
P.W.Jarvis	9	15	2	29*	132	10.15	–	–	2
N.V.Knight	12	21	–	113	585	27.85	1	4	21
M.N.Lathwell	2	4	–	33	78	19.50	–	–	–
C.C.Lewis	32	51	3	117	1105	23.02	1	4	25
M.J.McCague	3	5	–	11	21	4.20	–	–	1
D.E.Malcolm	40	58	19	29	236	6.05	–	–	7
P.J.Martin	8	13	–	29	115	8.84	–	–	6
M.P.Maynard	4	8	–	35	87	10.87	–	–	3
J.E.Morris	3	5	2	32	71	23.66	–	–	3
A.D.Mullally	13	19	4	24	99	6.60	–	–	3
T.A.Munton	2	2	1	25*	25	25.00	–	–	–
P.J.Newport	3	5	1	40*	110	27.50	–	–	1
M.M.Patel	2	2	–	27	45	22.50	–	–	–
M.R.Ramprakash	34	61	5	154	1574	28.10	1	9	25
S.J.Rhodes	11	17	5	65*	294	24.50	–	1	46/3
R.T.Robinson	29	49	5	175	1601	36.38	4	6	8
R.C.Russell	54	86	16	128*	1897	27.10	2	6	153/12
I.D.K.Salisbury	12	22	2	50	284	14.20	–	1	5

TEST   ENGLAND – BATTING AND FIELDING (continued)

	M	I	NO	HS	Runs	Avge	100	50	Ct/St
C.E.W.Silverwood	1	1	–	0	0	0.00	–	–	1
G.C.Small	17	24	7	59	263	15.47	–	1	9
A.M.Smith	1	2	1	4*	4	4.00	–	–	–
R.A.Smith	62	112	15	175	4236	43.67	9	28	39
J.P.Stephenson	1	2	–	25	36	18.00	–	–	–
A.J.Stewart	86	156	11	190	5968	41.15	12	30	155/7
P.M.Such	10	15	5	14*	67	6.70	–	–	3
J.P.Taylor	2	4	2	17*	34	17.00	–	–	–
G.P.Thorpe	53	97	11	138	3452	40.13	6	24	48
A.J.Tudor	2	4	1	18*	35	11.66	–	–	–
P.C.R.Tufnell	34	47	23	22*	123	5.12	–	–	12
S.L.Watkin	3	5	–	13	25	5.00	–	–	1
M.Watkinson	4	6	1	82*	167	33.40	–	1	1
A.P.Wells	1	2	1	3*	3	3.00	–	–	–
J.J.Whitaker	1	1	–	11	11	11.00	–	–	1
C.White	8	12	–	51	166	13.83	–	1	3

ENGLAND – BOWLING

	O	R	W	Avge	Best	5wI	10wM
M.A.Atherton	68	302	2	151.00	1- 20	–	–
K.J.Barnett	6	32	0				
J.E.Benjamin	28	80	4	20.00	4- 42	–	–
M.P.Bicknell	87	263	4	65.75	3- 99	–	–
S.J.E.Brown	33	138	2	69.00	1- 60	–	–
M.A.Butcher	32	83	0				
A.R.Caddick	768.2	2394	74	32.35	6- 65	5	–
D.G.Cork	993.5	3118	98	31.81	7- 43	5	–
R.D.B.Croft	579.5	1380	36	38.33	5- 95	1	–
P.A.J.DeFreitas	1639.4	4700	140	33.57	7- 70	4	–
M.A.Ealham	176.4	488	17	28.70	4- 21	–	–
N.H.Fairbrother	2	9	0				
A.Flintoff	35	112	1	112.00	1- 52	–	–
A.R.C.Fraser	1812.4	4836	177	27.32	8- 53	13	2
J.E.R.Gallian	14	62	0				
A.F.Giles	36	106	1	106.00	1-106	–	–
D.Gough	1116	3578	125	28.62	6- 42	5	–
D.W.Headley	446.2	1482	56	26.46	6- 60	1	–
G.A.Hick	496.3	1248	22	56.72	4-126	–	–
A.J.Hollioake	24	67	2	33.50	2- 31	–	–
B.C.Hollioake	42	199	4	49.75	2-105	–	–
R.K.Illingworth	247.3	615	19	32.36	4- 96	–	–
M.C.Ilott	173.4	542	12	45.16	3- 48	–	–
R.C.Irani	21	74	2	37.00	1- 22	–	–
P.W.Jarvis	318.4	965	21	45.95	4-107	–	–
C.C.Lewis	1142	3490	93	37.52	6-111	3	–
M.J.McCague	98.5	390	6	65.00	4-121	–	–
D.E.Malcolm	1413.2	4748	128	37.09	9- 57	5	2
P.J.Martin	242	580	17	34.11	4- 60	–	–
A.D.Mullally	554	1291	40	32.27	5-105	1	–
T.A.Munton	67.3	200	4	50.00	2- 22	–	–
P.J.Newport	111.3	417	10	41.70	4- 87	–	–
M.M.Patel	46	180	1	180.00	1-101	–	–
M.R.Ramprakash	139.1	444	4	111.00	1- 2	–	–
R.T.Robinson	1	0	0				
I.D.K.Salisbury	346.2	1346	19	70.84	4-163	–	–

TEST   **ENGLAND – BOWLING (continued)**

	O	R	W	Avge	Best	5wI	10wM
C.E.W.Silverwood	25	71	4	17.75	3-63	–	–
G.C.Small	654.3	1871	55	34.01	5-48	2	–
A.M.Smith	23	89	0				
R.A.Smith	4	6	0				
A.J.Stewart	3.2	13	0				
P.M.Such	479.4	1128	33	34.18	6-67	2	–
J.P.Taylor	48	156	3	52.00	1-18	–	–
G.P.Thorpe	23	37	0				
A.J.Tudor	42.2	180	7	25.71	4-89	–	–
P.C.R.Tufnell	1538.2	3636	100	36.36	7-47	5	2
S.L.Watkin	89	305	11	27.72	4-65	–	–
M.Watkinson	112	348	10	34.80	3-64	–	–
C.White	135.1	452	11	41.09	3-18	–	–

AUSTRALIA – BATTING AND FIELDING

	M	I	NO	HS	Runs	Avge	100	50	Ct/St
M.G.Bevan	18	30	3	91	785	29.07	–	6	8
A.J.Bichel	3	5	–	18	47	9.40	–	–	1
G.S.Blewett	31	53	2	214	1843	36.13	4	10	36
D.C.Boon	107	190	20	200	7422	43.65	21	32	99
S.H.Cook	2	2	2	3*	3	–	–	–	–
A.C.Dale	1	1	–	5	5	5.00	–	–	–
M.T.G.Elliott	17	28	1	199	1102	40.81	3	4	11
D.W.Fleming	10	10	1	71*	143	15.88	–	1	7
J.N.Gillespie	10	15	3	28*	97	12.12	–	–	3
M.L.Hayden	7	12	–	125	261	21.75	1	–	8
I.A.Healy	111	169	23	161*	4273	29.26	4	22	353/28
B.P.Julian	7	9	1	56*	128	16.00	–	1	4
M.S.Kasprowicz	14	18	2	25	180	11.25	–	–	5
J.L.Langer	16	27	1	179*	919	35.34	2	6	12
S.G.Law	1	1	1	54*	54	–	–	1	1
D.S.Lehmann	5	8	–	98	228	28.50	–	2	3
S.C.G.MacGill	8	10	1	43	133	14.77	–	–	7
G.D.McGrath	45	54	16	24	172	4.52	–	–	13
C.R.Miller	6	7	2	11	20	4.00	–	–	1
M.J.Nicholson	1	2	–	9	14	7.00	–	–	–
R.T.Ponting	22	35	2	127	1209	36.63	2	7	21
P.R.Reiffel	35	50	14	79*	955	26.52	–	6	15
G.R.Robertson	4	7	1	57	140	20.00	–	1	1
M.J.Slater	45	80	3	219	3515	45.64	11	12	17
M.A.Taylor	104	186	13	334*	7525	43.49	19	40	157
S.K.Warne	68	95	11	74*	1240	14.76	–	2	48
M.E.Waugh	86	143	10	153*	5840	43.90	16	33	100
S.R.Waugh	111	177	34	200	7213	50.44	17	40	78
P.Wilson	1	2	2	0*	0	–	–	–	–
S.Young	1	2	1	4*	4	4.00	–	–	–

AUSTRALIA – BOWLING

	O	R	W	Avge	Best	5wI	10wM
M.G.Bevan	214.1	703	29	24.24	6-82	1	1
A.J.Bichel	86.2	297	2	148.50	1-31	–	–
G.S.Blewett	178.2	520	9	57.77	2-25	–	–
D.C.Boon	6	14	0				
S.H.Cook	37.2	142	7	20.28	5-39	1	–
A.C.Dale	28	92	3	30.66	3-71	–	–

TEST **AUSTRALIA – BOWLING (continued)**

	O	R	W	Avge	Best	5wI	10wM
M.T.G.Elliott	2	4	0				
D.W.Fleming	355.2	1007	37	27.21	5-46	1	–
J.N.Gillespie	250.4	824	39	21.12	7-37	3	–
B.P.Julian	183	599	15	39.93	4-36	–	–
M.S.Kasprowicz	463.2	1344	38	35.36	7-36	2	–
S.G.Law	3	9	0				
D.S.Lehmann	17	45	2	22.50	1- 6	–	–
S.C.G.MacGill	349	1024	47	21.78	7-50	3	1
G.D.McGrath	1792.2	4736	202	23.44	8-38	11	–
C.R.Miller	220	567	17	33.35	3-57	–	–
M.J.Nicholson	25	115	4	28.75	3-56	–	–
R.T.Ponting	14.5	31	3	10.33	1- 0	–	–
P.R.Reiffel	1067.1	2804	104	26.96	6-71	5	–
G.R.Robertson	149.4	515	13	39.61	4-72	–	–
M.J.Slater	1.1	4	1	4.00	1- 4	–	–
M.A.Taylor	7	26	1	26.00	1-11	–	–
S.K.Warne	3337.3	7866	315	24.97	8-71	14	4
M.E.Waugh	663	1928	48	40.16	5-40	1	–
S.R.Waugh	1174.5	3105	89	34.88	5-28	3	–
P.Wilson	12	50	0				
S.Young	8	13	0				

SOUTH AFRICA – BATTING AND FIELDING

	M	I	NO	HS	Runs	Avge	100	50	Ct/St
H.D.Ackerman	4	8	–	57	161	20.12	–	1	1
P.R.Adams	21	27	6	29	107	5.09	–	–	16
A.M.Bacher	17	31	1	96	783	26.10	–	5	10
M.V.Boucher	16	23	2	100	502	23.90	1	3	69/2
W.J.Cronje	56	97	9	135	3363	38.21	6	20	28
D.J.Cullinan	45	77	6	168	2680	37.74	6	15	38
P.S.de Villiers	18	26	7	67*	359	18.89	–	2	11
A.A.Donald	52	70	26	34	504	11.45	–	–	13
S.Elworthy	1	2	–	48	58	29.00	–	–	1
H.H.Gibbs	11	21	–	54	433	20.61	–	2	8
A.C.Hudson	35	63	3	163	2007	33.45	4	13	36
J.H.Kallis	24	40	4	132	1327	36.86	3	7	23
G.Kirsten	50	91	8	210	3231	38.92	8	17	41
L.Klusener	17	26	5	102*	585	27.85	1	2	10
G.F.J.Liebenberg	5	8	–	45	104	13.00	–	–	1
B.M.McMillan	38	62	12	113	1968	39.36	3	13	49
M.Ntini	4	5	4	4*	9	9.00	–	–	1
S.M.Pollock	30	48	9	92	1143	29.30	–	5	13
J.N.Rhodes	41	66	7	117	2048	34.71	3	11	21
D.J.Richardson	42	64	8	109	1359	24.26	1	8	150/2
B.N.Schultz	9	8	2	6	9	1.50	–	–	2
P.L.Symcox	20	27	1	108	741	28.50	1	4	5
D.J.Terbrugge	4	5	5	4*	14	–	–	–	2

SOUTH AFRICA – BOWLING

	O	R	W	Avge	Best	5wI	10wM
P.R.Adams	742.3	2039	66	30.89	6-55	1	–
A.M.Bacher	1	4	0				
W.J.Cronje	507.1	1031	29	35.55	3-19	–	–
D.J.Cullinan	14	46	1	46.00	1-32	–	–
P.S.de Villiers	800.5	2063	85	24.27	6-23	5	2

174

TEST SOUTH AFRICA – BOWLING (continued)

	O	R	W	Avge	Best	5wI	10wM
A.A.Donald	1951.3	5628	260	21.64	8-71	17	2
S.Elworthy	31	79	1	79.00	1-41	–	–
J.H.Kallis	480.2	1103	41	26.90	5-90	1	–
G.Kirsten	54.1	135	2	67.50	1- 0	–	–
L.Klusener	496.1	1474	45	32.75	8-64	1	–
B.M.McMillan	1008	2537	75	33.82	4-65	–	–
M.Ntini	125.2	358	10	35.80	4-72	–	–
S.M.Pollock	1091.5	2657	120	22.14	7-87	8	–
J.N.Rhodes	2	5	0				
B.N.Schultz	288.5	749	37	20.24	5-48	2	–
P.L.Symcox	593.3	1603	37	43.32	4-69	–	–
D.J.Terbrugge	100	253	9	28.11	3-27	–	–

WEST INDIES – BATTING AND FIELDING

	M	I	NO	HS	Runs	Avge	100	50	Ct/St
J.C.Adams	33	52	11	208*	2104	51.31	5	10	32
C.E.L.Ambrose	84	122	26	53	1244	12.95	–	1	16
K.C.G.Benjamin	26	36	8	43*	222	7.92	–	–	2
I.R.Bishop	43	63	11	48	632	12.15	–	–	8
S.L.Campbell	30	51	2	208	1814	37.02	2	12	19
S.Chanderpaul	35	58	7	137*	2145	42.05	2	17	15
M.Dillon	6	11	1	36	84	8.40	–	–	1
D.Ganga	3	6	–	28	75	12.50	–	–	3
O.D.Gibson	2	4	–	37	93	23.25	–	–	–
R.I.C.Holder	10	15	2	91	376	28.92	–	2	9
C.L.Hooper	78	132	13	178*	4063	34.14	9	18	89
R.D.Jacobs	5	10	3	78	317	45.28	–	2	20
R.D.King	1	2	1	2*	2	2.00	–	–	1
C.B.Lambert	5	9	–	104	284	31.55	1	1	8
B.C.Lara	59	101	3	375	4860	49.59	10	26	80
R.N.Lewis	3	6	–	12	26	4.33	–	–	–
N.A.M.McLean	8	12	1	39	187	17.00	–	–	3
J.R.Murray	31	42	4	101*	917	24.13	1	3	96/3
D.Ramnarine	2	2	–	19	19	9.50	–	–	2
F.L.Reifer	4	8	–	29	63	7.87	–	–	4
F.A.Rose	11	14	2	34	125	10.41	–	–	1
P.V.Simmons	26	47	2	110	1002	22.26	1	4	26
P.A.Wallace	7	13	–	92	279	21.46	–	2	9
C.A.Walsh	106	142	47	30*	812	8.54	–	–	24
D.Williams	11	19	1	65	242	13.44	–	1	40/2
S.C.Williams	28	49	2	128	1092	24.26	1	3	26

WEST INDIES – BOWLING

	O	R	W	Avge	Best	5wI	10wM
J.C.Adams	214.3	673	16	42.06	5- 17	1	–
C.E.L.Ambrose	3122.5	7442	350	21.26	8- 45	21	3
K.C.G.Benjamin	855.2	2785	92	30.27	6- 66	4	1
I.R.Bishop	1401.1	3909	161	24.27	6- 40	6	–
S.Chanderpaul	219	654	5	130.80	1- 2	–	–
M.Dillon	194.3	616	18	34.22	5-111	1	–
O.D.Gibson	78.4	275	3	91.66	2- 81	–	–
C.L.Hooper	1675.5	4219	88	47.94	5- 26	4	–
R.D.King	28	130	0				
C.B.Lambert	1.4	5	1	5.00	1- 4	–	–
B.C.Lara	10	28	0				

TEST **WEST INDIES – BOWLING (continued)**

	O	R	W	Avge	Best	5wI	10wM
R.N.Lewis	97.3	318	1	318.00	1-67	–	–
N.A.M.McLean	207.2	660	17	38.82	3-53	–	–
D.Ramnarine	91	148	9	16.44	4-29	–	–
F.A.Rose	282.1	853	34	25.08	7-84	2	–
P.V.Simmons	104	257	4	64.25	2-34	–	–
C.A.Walsh	3829.5	10084	397	25.40	7-37	16	2
S.C.Williams	3	19	0				

NEW ZEALAND – BATTING AND FIELDING

	M	I	NO	HS	Runs	Avge	100	50	Ct/St
G.I.Allott	6	10	3	8*	18	2.57	–	–	1
N.J.Astle	22	41	3	125	1251	32.92	4	5	19
M.D.Bell	2	4	–	25	29	7.25	–	–	2
C.L.Cairns	35	61	2	126	1634	27.69	2	13	12
H.T.Davis	5	7	4	8*	20	6.66	–	–	4
S.B.Doull	26	40	9	31*	389	12.54	–	–	16
S.P.Fleming	39	69	3	176*	2426	36.75	2	18	65
C.Z.Harris	14	28	3	71	390	15.60	–	2	12
M.J.Horne	13	24	1	157	849	36.91	2	2	11
C.D.McMillan	10	18	1	142	834	49.05	2	6	5
D.J.Nash	18	27	9	89*	452	25.11	–	3	9
S.B.O'Connor	6	10	5	7	26	5.20	–	–	4
A.C.Parore	46	81	9	100*	1979	27.48	1	12	96/3
B.A.Pocock	15	29	–	85	665	22.93	–	6	5
M.W.Priest	3	4	–	26	56	14.00	–	–	–
D.G.Sewell	1	1	1	1*	1	–	–	–	–
C.M.Spearman	8	16	–	112	508	31.75	1	1	6
R.G.Twose	9	15	1	94	436	31.14	–	4	2
D.L.Vettori	16	26	5	90	377	17.95	–	2	9
P.J.Wiseman	5	8	2	23	45	7.50	–	–	–
B.A.Young	33	64	3	267*	1954	32.03	2	11	53

NEW ZEALAND – BOWLING

	O	R	W	Avge	Best	5wI	10wM
G.I.Allott	200.3	667	11	60.63	4-74	–	–
N.J.Astle	228.5	561	13	43.15	2-26	–	–
C.L.Cairns	1070.4	3568	109	32.73	6-52	5	–
H.T.Davis	168.2	499	17	29.35	5-63	1	–
S.B.Doull	858.5	2450	95	25.78	7-65	6	–
C.Z.Harris	224.4	613	9	68.11	2-57	–	–
M.J.Horne	11	26	0				
C.D.McMillan	109.4	318	8	39.75	2-27	–	–
D.J.Nash	579	1547	57	27.14	6-76	2	1
S.B.O'Connor	195.1	637	18	35.38	4-52	–	–
B.A.Pocock	4	20	0				
M.W.Priest	62.5	158	3	52.66	2-42	–	–
D.G.Sewell	23	90	0				
R.G.Twose	35.1	130	3	43.33	2-36	–	–
D.L.Vettori	675.5	1758	54	32.55	6-64	2	–
P.J.Wiseman	156.5	504	13	38.76	5-82	1	–

INDIA – BATTING AND FIELDING

	M	I	NO	HS	Runs	Avge	100	50	Ct/St
A.B.Agarkar	1	2	–	5	9	4.50	–	–	–
M.Azharuddin	94	137	9	199	5860	45.78	21	19	103
R.K.Chauhan	21	17	3	23	98	7.00	–	–	12
R.Dravid	25	41	4	190	2126	57.45	4	15	30
S.C.Ganguly	23	37	3	173	1731	50.91	6	5	6
Harbhajan Singh	3	6	3	15*	21	7.00	–	–	2
Harvinder Singh	2	3	1	0*	0	0.00	–	–	–
A.Jadeja	13	20	1	96	538	28.31	–	4	4
N.M.Kulkarni	2	1	1	1*	0	–	–	–	1
A.Kumble	49	60	10	88	905	18.10	–	3	23
A.Kuruvilla	10	11	1	35*	66	6.60	–	–	–
V.V.S.Laxman	10	16	2	95	405	28.92	–	4	9
D.S.Mohanty	2	1	1	0*	0	–	–	–	–
N.R.Mongia	36	54	6	152	1245	25.93	1	5	81/6
B.K.V.Prasad	20	27	10	30*	117	6.88	–	–	5
S.L.V.Raju	27	33	10	31	236	10.26	–	–	6
N.S.Sidhu	51	78	2	201	3202	42.13	9	15	9
R.Singh	1	1	–	0	0	0.00	–	–	1
R.R.Singh	1	2	–	15	27	13.50	–	–	5
J.Srinath	35	48	14	76	609	17.91	–	4	15
S.R.Tendulkar	64	97	9	179	4820	54.77	17	20	48

INDIA – BOWLING

	O	R	W	Avge	Best	5wI	10wM
A.B.Agarkar	34	100	2	50.00	1- 40	–	–
M.Azharuddin	2.1	16	0				
R.K.Chauhan	791.3	1857	47	39.51	4- 48	–	–
R.Dravid	3	6	0				
S.C.Ganguly	165.3	535	17	31.47	3- 28	–	–
Harbhajan Singh	94	314	7	44.85	3- 64	–	–
Harvinder Singh	23	98	2	49.00	1- 28	–	–
N.M.Kulkarni	70	195	1	195.00	1-195	–	–
A.Kumble	2526.5	6072	213	28.50	7- 59	11	1
A.Kuruvilla	294.1	892	25	35.68	5- 68	1	–
V.V.S.Laxman	17	51	0				
D.S.Mohanty	71.4	239	4	59.75	4- 78	–	–
B.K.V.Prasad	748.4	2122	63	33.68	6-104	5	1
S.L.V.Raju	1231	2736	92	29.73	6- 12	5	1
N.S.Sidhu	1	9	0				
R.Singh	40	176	3	58.66	2- 74	–	–
R.R.Singh	10	32	0				
J.Srinath	1363	3868	124	31.19	6- 21	3	–
S.R.Tendulkar	124	365	9	40.55	2- 7	–	–

PAKISTAN – BATTING AND FIELDING

	M	I	NO	HS	Runs	Avge	100	50	Ct/St
Aamir Sohail	45	79	3	205	2777	36.53	5	13	34
Ali Naqvi	5	9	1	115	242	30.25	1	–	1
Ali Rizvi	1	–	–	–	–	–	–	–	–
Aqib Javed	22	27	7	28*	101	5.05	–	–	2
Arshad Khan	2	2	–	7	11	5.50	–	–	–
Azhar Mahmood	14	21	4	136	687	40.41	3	1	10
Fazal-e-Akber	1	2	1	0*	0	0.00	–	–	1
Hasan Raza	2	2	–	27	30	15.00	–	–	–
Ijaz Ahmed	50	74	4	155	2799	39.98	10	11	35
Inzamam-ul-Haq	51	84	10	177	3160	42.70	6	21	46
Mohammad Hussain	2	3	–	17	18	6.00	–	–	1
Mohammad Ramzan	1	2	–	29	36	18.00	–	–	1
Mohammad Wasim	11	16	2	192	463	33.07	2	–	15/2
Mohammad Zahid	4	4	1	6*	7	2.33	–	–	–
Moin Khan	42	62	6	117*	1683	30.05	3	9	74/11
Mushtaq Ahmed	41	59	12	59	592	12.59	–	2	17
Naved Ashraf	1	1	–	32	32	32.00	–	–	–
Rashid Latif	22	34	5	68*	659	22.72	–	3	72/8
Saeed Anwar	36	60	1	176	2693	45.64	7	17	15
Salim Malik	100	148	22	237	5641	44.76	15	29	64
Saqlain Mushtaq	17	25	6	79	315	16.57	–	2	5
Shahid Afridi	1	2	–	10	16	8.00	–	–	2
Shahid Nazir	7	8	2	18	45	7.50	–	–	2
Shakeel Ahmed	1	1	–	1	1	1.00	–	–	1
Shoaib Akhtar	8	9	4	11	38	7.60	–	–	4
Waqar Younis	55	72	14	45	587	10.12	–	–	7
Wasim Akram	83	115	15	257*	2111	21.11	2	4	31
Yousuf Youhana	7	12	1	120*	448	40.72	1	4	8

PAKISTAN – BOWLING

	O	R	W	Avge	Best	5wI	10wM
Aamir Sohail	354.5	950	20	47.50	4- 54	–	–
Ali Naqvi	2	11	0	–	–	–	–
Ali Rizvi	18.3	72	2	36.00	2- 72	–	–
Aqib Javed	653	1874	54	34.70	5- 84	1	–
Arshad Khan	107	245	5	49.00	3- 72	–	–
Azhar Mahmood	348.4	941	25	37.64	4- 53	–	–
Fazal-e-Akber	13	32	3	10.66	2- 16	–	–
Ijaz Ahmed	28	69	2	34.50	1- 9	–	–
Inzamam-ul-Haq	1.3	8	0	–	–	–	–
Mohammad Hussain	30	87	3	29.00	2- 66	–	–
Mohammad Zahid	107	394	13	30.30	7- 66	1	1
Mushtaq Ahmed	1706.4	4788	165	29.01	7- 56	10	3
Rashid Latif	2	10	0	–	–	–	–
Saeed Anwar	8	23	0	–	–	–	–
Salim Malik	122.2	415	5	83.00	1- 3	–	–
Saqlain Mushtaq	773	2107	65	32.41	5- 32	4	–
Shahid Afridi	41.3	101	5	20.20	5- 52	1	–
Shahid Nazir	154.2	494	16	30.87	5- 53	1	–
Shakeel Ahmed	54.1	139	4	34.75	4- 91	–	–
Shoaib Akhtar	248.4	789	18	43.83	5- 43	1	–
Waqar Younis	1849.1	5931	275	21.56	7- 76	21	5
Wasim Akram	3132	8092	354	22.85	7-119	22	4

SRI LANKA – BATTING AND FIELDING

	M	I	NO	HS	Runs	Avge	100	50	Ct/St
S.D.Anurasiri	18	22	5	24	91	5.35	–	–	4
R.P.Arnold	3	6	–	50	138	23.00	–	1	4
M.S.Atapattu	20	36	2	223	1005	29.55	2	3	12
C.M.Bandara	1	2	1	0*	0	0.00	–	–	1
M.R.C.N.Bandaratilake	3	5	–	20	52	10.40	–	–	–
K.S.C.de Silva	6	9	5	6	19	4.75	–	–	2
P.A.de Silva	74	128	9	267	5129	43.10	17	18	36
S.K.L.de Silva	3	4	2	20*	36	18.00	–	–	1
H.D.P.K.Dharmasena	20	35	5	62*	660	22.00	–	2	11
S.T.Jayasuriya	38	64	7	340	2612	45.82	5	14	35
D.P.M.D.Jayawardena	6	9	–	167	398	44.22	1	3	11
R.S.Kalpage	10	17	1	63	292	18.25	–	2	9
R.S.Kaluwitharana	24	39	2	132*	1191	32.18	2	7	47/11
R.S.Mahanama	52	89	1	225	2576	29.27	4	11	56
M.Muralitharan	42	57	24	39	458	13.87	–	–	23
A.S.A.Perera	1	1	1	43*	43	–	–	–	–
K.R.Pushpakumara	18	24	11	23	93	7.15	–	–	8
A.Ranatunga	82	138	8	135*	4595	35.34	4	33	35
K.J.Silva	7	4	1	6*	6	2.00	–	–	1
H.P.Tillekeratne	53	87	13	126*	2879	38.90	6	15	85
W.P.U.C.J.Vaas	26	39	5	57	580	17.05	–	2	10
G.P.Wickremasinghe	31	50	5	51	481	10.68	–	1	11
D.N.T.Zoysa	4	7	1	16*	57	9.50	–	–	1

SRI LANKA – BOWLING

	O	R	W	Avge	Best	5wI	10wM
S.D.Anurasiri	662.1	1548	41	37.75	4- 71	–	–
R.P.Arnold	13	31	0				
M.S.Atapattu	8	24	1	24.00	1- 9	–	–
C.M.Bandara	21	79	0				
M.R.C.N.Bandaratilake	160	338	16	21.12	5- 36	1	–
K.S.C.de Silva	195.3	636	13	48.92	5- 85	1	–
P.A.de Silva	313.5	904	24	37.66	3- 30	–	–
H.D.P.K.Dharmasena	791.3	1893	50	37.86	6- 72	3	–
S.T.Jayasuriya	414	1145	25	45.80	4- 53	–	–
D.P.M.D.Jayawardena	16	50	0				
R.S.Kalpage	226.5	607	8	75.87	2- 27	–	–
R.S.Mahanama	6	30	0				
M.Muralitharan	2173.3	5464	203	26.91	9- 65	16	2
A.S.A.Perera	51	126	1	126.00	1-104	–	–
K.R.Pushpakumara	484.1	1837	47	39.08	7-116	3	–
A.Ranatunga	393.3	1027	16	64.18	2- 17	–	–
K.J.Silva	255.2	647	20	32.35	4- 16	–	–
H.P.Tillekeratne	5.4	14	0				
W.P.U.C.J.Vaas	925.5	2409	83	29.02	6- 87	4	1
G.P.Wickremasinghe	921.1	2786	60	46.43	5- 73	1	–
D.N.T.Zoysa	104.4	307	8	38.37	3- 47	–	–

ZIMBABWE – BATTING AND FIELDING

	M	I	NO	HS	Runs	Avge	100	50	Ct/St
A.D.R.Campbell	33	59	2	99	1589	27.87	–	11	33
C.N.Evans	2	4	–	11	25	6.25	–	–	1
A.Flower	33	58	10	156	2090	43.54	5	13	80/5
G.W.Flower	32	58	3	201*	2061	37.47	5	8	15
M.W.Goodwin	9	17	2	166*	804	53.60	1	6	6
D.L.Houghton	22	36	2	266	1465	43.08	4	4	17
A.G.Huckle	8	14	3	28*	74	6.72	–	–	3
N.C.Johnson	3	4	–	107	126	31.50	1	–	4
T.N.Madondo	2	3	–	14	16	5.33	–	–	–
E.Matambanadzo	2	3	1	7	11	5.50	–	–	–
M.Mbangwa	9	15	3	4	16	1.33	–	–	2
H.K.Olonga	10	13	1	7	30	2.50	–	–	7
G.J.Rennie	10	20	1	84	499	26.26	–	5	8
J.A.Rennie	4	6	1	22	62	12.40	–	–	1
B.C.Strang	13	23	7	53	223	13.93	–	1	9
P.A.Strang	20	34	7	106*	747	27.66	1	2	12
H.H.Streak	26	41	7	53	533	15.67	–	2	7
D.P.Viljoen	1	2	–	0	0	0.00	–	–	1
A.R.Whittall	9	17	3	17	106	7.57	–	–	8
G.J.Whittall	25	43	3	203*	1072	26.80	2	4	12
C.B.Wishart	11	20	1	63	292	15.36	–	2	5

ZIMBABWE – BOWLING

	O	R	W	Avge	Best	5wI	10wM
A.D.R.Campbell	7	20	0				
C.N.Evans	9	35	0				
A.Flower	0.1	0	0				
G.W.Flower	126	354	3	118.00	1- 4	–	–
M.W.Goodwin	17.5	58	0				
D.L.Houghton	0.5	0	0				
A.G.Huckle	261.1	872	25	34.88	6-109	2	1
N.C.Johnson	80.5	265	7	37.85	3- 41	–	–
E.Matambanadzo	33	155	2	77.50	2- 62	–	–
M.Mbangwa	258.2	590	24	24.58	3- 23	–	–
H.K.Olonga	222.4	749	25	29.96	5- 70	1	–
J.A.Rennie	120.4	293	3	97.66	2- 22	–	–
B.C.Strang	438.5	980	32	30.62	5-101	1	–
P.A.Strang	808.1	2154	57	37.78	5-106	3	–
H.H.Streak	993.3	2633	106	24.83	6- 90	3	–
D.P.Viljoen	3.3	14	1	14.00	1- 14	–	–
A.R.Whittall	225.2	631	6	105.16	3- 73	–	–
G.J.Whittall	506.5	1314	36	36.50	4- 18	–	–

FIRST-CLASS CRICKET RECORDS

To 21 September 1998

TEAM RECORDS

HIGHEST INNINGS TOTALS

1107	Victoria v New South Wales	Melbourne	1926-27
1059	Victoria v Tasmania	Melbourne	1922-23
952-6d	Sri Lanka v India	Colombo	1997-98
951-7d	Sind v Baluchistan	Karachi	1973-74
944-6d	Hyderabad v Andhra	Secunderabad	1993-94
918	New South Wales v South Australia	Sydney	1900-01
912-8d	Holkar v Mysore	Indore	1945-46
910-6d	Railways v Dera Ismail Khan	Lahore	1964-65
903-7d	England v Australia	The Oval	1938
887	Yorkshire v Warwickshire	Birmingham	1896
863	Lancashire v Surrey	The Oval	1990
860-6d	Tamil Nadu v Goa	Panjim	1988-89

Excluding penalty runs in India, there have been 30 innings totals of 800 runs or more in first-class cricket. Tamil Nadu's total of 860-6d was boosted to 912 by 52 penalty runs.

HIGHEST SECOND INNINGS TOTAL

770	New South Wales v South Australia	Adelaide	1920-21

HIGHEST FOURTH INNINGS TOTAL

654-5	England v South Africa	Durban	1938-39

HIGHEST MATCH AGGREGATE

2376	Maharashtra v Bombay	Poona	1948-49

RECORD MARGIN OF VICTORY

Innings and 851 runs: Railways v Dera Ismail Khan   Lahore   1964-65

MOST RUNS IN A DAY

721	Australians v Essex	Southend	1948

MOST HUNDREDS IN AN INNINGS

6	Holkar v Mysore	Indore	1945-46

LOWEST INNINGS TOTALS

12	†Oxford University v MCC and Ground	Oxford	1877
12	Northamptonshire v Gloucestershire	Gloucester	1907
13	Auckland v Canterbury	Auckland	1877-78
13	Nottinghamshire v Yorkshire	Nottingham	1901
14	Surrey v Essex	Chelmsford	1983
15	MCC v Surrey	Lord's	1839
15	†Victoria v MCC	Melbourne	1903-04
15	†Northamptonshire v Yorkshire	Northampton	1908
15	Hampshire v Warwickshire	Birmingham	1922

† *Batted one man short*

There have been 26 instances of a team being dismissed for under 20.

LOWEST MATCH AGGREGATE BY ONE TEAM

34 (16 and 18) Border v Natal East London 1959-60

LOWEST COMPLETED MATCH AGGREGATE BY BOTH TEAMS

105 MCC v Australians Lord's 1878

FEWEST RUNS IN AN UNINTERRUPTED DAY'S PLAY

95 Australia (80) v Pakistan (15-2) Karachi 1956-57

TIED MATCHES

Before 1949 a match was considered to be tied if the scores were level after the fourth innings, even if the side batting last had wickets in hand when play ended. Law 22 was amended in 1948 and since then a match has been tied only when the scores are level after the fourth innings has been completed. There have been 53 tied first-class matches, five of which would not have qualified under the current law. The most recent is:

Worcestershire (203/325-8d) v Nottinghamshire (233/295) Nottingham 1993

BATTING RECORDS
HIGHEST INDIVIDUAL INNINGS

501*	B.C.Lara	Warwickshire v Durham	Birmingham	1994
499	Hanif Mohammad	Karachi v Bahawalpur	Karachi	1958-59
452*	D.G.Bradman	New South Wales v Queensland	Sydney	1929-30
443*	B.B.Nimbalkar	Maharashtra v Kathiawar	Poona	1948-49
437	W.H.Ponsford	Victoria v Queensland	Melbourne	1927-28
429	W.H.Ponsford	Victoria v Tasmania	Melbourne	1922-23
428	Aftab Baloch	Sind v Baluchistan	Karachi	1973-74
424	A.C.MacLaren	Lancashire v Somerset	Taunton	1895
405*	G.A.Hick	Worcestershire v Somerset	Taunton	1988
385	B.Sutcliffe	Otago v Canterbury	Christchurch	1952-53
383	C.W.Gregory	New South Wales v Queensland	Brisbane	1906-07
377	S.V.Manjrekar	Bombay v Hyderabad	Bombay	1990-91
375	B.C.Lara	West Indies v England	St John's	1993-94
369	D.G.Bradman	South Australia v Tasmania	Adelaide	1935-36
366	N.H.Fairbrother	Lancashire v Surrey	The Oval	1990
366	M.V.Sridhar	Hyderabad v Andhra	Secunderabad	1993-94
365*	C.Hill	South Australia v NSW	Adelaide	1900-01
365*	G.St A.Sobers	West Indies v Pakistan	Kingston	1957-58
364	L.Hutton	England v Australia	The Oval	1938
359*	V.M.Merchant	Bombay v Maharashtra	Bombay	1943-44
359	R.B.Simpson	New South Wales v Queensland	Brisbane	1963-64
357*	R.Abel	Surrey v Somerset	The Oval	1899
357	D.G.Bradman	South Australia v Victoria	Melbourne	1935-36
356	B.A.Richards	South Australia v W Australia	Perth	1970-71
355*	G.R.Marsh	W Australia v S Australia	Perth	1989-90
355	B.Sutcliffe	Otago v Auckland	Dunedin	1949-50
352	W.H.Ponsford	Victoria v New South Wales	Melbourne	1926-27
350	Rashid Israr	Habib Bank v National Bank	Lahore	1976-77

There have been 121 triple hundreds in first-class cricket, W.V.Raman (313) and Arjan Kripal Singh (302*) for Tamil Nadu v Goa at Panjim in 1988-89 providing the only instance of two batsmen scoring 300 in the same innings.

MOST HUNDREDS IN SUCCESSIVE INNINGS

6	C.B.Fry	Sussex and Rest of England	1901
6	D.G.Bradman	South Australia and D.G.Bradman's XI	1938-39
6	M.J.Procter	Rhodesia	1970-71

TWO DOUBLE HUNDREDS IN A MATCH

244 202* A.E.Fagg   Kent v Essex   Colchester   1938

TRIPLE HUNDRED AND HUNDRED IN A MATCH

333 123   G.A.Gooch   England v India   Lord's   1990

DOUBLE HUNDRED AND HUNDRED IN A MATCH MOST TIMES

4   Zaheer Abbas   Gloucestershire   1976-81

TWO HUNDREDS IN A MATCH MOST TIMES

8   Zaheer Abbas   Gloucestershire and PIA   1976-82
7   W.R.Hammond   Gloucestershire, England and MCC   1927-45

MOST HUNDREDS IN A SEASON

18   D.C.S.Compton   1947   16   J.B.Hobbs   1925

100 HUNDREDS IN A CAREER

	Total Hundreds	Inns	100th Hundred Season	Inns
J.B.Hobbs	197	1315	1923	821
E.H.Hendren	170	1300	1928-29	740
W.R.Hammond	167	1005	1935	679
C.P.Mead	153	1340	1927	892
G.Boycott	151	1014	1977	645
H.Sutcliffe	149	1088	1932	700
F.E.Woolley	145	1532	1929	1031
L.Hutton	129	814	1951	619
G.A.Gooch	128	988	1992-93	820
W.G Grace	126	1493	1895	1113
D.C.S.Compton	123	839	1952	552
T.W.Graveney	122	1223	1964	940
D.G.Bradman	117	338	1947-48	295
I.V.A.Richards	114	796	1988-89	658
Zaheer Abbas	108	768	1982-83	658
A.Sandham	107	1000	1935	871
M.C.Cowdrey	107	1130	1973	1035
T.W.Hayward	104	1138	1913	1076
G.A.Hick	103	595	1998	574
G.M.Turner	103	792	1982	779
J.H.Edrich	103	979	1977	945
L.E.G.Ames	102	951	1950	915
G.E.Tyldesley	102	961	1934	919
D.L.Amiss	102	1139	1986	1081

MOST 400s: 2 – W.H.Ponsford
MOST 300s or more: 6 – D.G.Bradman; 4 – W.R.Hammond
MOST 200s or more: 37 – D.G.Bradman; 36 – W.R.Hammond; 22 – E.H.Hendren

MOST RUNS IN A MONTH

1294 (avge 92.42)   L.Hutton   Yorkshire   June 1949

MOST RUNS IN A SEASON

Runs			I	NO	HS	Avge	100	Season
3816	D.C.S.Compton	Middlesex	50	8	246	90.85	18	1947
3539	W.J.Edrich	Middlesex	52	8	267*	80.43	12	1947
3518	T.W.Hayward	Surrey	61	8	219	66.37	13	1906

The feat of scoring 3000 runs in a season has been achieved 28 times, the most recent instance being by W.E.Alley (3019) in 1961. The highest aggregate in a season since 1969 is 2755 by S.J.Cook in 1991.

1000 RUNS IN A SEASON MOST TIMES

28   W.G.Grace (Gloucestershire), F.E.Woolley (Kent)

HIGHEST BATTING AVERAGE IN A SEASON

(Qualification: 12 innings)

Avge			I	NO	HS	Runs	100	Season
115.66	D.G.Bradman	Australians	26	5	278	2429	13	1938
102.53	G.Boycott	Yorkshire	20	5	175*	1538	6	1979
102.00	W.A.Johnston	Australians	17	16	28*	102	–	1953
101.70	G.A.Gooch	Essex	30	3	333	2746	12	1990
100.12	G.Boycott	Yorkshire	30	5	233	2503	13	1971

FASTEST HUNDRED AGAINST AUTHENTIC BOWLING

| 35 min | P.G.H.Fender | Surrey v Northamptonshire | Northampton | 1920 |

FASTEST DOUBLE HUNDRED

| 113 min | R.J.Shastri | Bombay v Baroda | Bombay | 1984-85 |

FASTEST TRIPLE HUNDRED

| 181 min | D.C.S.Compton | MCC v NE Transvaal | Benoni | 1948-49 |

MOST SIXES IN AN INNINGS

| 16 | A.Symonds | Gloucestershire v Glamorgan | Abergavenny | 1995 |

MOST SIXES IN A MATCH

| 20 | A.Symonds | Gloucestershire v Glamorgan | Abergavenny | 1995 |

MOST SIXES IN A SEASON

| 80 | I.T.Botham | Somerset and England | | 1985 |

MOST FOURS IN AN INNINGS

| 72 | B.C.Lara | Warwickshire v Durham | Birmingham | 1994 |

MOST RUNS OFF ONE OVER

| 36 | G.St A.Sobers | Nottinghamshire v Glamorgan | Swansea | 1968 |
| 36 | R.J.Shastri | Bombay v Baroda | Bombay | 1984-85 |

Both batsmen hit for six all six balls of overs bowled by M.A.Nash and Tilak Raj respectively.

MOST RUNS IN A DAY

| 390* | B.C.Lara | Warwickshire v Durham | Birmingham | 1994 |

There have been 19 instances of a batsman scoring 300 or more runs in a day.

HIGHEST PARTNERSHIPS FOR EACH WICKET

First Wicket
561	Waheed Mirza/Mansoor Akhtar	Karachi W v Quetta	Karachi	1976-77
555	P.Holmes/H.Sutcliffe	Yorkshire v Essex	Leyton	1932
554	J.T.Brown/J.Tunnicliffe	Yorkshire v Derbys	Chesterfield	1898

Second Wicket
576	S.T.Jayasuriya/R.S.Mahanama	Sri Lanka v India	Colombo (RPS)	1997-98
475	Zahir Alam/L.S.Rajput	Assam v Tripura	Gauhati	1991-92
465*	J.A.Jameson/R.B.Kanhai	Warwickshire v Glos	Birmingham	1974

Third Wicket
467	A.H.Jones/M.D.Crowe	N Zealand v Sri Lanka	Wellington	1990-91
456	Khalid Irtiza/Aslam Ali	United Bank v Multan	Karachi	1975-76
451	Mudassar Nazar/Javed Miandad	Pakistan v India	Hyderabad	1982-83
445	P.E.Whitelaw/W.N.Carson	Auckland v Otago	Dunedin	1936-37
438	G.A.Hick/T.M.Moody	Worcestershire v Hants	Southampton	1997

Fourth Wicket
577	V.S.Hazare/Gul Mahomed	Baroda v Holkar	Baroda	1946-47
574*	C.L.Walcott/F.M.M.Worrell	Barbados v Trinidad	Port-of-Spain	1945-46
502*	F.M.M.Worrell/J.D.C.Goddard	Barbados v Trinidad	Bridgetown	1943-44
470	A.I.Kallicharran/G.W.Humpage	Warwickshire v Lancs	Southport	1982

Fifth Wicket
464*	M.E.Waugh/S.R.Waugh	NSW v W Australia	Perth	1990-91
405	S.G.Barnes/D.G.Bradman	Australia v England	Sydney	1946-47
401	M.B.Loye/D.Ripley	Northants v Glamorgan	Northampton	1998

Sixth Wicket
487*	G.A.Headley/C.C.Passailaigue	Jamaica v Tennyson's	Kingston	1931-32
428	W.W.Armstrong/M.A.Noble	Australians v Sussex	Hove	1902
411	R.M.Poore/E.G.Wynyard	Hampshire v Somerset	Taunton	1899

Seventh Wicket
460	Bhupinder Singh jr/P.Dharmani	Punjab v Delhi	Delhi	1994-95
347	D.St E.Atkinson/C.C.Depeiza	W Indies v Australia	Bridgetown	1954-55
344	K.S.Ranjitsinhji/W.Newham	Sussex v Essex	Leyton	1902

Eighth Wicket
433	V.T.Trumper/A.Sims	Australians v C'bury	Christchurch	1913-14
313	Wasim Akram/Saqlain Mushtaq	Pakistan v Zimbabwe	Sheikhupura	1996-97
292	R.Peel/Lord Hawke	Yorkshire v Warwicks	Birmingham	1896

Ninth Wicket
283	J.Chapman/A.Warren	Derbys v Warwicks	Blackwell	1910
268	J.B.Commins/N.Boje	SA 'A' v Mashonaland	Harare	1994-95
251	J.W.H.T.Douglas/S.N.Hare	Essex v Derbyshire	Leyton	1921

Tenth Wicket
307	A.F.Kippax/J.E.H.Hooker	NSW v Victoria	Melbourne	1928-29
249	C.T.Sarwate/S.N.Banerjee	Indians v Surrey	The Oval	1946
235	F.E.Woolley/A.Fielder	Kent v Worcs	Stourbridge	1909

35000 RUNS IN A CAREER

	Career	I	NO	HS	Runs	Avge	100
J.B.Hobbs	1905-34	1315	106	316*	**61237**	50.65	197
F.E.Woolley	1906-38	1532	85	305*	**58969**	40.75	145
E.H.Hendren	1907-38	1300	166	301*	**57611**	50.80	170
C.P.Mead	1905-36	1340	185	280*	**55061**	47.67	153
W.G.Grace	1865-1908	1493	105	344	**54896**	39.55	126
W.R.Hammond	1920-51	1005	104	336*	**50551**	56.10	167
H.Sutcliffe	1919-45	1088	123	313	**50138**	51.95	149
G.Boycott	1962-86	1014	162	261*	**48426**	56.83	151
T.W.Graveney	1948-71/72	1223	159	258	**47793**	44.91	122
G.A.Gooch	1973-97	988	75	333	**44841**	49.11	128
T.W.Hayward	1893-1914	1138	96	315*	**43551**	41.79	104
D.L.Amiss	1960-87	1139	126	262*	**43423**	42.86	102
M.C.Cowdrey	1950-76	1130	134	307	**42719**	42.89	107
A.Sandham	1911-37/38	1000	79	325	**41284**	44.82	107
L.Hutton	1934-60	814	91	364	**40140**	55.51	129
M.J.K.Smith	1951-75	1091	139	204	**39832**	41.84	69
W.Rhodes	1898-1930	1528	237	267*	**39802**	30.83	58
J.H.Edrich	1956-78	979	104	310*	**39790**	45.47	103
R.E.S.Wyatt	1923-57	1141	157	232	**39405**	40.04	85
D.C.S.Compton	1936-64	839	88	300	**38942**	51.85	123
G.E.Tyldesley	1909-36	961	106	256*	**38874**	45.46	102
J.T.Tyldesley	1895-1923	994	62	295*	**37897**	40.60	86
K.W.R.Fletcher	1962-88	1167	170	228*	**37665**	37.77	63
C.G.Greenidge	1970-92	889	75	273*	**37354**	45.88	92
J.W.Hearne	1909-36	1025	116	285*	**37252**	40.98	96
L.E.G.Ames	1926-51	951	95	295	**37248**	43.51	102
D.Kenyon	1946-67	1159	59	259	**37002**	33.63	74
W.J.Edrich	1934-58	964	92	267*	**36965**	42.39	86
J.M.Parks	1949-76	1227	172	205*	**36673**	34.76	51
M.W.Gatting	1975-97	861	123	258	**36549**	49.52	94
D.Denton	1894-1920	1163	70	221	**36479**	33.37	69
G.H.Hirst	1891-1929	1215	151	341	**36323**	34.13	60
I.V.A.Richards	1971/72-93	796	63	322	**36212**	49.40	114
A.Jones	1957-83	1168	72	204*	**36049**	32.89	56
W.G.Quaife	1894-1928	1203	185	255*	**36012**	35.37	72
R.E.Marshall	1945/46-72	1053	59	228*	**35725**	35.94	68
G.Gunn	1902-32	1061	82	220	**35208**	35.96	62

BOWLING RECORDS
ALL TEN WICKETS IN AN INNINGS

This feat has been achieved 76 times in first-class matches (excluding 12-a-side fixtures).
Three Times: A.P.Freeman (1929, 1930, 1931)
Twice: V.E.Walker (1859, 1865); H.Verity (1931, 1932); J.C.Laker (1956)

Instances since 1945:

W.E.Hollies	Warwickshire v Notts	Birmingham	1946
J.M.Sims	East v West	Kingston on Thames	1948
J.K.R.Graveney	Gloucestershire v Derbyshire	Chesterfield	1949
T.E.Bailey	Essex v Lancashire	Clacton	1949
R.Berry	Lancashire v Worcestershire	Blackpool	1953
S.P.Gupte	President's XI v Combined XI	Bombay	1954-55
J.C.Laker	Surrey v Australians	The Oval	1956
K.Smales	Nottinghamshire v Glos	Stroud	1956

G.A.R.Lock	Surrey v Kent	Blackheath	1956
J.C.Laker	England v Australia	Manchester	1956
P.M.Chatterjee	Bengal v Assam	Jorhat	1956-57
J.D.Bannister	Warwicks v Combined Services	Birmingham (M & B)	1959
A.J.G.Pearson	Cambridge U v Leicestershire	Loughborough	1961
N.I.Thomson	Sussex v Warwickshire	Worthing	1964
P.J.Allan	Queensland v Victoria	Melbourne	1965-66
I.J.Brayshaw	Western Australia v Victoria	Perth	1967-68
Shahid Mahmood	Karachi Whites v Khairpur	Karachi	1969-70
E.E.Hemmings	International XI v W Indians	Kingston	1982-83
P.Sunderam	Rajasthan v Vidarbha	Jodhpur	1985-86
S.T.Jefferies	Western Province v OFS	Cape Town	1987-88
Imran Adil	Bahawalpur v Faisalabad	Faisalabad	1989-90
G.P.Wickremasinghe	Sinhalese v Kalutara	Colombo	1991-92
R.L.Johnson	Middlesex v Derbyshire	Derby	1994
Naeem Akhtar	Rawalpindi B v Peshawar	Peshawar	1995-96

MOST WICKETS IN A MATCH

19	J.C.Laker	England v Australia	Manchester	1956

MOST WICKETS IN A SEASON

Wkts		Career	Matches	Overs	Mdns	Runs	Avge
304	A.P.Freeman	1928	37	1976.1	423	5489	18.05
298	A.P.Freeman	1933	33	2039	651	4549	15.26

The feat of taking 250 wickets in a season has been achieved on 12 occasions, the last instance being by A.P.Freeman in 1933. 200 or more wickets in a season have been taken on 59 occasions, the last being by G.A.R.Lock (212 wickets, average 12.02) in 1957.

The highest aggregates of wickets taken in a season since the reduction of County Championship matches in 1969 are as follows:

Wkts		Season	Matches	Overs	Mdns	Runs	Avge
134	M.D.Marshall	1982	22	822	225	2108	15.73
131	L.R.Gibbs	1971	23	1024.1	295	2475	18.89
125	F.D.Stephenson	1988	22	819.1	196	2289	18.31
121	R.D.Jackman	1980	23	746.2	220	1864	15.40

Since 1969 there have been 49 instances of bowlers taking 100 wickets in a season.

MOST HAT-TRICKS IN A CAREER

7	D.V.P.Wright
6	T.W.J.Goddard, C.W.L.Parker
5	S.Haigh, V.W.C.Jupp, A.E.G.Rhodes, F.A.Tarrant

2000 WICKETS IN A CAREER

	Career	Runs	Wkts	Avge	100w
W.Rhodes	1898-1930	69993	**4187**	16.71	23
A.P.Freeman	1914-36	69577	**3776**	18.42	17
C.W.L.Parker	1903-35	63817	**3278**	19.46	16
J.T.Hearne	1888-1923	54352	**3061**	17.75	15
T.W.J.Goddard	1922-52	59116	**2979**	19.84	16
W.G.Grace	1865-1908	51545	**2876**	17.92	10
A.S.Kennedy	1907-36	61034	**2874**	21.23	15
D.Shackleton	1948-69	53303	**2857**	18.65	20
G.A.R.Lock	1946-70/71	54709	**2844**	19.23	14
F.J.Titmus	1949-82	63313	**2830**	22.37	16
M.W.Tate	1912-37	50571	**2784**	18.16	13+1
G.H.Hirst	1891-1929	51282	**2739**	18.72	15

	Career	Runs	Wkts	Avge	100w
C.Blythe	1899-1914	42136	2506	16.81	14
D.L.Underwood	1963-87	49993	2465	20.28	10
W.E.Astill	1906-39	57783	2431	23.76	9
J.C.White	1909-37	43759	2356	18.57	14
W.E.Hollies	1932-57	48656	2323	20.94	14
F.S.Trueman	1949-69	42154	2304	18.29	12
J.B.Statham	1950-68	36999	2260	16.37	13
R.T.D.Perks	1930-55	53771	2233	24.07	16
J.Briggs	1879-1900	35431	2221	15.95	12
D.J.Shepherd	1950-72	47302	2218	21.32	12
E.G.Dennett	1903-26	42571	2147	19.82	12
T.Richardson	1892-1905	38794	2104	18.43	10
T.E.Bailey	1945-67	48170	2082	23.13	9
R.Illingworth	1951-83	42023	2072	20.28	10
F.E.Woolley	1906-38	41066	2068	19.85	8
N.Gifford	1960-88	48731	2068	23.56	4
G.Geary	1912-38	41339	2063	20.03	11
D.V.P.Wright	1932-57	49307	2056	23.98	10
J.A.Newman	1906-30	51111	2032	25.15	9
A.Shaw	1864-97	24580	2026+1	12.12	9
S.Haigh	1895-1913	32091	2012	15.94	11

ALL-ROUND RECORDS
THE 'DOUBLE'

3000 runs and 100 wickets: J.H.Parks (1937)

2000 runs and 200 wickets: G.H.Hirst (1906)

2000 runs and 100 wickets: F.E.Woolley (4), J.W.Hearne (3), W.G.Grace (2), G.H.Hirst (2), W.Rhodes (2), T.E.Bailey, D.E.Davies, G.L.Jessop, V.W.C.Jupp, J.Langridge, F.A.Tarrant, C.L.Townsend, L.F.Townsend

1000 runs and 200 wickets: M.W.Tate (3), A.E.Trott (2), A.S.Kennedy

Most Doubles: 16 – W.Rhodes; 14 – G.H.Hirst; 10 – V.W.C.Jupp

Double in Debut Season: D.B.Close (1949) – the youngest (18) to achieve this feat.

The feat of scoring 1000 runs and taking 100 wickets in a season has been achieved on 305 occasions, R.J.Hadlee (1984) and F.D.Stephenson (1988) being the only players to complete the 'double' since the reduction of County Championship matches in 1969.

WICKET-KEEPING RECORDS
EIGHT DISMISSALS IN AN INNINGS

9	(8ct, 1st)	Tahir Rashid	Habib Bank v PACO	Gujranwala	1992-93
9	(7ct, 2st)	W.R.James	Matabeleland v Mashonaland CD	Bulawayo	1995-96
8	(8ct)	A.T.W.Grout	Queensland v W Australia	Brisbane	1959-60
8	(8ct)	D.E.East	Essex v Somerset	Taunton	1985
8	(8ct)	S.A.Marsh	Kent v Middlesex	Lord's	1991
8	(6ct, 2st)	T.J.Zoehrer	Australians v Surrey	The Oval	1993
8	(7ct, 1st)	D.S.Berry	Victoria v South Australia	Melbourne	1996-97

TWELVE DISMISSALS IN A MATCH

13	(11ct, 2st)	W.R.James	Matabeleland v Mashonaland CD	Bulawayo	1995-96
12	(8ct, 4st)	E.Pooley	Surrey v Sussex	The Oval	1868
12	(9ct, 3st)	D.Tallon	Queensland v NSW	Sydney	1938-39
12	(9ct, 3st)	H.B.Taber	NSW v South Australia	Adelaide	1968-69

MOST DISMISSALS IN A SEASON

128 (79ct, 49st) L.E.G.Ames 1929

1000 DISMISSALS IN A CAREER

	Career	Dismissals	Ct	St
R.W.Taylor	1960-88	**1649**	1473	176
J.T.Murray	1952-75	**1527**	1270	257
H.Strudwick	1902-27	**1497**	1242	255
A.P.E.Knott	1964-85	**1344**	1211	133
F.H.Huish	1895-1914	**1310**	933	377
B.Taylor	1949-73	**1294**	1083	211
D.Hunter	1889-1909	**1253**	906	347
H.R.Butt	1890-1912	**1228**	953	275
J.H.Board	1891-1914/15	**1207**	852	355
H.Elliott	1920-47	**1206**	904	302
J.M.Parks	1949-76	**1181**	1088	93
R.Booth	1951-70	**1126**	948	178
L.E.G.Ames	1926-51	**1121**	703	418
D.L.Bairstow	1970-90	**1099**	961	138
G.Duckworth	1923-47	**1096**	753	343
R.C.Russell	1981-98	**1083**	972	111
H.W.Stephenson	1948-64	**1082**	748	334
J.G.Binks	1955-75	**1071**	895	176
T.G.Evans	1939-69	**1066**	816	250
A.Long	1960-80	**1046**	922	124
G.O.Dawkes	1937-61	**1042**	895	147
R.W.Tolchard	1965-83	**1037**	912	125
W.L.Cornford	1921-47	**1017**	675	342

FIELDING RECORDS

MOST CATCHES IN AN INNINGS

| 7 | M.J.Stewart | Surrey v Northamptonshire | Northampton | 1957 |
| 7 | A.S.Brown | Gloucestershire v Nottinghamshire | Nottingham | 1966 |

MOST CATCHES IN A MATCH

| 10 | W.R.Hammond | Gloucestershire v Surrey | Cheltenham | 1928 |

MOST CATCHES IN A SEASON

| 78 | W.R.Hammond | 1928 | 77 | M.J.Stewart | 1957 |

750 CATCHES IN A CAREER

1018	F.E.Woolley	1906-38	784	J.G.Langridge	1928-55
887	W.G.Grace	1865-1908	764	W.Rhodes	1898-1930
830	G.A.R.Lock	1946-70/71	758	C.A.Milton	1948-74
819	W.R.Hammond	1920-51	754	E.H.Hendren	1907-38
813	D.B.Close	1949-86			

LIMITED-OVERS INTERNATIONALS RESULTS SUMMARY
1970-71 to 25 September 1998

Opponents	Matches	E	A	SA	WI	NZ	I	P	SL	Z	B	C	EA	H	K	UAE	Tied	NR
England Australia	60	29	29	–	–	–	–	–	–	–	–	–	–	–	–	–	1	1
South Africa	16	6	–	10	–	–	–	–	–	–	–	–	–	–	–	–	–	–
West Indies	58	25	–	–	31	–	–	–	–	–	–	–	–	–	–	–	–	2
New Zealand	47	23	–	–	–	20	–	–	–	–	–	–	–	–	–	–	1	3
India	33	19	–	–	–	–	13	–	–	–	–	–	–	–	–	–	–	1
Pakistan	41	26	–	–	–	–	–	14	–	–	–	–	–	–	–	–	–	1
Sri Lanka	14	9	–	–	–	–	–	–	5	–	–	–	–	–	–	–	–	–
Zimbabwe	6	1	–	–	–	–	–	–	–	5	–	–	–	–	–	–	–	–
Canada	1	1	–	–	–	–	–	–	–	–	–	0	–	–	–	–	–	–
East Africa	1	1	–	–	–	–	–	–	–	–	–	–	0	–	–	–	–	–
Holland	1	1	–	–	–	–	–	–	–	–	–	–	–	0	–	–	–	–
U A Emirates	1	1	–	–	–	–	–	–	–	–	–	–	–	–	–	0	–	–
Australia South Africa	37	–	18	19	–	–	–	–	–	–	–	–	–	–	–	–	–	–
West Indies	84	–	33	–	49	–	–	–	–	–	–	–	–	–	–	–	1	1
New Zealand	73	–	51	–	–	20	–	–	–	–	–	–	–	–	–	–	–	2
India	53	–	29	–	–	–	21	–	–	–	–	–	–	–	–	–	–	3
Pakistan	46	–	22	–	–	–	–	21	–	–	–	–	–	–	–	–	1	2
Sri Lanka	35	–	22	–	–	–	–	–	11	–	–	–	–	–	–	–	–	2
Zimbabwe	11	–	10	–	–	–	–	–	–	1	–	–	–	–	–	–	–	–
Bangladesh	1	–	1	–	–	–	–	–	–	–	0	–	–	–	–	–	–	–
Canada	1	–	1	–	–	–	–	–	–	–	–	0	–	–	–	–	–	–
Kenya	1	–	1	–	–	–	–	–	–	–	–	–	–	–	0	–	–	–
S Africa West Indies	10	–	–	5	5	–	–	–	–	–	–	–	–	–	–	–	–	–
N Zealand	12	–	–	7	–	5	–	–	–	–	–	–	–	–	–	–	–	–
India	27	–	–	18	–	–	8	–	–	–	–	–	–	–	–	–	–	1
Pakistan	21	–	–	14	–	–	–	7	–	–	–	–	–	–	–	–	–	–
Sri Lanka	14	–	–	7	–	–	–	–	6	–	–	–	–	–	–	–	–	1
Zimbabwe	7	–	–	6	–	–	–	–	–	0	–	–	–	–	–	–	–	1
Holland	1	–	–	1	–	–	–	–	–	–	–	–	–	0	–	–	–	–
Kenya	1	–	–	1	–	–	–	–	–	–	–	–	–	–	0	–	–	–
U A Emirates	1	–	–	1	–	–	–	–	–	–	–	–	–	–	–	0	–	–
W Indies New Zealand	24	–	–	–	18	4	–	–	–	–	–	–	–	–	–	–	–	2
India	56	–	–	–	36	–	19	–	–	–	–	–	–	–	–	–	1	–
Pakistan	83	–	–	–	55	–	–	26	–	–	–	–	–	–	–	–	2	–
Sri Lanka	29	–	–	–	20	–	–	–	8	–	–	–	–	–	–	–	–	1
Zimbabwe	5	–	–	–	5	–	–	–	–	0	–	–	–	–	–	–	–	–
Kenya	1	–	–	–	0	–	–	–	–	–	–	–	–	–	1	–	–	–
N Zealand India	46	–	–	–	–	19	25	–	–	–	–	–	–	–	–	–	–	2
Pakistan	48	–	–	–	–	18	–	28	–	–	–	–	–	–	–	–	1	1
Sri Lanka	39	–	–	–	–	24	–	–	12	–	–	–	–	–	–	–	1	2
Zimbabwe	16	–	–	–	–	12	–	–	–	3	–	–	–	–	–	–	1	–
Bangladesh	1	–	–	–	–	1	–	–	–	–	0	–	–	–	–	–	–	–
East Africa	1	–	–	–	–	1	–	–	–	–	–	–	0	–	–	–	–	–
Holland	1	–	–	–	–	1	–	–	–	–	–	–	–	0	–	–	–	–
U A Emirates	1	–	–	–	–	1	–	–	–	–	–	–	–	–	–	0	–	–
India Pakistan	71	–	–	–	–	–	25	42	–	–	–	–	–	–	–	–	–	4
Sri Lanka	55	–	–	–	–	–	28	–	22	–	–	–	–	–	–	–	–	5
Zimbabwe	18	–	–	–	–	–	14	–	–	2	–	–	–	–	–	–	2	–
Bangladesh	7	–	–	–	–	–	7	–	–	–	0	–	–	–	–	–	–	–
East Africa	1	–	–	–	–	–	1	–	–	–	–	–	0	–	–	–	–	–
Kenya	4	–	–	–	–	–	3	–	–	–	–	–	–	–	1	–	–	–
U A Emirates	1	–	–	–	–	–	1	–	–	–	–	–	–	–	–	0	–	–
Pakistan Sri Lanka	71	–	–	–	–	–	–	46	23	–	–	–	–	–	–	–	–	2
Zimbabwe	16	–	–	–	–	–	–	14	–	1	–	–	–	–	–	–	1	–
Bangladesh	5	–	–	–	–	–	–	5	–	–	0	–	–	–	–	–	–	–
Canada	1	–	–	–	–	–	–	1	–	–	–	0	–	–	–	–	–	–
Holland	1	–	–	–	–	–	–	1	–	–	–	–	–	0	–	–	–	–
Kenya	1	–	–	–	–	–	–	1	–	–	–	–	–	–	0	–	–	–
U A Emirates	2	–	–	–	–	–	–	2	–	–	–	–	–	–	–	0	–	–
Sri Lanka Zimbabwe	13	–	–	–	–	–	–	–	11	2	–	–	–	–	–	–	–	–
Bangladesh	5	–	–	–	–	–	–	–	5	–	0	–	–	–	–	–	–	–

Opponents	Matches						Won by									Tied	NR
		E	A	SA	WI	NZ	I	P	SL	Z	B	C	EA	H	K UAE		
	Kenya	2	–	–	–	–	–	–	2	–	–	–	–	–	–	0	–
Zimbabwe	Kenya	6	–	–	–	–	–	–	5	–	–	–	–	–	–	0	– 1
	Bangladesh	2	–	–	–	–	–	2	0	–	–	–	–	–	–	–	–
Kenya	Bangladesh	4	–	–	–	–	–	–	–	–	1	–	–	–	–	3	–
Holland	U A Emirates	1	–	–	–	–	–	–	–	–	–	–	–	0	–	1	–
		1353	142	217	89	219	126	165	208	105	21	1	0	0	0	5 1	13 41

	Matches	Won	Lost	Tied	No Result	% Won (exc NR)
West Indies	350	219	121	4	6	63.66
South Africa	147	89	55	–	3	61.80
Australia	402	217	171	3	11	55.49
England	279	142	127	2	8	52.398
Pakistan	407	208	184	5	10	52.392
India	372	165	188	3	16	46.34
New Zealand	309	126	167	4	12	42.42
Sri Lanka	277	105	158	1	13	39.77
Kenya	20	5	14	–	1	26.31
Zimbabwe	100	21	73	4	2	21.42
United Arab Emirates	7	1	6	–	–	14.28
Bangladesh	25	1	24	–	–	4.00
Canada	3	–	3	–	–	–
East Africa	3	–	3	–	–	–
Holland	5	–	5	–	–	–

LOI RECORDS

To 25 September 1998

TEAM RECORDS

HIGHEST TOTALS

398-5	(50 overs)	Sri Lanka v Kenya	Kandy	1995-96
371-9	(50 overs)	Pakistan v Sri Lanka	Nairobi	1996-97
363-7	(55 overs)	England v Pakistan	Nottingham	1992
360-4	(50 overs)	West Indies v Sri Lanka	Karachi	1987-88
349-9	(50 overs)	Sri Lanka v Pakistan	Singapore	1995-96
348-8	(50 overs)	New Zealand v India	Nagpur	1995-96
347-3	(50 overs)	Kenya v Bangladesh	Nairobi	1997-98
339-4	(50 overs)	Sri Lanka v Pakistan	Chandigarh	1996-97
338-4	(50 overs)	New Zealand v Bangladesh	Sharjah	1989-90
338-5	(60 overs)	Pakistan v Sri Lanka	Swansea	1983
334-4	(60 overs)	England v India	Lord's	1975
333-7	(50 overs)	West Indies v Sri Lanka	Sharjah	1995-96
333-8	(45 overs)	West Indies v India	Jamshedpur	1983-84
333-9	(60 overs)	England v Sri Lanka	Taunton	1983
332-3	(50 overs)	Australia v Sri Lanka	Sharjah	1989-90
330-6	(60 overs)	Pakistan v Sri Lanka	Nottingham	1975

The highest for South Africa is 328-3 (v Holland, Rawalpindi, 1995-96); for India 309-5 (v Australia, Cochin, 1997-98); and for Zimbabwe 312-4 (v Sri Lanka, New Plymouth, 1991-92).

HIGHEST TOTALS BATTING SECOND

WINNING:	316-7	(47.5 overs)	India v Pakistan	Dhaka	1997-98
LOSING:	329	(49.3 overs)	Sri Lanka v West Indies	Sharjah	1995-96

HIGHEST MATCH AGGREGATES

664-19	(99.4 overs)	Pakistan v Sri Lanka	Singapore	1995-96
662-17	(99.3 overs)	West Indies v Sri Lanka	Sharjah	1995-96
652-12	(100 overs)	Sri Lanka v Kenya	Kandy	1995-96

LARGEST MARGINS OF VICTORY

232 runs	Australia beat Sri Lanka	Adelaide	1984-85
206 runs	New Zealand beat Australia	Adelaide	1985-86
202 runs	England beat India	Lord's	1975

LOWEST TOTALS (Excluding reduced innings)

43	(19.5 overs)	Pakistan v West Indies	Cape Town	1992-93
45	(40.3 overs)	Canada v England	Manchester	1979
55	(28.3 overs)	Sri Lanka v West Indies	Sharjah	1986-87
63	(25.5 overs)	India v Australia	Sydney	1980-81
64	(35.5 overs)	New Zealand v Pakistan	Sharjah	1985-86
69	(28 overs)	South Africa v Australia	Sydney	1993-94
70	(25.2 overs)	Australia v England	Birmingham	1977
70	(26.3 overs)	Australia v New Zealand	Adelaide	1985-86

The lowest for England is 93 (v Australia, Leeds, 1975); for West Indies 87 (v Australia, Sydney, 1992-93); and for Zimbabwe 94 (v Pakistan, Sharjah, 1996-97).

LOWEST MATCH AGGREGATE

88-13	(32.2 overs)	West Indies v Pakistan	Cape Town	1992-93

BATTING RECORDS
HIGHEST INDIVIDUAL INNINGS

194	Saeed Anwar	Pakistan v India	Madras	1996-97
189*	I.V.A.Richards	West Indies v England	Manchester	1984
188*	G.Kirsten	South Africa v UAE	Rawalpindi	1995-96
181	I.V.A.Richards	West Indies v Sri Lanka	Karachi	1987-88
175*	Kapil Dev	India v Zimbabwe	Tunbridge Wells	1983
171*	G.M.Turner	New Zealand v East Africa	Birmingham	1975
169*	D.J.Callaghan	South Africa v New Zealand	Pretoria	1994-95
169	B.C.Lara	West Indies v Sri Lanka	Sharjah	1995-96
167*	R.A.Smith	England v Australia	Birmingham	1993
161	A.C.Hudson	South Africa v Holland	Rawalpindi	1995-96
158	D.I.Gower	England v New Zealand	Brisbane	1982-83
153*	I.V.A.Richards	West Indies v Australia	Melbourne	1979-80
153*	M.Azharuddin	India v Zimbabwe	Cuttack	1997-98
153	B.C.Lara	West Indies v Pakistan	Sharjah	1993-94
152*	D.L.Haynes	West Indies v India	Georgetown	1988-89
151*	S.T.Jayasuriya	Sri Lanka v India	Bombay	1996-97

The highest for Australia is 145 by D.M.Jones (v E, Brisbane, 1990-91) and 145 by R.T.Ponting (v Z, Delhi, 1997-98); and for Zimbabwe 142 by D.L.Houghton (v NZ, Hyderabad, 1987-88).

Fastest 100	37 balls	Shahid Afridi (102)	P v SL	Nairobi	1996-97
Fastest 50	17 balls	S.T.Jayasuriya (134)	SL v P	Singapore	1995-96

HIGHEST PARTNERSHIP FOR EACH WICKET

1st	252	S.C.Ganguly/S.R.Tendulkar	India v Sri Lanka	Colombo (RPS)	1997-98
2nd	263	Aamir Sohail/Inzamam-ul-Haq	Pakistan v New Zealand	Sharjah	1993-94
3rd	230	Saeed Anwar/Ijaz Ahmed	Pakistan v India	Dhaka	1997-98
4th	275*	M.Azharuddin/A.Jadeja	India v Zimbabwe	Cuttack	1997-98
5th	223	M.Azharuddin/A.Jadeja	India v Sri Lanka	Colombo (RPS)	1997-98
6th	154	R.B.Richardson/P.J.L.Dujon	West Indies v Pakistan	Sharjah	1991-92
7th	119	T.Odoyo/A.Suji	Kenya v Zimbabwe	Nairobi	1997-98
8th	119	P.R.Reiffel/S.K.Warne	Australia v South Africa	Port Elizabeth	1993-94
9th	126*	Kapil Dev/S.M.H.Kirmani	India v Zimbabwe	Tunbridge Wells	1983
10th	106*	I.V.A.Richards/M.A.Holding	West Indies v England	Manchester	1984

4000 RUNS IN A CAREER

		LOI	I	NO	HS	Runs	Avge	100	50
D.L.Haynes	WI	238	237	28	152*	8648	41.37	17	57
M.Azharuddin	I	296	273	51	153*	8479	38.19	7	51
P.A.de Silva	SL	241	234	24	145	7684	36.59	11	51
Javed Miandad	P	233	218	41	119*	7381	41.70	8	50
S.R.Tendulkar	I	197	190	17	142	7146	41.30	17	43
Salim Malik	P	273	247	37	102	7030	33.47	5	46
A.Ranatunga	SL	244	230	45	131*	6870	37.13	4	46
I.V.A.Richards	WI	187	167	24	189*	6721	47.00	11	45
A.R.Border	A	273	252	39	127*	6524	30.62	3	39
R.B.Richardson	WI	224	217	30	122	6248	33.41	5	44
D.M.Jones	A	164	161	25	145	6068	44.61	7	46
D.C.Boon	A	181	177	16	122	5964	37.04	5	37
Ramiz Raja	P	198	197	15	119*	5841	32.09	9	31
Saeed Anwar	P	158	156	14	194	5754	40.52	15	26
S.R.Waugh	A	245	222	44	102*	5640	31.68	1	34
B.C.Lara	WI	130	128	12	169	5448	46.96	12	36
M.E.Waugh	A	158	153	12	130	5385	38.19	11	32
Inzamam-ul-Haq	P	168	158	21	137*	5298	38.67	5	37
Ijaz Ahmed	P	209	192	26	139*	5252	31.63	7	29
C.G.Greenidge	WI	128	127	13	133*	5134	45.03	11	31
R.S.Mahanama	SL	195	180	22	119*	4841	30.63	4	33
M.D.Crowe	NZ	143	141	19	107*	4704	38.55	4	34
Aamir Sohail	P	142	141	5	134	4491	33.02	5	30
N.S.Sidhu	I	136	127	8	134*	4414	37.09	6	33
S.T.Jayasuriya	SL	164	156	6	151*	4359	29.06	7	26
G.R.Marsh	A	117	115	6	126*	4357	39.97	9	22
G.A.Gooch	E	125	122	6	142	4290	36.98	8	23
W.J.Cronje	SA	142	132	23	112	4262	39.10	2	28
C.L.Hooper	WI	167	151	35	113*	4174	35.98	5	23
K.Srikkanth	I	146	145	4	123	4092	29.02	4	27
A.J.Lamb	E	122	118	16	118	4010	39.31	4	26

The highest for Zimbabwe is 2647 in 76 innings by G.W.Flower.

TEN HUNDREDS IN A CAREER

		LOI	100	E	A	SA	WI	NZ	I	P	SL	Z	K
D.L.Haynes	WI	238	17	2	6	–	–	2	2	4	1	–	–
Saeed Anwar	P	158	15	–	1	–	2	2	3	–	6	1	–
S.R.Tendulkar	I	197	17	–	4	1	3	1	–	2	4	1	2
B.C.Lara	WI	130	12	1	2	2	–	2	–	4	1	–	–
C.G.Greenidge	WI	128	11	–	1	–	–	3	3	2	1	–	–
M.E.Waugh	A	158	11	1	–	–	2	1	3	1	1	1	1
I.V.A.Richards	WI	187	11	3	3	–	–	1	3	–	1	–	–
P.A.de Silva	SL	241	11	–	2	–	–	3	1	–	4	1	–

The most for England is 8 by G.A.Gooch; for South Africa 8 by G.Kirsten; for New Zealand 5 by N.J.Astle; and for Zimbabwe 2 by A.D.R.Campbell and G.W.Flower.

BOWLING RECORDS
BEST ANALYSES

7-37	Aqib Javed	Pakistan v India	Sharjah	1991-92
7-51	W.W.Davis	West Indies v Australia	Leeds	1983
6-12	A.Kumble	India v West Indies	Calcutta	1993-94
6-14	G.J.Gilmour	Australia v England	Leeds	1975
6-14	Imran Khan	Pakistan v India	Sharjah	1984-85
6-15	C.E.H.Croft	West Indies v England	Kingstown	1980-81
6-20	B.C.Strang	Zimbabwe v Bangladesh	Nairobi	1997-98
6-23	A.A.Donald	South Africa v Kenya	Nairobi	1996-97
6-26	Waqar Younis	Pakistan v Sri Lanka	Sharjah	1989-90
6-29	B.P.Patterson	West Indies v India	Nagpur	1987-88

6-29	S.T.Jayasuriya	Sri Lanka v England	Moratuwa	1992-93
6-30	Waqar Younis	Pakistan v New Zealand	Auckland	1993-94
6-39	K.H.Macleay	Australia v India	Nottingham	1983
6-41	I.V.A.Richards	West Indies v India	Delhi	1989-90
6-44	Waqar Younis	Pakistan v New Zealand	Sharjah	1996-97
6-49	L.Klusener	South Africa v Sri Lanka	Lahore	1997-98
6-50	A.H.Gray	West Indies v Australia	Port-of-Spain	1990-91

The best for England is 5-20 by V.J.Marks (v New Zealand, Wellington, 1983-84); and for New Zealand 5-22 by M.N.Hart (v West Indies, Margao, 1994-95).

100 WICKETS IN A CAREER

		LOI	O	R	W	Avge	Best	4w	R/Over
Wasim Akram	P	247	2127.2	8116	356	22.79	5-15	20	3.81
Waqar Younis	P	171	1418.5	6496	281	23.11	6-26	21	4.57
Kapil Dev	I	224	1867	6945	253	27.45	5-43	4	3.71
C.E.L.Ambrose	WI	151	1341.5	4720	204	23.13	5-17	10	3.51
C.A.Walsh	WI	185	1628.4	6312	204	30.94	5- 1	6	3.87
C.J.McDermott	A	138	1243.3	5018	203	24.71	5-44	5	4.03
A.Kumble	I	146	1311.1	5374	199	27.00	6-12	7	4.09
J.Srinath	I	140	1215.1	5237	189	27.70	5-23	5	4.30
S.R.Waugh	A	245	1388.3	6285	184	34.15	4-33	3	4.52
A.A.Donald	SA	107	951	3863	182	21.22	6-23	9	4.06
Imran Khan	P	175	1243.3	4845	182	26.62	6-14	4	3.89
Aqib Javed	P	162	1326.3	5674	181	31.34	7-37	6	4.27
Saqlain Mushtaq	P	82	714.5	3067	163	18.81	5-29	12	4.29
R.J.Hadlee	NZ	115	1030.2	3407	158	21.56	5-25	6	3.30
M.Prabhakar	I	129	1060	4534	157	28.87	5-33	6	4.27
M.D.Marshall	WI	136	1195.5	4233	157	26.96	4-18	6	3.53
S.K.Warne	A	96	899.3	3703	150	24.68	5-33	10	4.11
C.L.Hooper	WI	167	1142.1	4934	148	33.33	4-34	2	4.31
J.Garner	WI	98	888.2	2752	146	18.84	5-31	5	3.09
I.T.Botham	E	116	1045.1	4139	145	28.54	4-31	3	3.96
Mushtaq Ahmed	P	130	1121.1	4842	144	33.62	5-36	3	4.31
S.T.Jayasuriya	SL	164	983.4	4801	144	33.34	6-29	6	4.88
M.A.Holding	WI	102	912.1	3034	142	21.36	5-26	6	3.32
E.J.Chatfield	NZ	114	1010.5	3618	140	25.84	5-34	4	3.57
M.Muralitharan	SL	99	898.5	3796	135	28.11	5-23	5	4.22
Abdul Qadir	P	104	850	3453	132	26.15	5-44	6	4.06
R.J.Shastri	I	150	1102.1	4650	129	36.04	5-15	3	4.21
D.K.Morrison	NZ	96	764.2	3470	126	27.53	5-34	3	4.53
I.R.Bishop	WI	84	722	3127	118	26.50	5-25	9	4.33
I.V.A.Richards	WI	187	940.4	4228	118	35.83	6-41	3	4.49
B.K.V.Prasad	I	98	817.5	3894	116	33.56	4-17	3	4.76
P.A.J.DeFreitas	E	103	952	3775	115	32.82	4-35	1	3.96
M.C.Snedden	NZ	93	754.1	3237	114	28.39	4-34	1	4.29
C.Z.Harris	NZ	113	886.1	3752	113	33.50	5-42	1	4.23
W.P.U.C.J.Vaas	SL	89	701.1	2841	111	25.59	4-20	3	4.05
Mudassar Nazar	P	122	809.1	3432	111	30.91	5-28	2	4.24
S.P.O'Donnell	A	87	725	3102	108	28.72	5-13	6	4.27
D.K.Lillee	A	63	598.5	2145	103	20.82	5-34	6	3.58
C.Pringle	NZ	64	552.2	2455	103	23.83	5-45	4	4.44
W.K.M.Benjamin	WI	85	740.2	3079	100	30.79	5-22	1	4.15
R.A.Harper	WI	105	862.3	3431	100	34.31	4-40	5	3.97

The most for Zimbabwe is 71 in 58 matches by H.H.Streak.

HAT-TRICKS

Jalaluddin	Pakistan v Australia	Hyderabad	1982-83
B.A.Reid	Australia v New Zealand	Sydney	1985-86
C.Sharma	India v New Zealand	Nagpur	1987-88
Wasim Akram	Pakistan v West Indies	Sharjah	1989-90

Wasim Akram	Pakistan v Australia	Sharjah	1989-90
Kapil Dev	India v Sri Lanka	Calcutta	1990-91
Aqib Javed	Pakistan v India	Sharjah	1991-92
D.K.Morrison	New Zealand v India	Napier	1993-94
Waqar Younis	Pakistan v New Zealand	East London	1994-95
Saqlain Mushtaq	Pakistan v Zimbabwe	Peshawar	1996-97
E.A.Brandes	Zimbabwe v England	Harare	1996-97
A.M.Stuart	Australia v Pakistan	Melbourne	1996-97

WICKET-KEEPING RECORDS
FIVE DISMISSALS IN AN INNINGS

5 – R.W.Marsh (Australia); D.J.Richardson (2) (South Africa); C.O.Browne, J.C.Adams, R.D.Jacobs (West Indies); A.C.Parore (New Zealand); S.M.H.Kirmani, S.Viswanath, K.S.More, N.R.Mongia (2) (India); Moin Khan, Rashid Latif (Pakistan); R.G.de Alwis, H.P.Tillekeratne, R.S.Kaluwitharana (Sri Lanka); A.Flower (2) (Zimbabwe).

100 DISMISSALS IN A CAREER

		LOI	Ct	St	Dis
I.A.Healy	Australia	168	195	39	234
P.J.L.Dujon	West Indies	169	183	21	204
D.J.Richardson	South Africa	122	149	16	165
Moin Khan	Pakistan	111	96	38	134
R.W.Marsh	Australia	92	120	4	124
N.R.Mongia	India	108	88	35	123
Rashid Latif	Pakistan	101	94	28	122
R.S.Kaluwitharana	Sri Lanka	96	62	42	104
A.J.Stewart	England	105	92	11	103
Salim Yousuf	Pakistan	86	80	22	102

FIELDING RECORDS
FIVE CATCHES IN AN INNINGS

| 5 | J.N.Rhodes | South Africa v West Indies | Bombay | 1993-94 |

100 CATCHES IN A CAREER
(Excluding catches taken while keeping wicket)

		LOI	Ct
M.Azharuddin	India	296	144
A.R.Border	Australia	273	127
I.V.A.Richards	West Indies	187	101

ALL-ROUND RECORDS
1000 RUNS AND 100 WICKETS

		LOI	Runs	Wkts
I.T.Botham	England	116	2113	145
R.J.Hadlee	New Zealand	115	1751	158
C.Z.Harris	New Zealand	113	2064	112
C.L.Hooper	West Indies	167	4174	148
Imran Khan	Pakistan	175	3709	182
S.T.Jayasuriya	Sri Lanka	164	4359	144
Kapil Dev	India	225	3783	253
Mudassar Nazar	Pakistan	122	2653	111
S.P.O'Donnell	Australia	87	1242	108
M.Prabhakar	India	130	1858	157
I.V.A.Richards	West Indies	187	6721	118
R.J.Shastri	India	150	3108	129
Wasim Akram	Pakistan	247	2384	356
S.R.Waugh	Australia	245	5640	184

WOMEN'S TEST CRICKET RECORDS

1934 to 30 June 1999

Compiled by Marion Collin

RESULTS SUMMARY

	Opponents	Tests	E	A	SA	Won by WI	NZ	I	P	SL	Drawn
England	Australia	36	6	7	–	–	–	–	–	–	23
	South Africa	4	1	–	0	–	–	–	–	–	3
	West Indies	3	2	–	–	0	–	–	–	–	1
	New Zealand	22	6	–	–	–	0	–	–	–	16
	India	6	1	–	–	–	–	0	–	–	5
Australia	West Indies	2	–	0	–	0	–	–	–	–	2
	New Zealand	13	–	4	–	–	1	–	–	–	8
	India	8	–	3	–	–	–	0	–	–	5
South Africa	New Zealand	3	–	–	0	–	1	–	–	–	2
New Zealand	India	5	–	–	–	–	0	0	–	–	5
Pakistan	Sri Lanka	1	–	–	–	–	–	–	0	1	–
		103	16	14	0	0	2	0	0	1	70

	Tests	Won	Lost	Drawn	Toss Won
England	71	16	7	48	44
Australia	59	14	7	38	18
South Africa	7	–	2	5	4
West Indies	5	–	2	3	4
New Zealand	43	2	10	31	21
India	19	–	4	15	11
Pakistan	1	–	1	–	–
Sri Lanka	1	1	–	–	1

TEAM RECORDS
HIGHEST INNINGS TOTALS

569-6d	Australia v England	Guildford	1998
525	Australia v India	Ahmedabad	1983-84
517-8d	New Zealand v England	Scarborough	1996
503-5d	England v New Zealand	Christchurch	1934-35
427-4d	Australia v England	Worcester	1998
426-9d	India v England	Blackpool	1986
414	England v New Zealand	Scarborough	1996
414	England v Australia	Guildford	1998
403-8d	New Zealand v India	Nelson	1994-95

LOWEST INNINGS TOTALS

35	England v Australia	Melbourne	1957-58
38	Australia v England	Melbourne	1957-58
44	New Zealand v England	Christchurch	1934-35
47	Australia v England	Brisbane	1934-35

BATTING RECORDS
HIGHEST INDIVIDUAL INNINGS

204	K.E.Flavell	NZ v E	Scarborough	1996
200	J.Broadbent	A v E	Guildford	1998
193	D.A.Annetts	A v E	Collingham	1987
190	S.Agarwal	I v E	Worcester	1986
189	E.A.Snowball	E v NZ	Lancaster	1934-35
179	R.Heyhoe-Flint	E v A	The Oval	1976
176*	K.Rolton	A v E	Worcester	1998
167	J.A.Brittin	E v A	Harrogate	1998
161*	E.C.Drumm	E v A	Christchurch	1994-95
160	B.A.Daniels	E v NZ	Scarborough	1996
158*	C.A.Hodges	E v NZ	Canterbury	1984
155*	P.F.McKelvey	NZ v E	Wellington	1968-69

HIGHEST PARTNERSHIP FOR EACH WICKET

1st	178	B.J.Haggett/B.J.Clark	A v I	Sydney	1990-91
2nd	235	E.A.Snowball/M.E.Hide	E v NZ	Christchurch	1934-35
3rd	309	L.A.Reeler/D.A.Annetts	A v E	Collingham	1987
4th	222	D.A.Annetts/L.A.Larsen	A v E	Sydney	1981-82
5th	135	E.R.Wilson/V.Batty	A v E	Adelaide	1957-58
6th	132	B.A.Daniels/K.Leng	E v NZ	Scarborough	1996
7th	110	K.Smithies/J.Chamberlain	E v A	Hove	1987
8th	181	S.J.Griffiths/D.L.Wilson	A v NZ	Auckland	1989-90
9th	107	B.Botha/M.Payne	SA v NZ	Cape Town	1971-72
10th	78	E.Barker/H.Hegarty	E v A	Adelaide	1957-58
	78	S.Gupta/S.Chakraborty	I v A	Lucknow	1983-84

1000 RUNS IN TESTS

Runs			M	I	NO	HS	Avge	100
1935	J.A.Brittin	England	27	44	5	167	49.61	5
1594	R.Heyhoe-Flint	England	22	38	3	179	45.54	3
1301	D.A.Hockley	New Zealand	19	29	4	126*	52.04	4
1164	C.A.Hodges	England	18	31	2	158*	40.13	2
1110	S.Agarwal	India	13	23	1	190	50.45	4
1078	E.Bakewell	England	12	22	4	124	59.88	4
1007	M.E.Maclagan	England	14	25	1	119	41.95	2

5 HUNDREDS

		M	I	E	A	SA	*Opponents* WI	NZ	I	P	SL
5	J.A.Brittin (E)	27	44	–	3	–	–	1	1	–	–

BOWLING RECORDS
SEVEN WICKETS IN AN INNINGS

8-53	N.David	I v E	Jamshedpur	1995-96
7- 6	M.B.Duggan	E v A	Melbourne	1957-58
7- 7	E.R.Wilson	A v E	Melbourne	1957-58
7-10	M.E.Maclagan	E v A	Brisbane	1934-35
7-18	A.Palmer	A v E	Brisbane	1934-35
7-24	L.Johnston	A v NZ	Melbourne	1971-72
7-34	G.E.McConway	E v I	Worcester	1986
7-41	J.Burley	NZ v E	The Oval	1966
7-61	E.Bakewell	E v WI	Birmingham	1979

TEN WICKETS IN A TEST

11- 16	E.R.Wilson	A v E	Melbourne	1957-58
11- 63	J.Greenwood	E v WI	Canterbury	1979
10- 65	E.R.Wilson	A v NZ	Wellington	1947-48
10- 75	E.Bakewell	E v WI	Birmingham	1979
10-107	K.Price	A v I	Lucknow	1983-84
10-118	D.A.Gordon	A v E	Melbourne	1968-69
10-137	J.Lord	NZ v A	Melbourne	1978-79

50 WICKETS IN TESTS

Wkts			M	Balls	Runs	Avge	Best
77	M.B.Duggan	E	17	3734	1039	13.49	7- 6
68	E.R.Wilson	A	11	2885	803	11.80	7- 7
60	M.E.Maclagan	E	14	3432	935	15.58	7- 10
57	R.H.Thompson	A	16	4304	1040	18.24	5- 33
55	J.Lord	NZ	15	3108	1049	19.07	6-119
50	E.Bakewell	E	12	2697	831	16.62	7- 61

HAT-TRICK

E.R.Wilson	Australia v England	Melbourne	1957-58

WICKET-KEEPING AND FIELDING RECORDS
SIX DISMISSALS IN AN INNINGS

8 (6ct, 2st)	L.Nye	E v NZ	New Plymouth	1991-92
6 (2ct, 4st)	B.Brentnall	NZ v SA	Johannesburg	1971-72

EIGHT DISMISSALS IN A TEST

9 (8ct, 1 st)	C.Matthews	A v I	Adelaide	1990-91
8 (6ct, 2st)	L.Nye	E v NZ	New Plymouth	1991-92

25 DISMISSALS IN TESTS

Total			Tests	Ct	St
58	C.Matthews	Australia	20	46	12
36	S.A.Hodges	England	11	19	17
28	B.Brentnall	New Zealand	10	16	12

20 CATCHES IN THE FIELD IN TESTS

Total			Tests
25	C.A.Hodges	England	18
20	L.A.Fullston	Australia	12

APPEARANCE RECORDS
25 TEST MATCH APPEARANCES

27	J.A.Brittin	England	1979-98

TEST MATCHES
RESULTS SUMMARY

To 30 September 1998

	Opponents	Tests	E	A	SA	WI	NZ	I	P	SL	Z	Tied	Drawn
England	Australia	291	92	114	–	–	–	–	–	–	–	–	85
	South Africa	115	49	–	21	–	–	–	–	–	–	–	45
	West Indies	121	28	–	–	51	–	–	–	–	–	–	42
	New Zealand	78	36	–	–	–	4	–	–	–	–	–	38
	India	84	32	–	–	–	–	14	–	–	–	–	38
	Pakistan	55	14	–	–	–	–	–	9	–	–	–	32
	Sri Lanka	6	3	–	–	–	–	–	–	2	–	–	1
	Zimbabwe	2	0	–	–	–	–	–	–	–	0	–	2
Australia	South Africa	65	–	34	14	–	–	–	–	–	–	–	17
	West Indies	86	–	35	–	29	–	–	–	–	–	1	21
	New Zealand	35	–	15	–	–	7	–	–	–	–	–	13
	India	54	–	25	–	–	–	11	–	–	–	1	17
	Pakistan	40	–	14	–	–	–	–	11	–	–	–	15
	Sri Lanka	10	–	7	–	–	–	–	–	0	–	–	3
South Africa	West Indies	1	–	–	0	1	–	–	–	–	–	–	–
	New Zealand	21	–	–	12	–	3	–	–	–	–	–	6
	India	10	–	–	4	–	–	2	–	–	–	–	4
	Pakistan	7	–	–	3	–	–	–	1	–	–	–	3
	Sri Lanka	5	–	–	3	–	–	–	–	0	–	–	2
	Zimbabwe	1	–	–	1	–	–	–	–	–	0	–	–
West Indies	New Zealand	28	–	–	–	10	4	–	–	–	–	–	14
	India	70	–	–	–	28	–	7	–	–	–	–	35
	Pakistan	34	–	–	–	12	–	–	10	–	–	–	12
	Sri Lanka	3	–	–	–	1	–	–	–	0	–	–	2
New Zealand	India	35	–	–	–	–	6	13	–	–	–	–	16
	Pakistan	39	–	–	–	–	5	–	18	–	–	–	16
	Sri Lanka	18	–	–	–	–	7	–	–	4	–	–	7
	Zimbabwe	8	–	–	–	–	3	–	–	–	0	–	5
India	Pakistan	44	–	–	–	–	–	4	7	–	–	–	33
	Sri Lanka	19	–	–	–	–	–	7	–	1	–	–	11
	Zimbabwe	2	–	–	–	–	–	1	–	–	0	–	1
Pakistan	Sri Lanka	19	–	–	–	–	–	–	9	3	–	–	7
	Zimbabwe	10	–	–	–	–	–	–	6	–	1	–	3
Sri Lanka	Zimbabwe	7	–	–	–	–	–	–	–	4	0	–	3
		1423	254	244	58	132	39	59	71	14	1	2	549

	Tests	Won	Lost	Drawn	Tied	Toss Won
England	752	254	215	283	–	368
Australia	581	244	164	171	2	289
South Africa	225	58	90	77	–	109
West Indies	343	132	84	126	1	179
New Zealand	262	39	108	115	–	133
India	318	59	103	155	1	164
Pakistan	248	71	56	121	–	120
Sri Lanka	87	14	37	36	–	42
Zimbabwe	30	1	15	14	–	19

TEST CRICKET RECORDS

To 30 September 1998

TEAM RECORDS

HIGHEST INNINGS TOTALS

952-6d	Sri Lanka v India	Colombo (RPS)	1997-98
903-7d	England v Australia	The Oval	1938
849	England v West Indies	Kingston	1929-30
790-3d	West Indies v Pakistan	Kingston	1957-58
758-8d	Australia v West Indies	Kingston	1954-55
729-6d	Australia v England	Lord's	1930
708	Pakistan v England	The Oval	1987
701	Australia v England	The Oval	1934
699-5	Pakistan v India	Lahore	1989-90
695	Australia v England	The Oval	1930
692-8d	West Indies v England	The Oval	1995
687-8d	West Indies v England	The Oval	1976
681-8d	West Indies v England	Port-of-Spain	1953-54
676-7	India v Sri Lanka	Kanpur	1986-87
674-6	Pakistan v India	Faisalabad	1984-85
674	Australia v India	Adelaide	1947-48
671-4	New Zealand v Sri Lanka	Wellington	1990-91
668	Australia v West Indies	Bridgetown	1954-55
660-5d	West Indies v New Zealand	Wellington	1994-95
659-8d	Australia v England	Sydney	1946-47
658-8d	England v Australia	Nottingham	1938
657-8d	Pakistan v West Indies	Bridgetown	1957-58
656-8d	Australia v England	Manchester	1964
654-5	England v South Africa	Durban	1938-39
653-4d	England v India	Lord's	1990
653-4d	Australia v England	Leeds	1993
652-7d	England v India	Madras	1984-85
652-8d	West Indies v England	Lord's	1973
652	Pakistan v India	Faisalabad	1982-83
650-6d	Australia v West Indies	Bridgetown	1964-65

The highest for South Africa is 622-9d (v A, Durban, 1969-70) and for Zimbabwe 544-4d (v P, Harare, 1994-95).

LOWEST INNINGS TOTALS

26	New Zealand v England	Auckland	1954-55
30	South Africa v England	Port Elizabeth	1895-96
30	South Africa v England	Birmingham	1924
35	South Africa v England	Cape Town	1898-99
36	Australia v England	Birmingham	1902
36	South Africa v Australia	Melbourne	1931-32
42	Australia v England	Sydney	1887-88
42	New Zealand v Australia	Wellington	1945-46
42	India v England	Lord's	1974
43	South Africa v England	Cape Town	1888-89
44	Australia v England	The Oval	1896
45	England v Australia	Sydney	1886-87
45	South Africa v Australia	Melbourne	1931-32
46	England v West Indies	Port-of-Spain	1993-94
47	South Africa v England	Cape Town	1888-89
47	New Zealand v England	Lord's	1958

The lowest for West Indies is 53 (v P, Faisalabad, 1986-87); for Pakistan 62 (v A, Perth, 1981-82); for Sri Lanka 71 (v P, Kandy, 1994-95); and for Zimbabwe 127 (v SL, RPS Colombo, 1996-97).

BATTING RECORDS
HIGHEST INDIVIDUAL INNINGS

375	B.C.Lara	WI v E	St John's	1993-94
365*	G.St A.Sobers	WI v P	Kingston	1957-58
364	L.Hutton	E v A	The Oval	1938
340	S.T.Jayasuriya	SL v I	Colombo (RPS)	1997-98
337	Hanif Mohammed	P v WI	Bridgetown	1957-58
336*	W.R.Hammond	E v NZ	Auckland	1932-33
334	D.G.Bradman	A v E	Leeds	1930
333	G.A.Gooch	E v I	Lord's	1990
325	A.Sandham	E v WI	Kingston	1929-30
311	R.B.Simpson	A v E	Manchester	1964
310*	J.H.Edrich	E v NZ	Leeds	1965
307	R.M.Cowper	A v E	Melbourne	1965-66
304	D.G.Bradman	A v E	Leeds	1934
302	L.G.Rowe	WI v E	Bridgetown	1973-74
299*	D.G.Bradman	A v SA	Adelaide	1931-32
299	M.D.Crowe	NZ v SL	Wellington	1990-91
291	I.V.A.Richards	WI v E	The Oval	1976
287	R.E.Foster	E v A	Sydney	1903-04
285*	P.B.H.May	E v WI	Birmingham	1957
280*	Javed Miandad	P v I	Hyderabad	1982-83
278	D.C.S.Compton	E v P	Nottingham	1954
277	B.C.Lara	WI v A	Sydney	1992-93
274	R.G.Pollock	SA v A	Durban	1969-70
274	Zaheer Abbas	P v E	Birmingham	1971
271	Javed Miandad	P v NZ	Auckland	1988-89
270*	G.A.Headley	WI v E	Kingston	1934-35
270	D.G.Bradman	A v E	Melbourne	1936-37
268	G.N.Yallop	A v P	Melbourne	1983-84
267*	B.A.Young	NZ v SL	Dunedin	1996-97
267	P.A.de Silva	SL v NZ	Wellington	1990-91
266	W.H.Ponsford	A v E	The Oval	1934
266	D.L.Houghton	Z v SL	Bulawayo	1994-95
262*	D.L.Amiss	E v WI	Kingston	1973-74
261	F.M.M.Worrell	WI v E	Nottingham	1950
260	C.C.Hunte	WI v P	Kingston	1957-58
260	Javed Miandad	P v E	The Oval	1987
259	G.M.Turner	NZ v WI	Georgetown	1971-72
258	T.W.Graveney	E v WI	Nottingham	1957
258	S.M.Nurse	WI v NZ	Christchurch	1968-69
257*	Wasim Akram	P v Z	Sheikhupura	1996-97
256	R.B.Kanhai	WI v I	Calcutta	1958-59
256	K.F.Barrington	E v A	Manchester	1964
255*	D.J.McGlew	SA v NZ	Wellington	1952-53
254	D.G.Bradman	A v E	Lord's	1930
251	W.R.Hammond	E v A	Sydney	1928-29
250	K.D.Walters	A v NZ	Christchurch	1976-77
250	S.F.A.F.Bacchus	WI v I	Kanpur	1978-79

The highest for India is 236* by S.M.Gavaskar (v WI, Madras, 1983-84).

750 RUNS IN A SERIES

Runs			Series	M	I	NO	HS	Avge	100	50
974	D.G.Bradman	A v E	1930	5	7	–	334	139.14	4	–
905	W.R.Hammond	E v A	1928-29	5	9	1	251	113.12	4	–
839	M.A.Taylor	A v E	1989	6	11	1	219	83.90	2	5
834	R.N.Harvey	A v SA	1952-53	5	9	–	205	92.66	4	3
829	I.V.A.Richards	WI v E	1976	4	7	–	291	118.42	3	2
827	C.L.Walcott	WI v A	1954-55	5	10	–	155	82.70	5	2
824	G.St A.Sobers	WI v P	1957-58	5	8	2	365*	137.33	3	3
810	D.G.Bradman	A v E	1936-37	5	9	–	270	90.00	3	1
806	D.G.Bradman	A v SA	1931-32	5	5	1	299*	201.50	4	–
798	B.C.Lara	WI v E	1993-94	5	8	–	375	99.75	2	2
779	E.de C.Weekes	WI v I	1948-49	5	7	–	194	111.28	4	2
774	S.M.Gavaskar	I v WI	1970-71	4	8	3	220	154.80	4	3
765	B.C.Lara	WI v E	1995	6	10	1	179	85.00	3	3
761	Mudassar Nazar	P v I	1982-83	6	8	2	231	126.83	4	1
758	D.G.Bradman	A v E	1934	5	8	–	304	94.75	2	1
753	D.C.S.Compton	E v SA	1947	5	8	–	208	94.12	4	2
752	G.A.Gooch	E v I	1990	3	6	–	333	125.33	3	2

HIGHEST PARTNERSHIP FOR EACH WICKET

1st	413	V.Mankad/Pankaj Roy	I v NZ	Madras	1955-56
2nd	576	S.T.Jayasuriya/R.S.Mahanama	SL v I	Colombo (RPS)	1997-98
3rd	467	A.H.Jones/M.D.Crowe	NZ v SL	Wellington	1990-91
4th	411	P.B.H.May/M.C.Cowdrey	E v WI	Birmingham	1957
5th	405	S.G.Barnes/D.G.Bradman	A v E	Sydney	1946-47
6th	346	J.H.W.Fingleton/D.G.Bradman	A v E	Melbourne	1936-37
7th	347	D.St E.Atkinson/C.C.Depeiza	WI v A	Bridgetown	1954-55
8th	313	Wasim Akram/Saqlain Mushtaq	P v Z	Sheikhupura	1996-97
9th	195	M.V. Boucher/P.L.Symcox	SA v P	Johannesburg	1997-98
10th	151	B.F.Hastings/R.O.Collinge	NZ v P	Auckland	1972-73
	151	Azhar Mahmood/Mushtaq Ahmed	P v SA	Rawalpindi	1997-98

WICKET PARTNERSHIPS OF OVER 350

576	2nd	S.T.Jayasuriya/R.S.Mahanama	SL v I	Colombo (RPS)	1997-98
467	3rd	A.H.Jones/M.D.Crowe	NZ v SL	Wellington	1990-91
451	2nd	W.H.Ponsford/D.G.Bradman	A v E	The Oval	1934
451	3rd	Mudassar Nazar/Javed Miandad	P v I	Hyderabad	1982-83
446	2nd	C.C.Hunte/G.St A.Sobers	WI v P	Kingston	1957-58
413	1st	V.Mankad/Pankaj Roy	I v NZ	Madras	1955-56
411	4th	P.B.H.May/M.C.Cowdrey	E v WI	Birmingham	1957
405	5th	S.G.Barnes/D.G.Bradman	A v E	Sydney	1946-47
399	4th	G.St A.Sobers/F.M.M.Worrell	WI v E	Bridgetown	1959-60
397	3rd	Qasim Omar/Javed Miandad	P v SL	Faisalabad	1985-86
388	4th	W.H.Ponsford/D.G.Bradman	A v E	Leeds	1934
387	1st	G.M.Turner/T.W.Jarvis	NZ v WI	Georgetown	1971-72
385	5th	S.R.Waugh/G.S.Blewett	A v SA	Johannesburg	1996-97
382	2nd	L.Hutton/M.Leyland	E v A	The Oval	1938
382	1st	W.M.Lawry/R.B.Simpson	A v WI	Bridgetown	1964-65
370	3rd	W.J.Edrich/D.C.S.Compton	E v SA	Lord's	1947
369	2nd	J.H.Edrich/K.F.Barrington	E v NZ	Leeds	1965
359	1st	L.Hutton/C.Washbrook	E v SA	Johannesburg	1948-49
351	2nd	G.A.Gooch/D.I.Gower	E v A	The Oval	1985
350	4th	Mushtaq Mohammed/Asif Iqbal	P v NZ	Dunedin	1972-73

4000 RUNS IN A TEST CAREER

Runs			M	I	NO	HS	Avge	100	50
11174	A.R.Border	A	156	265	44	205	50.56	27	63
10122	S.M.Gavaskar	I	125	214	16	236*	51.12	34	45
8900	G.A.Gooch	E	118	215	6	333	42.58	20	46
8832	Javed Miandad	P	124	189	21	280*	52.57	23	43
8540	I.V.A.Richards	WI	121	182	12	291	50.23	24	45
8231	D.I.Gower	E	117	204	18	215	44.25	18	39
8114	G.Boycott	E	108	193	23	246*	47.72	22	42
8032	G.St A.Sobers	WI	93	160	21	365*	57.78	26	30
7624	M.C.Cowdrey	E	114	188	15	182	44.06	22	38
7558	C.G.Greenidge	WI	108	185	16	226	44.72	19	34
7515	C.H.Lloyd	WI	110	175	14	242*	46.67	19	39
7487	D.L.Haynes	WI	116	202	25	184	42.29	18	39
7422	D.C.Boon	A	107	190	20	200	43.65	21	32
7249	W.R.Hammond	E	85	140	16	336*	58.45	22	24
7110	G.S.Chappell	A	87	151	19	247*	53.86	24	31
6996	D.G.Bradman	A	52	80	10	334	99.94	29	13
6971	L.Hutton	E	79	138	15	364	56.67	19	33
6868	D.B.Vengsarkar	I	116	185	22	166	42.13	17	35
6806	K.F.Barrington	E	82	131	15	256	58.67	20	35
6784	M.A.Taylor	A	96	171	12	219	42.66	18	36
6480	S.R.Waugh	A	103	162	29	200	48.72	14	38
6227	R.B.Kanhai	WI	79	137	6	256	47.53	15	28
6149	R.N.Harvey	A	79	137	10	205	48.41	21	24
6080	G.R.Viswanath	I	91	155	10	222	41.93	14	35
5949	R.B.Richardson	WI	86	146	12	194	44.39	16	27
5935	M.A.Atherton	E	84	155	6	185*	39.83	12	37
5807	D.C.S.Compton	E	78	131	15	278	50.06	17	28
5697	M.Azharuddin	I	91	132	8	199	45.94	20	19
5652	A.J.Stewart	E	81	146	10	190	41.55	11	28
5528	Salim Malik	P	96	142	21	237	45.68	15	28
5444	M.D.Crowe	NZ	77	131	11	299	45.36	17	18
5410	J.B.Hobbs	E	61	102	7	211	56.94	15	28
5357	K.D.Walters	A	74	125	14	250	48.26	15	33
5345	I.M.Chappell	A	75	136	10	196	42.42	14	26
5334	J.G.Wright	NZ	82	148	7	185	37.82	12	23
5248	Kapil Dev	I	131	184	15	163	31.05	8	27
5234	W.M.Lawry	A	67	123	12	210	47.15	13	27
5219	M.E.Waugh	A	78	128	7	153*	43.13	14	32
5200	I.T.Botham	E	102	161	6	208	33.54	14	22
5138	J.H.Edrich	E	77	127	9	310*	43.54	12	24
5129	P.A.de Silva	SL	74	128	9	267	43.10	17	19
5062	Zaheer Abbas	P	78	124	11	274	44.79	12	20
4882	T.W.Graveney	E	79	123	13	258	44.38	11	20
4869	R.B.Simpson	A	62	111	7	311	46.81	10	27
4737	I.R.Redpath	A	66	120	11	171	43.45	8	31
4656	A.J.Lamb	E	79	139	10	142	36.09	14	18
4595	A.Ranatunga	SL	82	138	8	135*	35.34	4	33
4555	H.Sutcliffe	E	54	84	9	194	60.73	16	23
4552	S.R.Tendulkar	I	61	92	9	179	54.84	16	19
4550	B.C.Lara	WI	54	91	3	375	51.70	10	23
4537	P.B.H.May	E	66	106	9	285*	46.77	13	22
4502	E.R.Dexter	E	62	102	8	205	47.89	9	27
4455	E.de C.Weekes	WI	48	81	5	207	58.61	15	19
4415	K.J.Hughes	A	70	124	6	213	37.41	9	22

Runs			M	I	NO	HS	Avge	100	50
4409	M.W.Gatting	E	79	138	14	207	35.55	10	21
4399	A.I.Kallicharran	WI	66	109	10	187	44.43	12	21
4389	A.P.E.Knott	E	95	149	15	135	32.75	5	30
4378	M.Amarnath	I	69	113	10	138	42.50	11	24
4334	R.C.Fredericks	WI	59	109	7	169	42.49	8	26
4236	R.A.Smith	E	62	112	15	175	43.67	9	28
4114	Mudassar Nazar	P	76	116	8	231	38.09	10	17

The highest for South Africa is 3471 by B.Mitchell (80 innings) and for Zimbabwe 1991 by G.W.Flower (54).

18 HUNDREDS

							Opponents					
			200	I	E	A	SA	WI	NZ	I	P	SL	Z
34	S.M.Gavaskar	I	4	214	4	8	–	13	2	–	5	2	–
29	D.G.Bradman	A	12	80	19	–	4	2	–	4	–	–	–
27	A.R.Border	A	2	265	8	–	–	3	5	4	6	1	–
26	G.St A.Sobers	WI	2	160	10	4	–	–	1	8	3	–	–
24	G.S.Chappell	A	4	151	9	–	–	5	3	1	6	–	–
24	I.V.A.Richards	WI	3	182	8	5	–	–	1	8	2	–	–
23	Javed Miandad	P	6	189	2	6	–	2	7	5	–	1	–
22	W.R.Hammond	E	7	140	–	9	6	1	4	2	–	–	–
22	M.C.Cowdrey	E	–	188	–	5	3	6	2	3	3	–	–
22	G.Boycott	E	1	193	–	7	1	5	2	4	3	–	–
21	R.N.Harvey	A	2	137	6	–	8	–	3	–	4	–	–
21	D.C.Boon	A	1	190	7	–	–	3	3	6	1	1	–
20	K.F.Barrington	E	1	131	–	5	2	3	3	3	4	–	–
20	M.Azharuddin	I	–	132	6	2	3	–	1	–	3	5	–
20	G.A.Gooch	E	2	215	–	4	–	5	4	5	1	1	–
19	C.G.Greenidge	WI	4	185	7	4	–	–	2	5	1	–	–
19	L.Hutton	E	4	138	–	5	4	5	3	2	–	–	–
19	C.H.Lloyd	WI	1	175	5	6	–	–	–	7	1	–	–
18	M.A.Taylor	A	1	171	6	–	2	1	2	2	3	2	–
18	D.I.Gower	E	2	204	–	9	–	1	4	2	2	–	–
18	D.L.Haynes	WI	–	202	5	5	–	–	3	2	3	–	–

The most for South Africa is 9 by A.D.Nourse (62 innings); for New Zealand 17 by M.D.Crowe (131); for Sri Lanka 17 by P.A.de Silva (128); for Zimbabwe 5 A.Flower (53) and by G.W.Flower (54). The most double hundreds by batsmen not included above is 4 by Zaheer Abbas (12 hundreds for Pakistan) and 3 by R.B.Simpson (10 for Australia).

BOWLING RECORDS

NINE WICKETS IN AN INNINGS

10- 53	J.C.Laker	E v A	Manchester	1956
9- 28	G.A.Lohmann	E v SA	Johannesburg	1895-96
9- 37	J.C.Laker	E v A	Manchester	1956
9- 52	R.J.Hadlee	NZ v A	Brisbane	1985-86
9- 56	Abdul Qadir	P v E	Lahore	1987-88
9- 57	D.E.Malcolm	E v SA	The Oval	1994
9- 65	M.Muralitharan	SL v E	The Oval	1998
9- 69	J.M.Patel	I v A	Kanpur	1959-60
9- 83	Kapil Dev	I v WI	Ahmedabad	1983-84
9- 86	Sarfraz Nawaz	P v A	Melbourne	1978-79
9- 95	J.M.Noreiga	WI v I	Port-of-Spain	1970-71
9-102	S.P.Gupte	I v WI	Kanpur	1958-59
9-103	S.F.Barnes	E v SA	Johannesburg	1913-14

9-113	H.J.Tayfield	SA v E	Johannesburg	1956-57
9-121	A.A.Mailey	A v E	Melbourne	1920-21

The best analysis for Zimbabwe is 6-90 by H.H.Streak (v P, Harare, 1994-95).

15 WICKETS IN A TEST († *On debut*)

19- 90	J.C.Laker	E v A	Manchester	1956
17-159	S.F.Barnes	E v SA	Johannesburg	1913-14
16-136†	N.D.Hirwani	I v WI	Madras	1987-88
16-137†	R.A.L.Massie	A v E	Lord's	1972
16-220	M.Muralitharan	SL v E	The Oval	1998
15- 28	J.Briggs	E v SA	Cape Town	1888-89
15- 45	G.A.Lohmann	E v SA	Port Elizabeth	1895-96
15- 99	C.Blythe	E v SA	Leeds	1907
15-104	H.Verity	E v A	Lord's	1934
15-123	R.J.Hadlee	NZ v A	Brisbane	1985-86
15-124	W.Rhodes	E v A	Melbourne	1903-04

The best analysis for South Africa is 13-165 by H.J.Tayfield (v A, Melbourne, 1952-53); for West Indies 14-149 by M.A.Holding (v E, The Oval, 1976); for Pakistan 14-116 by Imran Khan (v SL, Lahore, 1981-82); and for Zimbabwe 11-255 by A.G.Huckle (v NZ, Bulawayo, 1997-98).

35 WICKETS IN A SERIES

Wkts			Series	M	Balls	Runs	Avge	5wI	10wM
49	S.F.Barnes	E v SA	1913-14	4	1356	536	10.93	7	3
46	J.C.Laker	E v A	1956	5	1703	442	9.60	4	2
44	C.V.Grimmett	A v SA	1935-36	5	2077	642	14.59	5	3
42	T.M.Alderman	A v E	1981	6	1950	893	21.26	4	–
41	R.M.Hogg	A v E	1978-79	6	1740	527	12.85	5	2
41	T.M.Alderman	A v E	1989	6	1616	712	17.36	6	1
40	Imran Khan	P v I	1982-83	6	1339	558	13.95	4	2
39	A.V.Bedser	E v A	1953	5	1591	682	17.48	5	1
39	D.K.Lillee	A v E	1981	6	1870	870	22.30	2	1
38	M.W.Tate	E v A	1924-25	5	2528	881	23.18	5	1
37	W.J.Whitty	A v SA	1910-11	5	1395	632	17.08	2	–
37	H.J.Tayfield	SA v E	1956-57	5	2280	636	17.18	4	1
36	A.E.E.Vogler	SA v E	1909-10	5	1349	783	21.75	4	1
36	A.A.Mailey	A v E	1920-21	5	1465	946	26.27	4	2
36	G.D.McGrath	A v E	1997	6	1499	701	19.47	2	–
35	G.A.Lohmann	E v SA	1895-96	3	520	203	5.80	4	2
35	B.S.Chandrasekhar	I v E	1972-73	5	1747	662	18.91	4	1
35	M.D.Marshall	WI v E	1988	5	1219	443	12.65	3	1

The most for New Zealand is 33 by R.J.Hadlee (v A, 1985-86); for Sri Lanka 20 by R.J.Ratnayake (v I, 1985-86); and for Zimbabwe 22 by H.H.Streak (v P, 1994-95).

200 WICKETS IN TESTS

Wkts			M	Balls	Runs	Avge	5wI	10wM
434	Kapil Dev	I	131	27740	12867	29.64	23	2
431	R.J.Hadlee	NZ	86	21918	9611	22.29	36	9
383	I.T.Botham	E	102	21815	10878	28.40	27	4
376	M.D.Marshall	WI	81	17584	7876	20.94	22	4
375	C.A.Walsh	WI	102	22026	9668	25.78	15	2
362	Imran Khan	P	88	19458	8258	22.81	23	6
355	D.K.Lillee	A	70	18467	8493	23.92	23	7

Wkts			M	Balls	Runs	Avge	5 wI	10 wM
341	Wasim Akram	P	79	17922	7706	22.59	21	4
337	C.E.L.Ambrose	WI	80	17988	7133	21.16	20	3
325	R.G.D.Willis	E	90	17357	8190	25.20	16	–
313	S.K.Warne	A	67	19791	7756	24.77	14	4
309	L.R.Gibbs	WI	79	27115	8989	29.09	18	2
307	F.S.Trueman	E	67	15178	6625	21.57	17	3
297	D.L.Underwood	E	86	21862	7674	25.83	17	6
291	C.J.McDermott	A	71	16586	8332	28.63	14	2
267	Waqar Younis	P	53	10798	5748	21.53	21	5
266	B.S.Bedi	I	67	21364	7637	28.71	14	1
259	J.Garner	WI	58	13169	5433	20.97	7	–
252	J.B.Statham	E	70	16056	6261	24.84	9	1
249	M.A.Holding	WI	60	12680	5898	23.68	13	2
248	R.Benaud	A	63	19108	6704	27.03	16	1
246	G.D.McKenzie	A	60	17681	7328	29.78	16	3
242	B.S.Chandrasekhar	I	58	15963	7199	29.74	16	2
237	A.A.Donald	SA	47	11005	5233	22.08	15	2
236	A.V.Bedser	E	51	15918	5876	24.89	15	5
236	Abdul Qadir	P	67	17126	7742	32.80	15	5
235	G.St A.Sobers	WI	93	21599	7999	34.03	6	–
228	R.R.Lindwall	A	61	13650	5251	23.03	12	–
216	C.V.Grimmett	A	37	14513	5231	24.21	21	7
212	M.G.Hughes	A	53	12285	6017	28.38	7	1
203	M.Muralitharan	SL	42	13041	5464	26.91	16	2
202	A.M.E.Roberts	WI	47	11136	5174	25.61	11	2
202	J.A.Snow	E	49	12021	5387	26.66	8	1
200	J.R.Thomson	A	51	10535	5601	28.00	8	–

The highest aggregates for Zimbabwe is 94 in 23 Tests by H.H.Streak.

HAT-TRICKS

F.R.Spofforth	Australia v England	Melbourne	1878-79
W.Bates	England v Australia	Melbourne	1882-83
J.Briggs	England v Australia	Sydney	1891-92
G.A.Lohmann	England v South Africa	Port Elizabeth	1895-96
J.T.Hearne	England v Australia	Leeds	1899
H.Trumble	Australia v England	Melbourne	1901-02
H.Trumble	Australia v England	Melbourne	1903-04
T.J.Matthews (2)**	Australia v South Africa	Manchester	1912
M.J.C.Allom*†	England v New Zealand	Christchurch	1929-30
T.W.J.Goddard	England v South Africa	Johannesburg	1938-39
P.J.Loader	England v West Indies	Leeds	1957
L.F.Kline	Australia v South Africa	Cape Town	1957-58
W.W.Hall	West Indies v Pakistan	Lahore	1958-59
G.M.Griffin	South Africa v England	Lord's	1960
L.R.Gibbs	West Indies v Australia	Adelaide	1960-61
P.J.Petherick*	New Zealand v Pakistan	Lahore	1976-77
C.A.Walsh‡	West Indies v Australia	Brisbane	1988-89
M.G.Hughes‡	Australia v West Indies	Perth	1988-89
D.W.Fleming*	Australia v Pakistan	Rawalpindi	1994-95
S.K.Warne	Australia v England	Melbourne	1994-95
D.G.Cork	England v West Indies	Manchester	1995

*On debut ** Hat-trick in each innings † Four wickets in five balls ‡ Involving both innings*

WICKET-KEEPING RECORDS
SEVEN DISMISSALS IN AN INNINGS

7	Wasim Bari	Pakistan v New Zealand	Auckland	1978-79
7	R.W.Taylor	England v India	Bombay	1979-80
7	I.D.S.Smith	New Zealand v Sri Lanka	Hamilton	1990-91

FIVE STUMPINGS IN AN INNINGS

| 5 | K.S.More | India v West Indies | Madras | 1987-88 |

TEN DISMISSALS IN A TEST

| 11 | R.C.Russell | England v South Africa | Johannesburg | 1995-96 |
| 10 | R.W.Taylor | England v India | Bombay | 1979-80 |

25 DISMISSALS IN A SERIES

28	R.W.Marsh	Australia v England		1982-83
27 (inc 2st)	R.C.Russell	England v South Africa		1995-96
27 (inc 2st)	I.A.Healy	Australia v England (6 Tests)		1997
26 (inc 3st)	J.H.B.Waite	South Africa v New Zealand		1961-62
26	R.W.Marsh	Australia v West Indies (6 Tests)		1975-76
26 (inc 5st)	I.A.Healy	Australia v England (6 Tests)		1993
26 (inc 1st)	M.V.Boucher	South Africa v England		1998
25 (inc 2st)	I.A.Healy	Australia v England		1994-95

100 DISMISSALS IN TESTS

Total			Tests	Ct	St
355	R.W.Marsh	Australia	96	343	12
353	I.A.Healy	Australia	103	328	25
272†	P.J.L.Dujon	West Indies	81	267	5
269	A.P.E.Knott	England	95	250	19
228	Wasim Bari	Pakistan	81	201	27
219	T.G.Evans	England	91	173	46
198	S.M.H.Kirmani	India	88	160	38
189	D.L.Murray	West Indies	62	181	8
187	A.T.W.Grout	Australia	51	163	24
176	I.D.S.Smith	New Zealand	63	168	8
174	R.W.Taylor	England	57	167	7
165	R.C.Russell	England	54	153	12
152	D.J.Richardson	South Africa	42	150	2
151†	A.J.Stewart	England	81	144	7
141	J.H.B.Waite	South Africa	50	124	17
130	K.S.More	India	49	110	20
130	W.A.S.Oldfield	Australia	54	78	52
114†	J.M.Parks	England	46	103	11
104	Salim Yousuf	Pakistan	32	91	13

The most for Sri Lanka is 58 by R.S.Kaluwitharana (24 Tests) and for Zimbabwe 76† by A.Flower (30 Tests).

† *Including catches taken in the field*

FIELDING RECORDS
FIVE CATCHES IN AN INNINGS

5	V.Y.Richardson	Australia v South Africa	Durban	1935-36
5	Yajurvindra Singh	India v England	Bangalore	1976-77
5	M.Azharuddin	India v Pakistan	Karachi	1989-90
5	K.Srikkanth	India v Australia	Perth	1991-92
5	S.P.Fleming	New Zealand v Zimbabwe	Harare	1997-98

SEVEN CATCHES IN A TEST

7	G.S.Chappell	Australia v England	Perth	1974-75
7	Yajurvindra Singh	India v England	Bangalore	1976-77
7	H.P.Tillekeratne	Sri Lanka v New Zealand	Colombo (SSC)	1992-93
7	S.P.Fleming	New Zealand v Zimbabwe	Harare	1997-98

15 CATCHES IN A SERIES

15	J.M.Gregory	Australia v England	1920-21

100 CATCHES IN TESTS

Total			Tests	Total			Tests
156	A.R.Border	Australia	156	110	W.R.Hammond	England	85
144	M.A.Taylor	Australia	96	109	G.St A.Sobers	West Indies	93
122	G.S.Chappell	Australia	87	108	S.M.Gavaskar	India	125
122	I.V.A.Richards	West Indies	121	105	I.M.Chappell	Australia	75
120	I.T.Botham	England	102	103	G.A.Gooch	England	118
120	M.C.Cowdrey	England	114	101	M.Azharuddin	India	91
110	R.B.Simpson	Australia	62				

The most for South Africa is 56 by B.Mitchell (42 Tests); for New Zealand 71 by M.D.Crowe (77 Tests); for Pakistan 93 by Javed Miandad (124 Tests); for Sri Lanka 56 by R.S.Mahanama (52 Tests); and for Zimbabwe 29 by A.D.R.Campbell (30 Tests).

APPEARANCE RECORDS
100 TEST MATCH APPEARANCES

156	A.R.Border	Australia		114	M.C.Cowdrey	England
131	Kapil Dev	India		110	C.H.Lloyd	West Indies
125	S.M.Gavaskar	India		108	G.Boycott	England
124	Javed Miandad	Pakistan		108	C.G.Greenidge	West Indies
121	I.V.A.Richards	West Indies		107	D.C.Boon	Australia
118	G.A.Gooch	England		103	I.A.Healy	Australia
117	D.I.Gower	England		103	S.R.Waugh	Australia
116	D.L.Haynes	West Indies		102	I.T.Botham	England
116	D.B.Vengsarkar	India		102	C.A.Walsh	West Indies

The most for South Africa is 51 by W.J.Cronje; for New Zealand 86 by R.J.Hadlee; for Sri Lanka 82 by A.Ranatunga; and for Zimbabwe 30 by A.D.R.Campbell, A.Flower and G.W.Flower.

100 CONSECUTIVE TEST APPEARANCES

153	A.R.Border	Australia	March 1979 to March 1994
106	S.M.Gavaskar	India	January 1975 to February 1987

75 TESTS AS CAPTAIN

93	A.R.Border	Australia	December 1984 to March 1994

50 TEST UMPIRING APPEARANCES

66	H.D.Bird	July 1973 to June 1996

SRI LANKA v ZIMBABWE (1st Test)

At Asgiriya Stadium, Kandy on 7, 8, 9, 10, 11 January 1998.
Toss: Sri Lanka. Result: **SRI LANKA** won by 8 wickets.
Debuts: Zimbabwe – M.W.Goodwin.

SRI LANKA

S.T.Jayasuriya	lbw b Streak	6	lbw b Streak	0
M.S.Atapattu	c Campbell b P.A.Strang	223	not out	6
R.S.Mahanama	c Campbell b Streak	7	b Streak	0
P.A.de Silva	c Whittall b Huckle	75	not out	4
*A.Ranatunga	b Whittall	27		
H.P.Tillekeratne	c and b Whittall	44		
†R.S.Kaluwitharana	c and b Whittall	29		
W.P.U.C.J.Vaas	c Rennie b P.A.Strang	26		
M.Muralitharan	c B.C.Strang b P.A.Strang	17		
K.R.Pushpakumara	not out	2		
K.J.Silva				
Extras	(B 2, LB 2, NB 9)	13		
Total	(9 wickets declared)	**469**	(2 wickets)	**10**

ZIMBABWE

G.J.Rennie	c De Silva b Silva	53	lbw b Muralitharan	24
G.W.Flower	b Muralitharan	4	b De Silva	38
M.W.Goodwin	lbw b Silva	2	b Muralitharan	70
†A.Flower	lbw b Vaas	8	(5) c Mahanama b Muralitharan	67
*A.D.R.Campbell	c Mahanama b Pushpakumara	7	(6) lbw b Vaas	40
C.B.Wishart	c Mahanama b Muralitharan	3	(7) b Muralitharan	0
P.A.Strang	c De Silva b Muralitharan	35	(8) c sub (R.P.Arnold) b Muralitharan	33
H.H.Streak	b Muralitharan	5	(9) c Kaluwitharana b Pushpakumara	13
A.R.Whittall	not out	6	(4) b Muralitharan	14
B.C.Strang	b Muralitharan	2	not out	15
A.G.Huckle	lbw b Silva	0	lbw b Muralitharan	0
Extras	(B 6, LB 2, NB 7)	15	(B 5, LB 11, NB 8)	24
Total		**140**		**338**

ZIMBABWE	O	M	R	W		O	M	R	W
Streak	34	11	96	2		1	0	4	2
B.C.Strang	30	7	78	0		0.5	0	6	0
P.A.Strang	35.3	10	123	3					
Whittall	30	3	73	3					
Huckle	21	2	88	1					
Goodwin	4	2	7	0					

SRI LANKA	O	M	R	W		O	M	R	W
Vaas	17	4	36	1		24	3	65	1
Pushpakumara	14	5	34	1		19	2	64	1
Muralitharan	29	18	23	5		43	12	94	7
Silva	19.4	9	27	3	(5)	11	2	35	0
De Silva	5	0	12	0	(4)	13	5	25	1
Jayasuriya	1	1	0	0		16	0	38	0
Atapattu						1	0	1	0

FALL OF WICKETS

	SL	Z	Z	SL
Wkt	1st	1st	2nd	2nd
1st	16	29	68	0
2nd	33	36	69	0
3rd	173	46	103	–
4th	226	72	185	–
5th	321	75	261	–
6th	383	119	261	–
7th	440	127	271	–
8th	461	134	297	–
9th	469	136	334	–
10th	–	140	338	–

Umpires: B.C.Cooray (13) and M.J.Kitchen (*England*) (16).
Referee: R.Subba Row (*England*) (25). Test No. 1395/6 (SL 80/Z 25)

SRI LANKA v ZIMBABWE (2nd Test)

At Sinhalese Sports Club, Colombo on 14, 15, 16, 17, 18 January 1998.
Toss: Zimbabwe. Result: **SRI LANKA** won by 5 wickets.
Debuts: None.

ZIMBABWE

G.J.Rennie	c Kaluwitharana b Muralitharan	50
G.W.Flower	b Pushpakumara	41
M.W.Goodwin	b Anurasiri	73
G.J.Whittall	run out	11
†A.Flower	c and b Anurasiri	8
*A.D.R.Campbell	c Kaluwitharana b Vaas	44
C.B.Wishart	lbw b Muralitharan	2
P.A.Strang	c Pushpakumara b Anurasiri	5
H.H.Streak	b Vaas	3
A.R.Whittall	not out	1
M.Mbangwa	b Pushpakumara	0
Extras	(LB 3, W 1, NB 9)	13
Total		**251**

	c Kaluwitharana b De Silva	12
	b Jayasuriya	52
(4)	b Jayasuriya	39
(5)	c sub‡ b Muralitharan	17
(6)	not out	105
(7)	c Kaluwitharana b Anurasiri	37
(8)	c Kaluwitharana b Pushpakumara	18
(9)	b Muralitharan	3
(10)	run out	1
(3)	c Tillekeratne b De Silva	2
	c De Silva b Muralitharan	4
	(LB 6, W 1, NB 2)	9
		299

SRI LANKA

S.T.Jayasuriya	c G.J.Whittall b Streak	5
M.S.Atapattu	c A.Flower b Strang	48
R.S.Mahanama	b Mbangwa	8
P.A.de Silva	c and b Streak	27
*A.Ranatunga	c Streak b Strang	52
H.P.Tillekeratne	c Rennie b A.R.Whittall	7
†R.S.Kaluwitharana	c A.Flower b Strang	51
S.D.Anurasiri	not out	3
M.Muralitharan	c A.Flower b Mbangwa	11
K.R.Pushpakumara	b Strang	1
W.P.U.C.J.Vaas	absent ill	
Extras	(LB 11, W 1)	12
Total		**225**

	c A.Flower b Streak	68
	c A.Flower b Streak	0
	lbw b Mbangwa	0
	not out	143
(7)	not out	87
	lbw b Streak	0
(6)	c Campbell b Streak	4
	(B 11, LB 13)	24
	(5 wickets)	**326**

SRI LANKA	O	M	R	W		O	M	R	W
Vaas	12	1	35	2					
Pushpakumara	12.2	3	43	2	(1)	17	2	54	1
De Silva	7	1	33	0	(2)	23	4	61	2
Muralitharan	32	10	72	4	(3)	37.5	9	73	3
Anurasiri	27	8	65	3	(4)	19	5	41	1
Jayasuriya					(5)	29	8	64	2
ZIMBABWE									
Streak	15	5	28	2		25	6	84	4
Mbangwa	16	4	61	2		14	5	34	1
G.J.Whittall	3	0	18	0	(5)	7	1	12	0
Strang	18.5	2	77	4		24	4	75	0
A.R.Whittall	20	7	30	1	(3)	43	9	93	0
Goodwin						2	0	4	0

FALL OF WICKETS

	Z	SL	Z	SL
Wkt	1st	1st	2nd	2nd
1st	70	12	22	1
2nd	110	43	34	10
3rd	144	91	104	115
4th	174	91	117	115
5th	201	130	129	137
6th	206	198	204	–
7th	223	213	267	–
8th	240	224	284	–
9th	249	225	286	–
10th	251	–	299	–

Umpires: K.T.Francis (21) and Salim Badar (*Pakistan*) (5).   ‡ (D.R.M.D.Jayawardene)
Referee: R.Subba Row (*England*) (26).   Test No. 1396/7 (SL 81/Z 26)

SRI LANKA v ZIMBABWE 1997-98

SRI LANKA – BATTING AND FIELDING

	M	I	NO	HS	Runs	Avge	100	50	Ct/St
P.A.de Silva	2	4	2	143*	249	124.50	1	1	3
M.S.Atapattu	2	4	1	223	277	92.33	1	–	–
A.Ranatunga	2	3	1	87*	166	83.00	–	2	–
R.S.Kaluwitharana	2	3	–	51	84	28.00	–	1	6
W.P.U.C.J.Vaas	2	1	–	26	26	26.00	–	–	–
S.T.Jayasuriya	2	4	–	68	79	19.75	–	–	–
H.P.Tillekeratne	2	3	–	44	51	17.00	–	–	1
M.Muralitharan	2	2	–	17	28	14.00	–	–	–
R.S.Mahanama	2	4	–	8	15	3.75	–	–	3
K.R.Pushpakumara	2	2	1	2*	3	3.00	–	–	–

Played in one Test: S.D.Anurasiri 3* (1 ct); K.J.Silva did not bat.

SRI LANKA – BOWLING

	O	M	R	W	Avge	Best	5wI	10wM
M.Muralitharan	141.5	49	262	17	15.41	7-94	2	1
K.J.Silva	30.4	11	62	3	20.66	3-27	–	–
S.D.Anurasiri	46	12	106	4	26.50	3-65	–	–
W.P.U.C.J.Vaas	53	8	136	4	34.00	2-35	–	–
K.R.Pushpakumara	62.2	12	195	5	39.00	2-43	–	–
P.A.de Silva	48	10	131	3	43.66	2-61	–	–

Also bowled: M.S.Atapattu 1-0-1-0; S.T.Jayasuriya 46-10-102-2.

ZIMBABWE – BATTING AND FIELDING

	M	I	NO	HS	Runs	Avge	100	50	Ct/St
A.Flower	2	4	1	105*	188	62.66	1	1	5
M.W.Goodwin	2	4	–	73	184	46.00	–	2	–
G.J.Rennie	2	4	–	53	139	34.75	–	2	2
G.W.Flower	2	4	–	52	135	33.75	–	1	–
A.D.R.Campbell	2	4	–	44	128	32.00	–	–	3
P.A.Strang	2	4	–	35	76	19.00	–	–	–
A.R.Whittall	2	4	2	14	23	11.50	–	–	3
C.B.Wishart	2	4	–	18	23	5.75	–	–	–
H.H.Streak	2	4	–	13	22	5.50	–	–	2

Played in one Test: A.G.Huckle 0, 0; M.Mbangwa 0, 4; B.C.Strang 2, 15* (1 ct); G.J.Whittall 11, 17 (1 ct).

ZIMBABWE – BOWLING

	O	M	R	W	Avge	Best	5wI	10wM
H.H.Streak	75	22	212	10	21.20	4-84	–	–
M.Mbangwa	30	9	95	3	31.66	2-61	–	–
P.A.Strang	78.2	16	275	7	39.28	4-77	–	–
A.R.Whittall	93	19	196	4	49.00	3-73	–	–

Also bowled: M.W.Goodwin 4.5-2-11-0; A.G.Huckle 21-2-88-1; B.C.Strang 30.5-7-84-0; G.J.Whittall 10-1-30-0.

WEST INDIES v ENGLAND (1st Test)

At Sabina Park, Kingston, Jamaica on 29 January 1998.
Toss: England. Result: **MATCH DRAWN** (Abandoned – dangerous pitch).
Debuts: West Indies – N.A.M.McLean.

ENGLAND

*M.A.Atherton	c Campbell b Walsh	2
†A.J.Stewart	not out	9
M.A.Butcher	c S.C.Williams b Walsh	0
N.Hussain	c Hooper b Ambrose	1
G.P.Thorpe	not out	0
J.P.Crawley		
A.J.Hollioake		
A.R.Caddick		
D.W.Headley		
A.R.C.Fraser		
P.C.R.Tufnell		
Extras	(B 4, NB 1)	5
Total	(3 wickets)	**17**

WEST INDIES

S.L.Campbell
S.C.Williams
*B.C.Lara
S.Chanderpaul
C.L.Hooper
J.C.Adams
†D.Williams
N.A.M.McLean
I.R.Bishop
C.E.L.Ambrose
C.A.Walsh

WEST INDIES	O	M	R	W
Walsh	5.1	1	10	2
Ambrose	5	3	3	1

FALL OF WICKETS
E
Wkt 1st
1st   4
2nd   4
3rd   9
4th   –
5th   –
6th   –
7th   –
8th   –
9th   –
10th –

Umpires: S.A.Bucknor (34) and S.Venkataraghavan (*India*) (24).
Referee: B.N.Jarman (*Australia*) (9).   **Test No. 1397/116 (WI 338/E 741)**

WEST INDIES v ENGLAND (2nd Test)

At Queen's Park Oval, Port of Spain, Trinidad on 5, 6, 7, 8, 9 February 1998.
Toss: England. Result: **WEST INDIES** won by 3 wickets.
Debuts: None.

ENGLAND

*M.A.Atherton	c Lara b Ambrose	11	b Walsh		31
A.J.Stewart	lbw b Benjamin	50	c Hooper b McLean		73
J.P.Crawley	c S.C.Williams b Ambrose	17	lbw b McLean		22
N.Hussain	not out	61	c and b Walsh		23
G.P.Thorpe	c D.Williams b Hooper	8	c Lara b Walsh		39
A.J.Hollioake	run out	2	c Lara b Ambrose		12
†R.C.Russell	c S.C.Williams b McLean	0	lbw b Ambrose		8
A.R.Caddick	lbw b Walsh	8	c D.Williams b Ambrose		0
D.W.Headley	c D.Williams b Ambrose	11	not out		8
A.R.C.Fraser	c D.Williams b Benjamin	17	c Hooper b Ambrose		4
P.C.R.Tufnell	c Lara b Benjamin	0	c D.Williams b Ambrose		6
Extras	(B 6, LB 10, NB 13)	29	(B 5, LB 15, W 1, NB 11)		32
Total		**214**			**258**

WEST INDIES

S.L.Campbell	c Russell b Headley	1	c Stewart b Headley		10
S.C.Williams	c Atherton b Fraser	19	c Crawley b Fraser		62
*B.C.Lara	c Atherton b Fraser	55	c Russell b Fraser		17
C.L.Hooper	b Fraser	1	not out		94
S.Chanderpaul	c Thorpe b Fraser	34	c Thorpe b Tufnell		0
J.C.Adams	lbw b Fraser	1	c Stewart b Fraser		2
†D.Williams	lbw b Tufnell	16	c Thorpe b Headley		65
C.E.L.Ambrose	c and b Fraser	31	c Russell b Headley		1
K.C.G.Benjamin	b Fraser	0	not out		6
N.A.M.McLean	c Caddick b Fraser	2			
C.A.Walsh	not out	0			
Extras	(B 12, LB 5, NB 14)	31	(B 10, LB 8, NB 7)		25
Total		**191**	(7 wickets)		**282**

WEST INDIES	O	M	R	W		O	M	R	W		FALL OF WICKETS			
Walsh	27	7	55	1	(4)	29	5	67	3			E	WI	E	WI
Ambrose	26	16	23	3	(3)	19.5	3	52	5		*Wkt*	*1st*	*1st*	*2nd*	*2nd*
McLean	19	7	28	1	(2)	12	1	46	2		1st	26	16	91	10
Benjamin	24	5	68	2	(1)	15	3	40	0		2nd	87	42	143	68
Hooper	9	3	14	1		19	8	33	0		3rd	105	48	148	120
Adams	3	0	8	0							4th	114	126	202	121
Chanderpaul	1	0	2	0							5th	124	134	228	141
											6th	126	135	238	253
ENGLAND											7th	143	167	239	259
Headley	22	6	47	1		16	2	68	3		8th	172	177	239	–
Caddick	14	4	41	0		16	2	58	0		9th	214	190	246	–
Fraser	16.1	2	53	8	(4)	27	8	57	3		10th	214	191	258	–
Tufnell	21	8	33	1	(3)	34.2	9	69	1						
Hollioake						5	0	12	0						

Umpires: S.A.Bucknor (35) and S.Venkataraghavan (*India*) (25).
Referee: B.N.Jarman (*Australia*) (10). **Test No. 1398/117 (WI 339/E 742)**

WEST INDIES v ENGLAND (3rd Test)

At Queen's Park Oval, Port of Spain, Trinidad on 13, 14, 15, 16, 17 February 1998.
Toss: England. Result: **ENGLAND** won by 3 wickets.
Debuts: None.

WEST INDIES

S.L.Campbell	c Thorpe b Fraser	28		lbw b Fraser	13
S.C.Williams	c Thorpe b Caddick	24		c Atherton b Caddick	23
*B.C.Lara	c Russell b Fraser	42		lbw b Fraser	47
C.L.Hooper	c Butcher b Fraser	1	(5)	lbw b Headley	5
S.Chanderpaul	lbw b Fraser	28	(6)	c Russell b Headley	39
J.C.Adams	c Atherton b Caddick	11	(7)	c Atherton b Fraser	53
†D.Williams	b Caddick	0	(8)	lbw b Headley	0
C.E.L.Ambrose	b Caddick	4	(9)	b Headley	0
K.C.G.Benjamin	lbw b Caddick	0	(4)	c Russell b Fraser	1
N.A.M.McLean	c Headley b Fraser	11		c Stewart b Caddick	2
C.A.Walsh	not out	5		not out	1
Extras	(NB 5)	5		(LB 16, NB 10)	26
Total		**159**			**210**

ENGLAND

*M.A.Atherton	lbw b Ambrose	2		c D.Williams b Walsh	49
A.J.Stewart	c D.Williams b Hooper	44		c D.Williams b Walsh	83
J.P.Crawley	b Ambrose	1		run out	5
D.W.Headley	b Ambrose	0	(9)	not out	7
N.Hussain	c D.Williams b Walsh	0	(4)	lbw b Hooper	5
G.P.Thorpe	c D.Williams b Hooper	32	(5)	c D.Williams b Ambrose	19
M.A.Butcher	c and b Adams	28	(6)	not out	24
†R.C.Russell	not out	20	(7)	c Hooper b Ambrose	4
A.R.Caddick	run out	5	(8)	c D.Williams b Ambrose	0
A.R.C.Fraser	c and b Ambrose	5			
P.C.R.Tufnell	lbw b Ambrose	0			
Extras	(B 1, LB 4, NB 7)	12		(B 2, LB 15, NB 12)	29
Total		**145**		(7 wickets)	**225**

ENGLAND	O	M	R	W		O	M	R	W
Headley	14	0	40	0	(3)	26	3	77	4
Caddick	22	7	67	5	(1)	19	6	64	2
Fraser	20.4	8	40	5	(2)	25.3	11	40	4
Tufnell	9	5	11	0		15	6	13	0
Butcher	2	1	1	0					
WEST INDIES									
Walsh	17	4	35	1		38	11	69	2
Ambrose	15.4	5	25	5		33	6	62	3
McLean	9	2	23	0	(4)	4	0	17	0
Benjamin	13	3	34	0	(3)	11	3	24	0
Hooper	15	3	23	2	(6)	16	3	31	1
Adams	2	2	0	1	(5)	2	3	5	0

FALL OF WICKETS

Wkt	1st	1st	2nd	2nd
	WI	E	WI	E
1st	36	5	27	129
2nd	93	15	66	145
3rd	95	22	82	152
4th	100	27	92	168
5th	132	71	102	201
6th	132	101	158	213
7th	140	134	159	213
8th	140	135	159	–
9th	150	145	189	–
10th	159	145	210	–

Umpires: D.B.Hair (*Australia*) (23) and E.A.Nicholls (2).
Referee: B.N.Jarman (*Australia*) (11). **Test No. 1399/118 (WI 340/E 743)**

WEST INDIES v ENGLAND (4th Test)

At Bourda, Georgetown, Guyana on 27, 28 February, 1, 2 March 1998.
Toss: West Indies. Result: **WEST INDIES** won by 242 runs.
Debuts: West Indies – D.Ramnarine.

WEST INDIES

S.L.Campbell	c Russell b Headley	10	c Ramprakash b Fraser	17
S.C.Williams	c Thorpe b Fraser	13	c Stewart b Headley	0
*B.C.Lara	c Thorpe b Croft	93	c Butcher b Tufnell	30
S.Chanderpaul	c Thorpe b Fraser	118	run out	0
C.L.Hooper	c Hussain b Headley	43	lbw b Headley	34
J.C.Adams	lbw b Tufnell	28	lbw b Croft	18
†D.Williams	c Croft b Headley	0	c Tufnell b Ramprakash	15
I.R.Bishop	c Butcher b Croft	14	not out	44
C.E.L.Ambrose	c Headley b Tufnell	0	lbw b Croft	2
C.A.Walsh	not out	3	c Russell b Croft	0
D.Ramnarine	c Russell b Croft	0	c Russell b Headley	19
Extras	(B 4, LB 14, NB 12)	30	(B 1, LB 11, NB 6)	18
Total		**352**		**197**

ENGLAND

*M.A.Atherton	c Lara b Ambrose	0	lbw b Ambrose	1
A.J.Stewart	c D.Williams b Walsh	20	lbw b Walsh	12
M.A.Butcher	lbw b Bishop	11	lbw b Hooper	17
N.Hussain	lbw b Walsh	11	c Adams b Walsh	0
G.P.Thorpe	c D.Williams b Ramnarine	10	c Ramnarine b Ambrose	3
M.R.Ramprakash	not out	64	c D.Williams b Walsh	34
†R.C.Russell	lbw b Ramnarine	0	c Lara b Ambrose	17
R.D.B.Croft	c Lara b Hooper	26	c D.Williams b Hooper	14
D.W.Headley	c D.Williams b Hooper	0	c Chanderpaul b Ambrose	9
A.R.C.Fraser	c Lara b Ramnarine	0	c Walsh b Hooper	2
P.C.R.Tufnell	c Bishop b Ambrose	2	not out	0
Extras	(B 10, LB 2, NB 14)	26	(B 9, LB 2, W 1, NB 16)	28
Total		**170**		**137**

ENGLAND	O	M	R	W		O	M	R	W
Headley	31	7	90	3	(2)	13	5	37	3
Fraser	33	8	77	2	(1)	11	2	24	1
Butcher	3	0	15	0					
Croft	36.1	9	89	3	(3)	22	9	50	3
Tufnell	25	10	63	2	(4)	24	5	72	1
Ramprakash					(5)	2	1	2	1
WEST INDIES									
Walsh	27	7	47	2	(2)	15	4	25	3
Ambrose	12.1	5	21	2	(1)	14.1	3	38	4
Ramnarine	17	8	26	3	(5)	11	5	23	0
Bishop	13	4	34	1		3	1	4	0
Adams	3	2	1	0	(6)	1	0	5	0
Hooper	5	1	29	2	(3)	18	8	31	3

FALL OF WICKETS

	WI	E	WI	E
Wkt	1st	1st	2nd	2nd
1st	16	1	4	6
2nd	38	37	32	22
3rd	197	41	32	22
4th	295	65	75	28
5th	316	73	93	58
6th	320	75	123	90
7th	347	139	123	118
8th	349	139	127	125
9th	352	140	127	135
10th	352	170	197	137

Umpires: S.A.Bucknor (36) and D.B.Hair (*Australia*) (24).
Referee: B.N.Jarman (*Australia*) (12). **Test No. 1400/119 (WI 341/E 744)**

WEST INDIES v ENGLAND (5th Test)

At Kensington Oval, Bridgetown, Barbados on 12, 13, 14, 15, 16 March 1998.
Toss: West Indies. **MATCH DRAWN**.
Debuts: None.

ENGLAND

*M.A.Atherton	c Ambrose b Walsh	11	c Williams b Bishop		64
A.J.Stewart	c Williams b Walsh	12	c Lara b Bishop		48
M.A.Butcher	c Hooper b Ambrose	19	c Lambert b Ambrose		26
N.Hussain	c Lara b McLean	5	not out		46
G.P.Thorpe	c Lara b Hooper	103	not out		36
M.R.Ramprakash	c and b McLean	154			
†R.C.Russell	c Wallace b Hooper	32			
D.W.Headley	c Holder b Hooper	31			
A.R.Caddick	c Chanderpaul b Hooper	3			
A.R.C.Fraser	c Walsh b Hooper	3			
P.C.R.Tufnell	not out	1			
Extras	(LB 10, W 2, NB 17)	29	(B 1, LB 6, NB 6)		13
Total		**403**	(3 wickets declared)		**233**

WEST INDIES

C.B.Lambert	c Russell b Caddick	55	c Headley b Fraser		29
P.A.Wallace	lbw b Headley	45	lbw b Caddick		61
I.R.Bishop	c Russell b Tufnell	4			
*B.C.Lara	c Butcher b Headley	31	(3) not out		13
S.Chanderpaul	c Stewart b Fraser	45	(4) not out		3
R.I.C.Holder	b Ramprakash	10			
C.L.Hooper	lbw b Fraser	9			
†D.Williams	c Ramprakash b Caddick	2			
N.A.M.McLean	not out	7			
C.E.L.Ambrose	st Russell b Tufnell	26			
C.A.Walsh	c and b Headley	6			
Extras	(B 13, LB 2, NB 7)	22	(B 1, LB 5)		6
Total		**262**	(2 wickets)		**112**

WEST INDIES	O	M	R	W		O	M	R	W
Walsh	34	8	84	2		12	1	40	0
Ambrose	31	6	62	1		12	4	48	1
McLean	27	5	73	2	(6)	7	0	16	0
Hooper	37.5	7	80	5	(3)	21	5	58	0
Bishop	20	1	74	0	(4)	14	1	51	2
Chanderpaul	4	0	20	0	(5)	3	1	13	0
ENGLAND									
Headley	17.3	1	64	3	(2)	2	0	14	0
Fraser	22	5	80	2	(4)	11	3	33	1
Caddick	17	8	28	2	(1)	6	1	19	1
Tufnell	33	15	43	3	(3)	16.3	1	37	0
Ramprakash	18	7	32	1		2	1	3	0

FALL OF WICKETS

	E	WI	E	WI
Wkt	1st	1st	2nd	2nd
1st	23	82	101	72
2nd	24	91	128	108
3rd	33	134	173	–
4th	53	164	–	–
5th	131	190	–	–
6th	336	214	–	–
7th	382	221	–	–
8th	392	221	–	–
9th	402	255	–	–
10th	403	262	–	–

Umpires: C.J.Mitchley (*South Africa*) (23) and E.A.Nicholls (3).
Referee: B.N.Jarman (*Australia*) (13).   **Test No. 1401/120 (WI 342/E 745)**

WEST INDIES v ENGLAND (6th Test)

At Recreation Ground, St John's, Antigua on 20, 21, 22, 23, 24 March 1998.
Toss: West Indies. **WEST INDIES** won by an innings and 52 runs.
Debuts: None.

ENGLAND

*M.A.Atherton	c Ramnarine b Ambrose	15		lbw b Ambrose	13
A.J.Stewart	b Rose	22		c Wallace b Hooper	79
M.A.Butcher	c Lara b Ambrose	0		c Murray b Ambrose	0
D.W.Headley	c Lara b Ambrose	1	(8)	c Murray b Ramnarine	1
N.Hussain	c Holder b Ramnarine	37	(4)	run out	106
G.P.Thorpe	lbw b Ramnarine	5	(5)	not out	84
M.R.Ramprakash	c Chanderpaul b Walsh	14	(6)	b Ramnarine	0
†R.C.Russell	c Lambert b Ramnarine	0	(7)	lbw b Walsh	9
A.R.Caddick	c Walsh b Ramnarine	8		c Murray b Walsh	0
A.R.C.Fraser	b Walsh	9		c Chanderpaul b Walsh	4
P.C.R.Tufnell	not out	2		c Lambert b Walsh	0
Extras	(B 1, LB 2, NB 11)	14		(B 6, LB 4, W 1, NB 14)	25
Total		**127**			**321**

WEST INDIES

C.B.Lambert	c Thorpe b Ramprakash	104
P.A.Wallace	b Headley	92
*B.C.Lara	c Stewart b Caddick	89
S.Chanderpaul	lbw b Fraser	5
C.L.Hooper	not out	108
R.I.C.Holder	c and b Caddick	45
†J.R.Murray	c Hussain b Headley	4
F.A.Rose	lbw b Caddick	2
C.E.L.Ambrose	not out	19
D.Ramnarine		
C.A.Walsh		
Extras	(LB 14, NB 18)	32
Total	**(7 wickets declared)**	**500**

WEST INDIES	O	M	R	W		O	M	R	W
Walsh	25.5	8	52	2		31.2	7	80	4
Ambrose	17	6	28	3		20	5	66	2
Ramnarine	17	5	29	4	(4)	46	19	70	2
Hooper	1	1	0	0	(5)	39	18	56	1
Rose	9	4	14	1	(3)	11	2	39	0
Lambert	1	0	1	0					
ENGLAND									
Caddick	26	3	111	3					
Fraser	21	3	88	1					
Headley	30	4	109	2					
Tufnell	35	6	97	0					
Ramprakash	19	0	81	1					

FALL OF WICKETS

	E	WI	E
Wkt	1st	1st	2nd
1st	27	167	45
2nd	27	300	49
3rd	38	317	127
4th	57	324	295
5th	66	451	300
6th	105	458	312
7th	105	465	313
8th	105	–	316
9th	117	–	320
10th	127	–	321

Umpires: S.A.Bucknor (37) and C.J.Mitchley (*South Africa*) (24).
Referee: B.N.Jarman (*Australia*) (14).   **Test No. 1402/121 (WI 343/E 746)**

WEST INDIES v ENGLAND 1997-98

WEST INDIES – BATTING AND FIELDING

	M	I	NO	HS	Runs	Avge	100	50	Ct/St
P.A.Wallace	2	3	–	92	198	66.00	–	2	2
C.B.Lambert	2	3	–	104	188	62.66	1	1	3
B.C.Lara	6	9	1	93	417	52.12	–	3	13
C.L.Hooper	6	8	2	108*	295	49.16	1	1	5
S.Chanderpaul	6	9	1	118	272	34.00	1	–	4
I.R.Bishop	3	3	1	44*	62	31.00	–	–	1
R.I.C.Holder	2	2	–	45	55	27.50	–	–	2
S.C.Williams	4	6	–	62	141	23.50	–	1	3
J.C.Adams	4	6	–	53	113	18.83	–	1	2
D.Williams	5	7	–	65	98	14.00	–	–	19
S.L.Campbell	4	6	–	28	79	13.16	–	–	1
C.E.L.Ambrose	6	8	1	31	83	11.85	–	–	2
D.Ramnarine	2	2	–	19	19	9.50	–	–	2
C.A.Walsh	6	6	4	6	15	7.50	–	–	4
N.A.M.McLean	4	4	1	11	22	7.33	–	–	1
K.C.G.Benjamin	2	4	1	6*	7	2.33	–	–	–

Played in one Test: J.R.Murray 4 (3 ct); F.A.Rose 2.

WEST INDIES – BOWLING

	O	M	R	W	Avge	Best	5wI	10wM
C.E.L.Ambrose	205.5	62	428	30	14.26	5-25	2	–
D.Ramnarine	91	37	148	9	16.44	4-29	–	–
C.L.Hooper	190.5	61	355	15	23.66	5-80	1	–
C.A.Walsh	261.2	63	564	22	25.63	4-80	–	–
N.A.M.McLean	78	15	203	5	40.60	2-46	–	–

Also bowled: J.C.Adams 15-7-19-1; K.C.G.Benjamin 63-14-166-3; I.R.Bishop 50-7-163-3; S.Chanderpaul 10-3-35-0; C.B.Lambert 1-0-1-0; F.A.Rose 20-6-53-1.

ENGLAND – BATTING AND FIELDING

	M	I	NO	HS	Runs	Avge	100	50	Ct/St
M.R.Ramprakash	3	5	1	154	266	66.50	1	1	2
A.J.Stewart	6	11	1	83	452	45.20	–	4	6
G.P.Thorpe	6	11	3	103	339	42.37	1	1	9
N.Hussain	6	11	2	106	295	32.77	1	1	2
M.A.Atherton	6	11	–	64	199	18.09	–	1	5
M.A.Butcher	5	9	1	28	125	15.62	–	–	4
R.C.Russell	5	9	1	32	90	11.25	–	–	12/1
J.P.Crawley	3	4	–	22	45	11.25	–	–	1
D.W.Headley	6	9	2	31	69	9.85	–	–	4
A.J.Hollioake	2	2	–	12	14	7.00	–	–	–
A.R.C.Fraser	6	8	–	17	44	5.50	–	–	1
A.R.Caddick	5	7	–	8	19	2.71	–	–	2
P.C.R.Tufnell	6	8	3	6	11	2.20	–	–	–

Played in one Test: R.D.B.Croft 26, 14 (1 ct).

ENGLAND – BOWLING

	O	M	R	W	Avge	Best	5wI	10wM
A.R.C.Fraser	187.2	50	492	27	18.22	8-53	2	1
R.D.B.Croft	58.1	18	139	6	23.16	3-50	–	–
D.W.Headley	171.3	28	546	19	28.73	4-77	–	–
A.R.Caddick	120	31	388	13	29.84	5-67	1	–
P.C.R.Tufnell	212.5	67	438	7	62.57	2-43	–	–

Also bowled: M.A.Butcher 5-1-16-0; A.J.Hollioake 5-0-12-0; M.R.Ramprakash 41-9-118-3.

SOUTH AFRICA v PAKISTAN (1st Test)

At The Wanderers, Johannesburg on 14, 15, 16, 17 (*no play*), 18 February 1998.
Toss: Pakistan. Result: **MATCH DRAWN**
Debuts: None.

SOUTH AFRICA

A.M.Bacher	lbw b Waqar	46	(2) not out		20
*G.Kirsten	c Azhar b Waqar	3	(1) not out		20
J.H.Kallis	c Wasim b Shoaib	15			
D.J.Cullinan	b Waqar	16			
A.C.Hudson	b Mushtaq Ahmed	33			
H.H.Gibbs	lbw b Mushtaq Ahmed	4			
S.M.Pollock	c Mushtaq Ahmed b Azhar	21			
†M.V.Boucher	c Wasim b Saqlain	78			
L.Klusener	b Mushtaq Ahmed	6			
P.L.Symcox	c Shoaib b Saqlain	108			
A.A.Donald	not out	0			
Extras	(B 2, LB 21, W 4, NB 7)	34	(LB 4)		4
Total		**364**	(0 wickets)		**44**

PAKISTAN

Saeed Anwar	c Cullinan b Donald	2
*Aamir Sohail	c Boucher b Pollock	12
Ijaz Ahmed	c Pollock b Donald	34
Mohammad Wasim	c Boucher b Klusener	44
Inzamam-ul-Haq	b Klusener	0
†Moin Khan	c Gibbs b Klusener	46
Azhar Mahmood	c Donald b Pollock	136
Saqlain Mushtaq	c Boucher b Kallis	2
Mushtaq Ahmed	c Kirsten b Kallis	10
Waqar Younis	c Hudson b Klusener	10
Shoaib Akhtar	not out	4
Extras	(B 11, LB 7, W 3, NB 8)	29
Total		**329**

PAKISTAN	O	M	R	W	O	M	R	W
Waqar Younis	23	4	80	3	5.3	1	18	0
Shoaib Akhtar	21	1	84	1	5	0	22	0
Azhar Mahmood	20	1	52	1				
Mushtaq Ahmed	27	6	66	3				
Saqlain Mushtaq	12.2	0	47	2				
Aamir Sohail	1	0	12	0				

S AFRICA	O	M	R	W
Donald	23	4	89	2
Pollock	24.1	10	55	2
Klusener	24	6	93	4
Kallis	18	7	58	2
Symcox	5	0	16	0

FALL OF WICKETS

Wkt	SA 1st	P 1st	SA 2nd
1st	14	15	–
2nd	56	15	–
3rd	86	87	–
4th	91	91	–
5th	96	112	–
6th	149	219	–
7th	157	230	–
8th	166	255	–
9th	361	296	–
10th	364	329	–

Umpires: C.J.Mitchley (22) and P.Willey (*England*) (9).
Referee: J.R.Reid (*New Zealand*) (32). **Test No. 1403/5 (SA 216/P 244)**

SOUTH AFRICA v PAKISTAN (2nd Test)

At Kingsmead, Durban on 26, 27, 28 February, 1, 2 March 1998.
Toss: South Africa. Result: **PAKISTAN** won by 29 runs.
Debuts: South Africa – H.D.Ackerman; Pakistan – Fazal-e-Akber, Yousuf Youhana.

PAKISTAN

Saeed Anwar	lbw b Donald	43	lbw b Pollock	118
*Aamir Sohail	c Boucher b Pollock	17	c Boucher b Donald	36
Ijaz Ahmed	c De Villiers b Pollock	2	b De Villiers	24
Mohammad Wasim	c Kallis b Donald	12	run out	5
Yousuf Youhana	c Boucher b Donald	5	c Boucher b Pollock	1
†Moin Khan	c Donald b De Villiers	25	lbw b Pollock	5
Azhar Mahmood	b Donald	132	c Boucher b Pollock	1
Mushtaq Ahmed	c Kallis b Klusener	2	run out	20
Waqar Younis	c Hudson b Donald	6	c Klusener b Pollock	0
Shoaib Akhtar	c Boucher b Klusener	6	not out	1
Fazal-e-Akber	not out	0	c Klusener b Pollock	0
Extras	(B 2, LB 1, W 2, NB 4)	9	(LB 7, W 2, NB 6)	15
Total		**259**		**226**

SOUTH AFRICA

A.M.Bacher	c Moin b Fazal	17	(2) lbw b Fazal	0
G.Kirsten	c Azhar b Fazal	0	(1) c sub (Rashid Latif) b Mushtaq	25
J.H.Kallis	b Shoaib	43	c Moin b Mushtaq	22
H.D.Ackerman	c Mohammad Wasim b Mushtaq	57	lbw b Mushtaq	11
A.C.Hudson	lbw b Shoaib	0	c Fazal b Mushtaq	8
*W.J.Cronje	lbw b Mushtaq	3	c Moin b Waqar	11
S.M.Pollock	not out	70	st Moin b Mushtaq	30
†M.V.Boucher	b Shoaib	2	b Waqar	52
L.Klusener	b Shoaib	6	lbw b Mushtaq	2
P.S.de Villiers	b Shoaib	7	not out	46
A.A.Donald	lbw b Mushtaq	11	lbw b Waqar	0
Extras	(B 4, LB 2, W 3, NB 6)	15	(LB 15, NB 3)	18
Total		**231**		**225**

S AFRICA	O	M	R	W		O	M	R	W
Donald	19.2	4	79	5	(2)	10	2	20	1
De Villiers	18	5	55	1	(1)	16	1	51	1
Pollock	18	3	55	2		22.3	6	50	6
Klusener	18	3	67	2		9	1	32	0
Cronje						5	0	20	0
Kallis						17	1	46	0
PAKISTAN									
Waqar Younis	19	3	63	0		17.2	2	60	3
Fazal-e-Akber	8	2	16	2		5	2	16	1
Shoaib Akhtar	12	1	43	5		11	0	20	0
Mushtaq Ahmed	24	9	71	3		37	13	78	6
Azhar Mahmood	17	6	28	0		11	4	12	0
Aamir Sohail						1	1	24	0

FALL OF WICKETS				
	P	SA	P	SA
Wkt	1st	1st	2nd	2nd
1st	35	4	101	2
2nd	37	32	159	42
3rd	70	115	164	49
4th	82	115	182	76
5th	89	120	198	79
6th	127	139	203	110
7th	142	154	212	120
8th	153	166	220	153
9th	233	178	226	219
10th	259	231	226	225

Umpires: M.J.Kitchen (*England*) (17) and D.L.Orchard (5).
Referee: J.R.Reid (*New Zealand*) (33).   Test No. 1404/6 (SA 217/P 245)

SOUTH AFRICA v PAKISTAN (3rd Test)

At St.George's Park, Port Elizabeth on 6, 7 (*no play*), 8, 9, 10 March 1998.
Toss: Pakistan. Result: **SOUTH AFRICA** won by 259 runs.
Debuts: None.

SOUTH AFRICA

A.M.Bacher	lbw b Waqar	3	(2) c Rashid b Waqar		11
G.Kirsten	b Waqar	38	(1) c Rashid b Azhar		44
J.H.Kallis	b Waqar	10	c Rashid b Azhar		69
H.D.Ackerman	b Waqar	11	c Inzamam b Azhar		42
A.C.Hudson	c Moin b Mushtaq	42	b Waqar		4
*W.J.Cronje	lbw b Waqar	85	not out		7
S.M.Pollock	c Azhar b Wasim	38	b Waqar		7
†M.V.Boucher	c Rashid b Wasim	52	b Waqar		4
P.S.de Villiers	c Azhar b Waqar	1			
A.A.Donald	lbw b Wasim	1			
P.R.Adams	not out	2			
Extras	(LB 3, NB 7)	10	(B 1, LB 6, W 1, NB 10)		18
Total		**293**	(7 wickets declared)		**206**

PAKISTAN

Saeed Anwar	c Boucher b Donald	18	c Kallis b Donald		55
Aamir Sohail	c Hudson b Donald	3	(7) lbw b Adams		7
Ijaz Ahmed	c Boucher b Donald	0	(2) lbw b De Villiers		15
Inzamam-ul-Haq	c Boucher b Donald	6	(3) st Boucher b Adams		4
Moin Khan	c Boucher b De Villiers	17	lbw b Donald		1
Azhar Mahmood	c Adams b De Villiers	17	c Kirsten b Donald		41
Wasim Akram	not out	30	(5) c Boucher b Pollock		5
*†Rashid Latif	lbw b De Villiers	0	c Kallis b Adams		0
Waqar Younis	c Kirsten b De Villiers	7	c Boucher b Donald		3
Shoaib Akhtar	c Boucher b De Villiers	0	b De Villiers		2
Mushtaq Ahmed	c Boucher b De Villiers	5	not out		1
Extras	(LB 3)	3			0
Total		**106**			**134**

PAKISTAN	O	M	R	W		O	M	R	W
Wasim Akram	26	8	70	3		16	3	37	0
Waqar Younis	23	6	78	6		17.4	4	55	4
Azhar Mahmood	21	7	47	0	(4)	15	1	49	3
Shoaib Akhtar	13	4	30	0	(3)	16	1	58	0
Mushtaq Ahmed	16	1	65	1					
Aamir Sohail					(5)	1	1	0	0
S AFRICA									
Donald	13	3	47	4		15	4	27	4
Pollock	16	5	33	0		17	2	46	1
De Villiers	11.5	5	23	6		12.5	4	25	2
Adams						16	8	36	3

FALL OF WICKETS

	SA	P	SA	P
Wkt	1st	1st	2nd	2nd
1st	3	21	17	36
2nd	13	21	92	67
3rd	36	26	170	70
4th	81	29	185	75
5th	122	61	187	81
6th	200	62	198	93
7th	257	62	206	101
8th	263	84	–	120
9th	269	84	–	133
10th	293	106	–	134

Umpires: R.S.Dunne (*New Zealand*) (27) and R.E.Koertzen (5).
Referee: J.R.Reid (*New Zealand*) (34). **Test No. 1405/7 (SA 218/P 246)**

SOUTH AFRICA v PAKISTAN 1997-98

SOUTH AFRICA – BATTING AND FIELDING

	M	I	NO	HS	Runs	Avge	100	50	Ct/St
S.M.Pollock	3	5	–	70*	166	41.50	–	1	1
M.V.Boucher	3	5	–	78	188	37.60	–	3	17/1
W.J.Cronje	2	4	1	85	106	35.33	–	1	–
J.H.Kallis	3	5	–	69	159	31.80	–	1	4
H.D.Ackerman	2	4	–	57	121	30.25	–	1	–
P.S.de Villiers	2	3	1	46*	54	27.00	–	–	1
G.Kirsten	3	6	1	44	130	26.00	–	–	3
A.M.Bacher	3	6	–	46	97	19.40	–	–	–
A.C.Hudson	3	5	–	42	87	17.40	–	–	3
L.Klusener	2	3	–	6	14	4.66	–	–	2
A.A.Donald	3	4	1	11	12	4.00	–	–	2

Played in one Test: P.R.Adams 2* (1 ct); D.J.Cullinan 16 (1 ct); H.H.Gibbs 4 (1 ct); P.L.Symcox 108.

SOUTH AFRICA – BOWLING

	O	M	R	W	Avge	Best	5wI	10wM
P.R.Adams	16	8	36	3	12.00	3-36	–	–
P.S.de Villiers	58.4	15	154	10	15.40	6-23	1	–
A.A.Donald	80.2	17	262	16	16.37	5-79	1	–
S.M.Pollock	97.4	26	239	11	21.72	6-50	1	–
L.Klusener	51	10	192	6	32.00	4-93	–	–

Also bowled: W.J.Cronje 5-0-20-0; J.H.Kallis 35-8-104-2; P.L.Symcox 5-0-16-0.

PAKISTAN – BATTING AND FIELDING

	M	I	NO	HS	Runs	Avge	100	50	Ct/St
Azhar Mahmood	3	5	–	136	327	65.40	2	–	4
Saeed Anwar	3	5	–	118	236	47.20	1	1	–
Mohammad Wasim	2	3	–	44	61	20.33	–	–	3
Moin Khan	3	5	–	46	94	18.80	–	–	4/1
Aamir Sohail	3	5	–	36	75	15.00	–	–	–
Ijaz Ahmed	3	5	–	34	75	15.00	–	–	–
Mushtaq Ahmed	3	5	–	20	38	9.50	–	–	1
Waqar Younis	3	5	–	10	26	5.20	–	–	–
Shoaib Akhtar	3	5	2	6	13	4.33	–	–	1
Inzamam-ul-Haq	3	3	–	6	10	3.33	–	–	1

Played in one Test: Fazal-e-Akber 0*, 0 (1 ct); Rashid Latif 0, 0 (4 ct); Saqlain Mushtaq 2; Wasim Akram 30*, 5; Yousuf Youhana 5, 1.

PAKISTAN – BOWLING

	O	M	R	W	Avge	Best	5wI	10wM
Fazal-e-Akber	13	4	32	3	10.66	2-16	–	–
Mushtaq Ahmed	112	29	280	13	21.53	6-78	1	–
Waqar Younis	105.3	20	354	16	22.12	6-78	1	1
Wasim Akram	42	11	107	3	35.66	3-70	–	–
Shoaib Akhtar	78	7	257	6	42.83	5-43	1	–
Azhar Mahmood	84	19	188	4	47.00	3-49	–	–

Also bowled: Aamir Sohail 11-2-40-0; Saqlain Mushtaq 12.2-0-47-2.

NEW ZEALAND v ZIMBABWE (1st Test)

At Basin Reserve, Wellington on 19, 20, 21, 22 February 1998.
Toss: Zimbabwe. Result: **NEW ZEALAND** won by 10 wickets.
Debuts: None.

ZIMBABWE

G.J.Rennie	b Doull	13		lbw b Doull	15
G.W.Flower	b Nash	38		c and b Vettori	4
M.W.Goodwin	b Vettori	8	(4)	c Fleming b Cairns	72
G.J.Whittall	c Parore b O'Connor	6	(5)	c Astle b Nash	22
†A.Flower	c Parore b O'Connor	2	(6)	c O'Connor b Vettori	6
*A.D.R.Campbell	run out	37	(7)	c Horne b Cairns	56
P.A.Strang	c Young b Doull	1	(8)	b Cairns	0
H.H.Streak	lbw b O'Connor	39	(9)	not out	43
A.R.Whittall	c Parore b Cairns	1	(3)	run out	12
A.G.Huckle	c Parore b O'Connor	19		lbw b Vettori	0
M.Mbangwa	not out	0		lbw b Cairns	0
Extras	(LB 10, NB 6)	16		(B 6, LB 14)	20
Total		**180**			**250**

NEW ZEALAND

B.A.Young	c Strang b Streak	0	(2)	not out	10
M.J.Horne	c A.Flower b Mbangwa	44	(1)	not out	9
†A.C.Parore	c A.Flower b Huckle	78			
*S.P.Fleming	c Campbell b Huckle	36			
N.J.Astle	c A.Flower b Streak	42			
C.D.McMillan	c A.R.Whittall b Huckle	139			
C.L.Cairns	run out	0			
D.J.Nash	b Strang	41			
D.L.Vettori	b Strang	16			
S.B.Doull	c Goodwin b Strang	8			
S.B.O'Connor	not out	2			
Extras	(B 1, LB 4)	5		(LB 1)	1
Total		**411**		(0 wickets)	**20**

N ZEALAND	O	M	R	W		O	M	R	W
Cairns	16	2	50	1		24.3	6	56	4
O'Connor	18.3	7	52	4		14	3	39	0
Doull	17	8	18	2		13	1	47	1
Nash	14	7	11	1	(5)	9	6	10	1
Vettori	20	10	39	1	(4)	41	18	73	3
McMillan						5	1	5	0
ZIMBABWE									
Streak	22	6	74	2		2	0	13	0
Mbangwa	17	4	42	1					
Strang	49.1	13	126	3					
G.J.Whittall	5	2	12	0					
A.R.Whittall	12	0	50	0					
Huckle	40	10	102	3	(2)	1.5	0	6	0

FALL OF WICKETS

Wkt	Z 1st	NZ 1st	Z 2nd	NZ 2nd
1st	30	0	18	–
2nd	53	103	20	–
3rd	64	144	65	–
4th	70	179	110	–
5th	78	240	125	–
6th	89	254	155	–
7th	122	362	155	–
8th	131	388	249	–
9th	171	397	249	–
10th	180	411	250	–

Umpires: R.S.Dunne (26) and S.G.Randell (*Australia*) (34).
Referee: Hanumant Singh (*India*) (3).   **Test No. 1406/7 (NZ 258/Z 27)**

NEW ZEALAND v ZIMBABWE (2nd Test)

At Eden Park, Auckland on 26, 27, 28 February 1998.
Toss: Zimbabwe. Result: **NEW ZEALAND** won by an innings and 13 runs.
Debuts: None.

ZIMBABWE

G.J.Rennie	c Parore b Doull	0	(2) c Fleming b Cairns		0
G.W.Flower	c Parore b Doull	13	(1) c Young b Nash		32
M.W.Goodwin	c Young b Doull	28	c McMillan b Nash		14
*A.D.R.Campbell	c Astle b Doull	11	c Horne b Vettori		22
†A.Flower	c McMillan Nash	65	c Parore b Cairns		83
G.J.Whittall	c Young b Nash	1	lbw b Doull		10
H.H.Streak	c Fleming b Nash	12	lbw b Cairns		24
P.A.Strang	not out	30	not out		67
A.R.Whittall	lbw b Cairns	4	c Parore b Doull		3
A.G.Huckle	lbw b Cairns	0	b Doull		13
M.Mbangwa	b Cairns	0	c Fleming b Doull		0
Extras	(B 1, LB 3, NB 2)	6	(B 1, LB 6, NB 2)		9
Total		**170**			**277**

NEW ZEALAND

B.A.Young	b Streak	1
M.J.Horne	c G.J.Whittall b Mbangwa	157
†A.C.Parore	c A.Flower b Mbangwa	10
*S.P.Fleming	c Huckle b Mbangwa	19
N.J.Astle	c G.W.Flower b Streak	114
C.D.McMillan	c A.Flower b Strang	88
C.L.Cairns	c Strang b Streak	22
D.J.Nash	lbw b Strang	1
M.W.Priest	c Rennie b Strang	16
D.L.Vettori	c Campbell b Strang	0
S.B.Doull	not out	6
Extras	(B 8, LB 17, W 1)	26
Total		**460**

N ZEALAND	O	M	R	W		O	M	R	W
Doull	20	6	35	4		19.4	5	50	4
Cairns	16.5	4	56	3		29	9	81	3
Nash	18	4	41	3		10	5	13	2
Vettori	2	0	15	0		20	5	60	1
Astle	5	1	15	0					
Priest	1	0	4	0	(5)	14	0	51	0
McMillan					(6)	2	0	15	0
ZIMBABWE									
Streak	31	7	105	3					
Mbangwa	27	10	78	3					
G.J.Whittall	14	3	68	0					
Strang	18.1	0	54	4					
A.R.Whittall	11	1	37	0					
Huckle	13	1	66	0					
Goodwin	6	1	27	0					

FALL OF WICKETS

	Z	NZ	Z
Wkt	1st	1st	2nd
1st	1	2	4
2nd	32	40	29
3rd	53	69	71
4th	54	312	71
5th	55	322	90
6th	98	382	156
7th	157	405	227
8th	168	431	234
9th	170	433	277
10th	170	460	277

Umpires: D.B.Cowie (8) and S.G.Randell (*Australia*) (35).
Referee: Hanumant Singh (*India*) (4).   Test No. 1407/8 (NZ 259/Z 28)

NEW ZEALAND v ZIMBABWE 1997-98

NEW ZEALAND – BATTING AND FIELDING

	M	I	NO	HS	Runs	Avge	100	50	Ct/St
C.D.McMillan	2	2	–	139	227	113.50	1	1	2
M.J.Horne	2	3	1	157	210	105.00	1	–	2
N.J.Astle	2	2	–	114	156	78.00	1	–	2
A.C.Parore	2	2	–	78	88	44.00	–	1	8
S.P.Fleming	2	2	–	36	55	27.50	–	–	4
D.J.Nash	2	2	–	41	42	21.00	–	–	–
S.B.Doull	2	2	1	8	14	14.00	–	–	–
C.L.Cairns	2	2	–	22	22	11.00	–	–	–
D.L.Vettori	2	2	–	16	16	8.00	–	–	1
B.A.Young	2	3	1	10*	11	5.50	–	–	4

Played in one Test: S.B.O'Connor 2* (1 ct); M.W.Priest 16.

NEW ZEALAND – BOWLING

	O	M	R	W	Avge	Best	5wI	10wM
D.J.Nash	51	22	75	7	10.71	3-41	–	–
S.B.Doull	69.4	20	150	11	13.63	4-35	–	–
C.L.Cairns	86.2	18	243	11	22.09	4-56	–	–
S.B.O'Connor	32.3	10	91	4	22.75	4-52	–	–
D.L.Vettori	83	33	187	5	37.40	3-73	–	–

Also bowled: N.J.Astle 5-1-15-0; C.D.McMillan 7-1-20-0; M.W.Priest 15-0-55-0.

ZIMBABWE – BATTING AND FIELDING

	M	I	NO	HS	Runs	Avge	100	50	Ct/St
P.A.Strang	2	4	–	67*	98	49.00	–	1	2
H.H.Streak	2	4	1	43*	118	39.33	–	–	–
A.Flower	2	4	–	83	156	39.00	–	2	5
A.D.R.Campbell	2	4	–	56	126	31.50	–	1	2
M.W.Goodwin	2	4	–	72	122	30.50	–	1	1
G.W.Flower	2	4	–	38	87	21.75	–	–	1
G.J.Whittall	2	4	–	22	39	9.75	–	–	1
A.G.Huckle	2	4	–	19	32	8.00	–	–	1
G.J.Rennie	2	4	–	15	28	7.00	–	–	1
A.R.Whittall	2	4	–	12	20	5.00	–	–	1
M.Mbangwa	2	4	1	0*	0	0.00	–	–	–

ZIMBABWE – BOWLING

	O	M	R	W	Avge	Best	5wI	10wM
P.A.Strang	67.2	13	180	7	25.71	4-54	–	–
M.Mbangwa	44	14	120	4	30.00	3-78	–	–
H.H.Streak	55	13	192	5	38.40	3-105	–	–
A.G.Huckle	54.5	11	174	3	58.00	3-102	–	–

Also bowled: M.W.Goodwin 6-1-27-0; A.R.Whittall 23-1-87-0; G.J.Whittall 19-5-80-0.

INDIA v AUSTRALIA (1st Test)

At Chidambaram Stadium, Chepauk, Madras on 6, 7, 8, 9, 10 March 1998.
Toss: India. Result: **INDIA** won by 179 runs.
Debuts: India – Harvinder Singh; Australia – G.R.Robertson.

INDIA

†N.R.Mongia	c Healy b Kasprowicz	58	lbw b Blewett	18
N.S.Sidhu	run out	62	c Ponting b Robertson	64
R.Dravid	c Robertson b Warne	52	c Healy b Warne	56
S.R.Tendulkar	c Taylor b Warne	4	not out	155
*M.Azharuddin	c Reiffel b Warne	26	c S.R.Waugh b M.E.Waugh	64
S.C.Ganguly	lbw b Robertson	3	not out	30
A.Kumble	c S.R.Waugh b Robertson	30		
J.Srinath	c Taylor b Warne	1		
R.K.Chauhan	c Healy b Robertson	3		
Harvinder Singh	not out	0		
S.L.V.Raju	b Robertson	0		
Extras	(B 8, LB 6, NB 4)	18	(B 18, LB 6, NB 7)	31
Total		**257**	(4 wickets declared)	**418**

AUSTRALIA

*M.A.Taylor	c Mongia b Harvinder	12	(2) c Srinath b Kumble	13
M.J.Slater	c Dravid b Kumble	11	(1) b Srinath	13
M.E.Waugh	c Ganguly b Raju	66	(5) c Dravid b Kumble	18
S.R.Waugh	b Kumble	12	(6) c Dravid b Raju	27
R.T.Ponting	c Mongia b Raju	18	(7) lbw b Raju	2
G.S.Blewett	lbw b Chauhan	9	(3) c Dravid b Kumble	5
†I.A.Healy	c Ganguly b Raju	90	(8) not out	32
P.R.Reiffel	c Dravid b Kumble	15	(4) c Azharuddin b Raju	8
S.K.Warne	c Tendulkar b Kumble	17	c Kumble b Chauhan	35
G.R.Robertson	c Mongia b Srinath	57	b Chauhan	0
M.S.Kasprowicz	not out	11	c Srinath b Kumble	4
Extras	(B 1, LB 6, NB 3)	10	(B 4, LB 3, NB 4)	11
Total		**328**		**168**

AUSTRALIA	O	M	R	W		O	M	R	W		FALL OF WICKETS			
											I	A	I	A
Kasprowicz	21	8	44	1		14	6	42	0	Wkt	1st	1st	2nd	2nd
Reiffel	15	4	27	0		9	1	32	0	1st	122	16	43	18
Warne	35	11	85	4	(4) 30	7	122	1		2nd	126	44	115	30
Robertson	28.2	4	72	4	(3) 27	4	92	1		3rd	130	57	228	31
M.E.Waugh	1	0	4	0	(6) 9	0	44	1		4th	186	95	355	54
S.R.Waugh	4	1	11	0		4	0	27	0	5th	195	119	–	79
Blewett					(5) 10	2	35	1		6th	247	137	–	91
INDIA										7th	248	173	–	96
Srinath	17.3	3	46	1		6	4	9	0	8th	253	201	–	153
Harvinder Singh	11	4	28	1		2	0	9	0	9th	257	297	–	153
Kumble	45	10	103	4	(4) 23.5	7	51	4		10th	257	328	–	168
Chauhan	25	3	90	1	(3) 22	6	66	2						
Raju	32	8	54	3		14	2	57	3					

Umpires: G.Sharp (*England*) (6) and S.Venkataraghavan (26).
Referee: P.L.van der Merwe (*South Africa*) (20).   Test No. 1408/52 (I 316/A 579)

INDIA v AUSTRALIA (2nd Test)

At Eden Gardens, Calcutta on 18, 19, 20, 21 March 1998.
Toss: Australia. Result: **INDIA** won by an innings and 219 runs.
Debuts: Australia – P.Wilson.

AUSTRALIA

M.J.Slater	c Dravid b Srinath	0	(2) b Srinath		5
*M.A.Taylor	c Mongia b Ganguly	3	(1) run out		45
G.S.Blewett	b Srinath	0	lbw b Srinath		25
M.E.Waugh	lbw b Srinath	10	c Laxman b Kumble		0
S.R.Waugh	run out	80	(7) lbw b Kumble		33
R.T.Ponting	b Kumble	60	(5) c Srinath b Kumble		9
†I.A.Healy	c Laxman b Kumble	1	(6) lbw b Srinath		38
S.K.Warne	c Azharuddin b Kumble	11	c and b Kumble		0
G.R.Robertson	lbw b Ganguly	29	c Azharuddin b Kumble		0
M.S.Kasprowicz	c Azharuddin b Ganguly	25	c Raju b Chauhan		10
P.Wilson	not out	0	not out		0
Extras	(LB 2, NB 12)	14	(B 1, LB 3, NB 3)		7
Total		**233**			**181**

INDIA

V.V.S Laxman	c Healy b Robertson	95
N.S.Sidhu	lbw b M.E.Waugh	97
R.Dravid	c and b Blewett	86
S.R.Tendulkar	c Blewett b Kasprowicz	79
*M.Azharuddin	not out	163
S.C.Ganguly	c sub ‡ b Robertson	65
†N.R.Mongia	not out	30
A.Kumble		
J.Srinath		
R.K.Chauhan		
S.L.V.Raju		
Extras	(B 2, LB 7, NB 9)	18
Total	(5 wickets declared)	**633**

INDIA	O	M	R	W	O	M	R	W
Srinath	17	0	80	3	19	6	44	3
Ganguly	13.4	5	28	3	4	0	9	0
Kumble	28	11	44	3	31	10	62	5
Tendulkar	2	0	6	0				
Raju	17	2	42	0	16	7	20	0
Chauhan	11	2	30	0	(4) 18.4	4	42	1
Laxman	1	0	1	0				
AUSTRALIA								
Kasprowicz	34	6	122	1				
Wilson	12	2	50	0				
Blewett	20	3	65	1				
Warne	42	4	147	0				
Robertson	33	2	163	2				
M.E.Waugh	18	4	77	1				

FALL OF WICKETS

	A	I	A
Wkt	1st	1st	2nd
1st	0	191	7
2nd	1	207	55
3rd	15	347	56
4th	29	400	81
5th	141	558	91
6th	151	–	133
7th	168	–	158
8th	178	–	158
9th	232	–	181
10th	233	–	181

Umpires: B.C.Cooray (*Sri Lanka*) (14) and K.Parthasarathy (2). ‡ (D.S.Lehmann)
Referee: P.L.van der Merwe (*South Africa*) (21). **Test No. 1409/53 (I 317/A 580)**

INDIA v AUSTRALIA (3rd Test)

At Chinnaswamy Stadium, Bangalore on 25, 26, 27, 28 March 1998.
Toss: India. Result: **AUSTRALIA** won by 8 wickets.
Debuts: India – Harbhajan Singh; Australia – A.C.Dale, D.S.Lehmann.

INDIA

V.V.S Laxman	c Taylor b Kasprowicz	6	c Ponting b Warne	15
N.S.Sidhu	b Warne	74	c Lehmann b Warne	44
R.Dravid	b Warne	23	c Healy b Robertson	6
S.R.Tendulkar	b Dale	177	c and b Kasprowicz	31
*M.Azharuddin	c Healy b Lehmann	40	b Kasprowicz	18
S.C.Ganguly	lbw b Dale	17	b Robertson	16
†N.R.Mongia	c Ponting b Warne	18	not out	12
A.Kumble	c Waugh b Robertson	39	lbw b Robertson	9
Harvinder Singh	lbw b Dale	0	lbw b Kasprowicz	0
S.L.V.Raju	c Lehmann b Robertson	5	b Kasprowicz	2
Harbhajan Singh	not out	4	lbw b Kasprowicz	0
Extras	(B 6, LB 6, NB 9)	21	(B 5, LB 5, NB 6)	16
Total		**424**		**169**

AUSTRALIA

M.J.Slater	c Mongia b Harvinder	91	(2) c Azharuddin b Tendulkar	42
*M.A.Taylor	c Mongia b Kumble	14	(1) not out	102
G.S.Blewett	b Harbhajan	4	lbw b Kumble	5
M.E.Waugh	not out	153	not out	33
D.S.Lehmann	c Laxman b Harbhajan	52		
R.T.Ponting	c Tendulkar b Kumble	16		
†I.A.Healy	c Mongia b Kumble	4		
S.K.Warne	c Harbhajan b Raju	33		
G.R.Robertson	c Azharuddin b Kumble	4		
M.S.Kasprowicz	lbw b Kumble	4		
A.C.Dale	c Laxman b Kumble	5		
Extras	(B 12, LB 5, NB 3)	20	(B 8, LB 5)	13
Total		**400**	(2 wickets)	**195**

AUSTRALIA	O	M	R	W		O	M	R	W	FALL OF WICKETS
Kasprowicz	29	4	76	1		18	5	28	5	I A I A
Dale	23	6	71	3		5	1	21	0	Wkt 1st 1st 2nd 2nd
Warne	35	9	106	3		6	0	80	2	1st 24 68 50 91
Blewett	14	3	50	0	(5)	1	0	2	0	2nd 109 77 61 114
Robertson	11.2	1	58	2	(4)	12	2	28	3	3rd 110 143 92 –
Waugh	4	0	24	0						4th 249 249 111 –
Lehmann	7	1	27	1						5th 294 254 127 –
INDIA										6th 353 286 144 –
Harvinder Singh	7	0	44	1		3	0	17	0	7th 390 350 158 –
Ganguly	2	0	10	0						8th 390 378 159 –
Kumble	41.3	8	98	6	(2)	22.4	5	63	1	9th 415 394 163 –
Raju	37	7	118	1	(3)	15	4	37	0	10th 424 400 169 –
Harbhajan Singh	23	1	112	2	(4)	6	1	24	0	
Laxman	1	0	1	0						
Tendulkar					(5)	11.2	1	41	1	

Umpires: V.K.Ramaswamy (23) and D.R.Shepherd (*England*) (40).
Referee: P.L.van der Merwe (*South Africa*) (22).   **Test No. 1410/54 (I 318/A 581)**

INDIA v AUSTRALIA 1997-98

INDIA – BATTING AND FIELDING

	M	I	NO	HS	Runs	Avge	100	50	Ct/St
S.R.Tendulkar	3	5	1	177	446	111.50	2	1	2
M.Azharuddin	3	5	1	163*	311	77.75	1	1	6
N.S.Sidhu	3	5	–	97	341	68.20	–	4	–
N.R.Mongia	3	5	2	58	136	45.33	–	1	7
R.Dravid	3	5	–	86	223	44.60	–	3	6
V.V.S.Laxman	2	3	–	95	116	38.66	–	1	4
S.C.Ganguly	3	5	1	65	131	32.75	–	1	2
A.Kumble	3	3	–	39	78	26.00	–	–	2
R.K.Chauhan	2	1	–	3	3	3.00	–	–	–
S.L.V.Raju	3	3	–	5	7	2.33	–	–	1
J.Srinath	2	1	–	1	1	1.00	–	–	3
Harvinder Singh	2	3	1	0*	0	0.00	–	–	–

Played in one Test: Harbhajan Singh 4*, 0 (1 ct).

INDIA – BOWLING

	O	M	R	W	Avge	Best	5wI	10wM
S.C.Ganguly	19.4	5	47	3	15.66	3-28	–	–
A.Kumble	192	51	421	23	18.30	6-98	2	–
J.Srinath	59.3	13	179	8	22.37	3-44	–	–
S.L.V.Raju	131	32	297	7	42.42	3-26	–	–
R.K.Chauhan	76.4	15	228	4	57.00	2-66	–	–

Also bowled: Harvinder Singh 23-4-98-2; Harbhajan Singh 29-2-136-2; V.V.S.Laxman 2-0-2-0; S.R.Tendulkar 13.2-1-47-1.

AUSTRALIA – BATTING AND FIELDING

	M	I	NO	HS	Runs	Avge	100	50	Ct/St
M.E.Waugh	3	6	2	153*	280	70.00	1	1	1
I.A.Healy	3	5	1	90	165	41.25	–	1	6
S.R.Waugh	2	4	–	80	152	38.00	–	1	2
M.A.Taylor	3	6	1	102*	189	37.80	1	–	3
M.J.Slater	3	6	–	91	162	27.00	–	1	–
S.K.Warne	3	5	–	35	105	21.00	–	–	–
R.T.Ponting	3	5	–	60	105	21.00	–	1	3
G.R.Robertson	3	5	–	57	90	18.00	–	1	1
M.S.Kasprowicz	3	5	1	25	54	13.50	–	–	–
G.S.Blewett	3	6	–	25	48	8.00	–	–	2

Played in one Test: A.C.Dale 5; D.S.Lehmann 52 (2 ct); P.R.Reiffel 15, 8 (1 ct); P.Wilson 0*, 0*.

AUSTRALIA – BOWLING

	O	M	R	W	Avge	Best	5wI	10wM
A.C.Dale	28	7	92	3	30.66	3-71	–	–
G.R.Robertson	111.4	13	413	12	34.41	4-72	–	–
M.S.Kasprowicz	116	29	312	8	39.00	5-28	1	–
S.K.Warne	167	37	540	10	54.00	4-85	–	–

Also bowled: G.S.Blewett 45-8-152-2; D.S.Lehmann 7-1-27-1; P.R.Reiffel 24-5-59-0; M.E.Waugh 32-1-149-2; S.R.Waugh 12-1-38-0; P.Wilson 12-2-50-0.

ZIMBABWE v PAKISTAN (1st Test)

At Queens Sports Club, Bulawayo on 14, 15, 16, 17, 18 March 1998.
Toss: Zimbabwe. Result: **MATCH DRAWN**.
Debuts: Zimbabwe – T.N.Madondo, D.P.Viljoen.

ZIMBABWE

G.W.Flower	not out	156		lbw b Waqar	6
D.P.Viljoen	c Rashid b Waqar	0		lbw b Shoaib	0
M.W.Goodwin	c Rashid b Waqar	0	(4)	not out	166
*A.D.R.Campbell	c Rashid b Azhar	15	(5)	c Ijaz b Waqar	5
†A.Flower	c Rashid b Shoaib	44	(6)	not out	100
G.J.Whittall	lbw b Waqar	1			
T.N.Madondo	c Inzamam b Waqar	14			
H.H.Streak	c Ijaz b Azar	53			
P.A.Strang	c Inzamam b Shoaib	2			
A.R.Whittall	c Rashid b Azhar	17	(3)	c Yousuf b Shoaib	6
M.Mbangwa	c Rashid b Waqar	0			
Extras	(B 3, LB 13, W 2, NB 1)	19		(LB 14, W 1, NB 4)	19
Total		**321**		(4 wickets declared)	**302**

PAKISTAN

Saeed Anwar	c A.Flower b G.J.Whittall	33		c Goodwin b Strang	37
Ali Naqvi	c Campbell b Mbangwa	27		c Goodwin b Mbangwa	13
Ijaz Ahmed	c A.Flower b Mbangwa	23	(7)	not out	15
Inzamam-ul-Haq	c and b Strang	24		c A.Flower b Streak	12
Yousuf Youhana	b G.J.Whittall	60		c Viljoen b Streak	64
Moin Khan	c A.R.Whittall b G.J.Whittall	12		c Goodwin b Viljoen	97
Azhar Mahmood	lbw b Strang	0			
*†Rashid Latif	lbw b Streak	31			
Saqlain Mushtaq	lbw b Strang	34	(3)	c A.Flower b Streak	8
Waqar Younis	c Strang b G.J.Whittall	0			
Shoaib Akhtar	not out	7			
Extras	(LB 5)	5		(B 6, LB 6)	12
Total		**256**		(6 wickets)	**258**

PAKISTAN	O	M	R	W		O	M	R	W	FALL OF WICKETS
Waqar Younis	28.2	4	106	5		11	5	18	2		Z	P	Z	P
Azhar Mahmood	36	18	56	3	(3)	24	1	102	0	Wkt	1st	1st	2nd	2nd
Shoaib Akhtar	27	6	83	2	(2)	23.2	5	67	2	1st	9	58	0	28
Saqlain Mushtaq	20	1	60	0	(5)	14.3	0	63	0	2nd	15	80	15	54
Saeed Anwar	1	1	0	0	(6)	4	0	19	0	3rd	38	99	19	70
Ali Naqvi					(4)	2	0	11	0	4th	115	118	25	80
Inzamam-ul-Haq						1.3	0	6	0	5th	123	143	–	190
										6th	159	144	–	258
ZIMBABWE										7th	268	205		
Streak	24	5	74	1		18	6	42	3	8th	272	230		
Mbangwa	23	15	25	2		22	13	29	1	9th	321	230		
A.R.Whittall	7	1	29	0		8	3	28	0	10th	321	256		
G.J.Whittall	27	9	63	4		18	5	61	0					
Strang	26.1	8	54	3	(3)	27	5	69	1					
G.W.Flower	1	0	3	0										
Goodwin	1	0	3	0	(6)	2	0	3	0					
Viljoen						3.3	0	14	1					

Umpires: I.D.Robinson (18) and D.R.Shepherd (*England*) (39).
Referee: G.T.Dowling (*New Zealand*) (4). **Test No. 1411/9 (Z 29/P 247)**

ZIMBABWE v PAKISTAN (2nd Test)

At Harare Sports Club on 21, 22, 23, 24, 25 March 1998.
Toss: Zimbabwe. Result: **PAKISTAN** won by 3 wickets.
Debuts: None.

ZIMBABWE

G.W.Flower	c Rashid b Azhar	39		lbw b Wasim Akram	6
G.J.Rennie	c Rashid b Azhar	13		c Yousuf b Waqar	0
M.W.Goodwin	c Inzamam b Mushtaq	53		c Inzamam b Waqar	81
*A.D.R.Campbell	c Yousuf b Mushtaq	23		lbw b Azhar	14
†A.Flower	lbw b Waqar	1		c Inzamam b Mushtaq	49
G.J.Whittall	c Inzamam b Wasim Akram	62		c Rashid b Azhar	15
T.N.Madondo	run out	0		c Rashid b Azhar	2
H.H.Streak	c Mohd Wasim b Waqar	6		not out	37
B.C.Strang	c and b Waqar	53		c Yousuf b Mushtaq	21
A.G.Huckle	b Waqar	0		b Wasim Akram	0
M.Mbangwa	not out	0		lbw b Wasim Akram	3
Extras	(B 6, LB 14, W 1, NB 4)	25		(B 13, LB 15, NB 12)	40
Total		**277**			**268**

PAKISTAN

Saeed Anwar	lbw b Whittall	15		c sub‡ b Whittall	65
Ali Naqvi	c A.Flower b Whittall	13	(7)	c A.Flower b Huckle	8
Mohammad Wasim	c Mbangwa b Whittall	192		run out	8
Inzamam-ul-Haq	c and b Strang	13		st A.Flower b Huckle	10
Yousuf Youhana	c A.Flower b Mbangwa	9		c Goodwin b Whittall	52
Moin Khan	b Strang	12		c Campbell b Streak	21
Azhar Mahmood	c Whittall b Mbangwa	20	(2)	c Campbell b Streak	9
Wasim Akram	c Rennie b Mbangwa	0		not out	12
*†Rashid Latif	c sub (A.R.Whittall) b Strang	4		not out	1
Mushtaq Ahmed	c Campbell b Streak	57			
Waqar Younis	not out	8			
Extras	(LB 8, W 1, NB 2)	11		(B 2, LB 3, NB 1)	6
Total		**354**		(7 wickets)	**192**

PAKISTAN	O	M	R	W		O	M	R	W
Wasim Akram	20.5	6	67	1		33	8	70	3
Waqar Younis	20	7	47	4		25	3	60	2
Mushtaq Ahmed	20	2	74	2	(4)	37	6	84	2
Azhar Mahmood	22	6	69	2	(3)	16	7	26	3
ZIMBABWE									
Streak	31	8	83	1		13	5	40	2
Mbangwa	33	12	56	3	(3)	2	0	11	0
Strang	28	10	65	3	(5)	5	0	20	0
Whittall	32.5	4	78	3	(2)	15	4	35	2
Huckle	21	8	55	0	(4)	18.5	1	81	2
Goodwin	2	0	9	0					

FALL OF WICKETS

	Z	P	Z	P
Wkt	1st	1st	2nd	2nd
1st	47	31	7	14
2nd	75	46	9	59
3rd	141	61	38	77
4th	142	88	133	105
5th	143	119	166	138
6th	144	169	175	162
7th	153	169	205	186
8th	263	187	255	–
9th	263	334	255	–
10th	277	354	268	–

Umpires: S.G.Randell (*Australia*) (36) and R.B.Tiffin (6).
Referee: G.T.Dowling (*New Zealand*) (5).

‡ (A.R.Whittall)
Test No. 1412/10 (Z 30/P 248)

. 231

ZIMBABWE v PAKISTAN 1997-98

ZIMBABWE – BATTING AND FIELDING

	M	I	NO	HS	Runs	Avge	100	50	Ct/St
M.W.Goodwin	2	4	1	166*	300	100.00	1	2	4
G.W.Flower	2	4	–	156*	207	69.00	1	–	–
A.Flower	2	4	1	100*	194	64.66	1	–	7/1
H.H.Streak	2	3	1	53	96	48.00	–	1	–
G.J.Whittall	2	3	–	62	78	26.00	–	1	1
A.D.R.Campbell	2	4	–	23	57	14.25	–	–	4
T.N.Madondo	2	3	–	14	16	5.33	–	–	–
M.Mbangwa	2	3	1	3	5	2.50	–	–	1

Played in one Test: A.G.Huckle 0, 0; G.J.Rennie 13, 0 (1 ct); B.C.Strang 53, 21 (1 ct); P.A.Strang 2 (2 ct); D.P.Viljoen 0, 0 (1 ct); A.R.Whittall 17, 6 (1 ct).

ZIMBABWE – BOWLING

	O	M	R	W	Avge	Best	5wI	10wM
M.Mbangwa	80	40	121	6	20.16	3-56	–	–
G.J.Whittall	92.5	22	237	9	26.33	4-63	–	–
B.C.Strang	33	10	85	3	28.33	3-65	–	–
P.A.Strang	53.1	13	123	4	30.75	3-54	–	–
H.H.Streak	86	24	239	7	34.14	3-42	–	–

Also bowled: G.W.Flower 1-0-3-0; M.W.Goodwin 5-0-15-0; A.G.Huckle 39.5-9-136-2; D.P.Viljoen 3.3-0-14-1; A.R.Whittall 15-4-57-0.

PAKISTAN – BATTING AND FIELDING

	M	I	NO	HS	Runs	Avge	100	50	Ct/St
Yousuf Youhana	2	4	–	64	185	46.25	–	3	4
Saeed Anwar	2	4	–	65	150	37.50	–	1	–
Moin Khan	2	4	–	97	142	35.50	–	1	–
Rashid Latif	2	3	1	31	36	18.00	–	–	10
Ali Naqvi	2	4	–	27	61	15.25	–	–	–
Inzamam-ul-Haq	2	4	–	24	59	14.75	–	–	6
Azhar Mahmood	2	3	–	20	29	9.66	–	–	–
Waqar Younis	2	2	1	8*	8	8.00	–	–	1

Played in one Test: Ijaz Ahmed 23, 15* (2 ct); Mohammad Wasim 192, 8 (1 ct); Mushtaq Ahmed 57; Saqlain Mushtaq 34, 8; Shoaib Akhtar 7*; Wasim Akram 0, 12*.

PAKISTAN – BOWLING

	O	M	R	W	Avge	Best	5wI	10wM
Waqar Younis	84.2	19	231	13	17.76	5-106	1	–
Azhar Mahmood	98	32	253	8	31.62	3- 26	–	–
Wasim Akram	53.5	14	137	4	34.25	3- 70	–	–
Shoaib Akhtar	50.2	11	150	4	37.50	2- 67	–	–
Mushtaq Ahmed	57	8	158	4	39.50	2- 74	–	–

Also bowled: Ali Naqvi 2-0-11-0; Inzamam-ul-Haq 1.3-0-8-0; Saeed Anwar 5-1-19-0; Saqlain Mushtaq 34.3-1-123-0.

SOUTH AFRICA v SRI LANKA (1st Test)

At Newlands, Cape Town on 19, 20, 21, 22, 23 March 1998.
Toss: South Africa. Result: **SOUTH AFRICA** won by 70 runs.
Debuts: South Africa – M.Ntini.

SOUTH AFRICA

A.M.Bacher	c Mahanama b Wickremasinghe	6	(2) c Kaluwitharana b Vaas		0
G.Kirsten	lbw b Vaas	62	(1) c Mahanama b Vaas		15
H.D.Ackerman	c and b Muralitharan	23	(7) lbw b Muralitharan		8
D.J.Cullinan	b Wickremesinghe	113	c Tillekeratne b Muralitharan		68
*W.J.Cronje	c Mahanama b Vaas	49	c Muralitharan b Jayasuriya		74
J.H.Kallis	c Ranatunga b Muralitharan	3	(3) st Kaluwitharana b Jayasuriya		43
S.M.Pollock	lbw b Wickremesinghe	92	(8) st Kaluwitharana b Jayasuriya		6
†M.V.Boucher	run out	33	(6) c Jayasuriya b Muralitharan		10
A.A.Donald	b Muralitharan	12	c Pushpakumara b Jayasuriya		3
P.R.Adams	st Kaluwitharana b Muralitharan	3	c Kaluwitharana b Muralitharan		3
M.Ntini	not out	3	not out		0
Extras	(LB 8, NB 12)	20	(B 4, LB 3, W 1, NB 5)		13
Total		**418**			**264**

SRI LANKA

S.T.Jayasuriya	c Boucher b Donald	17	lbw Donald		0
M.S.Atapattu	c Cullinan b Adams	60	c and b Adams		71
R.S.Mahanama	c Boucher b Donald	9	c Kallis b Pollock		11
P.A.de Silva	c Boucher b Ntini	77	c Kallis b Adams		37
*A.Ranatunga	c Ackerman b Adams	22	c Kirsten b Kallis		43
H.P.Tillekeratne	c Boucher b Pollock	20	lbw b Donald		13
†R.S.Kaluwitharana	lbw b Pollock	13	b Pollock		45
W.P.U.C.J.Vaas	c Boucher b Pollock	30	c Boucher b Donald		0
G.P.Wickremasinghe	c sub (L.Klusener) b Pollock	11	b Ntini		51
M.Muralitharan	not out	15	run out		10
K.Pushpakumara	c Boucher b Donald	4	not out		9
Extras	(B 8, LB 7, W 1, NB 12)	28	(B 5, LB 3, NB 8)		16
Total		**306**			**306**

SRI LANKA	O	M	R	W		O	M	R	W		FALL OF WICKETS			
Vaas	21	2	75	2		11	3	41	2			SA	SL	SA	SL
Pushpakumara	20	3	81	0		8	0	24	0		Wkt	1st	1st	2nd	2nd
Wickremesinghe	28.4	7	75	3		8	1	24	0		1st	20	20	5	3
Muralitharan	45	8	135	4		41	10	108	4		2nd	60	36	18	27
Jayasuriya	6	1	29	0	(6)	33	7	53	4		3rd	155	165	134	98
De Silva	4	0	15	0	(5)	1	0	1	0		4th	251	194	146	171
Atapattu						1	0	7	0		5th	260	195	166	175
											6th	272	219	188	234
S AFRICA											7th	367	241	219	234
Donald	21.3	7	66	3		20	4	64	3		8th	402	270	256	239
Pollock	26	5	83	4		23	3	77	2		9th	414	300	260	287
Ntini	10	1	57	1	(4)	5.3	0	17	1		10th	418	306	264	306
Kallis	7	1	23	0	(3)	15	5	45	1						
Adams	20	2	62	2		27	3	90	2						
Cronje						5	3	5	0						

Umpires: R.S.Dunne (*New Zealand*) (28) and D.L.Orchard (6).
Referee: J.R.Reid (*New Zealand*) (35). **Test No. 1413/4 (SA 219/SL 82)**

233

SOUTH AFRICA v SRI LANKA (2nd Test)

At Centurion Park, Verwoerdburg, Pretoria on 27, 28, 29, 30 March 1998.
Toss: Sri Lanka. Result: **SOUTH AFRICA** won by 6 wickets.
Debuts: South Africa – G.F.J.Liebenburg.

SRI LANKA

S.T.Jayasuriya	c Boucher b Ntini	51	b Donald		16
M.S.Atapattu	run out	12	c Boucher b Donald		7
R.S.Mahanama	c Kallis b Cronje	50	lbw b Donald		0
P.A.de Silva	c Adams b Ntini	1	run out		41
*A.Ranatunga	lbw b Donald	73	c Boucher b Cronje		0
H.P.Tillekeratne	c Kirsten b Cronje	55	c sub (D.N.Crookes) b Cronje		0
†R.S.Kaluwitharana	c Boucher b Donald	9	run out		0
G.P.Wickremasinghe	c Adams b Donald	10	b Adams		21
D.N.T.Zoysa	lbw b Kallis	0	c Boucher b Donald		14
M.Muralitharan	c Boucher b Cronje	11	c Kirsten b Donald		15
K.R.Pushpakumara	not out	0	not out		0
Extras	(B 6, LB 14, W 3, NB 8)	31	(LB 5, NB 3)		8
Total		**303**			**122**

SOUTH AFRICA

G.F.J.Liebenberg	lbw b Pushpakumara	0	(2) lbw b Muralitharan		45
G.Kirsten	b Muralitharan	13	(1) not out		75
H.D.Ackerman	b Zoysa	7	b Muralitharan		2
D.J.Cullinan	c Wickremasinghe b Jayasuriya	103	lbw b Muralitharan		0
*W.J.Cronje	st Kaluwitharana b Muralitharan	10	c De Silva b Jayasuriya		82
J.H.Kallis	c Kaluwitharana b Wickremasinghe	12	not out		0
S.M.Pollock	b Muralitharan	1			
†M.V.Boucher	c Jayasuriya b Muralitharan	13			
A.A.Donald	b Muralitharan	6			
P.R.Adams	c and b Jayasuriya	12			
M.Ntini	not out	2			
Extras	(B 1, LB 6, W 6, NB 8)	21	(B 8, LB 3, NB 11)		22
Total		**200**	(4 wickets)		**226**

S AFRICA	O	M	R	W		O	M	R	W	FALL OF WICKETS
Donald	33	10	73	3		13.3	2	54	5	SL SA SL SA
Pollock	7.1	3	9	0						Wkt 1st 1st 2nd 2nd
Kallis	19	7	42	1		7	3	12	0	1st 53 0 19 89
Adams	22	6	77	0	(5)	7	1	25	1	2nd 66 11 19 99
Ntini	22.5	7	61	2	(2)	6	2	13	0	3rd 68 75 40 99
Cronje	14.3	3	21	3	(4)	8	3	13	2	4th 186 103 40 215
										5th 228 122 42 –
SRI LANKA										6th 240 137 42 –
Pushpakumara	16	2	55	1		7	2	27	0	7th 254 170 85 –
Zoysa	12	2	29	1		2	0	11	0	8th 255 182 98 –
Wickremasinghe	15	2	36	1		6	1	7	0	9th 290 186 118 –
Muralitharan	30	8	63	5	(5)	23.5	4	94	3	10th 303 200 122 –
Jayasuriya	5	2	10	2	(6)	19	6	62	1	
De Silva					(4)	5	1	14	0	

Umpires: Javed Akhtar (*Pakistan*) (16) and R.E.Koertzen (6).
Referee: J.R.Reid (*New Zealand*) (36). Test No. 1414/5 (SA 220/SL 83)

SOUTH AFRICA v SRI LANKA 1997-98

SOUTH AFRICA – BATTING AND FIELDING

	M	I	NO	HS	Runs	Avge	100	50	Ct/St
D.J.Cullinan	2	4	–	113	284	71.00	2	1	1
G.Kirsten	2	4	1	75*	165	55.00	–	2	3
W.J.Cronje	2	4	–	82	215	53.75	–	2	–
S.M.Pollock	2	3	–	92	99	33.00	–	1	–
J.H.Kallis	2	4	1	49	64	21.33	–	–	3
M.V.Boucher	2	3	–	33	56	18.66	–	–	13
A.A.Donald	2	3	–	18	36	12.00	–	–	–
H.D.Ackerman	2	4	–	23	40	10.00	–	–	1
P.R.Adams	2	3	–	12	17	5.66	–	–	3
M.Ntini	2	3	3	3*	5	–	–	–	–

Played in one Test: A.M.Bacher 6, 0; G.F.J.Liebenberg 0, 45.

SOUTH AFRICA – BOWLING

	O	M	R	W	Avge	Best	5wI	10wM
W.J.Cronje	27.3	9	39	5	7.80	3-21	–	–
A.A.Donald	88	23	257	14	18.35	5-54	1	–
S.M.Pollock	56.1	11	169	6	28.16	4-83	–	–
M.Ntini	44.2	10	148	4	37.00	2-61	–	–
P.R.Adams	76	12	254	5	50.80	2-62	–	–

Also bowled: J.H.Kallis 48-16-122-2.

SRI LANKA – BATTING AND FIELDING

	M	I	NO	HS	Runs	Avge	100	50	Ct/St
P.A.de Silva	2	4	–	77	156	39.00	–	1	1
M.S.Atapattu	2	4	–	71	150	37.50	–	2	–
A.Ranatunga	2	4	–	73	136	34.00	–	1	1
G.P.Wickremasinghe	2	4	–	51	93	23.25	–	1	1
H.P.Tillekeratne	2	4	–	55	90	22.50	–	1	1
S.T.Jayasuriya	2	4	–	51	84	21.00	–	1	3
R.S.Mahanama	2	4	–	50	70	17.50	–	1	3
M.Muralitharan	2	4	1	15*	51	17.00	–	–	2
R.S.Kaluwitharana	2	4	–	45	67	16.75	–	–	3/4
K.R.Pushpakumara	2	4	3	9*	13	13.00	–	–	1

Played in one Test: W.P.U.C.J.Vaas 30, 0; D.N.T.Zoysa 0, 14.

SRI LANKA – BOWLING

	O	M	R	W	Avge	Best	5wI	10wM
S.T.Jayasuriya	63	16	154	7	22.00	4-53	–	–
M.Muralitharan	139.5	30	400	16	25.00	5-63	1	–
W.P.U.C.J.Vaas	32	5	116	4	29.00	2-41	–	–
G.P.Wickremasinghe	57.4	11	142	4	35.50	3-75	–	–

Also bowled: M.S.Atapattu 1-0-7-0; P.A.de Silva 10-2-29-0; K.R.Pushpakumara 51-7-187-1; D.N.T.Zoysa 14-2-40-1.

SRI LANKA v NEW ZEALAND (1st Test)

At R.Premadasa Stadium, Khettarama, Colombo on 27, 28, 29, 30, 31 May 1998.
Toss: New Zealand. Result: **NEW ZEALAND** won by 167 runs.
Debuts: Sri Lanka – C.M.Bandara, M.R.C.N.Bandaratilake; New Zealand – P.J.Wiseman.

NEW ZEALAND

B.A.Young	c Kaluwitharana b Muralitharan	30	lbw b Bandaratilake	11
M.J.Horne	b Bandaratilake	15	c Ranatunga b Muralitharan	35
*S.P.Fleming	c Jayasuriya b Kalpage	78	not out	176
N.J.Astle	c Jayawardena b Kalpage	38	c Kaluwitharana b Jayasuriya	34
C.D.McMillan	lbw b Muralitharan	0	c Kalpage b Muralitharan	142
†A.C.Parore	c Jayasuriya b Wickremasinghe	67	c Kalpage b Muralitharan	1
C.L.Cairns	c Bandara b Muralitharan	19	c Jayawardena b Muralitharan	6
C.Z.Harris	lbw b Wickremasinghe	19	not out	14
D.L.Vettori	c Kalpage b Muralitharan	20		
P.J.Wiseman	c Jayawardena b Muralitharan	6		
S.B.Doull	not out	1		
Extras	(LB 10, W 1, NB 9)	20	(B 5, LB 8, NB 12)	25
Total		**305**	(6 wickets declared)	**444**

SRI LANKA

S.T.Jayasuriya	c Parore b Cairns	10	c Young b Wiseman	59
M.S.Atapattu	c Parore b Cairns	0	c Horne b Wiseman	16
D.P.M.D.Jayawardena	c Vettori c Wiseman	52	c Horne b Wiseman	54
P.A.de Silva	c Doull b McMillan	37	lbw b Vettori	71
*A.Ranatunga	b Cairns	49	c and b Vettori	9
†R.S.Kaluwitharana	b Vettori	72	c Parore b McMillan	39
R.S.Kalpage	b Wiseman	6	c Young b Vettori	16
G.P.Wickremasinghe	lbw b Vettori	27	(9) c Young b Cairns	0
M.R.C.N.Bandaratilake	run out	20	(8) c Horne b Wiseman	16
M.Muralitharan	b Vettori	0	not out	9
C.M.Bandara	not out	0	lbw b Wiseman	0
Extras	(LB 8, NB 4)	12	(B 1, LB 4, NB 3)	8
Total		**285**		**297**

SRI LANKA	O	M	R	W		O	M	R	W
Wickremasinghe	14	2	55	2		7	0	21	0
Jayawardena	3	0	10	0					
Bandaratilake	22	6	50	1	(2)	39	8	105	1
Muralitharan	38.2	9	90	5		36	5	139	4
Bandara	13	3	41	0		8	0	38	0
Kalpage	15	2	49	2		16	4	51	0
Jayasuriya						15	0	63	1
De Silva					(3)	2	0	14	0

N ZEALAND									
Doull	12.2	2	43	0		3	0	25	0
Cairns	15	0	59	3		19	6	64	1
Harris	7	1	27	0	(6)	4	1	16	0
Vettori	24	8	56	3		51	23	101	3
Wiseman	20	4	61	2	(3)	46.5	17	82	5
McMillan	12	4	31	1	(5)	6	4	12	1
Astle						2	0	2	0

FALL OF WICKETS

	NZ	SL	NZ	SL
Wkt	1st	1st	2nd	2nd
1st	25	6	11	70
2nd	97	21	68	89
3rd	141	101	160	194
4th	141	105	400	216
5th	188	206	404	216
6th	229	221	416	239
7th	269	237	–	277
8th	282	284	–	279
9th	296	284	–	289
10th	305	285	–	297

Umpires: K.T.Francis (22) and R.E.Koertzen (*South Africa*) (7).
Referee: Talat Ali (*Pakistan*) (3).   **Test No. 1415/16 (SL 84/NZ 260)**

SRI LANKA v NEW ZEALAND (2nd Test)

At Galle International Stadium on 3, 4, 5, 6, 7 June 1998.
Toss: New Zealand. Result: **SRI LANKA** won by an innings and 16 runs.
Debuts: None.

NEW ZEALAND

B.A.Young	c Jayasuriya b Bandaratilake	46		c Tillekeratne b Bandaratilake	11
M.J.Horne	c Kaluwitharana b Bandaratilake	1		lbw b Bandaratilake	3
*S.P.Fleming	lbw b Dharmasena	14		lbw b Muralitharan	10
N.J.Astle	c Tillekeratne b Dharmasena	53		b De Silva	13
D.L.Vettori	c Tillekeratne Bandaratilake	0	(9)	run out	0
C.D.McMillan	b Bandaratilake	13	(5)	c Jayasuriya b Bandaratilake	1
†A.C.Parore	c Jayasuriya b Dharmasena	30	(6)	not out	32
C.L.Cairns	c Jayasuriya b Dharmasena	0	(7)	c Tillekeratne b Bandaratilake	16
C.Z.Harris	c Bandaratilake b Dharmasena	4	(8)	c Jayawardena b Muralitharan	2
P.J.Wiseman	st Kaluwitharana b Dharmasena	23		c Tillekeratne b Bandaratilake	9
S.B.O'Connor	not out	0		c Jayasuriya b Muralitharan	0
Extras	(LB 7, NB 2)	9		(B 7, LB 7, W 1, NB 2)	17
Total		**193**			**114**

SRI LANKA

S.T.Jayasuriya	c Harris b Vettori	21
M.S.Atapattu	c Vettori b Wiseman	36
D.P.M.D.Jayawardena	lbw b Harris	167
P.A.de Silva	lbw b Vettori	10
*A.Ranatunga	c O'Connor b Vettori	36
H.P.Tillekeratne	b Wiseman	10
†R.S.Kaluwitharana	run out	3
H.D.P.K.Dharmasena	run out	12
G.P.Wickremasinghe	c Harris b Vettori	12
M.R.C.N.Bandaratilake	run out	4
M.Muralitharan	not out	2
Extras	(LB 8, NB 2)	10
Total		**323**

SRI LANKA	O	M	R	W		O	M	R	W
Wickremasinghe	7	1	20	0		2	0	6	0
Dharmasena	24.1	4	73	6	(4)	6	0	16	0
Bandaratilake	38	14	46	4	(2)	24	9	36	5
Muralitharan	23	9	33	0	(5)	16	7	24	3
Jayasuriya	4	1	8	0					
De Silva	5	2	6	0	(3)	7	2	18	1

N ZEALAND	O	M	R	W
O'Connor	4	0	13	0
Cairns	5	0	20	0
Wiseman	30	3	95	2
Vettori	26	4	88	4
Harris	25.4	6	56	1
McMillan	11	3	31	0
Astle	5	3	12	0

FALL OF WICKETS

	NZ	SL	NZ
Wkt	1st	1st	2nd
1st	5	44	18
2nd	21	106	21
3rd	90	135	40
4th	90	211	41
5th	110	262	69
6th	137	271	94
7th	137	301	103
8th	147	315	106
9th	190	319	109
10th	193	323	114

Umpires: B.C.Cooray (15) and D.L.Orchard (*South Africa*) (7).
Referee: Talat Ali (*Pakistan*) (4). **Test No. 1416/17 (SL 85/NZ 261)**

SRI LANKA v NEW ZEALAND (3rd Test)

At Sinhalese Sports Club, Colombo on 10, 11, 12, 13 June 1998.
Toss: Sri Lanka. Result: **SRI LANKA** won by 164 runs.
Debuts: None.

SRI LANKA

S.T.Jayasuryia	c Young b Cairns	13	c Parore b Cairns	8
M.S.Atapattu	c Vettori b Wiseman	48	lbw b Vettori	5
D.P.M.D.Jayawardena	c Parore b Cairns	16	c Horne b Vettori	11
P.A.de Silva	c Spearman b Cairns	4	c Astle b Vettori	3
*A.Ranatunga	run out	4	c Cairns b Priest	64
H.P.Tillekeratne	c Young b McMillan	43	b Vettori	40
†R.S.Kaluwitharana	b McMillan	28	lbw b Priest	88
H.D.P.K.Dharmasena	c Parore b Cairns	11	b McMillan	11
G.P.Wickremasinghe	not out	24	c Fleming b Vettori	0
M.R.C.N.Bandaratilake	lbw b Vettori	5	c Fleming b Vettori	7
M.Muralitharan	c Astle b Cairns	1	not out	26
Extras	(B 1, LB 8)	9	(B 8, LB 10, NB 1)	19
Total		**206**		**282**

NEW ZEALAND

B.A.Young	c Atapattu b Bandaratilake	2	st Kaluwitharana b Muralitharan	24
C.M.Spearman	c De Silva b Wickremasinghe	4	c and b Muralitharan	22
*S.P.Fleming	b Wickremasinghe	78	lbw b Dharmasena	3
N.J.Astle	c Atapattu b Dharmasena	16	c and b Muralitharan	16
M.J.Horne	c Tillekeratne b De Silva	35	c Kaluwitharana b Bandaratilake	12
C.D.McMillan	st Kaluwitharana b De Silva	2	c Jayawardena b Muralitharan	5
†A.C.Parore	lbw b De Silva	19	c b Bandaratilake	2
C.L.Cairns	run out	6	b Bandaratilake	26
M.W.Priest	c sub‡ b Muralitharan	12	b Bandaratilake	2
D.L.Vettori	c Jayasuriya b Muralitharan	0	b Muralitharan	3
P.J.Wiseman	not out	1	not out	0
Extras	(B 9, LB 4, NB 5)	18	(B 6, LB 10, NB 4)	20
Total		**193**		**131**

N ZEALAND	O	M	R	W		O	M	R	W
Cairns	17.4	1	62	5		17	0	75	1
Vettori	25	7	52	1		33	10	64	6
Priest	24	11	35	0	(6)	11.5	0	42	2
Wiseman	10	4	21	1		6	2	29	0
McMillan	12	5	27	2		14	2	46	1
Astle					(3)	3	0	8	0
SRI LANKA									
Wickremasinghe	6.3	3	7	2		6	2	5	0
Bandaratilake	20	6	48	1		17	3	52	4
Dharmasena	18	4	35	1	(4)	10	2	14	1
De Silva	18.5	7	30	3	(3)	3	0	14	0
Muralitharan	23.1	3	60	2		18.3	8	30	5

FALL OF WICKETS				
	SL	NZ	SL	NZ
Wkt	1st	1st	2nd	2nd
1st	23	5	12	44
2nd	52	7	16	57
3rd	56	30	24	63
4th	70	94	36	82
5th	102	98	138	84
6th	156	128	140	93
7th	163	143	188	105
8th	196	181	193	128
9th	201	183	211	131
10th	206	193	282	131

Umpires: P.Manuel (3) and V.K.Ramaswamy (*India*) (24).
Referee: Talat Ali (*Pakistan*) (5).   ‡ (A.S.A.Perera)
Test No. 1417/18 (SL 86/NZ 262)

SRI LANKA v NEW ZEALAND 1997-98

SRI LANKA – BATTING AND FIELDING

	M	I	NO	HS	Runs	Avge	100	50	Ct/St
D.R.M.D.Jayawardena	3	5	–	167	300	60.00	1	2	5
R.S.Kaluwitharana	3	5	–	88	230	46.00	–	2	4/3
A.Ranatunga	3	5	–	64	162	32.40	–	1	1
H.P.Tillekeratne	2	3	–	43	93	31.00	–	–	6
P.A.de Silva	3	5	–	71	125	25.00	–	1	1
S.T.Jayasuriya	3	5	–	59	111	22.20	–	1	8
M.S.Atapattu	3	5	–	48	104	20.80	–	–	2
M.Muralitharan	3	5	3	26*	38	19.00	–	–	2
G.P.Wickremasinghe	3	5	1	27	63	15.75	–	–	1
H.D.P.K.Dharmasena	2	3	–	12	34	11.33	–	–	–
M.R.C.N.Bandaratilake	3	5	–	20	52	10.40	–	–	–

Played in one Test: C.M.Bandara 0*, 0 (1 ct); R.S.Kalpage 6, 16 (3 ct).

SRI LANKA – BOWLING

	O	M	R	W	Avge	Best	5wI	10wM
H.D.P.K.Dharmasena	58.1	10	137	8	17.12	6-72	1	–
M.Muralitharan	155	41	376	19	19.78	5-30	2	–
P.A.de Silva	35.5	10	82	4	20.50	3-30	–	–
M.R.C.N.Bandaratilake	160	45	338	16	21.12	5-36	1	–
G.P.Wickremasinghe	42.3	8	114	4	28.50	2-7	–	–

Also bowled: D.R.M.D.Jayawardena 3-0-10-0; C.M.Bandara 21-3-79-0; R.S.Kalpage 31-6-100-2; S.T.Jayasuriya 19-1-71-1.

NEW ZEALAND – BATTING AND FIELDING

	M	I	NO	HS	Runs	Avge	100	50	Ct/St
S.P.Fleming	3	6	1	176*	359	71.80	1	2	2
A.C.Parore	3	6	1	67	151	30.20	–	1	6
N.J.Astle	3	6	–	53	162	27.00	–	1	2
C.D.McMillan	3	6	–	142	159	26.50	1	–	–
B.A.Young	3	6	–	46	124	20.66	–	–	5
M.J.Horne	3	6	–	35	101	16.83	–	–	4
C.Z.Harris	2	4	1	19	46	15.33	–	–	2
C.L.Cairns	3	6	–	26	73	12.16	–	–	1
P.J.Wiseman	3	5	2	23	32	10.66	–	–	–
D.L.Vettori	3	5	–	20	23	4.60	–	–	4

Played in one Test: S.B.Doull 1* (1 ct); S.B.O'Connor 0*, 0 (1 ct); M.W.Priest 12, 2; C.M.Spearman 4, 22 (1 ct).

NEW ZEALAND – BOWLING

	O	M	R	W	Avge	Best	5wI	10wM
D.L.Vettori	159	52	361	17	21.23	6-64	1	–
C.L.Cairns	73.4	7	280	10	28.00	5-62	1	–
P.J.Wiseman	112.5	30	288	10	28.80	5-82	1	–
C.D.McMillan	55	18	146	5	29.20	2-27	–	–

Also bowled: N.J.Astle 10-3-22-0; S.B.Doull 15.2-2-58-0; C.Z.Harris 36.4-8-99-1; S.B.O'Connor 4-0-13-0; M.W.Priest 35.5-11-77-2.

ENGLAND v SOUTH AFRICA (1st Test)

At Edgbaston, Birmingham on 4, 5, 6, 7, 8 (*no play*) June 1998.
Toss: South Africa. Result: **MATCH DRAWN**.
Debuts: None.

ENGLAND

M.A.Butcher	c Kallis b Adams	77		lbw b Pollock	11
M.A.Atherton	c Boucher b Donald	103		b Klusener	43
*†A.J.Stewart	c Cullinan b Klusener	49	(4)	b Donald	28
N.Hussain	lbw b Adams	35	(3)	lbw b Donald	0
G.P.Thorpe	b Pollock	10		b Klusener	43
M.R.Ramprakash	b Donald	49		c Kallis b Adams	11
M.A.Ealham	b Adams	5		c Pollock b Klusener	7
D.G.Cork	c Pollock b Donald	36		st Boucher b Adams	2
R.D.B.Croft	c Boucher b Donald	19		not out	1
D.Gough	not out	16			
A.R.C.Fraser	c Cronje b Pollock	9			
Extras	(B 18, LB 26, W 8, NB 2)	54		(B 10, LB 6, W 8)	24
Total		**462**		**(8 wickets)**	**170**

SOUTH AFRICA

G.Kirsten	c Butcher b Cork	12
G.F.J.Liebenberg	c sub (B.L.Spendlove) b Cork	3
J.H.Kallis	c Stewart b Cork	61
D.J.Cullinan	b Fraser	78
*W.J.Cronje	c sub (B.L.Spendlove) b Cork	1
J.N.Rhodes	c Stewart b Fraser	95
S.M.Pollock	c Croft b Fraser	16
†M.V.Boucher	c Stewart b Fraser	0
L.Klusener	c Stewart b Ealham	57
A.A.Donald	c and b Cork	7
P.R.Adams	not out	6
Extras	(LB 5, NB 2)	7
Total		**343**

S AFRICA	O	M	R	W		O	M	R	W
Donald	35	9	95	4		10	1	48	2
Pollock	42	12	92	2		12	2	43	1
Klusener	31	7	74	1		11	4	27	3
Cronje	11	3	28	0					
Adams	42	10	83	3	(4)	12.1	3	36	2
Kallis	20	7	46	0					
ENGLAND									
Fraser	34	6	103	4					
Cork	32.3	7	93	5					
Ealham	23	8	55	1					
Croft	27	3	85	0					
Butcher	1	0	2	0					

FALL OF WICKETS

	E	SA	E
Wkt	1st	1st	2nd
1st	179	6	24
2nd	249	38	31
3rd	309	119	80
4th	309	125	148
5th	329	191	153
6th	356	211	167
7th	411	224	167
8th	430	328	170
9th	437	328	–
10th	462	343	–

Umpires: D.R.Shepherd (41) and R.B.Tiffin (*Zimbabwe*) (7).
Referee: Javed Burki (*Pakistan*) (4).   **Test No. 1418/111 (E 747/SA 221)**

ENGLAND v SOUTH AFRICA (2nd Test)

At Lord's, London on 18, 19, 20, 21 June 1998.
Toss: England. Result: **SOUTH AFRICA** won by 10 wickets.
Debuts: England – S.P.James.

SOUTH AFRICA

A.M.Bacher	c Stewart b Cork	22		
G.Kirsten	b Cork	4	(1) not out	9
J.H.Kallis	b Cork	0		
D.J.Cullinan	c Stewart b Cork	16	(2) not out	5
*W.J.Cronje	c Ramprakash b Ealham	81		
J.N.Rhodes	c Stewart b Fraser	117		
S.M.Pollock	c Hussain b Cork	14		
†M.V.Boucher	c Stewart b Headley	35		
L.Klusener	b Headley	34		
A.A.Donald	not out	7		
P.R.Adams	c Stewart b Cork	3		
Extras	(B 1, LB 20, NB 6)	27	(NB 1)	1
Total		**360**	(0 wickets)	**15**

ENGLAND

S.P.James	c Boucher b Donald	10	(2) c Kallis b Pollock	0
M.A.Atherton	c Kirsten b Pollock	0	(1) c Kallis b Adams	44
N.Hussain	c Boucher b Donald	15	lbw b Klusener	105
*†A.J.Stewart	lbw b Pollock	14	(5) c Boucher b Kallis	56
D.W.Headley	c Boucher b Donald	2	(4) c Cronje b Adams	1
G.P.Thorpe	c Bacher b Kallis	10	lbw b Kallis	0
M.R.Ramprakash	c Boucher b Donald	12	b Klusener	0
M.A.Ealham	run out	8	b Kallis	4
D.G.Cork	c Klusener b Pollock	12	c Boucher b Kallis	2
R.D.B.Croft	not out	6	not out	16
A.R.C.Fraser	c Boucher b Donald	1	c Pollock b Adams	17
Extras	(B 8, LB 10, NB 2)	20	(B 1, LB 6, W 5, NB 7)	19
Total		**110**		**264**

ENGLAND	O	M	R	W	O	M	R	W
Fraser	31	8	78	1	1	0	10	0
Cork	31.1	5	119	6	0.1	0	5	0
Headley	22	2	69	2				
Ealham	15	2	50	1				
Croft	9	3	23	0				
S AFRICA								
Donald	15.3	5	32	5	24	6	82	0
Pollock	18	5	42	3	27	16	29	1
Klusener	8	5	10	0	23	5	54	2
Kallis	5	3	8	1	19	9	24	4
Adams					23	7	62	3
Cronje					4	2	6	0

FALL OF WICKETS

	SA	E	E	SA
Wkt	1st	1st	2nd	2nd
1st	8	15	8	–
2nd	16	15	102	–
3rd	43	40	106	–
4th	46	48	222	–
5th	230	49	224	–
6th	273	64	224	–
7th	283	74	225	–
8th	340	97	228	–
9th	353	109	233	–
10th	360	110	264	–

Umpires: D.B.Hair (*Australia*) (25) and G.Sharp (7).
Referee: Javed Burki (*Pakistan*) (5).

Test No. 1419/112 (E 748/SA 222)

ENGLAND v SOUTH AFRICA (3rd Test)

At Old Trafford, Manchester on 2, 3, 4, 5, 6 July 1998.
Toss: South Africa. Result: **MATCH DRAWN.**
Debuts: England – A.F.Giles.

SOUTH AFRICA

G.Kirsten	c Stewart b Fraser	210
G.F.J.Liebenberg	b Gough	16
J.H.Kallis	b Gough	132
D.J.Cullinan	b Giles	75
*W.J.Cronje	not out	69
J.N.Rhodes	c Cork b Gough	12
L.Klusener	not out	17
†M.V.Boucher		
A.A.Donald		
P.R.Adams		
M.Ntini		
Extras	(B 4, LB 10, W 1, NB 6)	21
Total	(5 wickets declared)	**552**

ENGLAND

N.V.Knight	c Boucher b Donald	11	c Boucher b Donald		1
M.A.Atherton	c Boucher b Ntini	41	c Ntini b Kallis		89
N.Hussain	c Boucher b Donald	4	b Kallis		5
*†A.J.Stewart	b Kallis	40	c Klusener b Donald		164
M.R.Ramprakash	c Boucher b Adams	30	lbw b Donald		34
D.G.Cork	c Cronje b Adams	6	(7) b Adams		1
R.D.B.Croft	b Ntini	11	(8) not out		37
G.P.Thorpe	lbw b Adams	0	(6) b Donald		0
A.F.Giles	not out	16	c sub ‡ b Donald		1
D.Gough	c Donald b Adams	6	c Kirsten b Donald		12
A.R.C.Fraser	lbw b Kallis	0	not out		0
Extras	(B 5, LB 12, NB 1)	18	(B 20, LB 2, W 1, NB 2)		25
Total		**183**	(9 wickets)		**369**

ENGLAND	O	M	R	W		O	M	R	W	FALL OF WICKETS
Gough	37	5	116	3						SA E E
Cork	35.5	7	109	0						*Wkt 1st 1st 2nd*
Fraser	35	11	87	1						1st 25 26 4
Croft	51	14	103	0						2nd 263 34 11
Giles	36	7	106	1						3rd 439 94 237
Ramprakash	5	0	17	0						4th 457 108 293
										5th 490 136 293
S AFRICA										6th – 155 296
Donald	13	3	28	2		40	14	88	6	7th – 156 323
Klusener	14	4	37	0	(5)	3	0	15	0	8th – 161 329
Ntini	16	7	28	2		29	11	67	0	9th – 179 367
Adams	31	10	63	4		51	22	90	1	10th – 183 –
Kallis	8.1	3	10	2	(2)	41	19	71	2	
Cronje						6	3	15	0	
Cullinan						1	0	1	0	

Umpires: D.B.Cowie (*New Zealand*) (9) and P.Willey (10).   ‡ (B.M.McMillan)
Referee: Javed Burki (*Pakistan*) (6).   **Test No. 1420/113 (E 749/SA 223)**

ENGLAND v SOUTH AFRICA (4th Test)

At Trent Bridge, Nottingham, on 23, 24, 25, 26, 27 July 1998.
Toss: England. Result: **ENGLAND** won by 8 wickets.
Debuts: England – A.Flintoff; South Africa – S.Elworthy.

SOUTH AFRICA

G.Kirsten	b Gough	7	lbw b Fraser		6
G.F.J.Liebenberg	c Stewart b Gough	13	lbw b Gough		0
J.H.Kallis	c Stewart b Flintoff	47	c Stewart b Cork		11
D.J.Cullinan	c Ramprakash b Fraser	30	c Ramprakash b Fraser		56
*W.J.Cronje	c Hick b Fraser	126	c Stewart b Cork		67
J.N.Rhodes	lbw b Fraser	24	c Stewart b Cork		2
S.M.Pollock	c Stewart b Fraser	50	c Stewart b Cork		7
†M.V.Boucher	lbw b Fraser	4	c Hussain b Fraser		35
S.Elworthy	c Ramprakash b Gough	48	lbw b Fraser		10
A.A.Donald	not out	4	not out		7
P.R.Adams	c Hick b Gough	0	c Stewart b Fraser		1
Extras	(B 9, LB 3, NB 9)	21	(B 1, LB 4, W 1)		6
Total		**374**			**208**

ENGLAND

M.A.Butcher	lbw b Donald	75	c Boucher b Pollock		22
M.A.Atherton	c Boucher b Donald	58	not out		98
N.Hussain	lbw b Elworthy	22	c Kallis b Donald		58
*†A.J.Stewart	c Kirsten b Kallis	19	not out		45
M.R.Ramprakash	not out	67			
I.D.K.Salisbury	b Donald	23			
G.A.Hick	b Donald	6			
A.Flintoff	c Boucher b Kallis	17			
D.G.Cork	c Boucher b Pollock	6			
D.Gough	c Boucher b Donald	2			
A.R.C.Fraser	lbw b Pollock	7			
Extras	(B 7, LB 13, W 1, NB 13)	34	(B 2, LB 11, W 2, NB 9)		24
Total		**336**	(2 wickets)		**247**

ENGLAND	O	M	R	W	O	M	R	W
Gough	30.2	4	116	4	16	4	56	1
Cork	17	2	65	0	(3) 20	4	60	4
Fraser	26	7	60	5	(2) 28.3	6	62	5
Flintoff	17	2	52	1	6	1	16	0
Salisbury	9	1	57	0	5	2	9	0
Butcher	4	1	12	0				
S AFRICA								
Donald	33	8	109	5	23	8	56	1
Pollock	35.5	12	75	2	26	3	79	1
Elworthy	22	8	41	1	(5) 9	1	38	0
Kallis	28	9	60	2	13	5	26	0
Adams	9	2	31	0	(3) 12	4	23	0
Cronje					4	1	12	0

FALL OF WICKETS

	SA	E	SA	E
Wkt	1st	1st	2nd	2nd
1st	21	145	3	40
2nd	26	150	17	192
3rd	68	191	21	–
4th	147	199	119	–
5th	196	244	122	–
6th	292	254	136	–
7th	302	285	189	–
8th	325	302	193	–
9th	374	307	200	–
10th	374	336	208	–

Umpires: R.S.Dunne (*New Zealand*) (29) and M.J.Kitchen (18).
Referee: A.Ebrahim (*Zimbabwe*) (1). Test No. 1421/114 (E 750/SA 224)

ENGLAND v SOUTH AFRICA (5th Test)

At Headingley, Leeds, on 6, 7, 8, 9, 10 August 1998.
Toss: England. Result: **ENGLAND** won by 23 runs.
Debuts: None.

ENGLAND

M.A.Butcher	b Pollock	116	c McMillan b Pollock	37
M.A.Atherton	c Kallis b Ntini	16	lbw b Donald	1
N.Hussain	c Boucher b Pollock	9	c Cronje b Pollock	94
*†A.J.Stewart	c Kallis b Donald	15	c Boucher b Pollock	35
M.R.Ramprakash	c Boucher b Donald	21	lbw b Pollock	25
G.A.Hick	c Rhodes b Ntini	2	(7) c Kirsten b Donald	1
A.Flintoff	c Liebenberg b Pollock	0	(8) c Boucher b Donald	0
D.G.Cork	not out	24	(9) c Boucher b Donald	10
I.D.K.Salisbury	b Ntini	0	(6) c Boucher b Pollock	4
D.Gough	c McMillan b Ntini	2	c Cullinan b Donald	5
A.R.C.Fraser	c Cullinan b Donald	4	not out	1
Extras	(B 4, LB 5, W 2, NB 10)	21	(B 14, LB 1, W 2, NB 10)	27
Total		**230**		**240**

SOUTH AFRICA

G.Kirsten	lbw b Fraser	6	c Atherton b Gough	3
G.F.J.Liebenberg	c Hick b Fraser	21	lbw b Gough	6
J.H.Kallis	c Ramprakash b Cork	40	lbw b Fraser	3
D.J.Cullinan	c Stewart b Gough	27	lbw b Gough	0
*W.J.Cronje	lbw b Frser	57	c Stewart b Fraser	0
J.N.Rhodes	c Stewart b Gough	32	c Flintoff b Gough	85
B.M.McMillan	c Salisbury b Cork	7	c Stewart b Cork	54
S.M.Pollock	c Salisbury b Fraser	31	not out	28
†M.V.Boucher	c Atherton b Gough	6	lbw b Gough	4
A.A.Donald	lbw b Fraser	0	c Stewart b Fraser	4
M.Ntini	not out	4	lbw b Gough	0
Extras	(LB 20, NB 1)	21	(LB 6, NB 2)	8
Total		**252**		**195**

S AFRICA	O	M	R	W		O	M	R	W
Donald	20.3	6	44	3	(2)	29.2	9	71	5
Pollock	24	8	51	3	(1)	35	14	53	5
Ntini	21	5	72	4	(4)	15	4	43	0
Kallis	9	4	30	0	(5)	15	6	31	0
McMillan	9	0	24	0	(3)	11	0	22	0
Cullinan						1	0	1	0
Cronje						4	1	4	0
ENGLAND									
Gough	24.3	7	58	3		23	6	42	6
Fraser	25	9	42	5		23	8	50	3
Cork	21	3	72	2		17	1	50	1
Flintoff	8	1	31	0		4	0	13	0
Salisbury	3	0	6	0		8	0	34	0
Butcher	9	4	23	0					

FALL OF WICKETS

	E	SA	E	SA
Wkt	1st	1st	2nd	2nd
1st	45	17	2	9
2nd	83	36	81	12
3rd	110	83	143	12
4th	181	120	200	12
5th	196	163	206	27
6th	196	184	207	144
7th	198	237	207	167
8th	200	242	229	175
9th	213	242	235	194
10th	230	252	240	195

Umpires: Javed Akhtar (*Pakistan*) (17) and P.Willey (11).
Referee: A.Ebrahim (*Zimbabwe*) (2).   **Test No. 1422/115 (E 751/SA 225)**

ENGLAND v SOUTH AFRICA 1998

ENGLAND – BATTING AND FIELDING

	M	I	NO	HS	Runs	Avge	100	50	Ct/St
M.A.Butcher	3	6	–	116	338	56.33	1	2	1
M.A.Atherton	5	10	1	103	493	54.77	1	3	2
A.J.Stewart	5	10	1	164	465	51.66	1	1	23
R.D.B.Croft	3	6	4	37*	90	45.00	–	–	1
N.Hussain	5	10	–	105	347	34.70	1	2	2
M.R.Ramprakash	5	9	1	67*	249	31.12	–	1	5
D.G.Cork	5	9	1	36	99	12.37	–	–	2
G.P.Thorpe	3	6	–	43	63	10.50	–	–	–
I.D.K.Salisbury	2	3	–	23	27	9.00	–	–	2
D.Gough	4	6	1	16*	43	8.60	–	–	–
A.R.C.Fraser	5	8	2	17	39	6.50	–	–	–
M.A.Ealham	2	4	–	8	24	6.00	–	–	–
A.Flintoff	2	3	–	17	17	5.66	–	–	1
G.A.Hick	2	3	–	6	9	3.00	–	–	3

Played in one Test: A.F.Giles 16*, 1; D.W.Headley 2, 1; S.P.James 10, 0; N.V.Knight 11, 1.

ENGLAND – BOWLING

	O	M	R	W	Avge	Best	5wI	10wM
A.R.C.Fraser	203.3	55	492	24	20.50	5- 42	3	1
D.Gough	130.5	26	388	17	22.82	6- 42	1	–
D.G.Cork	174.4	29	573	18	31.83	6-119	2	–

Also bowled: M.A.Butcher 14-5-37-0; R.D.B.Croft 87-20-211-0; M.A.Ealham 38-10-105-2; A.Flintoff 35-4-112-1; A.F.Giles 36-7-106-1; D.W.Headley 22-2-69-2; M.R.Ramprakash 5-0-17-0; I.D.K.Salisbury 25-3-106-0.

SOUTH AFRICA – BATTING AND FIELDING

	M	I	NO	HS	Runs	Avge	100	50	Ct/St
W.J.Cronje	5	7	1	126	401	66.83	1	4	4
L.Klusener	3	3	1	57	108	54.00	–	1	2
J.N.Rhodes	5	7	–	117	367	52.42	1	2	1
J.H.Kallis	5	7	–	132	294	42.00	1	1	7
D.J.Cullinan	5	8	1	78	287	41.00	–	3	3
G.Kirsten	5	8	1	210	257	36.71	1	–	4
S.M.Pollock	4	6	1	50	146	29.20	–	1	3
M.V.Boucher	5	6	–	35	84	14.00	–	–	25/1
G.F.Liebenberg	4	6	–	21	59	9.83	–	–	1
A.A.Donald	5	6	3	7*	29	9.66	–	–	1
M.Ntini	2	2	1	4*	4	4.00	–	–	1
P.R.Adams	4	4	1	6*	10	3.33	–	–	–

Played in one Test: A.M.Bacher 22 (1 ct); S.Elworthy 48, 10; B.M.McMillan 7, 54 (2 ct).

SOUTH AFRICA – BOWLING

	O	M	R	W	Avge	Best	5wI	10wM
A.A.Donald	243.2	69	653	33	19.78	6-88	4	–
S.M.Pollock	219.5	72	464	18	25.77	5-53	1	–
J.H.Kallis	158.1	65	306	11	27.81	4-24	–	–
P.R.Adams	180.1	58	388	13	29.84	4-63	–	–
M.Ntini	81	27	210	6	35.00	4-72	–	–
L.Klusener	90	25	217	6	36.16	3-27	–	–

Also bowled: W.J.Cronje 29-10-65-0; D.J.Cullinan 2-0-2-0; S.Elworthy 31-9-79-1; B.M.McMillan 20-0-46-0.

ENGLAND v SRI LANKA (Only Test)

At Kennington Oval, London, on 27, 28, 29, 30, 31 August 1998.
Toss: Sri Lanka. Result: **SRI LANKA** won by 10 wickets.
Debuts: Sri Lanka – A.S.A.Perera.

ENGLAND

M.A.Butcher	c Jayasuriya b Wickremasinghe	10	st Kaluwitharana b Muralitharan	15
S.P.James	c and b Muralitharan	36	c Jayawardena b Muralitharan	25
G.A.Hick	c Kaluwitharana b Wickremasinghe	107	lbw b Muralitharan	0
*†A.J.Stewart	c Tillekeratne b Perera	4	run out	32
M.R.Ramprakash	c Jayawardena b Muralitharan	53	c Tillekeratne b Muralitharan	42
J.P.Crawley	not out	156	b Muralitharan	14
B.C.Hollioake	c Atapattu b Muralitharan	14	lbw b Muralitharan	0
D.G.Cork	b Muralitharan	6	c Kaluwitharana b Muralitharan	8
I.D.K.Salisbury	b Muralitharan	2	lbw b Muralitharan	0
D.Gough	c Kaluwitharana b Muralitharan	4	b Muralitharan	15
A.R.C.Fraser	b Muralitharan	32	not out	0
Extras	(B 1, LB 11, W 2, NB 9)	23	(B 7, LB 8, W 1, NB 14)	30
Total		**445**		**181**

SRI LANKA

S.T.Jayasuriya	c Stewart b Hollioake	213	not out	24
M.S.Atapattu	lbw b Cork	15	not out	9
D.P.M.D.Jayawardena	c Hollioake b Fraser	2		
P.A.de Silva	c Stewart b Hollioake	152		
*A.Ranatunga	lbw b Gough	51		
H.P.Tillekeratne	lbw b Gough	0		
†R.S.Kaluwitharana	c Crawley b Cork	25		
H.D.P.K.Dharmasena	lbw b Fraser	13		
A.S.A.Perera	not out	43		
G.P.Wickremasinghe	b Fraser	0		
M.Muralitharan	c Stewart b Salisbury	30		
Extras	(B 15, LB 20, W 1, NB 4)	40	(LB 4)	4
Total		**591**	(0 wickets)	**37**

SRI LANKA	O	M	R	W		O	M	R	W	FALL OF WICKETS
Wickremasinghe	30	4	81	2		4	0	16	0	E SL E SL
Perera	40	10	104	1		11	2	22	0	Wkt 1st 1st 2nd 2nd
Dharmasena	18	3	55	0	(4)	19.3	13	12	0	1st 16 53 25 —
Muralitharan	59.3	14	155	7	(3)	54.2	27	65	9	2nd 78 85 25 —
Jayasuriya	11	0	38	0		28	14	30	0	3rd 81 328 78
De Silva						10.3	3	16	0	4th 209 450 93
Jayawardena						2	0	5	0	5th 230 450 116
ENGLAND										6th 277 488 116
Gough	30	5	102	2						7th 333 504 127
Fraser	23	3	95	3	(1)	2	0	19	0	8th 343 526 127
Hollioake	26	2	105	2		1	0	11	0	9th 356 532 180
Cork	36	5	128	2	(2)	2	0	3	0	10th 445 591 181
Salisbury	25.5	7	86	1						
Ramprakash	5	0	24	0						
Butcher	11	2	16	0						

Umpires: E.A.Nicholls (*West Indies*) (4) and D.R.Shepherd (42).
Referee: A.Ebrahim (*Zimbabwe*) (3). **Test No. 1423/6 (E 752/SL 87)**

PAKISTAN v AUSTRALIA (1st Test)

At Rawalpindi Cricket Stadium on 1, 2, 3, 4, 5 October 1998.
Toss: Pakistan. Result: **AUSTRALIA** won by an innings and 99 runs.
Debuts: Australia – C.R.Miller.

PAKISTAN

Saeed Anwar	c Langer b MacGill	145		lbw b Miller	19
*Aamir Sohail	c Healy b McGrath	4		b McGrath	13
Mohammad Wasim	c Healy b Fleming	1		lbw b Fleming	0
Inzamam-ul-Haq	c Langer b McGrath	14		lbw b Fleming	0
Salim Malik	c Taylor b Miller	10		not out	52
Azhar Mahmood	c McGrath b MacGill	16	(7)	c Langer b MacGill	1
†Moin Khan	c Fleming b MacGill	39	(6)	c Taylor b MacGill	18
Wasim Akram	c Fleming b MacGill	0		c Healy b Miller	15
Mohammad Hussain	b MacGill	1		c Miller b MacGill	17
Mushtaq Ahmed	run out	26		lbw b MacGill	0
Saqlain Mushtaq	not out	2		lbw b McGrath	7
Extras	(B 5, LB 2, NB 4)	11		(LB 3)	3
Total		**269**			**145**

AUSTRALIA

M.J.Slater	c Mohd Wasim b Hussain	108
*M.A.Taylor	c Moin b Wasim Akram	3
J.L.Langer	lbw b Wasim Akram	0
M.E.Waugh	lbw b Mushtaq Ahmed	0
S.R.Waugh	c Mohd Wasim b Aamir	157
D.S.Lehmann	b Hussain	98
†I.A.Healy	c Mohd Wasim b Saqlain	82
D.W.Fleming	b Wasim Akram	8
C.R.Miller	c and b Mushtaq Ahmed	3
S.C.G.MacGill	b Saqlain	21
G.D.McGrath	not out	3
Extras	(LB 19, NB 11)	30
Total		**513**

AUSTRALIA	O	M	R	W	O	M	R	W
McGrath	26	3	83	2	16.5	6	24	2
Fleming	20	3	39	1	15	4	38	2
Miller	23	4	65	1	21	8	30	2
MacGill	22	5	66	5	20	7	47	4
Lehmann	4	1	3	0	3	2	3	0
S.R.Waugh	2	0	6	0				

PAKISTAN	O	M	R	W
Wasim Akram	35	4	111	3
Azhar Mahmood	13	1	36	0
Mushtaq Ahmed	41	7	115	2
Saqlain Mushtaq	41.5	9	112	2
Mohammad Hussain	20	3	66	2
Aamir Sohail	23	3	54	1

FALL OF WICKETS

	P	A	P
Wkt	1st	1st	2nd
1st	13	11	24
2nd	18	11	32
3rd	35	28	32
4th	50	226	32
5th	81	352	66
6th	140	443	68
7th	140	459	94
8th	147	464	126
9th	267	504	128
10th	269	513	145

Umpires: Javed Akhtar (18) and P.Willey (*England*) (12).
Referee: P.L.van der Merwe (*South Africa*) (23).   Test No. 1424/41 (P 249/A 582)

PAKISTAN v AUSTRALIA (2nd Test)

At Arbab Niaz Stadium, Peshawar on 15, 16, 17, 18, 19 October 1998.
Toss: Australia. Result: **MATCH DRAWN**.
Debuts: None.

AUSTRALIA

*M.A.Taylor	not out	334	(2) b Aamir		92
M.J.Slater	c Azhar b Shoaib	2	(1) lbw b Mushtaq Ahmed		21
J.L.Langer	c Moin b Azhar	116	c Yousuf b Mushtaq		14
M.E.Waugh	c Salim b Aamir	42	b Shoaib		43
S.R.Waugh	c Moin b Shoaib	1	not out		49
R.T.Ponting	not out	76	lbw b Ijaz		43
†I.A.Healy			not out		14
D.W.Fleming					
C.R.Miller					
S.C.G.MacGill					
G.D.McGrath					
Extras	(LB 9, W 3, NB 16)	28	(LB 4, NB 9)		13
Total	(4 wickets declared)	**599**			**289**

PAKISTAN

Saeed Anwar	c Healy b Miller	126
*Aamir Sohail	c Fleming b McGrath	31
Ijaz Ahmed	c Healy b MacGill	155
Inzamam-ul-Haq	c Healy b S.R.Waugh	97
Salim Malik	c Taylor b McGrath	49
Yousuf Youhana	c S.R.Waugh b MacGill	28
†Moin Khan	c Healy b Ponting	0
Azhar Mahmood	c Langer b McGrath	26
Mushtaq Ahmed	not out	48
Mohammad Zahid	lbw b Fleming	1
Shoaib Akhtar		
Extras	(B 5, LB 9, W 1, NB 4)	19
Total	(9 wickets declared)	**580**

PAKISTAN	O	M	R	W		O	M	R	W	FALL OF WICKETS
Shoaib Akhtar	31	6	107	2		16	2	68	1	A P A
Mohammad Zahid	16	0	74	0	(4)	10	2	42	0	Wkt 1st 1st 2nd
Mushtaq Ahmed	46	3	153	0		20	1	59	2	1st 16 45 39
Azhar Mahmood	23	2	82	1	(2)	3	0	18	0	2nd 295 256 67
Aamir Sohail	42	8	111	1		10	1	35	1	3rd 418 371 170
Salim Malik	16	0	63	0		15	1	30	0	4th 431 454 179
Ijaz Ahmed						14	1	33	1	5th – 500 269
										6th – 501 –
AUSTRALIA										7th – 521 –
McGrath	36	8	131	3						8th – 571 –
Fleming	35.1	6	103	1						9th – 580 –
MacGill	42	5	169	2						10th – – –
Miller	38	12	99	1						
M.E.Waugh	8	0	32	0						
S.R.Waugh	8	1	19	1						
Ponting	5	1	13	1						

Umpires: S.A.Bucknor (*West Indies*) (38) and Mohammad Nazir jr (2).
Referee: P.L.van der Merwe (*South Africa*) (24). **Test No. 1425/42 (P 250/A 583)**

PAKISTAN v AUSTRALIA (3rd Test)

At National Stadium, Karachi on 22, 23, 24, 25, 26 October 1998.
Toss: Australia. Result: **MATCH DRAWN**.
Debuts: Pakistan – Shahid Afridi, Shakeel Ahmed.

AUSTRALIA

*M.A.Taylor	c Inzamam b Arshad	16	(2) b Arshad		68
M.J.Slater	st Moin b Arshad	96	(1) c Youhana b Arshad		11
J.L.Langer	lbw b Shoaib	30	run out		51
M.E.Waugh	c Inzamam b Shahid	26	st Moin b Shakeel		117
S.R.Waugh	lbw b Shahid	0	c Moin b Shakeel		28
D.S.Lehmann	b Shahid	3	c Ijaz b Wasim		26
†I.A.Healy	c Moin b Arshad	47	c Shahid b Shoaib		3
G.R.Robertson	c Yousuf b Shahid	5	c Wasim b Shakeel		45
C.R.Miller	b Wasim	0	c Shahid b Shakeel		0
S.C.G.MacGill	not out	23	run out		10
G.D.McGrath	c Shakeel b Shahid	6	not out		4
Extras	(B 1, LB 17, NB 10)	28	(B 4, LB 8, NB 15)		27
Total		**280**			**390**

PAKISTAN

*Aamir Sohail	c Langer b Miller	133	lbw b Miller		25
Shahid Afridi	c Taylor b McGrath	10	c Healy b Miller		6
Ijaz Ahmed	c Healy b McGrath	5	not out		120
Inzamam-ul-Haq	c Lehmann b McGrath	9	(7) not out		21
Salim Malik	c McGrath b MacGill	6	(4) lbw b Miller		0
Yousuf Youhana	b Robertson	9	(5) c M.E.Waugh b MacGill		11
†Moin Khan	c Slater b McGrath	20	(6) c MacGill b Lehmann		75
Wasim Akram	lbw b MacGill	35			
Shakeel Ahmed	c Langer b McGrath	1			
Arshad Khan	lbw b MacGill	7			
Shoaib Akhtar	not out	6			
Extras	(B 6, LB 5, W 1, NB 5)	17	(B 2, NB 2)		4
Total		**252**	(5 wickets)		**262**

PAKISTAN	O	M	R	W		O	M	R	W	FALL OF WICKETS
Wasim Akram	22	4	51	1		22	2	60	1		A P A P
Shoaib Akhtar	14.2	5	39	1		17	3	37	1	Wkt 1st 1st 2nd 2nd
Shakeel Ahmed	24.4	9	48	0	(5)	29.3	3	91	4	1st 38 26 27 20
Arshad Khan	41	14	72	3	(3)	56	14	141	2	2nd 105 40 135 33
Shahid Afridi	23.3	6	52	5	(4)	18	3	49	0	3rd 169 51 152 35
										4th 169 54 208 75
AUSTRALIA										5th 179 69 284 228
McGrath	25	6	66	5		18	11	40	0	6th 189 116 294 –
Miller	14	2	53	1		25	5	82	3	7th 210 214 357 –
MacGill	25.4	6	34	3		17	2	66	1	8th 211 239 357 –
Robertson	22	4	46	1	(5)	16	2	56	0	9th 266 240 369 –
Lehmann	1	0	6	0	(6)	2	0	6	1	10th 280 252 390 –
S.R.Waugh	2	0	6	0	(4)	8	5	10	0	

Umpires: D.L.Orchard (*South Africa*) (8) and Riazuddin (5).
Referee: P.L.van der Merwe (*South Africa*) (25). **Test No. 1426/43 (P 251/A 584)**

PAKISTAN v AUSTRALIA 1998-99

PAKISTAN – BATTING AND FIELDING

	M	I	NO	HS	Runs	Avge	100	50	Ct/St
Ijaz Ahmed	2	3	1	155	280	140.00	2	–	1
Saeed Anwar	2	3	–	145	290	96.66	2	–	–
Aamir Sohail	3	5	–	133	206	41.20	1	–	–
Mushtaq Ahmed	2	3	1	48*	74	37.00	–	–	1
Inzamam-ul-Haq	3	5	–	97	141	35.25	–	1	2
Moin Khan	3	5	–	75	152	30.40	–	1	5/2
Salim Malik	3	5	1	52*	111	27.75	–	1	1
Wasim Akram	2	3	–	35	50	16.66	–	–	1
Yousuf Youhana	2	3	–	28	48	16.00	–	–	3
Azhar Mahmood	2	3	–	26	43	14.33	–	–	1
Shoaib Akhtar	2	1	1	6*	6	–	–	–	–

Played in one Test: Arshad Khan 7; Mohammad Hussain 1, 17; Mohammad Wasim 1, 0 (3 ct); Mohammad Zahid 1; Saqlain Mushtaq 2*, 7; Shahid Afridi 10, 6 (2 ct); Shakeel Ahmed 1 (1 ct).

PAKISTAN – BOWLING

	O	M	R	W	Avge	Best	5wI	10wM
Shahid Afridi	41.3	9	101	5	20.20	5- 52	1	–
Shakeel Ahmed	54.1	12	139	4	34.75	4- 91	–	–
Arshad Khan	97	28	213	5	42.60	3- 72	–	–
Wasim Akram	79	10	222	5	44.40	3-111	–	–
Shoaib Akhtar	78.2	14	251	5	50.20	2-107	–	–
Mushtaq Ahmed	107	11	327	4	81.75	2- 59	–	–

Also bowled: Aamir Sohail 75-12-200-3; Azhar Mahmood 39-3-136-1; Ijaz Ahmed 14-1-33-1; Mohammad Hussain 20-3-66-2; Mohammad Zahid 26-2-116-0; Salim Malik 31-1-93-0; Saqlain Mushtaq 41.5-9-112-2.

AUSTRALIA – BATTING AND FIELDING

	M	I	NO	HS	Runs	Avge	100	50	Ct/St
M.A.Taylor	3	5	1	334*	513	128.25	1	2	4
S.R.Waugh	3	5	1	157	235	58.75	1	–	1
I.A.Healy	3	4	1	82	146	48.66	–	1	9
M.J.Slater	3	5	–	108	238	47.60	1	1	1
M.E.Waugh	3	5	–	117	228	45.60	1	1	1
D.S.Lehmann	2	3	–	98	127	42.33	–	1	1
J.L.Langer	3	5	–	116	211	42.20	1	1	6
S.C.G.MacGill	3	3	1	23*	54	27.00	–	–	1
G.D.McGrath	3	3	2	6	13	13.00	–	–	–
D.W.Fleming	2	1	–	8	8	8.00	–	–	3
C.R.Miller	3	3	–	3	3	1.00	–	–	1

Played in one Test: R.T.Ponting 76*, 43; G.R.Robertson 5, 45.

AUSTRALIA – BOWLING

	O	M	R	W	Avge	Best	5wI	10wM
S.C.G.MacGill	127.4	24	412	15	27.46	5-66	1	–
G.D.McGrath	120.5	34	344	12	28.66	5-66	1	–
C.R.Miller	121	31	329	8	41.12	3-82	–	–
D.W.Fleming	70.1	13	180	4	45.00	2-38	–	–

Also bowled: D.S.Lehmann 10-3-18-1; R.T.Ponting 5-1-13-1; G.R.Robertson 38-6-102-1; M.E.Waugh 8-0-32-0; S.R.Waugh 20-6-41-1.

ZIMBABWE v INDIA (Only Test)

At Harare Sports Club on 7, 8, 9, 10 October 1998.
Toss: India. Result: **ZIMBABWE** won by 61 runs.
Debuts: Zimbabwe – N.C.Johnson; India – A.B.Agarkar, R.R.Singh.

ZIMBABWE

G.J.Rennie	c sub ‡ b Agarkar	47		c R.R.Singh b Harbhajan	84
C.B.Wishart	c Harbhajan b Ganguly	21		c and b Kumble	63
M.W.Goodwin	lbw b Srinath	42		c and b Kumble	44
*A.D.R.Campbell	c Dravid b Srinath	0	(5)	c Azharuddin b Harbhajan	25
†A.Flower	c R.R.Singh b Srinath	30	(6)	not out	41
N.C.Johnson	c R.R.Singh b Kumble	4	(7)	c R.R.Singh b Kumble	1
C.N.Evans	c Mongia b Harbhajan	11	(8)	lbw b Kumble	4
H.H.Streak	c R.R.Singh b Harbhajan	8	(9)	c Dravid b Agarkar	3
H.K.Olonga	lbw b Kumble	5	(4)	c Azharuddin b Harbhajan	5
A.G.Huckle	not out	28		lbw b Srinath	1
M.Mbangwa	st Mongia b Kumble	2		b Srinath	0
Extras	(LB 1, W 2, NB 20)	23		(B 1, LB 12, NB 9)	22
Total		**221**			**293**

INDIA

†N.R.Mongia	b Olonga	1		c Wishart b Olonga	0
N.S.Sidhu	c Flower b Olonga	6		c Johnson b Streak	0
A.Kumble	b Streak	29	(8)	c Goodwin b Johnson	12
R.Dravid	c Johnson b Mbangwa	118	(3)	c Flower b Mbangwa	44
S.R.Tendulkar	c Campbell b Johnson	34	(4)	c Flower b Johnson	7
*M.Azharuddin	c Johnson b Olonga	1	(6)	c Campbell b Streak	7
S.C.Ganguly	lbw b Olonga	47	(6)	lbw b Huckle	36
R.R.Singh	lbw b Olonga	15	(7)	lbw b Johnson	12
A.B.Agarkar	c Flower b Streak	4		c Olonga b Mbangwa	5
J.Srinath	c sub (A.R.Whittall) b Streak	6		run out	23
Harbhajan Singh	not out	0		not out	15
Extras	(LB 4, W 4, NB 11)	19		(LB 3, W 1, NB 8)	12
Total		**280**			**173**

INDIA	O	M	R	W		O	M	R	W	FALL OF WICKETS
Srinath	21	3	59	3		23.3	7	43	2	
Agarkar	16	3	40	1		18	2	60	1	
Ganguly	5	1	21	1		4	1	10	0	
R.R.Singh	6	2	16	0	(6)	4	2	13	0	
Harbhajan Singh	15	2	42	2		20	4	64	3	
Kumble	17.4	3	42	3	(4)	36	4	87	4	
ZIMBABWE										
Streak	29	9	62	3	(2)	14	2	49	2	
Olonga	26	7	70	5	(1)	10	1	40	1	
Johnson	18	5	64	1		14.5	5	41	3	
Huckle	15	2	39	0	(5)	6	0	24	1	
Mbangwa	14.2	4	28	1	(4)	12	6	16	2	
Evans	3	0	8	0						
Goodwin	2	0	5	0						

		Z	I	Z	I
Wkt	1st	1st	2nd	2nd	
1st	42	2	138	3	
2nd	120	22	209	6	
3rd	120	49	223	29	
4th	122	124	223	37	
5th	140	127	246	104	
6th	163	215	249	112	
7th	180	259	257	124	
8th	181	268	288	129	
9th	214	280	293	133	
10th	221	280	293	173	

Umpires: R.E.Koertzen (*South Africa*) (8) and I.D.Robinson (19). ‡ (D.S.Mohanty).
Referee: A.C.Smith (*England*) (1). **Test No. 1427/3** (Z 31/I 319)

251

AUSTRALIA v ENGLAND (1st Test)

At Woolloongabba, Brisbane on 20, 21, 22, 23, 24 November 1998.
Toss: Australia. Result: **MATCH DRAWN.**
Debuts: None.

AUSTRALIA

*M.A.Taylor	c Hussain b Cork	46	(2) b Cork		0
M.J.Slater	c Butcher b Mullally	16	(1) c and b Fraser		113
J.L.Langer	lbw b Gough	8	c Mullally b Croft		74
M.E.Waugh	c Stewart b Mullally	31	not out		27
S.R.Waugh	c Stewart b Mullally	112	not out		16
R.T.Ponting	c Butcher b Cork	21			
†I.A.Healy	c Mullally b Fraser	134			
M.S.Kasprowicz	c Stewart b Mullally	0			
D.W.Fleming	not out	71			
S.C.G.MacGill	c Stewart b Mullally	20			
G.D.McGrath	c Atherton b Croft	5			
Extras	(LB 14, W 1, NB 6)	21	(B 1, LB 1, NB 5)		7
Total		**485**	(3 wickets declared)		**237**

ENGLAND

M.A.Butcher	c and b M.E.Waugh	116	lbw b MacGill		40
M.A.Atherton	c M.E.Waugh b McGrath	0	c Fleming b McGrath		28
N.Hussain	c Healy b Kasprowicz	59	b MacGill		47
*†A.J.Stewart	c Kasprowicz b MacGill	8	c Ponting b M.E.Waugh		9
G.P.Thorpe	c Langer b McGrath	77	c Langer b M.E.Waugh		14
M.R.Ramprakash	not out	69	st Healy b MacGill		21
D.G.Cork	c MacGill b McGrath	0	not out		4
R.D.B.Croft	b Kasprowicz	23			
D.Gough	lbw b McGrath	0			
A.D.Mullally	c Kasprowicz b McGrath	0			
A.R.C.Fraser	c M.E.Waugh b McGrath	1			
Extras	(B 1, LB 9, NB 12)	22	(LB 3, W 1, NB 9)		13
Total		**375**	(6 wickets)		**179**

ENGLAND	O	M	R	W		O	M	R	W
Gough	34	4	135	1		6	0	50	0
Cork	31	6	98	2		5	0	18	1
Mullally	40	10	105	5		14	4	38	0
Croft	23	6	55	1	(5)	20	2	71	1
Fraser	28	7	76	1	(4)	15	1	52	1
Ramprakash	2	1	2	0		2	0	6	0
AUSTRALIA									
McGrath	34.2	11	85	6		16	6	30	1
Fleming	27	5	83	0	(3)	7	2	12	0
Kasprowicz	29	7	82	2	(2)	8	3	28	0
MacGill	24	4	70	1		22	4	51	3
S.R.Waugh	3	0	17	0					
Ponting	3	0	10	0	(6)	1	1	0	0
M.E.Waugh	8	1	18	0	(5)	14	0	55	2

FALL OF WICKETS

	A	E	A	E
Wkt	1st	1st	2nd	2nd
1st	30	11	20	46
2nd	59	145	182	96
3rd	106	168	199	103
4th	106	240	–	133
5th	178	315	–	148
6th	365	319	–	161
7th	365	360	–	–
8th	420	373	–	–
9th	445	373	–	–
10th	485	375	–	–

Umpires: K.T.Francis (*Sri Lanka*) (23) and D.B.Hair (26).
Referee: J.R.Reid (*New Zealand*) (37). Test No. 1428/292 (A 585/E 753)

AUSTRALIA v ENGLAND (2nd Test)

At WACA Ground, Perth on 28, 29, 30 November 1998.
Toss: Australia. Result: **AUSTRALIA** won by 7 wickets.
Debuts: England – A.J.Tudor.

ENGLAND

M.A.Butcher	c Healy b Fleming	0		c Ponting b Fleming	1
M.A.Atherton	c Healy b McGrath	1		c Taylor b Fleming	35
N.Hussain	c Healy b McGrath	6		lbw b Fleming	1
*†A.J.Stewart	b McGrath	38		c Taylor b Fleming	0
M.R.Ramprakash	c Taylor b Fleming	26		not out	47
J.P.Crawley	c M.E.Waugh b Gillespie	4		c Langer b Miller	15
G.A.Hick	c Healy b Gillespie	0		c Ponting b Gillespie	68
D.G.Cork	c Taylor b Fleming	2		lbw b Gillespie	16
A.J.Tudor	not out	18		c Healy b Gillespie	0
D.Gough	c M.E.Waugh b Fleming	11		lbw b Gillespie	0
A.D.Mullally	c Healy b Fleming	0		b Gillespie	0
Extras	(LB 2, W 2, NB 2)	6		(NB 8)	8
Total		**112**			**191**

AUSTRALIA

*M.A.Taylor	c Stewart b Cork	61	(2)	c Hick b Mullally	3
M.J.Slater	c Butcher b Gough	34	(1)	c and b Gough	17
J.L.Langer	c Crawley b Ramprakash	15		c Atherton b Tudor	7
M.E.Waugh	c Butcher b Fleming	36		not out	17
J.N.Gillespie	c Stewart b Mullally	11			
S.R.Waugh	b Tudor	33	(5)	not out	15
R.T.Ponting	c Stewart b Tudor	11			
†I.A.Healy	lbw b Gough	12			
D.W.Fleming	c Hick b Gough	0			
C.R.Miller	not out	3			
G.D.McGrath	c Cork b Tudor	0			
Extras	(B 1, LB 10, NB 13)	24		(LB 3, NB 2)	5
Total		**240**		(3 wickets)	**64**

AUSTRALIA	O	M	R	W	O	M	R	W
McGrath	16	4	37	3	26	10	47	0
Fleming	14	3	46	5	19	7	45	4
Gillespie	7	0	23	2	15.2	2	88	5
Miller	2	0	4	0	10	4	11	1
ENGLAND								
Gough	25	9	43	3	9	5	18	1
Cork	21	5	49	1				
Tudor	20.2	5	89	4	5	0	19	1
Mullally	21	10	36	1	(2) 9	0	24	1
Ramprakash	2	0	12	1				

FALL OF WICKETS				
	E	A	E	A
Wkt	1st	1st	2nd	2nd
1st	2	81	5	16
2nd	4	115	11	24
3rd	19	138	15	36
4th	62	165	40	–
5th	74	209	67	–
6th	74	214	158	–
7th	81	228	189	–
8th	90	228	189	–
9th	108	239	189	–
10th	112	240	191	–

Umpires: D.J.Harper (1) and S.Venkataraghavan (*India*) (27).
Referee: J.R.Reid (*New Zealand*) (38). **Test No. 1429/293 (A 586/E 754)**

AUSTRALIA v ENGLAND (3rd Test)

At Adelaide Oval on 11, 12, 13, 14, 15 December 1998.
Toss: Australia. Result: **AUSTRALIA** won by 205 runs.
Debuts: None.

AUSTRALIA

M.J.Slater	c Stewart b Headley	17	(2) lbw b Gough	103
*M.A.Taylor	c Hussain b Such	59	(1) lbw b Such	29
J.L.Langer	not out	179	c sub (B.C.Hollioake) b Such	52
M.E.Waugh	c and b Such	7	not out	51
S.R.Waugh	c Hick b Gough	59	c Hick b Headley	7
R.T.Ponting	c Hick b Gough	5	b Gough	10
†I.A.Healy	c Ramprakash b Headley	13	not out	7
D.W.Fleming	lbw b Headley	12		
S.C.G.MacGill	b Such	0		
C.R.Miller	lbw b Headley	11		
G.D.McGrath	c Stewart b Gough	10		
Extras	(LB 6, NB 13)	19	(LB 12, W 1, NB 6)	19
Total		391	(5 wickets declared)	278

ENGLAND

M.A.Butcher	lbw b Miller	6	c Healy b Fleming	19
M.A.Atherton	c Taylor b MacGill	41	c M.E.Waugh b Miller	5
N.Hussain	not out	89	lbw b Miller	41
*†A.J.Stewart	c Slater b Miller	0	(6) not out	63
M.R.Ramprakash	c M.E.Waugh b McGrath	61	(4) b Fleming	57
J.P.Crawley	b McGrath	5	(7) c M.E.Waugh b McGrath	13
G.A.Hick	c Taylor b MacGill	0	(8) c Ponting b McGrath	0
D.W.Headley	lbw b MacGill	0	(5) c M.E.Waugh b Miller	2
D.Gough	c Healy b MacGill	0	c Healy b McGrath	3
A.D.Mullally	b Fleming	0	c Healy b Fleming	4
P.M.Such	lbw b Fleming	0	lbw b McGrath	0
Extras	(B 1, LB 3, W 1, NB 5)	10	(B 7, LB 9, NB 14)	30
Total		227		237

ENGLAND	O	M	R	W	O	M	R	W	FALL OF WICKETS
Gough	29.5	4	103	3	22	2	76	2		A	E	A	E
Mullally	26	5	59	0	16	6	18	0	Wkt	1st	1st	2nd	2nd
Headley	23	1	97	4	18	1	78	1	1st	28	18	54	27
Such	38	8	99	3	29	5	66	2	2nd	140	83	188	31
Ramprakash	9	1	27	0	12	1	27	0	3rd	156	84	216	120
Hick					1	0	1	0	4th	264	187	230	122
									5th	274	195	268	163
AUSTRALIA									6th	311	210	–	221
McGrath	18	4	48	2	17	0	50	4	7th	338	210	–	221
Fleming	10.5	2	34	2	21	3	56	3	8th	339	226	–	231
Miller	23	6	71	2	24	1	57	3	9th	354	227	–	236
MacGill	28	6	53	4	25	8	55	0	10th	391	227	–	237
M.E.Waugh	3	0	17	0									
S.R.Waugh					(5) 2	1	3	0					

Umpires: S.A.Bucknor (*West Indies*) (39) and S.J.Davis (2).
Referee: J.R.Reid (*New Zealand*) (39).   **Test No. 1430/294 (A 587/E 755)**

AUSTRALIA v ENGLAND (4th Test)

At Melbourne Cricket Ground on 26 (*no play*), 27, 28, 29 December 1998.
Toss: Australia. Result: **ENGLAND** won by 12 runs.
Debuts: Australia – M.J.Nicholson; England – W.K.Hegg.

ENGLAND

M.A.Atherton	c Healy b McGrath	0		b Fleming	0
*A.J.Stewart	b MacGill	107		c Slater b MacGill	52
M.A.Butcher	c Langer b McGrath	0		c Slater b MacGill	14
N.Hussain	c Healy b Nicholson	19	(5)	c Slater b Nicholson	50
M.R.Ramprakash	c McGrath b S.R.Waugh	63	(6)	b Nicholson	14
G.A.Hick	c Fleming b MacGill	39	(7)	b Fleming	60
†W.K.Hegg	c Healy b S.R.Waugh	3	(8)	c MacGill b Nicholson	9
D.W.Headley	c Taylor b McGrath	14	(4)	b McGrath	1
D.Gough	b MacGill	11		c Slater b MacGill	4
A.R.C.Fraser	not out	0		not out	7
A.D.Mullally	lbw b MacGill	0		c and b McGrath	16
Extras	(LB 7, W 1, NB 6)	14		(B 2, LB 4, NB 11)	17
Total		**270**			**244**

AUSTRALIA

*M.A.Taylor	c Hick b Gough	7	(2)	c Headley b Mullally	19
M.J.Slater	lbw b Gough	1	(1)	lbw b Headley	18
J.L.Langer	c Hussain b Gough	44		c Ramprakash b Mullally	30
M.E.Waugh	lbw b Fraser	36		c Hick b Headley	43
S.R.Waugh	not out	122		not out	30
D.S.Lehmann	c Hegg b Gough	13		c Hegg b Headley	4
†I.A.Healy	c Headley b Fraser	36		c Hick b Headley	0
D.W.Fleming	c Hick b Mullally	12		lbw b Headley	0
M.J.Nicholson	b Gough	5		c Hegg b Headley	9
S.C.G.MacGill	c Hegg b Mullally	43		b Gough	0
G.D.McGrath	b Mullally	0		lbw b Gough	0
Extras	(B 4, LB 6, NB 11)	21		(B 4, LB 1, NB 4)	9
Total		**340**			**162**

AUSTRALIA	O	M	R	W	O	M	R	W
McGrath	22	5	64	3	20.2	5	56	2
Fleming	19	3	71	0	17	4	45	2
Nicholson	10	0	59	1	15	4	56	3
MacGill	19	2	61	4	27	3	81	3
S.R.Waugh	6	2	8	2				
M.E.Waugh					(5) 1	1	0	0
ENGLAND								
Gough	28	7	96	5	15.4	2	54	2
Headley	25	3	86	0	17	5	60	6
Mullally	21.3	5	64	3	10	4	20	2
Ramprakash	2	0	6	0				
Fraser	22	0	78	2	(4) 4	0	23	0

FALL OF WICKETS
	E	A	E	A
Wkt	1st	1st	2nd	2nd
1st	0	13	5	31
2nd	4	26	61	41
3rd	81	98	66	103
4th	200	127	78	130
5th	202	151	127	140
6th	206	209	178	140
7th	244	235	207	140
8th	266	252	221	161
9th	270	340	221	162
10th	270	340	244	162

Umpires: S.A.Bucknor (*West Indies*) (40) and D.J.Harper (2).
Referee: J.R.Reid (*New Zealand*) (40). **Test No. 1431/295 (A 588/E 756)**

AUSTRALIA v ENGLAND (5th Test)

At Sydney Cricket Ground on 2, 3, 4, 5 January 1999.
Toss: Australia. Result: **AUSTRALIA** won by 98 runs.
Debuts: None.

AUSTRALIA

*M.A.Taylor	c Hick b Headley	2	(2) c Stewart b Gough	2
M.J.Slater	c Hegg b Headley	18	(1) c Hegg b Headley	123
J.L.Langer	c Ramprakash b Tudor	26	lbw b Headley	0
M.E.Waugh	c Hegg b Headley	121	c Ramprakash b Headley	24
S.R.Waugh	b Such	96	(7) b Headley	8
D.S.Lehmann	c Hussain b Tudor	32	(5) c Crawley b Such	0
†I.A.Healy	c Hegg b Gough	14	(6) c Crawley b Such	5
S.K.Warne	not out	2	c Ramprakash b Such	8
S.C.G.MacGill	b Gough	0	c Butcher b Such	6
C.R.Miller	b Gough	0	not out	3
G.D.McGrath	c Hick b Headley	0	c Stewart b Such	0
Extras	(LB 2, NB 9)	11	(B 3, LB 1)	4
Total		**322**		**184**

ENGLAND

M.A.Butcher	lbw b Warne	36	st Healy b Warne	27
*A.J.Stewart	c Warne b McGrath	3	st Healy b MacGill	42
N.Hussain	c M.E.Waugh b Miller	42	c and b MacGill	53
M.R.Ramprakash	c MacGill b McGrath	14	c Taylor b McGrath	14
G.A.Hick	c Warne b MacGill	23	b MacGill	7
J.P.Crawley	c Taylor b MacGill	44	b MacGill	5
†W.K.Hegg	b Miller	15	c Healy b MacGill	3
A.J.Tudor	b MacGill	14	b MacGill	3
D.W.Headley	c McGrath b MacGill	8	c Healy b MacGill	16
D.Gough	lbw b MacGill	0	not out	7
P.M.Such	not out	0	c and b MacGill	2
Extras	(B 8, LB 8, W 1, NB 4)	21	(LB 5, W 1, NB 3)	9
Total		**220**		**188**

ENGLAND	O	M	R	W		O	M	R	W	FALL OF WICKETS
Gough	17	4	61	3	(2)	15	3	51	1		A	E	A	E
Headley	19.3	3	62	4	(1)	19	7	40	4	Wkt	1st	1st	2nd	2nd
Tudor	12	1	64	2	(4)	5	2	8	0	1st	4	18	16	57
Such	24	6	77	1	(3)	25.5	5	81	5	2nd	52	56	25	77
Ramprakash	15	0	56	0						3rd	52	88	64	110
AUSTRALIA										4th	242	137	73	131
McGrath	17	7	35	2		10	1	40	1	5th	284	139	91	150
Miller	23	6	45	2		17	1	50	1	6th	319	171	110	157
MacGill	20.1	1	57	5		20.1	4	50	7	7th	321	204	141	164
Warne	20	4	67	1		19	3	43	1	8th	321	213	180	175
										9th	321	213	184	180
										10th	322	220	184	188

Umpires: R.S.Dunne (*New Zealand*) (30) and D.B.Hair (28).
Referee: J.R.Reid (*New Zealand*) (41). **Test No. 1432/296 (A 589/E 757)**

AUSTRALIA v ENGLAND 1998-99

AUSTRALIA – BATTING AND FIELDING

	M	I	NO	HS	Runs	Avge	100	50	Ct/St
S.R.Waugh	5	10	4	122*	498	83.00	2	2	–
M.E.Waugh	5	10	3	121	393	56.14	1	–	10
J.L.Langer	5	10	1	179*	436	48.44	1	2	4
M.J.Slater	5	10	–	123	460	46.00	3	–	5
I.A.Healy	5	8	1	134	221	31.57	1	–	16/3
D.W.Fleming	4	5	1	71*	93	23.75	–	1	2
M.A.Taylor	5	10	–	61	228	22.80	–	2	9
D.S.Lehmann	2	4	–	32	49	12.25	–	–	–
R.T.Ponting	3	4	–	21	47	11.75	–	–	4
S.C.G.MacGill	4	6	–	43	69	11.50	–	–	5
C.R.Miller	3	4	2	11	17	8.50	–	–	–
G.D.McGrath	5	7	–	10	15	2.14	–	–	3

Played in one Test: J.N.Gillespie 11; M.S.Kasprowicz 0 (2 ct); M.J.Nicholson 5, 9; S.K.Warne 2*, 8 (2 ct).

AUSTRALIA – BOWLING

	O	M	R	W	Avge	Best	5wI	10wM
J.N.Gillespie	22.2	2	111	7	15.85	5-88	1	–
S.C.G.MacGill	185.2	33	478	27	17.70	7-50	2	1
G.D.McGrath	196.4	53	492	24	20.50	6-85	1	–
D.W.Fleming	134.5	29	392	16	24.50	5-46	1	–
C.R.Miller	99	18	238	9	26.44	3-57	–	–

Also bowled: M.S.Kasprowicz 37-10-110-2; M.J.Nicholson 25-4-115-4; R.T.Ponting 4-1-10-0; S.K.Warne 39-7-110-2; M.E.Waugh 26-2-90-3; S.R.Waugh 11-3-28-2.

ENGLAND – BATTING AND FIELDING

	M	I	NO	HS	Runs	Avge	100	50	Ct/St
M.R.Ramprakash	5	10	2	69*	379	47.37	–	4	5
N.Hussain	5	10	1	89*	407	45.22	–	4	4
A.J.Stewart	5	10	1	107	316	35.11	1	2	11
M.A.Butcher	5	10	–	116	259	25.90	1	–	5
G.A.Hick	4	8	–	68	205	25.62	–	2	11
J.P.Crawley	3	6	–	44	86	14.33	–	–	3
M.A.Atherton	4	8	–	41	110	13.75	–	–	2
D.G.Cork	2	4	1	21*	39	13.00	–	–	1
A.J.Tudor	2	3	–	18*	35	11.66	–	–	–
A.R.C.Fraser	2	3	2	7*	8	8.00	–	–	1
W.K.Hegg	2	4	–	15	30	7.50	–	–	8
D.W.Headley	3	6	–	16	41	6.83	–	–	2
D.Gough	5	9	1	11	43	5.37	–	–	1
A.D.Mullally	4	7	–	16	20	2.85	–	–	2
P.M.Such	2	4	1	2	2	0.66	–	–	1

Played in one Test: R.D.B.Croft 23, 4*; G.P.Thorpe 77, 9.

ENGLAND – BOWLING

	O	M	R	W	Avge	Best	5wI	10wM
D.W.Headley	121.3	20	423	19	22.26	6- 60	1	–
A.J.Tudor	42.2	8	180	7	25.71	4- 89	–	–
P.M.Such	116.5	24	323	11	29.36	5- 81	1	–
A.D.Mullally	157.3	44	364	12	30.33	5-105	1	–
D.Gough	201.3	40	687	21	32.71	5- 96	1	–

Also bowled: D.G.Cork 57-11-165-4; R.D.B.Croft 43-8-126-2; A.R.C.Fraser 69-8-229-4; G.A.Hick 1-0-1-0; M.R.Ramprakash 44-3-136-1.

SOUTH AFRICA v WEST INDIES (1st Test)

At The Wanderers, Johannesburg on 26, 27, 28, 29, 30 November 1998.
Toss: West Indies. Result: **SOUTH AFRICA** won by 4 wickets.
Debuts: South Africa – D.J.Terbrugge; West Indies – R.D.Jacobs.

WEST INDIES

C.B.Lambert	c Boucher b Pollock	8		c Boucher b Symcox	33
P.A.Wallace	b Pollock	16		b Pollock	14
*B.C.Lara	b Pollock	11		lbw b Donald	7
S.Chanderpaul	lbw b Donald	74		lbw b Pollock	1
C.L.Hooper	c Cullinan b Donald	44	(7)	lbw b Pollock	34
S.C.Williams	c Cronje b Terbrugge	35	(5)	c Kallis b Terbrugge	12
†R.D.Jacobs	c Cronje b Kallis	14	(6)	c Terbrugge b Symcox	42
N.A.M.McLean	c Boucher b Pollock	28	(9)	c Cullinan b Symcox	11
R.N.Lewis	c Terbrugge b Donald	12	(8)	lbw b Pollock	10
C.E.L.Ambrose	c Boucher b Pollock	0		not out	0
C.A.Walsh	not out	5		lbw b Pollock	0
Extras	(LB 7, W 2, NB 5)	14		(B 1, NB 5)	6
Total		**261**			**170**

SOUTH AFRICA

G.Kirsten	b McLean	62		c Jacobs b Ambrose	7
A.M.Bacher	c Jacobs b Walsh	1		c Wallace b Walsh	6
J.H.Kallis	c Williams b Walsh	53		not out	57
D.J.Cullinan	c Jacobs b Walsh	8		c Williams b McLean	35
*W.J.Cronje	b Ambrose	41		c McLean b Walsh	31
J.N.Rhodes	lbw b McLean	17		c Jacobs b Walsh	9
S.M.Pollock	b Walsh	11		c Chanderpaul b Ambrose	9
†M.V.Boucher	c Lara b Lewis	12		not out	1
P.L.Symcox	run out	25			
A.A.Donald	c Jacobs b Ambrose	7			
D.J.Terbrugge	not out	3			
Extras	(B 1, LB 5, W 1, NB 21)	28		(LB 2, NB 7)	9
Total		**268**		(6 wickets)	**164**

S AFRICA	O	M	R	W		O	M	R	W
Donald	23	4	91	3		15	6	28	1
Pollock	23	4	54	5		20.3	4	49	4
Kallis	15	5	37	1	(4)	14	5	26	1
Terbrugge	16	5	32	1	(3)	14	5	23	1
Cronje	1	0	3	0					
Symcox	19	5	37	0	(5)	18	9	43	2
WEST INDIES									
Ambrose	28	5	63	2		15.4	3	42	2
Walsh	25	5	66	4		21	9	45	3
McLean	17	1	66	2	(5)	5	0	17	1
Lewis	23.5	4	67	1	(3)	17	4	45	0
Hooper					(4)	4	0	13	0

FALL OF WICKETS

	WI	SA	WI	SA
Wkt	1st	1st	2nd	2nd
1st	17	10	24	14
2nd	24	102	33	14
3rd	41	111	38	58
4th	132	154	53	124
5th	177	185	80	146
6th	198	209	148	163
7th	235	229	148	–
8th	255	230	170	–
9th	255	243	170	–
10th	261	268	170	–

Umpires: C.J.Mitchley (25) and D.R.Shepherd (*England*) (43).
Referee: R.S.Madugalle (*Sri Lanka*) (14). **Test No. 1433/2 (SA 226/WI 344)**

SOUTH AFRICA v WEST INDIES (2nd Test)

At St George's Park, Port Elizabeth on 10, 11, 12 December 1998.
Toss: West Indies. Result: **SOUTH AFRICA** won by 178 runs.
Debuts: None.

SOUTH AFRICA

G.Kirsten	c Jacobs b Walsh	29	c Jacobs b Walsh	2
H.H.Gibbs	b Walsh	2	c Lambert b Ambrose	4
J.H.Kallis	c Hooper b Walsh	30	c Jacobs b Ambrose	3
D.J.Cullinan	b Dillon	4	c Lambert b Walsh	10
*W.J.Cronje	run out	21	run out	24
J.N.Rhodes	c Hooper b Ambrose	17	c Jacobs b Ambrose	64
S.M.Pollock	c Williams b Ambrose	28	c Dillon b Ambrose	42
†M.V.Boucher	c Hooper b McLean	17	c Hooper b Ambrose	1
P.L.Symcox	b McLean	36	c Lambert b Ambrose	16
A.A.Donald	c Hooper b Walsh	34	b Walsh	11
D.J.Terbrugge	not out	2	not out	3
Extras	(B 4, LB 6, W 1, NB 14)	25	(B 1, LB 5, NB 9)	15
Total		**245**		**195**

WEST INDIES

S.C.Williams	b Terbrugge	37	(8) lbw b Donald	8
C.B.Lambert	c Cronje b Pollock	0	(1) c Boucher b Donald	2
*B.C.Lara	c Cullinan b Donald	4	(5) c Kirsten b Donald	39
C.L.Hooper	b Terbrugge	15	run out	8
S.Chanderpaul	lbw b Pollock	4	(2) c Kallis b Pollock	16
F.L.Reifer	c Boucher b Pollock	0	c Cullinan b Donald	9
†R.D.Jacobs	b Terbrugge	1	(3) lbw b Kallis	22
N.A.M.McLean	c Cronje b Donald	31	(7) run out	0
C.E.L.Ambrose	b Pollock	12	c Pollock b Donald	16
M.Dillon	c Rhodes b Pollock	9	b Pollock	9
C.A.Walsh	not out	2	not out	0
Extras	(LB 1, NB 5)	6	(LB 2, NB 9)	11
Total		**121**		**141**

WEST INDIES	O	M	R	W		O	M	R	W
Ambrose	17	6	28	2		19	4	51	6
Walsh	23.4	0	87	4		23.5	5	58	3
McLean	19	4	66	2	(5)	5	0	19	0
Dillon	11	1	54	1	(3)	9	2	26	0
Hooper					(4)	7	0	35	0
S AFRICA									
Donald	10	1	33	2		14.2	4	49	5
Pollock	13.3	2	43	5		13	1	46	2
Terbrugge	9	4	27	3	(4)	5	1	27	0
Kallis	3	1	8	0	(3)	6	2	17	1
Symcox	2	0	9	0					

FALL OF WICKETS

	SA	WI	SA	WI
Wkt	1st	1st	2nd	2nd
1st	6	0	5	3
2nd	52	31	9	40
3rd	67	58	11	54
4th	67	63	47	57
5th	89	63	53	68
6th	138	67	145	69
7th	142	75	151	77
8th	175	103	173	132
9th	241	112	183	141
10th	245	121	195	141

Umpires: R.E.Koertzen (9) and D.R.Shepherd (*England*) (44).
Referee: R.S.Madugalle (*Sri Lanka*) (15).   Test No. 1434/3 (SA 227/WI 345)

SOUTH AFRICA v WEST INDIES (3rd Test)

At Kingsmead, Durban on 26, 27, 28, 29 December 1998.
Toss: South Africa. Result: **SOUTH AFRICA** won by 9 wickets.
Debuts: West Indies – D.Ganga.

WEST INDIES

P.A.Wallace	c Cullinan b Kallis	21	c Boucher b Donald		1
J.R.Murray	lbw b Terbrugge	29	c Gibbs b Kallis		29
S.Chanderpaul	c Boucher b Kallis	4	c and b Pollock		75
*B.C.Lara	c Cronje b Terbrugge	51	c Gibbs b Terbrugge		79
C.L.Hooper	c Cullinan b Kallis	10	c Boucher b Pollock		2
D.Ganga	b Pollock	28	c Gibbs b Pollock		5
†R.D.Jacobs	b Cronje	39	not out		15
R.N.Lewis	c Cullinan b Cronje	0	c Boucher b Donald		0
F.A.Rose	c Kallis b Cronje	6	c Gibbs b Pollock		22
C.E.L.Ambrose	run out	0	c Cronje b Pollock		5
C.A.Walsh	not out	0	b Donald		3
Extras	(LB 5, NB 5)	10	(LB 12, W 2, NB 9)		23
Total		**198**			**259**

SOUTH AFRICA

G.Kirsten	c Hooper b Rose	26	not out	71
H.H.Gibbs	c Wallace b Rose	35	lbw b Hooper	49
J.H.Kallis	c Jacobs b Rose	11	not out	23
D.J.Cullinan	run out	40		
*W.J.Cronje	b Walsh	30		
J.N.Rhodes	c and b Walsh	87		
S.M.Pollock	c Hooper b Rose	30		
†M.V.Boucher	b Rose	0		
P.L.Symcox	b Rose	12		
A.A.Donald	b Rose	13		
D.J.Terbrugge	not out	2		
Extras	(B 4, LB 8, W 1, NB 13)	26	(LB 1, NB 3)	4
Total		**312**	(1 wicket)	**147**

WEST INDIES	O	M	R	W	O	M	R	W
Donald	13.4	1	55	0	20.2	4	62	3
Pollock	23.2	8	45	1	27	6	83	5
Terbrugge	12	2	39	2	13	4	28	1
Kallis	10	3	18	3	10	1	31	0
Symcox	8	1	17	0	12	3	43	0
Cronje	4.1	0	19	3				
S AFRICA								
Ambrose	17	1	60	0	(2) 4	0	16	0
Walsh	29	6	68	2	(3) 4	1	6	0
Rose	28	6	84	7	(1) 9	0	31	0
Lewis	20	2	70	0	(5) 12.4	0	43	0
Hooper	4	0	18	0	(4) 19	4	50	1

FALL OF WICKETS

	WI	SA	WI	SA
Wkt	1st	1st	2nd	2nd
1st	50	57	17	97
2nd	52	79	41	–
3rd	57	80	201	–
4th	105	140	201	–
5th	133	182	204	–
6th	178	262	213	–
7th	179	262	214	–
8th	185	284	245	–
9th	186	295	252	–
10th	198	312	259	–

Umpires: D.L.Orchard (9) and R.B.Tiffin (*Zimbabwe*) (8).
Referee: R.S.Madugalle (*Sri Lanka*) (16).   Test No. 1435/4 (SA 228/WI 346)

SOUTH AFRICA v WEST INDIES (4th Test)

At Newlands, Cape Town on 2, 3, 4, 5, 6 January 1999.
Toss: South Africa. Result: **SOUTH AFRICA** won by 149 runs.
Debuts: None.

SOUTH AFRICA

G.Kirsten	c Jacobs b Ambrose	0	c Murray b McLean	5
H.H.Gibbs	c Wallace b Dillon	42	c Jacobs b Dillon	25
J.H.Kallis	c Jacobs b Gibson	110	not out	88
D.J.Cullinan	c Jacobs b McLean	168	lbw b McLean	0
*W.J.Cronje	c Jacobs b McLean	0	c Hooper b Dillon	54
J.N.Rhodes	b Hooper	34	lbw b Hooper	23
S.M.Pollock	c Lara b Dillon	9	c Lara b Hooper	3
†M.V.Boucher	not out	15	c and b McLean	22
A.A.Donald	c Wallace b Dillon	0	not out	0
D.J.Terbrugge	not out	4		
P.R.Adams				
Extras	(LB 3, W 1, NB 20)	24	(LB 4, W1, NB 1)	6
Total	**(8 wickets declared)**	**406**	**(7 wickets declared)**	**226**

WEST INDIES

P.A.Wallace	c Cullinan b Donald	8	c Gibbs b Pollock	0
J.R.Murray	c Boucher b Donald	0	lbw b Kallis	7
S.Chanderpaul	c Rhodes b Terbrugge	6	c Cullinan b Kallis	5
*B.C.Lara	hit wkt b Donald	4	c and b Adams	33
C.L.Hooper	run out	86	b Kallis	20
D.Ganga	c Kirsten b Pollock	17	lbw b Pollock	16
†R.D.Jacobs	c Kallis b Pollock	29	not out	69
O.D.Gibson	c Kirsten b Kallis	37	run out	13
N.A.M.McLean	c Cronje b Adams	14	b Adams b Kallis	39
C.E.L.Ambrose	not out	4	c Kirsten b Adams	19
M.Dillon	c Boucher b Kallis	0	c Cronje b Kallis	36
Extras	(LB 2, W 2, NB 3)	7	(LB 2, NB 12)	14
Total		**212**		**271**

WEST INDIES	O	M	R	W		O	M	R	W	FALL OF WICKETS
Ambrose	24.1	7	49	1						SA WI SA WI
McLean	25.5	7	76	2	(1) 16	1	53	3		Wkt 1st 1st 2nd 2nd
Gibson	30	4	92	1	(2) 14.4	2	51	0		1st 0 1 31 0
Dillon	33.5	6	99	3	(3) 17	2	37	2		2nd 74 10 31 1
Hooper	27	6	60	1	(4) 28	2	52	2		3rd 309 14 31 15
Chanderpaul	6	0	27	0	(5) 12	4	29	0		4th 312 34 125 47
										5th 376 108 174 87
S AFRICA										6th 380 146 190 87
Donald	6	1	20	3						7th 397 164 222 108
Pollock	22	9	35	2	(1) 25	3	49	2		8th 397 199 – 173
Terbrugge	20	8	37	1	(4) 11	4	40	0		9th – 210 – 207
Kallis	15	5	34	2	(2) 27.4	4	90	5		10th – 212 – 271
Adams	16	2	61	1	23	5	80	2		
Cronje	6	1	23	0	(3) 1	1	0	0		
Cullinan					(6) 4	1	10	0		

Umpires: D.L.Orchard (10) and S.Venkataraghavan (*India*) (28).
Referee: R.S.Madugalle (*Sri Lanka*) (17).   Test No. 1436/5 (SA 229/WI 347)

SOUTH AFRICA v WEST INDIES (5th Test)

At Centurion Park, Centurion, Pretoria on 15, 16, 17, 18 January 1999.
Toss: West Indies. Result: **SOUTH AFRICA** won by 351 runs.
Debuts: West Indies – R.D.King.

SOUTH AFRICA

G.Kirsten	c Jacobs b Walsh	0	c Ganga b Hooper	134
H.H.Gibbs	c Reifer b Walsh	2	c Wallace b Hooper	51
J.H.Kallis	c Chanderpaul b Hooper	83	c Jacobs b Hooper	27
D.J.Cullinan	c Wallace b McLean	9	c Ganga b Dillon	4
*W.J.Cronje	c Jacobs b Dillon	25	c Ganga b McLean	58
J.N.Rhodes	c King b Dillon	24	not out	103
S.M.Pollock	c Lara b Walsh	13	not out	3
†M.V.Boucher	c Lara b Walsh	100		
L.Klusener	c Jacobs b Walsh	12		
A.A.Donald	not out	12		
P.R.Adams	c Jacobs b Walsh	7		
Extras	(B 4, LB 3, NB 19)	26	(B 3, LB 2, W 1, NB 13)	19
Total		**313**	(5 wickets declared)	**399**

WEST INDIES

P.A.Wallace	b Donald	4	c Boucher b Donald	4
D.Ganga	c Kallis b Pollock	0	c Rhodes b Pollock	9
S.Chanderpaul	c Donald b Klusener	38	c Cronje b Kallis	43
*B.C.Lara	c Kallis b Donald	68	lbw b Adams	14
C.L.Hooper	b Klusener	0	lbw b Klusener	10
F.L.Reifer	c Rhodes b Pollock	0	c Kallis b Adams	6
†R.D.Jacobs	not out	8	c Boucher b Kallis	78
N.A.M.McLean	c Cronje b Donald	8	b Adams	33
M.Dillon	c Adams b Donald	0	b Cullinan	5
R.D.King	lbw b Donald	0	not out	2
C.A.Walsh	lbw b Kallis	2	b Adams	0
Extras	(LB 1, NB 7)	8	(LB 5, NB 8)	13
Total		**144**		**217**

WEST INDIES	O	M	R	W		O	M	R	W
Walsh	24.5	6	80	6		7.3	4	6	0
McLean	18	1	71	1		23.3	3	89	1
King	11	1	50	0		17	1	80	0
Dillon	17	2	62	2		23	0	79	1
Hooper	17	5	27	1		36.2	4	117	3
Chanderpaul	5	1	16	0		8	1	23	0

S AFRICA									
Donald	13	2	49	5		2	0	8	1
Pollock	14	2	41	2		16	5	38	1
Klusener	13	3	27	2		16	4	50	1
Kallis	7.1	1	26	1	(6)	8	5	12	2
Adams					(4)	21.2	6	64	4
Cronje					(5)	5	3	8	0
Cullinan						7	1	32	1

FALL OF WICKETS				
	SA	WI	SA	WI
Wkt	1st	1st	2nd	2nd
1st	0	1	82	4
2nd	5	5	140	46
3rd	18	102	149	68
4th	65	122	256	86
5th	98	125	371	86
6th	123	126	–	117
7th	215	140	–	198
8th	270	140	–	209
9th	302	140	–	216
10th	313	144	–	217

Umpires: R.E.Koertzen (10) and S.Venkataraghavan (*India*) (29).
Referee: R.S.Madugalle (*Sri Lanka*) (18). **Test No. 1437/6 (SA 230/WI 348)**

SOUTH AFRICA v WEST INDIES 1998-99

SOUTH AFRICA – BATTING AND FIELDING

	M	I	NO	HS	Runs	Avge	100	50	Ct/St
J.H.Kallis	5	10	3	110	485	69.28	1	4	7
J.N.Rhodes	5	9	1	103*	378	47.25	1	2	4
G.Kirsten	5	10	1	134	336	37.33	1	2	4
W.J.Cronje	5	9	–	58	284	31.55	–	2	10
D.J.Cullinan	5	9	–	168	278	30.88	1	–	9
M.V.Boucher	5	8	2	100	168	28.00	1	–	14
H.H.Gibbs	4	8	–	51	210	26.25	–	1	5
P.L.Symcox	3	4	–	36	89	22.25	–	–	–
S.M.Pollock	5	9	1	42	148	18.50	–	–	2
A.A.Donald	5	7	2	34	77	15.40	–	–	1
P.R.Adams	2	1	–	7	7	7.00	–	–	3
D.J.Terbrugge	4	5	1	5*	14	–	–	–	2

Played in one Test: A.M.Bacher 1, 6; L.Klusener 12.

SOUTH AFRICA – BOWLING

	O	M	R	W	Avge	Best	5wI	10wM
S.M.Pollock	197.2	44	483	29	16.65	5-43	3	–
A.A.Donald	117.2	23	395	23	17.17	5-49	2	–
J.H.Kallis	115.5	32	299	17	17.58	5-90	1	–
D.J.Terbrugge	100	33	253	9	28.11	3-27	–	–
P.R.Adams	60.2	13	205	7	29.28	4-64	–	–

Also bowled: W.J.Cronje 17.1-5-53-3; D.J.Cullinan 11-2-42-1; L.Klusener 29-7-77-3; P.L.Symcox 59-18-149-3.

WEST INDIES – BATTING AND FIELDING

	M	I	NO	HS	Runs	Avge	100	50	Ct/St
R.D.Jacobs	5	10	3	78	317	45.28	–	2	20
B.C.Lara	5	10	–	79	310	31.00	–	3	5
S.Chanderpaul	5	10	–	75	266	26.60	–	2	2
C.L.Hooper	5	10	–	86	237	23.70	–	1	8
S.C.Williams	2	4	–	37	92	23.00	–	–	3
N.A.M.McLean	4	8	–	39	165	20.62	–	–	2
J.R.Murray	2	4	–	29	65	16.25	–	–	1
D.Ganga	3	6	–	28	75	12.50	–	–	3
C.B.Lambert	2	4	–	33	43	10.75	–	–	1
M.Dillon	3	6	–	36	59	9.83	–	–	1
C.E.L.Ambrose	4	8	2	19	56	9.33	–	–	–
P.A.Wallace	4	8	–	21	68	8.50	–	–	6
R.N.Lewis	2	4	–	12	22	5.50	–	–	–
F.L.Reifer	2	4	–	9	15	3.75	–	–	1
C.A.Walsh	4	8	4	5*	12	3.00	–	–	1

Played in one Test: O.D.Gibson 37, 13; R.D.King 0, 2* (1 ct); F.A.Rose 6, 22.

WEST INDIES – BOWLING

	O	M	R	W	Avge	Best	5wI	10wM
F.A.Rose	37	6	115	7	16.42	7- 84	1	–
C.A.Walsh	158.5	36	416	22	18.90	6- 80	1	–
C.E.L.Ambrose	124.5	26	309	13	23.76	6- 51	1	–
N.A.M.McLean	129.2	17	457	12	38.08	3- 53	–	–
M.Dillon	110.5	13	357	9	39.66	3- 99	–	–
C.L.Hooper	142.2	21	372	8	46.50	3-117	–	–

Also bowled: S.Chanderpaul 31-6-95-0; O.D.Gibson 44.4-6-143-1; R.D.King 28-2-130-0; R.N.Lewis 73.3-10-225-1.

NEW ZEALAND v INDIA (2nd Test)

At Basin Reserve, Wellington on 26, 27, 28, 29, 30 December 1998.
Toss: India. Result: **NEW ZEALAND** won by 4 wickets.
Debuts: New Zealand – M.D.Bell.

INDIA

N.S.Sidhu	c Fleming b Doull	0	(2) lbw b Doull		34
A.Jadeja	lbw b Doull	10	(1) b Nash		22
R.Dravid	lbw b Doull	0	b Wiseman		28
S.C.Ganguly	c Parore b Doull	5	c Bell b Wiseman		48
S.R.Tendulkar	c Bell b Doull	47	c Fleming b Nash		113
*M.Azharuddin	not out	103	c Parore b Nash		48
†N.R.Mongia	c Astle b Doull	0	c Fleming b Doull		2
A.Kumble	c McMillan b Doull	11	c Nash b Vettori		23
J.Srinath	c Fleming b Nash	7	not out		27
B.K.V.Prasad	c Fleming b Vettori	15	c and b Astle		0
Harbhajan Singh	c Astle b McMillan	1	c Horne b McMillan		0
Extras	(LB 3, NB 6)	9	(B 3, LB 1, W 1, NB 5)		10
Total		**208**			**356**

NEW ZEALAND

M.D.Bell	c Mongia b Prasad	4	c Dravid b Srinath		0
M.J.Horne	b Kumble	38	lbw b Kumble		31
*S.P.Fleming	run out	42	b Kumble		17
N.J.Astle	b Kumble	56	retired hurt		1
C.D.McMillan	c Dravid b Srinath	24	not out		74
†A.C.Parore	lbw b Kumble	2	run out		1
C.L.Cairns	c Tendulkar b Prasad	3	(8) c Jadeja b Srinath		61
D.J.Nash	not out	89	(9) not out		4
D.L.Vettori	b Tendulkar	57			
P.J.Wiseman	b Tendulkar	0	(7) lbw b Srinath		0
S.B.Doull	lbw b Kumble	0			
Extras	(B 13, LB 19, NB 5)	37	(B 9, LB 9, NB 8)		26
Total		**352**	(6 wickets)		**215**

N ZEALAND	O	M	R	W		O	M	R	W		FALL OF WICKETS
Doull	24	7	65	7		25	10	49	2		

											I	NZ	I	NZ
Cairns	17	3	69	0		19	2	68	0	Wkt	1st	1st	2nd	2nd
Nash	14	1	46	1		15	9	20	3	1st	0	7	41	0
Vettori	7	0	20	1		20	6	92	1	2nd	2	79	74	42
Astle	2	0	5	0	(7)	7	3	7	1	3rd	15	112	112	51
McMillan	1.4	1	0	1	(5)	10	2	26	1	4th	16	162	200	67
Wiseman					(6)	19	4	90	2	5th	99	172	297	74
										6th	99	179	304	211
INDIA										7th	132	208	304	–
Srinath	36	6	89	1		19.3	1	82	2	8th	149	345	346	–
Prasad	30	8	67	2		10	3	26	0	9th	207	349	349	–
Kumble	45.4	18	83	4		23	6	70	2	10th	208	352	356	–
Harbhajan Singh	25	6	61	0		5	1	11	0					
Ganguly	6	0	13	0										
Tendulkar	6	2	7	2	(5)	3	0	8	0					

Umpires: E.A.Nicholls (*West Indies*) (5) and E.A.Watkin (1).
Referee: B.N.Jarman (*Australia*) (15). **Test No. 1440/36 (NZ 263/I 320)**
The First Test at Carisbrook, Dunedin, scheduled for 18, 19, 20, 21, 22 December was
abandoned on the third day without a ball being bowled because of rain.

NEW ZEALAND v INDIA (3rd Test)

At Seddon Park, Hamilton on 2, 3, 4, 5, 6 January 1999.
Toss: India. Result: **MATCH DRAWN**.
Debuts: India – R.Singh.

NEW ZEALAND

M.D.Bell	c Mongia b Srinath	0		lbw b Tendulkar	25
M.J.Horne	b Srinath	63		c Mongia b Srinath	26
*S.P.Fleming	c Dravid b Srinath	0		b Prasad	18
R.G.Twose	c Mongia b Prasad	87		lbw b Tendulkar	4
C.D.McMillan	c Prasad b Kumble	92		c Mongia b Singh	84
†A.C.Parore	c sub (V.V.S.Laxman) b Prasad	21		c Singh b Kumble	50
P.J.Wiseman	c Ganguly b Singh	13			
C.L.Cairns	b Singh	2	(7)	c Dravid b Kumble	126
D.J.Nash	not out	18	(8)	run out	63
D.L.Vettori	c Srinath	24	(9)	not out	43
S.B.Doull	c Kumble b Srinath	6			
Extras	(B 5, LB 19, W 2, NB 14)	40		(B 9, LB 7, W 1, NB 8)	25
Total		**366**		(8 wickets declared)	**464**

INDIA

N.S.Sidhu	c Parore b Cairns	1	(2)	b Cairns	13
A.Jadeja	c Nash b Doull	12	(1)	c Parore b Cairns	21
R.Dravid	c McMillan b Cairns	190		not out	103
S.R.Tendulkar	lbw b Nash	67			
S.C.Ganguly	c Fleming b Doull	11	(4)	not out	101
*M.Azharuddin	c Fleming b Cairns	4			
†N.R.Mongia	b Horne b Nash	7			
A.Kumble	c Parore b Doull	0			
J.Srinath	c Twose b Wiseman	76			
B.K.V.Prasad	not out	30			
R.Singh	c Fleming b Cairns	0			
Extras	(B 2, LB 4, W 8, NB 4)	18		(LB 9, NB 2)	11
Total		**416**		(2 wickets)	**249**

INDIA	O	M	R	W		O	M	R	W	FALL OF WICKETS
Srinath	32.2	10	95	5	(3)	27	6	90	1		NZ	I	NZ	I
Prasad	33	10	61	2	(1)	33	8	75	1	Wkt	1st	1st	2nd	2nd
Kumble	27	7	64	1	(4)	45.5	13	124	2	1st	0	17	46	33
Singh	21	5	74	2	(2)	19	3	102	1	2nd	0	17	69	55
Ganguly	5	3	25	0	(6)	1	0	27	0	3rd	95	126	159	–
Tendulkar	3	0	23	0	(5)	7	0	30	2	4th	164	168	85	–
										5th	278	195	225	–
N ZEALAND										6th	311	204	225	–
Doull	36	15	64	3		4	0	17	0	7th	314	211	372	–
Cairns	22.3	3	107	4		9	1	30	2	8th	315	355	464	–
Nash	37	10	98	2						9th	356	416	–	–
Vettori	16	2	71	0						10th	366	416	–	–
McMillan	4	0	24	0	(3)	17	4	59	0					
Wiseman	13	2	46	1	(4)	12	0	80	0					
Twose					(5)	9.1	0	50	0					
Horne					(6)	1	0	4	0					

Umpires: D.B.Cowie (10) and R.E.Koertzen (*South Africa*) (11).
Referee: B.N.Jarman (*Australia*) (16). **Test No. 1441/37 (NZ 264/I 321)**

NEW ZEALAND v INDIA 1998-99

NEW ZEALAND – BATTING AND FIELDING

	M	I	NO	HS	Runs	Avge	100	50	Ct/St
D.J.Nash	2	4	3	89*	174	174.00	–	2	2
C.D.McMillan	2	4	1	92	274	91.33	–	3	2
D.L.Vettori	2	3	1	57	124	62.00	–	1	–
C.L.Cairns	2	4	–	126	192	48.00	1	1	–
M.J.Horne	2	4	–	63	158	39.50	–	1	2
S.P.Fleming	2	4	–	42	77	19.25	–	–	8
A.C.Parore	2	4	–	50	74	18.50	–	1	5
M.D.Bell	2	4	–	25	29	7.25	–	–	2
P.J.Wiseman	2	3	–	13	13	4.33	–	–	–
S.B.Doull	2	2	–	6	6	3.00	–	–	–

Played in one Test: N.J.Astle 56, 1* (3 ct); R.G.Twose 87, 4 (1 ct).

NEW ZEALAND – BOWLING

	O	M	R	W	Avge	Best	5wI	10wM
S.B.Doull	89	32	195	12	16.25	7- 65	1	–
D.J.Nash	66	20	164	6	27.33	3- 20	–	–
C.L.Cairns	67.3	9	274	6	45.66	4-107	–	–
C.D.McMillan	32.4	7	109	2	54.50	1- 0	–	–
P.J.Wiseman	44	3	216	3	72.00	2- 90	–	–
D.L.Vettori	43	8	183	2	91.50	1- 20	–	–

Also bowled: N.J.Astle 9-3-12-1; M.J.Horne 1-0-4-0; R.G.Twose 9.1-0-50-0.

INDIA – BATTING AND FIELDING

	M	I	NO	HS	Runs	Avge	100	50	Ct/St
R.Dravid	2	4	1	190	321	107.00	2	–	4
M.Azharuddin	2	3	1	103*	155	77.50	1	1	1
S.R.Tendulkar	2	3	–	113	227	75.66	1	1	1
J.Srinath	2	3	1	76	110	55.00	–	1	–
S.C.Ganguly	2	4	1	101*	165	55.00	1	–	1
B.K.V.Prasad	2	3	1	30*	45	22.50	–	–	1
A.Jadeja	2	4	–	22	65	16.25	–	–	1
N.S.Sidhu	2	4	–	34	48	12.00	–	–	–
A.Kumble	2	3	–	23	34	11.33	–	–	1
N.R.Mongia	2	3	–	7	9	3.00	–	–	5

Played in one Test: Harbhajan Singh 1, 1; R.Singh 0 (1 ct).

INDIA – BOWLING

	O	M	R	W	Avge	Best	5wI	10wM
S.R.Tendulkar	19	2	68	4	17.00	2- 7	–	–
J.Srinath	114.5	23	356	10	35.60	5-95	1	–
A.Kumble	141.3	44	341	9	37.88	4-83	–	–
B.K.V.Prasad	106	29	229	5	45.80	2-61	–	–
R.Singh	40	8	176	3	58.66	2-74	–	–

Also bowled: S.C.Ganguly 17-4-65-0; Harbhajan Singh 30-7-72-0.

PAKISTAN v ZIMBABWE (1st Test)

At Arbab Niaz Stadium, Peshawar on 27, 28, 29, 30 November 1998.
Toss: Zimbabwe. Result: **ZIMBABWE** won by 7 wickets.
Debuts: None.

PAKISTAN

Saeed Anwar	b Johnson	36	(7) c A.Flower b Olonga		31
*Aamir Sohail	c A.Flower b Mbangwa	15	(1) c and b Olonga		2
Ijaz Ahmed	c Whittall b Mbangwa	87	c Campbell b Streak		0
Inzamam-ul-Haq	lbw b Mbangwa	19	b Olonga		2
Yousuf Youhana	c Campbell b Streak	75	b Mbangwa		14
†Moin Khan	c Mbangwa b Olonga	15	b Mbangwa		6
Azhar Mahmood	c A.Flower b Streak	11	(2) c A.Flower b Olonga		5
Wasim Akram	b Olonga	10	c Olonga b Mbangwa		31
Mushtaq Ahmed	lbw b Streak	0	run out		0
Waqar Younis	lbw b Streak	6	not out		1
Aqib Javed	not out	1	c Wishart b Streak		0
Extras	(B 4, LB 6, NB 11)	21	(B 4, LB 2, NB 5)		11
Total		**296**			**103**

ZIMBABWE

G.J.Rennie	lbw b Wasim	2	c Ijaz b Wasim	6
G.W.Flower	c Azhar b Waqar	15	c Moin b Wasim	31
M.W.Goodwin	lbw b Waqar	29	not out	73
*A.D.R.Campbell	lbw b Wasim	16	c Ijaz b Wasim	12
†A.Flower	b Waqar	0	not out	17
N.C.Johnson	c Azhar b Wasim	107		
C.B.Wishart	b Wasim	3		
H.H.Streak	b Mushtaq	24		
A.R.Whittall	c Azhar b Waqar	13		
H.K.Olonga	lbw b Wasim	3		
M.Mbangwa	not out	1		
Extras	(LB 6, NB 19)	25	(B 4, LB 8, W 2, NB 9)	23
Total		**238**	(3 wickets)	**162**

ZIMBABWE	O	M	R	W	O	M	R	W
Streak	22.5	2	93	4	12.5	3	19	2
Olonga	17	3	47	2	11	1	42	4
Johnson	18	2	76	1	(4) 6	2	13	0
Mbangwa	23	9	40	3	(3) 7	2	23	3
Whittall	5	0	30	0				
PAKISTAN								
Wasim Akram	23	5	52	5	17	6	47	3
Waqar Younis	20.3	2	78	4	11	1	51	0
Aqib Javed	14	2	52	0	13.2	4	36	0
Azhar Mahmood	6	0	28	0	3	1	3	0
Mushtaq Ahmed	5	0	22	1	2	0	13	0

FALL OF WICKETS

	P	Z	P	Z
Wkt	1st	1st	2nd	2nd
1st	45	3	7	13
2nd	56	58	12	94
3rd	92	63	12	130
4th	210	63	15	–
5th	233	106	34	–
6th	268	115	41	–
7th	283	218	98	–
8th	283	218	102	–
9th	288	236	102	–
10th	296	238	103	–

Umpires: Athar Zaidi (5) and G.Sharp (*England*) (8).
Referee: C.W.Smith (*West Indies*) (18).   **Test No. 1438/11 (P 252/Z 32)**

PAKISTAN v ZIMBABWE (2nd Test)

At Gaddafi Stadium, Lahore on 10, 11, 12, 13, 14 December 1998.
Toss: Pakistan. Result: **MATCH DRAWN**.
Debuts: Pakistan – Naved Ashraf.

ZIMBABWE

G.J.Rennie	c Ijaz b Waqar	3	not out	16
G.W.Flower	lbw b Waqar	7	not out	17
M.W.Goodwin	c Moin b Waqar	10		
*A.D.R.Campbell	c Yousuf b Waqar	5		
†A.Flower	not out	60		
N.C.Johnson	c and b Shoaib	14		
C.B.Wishart	c Salim b Saqlain	28		
H.H.Streak	c Wasim b Saqlain	19		
H.K.Olonga	c Shoaib b Saqlain	3		
A.G.Huckle	c Saeed b Saqlain	13		
M.Mbangwa	c Ijaz b Saqlain	2		
Extras	(B 4, LB 3, NB 12)	19	(LB 5, NB 10)	15
Total		**183**	(0 wickets)	**48**

PAKISTAN

Saeed Anwar	c A.Flower b Johnson	75
Naved Ashraf	b Streak	32
Ijaz Ahmed	c Huckle b Johnson	16
Salim Malik	run out	2
Yousuf Youhana	not out	120
Hasan Raza	c Rennie b Huckle	3
*†Moin Khan	lbw b Olonga	25
Wasim Akram	c Johnson b Olonga	2
Saqlain Mushtaq	b Olonga	0
Shoaib Akhtar	b Huckle	11
Waqar Younis	not out	24
Extras	(LB 10, NB 5)	15
Total	(9 wickets declared)	**325**

PAKISTAN	O	M	R	W		O	M	R	W
Wasim Akram	20	6	42	0		6	0	23	0
Waqar Younis	18	3	54	4					
Shoaib Akhtar	15	1	48	1	(2)	5	1	15	0
Saqlain Mushtaq	13.5	3	32	5	(3)	1	0	5	0
ZIMBABWE									
Streak	33	8	75	1					
Olonga	25	9	63	3					
Mbangwa	24	4	66	0					
Johnson	24	2	71	2					
Huckle	7	0	40	2					

FALL OF WICKETS

	Z	P	Z
Wkt	1st	1st	2nd
1st	3	69	–
2nd	16	121	–
3rd	22	129	–
4th	28	132	–
5th	55	147	–
6th	104	213	–
7th	136	215	–
8th	140	215	–
9th	170	275	–
10th	183	–	–

Umpires: D.B.Hair (*Australia*) (27) and Mian Mohammad Aslam (5).
Referee: C.W.Smith (*West Indies*)(19). **Test No. 1439/12 (P 253/Z 34)**
The Third Test at Iqbal Stadium, Faisalabad, scheduled for 17, 18, 19, 20, 21 December was abandoned on the fourth day without a ball being bowled because of fog.

PAKISTAN v ZIMBABWE 1998-99

PAKISTAN – BATTING AND FIELDING

	M	I	NO	HS	Runs	Avge	100	50	Ct/St
Yousuf Youhana	2	3	1	120*	209	104.50	1	1	1
Saeed Anwar	2	3	–	75	142	47.33	–	1	1
Ijaz Ahmed	2	3	–	87	103	34.33	–	1	4
Waqar Younis	2	3	2	24*	31	31.00	–	–	–
Moin Khan	2	3	–	25	46	15.33	–	–	2
Wasim Akram	2	3	–	31	43	14.33	–	–	–

Played in one Test: Aamir Sohail 15, 2; Aqib Javed 1*, 0; Azhar Mahmood 11, 5 (3 ct); Hasan Raza 3; Inzamam-ul-Haq 19, 2; Mushtaq Ahmed 0, 0; Naved Ashraf 32; Salim Malik 2 (1 ct); Saqlain Mushtaq 0; Shoaib Akhtar 11 (2 ct).

PAKISTAN – BOWLING

	O	M	R	W	Avge	Best	5wI	10wM
Saqlain Mushtaq	14.5	3	37	5	7.40	5-32	1	–
Wasim Akram	66	17	164	8	20.50	5-52	1	–
Waqar Younis	49.3	6	183	8	22.87	4-54	–	–

Also bowled: Aqib Javed 27.2-6-88-0; Azhar Mahmood 9-1-31-0; Mushtaq Ahmed 9-2-35-1; Shoaib Akhtar 20-2-63-1.

ZIMBABWE – BATTING AND FIELDING

	M	I	NO	HS	Runs	Avge	100	50	Ct/St
A.Flower	2	3	2	60*	77	77.00	–	1	5
N.C.Johnson	2	2	–	107	121	60.50	1	–	1
M.W.Goodwin	2	3	1	73*	112	56.00	–	1	–
G.W.Flower	2	4	1	31	70	23.33	–	–	–
H.H.Streak	2	2	–	24	43	21.50	–	–	–
C.B.Wishart	2	2	–	28	31	15.50	–	–	1
A.D.R.Campbell	2	3	–	16	33	11.00	–	–	2
G.J.Rennie	2	4	1	16*	27	9.00	–	–	1
H.K.Olonga	2	2	–	3	6	3.00	–	–	2
M.Mbangwa	2	2	1	2	3	3.00	–	–	1

Played in one Test: A.G.Huckle 13 (1 ct); A.R.Whittall 13 (1 ct).

ZIMBABWE – BOWLING

	O	M	R	W	Avge	Best	5wI	10wM
H.K.Olonga	53	13	152	9	16.88	4-42	–	–
M.Mbangwa	54	15	129	6	21.50	3-23	–	–
H.H.Streak	68.4	19	187	7	26.71	4-93	–	–
N.C.Johnson	48	6	160	3	53.33	2-71	–	–

Also bowled: A.G.Huckle 7-0-40-2; A.R.Whittall 5-0-30-0.

ECB TOURS PROGRAMME

1999
World Cup/New Zealand (4)
Sri Lanka A

1999-2000
South Africa (5)/Zimbabwe (4 LOI)

2000
Zimbabwe (2)/West Indies (5)

2000-01
Pakistan (3)/Sri Lanka (3)

2001
Pakistan (2)/Australia (5)

2001-02
†India (3)/†New Zealand (3)

2002
†Sri Lanka (2 or 3)/†India (4 or 5)

2002-03
Australia/World Cup (South Africa)

2003
South Africa/†New Zealand

2003-04
†West Indies

2004
Zimbabwe/Pakistan

2004-05
†South Africa

2005
Australia

2006
†West Indies

† To be confirmed   No of Tests in brackets (where confirmed)
Schedule subject to the possible introduction of a world championship of Test cricket.

YOUNG CRICKETER OF THE YEAR

This annual award, made by The Cricket Writers' Club (founded in 1946), is currently restricted to players qualified for England, Symonds meeting that requirement at the time of his award, and under the age of 23 on 1 May. In 1986 their ballot resulted in a dead heat. Only seven of their selections (marked †) have failed to win an England cap.

1950	R.Tattersall	1975	†A.Kennedy
1951	P.B.H.May	1976	G.Miller
1952	F.S.Trueman	1977	I.T.Botham
1953	M.C.Cowdrey	1978	D.I.Gower
1954	P.J.Loader	1979	P.W.G.Parker
1955	K.F.Barrington	1980	G.R.Dilley
1956	†B.Taylor	1981	M.W.Gatting
1957	M.J.Stewart	1982	N.G.Cowans
1958	†A.C.D.Ingleby-Mackenzie	1983	N.A.Foster
1959	G.Pullar	1984	R.J.Bailey
1960	D.A.Allen	1985	D.V.Lawrence
1961	P.H.Parfitt	1986	†A.A.Metcalfe
1962	P.J.Sharpe		J.J.Whitaker
1963	G.Boycott	1987	R.J.Blakey
1964	J.M.Brearley	1988	M.P.Maynard
1965	A.P.E.Knott	1989	N.Hussain
1966	D.L.Underwood	1990	M.A.Atherton
1967	A.W.Greig	1991	M.R.Ramprakash
1968	R.M.H.Cottam	1992	I.D.K.Salisbury
1969	A.Ward	1993	M.N.Lathwell
1970	C.M.Old	1994	J.P.Crawley
1971	†J.Whitehouse	1995	†A.Symonds
1972	†D.R.Owen-Thomas	1996	C.E.W.Silverwood
1973	M.Hendrick	1997	B.C.Hollioake
1974	P.H.Edmonds	1998	A.Flintoff

SECOND XI FIXTURES 1999

Abbreviations: Second XI Championship matches
(Three days unless marked* which are four days)
AON Trophy (One day; marked†)

APRIL
Tue 20 Riverside *Durham v Northants
Canterbury *Kent v Somerset
Trent Bridge *Notts v Middx
Wed 21 Cardiff Glam v Essex
Bristol †Glos v Glam
Tue 27 Southampton *Hants v Kent
The Oval *Surrey v Essex
Wed 28 Hove Sussex v Glos
Knowle & Dorridge Warwks v Notts
Worcester Worcs v Leics
York Yorks v Somerset
MAY
Wed 5 Cheadle Derbys v Sussex
Chester-le-Street Durham v Glos
Haslingden Lancs v Glam
North Perrott Somerset v Essex
Headingley Yorks v Middx
Mon 10 Maidstone *Kent v Essex
Eastbourne Sussex v Durham
Portsmouth †Hants v Glam
Tue 11 Middleton *Lancs v Yorks
Wed 12 Abbotsholme S Derbys v Hants
Moseley Warwks v Glos
Sun 16 Panteg Glam v Worcs
Mon 17 Middleton SC Sussex v Lancs
Tue 18 Harrogate *Yorks v Essex
Wed 19 Ashford Kent v Middx
Boots Ground Notts v Somerset
Cheam Surrey v Warwks
Mon 24 Cardiff *Glam v Glos
Shenley †MCC YC v Essex
Doncaster †Yorks v Derbys
Tue 25 Hove *Sussex v Surrey
Rotherham *Yorks v Derbys
Milton Keynes †MCCA U25 v Middx
Wed 26 Bristol Glos v Notts
Blackpool Lancs v Kent
Ealing Middx v Kent
Fri 28 Solihull †Warwks v MCCA U25
Mon 31 Duffield †Derbys v Yorks
Worcester †Worcs v Glos
JUNE
Tue 1 Dunstall CC *Derbys v Middx
Cheltenham C *Glos v Glam
Southampton *Hants v Northants
Taunton *Somerset v Sussex
Kidderminster *Worcs v Warwks
Saffron Walden †Essex v MCC YC
Wed 2 Saffron Walden Essex v Leics
Canterbury Kent v Durham
Mon 7 Hinckley Leics v Surrey

Dunstable †MCCA U25 v Northants
Bath Rec. †Somerset v Glos
Tue 8 Maidstone *Kent v Sussex
Boots Ground *Notts v Derbys
Taunton *Somerset v Worcs
Middlesbrough *Yorks v Lancs
Hartlepool Durham v Glam
Banbury †MCCA U25 v Warwks
Wed 9 Bristol Glos v Northants
Bournemouth SC Hants v Warwks
Mon 14 Riverside *Durham v Yorks
Hinckley *Leics v Glam
Hatherley & Reddings †Glos v Hants
Shenley †MCC YC v Surrey
Harrow †Middx v Northants
Tue 15 Finchampstead Hants v Notts
Northampton *Northants v Worcs
Stratford-upon-Avon *Warwks v Lancs
Harrow †Middx v MCCA U25
Wed 16 Oxted Surrey v Derbys
Mon 21 Chelmsford *Essex v Warwks
Abergavenny *Glam v Hants
Old Trafford Lancs v Leics
Bristol †Glos v Worcs
Tue 22 The Oval *Surrey v Notts
Bristol Glos v Derbys
Elland Yorks v Kent
Wed 23 Oundle S Northants v Somerset
Worcester Worcs v Middx
Fri 25 Shenley †MCC YC v Sussex
Todmorden †Yorks v Lancs
Mon 28 Chelmsford Essex v Surrey
Southampton †Hants v Somerset
Fleetwood *Lancs v Durham
Milton Keynes †Northants v Leics
Unity Casuals †Notts v Yorks
Middleton SC †Sussex v MCC YC
Worcester †Worcs v Glam
Tue 29 Cardiff *Glam v Somerset
Lutterworth †Leics v Middx
Shenley †MCC YC v Kent
Farnsfield †Notts v Derbys
Marske †Yorks v Durham
Wed 30 Southampton †Hants v Glos
Canterbury †Kent v Essex
Littleborough †Lancs v Derbys
Hove †Sussex v Surrey
Coventry & N Warwick †Warwks v Middx
Ombersley †Worcs v Somerset
JULY
Thurs 1 Seaton Carew †Durham v Derbys
Newport †Glam v Worcs

	Lutterworth	†Leics v Warwks		Castleford	*Yorks v Warwks
	Bingley	†Yorks v Notts		Bournemouth SC	Hants v Essex
Fri 2	Repton S	†Derbys v Lancs	Wed 28	Milton Keynes	Northants v Surrey
	Riverside	†Durham v Notts		Boots Ground	Notts v Worcs
	Canterbury	†Kent v Surrey		Clevedon	Somerset v Derbys
	Hove	†Sussex v Essex	AUGUST		
	Barnt Green	†Worcs v Hants	Mon 2	Heanor	*Derbys v Durham
Mon 5	Boldon	†Durham v Yorks	Tue 3	Chelmsford	*Essex v Middx
	Bristol	†Glos v Somerset		Usk	*Glam v Surrey
	Southampton	†Hants v Worcs		Taunton	*Somerset v Glos
	Canterbury	†Kent v Sussex		Hove	*Sussex v Leics
	Old Trafford	†Lancs v Notts		Worcester	*Worcs v Lancs
	Ealing	†Middx v Leics	Wed 4	Southampton	Hants v Yorks
	The Oval	†Surrey v Essex		Worksop C	Notts v Kent
Tue 6	Belper Meadows	†Derbys v Notts	Mon 9	Oakham S	*Leics v Notts
	Taunton	†Somerset v Worcs		Hastings	*Sussex v Hants
	The Oval	†Surrey v Kent		South Shields	Durham v Surrey
	W.Brom Dartmouth	†Warwks v Leics	Tue 10	Studley	*Warwks v Northants
Wed 7	Ebbw Vale	†Glam v Hants		Hatherley & Reddings	Glos v Essex
	Old Trafford	†Lancs v Yorks	Wed 11	Pontarddulais	Glam v Yorks
	Ealing	†Middx v Warwks		Taunton	Somerset v Lancs
	Welbeck	†Notts v Durham	Mon 16	†AON Semi-Finals (One day)	
	Hayward's Heath	†Sussex v Kent	or Tue 17		
Thurs 8	Glossop	†Derbys v Durham	Wed 18	Halstead	Essex v Durham
	Isham	†Northants v MCCA U25		Bristol	Glos v Yorks
	Worksop C	†Notts v Lancs		Folkestone	Kent v Warwks
	Taunton	†Somerset v Glam		Hinckley	Leics v Northants
	The Oval	†Surrey v MCC YC		Whitgift S	Surrey v Hants
Fri 9	Billericay	†Essex v Sussex		Worcester	Worcs v Sussex
	Maidstone	†Kent v MCC YC	Mon 23	Lytham	*Lancs v Derbys
	North Runcton	†MCCA U25 v Leics	Tue 24	Bristol	*Glos v Leics
	Taunton	†Somerset v Hants		Uxbridge (RAF)	*Middx v Surrey
	Leamington	†Warwks v Northants		Northampton	*Northants v Kent
Mon 12	Coggeshall	†Essex v Kent		Edgbaston	*Warwks v Glam
	Northampton	†Northants v Warwks		Saffron Walden	Essex v Notts
Tue 13	Coggeshall	*Essex v Derbys	Wed 25	Headingley	Yorks v Sussex
	Bristol	*Glos v Hants	Mon 30	Liverpool	*Lancs v Glos
	Eton C	*Middx v Sussex	Tue 31	Trent Bridge	*Notts v Yorks
	The Oval	*Surrey v Somerset		Southampton	Hants v Somerset
	Kidderminster	*Worcs v Yorks		Colchester	Essex v Worcs
	Leicester	†Leics v Northants	SEPTEMBER		
Wed 14	Ammanford	Glam v Kent	Wed 1	Eltham	Kent v Surrey
	Nottingham HS	Notts v Northants		Harrow	Middx v Northants
Thurs 15	Sunderland	†Durham v Lancs		Kenilworth Wardens	Warwks v Derbys
	Leicester	†Leics v MCCA U25	Mon 6	†AON Trophy Final	
Mon 19	Northampton	*Northants v Yorks		(Reserve day Tue 7 Sept)	
	The Oval	†Surrey v Sussex	Tue 7	Worcester	*Worcs v Durham
Tue 20	Heanor	*Derbys v Lancs		(Play starts Wed 8 if either team in AON Final)	
	Darlington	*Durham v Notts	Wed 8	Derby	Derbys v Glam
	Cardiff	*Glam v Somerset		Wickford	Essex v Northants
	Southampton	*Hants v Worcs		Leicester	Leics v Yorks
	Walmley	Warwks v Middx		Southgate	Middx v Lancs
Wed 21	The Oval	Surrey v Lancs		Boots Ground	Notts v Surrey
Mon 26	Crosby	*Lancs v Durham		Horsham	Sussex v Warwks
	Oakham S	*Leics v Kent	Mon 13	Old Trafford	Lancs v Hants
	Wellingborough S	*Northants v Middx		Northampton	Northants v Derbys
Tue 27	Uxbridge (RAF)	*Middx v Glos			

MINOR COUNTIES CHAMPIONSHIP FIXTURES 1999

	Venue	*Match*
MAY		
Sun 23	Truro	(W) Cornwall v Wales
	Colwall	(W) Herefords v Berks
Sun 30	Carlisle	(E) Cumbria v Bedfords
	Dean Park	†(W) Dorset v Herefords
	Sleaford	†(E) Lincs v Herts
	Corsham	(W) Wilts v Devon
JUNE		
Sun 6	Wardown Park	(E) Bedfords v Bucks
	Tring Park CC	(E) Herts v Norfolk
Wed 9	Milton Keynes	†(E) Bucks v Staffs
	Wisbech	†(E) Cambs v Lincs
Sun 13	Bedford CC	(E) Bedfords v Suffolk
	Alderley Edge	(W) Cheshire v Wilts
	Millom	(W) Cumbria v Lincs
	Dean Park	(W) Dorset v Wales
	Jesmond	†(E) Northumberland v Norfolk
	Shipton under Wychwood	(W) Oxon v Shropshire
Tue 15	Reading	(W) Berks v Shropshire
	March	(E) Cambs v Norfolk
Sun 20	Marlow	(E) Bucks v Cambs
	Challow and Childrey	†(W) Oxon v Wilts
	Colwyn Bay	(W) Wales v Cheshire
JULY		
Sun 4	Hertford	†(E) Herts v Bedfords
	Lincoln Lindum	(E) Lincs v Suffolk
	St Georges	(W) Shropshire v Devon
Tue 6	Bowdon	(W) Cheshire v Devon
	Jesmond	†(E) Northumberland v Suffolk
Thu 8	Cannock	†(E) Staffs v Cambs
Sun 11	Southill Park	(E) Bedfords v Staffs
	Finchampstead	†(W) Berks v Dorset
	Beaconsfield	†(E) Bucks v Cumbria
	Shenley Park	†(E) Herts v Northumberland
	Pontarddulais	(W) Wales v Oxon
	South Wilts CC	(W) Wilts v Herefords
Tue 13	Beaconsfield	(E) Bucks v Northumberland
	Stevenage CC	(E) Herts v Cumbria
Sun 18	Hurst CC	(W) Berks v Wilts
	Exmouth	(W) Devon v Wales
	Jesmond	(E) Northumberland v Lincs
	Christ Church	(W) Oxon v Dorset
Mon 19	Oxton	†(W) Cheshire v Cornwall
Tue 20	Brewood	(E) Staffs v Northumberland
Wed 21	Fenner's	(E) Cambs v Herts
	Bridgnorth	†(W) Shropshire v Cornwall
Thu 22	Lakenham	(E) Norfolk v Suffolk
Sun 25	Weymouth	†(W) Dorset v Devon

273

	Venue	Match
	Kington	†(W) Herefords v Cheshire
	Long Warston	(E) Herts v Staffs
	Grimsby	(E) Lincs v Bucks
	Lakenham	†(E) Norfolk v Bedfords
	Banbury CC	(W) Oxon v Berks
	Oswestry	†(W) Shropshire v Wales
	Marlborough	(W) Wilts v Cornwall
AUGUST		
Sun 1	Dunstable	†(E) Bedfords v Lincs
	Torquay	†(W) Devon v Oxon
	Dean Park	(W) Dorset v Cornwall
	Lakenham	†(E) Norfolk v Cumbria
	Ransome's	†(E) Suffolk v Bucks
	Newport	†(W) Wales v Herefords
Tue 3	Falmouth	(W) Cornwall v Oxon
	Lakenham	(E) Norfolk v Bucks
	Ransome's	(E) Suffolk v Cumbria
Sun 8	Netherfield	(E) Cumbria v Northumberland
	Luctonians CC	(W) Herefords v Shropshire
	Thane CC	†(W) Oxon v Cheshire
Mon 9	Lakenham	(E) Norfolk v Staffs
Tue 10	Falkland CC	(W) Berks v Cheshire
	Westbury	†(W) Wilts v Shropshire
Wed 11	Fenner's	(E) Cambs v Bedfords
	Ipswich School	†(E) Suffolk v Staffs
Sun 15	Camborne	†(W) Cornwall v Berks
	Bovey Tracey	(W) Devon v Herefords
	Jesmond	(E) Northumberland v Cambs
	Sinful	(W) Shropshire v Dorset
	Mildenhall	(E) Suffolk v Herts
	Swansea	†(W) Wales v Wilts
Tue 17	Neston	(W) Cheshire v Dorset
	St Austell	(W) Cornwall v Herefords
	Barrow	†(E) Cumbria v Cambs
	Mount Wise, Plymouth	†(W) Devon v Berks
	Stone	(E) Staffs v Lincs
Sun 22	Wormsley	(E) Bucks v Herts
	Budleigh Salterton	(W) Devon v Cornwall
	Dean Park	(W) Dorset v Wilts
	Brockhampton	(W) Herefords v Oxon
	Grantham	(E) Lincs v Norfolk
	Jesmond	(E) Northumberland v Bedfords
	Wellington	(W) Shropshire v Cheshire
	Leek	(E) Staffs v Cumbria
	Bury St Edmunds	(E) Suffolk v Cambs
	St Fagans	(W) Wales v Berks
SEPTEMBER		
Sun 12	tba	*CHAMPIONSHIP FINAL* (three days)

† Match to be played under 'Grade' Rules

ECB 38 COUNTY COMPETITION FIXTURES 1999

	Venue	*Group*	*Match*
MAY			
Wed 5	Middleton CC (tbc)	(6)	Lancashire v Cheshire
Sun 9	Dean Park	(1)	Dorset v Devon
	Helston	(1)	Cornwall v Somerset
	Bedford CC	(3)	Bedfordshire v Surrey
	Abergavenny	(4)	Wales v Herefordshire
	Shrewsbury	(6)	Shropshire v Derbyshire
Sun 16	Sherborne School	(1)	Dorset v Cornwall
	Hungerford	(2)	Berkshire v Buckinghamshire
	K.E.S. Birmingham	(4)	Warwickshire v Wales
	Brockhampton	(4)	Herefordshire v Wiltshire
	Thame CC	(5)	Oxfordshire v Huntingdonshire
	Hinckley Town CC	(5)	Leicestershire v Nottinghamshire
	Penrith	(6)	Cumberland v Cheshire
	Lakenham	(7)	Norfolk v Cambridgeshire
	Gt Oakley CC	(7)	Northamptonshire v Suffolk
	Cleethorpes	(8)	Lincolnshire v Durham
	Tba	(8)	Yorkshire v Northumberland
Sun 23	Sidmouth	(1)	Devon v Gloucestershire
	Ascott Park	(2)	Buckinghamshire v Hampshire
	Hastings & St Leonards	(2)	Sussex v Kent
	Halesowen	(4)	Worcestershire v Wiltshire
	Kimbolton School	(5)	Huntingdonshire v Leicestershire
	Aston Rowant	(5)	Oxfordshire v Staffordshire
	Boughton Hall	(6)	Cheshire v Shropshire
	Lakenham	(7)	Norfolk v Suffolk
	Chester-le-Street (Ropery Lane)	(8)	Durham v Lincolnshire
Wed 26	New Brighton	(6)	Cheshire v Derbyshire
Thu 27	Metropolitan Police CC	(3)	Surrey v Middlesex
	Askam	(6)	Cumberland v Lancashire
Sun 30	Taunton (County Ground)	(1)	Somerset v Gloucestershire
	Ashford CC	(2)	Kent v Hampshire
	Ynysygerwn	(4)	Wales v Worcestershire
	Saffron Walden	(7)	Cambridgeshire v Essex
	Finedon Dolben CC	(7)	Northamptonshire v Norfolk
JUNE			
Sun 6	Bristol University	(1)	Gloucestershire v Cornwall
	Bath (Recreation Ground)	(1)	Somerset v Dorset
	Slough	(2)	Berkshire v Sussex
	K.E.S. Birmingham	(4)	Warwickshire v Herefordshire
	Swindon	(4)	Wiltshire v Wales
	Dunstall (tbc)	(5)	Staffordshire v Leicestershire
	Boots Ground	(5)	Nottinghamshire v Oxfordshire
	Exning CC	(7)	Suffolk v Cambridgeshire
	Chelmsford (County Ground)	(7)	Essex v Northamptonshire
	Bourne	(8)	Lincolnshire v Yorkshire
Tue 8	Chester-le-Street (Riverside)	(8)	Durham v Northumberland
Wed 9	Blackpool CC (tbc)	(6)	Lancashire v Shropshire

	Venue	*Group*	*Match*
Thu 10	Metropolitan Police CC	(3)	Surrey v Hertfordshire
	Elland CC	(8)	Yorkshire v Durham
Sun 13	Instow	(1)	Devon v Somerset
	Aylesbury (tbc)	(2)	Buckinghamshire v Kent
	Cove CC	(2)	Hampshire v Sussex
	Shenley	(3)	Middlesex v Hertfordshire
	Dales CC	(4)	Herefordshire v Worcestershire
	Kimbolton School	(5)	Huntingdonshire v Nottinghamshire
Thu 17	Richmond CC	(3)	Middlesex v Bedfordshire
	Denby CC	(6)	Derbyshire v Lancashire
Sun 20	Penzance	(1)	Cornwall v Devon
	Southampton (County Ground)	(2)	Hampshire v Berkshire
	Shenley Park	(3)	Hertfordshire v Bedfordshire
	Bromsgrove	(4)	Worcestershire v Warwickshire
	Boots Ground	(5)	Nottinghamshire v Staffordshire
	Whitchurch	(6)	Shropshire v Cumberland
	Chelmsford (County Ground)	(7)	Essex v Norfolk
	Jesmond	(8)	Northumberland v Lincolnshire
Sun 27	Bristol University	(1)	Gloucestershire v Dorset
	Canterbury (County Ground)	(2)	Kent v Berkshire
	Horsham	(2)	Sussex v Buckinghamshire
	Dunstable CC	(3)	Bedfordshire v Middlesex
	Shenley Park	(3)	Hertfordshire v Surrey
	Warminster	(4)	Wiltshire v Warwickshire
	Longton	(5)	Staffordshire v Huntingdonshire
	Oakham School	(5)	Leicestershire v Oxfordshire
	Denby CC	(6)	Derbyshire v Cumberland
	Copdock CC	(7)	Suffolk v Essex
	March	(7)	Cambridgeshire v Northamptonshire
	Jesmond	(8)	Northumberland v Yorkshire

JULY

Fri 16	**Quarter-Finals**	
	Match A	Winners of Group 4 v Winners of Group 1
	Match B	Winners of Group 8 v Winners of Group 6
	Match C	Winners of Group 7 v Winners of Group 5
	Match D	Winners of Group 2 v Winners of Group 3
Thu 29	**Semi-Finals**	
Fri 30	(Semi-Finals Reserve Day)	
	Match E	Winners of Match D v Winners of Match A
	Match F	Winners of Match B v Winners of Match C

SEPTEMBER

Wed 1	**FINAL at Lord's**	Winners of Match E v Winners of Match F
Thu 2	(Final Reserve Day)	

PRINCIPAL FIXTURES 1999

*Floodlit

Thursday 8 April
Fenner's:	Cambridge U v Lancs
The Parks:	Oxford U v Worcs

Monday 12 April
Trent Bridge:	Notts v Cambridge U

Tuesday 13 April
County Championship
Riverside:	Durham v Worcs
Chelmsford:	Essex v Leics
Old Trafford:	Lancs v Sussex
Lord's:	Middx v Kent
The Oval:	Surrey v Glos

Wednesday 14 April
The Parks:	Oxford U v Hants

County Championship
Edgbaston:	Warwks v Northants

Thursday 15 April
Fenner's:	Cambridge U v Somerset

Saturday 17 April
CGU National League Division One
Leicester:	Leics v Hants

Sunday 18 April
CGU National League Division One
Canterbury:	Kent v Lancs

CGU National League Division Two
Riverside:	Durham v Surrey
Lord's:	Middx v Notts

Monday 19 April
County Championship
Edgbaston:	Warwks v Somerset

Tuesday 20 April
County Championship
Derby:	Derbys v Glam
Leicester:	Leics v Notts
Lord's:	Middx v Lancs
Worcester:	Worcs v Surrey

Wednesday 21 April
County Championship
Southampton: Hants v Kent

Hove:	Sussex v Northants
Headingley:	Yorks v Glos

Other Match
Fenner's:	Cambridge U v Essex

Saturday 24 April
CGU National League Division Two
Taunton:	Somerset v Durham

Sunday 25 April
CGU National League Division One
Chelmsford:	Essex v Lancs
Southampton:	Hants v Kent
Edgbaston:	Warwks v Worcs
Headingley:	Yorks v Glos

CGU National League Division Two
Lord's:	Middx v Glam
The Oval:	Surrey v Northants
Hove:	Sussex v Derbys

Wednesday 28 April
County Championship
Riverside:	Durham v Hants
Chelmsford:	Essex v Warwks
Cardiff:	Glam v Sussex
Bristol:	Glos v Middx
Canterbury:	Kent v Derbys
Leicester:	Leics v Lancs
Northampton:	Northants v Surrey
Trent Bridge:	Notts v Worcs

Thursday 29 April
County Championship
Taunton:	Somerset v Yorks

Monday 3 May
CGU National League Division One
Bristol:	Glos v Lancs
Southampton:	Hants v Warwks
Canterbury:	Kent v Leics
Worcester:	Worcs v Yorks

CGU National League Division Two
Riverside:	Durham v Middx
Cardiff:	Glam v Derbys
Northampton:	Northants v Sussex
Trent Bridge:	Notts v Surrey

Tuesday 4 May
NatWest Trophy Round 1 (see page 285)

Wednesday 5 May
The Parks: Oxford U v Notts

Friday 7 May
World Cup Warm-up Matches
Canterbury: Kent v England
Leicester: Leics v India
Northampton: Northants v Sri Lanka
Taunton: Somerset v Kenya
Hove: Sussex v South Africa
Worcester: Worcs v Zimbabwe

Saturday 8 May
World Cup Warm-up Matches
Derby: Derbys v Pakistan
Riverside: Durham v Scotland
Chelmsford: Essex v Bangladesh
Cardiff: Glam v Australia
Bristol: Glos v West Indies
Southampton: Hants v New Zealand

Sunday 9 May
World Cup Warm-up Matches
Derby: Derbys v Zimbabwe
Chelmsford: Essex v England
Bristol: Glos v Kenya
Canterbury: Kent v South Africa
Trent Bridge: Notts v Sri Lanka
Harrogate: Yorks v India
Other Match
Fenner's: Cambridge U v Northants

Monday 10 May
World Cup Warm-up Matches
Riverside: Durham v Pakistan
Old Trafford: Lancs v Scotland
Southgate: Middx v Bangladesh
The Oval: Surrey v New Zealand
Edgbaston: Warwks v West Indies
Worcester: Worcs v Australia

Tuesday 11 May
World Cup Warm-up Matches
Cardiff: Glam v Kenya
Southampton: Hants v England
Leicester: Leics v Sri Lanka
Southgate: Middx v South Africa
Trent Bridge: Notts v India
Edgbaston: Warwks v Zimbabwe

Wednesday 12 May
World Cup Warm-up Matches
Old Trafford: Lancs v Pakistan
Northampton: Northants v Bangladesh
Taunton: Somerset v Australia

The Oval: Surrey v West Indies
Arundel: Sussex v New Zealand
Scarborough: Yorks v Scotland

Friday 14 May
County Championship
Stockton: Durham v Kent
Cardiff: Glam v Glos
Southampton: Hants v Worcs
Old Trafford: Lancs v Northants
Trent Bridge: Notts v Somerset
The Oval: Surrey v Essex
Edgbaston: Warwks v Derbys
Headingley: Yorks v Middx
World Cup Group Match
Lord's: England v Sri Lanka

Saturday 15 May
World Cup Group Matches
Hove: India v South Africa
Taunton: Zimbabwe v Kenya

Sunday 16 May
World Cup Group Matches
Bristol: West Indies v Pakistan
Worcester: Australia v Scotland
Other Match (1 day)
Fenner's: Cambridge U v Oxford U

Monday 17 May
World Cup Group Match
Chelmsford: Bangladesh v New Zealand

Tuesday 18 May
World Cup Group Match
Canterbury: England v Kenya
NatWest Trophy Round 2 (see page 286)

Wednesday 19 May
County Championship
Derby: Derbys v Northants
Chelmsford: Essex v Yorks
Old Trafford: Lancs v Notts
Lord's: Middx v Hants
Taunton: Somerset v Leics
Hove: Sussex v Glos
Edgbaston: Warwks v Worcs
NatWest Trophy Round 2 (see page 286)
Other Match
The Parks: Oxford U v Glam
World Cup Group Matches
Northampton: Sri Lanka v South Africa
Leicester: India v Zimbabwe

Thursday 20 May

World Cup Group Matches
Cardiff: Australia v New Zealand
Riverside: Pakistan v Scotland
Other Match
Fenner's: Cambridge U v Kent

Friday 21 May

World Cup Group Match
Dublin: West Indies v Bangladesh

Saturday 22 May

World Cup Group Matches
The Oval: England v South Africa
Worcester: Zimbabwe v Sri Lanka

Sunday 23 May

CGU National League Division One
Chelmsford: Essex v Yorks
Old Trafford: Lancs v Worcs
Edgbaston: Warwks v Kent
CGU National League Division Two
Derby: Derbys v Durham
Taunton: Somerset v Surrey
Hove: Sussex v Glam
World Cup Group Matches
Bristol: Kenya v India
Headingley: Australia v Pakistan

Monday 24 May

World Cup Group Matches
Southampton: West Indies v New Zealand
Edinburgh: Scotland v Bangladesh

Tuesday 25 May

World Cup Group Match
Trent Bridge: England v Zimbabwe
Other Match
The Parks: Oxford U v Warwks

Wednesday 26 May

County Championship
Gloucester: Glos v Essex
Canterbury: Kent v Leics
Lord's: Middx v Sussex
The Oval: Surrey v Somerset
Worcester: Worcs v Glam
World Cup Group Matches
Taunton: Sri Lanka v India
Amsterdam: South Africa v Kenya

Thursday 27 May

County Championship
Trent Bridge: Notts v Hants
Headingley: Yorks v Durham
World Cup Group Matches
Leicester: West Indies v Scotland
Riverside: Australia v Bangladesh

Friday 28 May

World Cup Group Match
Derby: New Zealand v Pakistan

Saturday 29 May

World Cup Group Matches
Chelmsford: Zimbabwe v South Africa
Edgbaston: England v India

Sunday 30 May

World Cup Group Matches
Southampton: Sri Lanka v Kenya
Old Trafford: West Indies v Australia

Monday 31 May

CGU National League Division One
Gloucester: Glos v Worcs
Leicester: Leics v Lancs
Edgbaston: Warwks v Essex
Headingley: Yorks v Hants
CGU National League Division Two
Cardiff: Glam v Northants
Lord's: Middx v Sussex
Trent Bridge: Notts v Somerset
The Oval: Surrey v Derbys
World Cup Group Matches
Edinburgh: Scotland v New Zealand
Northampton: Pakistan v Bangladesh

Wednesday 2 June

County Championship
Derby: Derbys v Yorks
Riverside: Durham v Somerset
Ilford: Essex v Hants
Bristol: Glos v Lancs
Tunbridge Wells: Kent v Surrey
Leicester: Leics v Glam
Northampton: Northants v Notts
Horsham: Sussex v Worcs
Edgbaston: Warwks v Middx
World Cup Super Six

Friday 4 June

The Oval: Group A – 2 v Group B – 2

Saturday 5 June
World Cup Super Six
Trent Bridge: Group A – 1 v Group B – 1

Sunday 6 June
CGU National League Division One
Ilford: Essex v Glos
Tunbridge Wells: Kent v Worcs
Leicester: Leics v Warwks
CGU National League Division Two
Derby: Derbys v Glam
Riverside: Durham v Somerset
Northampton: Northants v Middx
World Cup Super Six
Headingley: Group A – 3 v Group B – 3

Monday 7 June
Tourist Match (1 day) (prov)
Riverside: Durham v New Zealand

Tuesday 8 June
World Cup Super Six
Old Trafford: Group A – 2 v Group B – 1

Wednesday 9 June
World Cup Super Six
Lord's: Group A – 3 v Group B – 2
County Championship
Chelmsford: Essex v Derbys
Cardiff: Glam v Middx
Basingstoke: Hants v Yorks
Southport: Lancs v Warwks
Leicester: Leics v Surrey
Northampton: Northants v Durham
Bath: Somerset v Glos
Hove: Sussex v Kent
Vodafone Challenge Series (4 days)
Worcester: Worcs v New Zealand
(If New Zealand not in WC Super Six)

Thursday 10 June
World Cup Super Six
Edgbaston: Group A – 1 v Group B – 3

Friday 11 June
World Cup Super Six
The Oval: Group A – 3 v Group B – 1

Saturday 12 June
World Cup Super Six
Trent Bridge: Group A – 2 v Group B – 3

Sunday 13 June
World Cup Super Six
Headingley: Group A – 1 v Group B – 2
CGU National League Division One
Chelmsford: Essex v Kent
Bristol: Glos v Leics
Basingstoke: Hants v Yorks
Edgbaston: Warwks v Lancs
CGU National League Division Two
Northampton: Northants v Surrey
Bath: Somerset v Notts
Hove: Sussex v Durham
Tourist Match (1 day)
Cardiff: Glam v New Zealand
(If New Zealand not in WC Super Six)

Tuesday 15 June
County Championship
Southampton: Hants v Leicester
Canterbury: Kent v Glam
Trent Bridge: Notts v Warwks
The Oval: Surrey v Lancs
Worcester: Worcs v Somerset
Headingley: Yorks v Sussex
Other Match
Chelmsford: Essex v Oxford U
Vodafone Challenge Series
Bristol: Glos v New Zealand
(One-day match on Fri 18 June if New Zealand in Super Six but out of S-F)

Wednesday 16 June
World Cup
Old Trafford: *Semi-Final (1)*
Other Match
Fenner's: Cambridge U v Middx

Thursday 17 June
World Cup
Edgbaston: *Semi-Final (2)*

Saturday 19 June
CGU National League Division One
Southampton: Hants v Leics
Worcester: Worcs v Glos
Headingley: Yorks v Essex
CGU National League Division Two
Riverside: Durham v Northants
Trent Bridge: Notts v Middx
Taunton: Somerset v Derbys
The Oval: Surrey v Glam

Sunday 20 June
Lord's: **WORLD CUP FINAL**
(Reserve days Mon 21 and Tues 22)

Tourist Match (4 days)
The Parks: BUSA v New Zealand
(One-day match on Weds 23 June if New Zealand in World Cup Final)

Wednesday 23 June

NatWest Trophy Round 3 (see page 286)

Friday 25 June

Benson & Hedges Super Cup
First and Second Quarter-Finals
Old Trafford: Lancs v Sussex
Headingley: Yorks v Hants
(Reserve days Sat 26 to Mon 28 June)
Vodafone Challenge Series
Taunton: Somerset v New Zealand
University Match (3 days)
Lord's: Oxford U v Cambridge U

Saturday 26 June

Benson & Hedges Super Cup
Third Quarter-Final
(Reserve days 27 and 28 June)
Leicester: Leics v Warwks

Sunday 27 June

Benson & Hedges Super Cup
Fourth Quarter-Final
(Reserve day Mon 28 June)
Bristol: Glos v Surrey

Monday 28 June

CGU National League Division Two
Hove: *Sussex v Northants

Tuesday 29 June

County Championship
Old Trafford: Lancs v Essex
CGU National League Division One
Leicester: *Leics v Yorks

Wednesday 30 June

County Championship
Swansea: Glam v Hants
Bristol: Glos v Notts
Maidstone: Kent v Warwks
Lord's: Middx v Derbys
Northampton: Northants v Worcs
Taunton: Somerset v Sussex
The Oval: Surrey v Durham

Thursday 1 July

FIRST CORNHILL TEST MATCH
Edgbaston: **ENGLAND v NEW ZEALAND**

County Championship
Leicester: Leics v Yorks

Saturday 3 July

CGU National League Division One
Old Trafford: *Lancs v Essex

Sunday 4 July

CGU National League Division One
Maidstone: Kent v Warwks
Worcester: Worcs v Hants
CGU National League Division Two
Derby: Derbys v Surrey
Swansea: Glam v Sussex
Lord's: Middx v Durham
Northampton: Northants v Notts
Other Match (3 days)
Oakham S: ECB XI v Sri Lanka A

Tuesday 6 July

Women's International Match
Old Trafford: England v India (1st LOI)

Wednesday 7 July

NatWest Trophy Round 4 (see page 286)
Other Match (1 day)
Milton Keynes: New Zealand v Sri Lanka A

Friday 9 July

County Championship
Derby: Derbys v Somerset
Riverside: Durham v Notts
Cardiff: Glam v Essex
Lord's: Middx v Northants
Worcester: Worcs v Kent
Vodafone Challenge Series
Southampton/ Hants/Yorks v New
Headingley: Zealand
(Depending on B&H Super Cup Q-F)
Tourist Match (4 days)
Old Trafford/ Lancs/Sussex v Sri Lanka A
Hove:
(Depending on B&H Super Cup Q-F)
Women's International Match
Northampton: England v India (2nd LOI)

Sat 10 July

Benson & Hedges Super Cup
First Semi-Final
(Reserve days Sun 11 and Mon 12 July)

Sunday 11 July

Benson & Hedges Super Cup
Second Semi-Final

(Reserve day Mon 12 July)
Women's International Match
Trent Bridge: England v India (3rd LOI)

Tuesday 13 July

County Championship
Edgbaston: Warwks v Yorks
CGU National League Division Two
Riverside: *Durham v Derbys

Wednesday 14 July

County Championship
Southend: Essex v Middx
Cheltenham: Glos v Worcs
Blackpool: Lancs v Glam
Guildford: Surrey v Hants
Arundel: Sussex v Leics

Thursday 15 July

County Championship
Riverside: Durham v Derbys
Vodafone Challenge Series
Canterbury: Kent v New Zealand
Tourist Match (4 days)
Northampton: Northants v Sri Lanka A
Women's Test Match (4 days)
Shenley: England v India

Saturday 17 July

CGU National League Division One
Edgbaston: Warwks v Yorks

Sunday 18 July

CGU National League Division One
Southend: Essex v Hants
Cheltenham: Glos v Yorks
CGU National League Division Two
Trent Bridge: Notts v Glam
Guildford: Surrey v Somerset
Arundel: Sussex v Middx

Monday 19 July

CGU National League Division One
Old Trafford: *Lancs v Warwks
Tourist Match (1 day)
Cheltenham: Glos v Sri Lanka A

Tuesday 20 July

County Championship
Scarborough: Yorks v Northants
CGU National League Division One
Worcester: *Worcs v Leics

Wednesday 21 July

County Championship
Derby: Derbys v Sussex
Cheltenham: Glos v Durham
Portsmouth: Hants v Lancs
Trent Bridge: Notts v Kent
Taunton: Somerset v Middx
Edgbaston: Warwks v Surrey
Tourist Match (4 days)
Chelmsford: Essex v Sri Lanka A

Thursday 22 July

SECOND CORNHILL TEST MATCH
Lord's: **ENGLAND v NEW ZEALAND**
Worcester: Worcs v Leics

Sunday 25 July

CGU National League Division One
Cheltenham: Glos v Warwks
Portsmouth: Hants v Lancs
Scarborough: Yorks v Kent
CGU National League Division Two
Derby: Derbys v Northants
Pontypridd: Glam v Surrey
Cleethorpes: Notts v Sussex
Taunton: Somerset v Middx

Monday 26 July

Tourist Match (1 day)
Riverside: Durham v Sri Lanka A

Wednesday 28 July

NWT Quarter-Finals (see page 286)
Tourist Matches (1 day)
Derby/Bristol: Derbys/Glos v NZ
(Glos to play New Zealand if Derbys in NWT Quarter-Finals)
Headingley/ Yorks/Leics v Sri Lanka A
Leicester: (One day)
(Depending on NWT Quarter-Finals)

Friday 30 July

County Championship
Cardiff: Glam v Durham
Northampton: Northants v Essex
Trent Bridge: Notts v Derbys
Vodafone Challenge Series
Leicester/ Leics/Warwks v New
Edgbaston: Zealand
(Warwks to play New Zealand if Leics involved in B&H Super Cup Final)
Tourist Match (4 days)
Bristol: Glos/Surrey v Sri Lanka A
(Surrey to play Sri Lanka A if Glos involved in B&H Super Cup Final)

NatWest Under-19 International Match
Canterbury: England U19 v Australia
U19 (1st LOI)

Saturday 31 July

NatWest Under-19 International Match
Chelmsford: England U19 v Australia
U19 (2nd LOI)

Sunday 1 August

Lord's: B & H SUPER CUP FINAL
(Reserve day Mon 2 Aug)
CGU National League Division One
Worcester: Worcs v Kent

Monday 2 August

NatWest Under-19 International Match
Hove: England U19 v Australia
U19 (3rd LOI)

Tuesday 3 August

CGU National League Division One
Bristol: *Glos v Hants

Wednesday 4 August

County Championship
Derby: Derbys v Lancs
Riverside: Durham v Sussex
Canterbury: Kent v Essex
Southgate: Middx v Notts
Northampton: Northants v Somerset
The Oval: Surrey v Glam
Headingley: Yorks v Worcs
CGU National League Division One
Edgbaston: *Warwks v Leics

Thursday 5 August

THIRD CORNHILL TEST MATCH
Old Trafford: ENGLAND v NEW ZEALAND
County Championship
Bristol: Glos v Hants

Friday 6 August

County Championship
Leicester: Leics v Warwks

Sunday 8 August

CGU National League Division One
Canterbury: Kent v Essex
Headingley: Yorks v Worcs
CGU National League Division Two
Riverside: Durham v Sussex
Southgate: Middx v Somerset

Northampton: Northants v Derbys
The Oval: Surrey v Notts

Tuesday 10 August

CGU National League Division One
Southampton: Hants v Essex
Old Trafford: Lancs v Glos
Leicester: Leics v Durham
CGU National League Division Two
Cardiff: Glam v Durham
Southgate: Middx v Derbys
Trent Bridge: *Notts v Northants
Hove: *Sussex v Somerset
Tourist Match (4 days)
Worcester: Worcs v Sri Lanka A

Wednesday 11 August

Tourist Match (1 day)
Southgate: Middx v New Zealand

Thursday 12 August

CGU National League Division One
Chelmsford: Essex v Leics
Bristol: *Glos v Kent
Headingley: *Yorks v Lancs
CGU National League Division Two
Derby: Derbys v Somerset
Riverside: Durham v Notts
Northampton: Northants v Glam
Hove: *Sussex v Surrey

Friday 13 August

Vodafone Challenge Series
Chelmsford/   Essex/Northants v New
Northampton: Zealand
(Northants to play New Zealand if Essex in NWT Semi-Finals)

Saturday 14 August

NatWest Trophy First Semi-Final
(Reserve days Sun 15 and Mon 16 Aug)

Sunday 15 August

NatWest Trophy Second Semi-Final
(Reserve day Mon 16 Aug)
Tourist Match (1 day)
Taunton/   Somerset/Sussex v Sri
Hove: Lanka A
(Sussex to play Sri Lanka if Somerset in NWT Semi-Finals)
Women's Test Match (4 days)
Shenley: England v India

Monday 16 or Tuesday 17 August
Aon Trophy
Semi-Finals

Tuesday 17 August
County Championship
Southampton: Hants v Warwks
Northampton: Northants v Glos
CGU National League Division One
Old Trafford: *Lancs v Yorks
Tourist Match (4 days)
Shenley: MCC v Sri Lanka A
NatWest Under-19 International (4 days)
Edgbaston: England U19 v Australia U19 (1st Test)

Wednesday 18 August
County Championship
Colchester: Essex v Durham
Colwyn Bay: Glam v Notts
Southgate: Middx v Leics
Taunton: Somerset v Kent
Hove: Sussex v Surrey
Kidderminster: Worcs v Derbys

Thursday 19 August
FOURTH CORNHILL TEST MATCH
The Oval: ENGLAND v NEW ZEALAND
County Championship
Old Trafford: Lancs v Yorks

Sunday 22 August

CGU National League Division One
Colchester: Essex v Warwks
Southampton: Hants v Glos
Leicester: Leics v Worcs
CGU National League Division Two
Colwyn Bay: Glam v Notts
Southgate: Middx v Northants
Taunton: Somerset v Sussex

Monday 23 August
NatWest Under-19 International (4 days)
Bristol: England U19 v Australia U19 (2nd Test)

Tuesday 24 August
County Championship
Derby: Derbys v Surrey
Riverside: Durham v Middx
Chelmsford: Essex v Somerset
Cardiff: Glam v Warwks
Portsmouth: Hants v Sussex
Canterbury: Kent v Northants

Leicester: Leics v Glos
Trent Bridge: Notts v Yorks
Worcester: Worcs v Lancs

Sunday 29 August
CGU National League Division One
(Match involving NWT finalists to be re-arranged)
Canterbury: Kent v Yorks
Old Trafford: Lancs v Leics
Worcester: Worcs v Essex
CGU National League Division Two
Trent Bridge: Notts v Derbys
The Oval: Surrey v Durham
Lord's: NATWEST TROPHY FINAL
(Reserve day Mon 30 Aug)

Monday 30 August
CGU National League Division One
(Match involving NWT finalists to be re-arranged)
Canterbury: Kent v Hants
Leicester: Leics v Glos
Worcester: Worcs v Warwks
CGU National League Division Two
Derby: Derbys v Notts
Cardiff: Glam v Somerset
Northampton: Northants v Durham

Tuesday 31 August
County Championship
Eastbourne: Sussex v Essex
CGU National League Division One
Edgbaston: *Warwks v Glos
CGU National League Division Two
Lord's: Middx v Surrey
Taunton: *Somerset v Glam

Wednesday 1 September
County Championship
Old Trafford: Lancs v Derbys
Leicester: Leics v Hants
Northampton: Northants v Hants
The Oval: Surrey v Notts
Scarborough: Yorks v Kent
NatWest Under-19 International (4 days)
Riverside: England U19 v Australia U19 (3rd Test)

Thursday 2 September
County Championship
Taunton: Somerset v Glam
Edgbaston: Warwks v Glos

Sunday 5 September

CGU National League Division One
Chelmsford: Essex v Worcs
Scarborough: Yorks v Leics
CGU National League Division Two
Derby: Derbys v Middx

Monday 6 September

CGU National League Division One
Old Trafford: *Lancs v Hants
CGU National League Division Two
The Oval: *Surrey v Sussex
Aon Trophy Final (Reserve day Tues 7 Sept)

Tuesday 7 September

CGU National League Division Two
The Oval: *Surrey v Middx

Wednesday 8 September

County Championship
Riverside: Durham v Warwks
Chelmsford: Essex v Worcs
Bristol: Glos v Derbys
Southampton: Hants v Somerset
Old Trafford: Lancs v Kent
Northampton: Northants v Leics
Headingley: Yorks v Glam
CGU National League Division Two
Hove: *Sussex v Notts

Thursday 9 September

County Championship
Lord's: Middx v Surrey

Friday 10 September

County Championship
Hove: Sussex v Notts

Sunday 12 September

CGU National League Division One
Bristol: Glos v Essex
Southampton: Hants v Worcs
Old Trafford: Lancs v Kent
Headingley: Yorks v Warwks
CGU National League Division Two
Riverside: Durham v Glam
Northampton: Northants v Somerset

Wednesday 15 September

County Championship
Derby: Derbys v Hants
Cardiff: Glam v Northants
Canterbury: Kent v Glos
Leicester: Leics v Durham
Trent Bridge: Notts v Essex
Taunton: Somerset v Lancs
The Oval: Surrey v Yorks
Edgbaston: Warwks v Sussex
Worcester: Worcs v Middx

Sunday 19 September

CGU National League Division One
Canterbury: Kent v Glos
Leicester: Leics v Essex
Edgbaston: Warwks v Hants
Worcester: Worcs v Lancs
CGU National League Division Two
Derby: Derbys v Sussex
Cardiff: Glam v Middx
Trent Bridge: Notts v Durham
Taunton: Somerset v Northants

NATWEST TROPHY FIXTURES 1999

† Recreational Team from ECB's 38 Counties

Tuesday 4 May

First Round
1 Koninklijke UD (Deventer): Holland v Cambridgeshire†
2 Cheam: Surrey† v Norfolk†
3 Bury St Edmunds: Suffolk† v Hampshire†
4 Sleaford: Lincolnshire† v Wales†
5 West Lothian Cty (Linlithgow): Scotland v Nottinghamshire†
6 Mote Park (Maidstone): Kent† v Denmark
7 Netherfield (Kendal): Cumbria† v Cornwall†
8 Northampton: Northamptonshire† v Wiltshire†
9 Wardown Park (Luton): Bedfordshire† v Huntingdonshire†
10 Reading: Berkshire† v Warwickshire†
11 Radlett: Hertfordshire† v Leicestershire†

12	Hatherley & Reddings (Cheltenham):	Gloucestershire† v Yorkshire†
13	Jesmond:	Northumberland† v Ireland
14	Hartlepool:	Durham† v Oxfordshire†

Tuesday 18 May

Second Round
23	Taunton:	Somerset† v Bedfordshire†/Huntingdonshire†

Wednesday 19 May

Second Round
15	Liverpool:	Lancashire† v Holland/Cambridgeshire†
16	Cheam/Lakenham:	Surrey†/Norfolk† v Cheshire†
17	Wellington:	Shropshire† v Suffolk†/Hampshire†
18	Dunstall:	Derbyshire† v Lincolnshire†/Wales†
19	Hamilton Crescent (Glasgow)/Boots Ground:	Scotland/Nottinghamshire† v Dorset†
20	Maidstone/Worcester:	Kent†/Denmark v Worcestershire†
21	Southgate:	Middlesex† v Cumbria†/Cornwall†
22	Brockhampton:	Herefordshire† v Northamptonshire†/Wiltshire†
24	Torquay:	Devon† v Berkshire†/Warwickshire†
25	Hertford/Oakham School:	Hertfordshire†/Leicestershire† v Sussex†
26	Hatherley & Reddings (Cheltenham)/ Sheffield (Abbeydale):	Gloucestershire†/Yorkshire† v Buckinghamshire†
27	Jesmond/Belfast:	Northumberland†/Ireland† v Essex†
28	Gateshead Fell/Challow & Childrey:	Durham†/Oxfordshire† v Staffordshire†

Wednesday 23 June

Third Round (First-class counties in bold)
29	Lytham/Deventer/March:	Lancs†/Holland/Cambs† v **Durham**
30	Guildford/Lakenham/Bowdon:	Surrey†/Norfolk†/Cheshire† v **Kent**
31	St George's/Bury St Edmunds/Portsmouth:	Shropshire†/Suffolk†/Hants† v **Glam**
32	Derby/Grantham/St Helen's, Swansea:	Derbys†/Lincs†/Wales† v **Somerset**
33	Grange (Edinburgh)/Boots Ground/Deane Park:	Scotland/Notts†/Dorset† v **Surrey**
34	Canterbury/away/Kidderminster:	Kent†/Denmark/Worcs† v **Hants**
35	Southgate/Netherfield/Truro:	Middx†/Cumbria†/Cornwall† v **Sussex**
36	Kington/Old Northamptonians/South Wilts (Bemerton):	Herefords†/Northants†/Wilts† v **Yorks**
37	Taunton/Wardown Park (Luton)/Kimbolton Sch:	Somerset†/Bedfords†/Hunts† v **Derbys**
38	Exmouth/Finchampstead/Edgbaston:	Devon†/Berks†/Warwks† v **Worcs**
39	Radlett/Leicester/Hove:	Herts†/Leics†/Sussex† v **Lancs**
40	Bristol/Harrogate/Marlow:	Glos†/Yorks†/Bucks† v **Warwks**
41	Jesmond/Clontarf/Chelmsford (TBC):	Northumberland†/Ireland†/Essex† v **Leics**
42	Riverside/Challow & Childrey/Leek:	Durham†/Oxon†/Staffs† v **Glos**
43	Northampton:	**Northants** v **Essex**
44	Trent Bridge:	**Notts** v **Middx**

Wednesday 7 July

Fourth Round
45	Winner Match 38 v Winner Match 33
46	Winner Match 36 v Winner Match 41
47	Winner Match 31 v Winner Match 40
48	Winner Match 43 v Winner Match 44
49	Winner Match 34 v Winner Match 39
50	Winner Match 29 v Winner Match 30
51	Winner Match 42 v Winner Match 37
52	Winner Match 35 v Winner Match 32

Quarter-Finals:	Wednesday 28 July
Semi-Final (1):	Saturday 14 August
Semi-Final (2):	Sunday 15 August
Final:	Sunday 29 August

FIELDING CHART

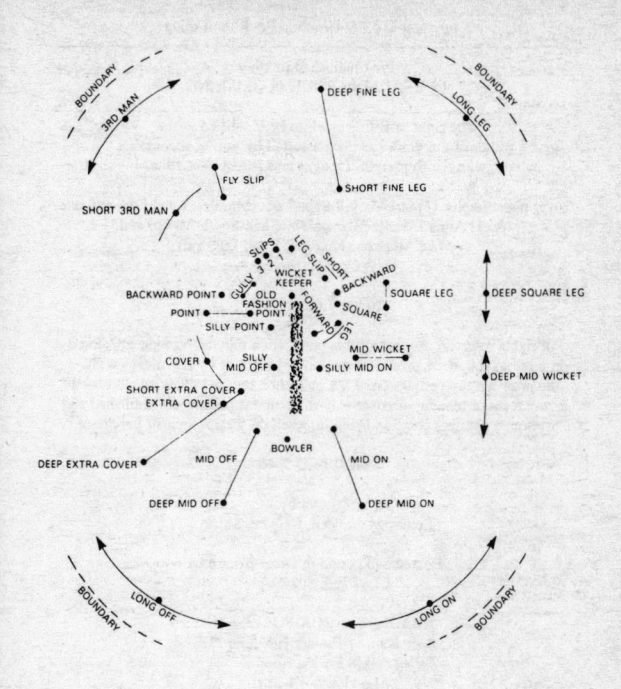

Copyright © 1999 Headline Book Publishing

First published in 1999
by HEADLINE BOOK PUBLISHING

The right of Bill Frindall to be identified as the
author of the Work has been asserted by him in accordance
with the Copyright, Designs and Patents Act 1988.

Cover photographs: (*Front*) Mark Ramprakash (Middlesex and England) and
(*back*) Allan Donald (Warwickshire and South Africa) and
Mike Atherton (Lancashire and England)
© Graham Morris

10 9 8 7 6 5 4 3 2 1

All rights reserved. No part of this publication may be reproduced, stored
in a retrieval system, or transmitted, in any form or by any means without
the prior written permission of the publisher, nor be otherwise circulated
in any form of binding or cover other than that in which it is published and
without a similar condition being imposed on the subsequent purchaser.

ISBN 0 7472 5946 1

Typeset by
Letterpart Limited, Reigate, Surrey

Printed and bound in Great Britain by
Clays Ltd, St Ives plc.

HEADLINE BOOK PUBLISHING
A division of Hodder Headline PLC
338 Euston Road
London NW1 3BH